Focus

This book presents a collection of writings on the issue of focus in its broadest sense. While commonly being considered as related to phenomena such as presupposition and anaphora, focusing is much more widespread, and it is this pervasiveness that the current collection addresses. The volume brings together theoretical, psychological, and descriptive approaches to focus, at the same time maintaining the overall interest in how these notions apply to the larger problem of evolving some formal representation of the semantic aspects of linguistic content.

The chapters in this volume have been reworked from a selection of original papers presented at a conference held in 1994 in Schloss Wolfsbrunnen in Germany.

Peter Bosch is the head of IBM's Institute for Logic and Linguistics in Heidelberg and holds the position of privatdozent at the Institute for Semantic Information Processing at the University of Osnabrück. Rob van der Sandt is a senior lecturer in logic and philosophy in the Department of Philosophy at the University of Nijmegen.

T0381636

Studies in Natural Language Processing

Douglas E. Appelt, *Planning English Sentences*

Madeleine Bates and Ralph M. Weischedel (eds.), *Challenges in Natural Language Processing*

Steven Bird, *Computational Phonology*

Peter Bosch and Rob van der Sandt, *Focus*

T. Briscoe, Ann Copestake, and Valeria Paiva (eds.), *Inheritance, Defaults and the Lexicon*

Ronald Cole, Joseph Mariani, Hans Uszkoreit, Giovanni Varile, Annie Zaenen, Antonio Zampolli, and Victor Zue (eds.), *Survey of the State of the Art in Human Language Technology*

David R. Dowty, Lauri Karttunen, and Arnold M. Zwicky (eds.), *Natural Language Parsing*

Ralph Grishman, *Computational Linguistics*

Graeme Hirst, *Semantic Interpretation and the Resolution of Ambiguity*

András Kornai, *Extended Finite State Models of Language*

Kathleen R. McKeown, *Text Generation*

Martha Stone Palmer, *Semantic Processing for Finite Domains*

Terry Patten, *Systemic Text Generation as Problem Solving*

Michael Rosner and Roderick Johnson (eds.), *Computational Linguistics and Formal Semantics*

Patrick Saint-Dizier and Evelyn Viegas (eds.), *Computational Lexical Semantics*

Focus

Linguistic, Cognitive, and Computational Perspectives

Edited by

Peter Bosch and **Rob van der Sandt**

CAMBRIDGE
UNIVERSITY PRESS

CAMBRIDGE UNIVERSITY PRESS
Cambridge, New York, Melbourne, Madrid, Cape Town, Singapore,
São Paulo, Delhi, Dubai, Tokyo, Mexico City

Cambridge University Press
The Edinburgh Building, Cambridge CB2 8RU, UK

Published in the United States of America by Cambridge University Press, New York

www.cambridge.org
Information on this title: www.cambridge.org/9780521168502

© Cambridge University Press 1999

First published 1999
First paperback edition 2010

A catalogue record for this publication is available from the British Library

Library of Congress Cataloguing in Publication Data
Focus: Linguistic, Cognitive, and Computational Perspectives / edited by Peter Bosch,
Rob van der Sandt.
    p. cm.
Rev. papers originally presented at a conference held 1994,
Schloss Wolfsbrunnen, Ger.
Includes bibliographical references and index.
ISBN 0-521-58305-5 (hardbound)
1. Focus (Linguistics) 2. Computational linguistics. I. Bosch, Peter.
II. Sandt, Rob A. van der.
P299.F63F63   1998
401'.41 - dc21 98-17211

ISBN 978-0-521-58305-3 Hardback
ISBN 978-0-521-16850-2 Paperback

Contents

List of Contributors   *page* ix

Preface   xi

Peter Bosch and Rob van der Sandt

Part I Surface Realization of Focus

1 Contrastive Stress, Contrariety, and Focus   3
   Kees van Deemter

2 The Processing of Information Structure   18
   Carsten Günther, Claudia Maienborn, Andrea Schopp

3 On the Limits of Focus Projection in English   43
   Carlos Gussenhoven

4 Informational Autonomy   56
   Joachim Jacobs

5 Subject-Prodrop in Yiddish   82
   Ellen F. Prince

Part II Semantic Interpretation of Focus Phenomena

6 What Is the Alternative? The Computation of Focus
   Alternatives from Lexical and Sortal Information   105
   Peter I. Blok and Kurt Eberle

7 The Treatment of Focusing Particles in Underspecified
   Discourse Representations   121
   Johan Bos

8 Topic   142
   Daniel Büring

9 Focus with Nominal Quantifiers   166
   Regine Eckardt

10   Topic, Focus, and Weak Quantifiers   187
     Gerhard Jäger

11   Focus, Quantification, and Semantics-Pragmatics Issues   213
     Barbara H. Partee

12   Association with Focus or Association with Presupposition?   232
     Mats Rooth

     Part III   The Function of Focus in Discourse

13   Discourse and the Focus/Background Distinction   247
     Nicholas Asher

14   Domain Restriction   268
     Bart Geurts and Rob van der Sandt

15   On Different Kinds of Focus   293
     Jeanette K. Gundel

16   Stressed and Unstressed Pronouns:
     Complementary Preferences   306
     Megumi Kameyama

17   Discourse Linking and Discourse Subordination   322
     Kjell Johan Sæbø

18   Position and Meaning: Time Adverbials in Context   336
     Henriëtte de Swart

     Name Index   363
     Subject Index   366

Contributors

Nicholas Asher, University of Texas, Austin
Peter I. Blok, University of Amsterdam
Johan Bos, University of the Saarland
Peter Bosch, IBM Germany, Heidelberg
Daniel Büring, University of Cologne
Kees van Deemter, Philips Electronic Labs, Eindhoven
Kurt Eberle, IBM Germany, Heidelberg
Regine Eckardt, University of Konstanz
Bart Geurts, University of Osnabrück
Jeanette K. Gundel, University of Minnesota
Carsten Günther, IBM Germany, Heidelberg
Carlos Gussenhoven, University of Nijmegen
Joachim Jacobs, University of Wuppertal
Gerhard Jäger, University of Pennsylvania
Megumi Kameyama, SRI International, Stanford
Claudia Maienborn, Humboldt University of Berlin
Barbara H. Partee, University of Massachusetts, Amherst
Ellen F. Prince, University of Pennsylvania
Mats Rooth, University of Stuttgart
Kjell Johan Sæbø, University of Oslo
Rob van der Sandt, University of Nijmegen
Andrea Schopp, University of Hamburg
Henriëtte de Swart, University of Utrecht

Preface

Some of the more exciting developments in theoretical linguistics as well as in natural language processing during the past decade have taken place in the study of discourse.

After a period of linguistic investigation that was characterized by the words (though not necessarily the spirit) of Richard Montague's title "English as a Formal Language," that is, a period that followed the paradigm of modeling natural languages after formal languages, the study of discourse started in the late 1970s to emphasize features of natural language that are not typically found in formal languages, without, of course, turning away from the formal methods that had been developed.

The particular excitement of this development derives from the fact that in discourse the "naturalness" of natural language becomes clearly visible. Many of the features of natural language that show up in discourse phenomena are not commonly features of formal languages, nor would it make much sense to incorporate them into formal languages. We are thinking here, first of all, of coherence phenomena. For what distinguishes a discourse from a set of sentences or utterances is crucially the requirement of coherence. And coherence has its semantic as well as, in a broad, Carnapian sense, its syntactic side. Logical and referential coherence, as in presupposition and anaphora, show up the semantic side, and the "grammaticalness" of a sequence of utterances with respect to word order and intonation shows up the syntactic side of coherence. In formal languages there is little reason to have anaphoric relations (except for the somewhat special case of variable binding). Similarly, there is probably no good reason for introducing presupposition into a formal language, unless the purpose is to have the formal language model certain aspects of a natural language. Word order in formal languages is a matter of right or wrong, but not a means of expression; and intonation, if you like, the phonological equivalent of word order in natural language, can have a place only in a spoken language – but not many of these are formal languages.

But what has all this to do with focus? From the point of view of natural language discourse, focusing is a means of structuring a series of utterances and, at the same time, from the point of view of processing discourse, it is a way of partitioning information. From a computational perspective the need for some such device is clear: the complexity and the amount of data relevant in processing discourse are too great for formal and computationally tractable approaches to cope with.

And of course, the human mind is no better off in this respect than the computer. There is, therefore, a need to find ways of partitioning the data according to the informational requirements of particular processing steps for the human mind as well as for the machine, that is, for one or the other form of focusing.

Focusing, along this line of thought, is, psychologically or computationally speaking, a matter of managing the working memory of the discourse processor. What is in focus – in this parlance – is what is in the working memory, occasionally also called *focused memory* by psychologists. Accordingly, if you permit continued simplification, a coherent discourse is one that is processed with greater ease because there is not much erratic swapping of the contents of the working memory, but rather a regular movement from *given* (i.e., focus) to *new*.

Not really different in content, but quite opposed in the wording, is the linguistic tradition, in which one thinks of coherence typically as topic continuity and where discourse moves ahead from *given* (i.e., topic) to *new* by adding new foci, often in what syntacticians call focus position and with a special intonation contour. What in the processing world is called "focus" is associated with Givenness and what most linguists call "focus" is associated with Newness.

It is mainly a historical accident, due to the fact that the phenomenon has attracted attention from diverse disciplines, that the term *focus* has come to be used in different and mutually opposed meanings. But the terminological opposition is no reason to think that the subject matter of the various approaches to *focus* should be different. It is rather that this blatant opposition in usage drives to an extreme what we can otherwise perceive as unclarity and incompleteness of definition in this area. Notions like *given* and *new*, *topic* and *focus*, *theme* and *rheme*, and even *subject* and *predicate* all suffer from this problem. At the root of it is not any lack of interest in clear and well-defined terminology, but rather the fact that precision can only be achieved with respect to particular sets of data or domains of application, and different researchers, at least for the time being, seem to have different data in mind.

There is not yet a complete theory that simultaneously handles all these notions in a coherent way, let alone a comprehensive theory that integrates the intonational and syntactic realization, the interpretation, and the discourse functions of focus. There are, however, clear signs that lead us to think that a more integrated approach to the subsets of phenomena treated in existing theories is feasible.

The motivation for bringing together the contributions in this volume lies in our conviction that only an integration of the approaches from various disciplines will do justice to the actual complexity of the phenomena and ultimately lead to an integrated theory that comprises the various subsets of data and outlooks from different disciplines. We therefore brought together researchers from different backgrounds and had them react to, and comment on, each other's work to give the reader a chance to make the links and prepare for the next steps.

We have classified the chapters according to where the actual emphasis of each contribution is into a section on *surface realization of focus*, on questions of *semantic interpretation of focus phenomena*, and on the *function of focus in discourse*. This rough division cannot, of course, do justice to the interrelations that hold among the chapters. Nearly all chapters in this volume show that the problems are too closely interconnected to allow for clean surgery. Just as several contributions in the first section relate intonational issues directly to semantics and discourse, most of those on semantics show that a proper semantic analysis cannot be obtained unless we take a closer look at its syntactic realization and the structure of the surrounding discourse. The following paragraphs, far from being a comprehensive survey, are intended to give the reader some guidance as to where some of the more interesting connections are found.

Surveys and comparisons of various approaches to focus are found in the contributions by Gundel and by Partee. *Gundel*'s chapter is the one we should recommend as the first to be read in this collection by anybody who either is new to focus research or has so far only been concerned with a narrow section of this subject matter. Gundel gives an overview of various notions of focus in linguistics, AI, and psychology and shows how they are interrelated. She distinguishes focus in the psychological sense of center of attention from semantic focus – in the sense of new information – and contrastive focus, which is closely related to linguistic prominence. While semantic focus is truth-conditionally relevant, it does not necessarily bring its object into the focus of attention; contrastive focus, on the other hand, is not truth-conditionally relevant, but always moves its objects into psychological focus.

Partee's contribution contains a comparison of recent work in formal semantics and the work done in the very different tradition of the Prague school. She also gives a summary of her earlier work on the way focus affects the interpretation of quantificational structures and thus brings up issues and sets the stage for some of the chapters (notably Eckardt's and Büring's) found in the second and third sections. Partee's is the only chapter in this volume that gives a central place to the Prague school approach to focus. Partee, having worked with Eva Hajičová and Petr Sgall for extended periods over several years, writes, as it were, her account of how to make sense of the Prague theory from the point of view of her own background in formal syntax and semantics and looks at ways of coming to a full understanding of the Prague work in the sense of incorporating its insights into formal approaches. The discussion shows that if we take the latter work seriously, focus phenomena force us to rethink the way the relations among syntax, semantics, and pragmatics are traditionally conceived of.

Intonational and syntactic issues and their connection with discourse are the main theme of Part I of this book. *Gussenhoven* discusses the phonological realization of focus and contrasts the major views on focus projection in English. Focus projection, or the ability of a pitch accent to mark a larger constituent than the word it is placed on as focused, has been given different treatments in the recent literature. Gussenhoven reviews the major points in the recent history of the controversy and argues in his chapter, on the basis of so-called focus ambiguity as well as a range of further empirical grounds, that focus projection is restricted to a sequence of an argument and its predicate. He shows that this view of focus projection not only provides a better empirical account than its competitors, but is also conceptually simpler.

The contributions by Jacobs and van Deemter interrelate intonation and semantics. *Jacobs*'s chapter investigates what he calls the informational autonomy of constituents. This notion is related to the way a constituent's interpretation is constrained by the meaning of constituents with which it combines. Jacobs demonstrates correlations of informational autonomy with sentence accent (and also with word accent in compound words) and with feature projection in syntax and works out the details of semantic processing of informational autonomy as well as the syntactic conditions that constrain informational autonomy. He shows that existing syntactic theories cannot account for the full range of syntactic and stress data as well as the observed semantic phenomena. *Van Deemter* draws attention to a number of cases of contrasting accents that elude treatments by theories of Given and New as well as theories that are based on the notion of syntactic or semantic parallelism. He develops an alternative that is based on the logical notion of contrariety. The chapter contains a detailed discussion of the notions of novelty and contrastiveness as the source of accents and gives a formalization of the notion of contrast based on the logical notion of contrariety.

The chapters by Kameyama and by Prince link intonation and syntax, respectively, to the requirements of the surrounding discourse. The theoretical background of both chapters is Centering Theory, which brings together previous work on discourse focusing and the modeling of attentional state in discourse. *Kameyama* offers a perspective on the interpretation of stressed pronouns that is well in line with the philosophy of Rooth's focus theory: that is, she views the semantics of focused constituents in the first place as a matter of contrast between a set of background options and the interpretation of the actually focused constituent. For focused, and hence stressed, pronouns this means that their reference options come, as it were, from the same pool as those for unstressed anaphoric pronouns, but that the pool is divided into the two complementary sets, one of which interprets focused pronouns and the other anaphoric pronouns. For practical purposes of pronoun resolution this means that once we have an algorithm for anaphoric pronouns, it is relatively easy to build an extension for the resolution of focused pronouns on top, as it were. Kameyama makes a detailed proposal for how this would work.

Prince's chapter on subject prodrop is probably the most strongly empirically oriented chapter in our collection. Subject prodrop has been studied fairly widely from both syntactic and discourse perspectives and for quite a variety of languages. The common assumption of virtually all these studies was that subject prodrop is a unitary phenomenon. Prince shows in her corpus-based study that this is certainly not true of Yiddish, where subject prodrop had not been studied. A highly plausible speculation one might link to Prince's chapter is that similar empirical work on

Italian, Spanish, and other prodrop languages may well show that also there the phenomenon may be less uniform than has hitherto been assumed.

Two central themes pervade Parts II and III. One of these themes is the relation between the topic/focus division and the presupposition/assertion dichotomy. Another is the way focus and presupposition affect the interpretation of quantified structures.

As for the first point it has often been remarked that there are nontrivial relations between the topic/focus dichotomy on the one hand and the presupposition/assertion dichotomy on the other. Both distinctions and their interrelations have been discussed since the 1950s, notably by Strawson, by the Prague school, and by a variety of authors after them. Take, for instance, the position of Jackendoff, who identifies focus with asserted information and uses the term *presupposition* for what is more commonly referred to as focal background. It has equally often been observed that in spite of their resemblances these dichotomies cannot be reduced to each other. This historical situation is reflected in various contributions that explore the interrelations between these pairs from current views on dynamic interpretation and information structure.

Rooth addresses the issue of whether the semantics of intonational focus can be strengthened so as to yield existential presupposition in the framework of alternative semantics. This would associate with focus constructions the same presupposition as is generally assumed for cleft sentences. Rooth points out that such an analysis can easily be accomplished in the framework of alternative semantics by requiring that at least one member of the set of alternatives derived from the focal structure is true. On the basis of a careful comparison between focus and cleft constructions in counterfactual environments he reaches a negative conclusion. It is argued that an existential presupposition semantics for focus is at odds with the flexibility in the licensing of focus we find in counterfactual environments.

Focus particles have attracted considerable attention from researchers in both focus and presupposition theory. Focus affects both the meaning and the presuppositions of sentences in which such particles occur. This phenomenon is analyzed in detail in the contribution by *Bos*, who presents a description language for underspecified discourse representations and shows how ambiguities arising from focus particles can be treated. His account incorporates and integrates ideas from Rooth's alternative semantics and from the presupposition-as-anaphora theory. After a detailed presentation of the formalism Bos applies his language to a small fragment of English and shows how scope ambiguities and focus adverbs can be treated in his framework.

A central issue in the recent literature on focus and presupposition concerns the interaction of focus and quantification, and quite a lot of this work centers on the observation made by a variety of authors that focus and presupposition affect the interpretation of quantificational domains. Quantifiers depend for their interpretation on context, and so does the interpretation of focus and presupposition. It is generally agreed that the domain of quantification is severely underdetermined by information provided by the restrictor; it is also uncontroversial that topicality and presupposition are among the crucial factors involved in determining the actual domain of quantification. There is no consensus, however, on how this determination is actually achieved.

As discussed in a series of papers by Partee and summarized in her contribution to this volume, the focus/background division and presuppositions triggered in the nuclear scope of a quantifier may influence the interpretation of the quantifier's domain. *Eckardt's* chapter focuses on cases where nominal quantifiers seem to associate with focus just as adverbial quantifiers do. The generalization is that backgrounded or presuppositional material in the quantifier's nuclear scope tends to be interpreted as if it originated in the restrictor while focused material remains part of its nuclear scope. Again there is a general consensus about the reality of this phenomenon, but there is no unanimity as to whether syntactic, semantic, or pragmatic processes are responsible for it. A tendency found in a number of chapters is that focus and presupposition are not directly responsible for the interpretation of quantificational domains but affect it in a more indirect way.

The issue how information structure affects the interpretation of quantifiers is discussed from various points of view in the contributions of Büring, Eckardt, Geurts and van der Sandt, Jäger, and Sæbø. Eckardt and Büring analyze the phenomenon building on Rooth's alternative semantics. Jäger implements his account in an extension of dynamic predicate logic, and Sæbø whereas Geurts and van der Sandt discuss it from the point of view of the presupposition-as-anaphora theory. The discussions show the intricate relationship among anaphoric processes, topicality, and presupposition.

Eckardt discusses cases where nominal quantifiers behave in the same way as adverbial quantifiers when focus is involved and argues that the interpretation of the arguments of a quantifier is not syntax but focus driven. She shows furthermore that the semantics of focus will do only part of the job. A further restriction of the context of interpretation is required. In the appendix to her paper she gives a formal account of the data discussed.

The analysis of focus as given in alternative semantics is extended by *Büring* to account for sentence topics. Büring then applies the resulting theory to the analysis of nominal quantifiers. He claims, just as Eckardt does, that the semantic effects observed in the literature don't result from the syntax. These effects can instead be attributed to the workings of the topic/focus/background structure. It is argued that partitive, proportional, and focus-affected readings can be derived by the topic/focus semantics given in conjunction with a Westerståhl-type use of domain variables.

Jäger's analysis of focus and quantification adopts a dynamic semantics in the Groenendijk/Stokhof/Veltman style. Like Büring, Jäger argues against postulating a syntactic or semantic ambiguity in weak quantifiers. The difference between the existential or weak reading and the presuppositional or strong one should instead be attributed to the information structure of the entire sentence. The strong reading is limited to environments where the quantifier is a topic. Jäger argues that the familiar distinction between established and new discourse referents is to account for the anaphoric reading of weak quantifiers. Building on this analysis he distinguishes between two types of discourse entities, which differ in terms of prominence or some related notion. On Jäger's account indefinites that are part of the comment introduce new discourse markers. Indefinite topics on the other hand merely activate old discourse referents. A formal account of the resulting theory is given in an appendix.

The contributions of Sæbø as well as Geurts and van der Sandt discuss quantification and domain restriction from the point of view of the presupposition-as-anaphora theory. *Sæbø's* chapter concentrates on the type of domain restriction that comes about as a result of anaphoric take-up of given information. His account of discourse linking and discourse subordination is given as a presuppositional extension of Kamp and Reyle's proposal to deal with dependent plural pronouns. It is argued that a generalization of Kamp and Reyle's proposal makes it applicable to a much wider range of data, while giving a more principled account of discourse subordination.

Geurts and van der Sandt argue that given a few independently motivated assumptions concerning the representation of quantifiers, and given a Jackendoff-type account of the interrelation between focus and presupposition, the presupposition-as-anaphora theory accounts for the three major ways in which quantificational domains may be restricted. It is shown that they may be restricted by anaphoric take-up of contextual information, by accommodation of presupposed material, and by means of focusing. They also respond to some criticisms that were raised with respect to their notion of (intermediate or restrictor) accommodation.

Both de Swart and Asher integrate their account in a wider framework of discourse and discourse structure. Their analyses build on earlier work on discourse structure by Asher and Lascarides and Asher. *De Swart* develops an analysis of phrasal and clausal time adverbials in a framework that, in contrast to the Reichenbachian view, does not make use of reference times. The interpretation of such adverbials is taken to reside in their presuppositional character. Inference rules about the presuppositional properties and the topic/focus structure determine the order in which they are processed. Preposed time adverbials are topical and thus set the stage for the interpretation of the main clause and the background for focus. Postposed time adverbials may or may not be in focus and thus create ambiguities. The analysis is extended to quantificational environments and to cases where temporal adverbs occur with focus adverbs like *only* or *even.*

Asher aims to integrate the semantic treatments of focus as found in work by, for example, Rooth and Krifka with the more informal pragmatic and discourse-related accounts found in the work of, for instance, Hopper and Givon. The basis of this analysis is the theory of discourse structure and discourse relations he developed in earlier work. His chapter focuses on a phenomenon that has proved to be notoriously difficult to incorporate in a purely semantic account, that is,

VP-ellipsis. Asher's central conclusion is that there is a nontrivial relation between discourse focus as found in the discourse-related analyses and sentential focus (as analyzed in, e.g., alternative semantics). He explores their interrelations in detail, thereby producing a unified theory that integrates the semantics in his theory of discourse structure.

Computational linguistics and machine translation enter the stage in the contributions by Günther, Maienborn, and Schopp and by Blok and Eberle. *Günther, Maienborn, and Schopp* report on an implemented system of speech production from their SYNPHONICS project. SYNPHONICS offers an integrated view of information structure in speech production from a cognitive perspective. This includes all processes and modules from the computation of information structure of utterances in discourse context to their phonetic realization. The major theoretical point of the chapter is that it shows how the processing requirement of incrementality can be reconciled with structural requirements. *Blok and Eberle* tackle the problem of how to make practical use of Rooth's notion of alternative semantics: given that the interpretation of focused constituents depends on the set of interpretation alternatives available, how do we compute this set of alternatives? Blok and Eberle look at this problem in the context of machine translation, where the alternatives are not only determined semantically or conceptually, but also crucially by the lexical material available in source and target language. Their proposal shows a piece of integrated processing of linguistic and nonlinguistic knowledge resources.

Peter Bosch
Rob van der Sandt

PART I

Surface Realization of Focus

1 Contrastive Stress, Contrariety, and Focus

KEES VAN DEEMTER

Abstract

Prosodically acceptable speech must contain accents at appropriate words. This chapter argues that many cases of accenting can be accounted for neither by a theory of given and new information nor by one that looks for syntactic and/or semantic parallelism. An account is attempted that makes use of the notion of *contrariety* that originates from traditional logic. It states, roughly speaking, that contrastive stress is required between sentences that stand in the relation of contrariety, modulo certain "identifying" substitutions.

1 Current Perspectives on Contrast

If speech generation systems are to generate prosodically acceptable speech, the generation of *accents*[1] is an important requirement. The importance of *information status* for accenting was demonstrated a long time ago (e.g., Halliday 1967, Chafe 1976). According to these accounts, which have now proved their validity for most Germanic languages, an expression that conveys new information tends to be focused by means of an accent. The exact place of the accent, within the focused constituent, is partly determined by syntactic structure. In this chapter, it is assumed that syntactic structure is accounted for through the mechanism of *Focus-Accent Theory*.[2]

Given that the connection between accent and new information is now well established, it would be tempting to explain all accents as caused by informational newness. Unfortunately, this is not always possible. Cruttenden, for example, cites various kinds of cases in which *given* information must be accented. For example, someone may, at some stage of a dialogue, say *I didn't go after all*, and someone else may reply *You didn't* $^+$*go?*,[3] where the verb *go* is accented even though it constitutes given information (Cruttenden 1986). In monologues, cases such as the following come to mind:

(1) $^+$Mozart wrote $^+$few fugues, but $^+$Bach wrote $^+$many fugues.

Thanks are due to Bob Ladd, Willem Rump, and Jacques Terken for useful conversations on the topic of this chapter. An earlier version has appeared in the proceedings of the *Journal of Semantics* conference on focus: P. Bosch and R. van der Sandt (eds.), "Focus & Natural Language Processing," December 1994, and in the IPO Annual Progress Report 1994.

3

(2)   John is neither [+]eager to please, nor [+]easy to please, nor [+]certain to please.

In all such examples, the accents tend to be as indicated, whether or not the focused entities constitute new information. For example, *Mozart* and *Bach* must be accented even if they have occurred just prior to the utterance of (1).[4] In cases like (1) and (2), it is common to speak of contrastive intonation, or more specifically of contrastive stress or contrastive accent, even though the term *contrast* has also been used in a much wider sense (see, e.g., Steedman 1994). Intuitively speaking, the accents indicated in (1) and (2) express a *contrast* (cf. the notion of contrast in visual perception) between different expressions. For example, *Mozart* and *Bach* are such contrasted expressions, and likewise, the two sentential conjuncts of (1) are also said to be in contrast. Chomsky wrote in connection with (2) that "in 'parallel constructions' ... contrastive intonation is necessary," but he added that it had never been made quite clear what this notion of "parallel constructions" signifies (Chomsky 1971). Also, there is no obvious physical difference that forms the basis of the distinction between contrastive and other accents. All of this makes *contrast* a somewhat problematic notion, which has so far largely defied formalization. The present chapter will stick to the intuitive label *contrast* and try to formalize the intuition behind it. In addition, it is assumed that all the expressions that are designated as contrasted must be accented in speech, and this is where our formalization makes its actual predictions. The possibility of a practical application is briefly mentioned in Section 4.

Imagine two expressions, a and b, that are, in principle, contrastable. (See Section 3 for details.) For example, expression a is a proper name that refers to the person x, and it does so in the context of the sentence S_a, while expression b refers to another person y, doing so in the context of the sentence S_b. It seems clear that a proper theory of contrastive stress has to specify under which conditions a and b can be contrasted. Yet, not much work seems to have been done toward formalizing the conditions that determine whether two sentences are contrastable.[5] One possibility for a theory of contrastive stress is to turn to theories of parallelism, as have come up in relation to other linguistic phenomena. By now, some partial formalizations of parallelism have been proposed. For example, Prüst has proposed a notion of parallelism to account for VP anaphora and several related phenomena (Prüst 1992).[6] Characteristically, however, his proposal implies a rather strict *syntactic* parallelism. This is no coincidence. The notion of parallelism seems hard to conceive of in a completely nonsyntactic way. Thus it may be that parallelism can account for such cases of contrastive stress as Rooth's (3) and possibly even for such cases as (2).

(3)   An [+]American farmer talked to a [+]Canadian farmer.

However, a theory based on parallelism cannot account for contrast between such syntactically dissimilar sentences as the two constituent sentences of the following pairs:

(4) $^+$Seven has no divisors; $^+$eight is a power of two.

(5) $^+$Grandma drives 200 m.p.h.; $^+$daddy never violates the speed limits.

(6)   I bought a $^+$novel from the bookshop, but Tom sold me an entire $^+$encyclo-pedia.

(Once more, the words that are marked as accented must be accented even if they constitute given information.) For example, consider (5). There is no more (syntactic) parallelism between the first and the second conjunct than there is between the first conjunct and, say, *daddy never knew that*, and yet the conjuncts in (5) require contrastive accent and those in (5′) do not:

(5′)   Grandma drives 200 m.p.h.; daddy never knew that.

We will assume that a properly formalized notion of parallelism is a sufficient, but not a necessary condition for contrastive stress. In what follows, one other sufficient condition for contrastive stress, which will be able to account for such cases as (4)–(6), will be explored. Yet other sources of contrastive accent must wait for further research.

Rooth observed that "in many examples, theoretical accounts based on a semantics of contrast are in competition with ones based on a semantics of anaphora," that is, on a semantics of givenness. Consequently, it is desirable to deal with contrast, novelty, and givenness in one framework. Therefore, we will now first sketch a little theory of novelty and givenness, and then indicate how contrastiveness fits in.

2   Novelty and Contrastiveness as Sources of Accent

A proposal for how given/new status of information may be relevant for noun phrase accenting has been put forward in van Deemter 1994 and van Deemter et al. 1994. The general idea is as follows. Much of what is said in a discourse can be interpreted in basically two ways, namely, as true of the entire domain of discourse or as true of some contextually determined subdomain. This holds, among other things, for the descriptive information contained in a noun phrase. For example, consider (7):

(7)   a. The children were upstairs.
         b. The girls were having fun.

Here the descriptive information that is contained in the NP *the girls* (roughly: 'The set x contains all the girls') may be true of the set that is introduced by it, but it may also be that it is only true "against the background" of an earlier-introduced set, namely, that of all the children that are mentioned in the first sentence. In the latter case, what it says is that the set contains all the girls that are *also* elements of this set of children, and the predicate *were having fun* in (7b) is used to assert that all of those (i.e., the elements of Girls ∩ Children) were having fun. Technically, this may be modeled through Dag Westerståhl's method of using *context sets* to restrict the first argument of a generalized quantifier (Westerståhl 1985, van Deemter 1992).

Let us stick to this second interpretation of the discourse for a while, and call it its "anaphoric" interpretation, stretching that notion somewhat beyond its traditional meaning. Now two possibilities may be distinguished: either all the children happen to be girls or some of them are boys. In the first case, we speak of *identity anaphora*, since the NP *the girls* refers to an already-introduced set of individuals. In the second case, we speak of *nonidentity anaphora*, because the set of girls is introduced through a relation with an already-familiar entity (hence the designation "anaphoric"), but this relation is not the relation of identity: the set of female children is carved out, so to speak, from the larger set of children. Now as it happens, there is a connection between having identity anaphora and appearing unaccented. More precisely, if an NP can be construed as standing in a relation of identity anaphora to another NP then it need not be accented, but in any other case (including the one where it has to be construed as standing in a relation of nonidentity anaphora), there is a strong tendency for the NP to be accented.

If a constituent is accented, Focus-Accent Theory offers rules that determine what word in the constituent the accent must trickle down to. These rules make use of so-called metrical trees, which represent the syntactic structure of a sentence in the form of a binary tree. For example, if the phrase *the author of a sonata* is used to introduce a new individual into the discourse, it needs to be accented. Focus-Accent Theory predicts that, normally, the accent will land on *sonata*. However, there can be several reasons why accent is prevented from going to that part of the syntax tree, and these are covered by the so-called *Default Accent* rule (Ladd 1980). In van Deemter 1994, it has been proposed that deaccenting of a word can take place for two reasons. The first is that the word is part of an NP that has identity anaphora to some other NP, as in (8), where it is assumed that *this sonata* refers to *this piece of music*:

(8)   Look at this piece of music. [The ⁺composer of [this ⁻sonata]] must have been a funny guy!

Suppose *The composer of this sonata* constitutes new information, so it has to be accented. If only syntax were taken into account, this would mean that *sonata* is accented, but since *this sonata* has identity anaphora to some already-established discourse entity, the Default Accent rule will move the accent to *composer*. Note that this happens even if the word *sonata* has not been mentioned before. The second reason for deaccenting occurs, roughly, when the word that would normally receive accent has occurred in the very recent past, or when a subsumed (i.e., extensionally included) word has done that. Note that this makes concept-givenness a nonsymmetrical relation, since a word may now be deaccented because of a subsumed word, but not the other way round. For example, in (9a), *string instruments* can be deaccented because of the extensionally included *viola*. In (9b), however, *viola* cannot be deaccented because of the subsuming (i.e., extensionally including) *string instruments*.

(9)   a. Bach wrote many pieces for $^+$viola; he must have loved $^-$string $^-$instruments.

        b. Bach wrote many pieces for $^+$string instruments; he must have loved the $^+$viola.

Note that some of the work that might be done by a theory of *contrast* can also be done by a theory of givenness, provided it allows for "anticipatory" deaccenting (Cruttenden 1986).[7] For example, consider (1), here repeated as (10).

(10) $^+$Mozart wrote $^+$few $^-$fugues, but $^+$Bach wrote $^+$many $^-$fugues.

The accent on *many* can be explained straightforwardly by making use of the Default Accent rule: *fugues* constitutes given information, and consequently, accent must land on *many*. Slightly harder to account for is the accenting on *few fugues*. It occurs earlier than *many fugues*, so *fugues* does not constitute given information yet. To account for the accent on *few*, one might define a notion of givenness that looks forward as well as backward. Note, however, that such a mechanism cannot account for contrastive accent in cases where there is little common material. One kind of case is illustrated by the occurrences of *Bach* and *Mozart* in (10), which are accented, but not as a result of an application of the *Default Accent* rule, since there is no common material to trigger this rule. Other kinds of cases are illustrated in (4–6). Once more, nothing is deaccented, and yet the accent lands on a word (*seven, eight, Grandma*, etc.) that might happen to express given information. This shows that, in addition to "givenness" accounts of accent, no matter how liberal, a genuine account of contrast has to be provided.[8]

Granted that both novelty and contrastiveness need accounting for, how are the two related? Space does not allow extensive discussion of this issue – and of the more general question of how all the different semantic factors involved in accenting interact – and these will be discussed elsewhere. What follows is a very rough outline.

I will assume that contrast is completely on a par with novelty: an expression can be marked as new (i.e., it is not identity anaphoric), and it can also be marked as contrasted with something. In either case, it is accented. Also in either case, the Default Accent rule may apply. For example, consider examples (1) and (2) again, with the phrases $^+$*few fugues*, $^+$*many fugues* and $^+$*eager to please*, $^+$*easy to please*, $^+$*certain to please*, respectively. In all these examples, the main accent has shifted away from the words (*fugues, please*) where it would normally go. As has already been noted, however, deaccenting occurs in both directions: In (10), the first occurrence of *fugues* is deaccented because of the second occurrence, just as the second occurrence is deaccented because of the first. Deaccenting has to become a bidirectional affair. The most interesting case is that of concept-givenness, where it seems that the nonsymmetry that has been noted in connection with (9a, b) disappears when deaccenting applies between two expressions that are parts of contrasted expressions. For example, in (11) the lack of an accent on *viola* does not seem warranted, precisely because not all instruments are violas.[9]

(11)*   Bach owned an $^+$old $^-$viola; Mozart owned a $^+$new $^-$instrument.

On the other hand, we have seen that bidirectional deaccenting within contrastive constructions does apply between words that have *the same* denotation. Thus, we will make the following hypothesis. Deaccenting of a word occurrence w that is part of an informationally new constituent c applies if w *subsumes* a recent word occurrence w', unless c is also contrasted with some other constituent. Deaccenting of a word occurrence w that is part of a constituent that is contrasted with some other constituent applies only if the word is extensionally *identical* with a recent word occurrence w'. (The precise meaning of *recent* is one of the things that have to be made more precise.) If a variety of this hypothesis is correct, it may be accounted for by taking the notion of 'anticipatory deaccenting' seriously, and by looking at w and w' separately: For w to be deaccented, it has to subsume w', but for w' to be deaccented by the future occurrence of w, w' has to subsume w. Consequently, bidirectional deaccenting is (correctly) predicted to occur only if w and w' are extensionally equal, as is the case in (10), for example.

After these remarks on deaccenting, we now turn to a formalization of the conditions under which two expressions are contrasted.

3   Toward a Formalization of the Notion of Contrast

We have seen that syntactic parallelism is one possible source of contrastive accent. I will now try to show how another source of contrast is related to the Aristotelian notion of *contrariety*. Two propositions are *contraries* if it is impossible for them to be true at the same time. Thus, *Mozart wrote (exactly) 23 string quartets* and *Mozart wrote (exactly) 24 string quartets* are contraries. Note that this definition causes contraries to include *contradictories*, which can be neither true at the same time nor false at the same time. Thus, *Mozart wrote at least 23 string quartets* will also be called a contrary of *Mozart wrote fewer than 23 string quartets*. Formally, if S denotes p and S' denotes p', we will write $C[S, S']$ (read: 'S and S' are contraries') to say that $\models p \rightarrow \neg p'$. In other words, $C[S, S']$ holds if $p \rightarrow \neg p'$ is a logical truth.[10]

Using contrariety as a direct formalization of contrast would account for some cases of contrastive accent, as in

(12)   It's not true that Mozart wrote $^+$24 string quartets; he wrote $^+$23 string quartets!

But when two propositions are contrasted, it is usually not these propositions themselves that are logical contraries, but some related propositions. For instance, in (13) the propositions expressed by the two conjuncts do not stand in the relation of contrariety.

(13) $^+$Bach was an organ mechanic; $^+$Mozart knew little about organs.

Note, however, that when *Mozart* replaces *Bach*, the two conjuncts do express contraries, at least under some plausible assumptions about organ mechanics (see section 4). Likewise, in (14) the propositions that are expressed in the two conjuncts do not stand in the relation of contrariety, but if *John* and *Peter* are replaced by an arbitrary constant as in (15), then the resulting conjuncts do express contraries at least in a monogamous society.

(14) $^+$John is married to $^+$Mary and $^+$Peter is married to $^+$Sally.

(15)   a is married to Mary and a is married to Sally.

More precisely, the two propositions p_1 and p_2 that are expressed by the two conjuncts of (15) are contraries given the assumption of monogamy (m). Thus, $m \models (p_1 \rightarrow \neg p_2)$. Now consider a polygamous society of the type where a man can have several wives but not the other way round. Then no contrariety is expressed by (15), and yet (14) would still tend to be uttered with contrastive stress as indicated. This is explained by the fact that another substitution can be made, resulting in (16).

(16)   John is married to b and Peter is married to b.

As is easy to see, (16) contains a contrariety, even in the new situation. Only in a society that allows several marital partners to both men and women would the substitution trick fail to predict the indicated accents, and then no accents are predicted, except of course as a result of other 'accent triggers' than contrariety, such as novelty of information or strong emotional involvement. Thus, we will consider contrastive stress as legitimized in a pair of sentences that are associated – through a substitution that causes a position in one sentence to be identical to one in another sentence – with a pair of sentences that stand in the relation of contrariety. The case in which the sentences themselves are contraries falls out as a boundary case.

Observe that, in the situation of a male-dominated polygamous society, (14) does not only have accents on *Mary* and *Sally*, but on *John* and *Peter* as well. The latter will be viewed as side effects of the contrariety induced by the substitution in (16). Our main task, at this point, is to predict in which cases two sentences are in contrast to each other. The question of where the accents will land will be briefly taken up at the end of this section.

An important question is, at what level the relation of contrast should be defined. Two options present themselves: the level of the actual sentence and the semantic level (i.e., that of the propositions expressed). We take it that the sentence level is the appropriate level, since this contains all kinds of details that are lost in semantic analysis, such as the words that are used. However, meaning *is* relevant, so let us assume that a sentence comes with a unique analysis, through which it is disambiguated. Thus, we assume that the syntactic constituents of the sentence are known, and so is its intended interpretation. Let $S_{x_1,\dots,x_k}$ be a way to partition a sentence S into nonoverlapping constituents $x_1, \dots, x_k$. We will assume that there are very few limitations as to what can count as a constituent. At one end of the scale, even *morphemes* can be contrasted (e.g., *The farmers practiced* (^+in)*tensive, rather than* (^+ex)*tensive agriculture*).[11] At the other end of the scale, there are entire sentences. We will assume that these, too, can be contrasted, but since the effect is probably indistinguishable from ordinary sentence stress, this is a less than crucial decision.

Now let $\bowtie$ denote the relation of contrast, and let $\bowtie$ be superscripted by the pair of expressions that stand in contrast to each other. Let a be an arbitrary constant of the right category. Then:

Contrastable sentences:

$$\left(S_{m_1, \dots, m_i, \dots, m_k} \overset{\langle m_i, n_y \rangle}{\bowtie} S'_{n_1, \dots, n_y, \dots, n_l} \right)$$

$$\Leftrightarrow_{Def} C \left[S_{m_1, \dots, a, \dots, m_k}, \; S'_{n_1, \dots, a, \dots, n_l} \right]$$

In other words, $(S_{m_1,\dots,m_i,\dots,m_k} \overset{\langle m_i,n_y \rangle}{\bowtie} S'_{n_1,\dots,n_y,\dots,n_l})$ means that a contrariety can be achieved between $S_{m_1,\dots,m_i,\dots,m_k}$ and $S'_{n_1,\dots,n_y,\dots,n_l}$ by means of an *identifying substitution* for the constituents m_i and n_y. An example is (13), here repeated as (17) with Bach $= m_i$ and Mozart $= n_y$.

(17) $^+$Bach was an organ mechanic; $^+$Mozart knew little about organs.

As has been indicated in section 1, conditions on contrastable *sentences* are not enough. A theory of contrastive stress must also say which expressions are contrastable *expressions*, or items. For example, two occurrences of the name *Mozart* are not normally contrastable. It will be assumed that *inequality of denotations* is the sole condition that determines whether expressions are contrastable. For example, two occurrences of the same name are not contrastable unless they are used as names for the same person. Likewise, a name and a pronoun cannot be contrasted if they corefer. Contrastability is tantamount to inequality of denotations. To save this claim from being falsified in epistemic contexts, however, one has to make the Fregean assumption that in such contexts, denotation equals meaning (or intension) rather than extension. Thus, in (18), *Bach* and *the composer of The Musical Offering* are contrastable items, because (18) is an epistemic context, even though Bach was the composer of *The Musical Offering*.

(18)   Mary knows that the composer of *The Musical* $^+$*Offering* was a genius, but she does not know that $^+$Bach was a genius.

Something analogous holds in a number of other contexts, including various kinds of quotation, as in (19) where *Theophilus* refers to the name "Theophilus," and *Amadeus* refers to the name "Amadeus."

(19)   Mozart's Christian name was $^+$Theophilus, not $^+$Amadeus.

The following formalization summarizes our proposal:[12]

> **Contrastive accent:** Two analyzed sentences α and α' stand in the relation of contrast in case their constituents can be grouped as $\alpha_{m_1,\dots,m_i,\dots,m_j,\dots,m_k}$ and $\alpha'_{n_1,\dots,n_x,\dots,n_y,\dots,n_l}$, respectively, while the following two conditions hold:
>
> (i)   the two elements of the pair $\langle m_i, n_y \rangle$ are contrastable items; and
>
> (ii) $(\alpha_{m_1,\dots,m_i,\dots,m_j,\dots,m_k} \overset{\langle m_i, n_y \rangle}{\bowtie} \alpha'_{n_1,\dots,n_x,\dots,n_y,\dots,n_l})$.
>
> If both conditions hold, $\langle m_i, n_y \rangle$ will be called a *contrast pair*.

If two analyzed sentences α and β stand in the relation of contrast, while $\langle w_1, w_2 \rangle$ is a contrast pair, then α and β must be accented to reflect the contrast. *Where* exactly the accents materialize is a question that cannot be answered in the present chapter, since it involves more details of Focus-Accent Theory than can be assumed at this point. Instead, we will sketch the procedure informally. Normally (but cf. Section 4), both elements of the contrast pair, w_1 and w_2, are accented. In addition, we will assume, for simplicity, that contrastability of items is not an issue, and then we claim that, in each of α and α', at least one additional accent has to occur. Because of its use of binary syntactic trees, Focus-Accent Theory allows a precise bipartition of any sentence in what may be termed a subject and a predicate. Now for each of α, α', the expression in the contrast pair (i.e., w_1 or w_2) must occur either in the subject or in the predicate. If it occurs in (or coincides with) the subject (as is the case in most of the examples in this chapter), then the additional accent must be located in the predicate; conversely, if the expression in the contrast pair occurs in the predicate (as in (16)), then the additional accent must be located in the subject. In both cases, the standard mechanism of Focus-Accent Theory (cf. Section 2 for an impression) determines the word within the subject/predicate where the accent lands.

For example, consider example (17). First, *Bach* and *Mozart* belong to the contrast pair and are therefore accented. Second, accents are located in the predicates. In the predicate *was an organ mechanic*, the accent trickles down to its normal place, *organ*, or else, if anticipatory deaccenting is applied, the accent shifts to *mechanic*. In the predicate *knew little about organs*, the word *organs* must be deaccented, and accent lands on *about*, or else on *little*, if the preposition *about* is prevented from carrying an accent. Thus, one derives the following possible accent patterns:

(17)   a.   Bach was an $^+$organ mechanic; $^+$Mozart knew little $^+$about organs.
         b.   Bach was an $^+$organ mechanic; $^+$Mozart knew $^+$little about organs.
         c. $^+$Bach was an organ $^+$mechanic; $^+$Mozart knew little $^+$about organs.
         d. $^+$Bach was an organ $^+$mechanic; $^+$Mozart knew $^+$little about organs.

A couple of remarks on *how* contrastive accents are realized are made in Section 4.

4   Remaining Issues

This concludes a modest attempt to conquer a piece of prosodic territory using formal weaponry. But a cautionary note should be added: intonation is a difficult area, and we are only beginning to get an understanding of how properties of intonation are connected with linguistic concepts. This seems mainly due to the intrinsic difficulty of these concepts, and perhaps partly to differences between individual speakers and hearers. Some useful abstractions are now beginning to emerge, especially in connection with intonational focusing, and I hope contrariety is becoming one of them. At the present stage, however, most work that connects intonation and semantics/pragmatics is necessarily of a rather tentative nature, and it is much in need of theoretical underpinning (witness, for example, the many different ways in which such key notions as *focus* are currently used), as well as of empirical verification. Proper empirical verification is not easy to accomplish, since it will have to involve more than a few isolated sentences, and since it is essential that the evaluation does not rely on the subjects' mastery of theory-laden terms (including the words *accent, stress,* and *prominence*). Perhaps the main asset of this chapter is the notion that different 'triggers' for accenting seem to operate in basically the same fashion: they cause constituents to be accented, while Focus-Accent Theory (in cooperation with a semantics-based deaccenting mechanism) determines at what exact word the accent must fall. Now for some remaining issues, which cannot be dealt with at length in this chapter and will be discussed in more detail elsewhere.

4.1   *Other Sources of Accent*

It has been claimed that contrariety (modulo identifying substitutions) is one factor that triggers accenting. It should be stressed that contrariety and novelty of information do not exhaust the set of accent triggers. One possible accent trigger that ought to be mentioned because of its similarity to the one that was discussed in this chapter is the following. Consider the following variant of sentence (4):

(4′) $^+$Seven is a prime number and so is $^+$thirteen.

Contrariety cannot explain this accent pattern, for if *thirteen* is replaced by *seven*, no contrariety results. However, another logical oddity does result, namely, redundancy of information:

(20)   Seven is a prime number and so is seven.

the two conjuncts of which are logically equivalent. What this type of example suggests is that equivalence (modulo identifying substitutions) works much as contrariety (modulo identifying substitutions) does. The same formal account can be used as in section 3, except that the notation $C[S_{m_1,...,a,...,m_k}, S'_{n_1,...,a,...,n_l}]$ is replaced by $E[S_{m_1,...,a,...,m_k}, S'_{n_1,...,a,...,n_l}]$, where E denotes logical equivalence.[13]

In the case of (4′), syntactic parallelism could provide an alternative explanation of the accent pattern, but more difficult examples, where no strict syntactic parallelism can be found, are easily constructed.

4.2   Interpretation and Implicature

There are many cases that do involve contrariety and yet are not covered directly by the mechanism of the previous section. Consider the example $^+$*Bach was an organ mechanic;* $^+$*Mozart knew little about organs.* Is there really a contrariety between being an organ mechanic and knowing little about organs? This is only true under certain assumptions. Taking the perspective of speech interpretation, one might take the following perspective: If a pair of sentences are uttered with stress, and if this stress cannot be explained through other factors, then it has to be a case of contrariety. If the sentences do not stand in the relation of "contrariety modulo identifying substitutions" that has been detailed in this chapter, assumptions have to be made that cause them to stand in this relation. For example, in the *organ* example, one assumption that does the trick says that 'being an x-mechanic' implies knowing much about x. This assumption has the status of an implicature, rather than that of an assertion. The choice of a suitable assumption might best be modeled through an *abduction* process as proposed by Hobbs and others (Hobbs et al. 1990), in which the epistemic "cost" of an assumption can be taken into account. Note that similar remarks apply to the semantic import of "information status"-type accenting. For example, if it is used anaphorically with the set Children as its antecedent, *the girls* (cf. Section 2) must always refer to the set Girls ∩ Children. Arguably, the import of an accent on *girls* is to express the *presupposition* that not all of the children are girls, and the reverse holds for the lack of an accent.

A final example of implicature arises when an accenting pattern suggests that some other sentence has been uttered, whereas in fact it has not. For example, if the speaker at a colloquium says (21), then if he or she stresses *decent*, there is a strong hint that some (contextually salient) colloquium organizer is not so decent.

(21)   Any decent colloquium organizer gives you a nice introduction.

Elliptic cases like this are obviously hard to resolve, but it is clear that accenting can play an important role in them.

A related case of indirect contrariety arises when one of the contrasted sentences is ambiguous, while some interpretations lead to contrariety and others do not. For example, in (22) the deaccenting of *financial institution* can only be explained (through concept-givenness) if *bank* is understood as denoting a financial institution.

(22)   John went to a bank. When $^+$I go to a $^-$financial $^-$institution, (etc.).

As a result, readings of the word *bank* that are incompatible with being a financial institution will be discarded. Stress can also cause a vague expression to become more precise. For example, this is the case in (23), which forces an interpretation on the vague quantifier *numerous* that exceeds 30.

(23) $^+$Mozart wrote fewer than $^+$30 string quartets, but $^+$Haydn wrote $^+$numerous string quartets.

4.3   Physical Realization

Little has been said in this chapter about the physical realization of contrastive accents. It has been assumed that all contrasted items have to be uttered as accented, and it has not been assumed that there are any physical properties that distinguish the different kinds of accent (cf. note 1). Regarding the first assumption, a qualification is needed, since the accent on the very first item (in a list of items contrasted) seems to be optional. Thus, if Mozart has been mentioned in the previous sentence, (1) may be uttered without accents on *Mozart* and *few*:

(1') $^-$Mozart wrote $^-$few $^+$fugues, but $^+$Bach wrote $^+$many fugues.

This can happen, for example, if the speaker has not planned on saying the second conjunct, or if he does not become fully aware of the contrariety until after the first conjunct has been uttered.

Regarding the issue of physical difference, it should be noted that no physical or even perceptual difference is excluded by our account. The issue of whether such a difference exists seems undecided at this point. Pierrehumbert and Hirschberg hypothesized that contrastive accents were characterized by so-called $L + H^*$ accents, in which pitch falls to a low (L) pitch level before it rises rapidly to a high (H) level, while novelty accents are characterized by a so-called H^* accent, in which pitch rises directly, and less steeply, to that same high level (Pierrehumbert and Hirschberg 1990). More recently, however, Bartels and Kingston were unable to confirm this hypothesis in experimental work, finding evidence instead that contrastive accents might be characterized by greater peak height than novelty accents (Bartels and Kingston 1994). Note that even if an individual "contrastive" accent would turn out to be indistinguishable from a "novelty" accent, as is often assumed (Ladd 1980), it may be that the pattern of accents in the entire utterance can help to determine whether a given accent is contrastive.[14] Be this as it may. If and when it is possible to measure whether a given intonation contour is a contrastive accent, as opposed to one that has a different source, it will become easier to verify a theory such as the one outlined in the present chapter, and it would also add to its potential for application in speech understanding systems.

4.4   A Possible Application

The work reported in this chapter has been done in the context of the 'Dial Your Disc' (DYD) project (Collier and Landsbergen 1995, van Deemter et al. 1994). In

DYD, spoken monologues are generated on the basis of a database of facts about the music of W. A. Mozart, in combination with syntactic templates that determine the basic structure of the sentences that can be generated. A concept-to-speech system like DYD forms an ideal test bed for theories of accenting, such as the one discussed in the present chapter. The current implementation of DYD involves accenting of new (i.e., other than identity-anaphoric) information, as well as the two types of deaccenting that were pointed out in Section 2 of the present chapter. Moreover, contrastive accents are hand-coded in the syntactic templates that form the basis of language generation in DYD. Although the current, alternative proposal for the treatment of contrastive accents involves semantic considerations that are difficult to mechanize, the notion of 'contrariety modulo identifying substitutions' should not be overly problematic in the setting of a Prolog theorem prover.

Notes

1   I will follow 't Hart et al. (1990) in considering accent as the phenomenon that speech melody can make some parts of an utterance stand out as prominent. Thus, accent is viewed as one single phenomenon, the linguistic properties of which can be studied without taking its different possible realizations into account. (Compare, e.g., Steedman 1996, this volume, for a different perspective, in which distinctions are made between various kinds of accents.) Since changes in (F_0) pitch have been found to be the single most prevalent determinant of accents, the expression *pitch accent* is often used in this tradition. See also Section 4 for a brief discussion.

2   See, for example, Baart (1987) and Dirksen (1992) for a version of Focus-Accent Theory. In van Deemter (1994), an integration is attempted of Dirksen's version of Focus-Accent Theory and the considerations of information status that are sketched in section 2. For an alternative to this version of Focus-Accent Theory, see, for example, Cinque (1993) or Jacobs, this volume.

3   In our examples, the notation $^+\alpha$ designates a pitch accent, no matter how it is realized. (See, e.g., 't Hart et al. 1990.) Conversely, $^-\alpha$ designates the absence of an accent. If a word is not marked by either of these notations, it is left open whether the word appears accented or not. Thus, our indication of accenting in example sentences is by no means intended to be complete.

4   For now, the discussion will focus on the contrast between *Bach* and *Mozart*. The accents on *few* and *many* are briefly discussed in Section 2 (see example (10)).

5   In Rooth's sketch of an account of contrast, for example, two items are predicted to trigger contrastive accent in case one of the two is an element of the set of alternatives that is associated with the other (Rooth 1992). But unless some constraints on what constitutes a contrastable position are added, such an account predicts contrastive accent on any proper name of a person, provided another person is named in the same discourse (e.g., ^+Bill *was talking to* ^+Harry, in a situation in which both *Bill* and *Harry* constitute given information).

6   Prüst's parallelism requires that the terms appearing in the semantic representations of two expressions must be sufficiently similar, or in his terms, "characteristically generalizable," which means that "they are generalizable to an object that exhibits important characteristics of both terms." The notion of an *important characteristic* defies complete formalization, according to Prüst, because what counts as an important

characteristic may vary from context to context. See also Dalrymple et al. (1991), where similar conclusions are drawn.

7   Something along the lines of anticipatory deaccenting will be necessary in our own account as well, as will become clear presently.

8   See Ladd (1980) for a more elaborate discussion of this issue, in terms of a figure/ground metaphor.

9   As several people pointed out to me, the indicated accent pattern *is* acceptable in case the second conjunct is used to say that Mozart owned a new *viola*. See Section 4 for a brief discussion of how contrastive stress can affect interpretation.

10 Thus, $\models p \rightarrow \neg p'$ means that p and p' are such that if p is true, p' has to be false. It follows that, conversely, if p' is true, p has to be false. Note that $C[S, S']$ will always hold if either or both of S and S' express a logical falsehood. It seems no serious limitation, however to exclude logical falsehoods from consideration and to focus on contingent propositions, with the semantics of which it is easier to come to grips. (Cf. Note 13.)

11 The question of what constitutes the smallest linguistic entity that can be accented because it stands in contrast to something else is discussed in van Heuven (1994). Many of his examples, however, rely on some form of quotation. If quotation contexts are allowed, then even phonemes are contrastable (*I said pit, not bit*; cf. van Heuven (1994:79), but quotation contexts are better viewed as a separate issue, as will be argued in connection with examples (18) and (19).

12 An alternative formulation would make contrastibility of items a part of the definition of contrastable sentences, so that the $\bowtie$ relation can only list pairs that are actually contrastable.

13 Logical equivalence between p and p' amounts, formally, to $\models p \leftrightarrow p'$. Note that the relation $E[S, S']$ will always hold if both of S and S' express logical truths, no matter their respective subject matter. As in the case of contrariety, however (Note 10), the limitation to contingent sentences seems both difficult to avoid and unproblematic.

14 For example, it may happen that all the items that are contrasted in a given utterance are of "type 5", that is, the type of a "fast, early, half-rise" ('t Hart et al. 1990), and it may be this pattern that causes the accents to stand out as contrastive.

References

Baart, J.L.G. 1987. Focus, Syntax and Accent Placement. Ph.D. thesis, Leyden University, The Netherlands.

Bartels, C., and J. Kingston. 1994. Salient Pitch Cues in the Perception of Contrastive Focus. In P. Bosch and R. van der Sandt (eds.), *Focus & Natural Language Processing*, Proceedings of the 'Journal of Semantics' conference on Focus. IBM Working Papers, TR-80.94-006.

Chafe, W.L. 1976. Givenness, Contrastiveness, Definiteness, Subjects, Topics and Points of View. In C.N.Li (ed.), *Subject and Topic*. Academic Press, New York.

Chomsky, N. 1971. Deep Structure, Surface Structure, and Semantic Interpretation. In D. Steinberg and L. Jakobovits, eds. 'Semantics: An interdisciplinary reader in Philosophy, Linguistics and Psychology', Cambridge University Press, Cambridge.

Cinque, G. 1993. A Null Theory of Phrase and Compound Stress. *Linguistic Inquiry*, 24(2): 239–297.

Collier, R., and J. Landsbergen. 1995. Language and Speech Generation. Philips Journal of Research. 49:419–437.

Cruttenden, A. 1986. *Intonation*. Cambridge University Press, Cambridge.

Dalrymple, M.; Schieber, S.; and Pereira, F. 1991. Ellipsis and Higher-Order Unification. *Linguistics and Philosophy* 14:399–452.

Deemter, K. van. 1992. Towards a Generalization of Anaphora. *Journal of Semantics* 9(1): 27–51.

Deemter, K. van. 1994. What's New? A Semantic Perspective on Sentence Accent. *Journal of Semantics* 11:1–31.

van Deemter, K., and Odijk, J. 1997. Context Modeling and the Generation of Spoken Discourse. Speech Communication 21, 101–121.

Dirksen, A. 1992. Accenting and Deaccenting: A Declarative Approach. *Proceedings of Coling Conference*, Nantes, France.

Halliday, M. A. K. 1967. Notes on Transitivity and Theme in English. *Journal of Linguistics* 3:199–244.

't Hart, J.; Collier, R.; and Cohen, A. 1990. *A Perceptual Study of Intonation: An Experimental Phonetic Approach to Speech Melody.* Cambridge University Press, Cambridge.

Heuven, V. J. van. 1994. What is the Smallest Prosodic Domain? In P.A. Keating (ed.), *Phonological Structure and Phonetic Form.* Papers in Laboratory Phonology III, Cambridge University Press, Cambridge.

Hobbs, J. R.; Stickel, M.; Appelt, D.; and Martin, P. 1990. Interpretation as Abduction. SRI International, Technical Note 499.

Jacobs, J. Informational Autonomy. (In this volume.)

Ladd, D. R. 1980. The Structure of Intonational Meaning: Evidence from English. Indiana University Press, Bloomington.

Pierrehumbert, J., and Hirschberg, J. 1990. The Meaning of Intonational Contours in the Interpretation of Discourse. In P. Cohen, J. Margan, and M. Pollack (Eds.), *Intentions in Communication.* MIT Press, Cambridge MA.

Prüst, H. 1992. On Discourse Structuring, VP Anaphora and Gapping. Ph.D. dissertation, University of Amsterdam.

Rooth, M. 1992. A Theory of Focus Interpretation. *Natural Language Semantics* 1:75–116.

Steedman, M. 1994. Remarks on Intonation and 'Focus'. In P. Bosch and R.v.d. Sandt (Eds.), *Focus and Natural Language Processing.* IBM Deutschland GmbH. Heidelberg. Vol. 1: 185–204.

Westerståhl, D. 1985. Determiners and Context Sets. In J. van Benthem and A. ter Meulen (Eds.), *Generalized Quantifiers in Natural Language.* Foris, GRASS-4, Dordrecht (Holland)/Cinna minson (USA).

2 The Processing of Information Structure

CARSTEN GÜNTHER, CLAUDIA MAIENBORN,
AND ANDREA SCHOPP

Abstract

This chapter sketches an integrated view on processing information structure in a cognitively motivated computational linguistic model of language production. The approach extends from computing the information structure of an utterance out of a conceptual structure and a relevant contextual embedding to its corresponding prosodic realization. Apparently conflicting requirements of structurally oriented theories of information structure, on the one hand, and incrementality as one major property of human language processing, on the other hand, are shown to be reconcilable within the language production system advocated here.

1 Introduction

Within theoretical linguistics, information structure is generally seen as a phenomenon that concerns propositional units. Current theories of information structure consider whole sentences as the relevant level at which relational notions such as focus/background structure and topic/comment structure are determined (cf., e.g., Jacobs 1992, this volume). From the viewpoint of language processing, however, the sentence level is surely ruled out as a primary processing unit. Research in psycholinguistics as well as in computational linguistics has shown that incrementality is an essential property of efficient language processing (cf., e.g., Kempen and Hoenkamp 1987, Levelt 1989). This means that the components of a processing system for language production or understanding are enabled to process fragmentary input (so-called increments) rather than processing only complete input structures. While increments pass sequentially through succeeding processing components, each component operates in parallel on a distinct fragment of the input structure.[1]

Thus, the question arises of how the declarative view on information structure taken within theoretical linguistics can be brought into accord with a procedural model of language processing pursued within psycholinguistics. That is, how is information structuring performed under the circumstances of incremental language

The work reported on here was carried out in a research project funded by the German Science Foundation (DFG) within the research program of Cognitive Linguistics under grant no. Ha 1237/4. We would like to thank Bernd Abb, Uta Arnold, Ingo Schröder, and Soenke Ziesche for their substantial contributions to the design and implementation of the SYNPHONICS system.

18

processing? An answer to this question might allow us to draw some conclusions about the validity of both theoretical linguistic models of information structure as well as psycholinguistic models of language processing.

In this chapter, we concentrate on focus/background structure, that is, the dimension of information structure that divides a proposition into an informationally more relevant (new) part, that is, the *focus*, and a less relevant part that is mutually known by the speaker and the hearer, that is, the *background*. The goal of the chapter is to provide a procedural account of focus/background structure within language production.[2] This comprises the issue of generating a focus/background structure in the course of building up the propositional content of an utterance and its subsequent grammatical realization. In a language like German, which we have chosen as output language, grammatical realization of focus/background structure is accomplished primarily by prosodic means. As concerns the semantic foundation of focus/background structure, emphasis will be placed on reconstructing the formal notion of *alternative sets* referred to in theoretical linguistic approaches to the semantics of focus since the work of Rooth (1985) in cognitive linguistic terms that are suitable for a psycholinguistically biased model of language production.

The computational linguistic model of language production proposed here is being developed within the SYNPHONICS project (*Syn*tactic and *Phon*ological realization of *I*ncrementally Generated *C*onceptual *S*tructures), which aims at linking psycholinguistic insights with well established assumptions in theoretical linguistics. In Section 2, we shall give a brief overview of the SYNPHONICS system with special emphasis on the basic foundations that are relevant for our present topic. Section 3 elaborates our account of incrementally computing focus/background structure. It will be shown how a global focus/background structure for a propositional unit is built up under recourse to local focus information of single propositional fragments. Section 4 deals with the incremental realization of information structuring in terms of accent assignment. Both processing steps, semantic computation as well as phonological realization of focus/background structure, will turn out to benefit crucially from independently motivated properties of the SYNPHONICS system.

For expository reasons, we will use rather simple examples in order to illustrate the procedural approach to the different configurations of information structure that are of interest here (viz. wide focus, narrow focus, contrastive focus, and double focus). The general account claims to have a broader coverage, though. It has proved to provide an adequate basis for dealing with more intricate cases of focus/background structure, which can be found, for instance, in the domain of adjuncts too (cf. Maienborn 1994).

2   Overview of the Language-Production System SYNPHONICS

The SYNPHONICS project adopts a cognitive approach to a computational linguistic model of language production that combines results from psycholinguistic research about the time course of human language production with recent developments in theoretical linguistics concerning the representation of semantic, syntactic, phonological, and phonetic knowledge. The aim of the project consists in developing a system that covers the incremental generation of utterances from prelinguistic conceptualization to the formation of phonological structures, which are in turn interpreted phonetically, yielding an articulatorically specified input to a speech synthesis module. Among the linguistic phenomena that are analyzed within the SYNPHONICS framework, emphasis is placed on investigations concerning the syntactic and prosodic realization of information structures that vary in accordance with conceptual and contextual variations. We argue in particular that certain meaning distinctions triggered by changes in information structure are reflected by prosodic means without any additional support from syntax (cf. Günther et al. 1993). Therefore, SYNPHONICS conjectures a direct semantics/phonology interface in addition to the commonly assumed syntax/semantics and syntax/phonology interfaces. This enables the phonological component directly to access semantic information.[3]

The grammar formalism used for encoding declarative linguistic knowledge is HPSG.[4] Its multidimensional constraint-based architecture provides suitable means for the representation of the dependencies among semantic, syntactic, and phonological structure that are crucial for an account of information structure. Conceptual and linguistic objects are represented formally as typed feature structures in ALE (Attribute Logic Engine, cf. Carpenter 1992).[5] Figure 2.1 gives an overview of the architecture of the SYNPHONICS system with its three central processing units: the Conceptualizer, which plans the conceptual representation of an intended utterance as preverbal message; the Formulator, which encodes the preverbal message in terms of grammatical structure; and the Articulator, which finally generates a speech signal. For a detailed description of the SYNPHONICS system compare Herweg (1992), Schopp (1993, 1994), Günther (1994a), and Abb et al. (1995).

The Conceptualizer operates on a conceptual knowledge base (CKB), which comprises facts and rules representing so-called world knowledge as well as episodic knowledge corresponding to a particular scene representation. One of the peculiarities of the SYNPHONICS system as opposed to other language production systems (cf., e.g., Levelt 1989) is that it acknowledges the influence that the context has on an utterance by distinguishing analytically two parts of the preverbal message: The Conceptualizer creates a conceptual structure (CS) that comprises the propositional content of the planned utterance and a contextual structure (CT) that contains the currently relevant parts of the contextual environment. Our central claim with respect to the notion of context is that context should not be viewed as just a collection of discourse information, monotonically increasing while discourse develops but rather as a result of an active construction process that selects only the relevant pieces of information according to the intended utterance (cf. Herweg and Maienborn 1992, Günther et al. 1993 for a discussion of this topic). We therefore favor a dynamic and selective view of context instead of a uniform allocation of the whole discourse information. The SYNPHONICS architecture reflects this view by assuming a bipartite output stream of the conceptualization process, CS and CT.[6]

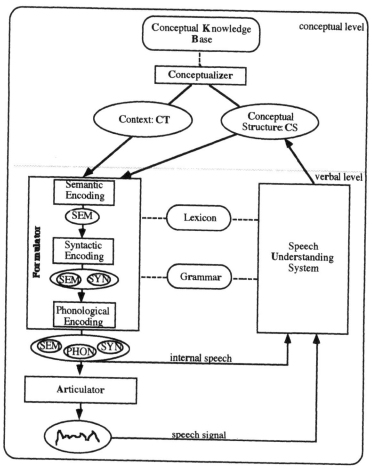

Fig. 2.1. The SYNPHONICS architecture

It is worthwhile to add that CS and CT comprise conceptual representations of the same formal type. Therefore, each conceptual entity might be assigned dynamically either to CS or to CT in the course of conceptual planning. Figure 2.2 shows a (slightly simplified) schematic representation of a corresponding conceptual entity.

$$
\begin{bmatrix}
\text{concpred: } \{\text{pred1}\} \\
\text{r\_pointer: r1} \\
\text{rel\_set: } \{\} \\
\textit{object\_refo}
\end{bmatrix}
$$

Fig. 2.2. Schematic representation of a referential object

Relevant information about conceptual entities is represented in terms of referential objects (*refo*), which are subclassified further into the subtypes *sit-refo* and *object-refo*, corresponding to the ontological distinction of situations and objects. Conceptual entities are characterized by referential, sortal, and relational information. The attribute *r-pointer* fixes the referential status of a refo, *concpred* (*conceptual predicate*) supplies sortal information, and *rel-set* specifies relational information about the refo in terms of, for example, thematic linkings to other *refos* relevant for the current utterance. CS and CT each are built up by a collection of *refos*.

Within the Formulator, a processing unit called "Semantic Encoder" generates a genuine linguistic meaning representation, namely, the semantic structure SEM (cf. Fig. 2.3), from the extralinguistic input structures CS and CT.[7] Within SYNPHONICS, SEM is divided into three major parts: Referential information is collected at a *ref_info* attribute that is mapped onto the partition of the lexicon that contains functional elements (determiner, complementizer, etc.) in the course of lexical access. The descriptive content of a *refo* is accounted for by *the core_info* attribute, which triggers the selection of suitable lemmata. And finally, information about the thematic embedding of a *refo* with regard to the actual CS configuration is collected in an *embed_info* attribute. The embedding information triggers in turn the selection of semantic/syntactic schemata (head-complement schema, head-adjunct schema) that build up the structural environment for the linguistic expression that is associated to a *refo*. In the course of semantic encoding, sortal information of CS is always mapped onto the *core_info* part of SEM, whereas relational information of CS may become part of *core_info* or of *embed_info*, depending on whether the relation expressed turns out to be an integral part of the *refo*'s semantic representation or not. That is, inherently relational expressions, as for instance verbs and relational nouns, assign thematic roles to their environment. The corresponding relational information is therefore mapped onto the *core_info* part. (We use the notion of *x-giver* and its ramifications *agent-giver*, *theme-giver*, and so on, to express this relational dependency.) Nonrelational nouns, on the other hand, have no relational content on their own but are assigned thematic roles (cf. the notion of *x-taker*). The corresponding relational information is thus mapped onto the *embed_info* part.

$$
\begin{bmatrix}
\mathrm{ref\_info:}\begin{bmatrix} \mathrm{r\_pointer:}\ [1]\mathrm{r1} \end{bmatrix} \\
\mathrm{core\_info:}\ \left\{ \begin{bmatrix} \mathrm{sempred:}\ []\mathrm{pred} \\ \mathrm{inst:}\ [1] \end{bmatrix} \right\} \\
\mathrm{embed\_info:}\ \left\{ \begin{bmatrix} \mathrm{r\_pointer:}\ \mathrm{s1} \\ \mathrm{rel:}\ \mathrm{x\_taker} \end{bmatrix} \right\} \\
\end{bmatrix}_{sem}
$$

Fig. 2.3. Schematic representation of a semantic structure

SEM is integrated into a complex HPSG sign that is successively augmented by the syntactic structure SYN and the phonological structure PHON, while passing subsequently the corresponding processing units of the Formulator. Finally, the Articulator interprets PHON phonetically and yields an articulatorically specified input to a speech synthesis module.

As we saw in Section 1, incremental language production presupposes that the system components are enabled to process fragmentary input. As soon as a particular component has passed on the results to its successor component, it is ready to process the next incoming increment. This processing mode allows information fragments to be minimal, always provided that the maintenance of the connections between increments is somehow ensured. In SYNPHONICS, this task of ensuring coherence is mainly accomplished by the conception of embedding information as illustrated for the case of thematic relations. Embedding information is – besides referential specification – the major means to guarantee that a coherent linking between refos and, thus, the global shape of a propositional unit are recoverable under the circumstances of processing incrementally fragmentary information. This overall system design has already been shown to cope with a multitude of linguistic phenomena (cf., e.g., Herweg 1992, Schopp 1993, 1994). In the following, it will be applied to the issue of incrementally computing focus/background structure.

3   Incremental Computation of Information Structure

Focus/background structure is a purely linguistic means of signaling the organization of information within a propositional unit. Yet, it originates from genuinely conceptual configurations. Thus, the computation of information structure in terms of focus/background structure must take place at the interface between language independent and language specific processing units. Therefore, this task is performed at the level of semantic encoding, in SYNPHONICS.

There are two subtasks that have to be carried out in order to establish the focus/background structure of an incrementally generated utterance. First, we have to determine the informational status of the increment that is currently being processed. Second, we need some hints about the informational status of the increment's environment, that is, information on how the focus/background structure of the increment fits into the focus/background structure of the whole utterance. As mentioned in Section 1, we are not entitled to assume a complete picture of the planned utterance, according to psycholinguistic evidence. This gives rise to the following questions: What kind of embedding information concerning focus/background structure turns out to be minimally necessary, and what is a psycholinguistically legitimate source for this type of information?

The approach taken in SYNPHONICS assumes that already a minimal amount of information about the environment of an increment suffices to handle focus/

background structure under the circumstances of incremental language production. We argue, in particular, that the only information needed, besides information about the focus/background structure of the increment itself, is information about whether a focused increment is part of a larger focus domain or not. In this section, we will show how this minimal amount of embedding information concerning focus/background structure is computed at the level of semantic encoding in the course of processing every single increment. In the next section, we will demonstrate that exactly this kind of information suffices for incremental realization of focus/background structure at the level of phonological encoding.

A solution for the issue of determining an increment's own informational status (viz. local focus information) as well as its focus/background embedding (viz. global focus information) can be provided by the notion of context established in SYNPHONICS for independent reasons (cf. Section 2). The context representation can be seen as expressing the informational demand that the speaker wants to fulfill with his utterance. This informational demand might originate from the previous discourse, from a question posed explicitly by the hearer, for instance, or it might result from other types of contextual influences, such as perceptions that the speaker wants to communicate to the hearer.[8] In any case, all contextual parameters that are relevant for the actual utterance are collected into the context representation CT. In order to be contextually adequate, an utterance has to meet the contextual requirements expressed by CT. Therefore, the structure of CT may give us some hints about the global shape of the utterance; it may facilitate inferences about the propositional content to be uttered that go beyond the fragmentary information supplied by an increment in isolation. Having identified the primary source for the construction of focus/background structure, let us proceed to the discussion of the concrete algorithm for computing focus/background structure employed in SYNPHONICS.

During semantic encoding, each increment is checked as to whether its information fulfills the informational demand expressed by CT – in this case it belongs to the focus of the utterance – or whether it pertains to the part of CT mutually known by speaker and hearer, that is, the background. In the focus case, we need to determine furthermore whether the currently processed increment fulfills the informational demand of the utterance exhaustively or only partially. In the former case, we are dealing with narrow focus; in the latter the information expressed by the increment is part of a larger focus domain: that is, we are dealing with wide focus. Finally, contrastive focus is given in case CT does not express an informational demand but rather a claim, which might have been established, for instance, by a previous assertion of the hearer. Here, the speaker's utterance is linked to CT by correcting the claim expressed in CT according to the speaker's own beliefs. The result of the computing algorithm consists of the classification of the increment's semantic representation as *widely focused, narrowly focused, contrastively focused*, or *non-focused* (i.e., *background*). In SYNPHONICS, this differentiation is expressed by a corresponding type of distinction of the semantic restriction elements. Notice that focus/background structure is thereby accounted for at the level of semantic representation.

Let us go now into some more detail, having a look at some illustrative examples. As we have seen, the Semantic Encoder determines the focus/background structure of an increment by matching it against CT. Let us assume that Figure 2.4 comprises an actual context selection that has to be taken into account by a speaker who plans an utterance. Figure 2.4 expresses that an object referent r1, *Peter*; an object referent r2, of type 'book'; and a situational referent 1, of type 'give' are given in the context. Furthermore, the situational referent establishes certain thematic relations to other referential entities, namely, *agent*, *experiencer*, and *theme*. Agent and theme role, are assigned to r1 and r2, respectively, whereas the experiencer role remains underspecified (*r_var* stands for an object variable).

CT:

$$
\left\{
\begin{array}{l}
\left[\begin{array}{l}
\text{concpred: \{peter\}} \\
\text{r\_ pointer: r1} \\
\text{rel\_set:} \left\{\left[\begin{array}{l}\text{r\_pointer: s1}\\\text{rel: agent\_taker}\end{array}\right]\right\} \\
\text{\_\_}obj\_refo
\end{array}\right],
\left[\begin{array}{l}
\text{concpred: \{book\}} \\
\text{r\_ pointer: r2} \\
\text{rel\_set:} \left\{\left[\begin{array}{l}\text{r\_pointer: s1}\\\text{rel: theme\_taker}\end{array}\right]\right\} \\
\text{\_\_}obj\_refo
\end{array}\right], \\[2em]
\left[\begin{array}{l}
\text{concpred: \{give\}} \\
\text{r\_ pointer: s1} \\
\text{rel\_set:} \left\{\left[\begin{array}{l}\text{r\_pointer: r1}\\\text{rel: agent\_giver}\end{array}\right],\left[\begin{array}{l}\text{r\_pointer: r2}\\\text{rel: theme\_giver}\end{array}\right],\left[\begin{array}{l}\text{r\_pointer: r\_var}\\\text{rel: experiencer\_giver}\end{array}\right]\right\} \\
\text{\_\_}sit\_refo
\end{array}\right]
\end{array}
\right\}
$$

Fig. 2.4. Sample context representation

Every context restricts possible utterances to a certain extent. The context representation assumed in Figure 2.4 turns out to be very restrictive, because it delimits precisely the informational demand that the utterance is supposed to fulfill, namely, information about the referent that is assigned the experiencer role. The context representation in Figure 2.4 may thus be seen as expressing the implicit question *To whom did Peter give the book?*[9] A plausible utterance that takes into account these contextual requirements could be an utterance with a propositional content corresponding to *Peter gave Mary the book*. Now, what happens if the first increment reaches the Semantic Encoder? Let us assume, for the time being, that the first increment comprises conceptual information about the topic of the utterance, namely, the referential object r1. Its conceptual structure is given in Figure 2.5.

In the course of semantic processing, the CS fragment is compared with CT. Since it matches exactly one of the CT elements, the conclusion can be drawn that the increment currently processed does not contribute any new information in the actual context setting but rather supplies background information. The increment's semantic representation is therefore assigned the informational status *non-focused* (cf. Fig. 2.6).

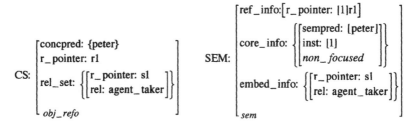

Fig. 2.5. CS increment 'Peter'   Fig. 2.6. Nonfocused semantic representation

What about the increment comprising conceptual information about the referential object *Mary* (cf. Fig. 2.7)? There is no element in CT that matches this CS fragment. On the contrary, the information supplied by CS fits exactly into one clearly shaped gap within the conceptual specification of s1, namely, the gap corresponding to the lack of information about the bearer of the experiencer role in s1. With respect to the context setting in Figure 2.4, the CS fragment in Figure 2.7 supplies new information that is suitable to fulfill exhaustively a precisely delimited informational demand in CT. Therefore, the increment's semantic representation is assigned the informational status *narrowly focused* (cf. Fig. 2.8).

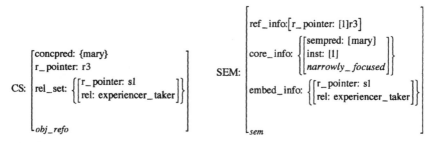

Fig. 2.7. CS increment 'Mary'   Fig. 2.8. Narrowly focused semantic representation

If the increment supplies more complex information about the bearer of the experiencer role, as in Figure 2.7′ each of the corresponding semantic restriction elements is assigned the informational status *narrowly focused* (cf. Fig. 2.8′).

In general terms, the structural configuration that is decisive for the assignment of narrow focus can be characterized as follows: CT contains a variable that is related to the contextual environment by a thematic link, and CS provides an instantiation of the variable equipped with a thematic linking that is compatible with the relation established in CT. The information that fills up the gap constitutes one single focus domain and thus qualifies as narrow focus. Under this view, multiple focus is

$$
\text{CS: } \begin{bmatrix} \text{concpred: } \{\text{young, lady}\} \\ \text{r\_pointer: r3} \\ \text{rel\_set: } \left\{ \begin{bmatrix} \text{r\_pointer: s1} \\ \text{rel: experiencer\_taker} \end{bmatrix} \right\} \\ \\ \text{obj\_refo} \end{bmatrix}
$$

$$
\text{SEM: } \begin{bmatrix} \text{ref\_info:} \begin{bmatrix} \text{r\_pointer: [1]r3} \end{bmatrix} \\ \text{core\_info: } \left\{ \begin{bmatrix} \text{sempred: } \lfloor\text{young}\rfloor \\ \text{inst: [1]} \\ \textit{narrowly\_focused} \end{bmatrix}, \begin{bmatrix} \text{sempred: } \lfloor\text{lady}\rfloor \\ \text{inst: [1]} \\ \textit{narrowly\_focused} \end{bmatrix} \right\} \\ \text{embed\_info: } \left\{ \begin{bmatrix} \text{r\_pointer: s1} \\ \text{rel: experiencer\_taker} \end{bmatrix} \right\} \\ \text{sem} \end{bmatrix}
$$

Fig. 2.7′. CS increment 'young lady'

Fig. 2.8′. Narrowly focused semantic representation

simply a phenomenon that originates from a contextual setting with two or more clearly shaped but distinct informational gaps. Each of the increments that supply information about one of the gaps qualifies as *narrowly focused*.

Having discussed so far the issues of background and narrow focus, let us turn now to the apparently more intricate problem of determining incrementally wide focus. In contrast to narrow focus, wide focus originates from contextual configurations that are less restrictive with regard to the propositional content of adequate utterances. If CT raises only few conditions that have to be met by the actual utterance, that is, the informational demand established by CT is more or less underspecified, there is a broader range of possible utterances and each utterance conveys a greater extent of new information, depending on the determinacy of CT. Take, for instance, the context representation in Figure 2.9, which is a slightly changed version of Figure 2.4.

$$
\text{CT: } \left\{ \begin{bmatrix} \text{concpred: } \{\text{peter}\} \\ \text{r\_pointer: r1} \\ \text{rel\_set: } \left\{ \begin{bmatrix} \text{r\_pointer: s1} \\ \text{rel: agent\_taker} \end{bmatrix} \right\} \\ \text{obj\_refo} \end{bmatrix}, \begin{bmatrix} \text{concpred: } \{\text{book}\} \\ \text{r\_pointer: r2} \\ \text{rel\_set: } \left\{ \begin{bmatrix} \text{r\_pointer: s1} \\ \text{rel: theme\_taker} \end{bmatrix} \right\} \\ \text{obj\_refo} \end{bmatrix}, \begin{bmatrix} \text{concpred: } \{\} \\ \text{r\_pointer: s1} \\ \text{rel\_set: } \left\{ \begin{bmatrix} \text{r\_pointer: r\_var} \\ \text{rel: agent\_giver} \end{bmatrix}, \begin{bmatrix} \text{r\_pointer: r\_var} \\ \text{rel: theme\_giver} \end{bmatrix} \right\} \\ \text{sit\_refo} \end{bmatrix} \right\}
$$

Fig. 2.9. Sample context representation

Again, r1, r2, and s1 are selected as contextually relevant discourse referents. But in this case, there is less information available about s1. The only thing we know about s1 is that it refers to a situation with at least one agent and one theme. The sortal type of the situation and possibly further participants remain, however, unspecified. That is, Figure 2.9 may be understood as expressing the implicit question *What has Peter done with the book?* The informational demand of this kind of context is not as sharply delimited as in Figure 2.4, because any kind of information may be suitable, provided it meets the minimal contextual requirements concerning referential identity and thematic linking.[10] Let us assume that, within the contextual setting of Figure 2.9, the speaker wants to say that Peter gave the book to Mary, and let us turn immediately to the semantic processing of the increment comprising conceptual information about Mary (cf. Fig. 2.7). This time, the only hint to an adequate integration of CS that is provided by CT concerns referential identity of the situation referents in CT and CS. We are therefore entitled to assume that the fragment supplied by CS constitutes one piece of information that conveys further information about the situation referent and thus is part of the focus of the utterance. In particular, no evidence is given whether the increment's information is the only new information communicated by the speaker, or whether it might be augmented by subsequent increments. Therefore, the corresponding semantic restriction element is assigned the type *widely focused* (Fig. 2.10).

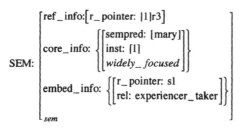

Fig. 2.10. Widely focused semantic representation

If, for instance, a subsequent increment conveys information about the location where the situation takes place, or any other kind of additional information about the situation referent, the same conditions concerning its contextual embedding may be applied. Therefore, the semantic structure is qualified as *widely focused*, too. The same holds true for an increment conveying sortal information about the situation referent. Thus, to sum up so far: If the informational content of a CS increment does not belong to the background specified in CT and it does not fit an exactly delimited CT gap either, the Semantic Encoder computes a semantic structure of type *widely focused*.[11] In the course of processing one increment after the other, the collection of restriction elements that were assigned wide focus builds up step by step a complete focus domain.

Finally, the structural configurations that trigger the assignment of contrastive focus remain to be accounted for. As we have seen, in the case of contrastive focus there is no informational demand expressed in CT, but rather a claim that the speaker wants to contradict. The refusal of CT may refer to any part of the conceptual information, that is, the referential (*this book vs. that book*), sortal (*book vs. newspaper* or *borrow vs. buy*), or relational part (*Peter gave the book to Mary vs. Mary gave the book to Peter*), whereas the remaining parts of the CS increment are presupposed to match with the corresponding CT opponent. Given for instance the CT in Figure 2.11, which expresses the claim that Peter borrowed the book from Mary, the speaker may want to correct this claim by uttering that it was the case that Peter bought the book from Mary. That is, the propositional content of CS differs from CT only with respect to the sortal information about the situational referent. Consequently, the corresponding semantic restriction element is marked as *contrastively focused* (cf. Figs. 2.12 and 2.13).

$$
\text{CT:} \left\{
\begin{bmatrix}
\text{concpred: } \{peter\} \\
\text{r\_pointer: r1} \\
\text{rel\_set: } \left\{ \begin{bmatrix} \text{r\_pointer: s1} \\ \text{rel: agent\_taker} \end{bmatrix} \right\} \\
\textit{obj\_refo}
\end{bmatrix},
\begin{bmatrix}
\text{concpred: } \{book\} \\
\text{r\_pointer: r2} \\
\text{rel\_set: } \left\{ \begin{bmatrix} \text{r\_pointer: s1} \\ \text{rel: theme\_taker} \end{bmatrix} \right\} \\
\textit{obj\_refo}
\end{bmatrix},
\begin{bmatrix}
\text{concpred: } \{mary\} \\
\text{r\_pointer: r3} \\
\text{rel\_set: } \left\{ \begin{bmatrix} \text{r\_pointer: s1} \\ \text{rel: experiencer\_taker} \end{bmatrix} \right\} \\
\textit{obj\_refo}
\end{bmatrix}
\right.
$$

$$
\begin{bmatrix}
\text{concpred: } \{borrow\} \\
\text{r\_pointer: s1} \\
\text{rel\_set: } \left\{ \begin{bmatrix} \text{r\_pointer: r1} \\ \text{rel: agent\_giver} \end{bmatrix}, \begin{bmatrix} \text{r\_pointer: r2} \\ \text{rel: theme\_giver} \end{bmatrix}, \begin{bmatrix} \text{r\_pointer: r3} \\ \text{rel: experiencer\_giver} \end{bmatrix} \right\} \\
\textit{sit\_refo}
\end{bmatrix}
$$

Fig. 2.11. Sample context representation

$$
\text{CS:} \begin{bmatrix}
\text{concpred: } \{buy\} \\
\text{r\_pointer: s1} \\
\text{rel\_set: } \left\{ \begin{bmatrix} \text{r\_pointer: r1} \\ \text{rel: agent\_giver} \end{bmatrix}, \begin{bmatrix} \text{r\_pointer: r2} \\ \text{rel: theme\_giver} \end{bmatrix}, \begin{bmatrix} \text{r\_pointer: r3} \\ \text{rel: experiencer\_giver} \end{bmatrix} \right\} \\
\textit{sit\_refo}
\end{bmatrix}
$$

Fig. 2.12. CS increment 'buy'

$$
\text{SEM:} \begin{bmatrix}
\text{ref\_info:} \begin{bmatrix} \text{r\_pointer: } [1|s1] \end{bmatrix} \\
\text{core\_info: } \left\{ \begin{bmatrix}
\text{sempred: } [buy] \\
\text{inst: } [1] \\
\text{reln: } \left\{ \begin{bmatrix} \text{r\_pointer: r1} \\ \text{rel: agent\_giver} \end{bmatrix}, \begin{bmatrix} \text{r\_pointer: r2} \\ \text{rel: theme\_giver} \end{bmatrix}, \begin{bmatrix} \text{r\_pointer: r3} \\ \text{rel: experiencer\_giver} \end{bmatrix} \right\} \\
\textit{contrastively\_focused}
\end{bmatrix} \right\} \\
\text{embed\_info: } \{ \, \} \\
\textit{sem}
\end{bmatrix}
$$

Fig. 2.13. Contrastively focused semantic representation

This completes the survey of the SYNPHONICS approach to the incremental computation of focus/background structure.[12] Local as well as global aspects of focus/background structure are determined by making intensive use of the CS-CT distinction developed in SYNPHONICS for independent reasons. We will now proceed with a sketch of the incremental realization of information structure.

4   Incremental Realization of Information Structure

Differences in focus/background partitioning of a semantic representation trigger different phonetic realizations by prosodic means. Generally speaking, focused constituents are realized more prominently than nonfocused constituents. The concrete phonetic realization of prominence is language and context dependent. In German, for instance, focus is prosodically marked essentially by an outstanding movement of fundamental frequency (F0), that is, the pitch accent, but also by lengthening and an intensity peak. Yet, it is not possible to map semantic focus features directly onto phonetic parameters. An abstract prosodic rule inventory is required, instead, that interprets focus-type information into an abstract prosodic feature representation in terms of accent pattern and accent tones. These abstract prosodic feature values are converted into concrete tonal, durational, and intensity parameters afterwards.

The accent placement and the corresponding tone contour on focused constituents depend on the assigned focus-type information and the argument/modifier status of the verb-adjacent constituent. In the case of narrow focus, the prosodic focus realization is restricted to the focused constituent. Figure 2.14 shows the analysis of the speech signal[13] of the utterance *Er hat den Mimen die MAHNUNG geschickt (He has sent the mimes the warning)*[14] as a possible answer to the question *What has the manager sent to the mimes?* With respect to this context setting, the constituent *die Mahnung* is marked as *narrowly_focused*, according to the computation of information structure explained earlier. Thus, it becomes the most prominent constituent of the utterance. Within a narrowly focused constituent, the metrically strongest word of the constituent (*Mahnung*) carries the nuclear accent, which is tonally realized by an initial dip and a following rise of the fundamental frequency (transcribed as a complex accent tone $L + H^*$) on the word accent bearing syllable. The nuclear accent is finally bound by a drop of the fundamental frequency onto the speaker's baseline (transcribed as a phrasal tone $L-$). If an utterance comprises multiple narrow foci, each focused constituent is assigned a nuclear accent, which will be realized in turn as an $L + H^*$ $L-$ tone contour.

In the case of wide focus, on the other hand, the prosodic realization of the information structure yields a more complex accent distribution and tone contour. Figure 2.15 shows the prosodic realization of the same utterance but with a different, less restricted context setting. This utterance is a possible answer to the question *What has the manager done?*, which causes a wide focusing of the complex constituent *[F den Mimen die Mahnung geschickt] (sent the mimes the warning)*. The f0-contour in Figure 2.15 shows two pitch accents on the arguments

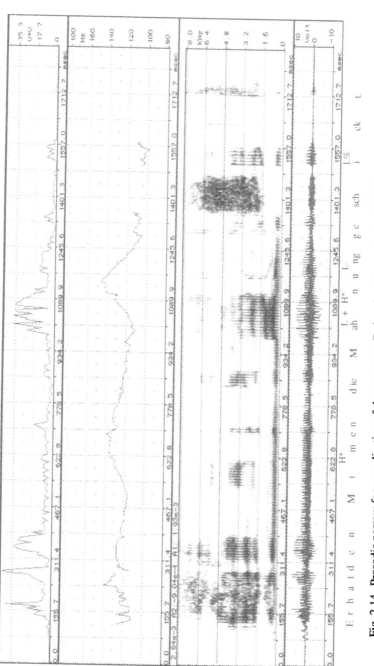

Fig. 2.14. Prosodic narrow focus realization of the utterance *Er hat den Mimen* [*F die MAHNUNG*] *geschickt*

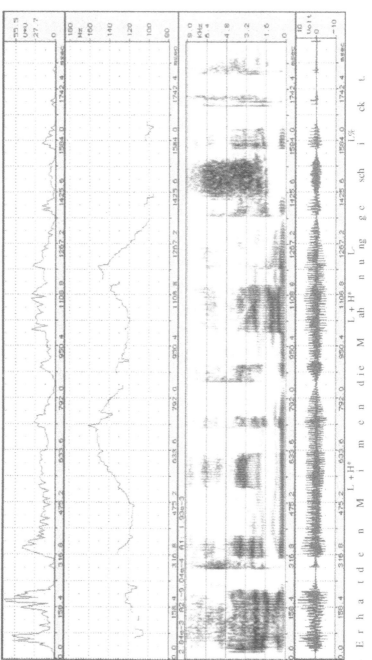

Fig. 2.15. Prosodic wide focus realization of the utterance *Er hat* [*F den MIMEN die MAHNUNG geschickt*]

of the verb. The second accent is perceived as the stronger because of its late position in the utterance and the immediately following strong fall. Because of this prominence distinction, the last accent will be called *nuclear accent* and the preceding ones *prenuclear accents*. Both accent types are realized tonally by a rising pitch accent L + H*, but the nuclear accent comprises additionally a low phrasal tone L−. Notice that the exact boundaries of the focus domain are not prosodically marked: The verb is part of the focus domain, yet, it does not carry a pitch accent due to its sentence-final position. The underdetermined marking of focus domains is the reason for the phenomenon of so-called focus ambiguities (cf. Jacobs 1991).

The nonaccenting of widely focused verbs in sentence-final position is restricted to argument-verb constellations. Syntactic constructions of verbs with a verb-adjacent adjunct exhibit a different accent pattern (cf., e.g., Jacobs 1991, Maienborn 1994). Figure 2.16 shows the accent distribution in the utterance *Sie hat auf der Wiese geschlafen. (She has slept in the meadow.)* Contrary to the accent pattern in Fig. 2.15, the V^0-constituent *geschlafen* carries the nuclear accent (L + H* L−) and the verb-adjacent adjunct *auf der Wiese* the prenuclear accent (L + H*), which is in turn realized on the noun in accordance with general metrical principles.

Generally speaking, in the case of wide focus on VP level (focusing of the verb and its arguments and adjuncts), the nuclear accent is assigned to the verb-adjacent arguments or, in the case of the occurrence of a verb-adjacent adjunct, to the verb itself.[15] Table 2.1 gives a summary of the prosodic realization of different focus-type information. Besides narrow and wide focus, contrastive focus is characterized by its outstanding tonal realization and the f_0-dip immediately on the accent-bearing syllable (transcribed as L* + H).

Table 2.1. *Prototypical prosodic realization of focus in German*

Semantic Focus Type	Accent Type	Pitch Accent
narrow focus	nuclear accent	accent tone: L+H* phrasal tone: L-
wide focus	prenuclear accent	accent tone: L+H*
	nuclear accent (assigned either to the verb-adjacent argument or to the verb itself)	accent tone: L+H* phrasal tone: L-
contrastive focus	contrastive accent	accent tone: L*+H phrasal tone: L-

In the following, we present the incremental derivation of different accent types, based on the semantic focus computation developed in Section 3. Dealing with incrementality as a characteristic processing property with regard to focus realization,

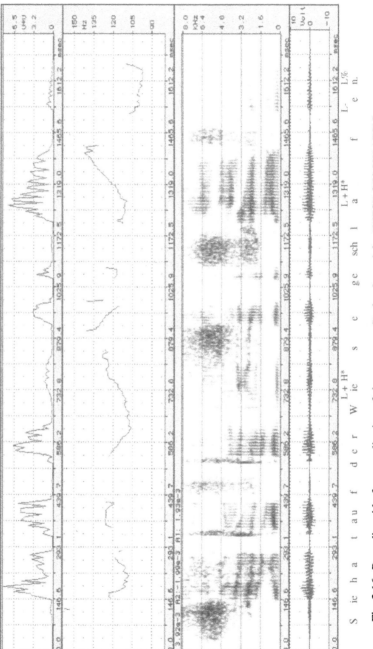

Fig. 2.16. Prosodic wide focus realization of the utterance *Sie hat* [F *auf der WIESE GESCHLAFEN*]

we have to bear in mind that the focus domain is not necessarily completely specified when single increments are processed.

Within the SYNPHONICS System, abstract prosodic planning of focus realization is part of the phonological encoding, whereas the acoustic parametrization takes place within the phonetic-articulatory planning module after a phonetic interpretation of sub- and suprasegmental structures (cf. Section 2). There is a current controversy about which aspects determine prosodic planning units and how the Phonology-Syntax interface should be designed (indirect or direct reference approach, cf. Inkelas & Zec 1990). The debate centers around the problem of how to ensure a uniform notion of the prosodic structure units either in syntactic terms (maximal phrasal projections according to the definition of Phonological Phrases, cf. Nespor & Vogel 1986) or in mere semantic terms (argument, predicate, modifier structuring, cf. Gussenhoven 1992; sense units, cf. Selkirk 1984). These theories, which might be termed structural approaches, do not take into account procedural aspects of language processing.

According to our incremental approach, we advocate a dynamic view on the Syntax-Phonology interface where structure units and increment size are determined essentially by procedural aspects. At this formulator-internal interface, structure units (single lemmata or constituents) are taken out (from left to right) from the semantic and syntactic structure built up so far, provided that they are exhaustively morpho-syntactically specified (in terms of case, gender, number, person, and tense information) as well as standing in a left-to-right gap-free order. A complete, category-dependent morpho-syntactic specification is necessary for a correct morphophonological generation of word forms (lemmata) to take place. These are the only requirements increments have to fulfill in order to enter the Phonological Encoder. Thus, prosodic increment size turns up as a procedural result of the encoding processes performed so far. In fact, we argue that prosodic planning units are defined in procedural terms (reflected by morpho-syntactic completeness and linear order), rather than in terms of semantic or syntactic constituent structure. Thus we can dispense with an explicit transformation of semantic and syntactic structures into prosodic structures. Such a dynamic view on prosodic planning units reflects the overwhelming variance of speech chunks in natural spoken dialogues.

These rather parsimonious requirements on increment properties of prosodic planning units ensure that prosodic planning takes place without presupposing completeness of focus domains. Such a strict incremental proceeding enables a phonetic realization of fragments of a wide focus domain even in the case that succeeding parts of the utterance are not yet semantically processed. Thus, as in the case of semantic focus calculation, prosodic focus realization can be considered from a local as well as from a global point of view. The local domain covers the focus realization within the actual increment selected by the Syntax-Phonology interface. The global perspective takes into account focus-type information that goes beyond one single increment (narrow or wide focus) as well as the structural information conveyed by the syntactic environment and serves to license the application of focus projection rules.

In the following, we will present focus realization rules that cover the determination of the accent distribution on constituents for different focus domain sizes. These rules are instantiations of one general focus realization principle that take into account different structural conditions and focus-type information. In this sense, these rules manifest the direct link between Semantics and Phonology within SYNPHONICS. They are applied along the verbal projection line during the incremental structure-building process. Prosody internal metrical principles inherit the abstract accent information to the most prominent lexeme (DTE = designated terminal element) of a constituent where the accent is realized by a special tone contour. The different kinds of rules (focus-accent mapping, accent inheritance, accent-tone mapping) represent declarative grammatical constraints that relate different types of grammatical knowledge. They are applied at different time points during the course of language production.

The case of narrow focus assignment on a single constituent does not exhibit a severe problem for an incremental approach to focus-accent mapping because of the locality of rule restrictions and effects. In the example mentioned (see Figs. 2.4–2.8) *Peter hat [$_F$ MARIA] das Buch gegeben. (Peter has given Mary the book.)*, the verbal argument *Maria* has been specified as *narrowly_focused*. The appropriate prosodic realization of this focus/background structure is guaranteed by the assignment of the nuclear accent to the narrowly focused constituent (cf. Table 2.1). This relation between semantic and prosodic structure is formulated according to the rule in Figure 2.17. The *Narrow-Focus Accent Rule*[16] checks the focus status of a constituent and assigns to the phonological feature PHON|ACC the value *nuclear_accent (nucl_acc)*[17] if this constituent is narrowly focused. The rule evaluates only local semantic-type information (*narrowly_focused*) and does not need any further semantic or syntactic structure information about preceding or following increments.

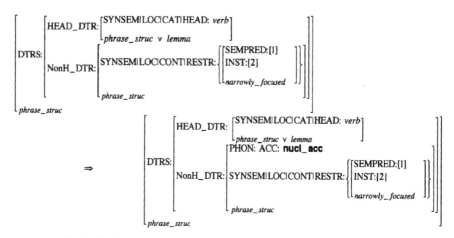

Fig. 2.17. Narrow-Focus Accent Rule

Likewise, the realization of contrastive focus is a local process, which leads, however, to a more prominent realization (contrastive accent, Table 2.1) during the subsequent acoustic realization than in the case of narrow focus (cf. Bartels and Kingston 1994).

The incremental realization of wide focus turns out to be a more intricate problem since global structural knowledge about the information structure of the whole utterance has to be taken into account at large. The complete focus domain is expressed by one nuclear accent and preceding prenuclear accents, but the exact accent placement depends on semantic and syntactic conditions. The nuclear accent will be realized either on the verb-adjacent complement or, in the case of the occurrence of a verb-adjacent adjunct, on the verb itself. Preceding constituents (whether complements or adjuncts) of the focus domain carry prenuclear accents. Thus, a focus-accent mapping that proceeds incrementally has to check first whether the currently processed focused constituent is in a verb-adjacent position. If this is not the case, the constituent will be marked for prenuclear accent. Therefore, in the example *Peter hat [F MARIA das BUCH gegeben]*, the non-verb-adjacent constituent *Maria* is assigned prenuclear accent. The rule in Figure 2.18 licenses assignment of prenuclear accent (*prenucl_acc*) to widely focused non-verb-adjacent constituents (NonH_DTR) by ensuring that the verbal head daughter (CAT:HEAD: *verb*) is not of category V[0].[18] Notice that this rule imposes minimal requirements on global information, ensuring incremental processing. For the prosodic processing of the structural increment *Maria*, it is only necessary to know that this increment is part of a larger focus domain and that the sister constituent is not the verbal head.

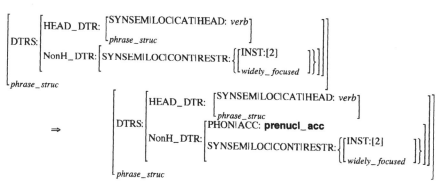

Fig. 2.18. Wide-Focus Accent Rule (for non-verb-adjacent constituents)

In the case that a verb-adjacent constituent is selected at the Syntax-Phonology interface, it must be checked whether this constituent is a complement or an adjunct. Figure 2.15 illustrates that verb-adjacent complements carry the nuclear accent. The rule in Figure 2.19 – usually termed the *Focus Projection Rule* – is applicable to a V[0]-complement configuration[19] and assigns to the verb-adjacent focus exponent the nuclear accent (PHON|ACC: nucl_acc).

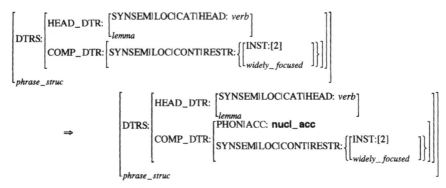

Fig. 2.19. Wide-Focus Accent Rule (for verb-adjacent complements)

In the case of widely focused verb-adjacent adjuncts, no focus projection takes place, and the nuclear accent is realized on the verbal head itself (cf. Fig. 2.16). This is ensured by the rule in Figure 2.20 that assigns a prenuclear accent to the adjunct and a nuclear accent to the verb, respectively.

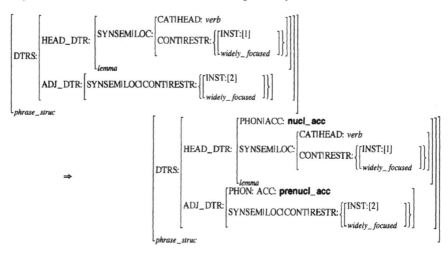

Fig. 2.20. Wide-Focus Accent Rule (for verb-adjacent adjuncts)

The subsequent prosodic encoding and its phonetic interpretation in terms of acoustic parameter settings ensure the appropriate acoustic realization of information structuring (cf. Günther 1994 for details). As presented in Table 2.1, the different accent types are associated with different tone contours. The accent tones are realized on the metrical strongest element of the focused constituents. The prosodic accent interpretation rules of Figures 2.21–2.23 evaluate the accent status (nuclear, prenuclear, and contrastive accent) of a given word (*lexeme*) and assign the appropriate tone information. The tone contour on a lexeme is postlexically specified in terms of accent, phrasal, and boundary tones whereby tonal focus realization is restricted to accent tone (ACC_TONE) and phrasal tone (PHRAS_TONE).

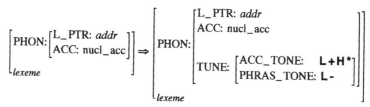

Fig. 2.21. Nuclear Accent Realization Rule

Fig. 2.22. Prenuclear Accent Realization Rule

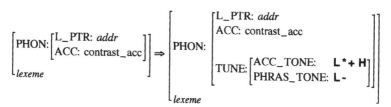

Fig. 2.23. Contrastive Accent Realization Rule

These abstract phonological tones are in turn interpreted phonetically, yielding concrete acoustic parameters as target values for the calculation and interpolation of the fundamental frequency contour.

To summarize the general approach to the processing of information structure within SYNPHONICS: Focus/background structure originates at the interface between the conceptual and the semantic levels as a result of comparing an actual conceptual fragment with its corresponding relevant context representation and is realized incrementally by prosodic means, thereby exploiting essential properties of the system, namely, the assumption of a conceptual representation, CS, and a relevant contextual environment, CT, as input for the linguistic components; the consideration of local information as well as global linkings of processing units by means of different types of embedding information; and, finally, the facility of a direct access of phonological processes to semantic representations by means of a direct semantics/phonology interface.

Notes

1   Current topics of research in computational linguistics as well as in psycholinguistics concern, in particular, the sequence and size of increments, their internal structure, as well as their interrelations.

2   Compare Günther et al. (1993) for a procedural account of topic/comment structure in a language production system.

3   The assumption of a direct semantics/phonology interface is currently becoming more popular; compare, for example, Engdahl & Vallduví (1994).

4   While adopting HPSG as grammar formalism, we deviate substantially from parts of the standard HPSG grammar theory; compare, for example, Abb and Maienborn (1994), Abb et al. (1995).

5   ALE lends itself as a formal description language for a language processing system because it supports a uniform formal specification of structural as well as rule knowledge.

6   For present purposes, we put aside the issue of giving a psycholinguistically supported account of the corresponding CT and CS selection processes. Therefore, in the following we will just deal with the question of how linguistic processing proceeds given a certain CS-CT configuration.

7   Compare Bierwisch and Schreuder (1992), Herweg and Maienborn (1992) for a motivation of the distinction between a linguistic (viz semantic) versus an extralinguistic (viz. conceptual) level of meaning representation from the perspective of language production.

8   Compare the notion of implicit question or *quaestio* in Klein and von Stutterheim (1987).

9   In the present chapter, we neglect issues concerning the referential specification of discourse referents in terms of definiteness, tense, and so on.

10 In fact, maximal focus over the whole utterance originates from a minimally restrictive CT that just provides a "naked" situation referent without any sortal or relational information, thus corresponding to the implicit question *What's going on?*

11 Notice that, given a contextual setting with a precisely delimited informational demand, if the speaker decides to supply further information compatible with, but not strictly required by, CT, the resulting utterance turns out to be less acceptable, because it contravenes at least slightly conditions of contextual appropriateness. Compare, for instance, the utterance *At the bus stop, Peter gave the book to Mary.* which is not well suited in the contextual setting of Figure 2.4, which expresses the implicit question *To whom did Peter give the book?* Besides fulfilling the specific informational demand expressed in Figure 2.4, this utterance supplies further new information (in terms of a locative adverbial) that is not properly asked for in CT. When we continue the utterance with, for example, ... *and in the subway, he gave it to Paul,* the utterance becomes acceptable again. But in this case the speaker plans his utterance with regard to a more complex context representation that comprises pairs of situation referents and experiencers. For lack of space, we cannot go into more detail here.

12 Compare Ziesche (1994) for documentation of the implementation realized in SYNPHONICS.

13 The speech analysis figures show the following information from top to bottom: intensity, fundamental frequency in the range of 80–180 Hz, frequency spectrum in the range of 0–8 kHz, and the speech signal.

14 We illustrate our focus-accent rules with German example sentences.

15 Actually, this is a slight simplification. Compare Maienborn (1994) for a specific type of verb-adjacent adjunct that might also bear a sentence accent.

16 The focus-type information originates from the specification of the semantic structure SEM (cf. Figs. 2.3 and 2.8). During lexical access, SEM is integrated into a complex

HPSG sign; the focus-type information then becomes part of the semantic restriction set (RESTR) of the CONTENT value of the corresponding HPSG sign. The hierarchical structure of a phrasal linguistic sign (*phrase_struc*) is coded as a binary branching tree (as the value of the daughters feature DTRS) whereby a phrasal sign branches into a head daughter (HEAD_DTR) and either a complement daugther (COMP_DTR) or an adjunct daughter (ADJ_DTR). In the case of narrow focus, the accent-type specification is independent of the argument/modifier status of a constituent. For the sake of a general presentation, the feature NonH_DTR is therefore an abbreviation for either a complement daughter or an adjunct daughter.

17 For the sake of illustration, only the focus-accent rules are presented. The determination of the metrical strongest constituent (DTE) within a complex PP or DP is not a topic of this chapter. This process is described in detail in Günther (1994).

18 In this case, the type of the head daughter must not be *lemma* but *phrase_struc*. (Terminal nodes of the syntactic tree structure are typed as *lemma*, whereas all hierarchically higher nodes are typed as *phrase_struc*.)

19 The type of the head daughter is *lemma*.

References

Abb, B., C. Günther, M. Herweg, K. Lebeth, C. Maienborn, and A. Schopp. 1995. Incremental syntactic and phonological encoding: An outline of the SYNPHONICS Formulator. In G. Adorni & M. Zock (eds.), *Trends in Natural Language Generation: An Artificial Intelligence Perspective*. Berlin: Springer.

Abb, B. and C. Maienborn. 1994. Adjuncts in HPSG. In H. Trost (ed.), *Conference Proceedings of KONVENS 94: Verarbeitung natürlicher Sprache. Wien, 28–30. September 1994*, Berlin: Springer, 13–22.

Bartels, C., and J. Kingston. 1994. Salient pitch cues in the perception of contrastive focus. In P. Bosch & R. van der Sandt (1994, eds.) Vol. 1, 1–10.

Bierwisch, M. and R. Schreuder. 1992. From concepts to lexical items. *Cognition* 42:23–60.

Bosch, P. and R. van der Sandt. 1994: Focus and Natural Language Processing. (Working Papers of the Institute for Logic and Linguistics) IBM Deutschland Heidelberg.

Carpenter, B. 1992. *The Logic of Typed Feature Structures*. Cambridge: Cambridge University Press.

Engdahl, E. and E. Vallduví. 1994. Information packaging and grammar architecture: A constraint-based approach. In: E. Engdahl (ed.), *Integrating Information Structure into Constraint-Based and Categorial Approaches* (DYANA-2 Report), ILLC: Amsterdam, 39–79.

Günther, C. 1994. *Planung und Repräsentation prosodischer und phonetisch-artikulatorischer Merkmale im Sprachproduktionssystem SYNPHONICS*. In: A. Schopp (ed.), 15–28.

Günther, C. ed. (1994a). *Hamburger Arbeitspapiere zur Sprachproduktion. VI*. GK-Kognitionswissenschaft, AP 20, Universität Hamburg.

Günther, C., C. Habel, C. Maienborn, and A. Schopp. 1993. *What's up with the printer? Context relative presentation of conceptual structure and its prosodic realization in a language production system*. In: A. Schopp (ed.), 5–16.

Gussenhoven, C. 1992. Sentence accents and argument structure. In I.M. Roca (ed.) *Thematic Structure: Its Role in Grammar*, Berlin, New York: Foris, 79–106.

Herweg, M., ed. 1992. *Hamburger Arbeitspapiere zur Sprachproduktion. I*. GK-Kognitionswissenschaft, AP 9, Universität Hamburg.

Herweg, M. and C. Maienborn. 1992. Konzept, Kontext, Bedeutung – Zur Rolle der Zwei-Ebenen-Semantik in einem Modell der Sprachproduktion. In: M. Herweg (ed.), 7–36.

Inkelas, S. and D. Zec. 1990. *The Phonology-Syntax Connection*. Chicago: University of Chicago Press.

Jacobs, J. 1991. Focus Ambiguities. *Journal of Semantics* 8, 1–36.

Jacobs, J., ed. 1992. *Informationsstruktur und Grammatik*. Opladen: Westdeutscher Verlag.

Kempen, G. and E. Hoenkamp. 1987. An Incremental Procedural Grammar for Sentence Formulation. *Cognitive Science* 11, 201–258.

Klein, W. and C. von Stutterheim. 1987: Quaestio und referentielle Bewegung in Erzählungen. *Linguistische Berichte* 109:163–183.

Levelt, W. J. 1989. *Speaking: From Intention to Articulation*. Cambridge, Mass.: MIT Press.

Maienborn, C. 1994. Fokus und Adjunktion: Überlegungen zum Fokusprojektionsverhalten von Adjunkten am Beispiel der Lokaladverbiale. In: A. Schopp (ed.), 29–66.

Nespor, M. and I. Vogel. 1986. *Prosodic Phonology*. Dordrecht: Foris.

Rooth, Mats E. 1985. Association with focus. Dissertation, University of Massachusetts, Amherst.

Schopp, A., ed. 1993. *Hamburg Working Papers on Language Production. II*. GK-Kognitionswissenschaft, AP 13, Universität Hamburg.

Schopp, A., ed. 1994. *Hamburger Arbeitspapiere zur Sprachproduktion. III*. GK-Kognitionswissenschaft, AP 15, Universität Hamburg.

Selkirk, E. O. 1984. *Phonology and Syntax: The Relation between Sound and Structure*. Cambridge, Mass.: MIT Press.

Ziesche, S. 1994. Der semantische Enkodierer im SYNPHONICS-Project. In: C. Günther (ed.), 53–112.

3   On the Limits of Focus Projection in English

CARLOS GUSSENHOVEN

Abstract

Focus projection, the ability of a pitch accent to mark a larger constituent than the word it is found on as focused, has been given different treatments in the recent literature. In one view, focus projection cannot extend beyond the confines of the word; in another it is restricted to a sequence of an argument and its predicate, while in a third it can extend all the way to the sentence (the latter two types of projection being subject to various conditions). This chapter argues on the basis of 'focus ambiguity' that the second view is to be preferred over the first as well as over the third. In particular, the third interpretation of focus projection, proposed by Selkirk, is shown to make the wrong predictions in a number of structures, while two arguments that have been put forward in support of the third view are shown to be flawed. By contrast, the second, more restricted view of focus projection is not only seen to make the correct predictions, in both simple sentences and sentences with embedded predicates, but is also conceptually simpler. It is argued that the cause of the failure of the sentence-wide view is the a priori assumption that the focus of the sentence must correspond to a single node in the syntactic tree. Unlike this view, Höhle's proposal that the focus may be discontinuous does appear to make the correct predictions.

1   Introduction

Like many languages, English expresses the focus of the sentence in the phonological structure. Most strikingly, pitch accents appear on focused constituents. The expectation, therefore, is that unaccented constituents are outside the focus. However, the situation is more complex than this. One of the most intriguing and widely debated issues in the expression of focus in English is what Chomsky (1972) called 'Focus Projection', the phenomenon that a pitch accent can serve to mark more than just the word it is placed on as focused (a phenomenon that is also to be found in the related languages German, Frisian, Dutch, and Afrikaans; see Schmerling 1976, Gussenhoven 1983, Ladd 1996). As a result, a sentence like (1) is ambiguous between a full-focus reading (as when it is an answer to "What

I thank Ad Foolen, Wus van Lessen Kloeke, and Erwin Marsi for useful discussion of the issues dealt with in this chapter. This is a revised version of the contribution to the Proceedings of the Focus Conference, which was entitled "Focus and Sentence Accents in English."

happened?") and a reading with focus just on the subject (as when it is an answer to "What did you say is gone?").

(1)   The BULB's gone.

No agreement has been reached on the extent of focus projection in English. The most restricted view, espoused by Bolinger (1972, 1985), is that there simply is no focus projection beyond the word the pitch accent is placed on. In this view, called the "radical Focus-To-Accent view" by Ladd (1996), the predicate *is gone* is outside the focus, because it is unaccented. A second view, introduced by Schmerling (1976), holds that arguments can project focus to adjacent predicates, such that predicates that are adjacent to one of their arguments may remain unaccented (cf. (1)). This view, espoused by Fuchs (1984), Gussenhoven (1983), Ladd (1983), Baart (1987), and others, will be referred to as "restricted focus projection". A third view, one that equally goes back to Schmerling (1976), allows for focus to be projected upward to larger constituents and ultimately to the sentence (Selkirk 1984, 1995, Steedman 1994). This view will be referred to as "extended focus projection". Both "restricted" and "extended" focus projection fall under what was called the "Focus-To-Accent" approach in Gussenhoven (1985).

This chapter briefly summarizes two representative descriptions in the "restricted" and "extended" traditions, Gussenhoven (1983, 1992) and Selkirk (1984, 1995), respectively. It is shown that the extended view, but not the restricted view, is compatible with the premise that the focus of the sentence is always a syntactic constituent. While this would at first sight appear to be a decisive advantage for the theory of extended focus projection, it will be shown that this conception of the focus of the sentence does not lead to a situation in which the focus of the sentence contains all and only the information sought by the (implied) question. This is because extended focus projection will lead to the presence of 'old information' inside the focus constituent, which requires the postulation of a set of focus interpretation rules, not needed in a theory of restricted focus projection, side by side with a set of focus projection rules. The restricted view of focus projection requires only a single statement of the relation between pitch accents and focus. In addition to this advantage, it will be argued that extended focus projection faces empirical difficulties. Moreover, the data on which two arguments in favor of extended focus projection have been based will be given alternative interpretations that are consistent with the restricted view.

2   The Restricted View of Focus Projection

This section summarizes the characterization of the focus-accent relation of Gussenhoven (1983, 1992). The Sentence Accent Assignment Rule (SAAR) is discussed, and it is pointed out that one implication of the limited extent of the focus projection is that sentences may have more than one obligatory accent. The difference between obligatory and optional accents is briefly discussed.

2.1 SAAR

In the restricted view, the predicate-argument structure of the sentence is inspected, and every focused argument (**A**), modifier (**M**), and predicate (**P**) is accented, with the exception of a predicate that is adjacent to one of its arguments. (Modifiers are adverbial constituents that are not specified in the argument positions of the verb.) This generalization was formalized in Gussenhoven (1983) as the Sentence Accent Assignment Rule (SAAR). In fact, in computer implementations of the rule (Marsi 1993) it has proved to be more convenient to implement its complement (cf. (2b)). This is mainly because many arguments and modifiers will have more than one pitch accent: in an accent assignment analysis, rules must be written that seek out the right locations for the pitch accents in longer, multi-accent constituents like *those THREE YELlow FLOWers*. Moreover, the potential absence of pitch accents as a result of rhythmic conditions (e.g. *those THREE yellow FLOWers*) will have to be taken into account somehow when accents are assigned. In an analysis in which all accentable syllables are marked as such in the input with an abstract placeholder for a pitch accent (indicated by capitalization in the examples), accents can be removed in one fell swoop from those constituents that are unaccented, while those that are accented will automatically have their accents in the right positions. In this view, the Rhythm Rule of English is an accent deletion rule, which turns *THIRTEEN MEN* into *THIRteen MEN* or – optionally – THREE YELLOW FLOWERS into THREE yellow FLOWERS. In a deletion analysis, accents are thus to be interpreted as abstract placeholders, marking locations that will be filled with a pitch accent like H*L if they survive the actions of various deletion rules (Gussenhoven 1991, van der Hulst 1996).

(2)   a. Deaccent every **A**, **P**, and **M** outside the focus constituent;
        b. Deaccent a focused **P** that is adjacent – disregarding any intervening nonfocused **A** or **M** – to an accented **A**.

The term *focus domain* was proposed for any constituent whose focus can be marked with a single pitch accent, such as a focused argument, a focused modifier, or a focused argument-predicate combination. That is, it defines the domain of focus projection.

There are many situations in which the focus projection postulated in (2b) cannot go through. One of these is word order (Stechow and Uhmann 1986); other deviations are listed in the appendix in Gussenhoven (1992). The discussion attempts to steer clear of these complications, none of which I believe obviously distinguish between the two views at issue here.

2.2 *Obligatory Prenuclear Pitch Accents*

Although both the theory of extended projection of Selkirk (1984, 1995) and the restricted focus projection sketched above make similar predictions here, it is pointed out that other versions of extended focus projection (Chomsky 1972, Cinque 1993) fail to account for the presence of obligatory prenuclear pitch accents. There is a widespread belief that the full-focus version of a sentence is always equivalent to a narrow focus version with the focus on the last pitch-accented word, as well as to a whole series of intermediate focus interpretations. A pitch accent on *feather*, in this view, would be sufficient to allow the whole sentence *John's tickling Mary with a feather* to have full focus. But this is not the case: sentences often have more than one obligatory pitch accent, and this particular example is a case in point. Consider the minimal pair in (3). Only (3a) is the appropriate rendering in the full-focus context given. That is, (3b) does not have the full-focus reading. Observe that (2) correctly characterizes the accent distribution in (3). In (3a), the focused arguments *John* and *Mary*, and the focused modifier *with a feather* are accented by (2a), while the predicate *is tickling* remains unaccented by (2b). In (3b), the focused modifier *with a feather* is accented, while no accents appear on the remaining nonfocused constituents by (2a).

(3)   a. (What's going on?)
            JOHN's tickling MARY with a FEATHER.
        b. (What's John tickling Mary with?)
            John's tickling Mary with a FEATHER.

Experimental work confirms that the meaningful presence versus absence of prenuclear pitch accents can be used by listeners to determine the focus structure of the sentence (Gussenhoven 1983a, Byrd and Clifton 1995). This important issue is somewhat obscured by the fact that English has a late rule that adds pitch accents to unfocused constituents to the left of the nuclear pitch accent.[1] As a result of (4), (3a), but not (3b), is ambiguous between a full-focus reading and a reading with narrow focus on *feather*. (Possibly, there is a phonetic distinction between obligatory and optional prenuclear accents: the prefinal pitch accents in the narrow focus version are not obligatory and, when present, may have reduced excursions.)

(4)   *Prefocal Pitch Accents*: Assign pitch accents to the constituents before the nuclear pitch accent. (Optional)

3   Extended Focus Projection

This section summarizes the theory of focus projection in Selkirk (1984, 1995). It is pointed out that this description faces empirical difficulties. The position that the focus of the sentence, defined as the information sought by a question, should correspond to a syntactic constituent is criticized, and instead it will be argued, with Höhle (1982), that the focus can be syntactically discontinuous. Two arguments for the extended approach are discussed, and the interpretation of the examples used is challenged.

3.1   *Selkirk (1984, 1995)*

In extended focus projection, focus can be passed on to larger constituents than an argument-predicate combination. Selkirk (1984, 1995) projects focus according to (5). Notationally, focus projection is indicated by labeling the node of the constituent to which focus is projected with "F", any such constituent being "F-marked". The highest constituent so marked is called the *focus*.

(5)   *Focus Projection* (Selkirk 1984)
       a. An accented word is F-marked
       b. F-marking of the head of a phrase licenses F-marking of the phrase
       c. F-marking of an internal argument of a head licenses F-marking of the head

In (6), the focus that the noun *Mary* receives by (5a) is passed on to the NP *Mary* by (5b), and from it to the head of the PP *to* by (5c), to the PP *to Mary* by (5b), to the head of the VP *sent* by (5c), to the VP *sent the book to Mary* by (5b), and finally to the S *She sent the book to Mary* by (5b). F is the label used for F-marked constituents and FOC is used to label the Focus.

(6)   [She [[sent]$_F$ a book [to [MARY]$_F$]$_F$]$_F$]$_{FOC}$

Sentence (6) is intended as a possible answer to the question "What did she do with the book?" That is, *a book*, which does not have a pitch accent, is typically *old information*. It is this type of situation that lies at the heart of the divergence within the structural Focus-To-Accent view between the restricted and extended approaches. The inclusion of this NP in the focus constituent *sent a book to Mary* and its evident status as old information in the discourse are in conflict to the extent that one and the same constituent would appear to be old information as well as be part of a constituent that represents new information. This situation is inevitable if the assumption is made that the focus of the sentence should be a constituent of the sentence: the predicate *sent* and the argument *to Mary* cannot form a constituent without also including the argument *the book*.

An important consequence of the presence of constituents that are old information in constituents that are new information is the need for rules that determine when an unaccented word is to be interpreted as new. These are the Focus Interpretation Principles, which Selkirk (1995) gives as (7).

(7)   *Focus Interpretation* (Selkirk, 1995)
       F-marked, but not a Focus: New
       Not F-marked (not a Focus): Given
       F-marked, and Focus: Given or New

Applied to (6), (7) yields (8).

(8)   She sent a book to MARY
        Focus: *She sent a book to Mary*
        New: *sent a book to Mary, sent, to Mary, Mary*
        Given: *She, a book*
        Given or New: *She sent a book to Mary*

In more complex structures, the number of F-marked constituents may be rather large, and the evaluation of the algorithm in (7) can be very difficult as a result. Indeed, since it would appear to be possible not to project the focus maximally according to (5), as in the case of a contrastively focused version of the sentence in (8), when it is a reply to "Who did she send a book to?" a number of intermediate focus projections are possible, each of which will have a corresponding set of interpretations. In the next section, we will deal with the way the restricted approach deals with cases like (6). For now, two empirical problems with this description are pointed out. First, the theory in (5) and (7) makes the wrong prediction in cases like (9). Following Selkirk's theory, we can pass the focus of the accented predicate on to the VP, and thence to the S, which suggests that the VP *sent a book to Mary* can be interpreted as new. However, (9) would clearly be inappropriate in a context "What did she do?"

(9)   [She [[SENT]$_F$ a book to Mary]$_F$]$_{FOC}$

The second problem is related to the solution Selkirk (1995) proposes for cases like (10). As indicated by the context, both the subject and the predicate are in focus. The algorithm in (5) does not allow a focus to be projected from the subject to the VP, and an additional provision is therefore required to account for such broad-focus "news sentences" (Schmerling 1976). Selkirk does this by first assuming, in line with current syntactic theories, that the surface subject is generated in the VP in deep structure, so that a VP-internal subject trace can be referred to by the Focus Interpretation Principles. The additional clause is given as (11), and the focus projections in (12). Here, the focus of *Johnson* licenses F-marking of the subject NP, which by (11) licenses F-marking of the trace, which in turn licenses F-marking of its predicate *died*, whence focus is projected to the entire sentence.

(10)   What happened?
        JOHNson died (Schmerling 1976)

(11)   F-marking of the antecedent of a trace left by NP- or *wh*-movement licenses the F-marking of the trace (Selkirk 1995)

(12) $_{FOC}$[[[JOHNSON]$_F$]$_F$ [[t]$_F$ [died]$_F$]$_F$]$_{FOC}$

As pointed out by Erwin Marsi (p.c.), the problem with this solution is that it does not discriminate between cases like (10), in which a single argument projects focus to its predicate, and cases like (13), where in addition to the argument in subject position, there is an argument in object position. Observe that (13) is not a possible reply to "What happened?"

(13)   MARY bought a book about bats

In a different way, this particular shortcoming is also a problem for the restricted treatment summarized in Section 2. For SAAR, (10) is no problem, since focus projection from an argument to a predicate can take place regardless of the argument's role. What then prevents the subject in (13) from passing on focus to its predicate? The answer would appear to lie in the morphological realization of the arguments and modifiers in the VP. As observed in Gussenhoven (1992), the subject argument cannot project focus to its predicate if some other constituent in the VP is realized by a major-class item. Thus, (14) can be a full focus sentence, but (15) cannot, even though the object argument is outside the focus. How this fact is to be accounted for, in either theory under discussion, is less clear.

(14)   (A: Why is SHE here?)
         B: Her HUSband beats her

(15)   (A: Why is SHE here?)
         B: *Her HUSband beats the poor soul

3.2   *The Restricted View: Discontinuous Focus*

In the restricted focus projection approach, the interpretation of (8) is directly given by the 'focus projection rule' (2). Since the pitch accent on *to Mary* can either express the focus for this argument by itself or for the combination of its predicate *sent* and itself – recall that predicate and argument may be separated by nonfocused constituents (2b) – the interpretation is either that *(to) Mary* is[+focus] or that *sent to Mary* is. Examples like (6) therefore do not pose an empirical problem for the 'restricted' view, but do highlight the implication that the focus of the sentence does not always coincide with a syntactic constituent. Clearly, if the inclusion of unfocused constituents in focused constituents is to be avoided, as it has to be if (2) is to work, then the assumption that the focus of the sentence is a syntactic constituent needs to be abandoned. An explicit proposal to this effect is made by Höhle (1982), who argues that focus can be discontinuous. The notion of *discontinuous focus* should be distinguished from the notion of *multiple foci*, the existence of more than one focus constituent in the sentence. A focus constituent is equated by Höhle with the answer to a question or an implied question (cf. Stechow and Uhmann 1986, and van Kuppevelt 1995, who uses the term *topic* for our *focus*). Thus, (16) and (17), which have identical distributions of pitch accents, provide a minimal pair illustrating the distinction between discontinuous focus (16) and multiple foci (17). In (17), the foci represent answers to separate questions. In (16), the unfocused *dem Kind* intervenes between two focused components of a single focus. The occurrence of discontinuous focus is the logical consequence of the fact that the answer to a single question need not form a syntactic constituent. That is, even though the focus will usually coincide with a syntactic constituent, there is no rule of syntax that requires the words conveying the answer to an (implied) question to be assigned to an exclusive constituent.

(16)   A: Was hat das Kind erlebt?
        B: KARL hat dem Kind einen FÜLLER geschenkt
        [*Karl. . .einen Füller geschenkt*]$_{FOC}$

(17)   a: Wer hat was hinsichtlich des Kindes getan?
        b: KARL hat dem Kind einen FÜLLER geschenkt
        [*Karl*]$_{FOC}$ [*einen Füller geschenkt*]$_{FOC}$ (cf. Höhle 1982)

The position that the focus of the sentence need not be a syntactic constituent makes focus a less tractable phenomenon in syntactic models. The important advantage of a theory with restricted focus projection, however, is that because of the less complex relation between accented words and the size of the focus domain, the need for a separate set of focus interpretation rules never arises. Indeed, focus projection principles should in themselves suffice to identify the focused (*new*) status of the constituents in a sentence. Such principles are formulated in order to characterize the nontrivial relation between sentence accents and focus. The adoption of the "focus-to-accent" view of sentence accentuation was called into being precisely to deal with the problem that not all focused constituents are accented, and to provide a way of characterizing unaccented constituents as being in the focus, and hence as being *new*, or the answer to an implied question. If the connection between the presence of a pitch accent and the interpretation of the status of the word it is placed on is mediated by two sets of rules, one taking pitch accents as input and the other taking focus as input, *focus* acquires the status of an auxiliary symbol that is devoid of both phonological and semantic content. That is, instead of (18b), the assumption must be that we make do with (18a). Moreover, the postulation of Focus Interpretation Principles incorrectly suggests that what we are interpreting is the meaning of focus. The interpretation of focus in a true sense is very different from the structural issue in (18a). It cannot be reduced to newness and givenness.

(18)   a. *Restricted Focus Projection:*
           Pitch Accent distribution ↔ Focus distribution
        b. *Extended Focus Projection:*
           Pitch Accent distribution ↔ Focus distribution ↔ Focus Interpretation

3.3   *Two Arguments for Extended Focus Projection Refuted*

Selkirk (1995) presents two arguments for the theory of extended focus projection in (5) and (7), which are here reproduced. It will be shown that alternative interpretations are available for the focus structure of the examples on which the arguments are based. The first argument is based on the interpretation of (19) as a full-focus sentence. Here, the pitch accent on the inflectional projection of the verb is said to license focus for the whole sentence.

(19)   A: Mary didn't buy a book about bats
         B: $_{FOC}$[[Mary] [$_F$[DID]$_F$ [buy a book about bats]]$_F$]$_{FOC}$ (Selkirk 1995)

However, it is not clear why full-sentence focus is a required interpretation here. Bolinger (1983) and Gussenhoven (1983) describe cases like these as having focus on the polarity of the sentence. The background, the information that Speaker A would like to see included in B's discourse model, is that 'Mary did not buy a book about bats'; the contribution Speaker B then makes is to remove the negative; that is, he focuses on the positive polarity. The need for assuming that the entire sentence is the focus is not evident: the implied question to which B's sentence is a reply is 'Which of the information contained in *NEG,PAST[Mary buy a book about bats]* is incorrect?' upon which NEG is taken as the focus.

A related case, (20), is given in Selkirk (1984), originally from Ladd (1980).

(20)   A: Has John read *Slaughterhouse Five?*
         B: John does not READ books (Ladd 1980)

Here again, polarity is under focus. In Gussenhoven (1983), I argued that cases like (20) differ from those in (19) in the *kind* of focus used. In (19) the speaker offers the focus (the positive polarity) as a contradiction of what the listener (Speaker A) said. Apart from the change in polarity, (20) differs from (19) in that Speaker B is now not rejecting an attempted contribution made by Speaker A, but is correcting a presupposition that Speaker A evidently has. Put differently, the negative polarity of Speaker A's proposition *NEG,PAST[Mary buy a book about bats]* in (19) was not admitted into B's discourse model, while in (20) Speaker B is concerned to debug A's version of the discourse model, which was found to contain erroneously the proposition *POSITIVE[John read books]*. That is, the [-focus] information is [John reads books], and the [+focus] information is that this is not the case. (20) is an example of "counterpresuppositional" focus, while (19) is an example of "counterassertive" focus. These examples make it clear that a definition of the focus as the answer to an implied question is not entirely satisfactory. In (20) the implied question is 'Are any of the propositions I am presupposing in my question *POSITIVE[John reads Slaughterhouse Five]* incorrect?', upon which the speaker identifies *POSITIVE[John read books]*, selects *POSITIVE* as the incorrect information, and hence focuses on *NEGATIVE* in his reply. The distinction between "counterassertive" and "counterpresuppositional" focus is formally expressed only if the focus is confined to the polarity in English, German, and Dutch, as illustrated in (21)–(24). Observe that the pitch accent does not always appear on equivalent words in these languages. In particular, Selkirk's account of (19) cannot be maintained for the

German translation, since *doch* is neither the head of the VP nor an argument of *liest*.

(21)   A: He doesn't read books
         B: He DOES read books/Er liest DOCH Bücher
                                        (counterassertive, POS)

(22)   A: He reads books
         B: He DOESN'T read books/Er liest KEINE Bücher
                                        (counterassertive, NEG)

(23)   A: If he read books, he would know this
         B: He READS (DOES READ) books/Er LIEST doch Bücher
                                        (counterpresupposional, POS)

(24)   A: Has John read *Slaughterhouse Five?*
         B: He doesn't READ books/Er LIEST keine Bücher
                                        (counterpresuppositional, NEG)

A second argument used in Selkirk (1995) is based on the claim that *only* can govern focus over the entire embedded sentence in (25).

(25)   A: I was thinking that bats eat mosquitoes
         B: I was only thinking that ₍FOC₎[MARY bought a BOOK about bats]₍FOC₎
                                        (Selkirk, 1995)

In the "extended" view, *(about) bats* is a given constituent in a focused constituent; in the "restricted" view, it would for that reason be excluded from the focus. The "extended" interpretation in (25) is arrived at via focus projection from *book* to the NP *a book about bats*, from this argument NP to the verb *bought*, from there to the VP, and then on to the entire embedded S. The argument for this interpretation is that because *only* dominates the embedded S, therefore S must be focus. However, the assumption that there is a necessary identity of the focus of the sentence and the syntactic position of *only* cannot be maintained. This position effectively predicts that there cannot be any distinctions of focus distribution in embedded sentences dominated by *only*. This prediction is clearly false. In (26a), which might have the context "Were you thinking they might all catch a cold or what?" it is reasonable to assume that the entire embedded clause is in focus. The homophonous (26b) is appropriate in a context like "Were you perhaps thinking they wouldn't fit in the spare bedroom?" and therefore has only *into a phone booth* in focus. The syntactic position of *only* is no different, but its focus clearly is.

(26)   a. I was only thinking ₍FOC₎[that they wouldn't fit into a PHONE booth]₍FOC₎
         b. I was only thinking that they wouldn't fit ₍FOC₎[into a PHONE booth]₍FOC₎

Examples (26a, b) demonstrate the incorrectness of Selkirk's premise that the position of *only* in the syntactic structure allows the focus it governs to be read off directly from that structure, and the argument she bases on (25) therefore cannot go through. Apparently, *only* can be raised into the "reporting" matrix sentence independently of the focus in the embedded sentence. Indeed, the sentence in (26) can be given yet another analysis, one in which only *phone* is focused (i.e., 'not a recording booth'). This analysis of (26) leaves the possibility open that the syntactic position of *only* is equivalent to its scope. In that interpretation, the syntactic scope of *only* cannot be coextensive with the focus, since the semantic scope of *only* includes (at least) the embedded sentence. König (1991) illustrates the distinction between scope and focus with the help of (27a, b), and comments, "[t]he focus of the particle [*sc.* also] is exactly the same in these two cases and can thus not be responsible for the difference in meaning" (1991:30).

(27)   a.   He also drinks WHISKEY very rarely
        b.   Very rarely does he also drink WHISKEY (König 1991)

In any event, these two examples do not lend support to the 'extended' view of focus projection.

4   "Restricted" Focus Projection in Complex Sentences

In this section, it is emphasized that the "restricted" focus projection of (2) can produce quite complex focus constituents. This is because, in embedded structures, (2b) can be satisfied at different levels of structure by the same surface sentence accent (Gussenhoven 1992). A case in point is provided by the original example used by Chomsky (1972), here given as (28a, b).

(28)   a.   (A: What ex-convict wearing something red was he warned to look out for?)
              B: He was warned to look out for an ex-convict in a red [SHIRT]$_{FOC}$
        b.   (A: What was going on?)
              B: [He was warned to look out for an ex-convict in a red SHIRT]$_{FOC}$

A complication here is the use of the complex argument *an ex-convict in a red shirt*. When focused, it is pronounced as in (29), on the principle that every lexical element in the argument or modifier is accented, barring the effects of the Compound Rule and the Rhythm Rule.

(29)   an EX-CONvict in a RED SHIRT

To circumvent this complication, I have replaced it with the single-accent expression *a maniac*. In (30), *for a maniac* is an argument of the predicate *to look out*, and hence *look out*, though focused, can be unaccented. The constituent *to look out for a maniac*, in its turn, is an argument of *was warned*, and so this predicate can remain unaccented. The sole accent on *maniac* thus serves to put the entire VP in (30) in focus.

(30)   (to look OUT)$_{Pred}$ (for a MANiac)$_{Arg}$
                                         out   *first cycle*
       (was   WARNED)$_{Pred}$ (to look out for a MANiac)$_{Arg}$
                 warned   *second cycle*
       He[was warned to look out for a MANiac]$_{FOC}$ *output*

Similarly, sentences like (31) can have everything except the subject of the matrix
sentence in focus, even though there is just an accent on *bird*. Since in the lowest
clause, *a bird* is an argument of *sing*, the latter predicate can remain unaccented.
Since *a bird sing* is an accented argument of the predicate *hear*, this predicate can
remain unaccented, while *to hear a bird sing* is an accented argument allowing
failed to be unaccented. Such embedded structures, therefore, allow multiple applications of (2), which explains why the "restricted view" can account for the
existence of quite long stretches of unaccented, focused speech.

(31)   A: Why weren't you admitted to the Poets' Club?
         B: I failed to hear a BIRD sing

The three applications of the focus projection to the predicates are shown in (32).

(32)   (a BIRD)$_{Arg}$ (SING)$_{Pred}$
                                                  sing   *first cycle*
                   (to HEAR)$_{Pred}$ (a BIRD   sing)$_{Arg}$
                          hear   *second cycle*
       (FAILED)$_{Pred}$ (to hear   BIRD   sing)$_{Arg}$
       failed   *third cycle*
       I [failed to hear a BIRD sing]FOC   *output*

Note

1   I am obliged to Charles Clifton for pointing out that the formulation in an earlier version
    of this chapter, according to which pitch accents are optionally added before the focus
    constituent, incorrectly predicts that optional pitch accents cannot be assigned to focused
    unaccented predicates before accented arguments (cf. *teaches* in *He teaches linGUIStics*,
    as a reply to "What does he do?").

References

Baart, J. L. G. 1987. *Focus, Syntax, and Accent Placement*. Dordrecht: ICG Printing.
Bolinger, D. 1972. Accent is predictable (if you're a mind reader). *Language* 48, 633–644.
Bolinger, D. 1983. Two views of accent. *Journal of Linguistics* 21, 79–123.
Bolinger, D. 1985. *Intonation and Its Parts*. London: Edward Arnold.
Byrd, S., and C. Clifton, Jr. 1995. Focus, accent, and argument structure: Effects on language
    comprehension. *Language & Speech* 38, 365–391.
Chomsky, N. 1972. Deep structure, surface structure, and semantic interpretation. In *Lin-
    guistics and Psychology*, ed. D.D. Steinberg and L.A. Jacobovits. *Semantics: An In-
    terdisciplinary Reader in Philosophy*. Cambridge: Cambridge University Press.

Cinque, G. 1993. A null theory of phrase and compound stress. *Linguistic Inquiry* 24, 239–297.

Fuchs, A. 1984. 'Deaccenting' and 'default accent'. In *Intonation, Accent and Rhythm: Studies in Discourse Phonology.* ed. D. Gibbon and H. Richter. Berlin/New York: De Gruyter. 134–164.

Gussenhoven, C. 1983. Focus, mode, and the nucleus. *Journal of Linguistics* 19, 377–419. Reprinted as Chapter 1 in Gussenhoven (1984).

Gussenhoven, C. 1983a. Testing the reality of focus domains. *Language and Speech* 26, 61–80. Reprinted as Chapter 4 in Gussenhoven (1984).

Gussenhoven, C. 1984. *On the Grammar and Semantics of Sentence Accents.* Dordrecht/Cinnaminson: Foris.

Gussenhoven, C. 1985. Two views of accent: A reply. *Journal of Linguistics* 21, 377–417.

Gussenhoven, C. 1991. The English Rhythm Rule as an accent assignment rule. *Phonology* 8, 1–35.

Gussenhoven, C. 1992. Sentence accents and argument structure. In I.M. Roca (ed.), *Thematic Structure: Its Role in Grammar.* Berlin, New York: Foris. 79–106.

Hayes, B., and A. Lahiri. 1991. Bengali intonational phonology. *NLLT* 9, 47–96.

Höhle, T. 1982. Explikationen für 'Normale Betonung' and 'Normale Wortstellung'. In W. Abraham (ed.), *Satzglieder im Deutschen.* Tübingen: Gunter Narr. 75–153.

Hulst, H. van der. 1996. Word accent. In H. van der Hulst (ed.), *Word Prosodic Systems in the Languages of Europe.* Berlin, New York: Mouton de Gruyter.

König, E. 1991. *The Meaning of Focus Particles.* London: Routledge.

Ladd, D.R. 1980. *The Structure of Intonational Meaning: Evidence from English.* Bloomington: Indiana University Press.

Ladd, D.R 1983. *Even,* focus, and normal stress. *Journal of Semantics* 2, 157–170.

Ladd, D.R. 1996. *Intonational Phonology.* Cambridge: Cambridge University Press.

Marsi, E. 1993. Evaluatie van linguistische theorie over syntaxis en intonatie door computationele implementatie. MA Thesis, University of Nijmegen.

Pierrehumbert, J., and M. Beckman. 1988. *Japanese Tone Structure.* Cambridge, Mass.: MIT Press.

Schmerling, S. 1976. *Aspects of English Sentence Stress.* Austin: Texas University Press.

Selkirk, E. 1984. *Phonology and Syntax: The Relation between Sound and Structure.* Cambridge, Mass.: MIT Press.

Selkirk, E. 1995. Sentence prosody: Intonation, stress and phrasing. In J. Goldsmith (ed.), *Handbook of Phonological Theory,* London: Blackwell. 550–569.

Stechow, A. von, and S. Uhmann. 1986. Some remarks on focus projection. In W. Abraham and S. de Meij (eds.), *Topic, Focus, and Configurationality: Papers from the 6th Groningen Grammar Talks 1984,* Amsterdam: Benjamins. 295–320.

Steedman, M. 1994. Remarks on Intonation and "Focus." In P. Bosch and R. van der Sandt (eds.), *Focus and Natural Language Processing.* Heidelberg: IBM Deutschland.

4   Informational Autonomy

JOACHIM JACOBS

Abstract

The concept of informational autonomy plays an important role in the analysis of various grammatical phenomena such as focus ambiguity, valency projection, and restrictions on extraction. I speculate that informational autonomy can be explicated on the basis of a partitioning of propositions into chunks corresponding to aspects of situations. With the help of a list of grammatical prerequisites of nonautonomy, several predictions about accentuation and extraction are derived.

1   Introduction

Informational autonomy is a relation between heads and their sister constituents. For example, the head daughters of (1a–c) are informationally autonomous in relation to their sisters:

(1)   a. [[Kommissar Meier] [hat den Bürgermeister verhaftet]$_{+ia}$]
           superintendent M. has the mayor   arrested
        b. [[einem Freund] [[ein Haus]   bauen]$_{+ia}$]
           for-a friend(dat) a house(acc) to-build
        c. [[schnell] [wegrennen]$_{+ia}$]
           quickly   to-run away
        d. [[weiß][-blau]$_{+ia}$]
           white -blue

In contrast, the head daughters of (2a–c) (in the most plausible reading of these examples) are informationally nonautonomous in relation to their sisters:

(2)   a. [[Die Polizei] [kommt]$_{-ia}$]
           the police   is-coming
        b. [[ein Haus]   [bauen]$_{-ia}$]
           a house(acc) to-build
        c. [[dunkel][blau]$_{-ia}$]
           dark   blue

Thus, in (1a) the VP *[hat den Bürgermeister verhaftet]* is autonomous in relation to

This chapter is a revised version of Jacobs 1993a. For helpful comments I thank Beatrice Primus, Manfred Krifka, Manfred Pinkal, and Kjell Johan Sæbø.

the subject, whereas the head of (2a), *kommt*, is informationally nonautonomous in relation to *[die Polizei]*. Occasionally, I will use different terminology (introduced in earlier work); in cases of informational nonautonomy, I will say that the non-head is *integrated* into the head.

In the first part of this chapter I argue that informational autonomy plays an important role in the grammar of German and English. It is a central concept in the theory of phrasal and compound stress, explaining, among other things, the phenomenon of focus ambiguity. Furthermore, it seems to be one of the crucial notions in the theory of feature projection. Nonautonomy (or integration) produces tight, wordlike structures that allow features to climb the tree even when they come from a non-head. This also has interesting consequences for the theory of extraction sites, provided that extraction is based on feature projection, as I will assume.

In the second part I will speculate about the nature of informational autonomy. Its role in grammar has become fairly clear through recent research, but the phenomenon itself is still mysterious, even though it has a rather simple intuitive basis: A head X of a constituent Y is informationally autonomous in relation to the non-head daughters of Y iff the semantic processing of Y involves an independent step of processing X. This is not the case in (2a), for example.[1] We do not start semantic processing of this sentence by referring to a certain group of policemen, then go on by processing the meaning of the head *kommt* in a second step and finally combine the results of the two steps. Rather, (2a) is semantically processed at one fell swoop, by referring holistically to an event of approaching policemen. Similarly, in (2c), we do not first refer to the property of being dark and then refer to the property of being blue. We obviously refer to only one property, although its quality is determined by combining the meanings of the two constituents. In (1a), on the other hand, it seems quite clear that semantic processing proceeds in several steps, namely, by first identifying a certain person, and then ascribing to this person a certain action, which itself is semantically processed independently, probably in several steps. Unfortunately, in many cases our intuitions about semantic processing are much less clear. Therefore, we need an explication of informational autonomy that correctly predicts the clear cases and decides the unclear ones. In a first attempt at such an explication, I will propose that informational autonomy could be represented by structuring the way we calculate the propositional content of sentences from the meanings of their parts in a certain way. I will conjecture that this structure has certain properties that could explain an important trait of informational nonautonomy, namely, its being restricted to deeply embedded heads. However, this proposal concerning the formal representation of informational autonomy will not lead to much more than a program for future research. Especially, it will not enable us to diagnose autonomy in all possible cases and independently of its intended grammatical applications. Therefore, in a second attempt at capturing informational autonomy, I will give a list of grammatical prerequisites of nonautonomy, which can help in deciding whether given heads are autonomous. After having introduced this list, I will show that it allows fine-grained predictions in the areas mentioned in the first section, namely, focus ambiguity, feature projection, and extraction. In the final section I will shortly address the question whether the concept of informational autonomy could be replaced by a simpler *syntactic* notion. Many of the examples we will discuss suggest that this could be done, and other researchers dealing with phenomena like focus ambiguity have indeed proposed that the crucial factor is syntactic. However, I will try to show that a purely syntactic approach is likely to fail.

2   The Role of Informational Autonomy in Grammar

2.1   Sentence Stress

In languages like German and English, sentence stress reacts to informational nonautonomy. Unless in narrow focus, informational nonautonomous heads in these languages are less prominent than their sisters in the metrical tree, as exemplified in (4a) and (4b):[2]

(4)   a.   b.

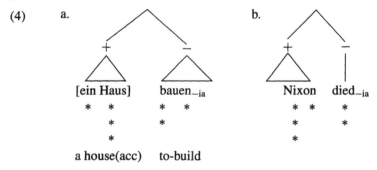

       a house(acc)   to-build

(5a, b), on the other hand, illustrate what happens in cases of informational autonomy:

(5)   a.   b.

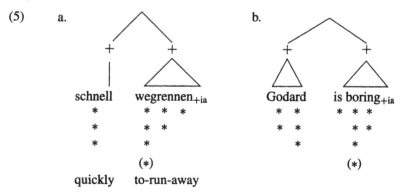

       quickly   to-run-away

When the head is autonomous it equals the non-head in prominence; that is, they both get a plus in the metrical tree. This is reflected in the metrical grid by equally high columns under the strongest syllables of the two constituents. However, an optional operation can add an asterisk to the last of the highest columns in the grid. Application of this rhythmical operation depends on tempo and other nongrammatical factors.

Note that there is an element of iconicity here: The destressing of a head indicates its nonautonomous status in semantic processing.

Other patterns can be observed when one of the constituents is *nonstressable*. There are two kinds of nonstressability: In the first type, constituents inherit this feature from the lexicon, where certain "small words" are marked as being inherently nonstressable. The second type of nonstressability is the result of contextual predictability. (6a) and (6b) are examples of lexically and contextually induced nonstressability, respectively:[3]

(6)   a.   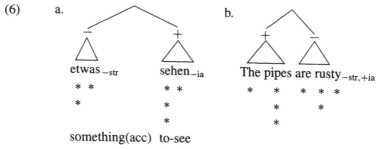   b.

The indefinite pronoun *etwas* is inherently −str. The predicate *are rusty* becomes −str when uttered in a context that makes its content predictable, for example when (6b) is used as an answer to the question *Why does the water from the tap come out brown?*[4]

In these cases the difference between autonomous and nonautonomous heads is neutralized: A nonstressable constituent (unless it is in narrow focus) is always less prominent than its stressable sister, no matter whether the head is +ia or −ia. Therefore, when discussing the effects of autonomy on stress patterns, we will have to make sure that these effects are not blurred by nonstressability.

The metrical grids assigned by these rules are not only intended to reflect rhythmical intuitions. They also indicate the possible positions of *pitch accents*. Suppose that the grid is such that its n ($1 \leq n$) highest columns are assigned to the syllables $s_1, \ldots, s_n$; then in German (and probably also in English and Dutch), the last of these syllables, s_n, must be associated with a pitch accent, and no syllable following s_n can be associated with a pitch accent. In addition, syllables preceding s_n can be associated with a pitch accent if they have at least three "*" in the grid.[5] Thus, in many cases more than one pitch accent pattern is possible for given expressions. For example, (5b) may be pronounced with just one pitch accent on *bor-*, or alternatively with two accents on *-dard* and *bor-*. (4b), however, can get only one pitch accent (*on Nix-*).[6]

This analysis of stress patterns and pitch accent positions in terms of informational autonomy yields an explanation of the fact that certain accentuations are ambiguous with respect to (w.r.t.) the placement of focus, a phenomenon that has been called *focus projection* in parts of the literature. Compare (4) and (5) with (7) and (8):

(7)   a.

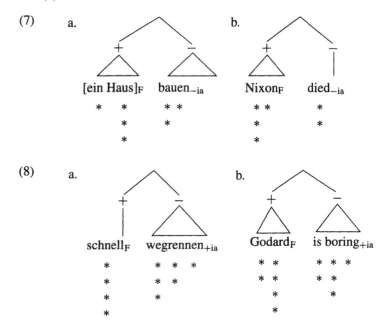

In (7) and (8), the non-head constituent is marked with the feature F, which means that it is in narrow focus. In (4) and (5), on the other hand, none of the daughters is in narrow focus. What is the influence of F on the accentuation? For simple cases like (7) and (8), this question can be answered as follows: A constituent that is F or dominates a constituent that is F must get a plus in the metrical tree, and its sister constituent must get a minus (regardless of the ±ia- and ±str-values of these constituents).[7] This is the pattern we see in (7) and (8).

But now note that there is a remarkable difference between (4) and (7) on the one hand and (5) and (8) on the other: The examples with autonomous heads, (5) and (8), have different stress patterns, depending on whether the nonhead is F or not. But in the examples with nonautonomous heads, that is, in (4) and (7), we have the same stress pattern, no matter whether the non-head is F or not. In other words, these examples, when stressed as indicated, are ambiguous with respect to the presence or absence of F on the non-head. The reason for this kind of focus ambiguity lies in the fact that both nonautonomy of the head and narrow focus on the non-head result in a plus-minus pattern in the metrical tree.

This autonomy-based explanation of focus ambiguity also applies to more difficult examples. For example, in double-object constructions only one of the objects is predicted to be a possible source of focus projection. Consider (9):

(9)

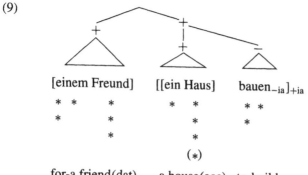

[einem Freund]	[[ein Haus]	bauen$_{-ia}$]$_{+ia}$
for-a friend(dat)	a house(acc)	to-build

Again, the head verb is nonautonomous. Therefore, a minus-plus pattern is assigned to the verb and its sister. The phrase consisting of the verb and the direct object, however, is informationally autonomous, due to its syntactic complexity (see below). Thus, a plus-plus pattern is assigned to this phrase and its sister, the indirect object. Accordingly, the grid assigns equally high columns to each of the objects, but the last of these highest columns again can (and normally will) receive an additional "*". This analysis correctly predicts that only an F on the direct object can give rise to focus ambiguity here. For if we compare (9) with (10a, b), where the direct object and the indirect object are F, respectively, we see that only in the former case does the same grid pattern arise as in (9):

(10)   a.

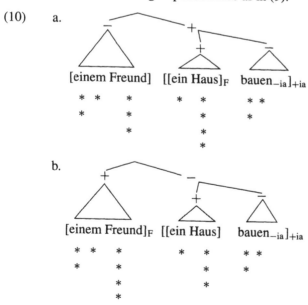

[einem Freund]	[[ein Haus]$_F$	bauen$_{-ia}$]$_{+ia}$

b.

[einem Freund]$_F$	[[ein Haus]	bauen$_{-ia}$]$_{+ia}$

The grid of (10a) is identical with the grid of (9) (provided that the last of the strongest syllables has been strengthened). In contrast, the grid of (10b) is different from the pattern emerging in the absence of internal foci. Therefore, this case is not ambiguous w.r.t. the position of focus. Main stress on the indirect object can only be interpreted as a narrow focus on this object. (A more detailed discussion of the relation between autonomy and focus ambiguity can be found in Jacobs 1991.)

Another phenomenon that the autonomy-based theory of sentence stress explains without additional assumptions is the *difference between the stress patterns of head-final and non–head-final constructions or languages*, a difference that has been noted in the typological literature, but has not yet been explained. It can be observed in cases of neutral stress, that is, when no internal foci are present. When the head is in final position, the neutral stress patterns of complex constituents will depend on certain grammatical relations between the daughter constituents. In contrast, when the head is in a nonfinal position, no influence of grammatical relations on neutral stress patterns can be observed. Compare, for example, (4) and (5) on the one hand with (11) on the other. In (4) and (5), where the second of the daughter constituents is the head, the neutral stress pattern is sensitive to the grammatical relation between the non-head and the head. A non-head that is an object or a special kind of subject, as in (4), will trigger a stress pattern that is different from the pattern that arises when the non-head is an adjunct or a different kind of subject, as in (5). These differences, according to our theory, reflect the autonomy or nonautonomy of the head. But now note what happens in cases with nonfinal heads, as in (11):

(11)   a.   b.

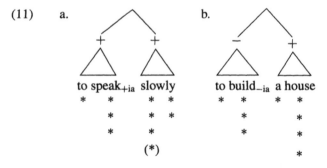

In such cases there is practically no difference between the grids of adjunct-verb combinations and those of object-verb combinations, provided that the usual strengthening of the last strongest syllable applies. In both cases, the nonhead will emerge as the rhythmically most prominent constituent. That is why researchers concentrating on languages or constructions with the head in second or first position tend to ignore influences of grammatical or semantic relations on neutral stress.[8] Note that our autonomy-based rules predict these differences between head-final and non–head-final structures without any language-specific or construction-specific rules, provided that the nonautonomy of heads is marked by destressing them and that the last of several strongest syllables is normally strengthened.[9]

A further application of the autonomy-based theory of stress is the accentuation of *compounds*. As is well known from segmental phonology, compounds in many languages behave like syntactic phrases in regard to many phonological processes, for instance, assimilations. However, the traditional and still prevailing accounts of their stress patterns treat them as nonphrasal.[10] In contrast, the autonomy-based theory allows for an analysis of compounds as phonologically phrasal also in regard to their stress patterns. Consider (12a, b):

(12)

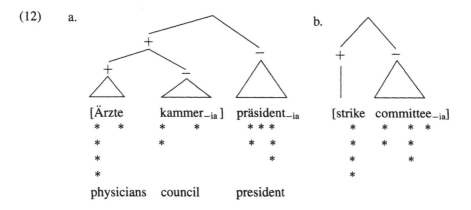

If we assume that all head constituents of these examples are nonautonomous – an assumption that is in line with the intuitive characterization of nonautonomy above – the stress patterns depicted in (12) follow from the minus-marking of nonautonomy (which in (12a) is applied recursively). For the analysis of more complex cases like (13) we have to remember that nonautonomy requires heads to be noncomplex; compare our discussion of double-object examples like (10). This assumption yields intuitively correct stress patterns for cases like (13):

(13)

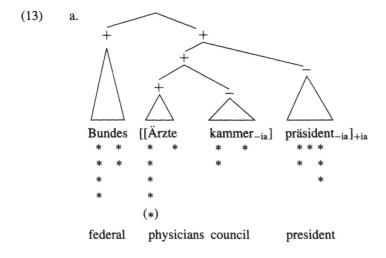

b.

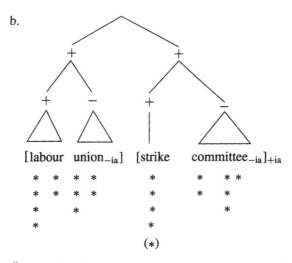

[labour union$_{-ia}$] [strike committee$_{-ia}$]$_{+ia}$

Because *Ärztekammerpräsident* and *strike committee* are informationally autonomous, they will equal their sister constituents in prominence, yielding equally
high columns under the strongest syllables of these constituents in the metrical
grid. As a result of strengthening the last of these strongest syllables, *ärzte-* and
strike emerge as the rhythmically strongest positions. This pattern, of course,
would also have been assigned by Chomsky and Halle's (1968) Compound Stress
Rule or by any of its metrical reformulations (e.g., in Liberman and Prince 1977).
But note that in our derivation we didn't use any rules or assumptions that are
specific for compounds. Rather, we applied exactly the same principles as in the
analysis of syntactic phrases like (10). Thus, we can now claim that compounds
are phrasal not only in regard to their segmental phonology but also w.r.t. their
stress patterns.

One of the problems of this analysis is that stress patterns of compounds aren't
always calculated from their internal structure. Rather, in many cases they are
idiosyncratic or assigned through analogy to other words (just as the meanings of
compounds are often the result of idiosyncrasies or analogies). But to the extent
that the stress patterns are "compositional", the autonomy-based theory will predict
them quite accurately, as I argue in more detail in Jacobs (1993a, b).

2.2   Valency Projection

Informational autonomy also plays a role in syntax (discussed in detail in Jacobs
1992b). The basic fact is that nonautonomy or integration, through combining
sister constituents to form semantically tight, wordlike structures, assimilates these
structures to words also in regard to feature projection, especially the projection
of the *syntactic valency* of constituents (which I assume to be a syntactic feature).
It is well known that within words the syntactic valency of a daughter constituent

can be projected from a non-head (provided that certain independent conditions are met), as illustrated in (14), where the dative valency slot (symbolized by /dat) of the non-head verb stem is projected to the adjectival mother node (cf. *weil das den Leuten zumutbar ist* 'because this of-these people(dat) expectable is'):

(14)

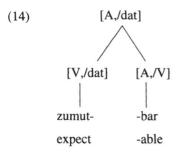

In syntactic phrases, on the other hand, valency normally cannot be projected from a non-head, as (15a, b) exemplify:

(15) a. *   [V,infl,/dat]

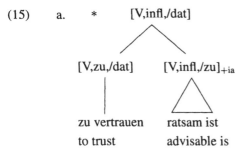

b.   [V,zu,/dat]

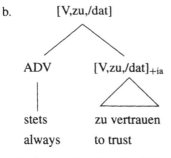

Ungrammatical examples like *weil dem Kanzler [wahrscheinlich [zu vertrauen ratsam ist]]* ('because the chancellor(dat) probably to trust advisable is') show that, as a result of the non-head position of *zu vertrauen* in (15a), the dative slot of this verb cannot be projected to the mother node. Only if the verb is in head position, as in (15b), will the dative slot be able to climb the tree; compare *[Dem Kanzler [stets [zu vertrauen]]] ist ratsam* ('The chancellor(dat) always to trust is advisable').

Now consider (16). Here, *zu vertrauen* again is in a non-head position, but now the head is nonautonomous in relation to the non-head, because the latter is the logical object of the head. (The relation between objecthood and informational nonautonomy will be discussed later.)

(16)

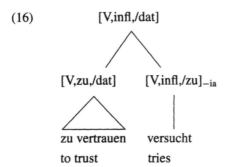

In this case the valency of *zu vertrauen* can be projected without problems, as is illustrated by grammatical sentences like *weil er dem Kanzler [leider [zu vertrauen versucht]]* ('because he the chancellor(dat) unfortunately to trust tries'). In other words, with respect to valency projection, (16) patterns with (14), not with (15); that is, it behaves like a complex word, not as a phrase. I hypothesize that this is a result of the fact that the non-head of (16) is integrated into the head.

This idea has far-reaching consequences (e.g., in the analysis of raising constructions), which become even more far-reaching when we combine it with another idea, originating in categorial grammar: If we represent *movement traces* by additional slots in the valency of their mother node, which are then projected up the tree until they are saturated by the antecedent, structures like (17) will emerge:

(17)   a.

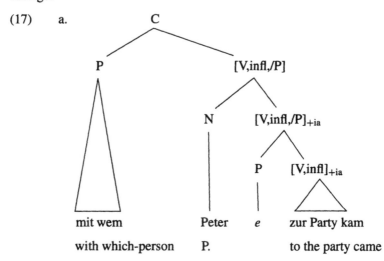

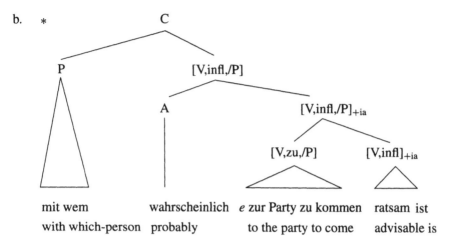

b. *

If we assume that valency places marking empty nodes and valency places induced by the lexicon are subject to the same principles, the contrast between (17a) and (17b) can be predicted without further assumptions: (17a) is grammatical, because here the projection of the valency place marking the empty prepositional adjunct involves only head nodes. In (17b), on the other hand, this valency place is projected from a non-head node. This is correctly predicted to be ungrammatical. As we have seen in (15b), valency places cannot be projected from non-head daughters of syntactic phrases.

But as we saw in (16), this restriction is cancelled when the head of the phrase is nonautonomous. Therefore, we should expect examples like (18) to be grammatical, where the trace is contained in the sister of a nonautonomous head – and indeed they are grammatical:

(18)

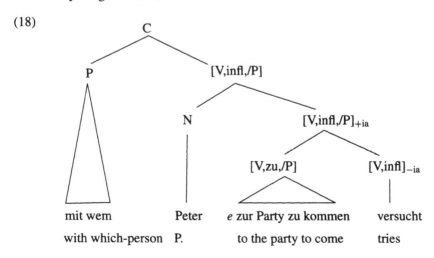

In other words: If we combine our proposals concerning the role of informational autonomy in valency projection with a valency projection theory of movement, some well known facts about extraction domains can be derived without further stipulations. We predict that objecthood – more precisely: integration – is a prerequisite for the non-head to be a possible extraction domain. Thus, it follows that (certain) subjects and adjuncts, due to the informational autonomy of their head sisters, are islands for movement, while objects, when they are integrated, are not. Note that this result is not stipulated in a definition of extraction barriers, as it is in all versions of Chomskyan generative grammar, for example, in Chomsky's (1986) definition of *blocking category*, which states that direct objects cannot be blocking categories. Rather, the asymmetries between (certain) subjects and adjuncts on the one hand and (certain) objects on the other follow from the independently motivated principle that projection of valency places can start from non-heads only in tight, wordlike structures.[11]

Note finally that this view of movement explains hitherto unexplained *relations between movement and accentuation*. For example, we predict that in a head-final construction, a non-head is a possible extraction domain only if putting the main stress on it will lead to focus ambiguity. Thus we correctly predict that in (9) only the object that is a source of focus projection, that is, the direct object (cf. (10)), is a possible extraction domain. This is illustrated by examples like *was_i hat er seinem Freund [e_i für ein Haus] bauen wollen* versus **was_i hat er [e_i für einem Freund] ein Haus bauen wollen*. This cross-level prediction follows directly from the role informational autonomy plays in sentence phonology and in the theory of movement, as the reader may easily verify.

3   Informational Autonomy and the Representation of Meaning

Now that we have seen that informational autonomy is an important notion in several parts of the grammar, we must begin to ask how this notion can be explicated. Remember the intuitive characterization of informational autonomy given earlier: A head X of a constituent Y is informationally autonomous in relation to its sister nodes iff the semantic processing of Y involves an independent step of processing X. Thus, the locus of informational autonomy seems to be the way we compose the meanings of daughters to calculate the meaning of their mother. But unfortunately, if we rely on the usual explications of meaning composition, we will not be able to distinguish autonomous from nonautonomous heads in a general way. Compare examples (1a) and (2a). According to the usual analysis, the meaning of both of these sentences is derived by applying a predicate to an argument, as shown in (M1a) and (M2a):

(M1a) [hat den Bürgermeister verhaftet]′([Kommissar M.]′)
(M2a) kommt′([die Polizei]′)

Thus, in both cases two semantic entities are combined to form a third semantic entity. But, according to our intuitive characterization, the crucial difference between (2a) and (1a) is that in the former processing proceeds in just one step, whereas in (1a) several steps are involved. Note that this problem cannot be solved by switching to a generalized quantifier analysis. This would only reverse the position of predicate and argument, but it will not reduce the number of steps involved in the analysis of (2a). And even a Davidsonian reformulation will not help, although by adding an event variable to the meaning of the verb phrase we would introduce into the formal representation the kind of entity we have referred to in our intuitive description of (2a). But still, there will be too many entities, because now, not only a predicate and an argument, but also an event will be involved in the semantic analysis of (2a).

Note finally that we cannot solve this problem by simply assuming that expressions like (2a) are semantically noncomplex. Just like (1a), also (2a) conveys a complex meaning that is calculated from two less complex meanings (or else we wouldn't understand it). The difference, as we have described it, does not lie in the number of *meanings* involved, but rather in the number of *steps* that are taken in the calculation. Thus, we need a representation that separates information concerning the number of meanings from information about the number of steps. In other words, we need something like (CM1a) and (CM2a) (where C stands for calculation):

(CM1a) $\downarrow\downarrow$[hat den Bürgermeister verhaftet]$'\downarrow$($\downarrow$[Kommissar M.]$'\downarrow$)$\downarrow$
(CM2a) $\downarrow$kommt$'$ ([die Polizei]$'$)$\downarrow$

Here, each pair of downward arrows indicates that the material enclosed corresponds to a step on the relevant level of semantic calculation. (CM2a) contains only one pair of arrows and therefore indicates that only one step is involved, while (CM1a) is made up of three pairs of arrows, one enclosing the predicate, one enclosing the argument, and one enclosing the whole proposition. Thus we get a direct representation of what we think is the crucial difference between (1a) and (2a), without abandoning more traditional assumptions about the way the meaning of these sentences is composed.

Having introduced this simple notation, we can speculate a little about its role in semantic representations. Given our intuitive interpretation of the downward arrows, it is natural to assume that complex constituents with a non-head daughter X and a nonautonomous head Y will have semantic representations of the general form (CM19) (where h marks the head):

(CM19) $\downarrow$ X$'$ Δ Y$'_h$ $\downarrow$

X$'$ and Y$'$ represent the meanings of X and Y, respectively. Δ is the operation applied to combine the two meanings. For example, in (CM2a), Δ is function application. In other cases, it could be function composition, generalized conjunction, and so on. Y$'$ is presupposed not to contain internal arrows.

On the other hand, constituents with informationally autonomous heads can be expected to have representations of the general form (CM20) in the typical case, exemplified by (CM1a):

$$(CM20) \downarrow\downarrow X' \downarrow \Delta \downarrow Y'_h \downarrow\downarrow$$

But there are other theoretical possibilities of placing downward arrows into semantic representations, such as the one shown in (CM21):

$$(CM21) \downarrow X' \Delta \downarrow Y'_h \downarrow\downarrow$$

Are there instantiations of (CM21), that is, complex constituents whose meaning is calculated such that only the head corresponds to a substep in the calculation? I don't think that we can answer this question without an exact interpretation of the downward arrows. But even though we have not yet discussed matters of interpretation (see below), we can expect that instantiations of (CM21), if they exist, are cases of informational autonomy, because they clearly involve an independent step of processing the head meaning.

The fact that both (CM20) and (CM21) are instances of informational autonomy has interesting consequences when the arrow notation is applied recursively. Consider (1b) and (2b). According to our assumptions, (2b), having a nonautonomous head, will be represented by (CM2b):

$$(CM2b) \downarrow \text{bauen}'([\text{ein Haus}]') \downarrow$$

Now consider (1b). This VP properly contains (2b). Therefore, its CM representation should be composed of (CM2b) and of the CM representation of the dative object. Accordingly, it will have one of the representations in (CM1b), depending on whether we assume an independent step for the dative object or not:

$$(CM1b) \downarrow\downarrow \text{bauen}'([\text{ein Haus}]') \downarrow (\downarrow[\text{einem Freund}]'\downarrow)\downarrow$$
$$\downarrow\downarrow \text{bauen}'([\text{ein Haus}]')\downarrow([\text{einem Freund}]')\downarrow$$

Both versions of (CM1b) are cases of autonomy, the first of type (CM20), the second of type (CM21): In both cases, the head daughter of (1b), the inner VP *ein Haus bauen*, is represented as an independent step in the calculation. This follows from the assumption that the CM-representations of complex expressions are built up compositionally from the CM-representations of their parts. Thus, we have here the core of an explanation of the requirement (anticipated in the analysis of some of our examples above) that nonautonomous heads be syntactically noncomplex. This restriction seems to be a logical consequence of the fact that the CM representation of a constituent with a complex head, provided that it is composed of the CM representations of its parts, will always contain an arrowed head meaning, thereby instantiating either (CM20) or (CM21). (Of course, this will also happen when a complex head has an autonomous head itself, as when (CM1a) becomes the head of a more complex sentence.)

But there is a hidden premise in this explanation. We have to assume that every time the meanings of two sisters are composed, the result will be arrowed, that is, will correspond to a step on the relevant level of semantic calculation. While this assumption seems natural when the meanings of constituents with full lexical content are combined, it is less plausible when the meaning of a *functional element* is added to the meaning of its sister constituent. Indeed, the data seem to require that we assume that functional elements never add arrows. In other words, the CM-representation of a constituent with daughters X and Y, where X or Y is a functional element, will probably have the general form (CM22), where only the meaning of the nonfunctional daughter may contain internal arrows:

$$(\text{CM22}) \ X' \ \Delta \ Y'_h$$

Of course, all of this is largely speculative as long as we don't know exactly what the arrows mean. Very roughly, an interpretation of the arrows could be based on the idea that every sentence, besides conveying a proposition, indicates the way a situation corresponding to this proposition is built up in the mind of the speaker/hearer by composing certain aspects of the situation in a step-by-step fashion. Thus, the entities that could be used in the interpretation of the arrows are situations (of different types: events, states, etc.) and aspects of situations: individuals with certain roles, activities, properties, and so on, which themselves may be built up in the mind of the speaker/hearer in several steps by combining subaspects of the situation. Note that an interpretation of this kind could explain why functional elements don't add arrows: They don't correspond to aspects of situations but rather help to locate situations and aspects thereof with respect to spatiotemporal parameters, to possible worlds, and so forth. Note further that autonomy, viewed in this perspective, is independent of *focus-background structure* if, as I have argued in several papers,[12] the latter manifests itself semantically as a structure that is imposed on the *propositional content* of expressions (and not on the way this content is calculated).[13]

Unfortunately, I cannot give a more precise characterization of the intended interpretation of the arrows here, as this would require a lot of additional research. So, although we now have a rough idea of what the role of informational autonomy in the structure of meaning could be, we still don't have general diagnostic criteria for deciding whether a given constituent is informationally autonomous. Therefore, I will now present a list of what I think are the necessary grammatical conditions of nonautonomy. This list, however, is fully compatible with our speculations about the role autonomy plays in semantic structures and in part repeats assumptions we made in the preceding discussion.

4   Grammatical Prerequisites of Nonautonomy

A head X of a complex constituent is informationally nonautonomous in relation to its sister Y only if

a. Y is an argument of X;
b. if X assigns a Θ-role to Y then
    (i)   X does not ascribe to Y a spatiotemporally unlimited property and
    (ii) Y is associated with protopatient entailments;
c. X does not contain more than one constituent with a full lexical meaning.

The first condition excludes heads that are *coordinated with* or *modified by* their sisters, as coordination and modification are incompatible with a functor argument relation between a head and its sister. In other words, coordination and modification always create autonomous heads.

For coordination, this seems to be essential. It is well known that the semantic difference between coordination and other constructions cannot be fully reduced to a difference in truth-conditions. Researchers in the semantics of coordination (e.g. Lang 1988) have pointed out that coordination involves a specific way of semantic processing. It seems that one of the essential properties of this specific way of processing is that it proceeds step by step. This, of course, is reflected in the stress patterns of coordinations. They are stressed exactly as the rules sketched earlier predict, given that their heads are autonomous. However, one might suspect that the possibility of extraction from coordinated structures is incompatible with our assumption that extraction from sisters of autonomous heads is blocked. But, in fact, it's not, because these sisters are heads themselves. (Remember that heads are always possible extraction sites.) And even if we assume that coordination is single-headed we could explain their extraction behavior by assuming that the gaps in the non-heads are parasitic. (Both views predict that extraction from coordination must be across the board.)

In the case of modification, matters are less clear. However, traditional grammarians have always assumed that modification, like coordination, is a way of adding information to constituents that do not necessarily require this additional information. So at least it is not unnatural to assume that modified heads are informationally autonomous. The phonological and syntactic behavior of modifiers is exactly as we expect from this: Stressing them does not lead to focus ambiguity in head-final structures, they don't project their valency to the mother node (that is why modifiers have to be maximal projections), and they are islands for movement.

The requirement that integrated non-heads be arguments seems to apply to compounds, too. In (23a), the daughters are coordinated, in (23b), the non-head is a modifier of the head:

(23)   a. [[weiß][-blau]$_{+ia}$]
        b. [[long] [suffering]$_{+ia}$]

As expected, these compounds show the signs of informational autonomy, especially in their stress pattern; compare (24):

(24)   a.   b.

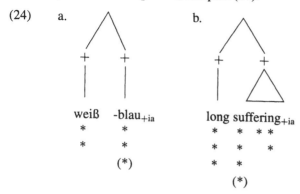

However, many German compounds have a plus-minus stress pattern although their first immediate constituent is not an argument of the second. For example, the German equivalents of *tóy factory* ('a factory that makes toys') and *toy fáctory* ('a factory that is a toy') have exactly the same pronounciation, namely, (25):

(25)

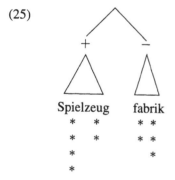

('factory that makes toys' or 'factory that is a toy')

Therefore, the first condition in our list of prerequisites of nonautonomy may have to be parametrized in some way. For the head of a German compound to be nonautonomous, it seems to be sufficient that its sister non-head is a restrictive qualifier, while in English it must be an argument. (Note that this still predicts that the head of *weiß-blau* is autonomous: *weiß* is not a restrictive qualifier here.)

Clause b tells us which kinds of arguments nonautonomous heads can have, as not every head of a predicate-argument phrase qualifies for being nonautonomous. These further restrictions only concern heads that assign a Θ-role to their argument. If they don't, that is, if they have a purely functional meaning, they are always nonautonomous, provided that the other conditions are met. (This seems to follow from our assumption that every step on the relevant level of semantic calculation is related to an aspect of a situation: Functional heads don't refer to aspects of situations, compare the above.)

Condition (b.i) prohibits from being nonautonomous those Θ-assigning heads that specify a property that the argument has regardless of its changing spatiotemporal conditions, compare (26a). This includes generic properties; compare (26b):

(26)   a. daß [[Peter] [ehrgeizig ist]$_{+ia}$]
        that P.   ambitious is
      b. daß [[Hunde] [[Katzen] [jagen]$_{\pm ia}$]$_{+ia}$]
        that dogs   cats   chase

Note that the property assigned generically to the subject in (26b) can itself be split into an argument and a generic property in one reading of the sentence, namely, in the reading 'it is typical for dogs and typical for cats that the former chase the latter'. In this interpretation there are two autonomous heads, resulting in the pronunciation (27b), whereas if we interpret (26b) as 'it is typical for dogs that they chase some cats', we get (27a):

(27)   a.   b.

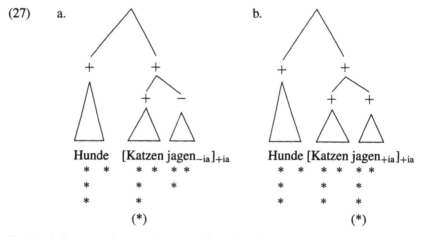

The fact that constituents that describe situations without clear spatiotemporal boundaries cannot have nonautonomous heads might be related to cognitive limitations of calculating situations of this kind at one fell swoop.

Cognitive restrictions might also be at the bottom of subcondition (b.ii), which makes every head autonomous whose sister-argument has a Θ-role that is untypical for objects, in the sense of Dowty (1991). Actually, Dowty eliminates traditional Θ-roles from the grammar and replaces them with sets of entailments lexically associated with the argument. The extent to which these entailments are prototypical for agents or patients determines whether the argument will behave more like a subject or more like an object. Here is a version of Dowty's list of protopatient entailments that includes some of the modifications proposed in Primus (1994) (Y: the argument under discussion):

a. Y undergoes a change of state
b. Y is an incremental theme
c. Y is causally affected by another participant
d. the event causes Y to exist or to be perceived.

Although this list still needs some refinements,[14] it already enables us to make rather fine-grained predictions. For example, we predict that syntactic *subjects* may be integrated provided that they have at least one protopatient-property. This applies to subjects of passive or unaccusative verbs, but it also covers cases like (28),

(28)   daß [[ein Freund] [angerufen hat]$_{-ia}$]
           a   friend   called   has

where the verb describes an action of the subject. This action causes the subject to be perceived. Therefore, condition (b.ii) is met here. As the other conditions are fulfilled, too, we predict that the head can be nonautonomous. Thus, we explain the thetic stress pattern in (29) and the fact that the subject, although it is an external argument, is a possible extraction domain in German; compare (30):

(29)

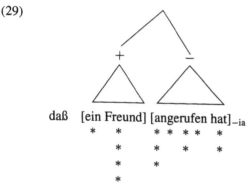

daß   [ein Freund]   [angerufen hat]$_{-ia}$
         *   *   * * *   *
              *   * *   *
              *   *
              *

(30)   von dem$_i$ gerade [[ein Freund e$_i$] [angerufen hat]$_{-ia}$]
           of whom just   a   friend   called   has

Head sisters of syntactic *objects*, on the other hand, do not always fulfill condition (b.ii). For example, the verbal complex *angeödet hat* 'has bored to death' of (31) fails to do so, because its sister object isn't associated with any protopatient entailments. Rather it has the traditional role of an experiencer:[15]

(31)   daß [[das Stück] [[einen Kritiker] [angeödet   hat]$_{+ia}$]$_{+ia}$]
           the play   a   critic(acc)bored-to-death has

This explains why putting the main stress on the direct object in this case does not result in focus ambiguity. As a consequence of the autonomous verbal complex, the neutral stress pattern of (31) is (32), where after strengthening the last strongest syllable the *verb* becomes rhythmically most prominent:

(32)

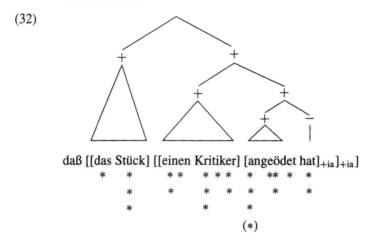

daß [[das Stück] [[einen Kritiker] [angeödet hat]$_{+ia}$]$_{+ia}$]
        *   *   * *   * * *   * ** *   *
        *   *   *   *   *   *   *
        *   *   *
(*)

Furthermore, we correctly predict that the direct object in this case is a bad extraction site; compare (33):

(33)
*von welcher Zeitung$_i$ [[das Stück] [[einen Kritiker e$_i$] [angeödet   hat]$_{+ia}$]$_{+ia}$]
of which newspaper the play   a   critic   bored-to-death has

Examples like this show clearly that each of the subconditions (b.i) and (b.ii) is independently motivated. The object of *angeödet hat* is a 'stage level' argument. Therefore the fact that it cannot be integrated is not predicted by condition (b.i).[16]

The last clause in the list repeats our assumption that heads exceeding a certain syntactic complexity will always be autonomous. We have seen the consequences of this already in several examples, for example, in (9) and (13). Note that this condition does not restrict the number of *functional* elements contained in X, in accordance with our observation that functional elements never add to the complexity in the relevant sense. Note furthermore that the *kind* of functional elements possibly present in X isn't restricted either. Thus, a nonautonomous X may contain not only functional heads, but also functional arguments, as in (34),

(34)   daß [[ein Freund] [uns angerufen hat]$_{-ia}$]
           a friend   us   called   has

where an argument pronoun is part of the head VP. (I assume that pronouns like *uns* don't have full lexical meanings.) As expected, (34) does not differ dramatically from (28) in its neutral stress pattern – compare (36a) – and in its behavior under movement – compare (37a) – whereas a corresponding sentence with a full lexical object, like (35), does:

(35)   daß [[ein Freund] [[den lokalen Fernsehsender angerufen hat]$_{+ia}$]
           a friend   the local TV station   called   has

The presence of the full object blocks focus projection and extraction from the subject; compare (36b) and (37b):

(36)   a.

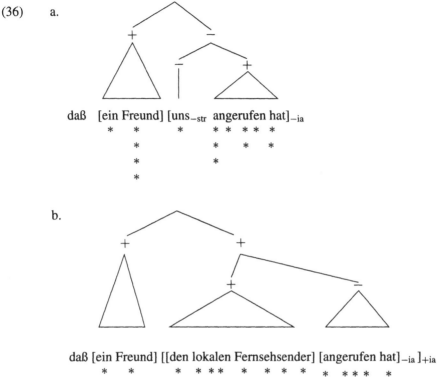

daß   [ein Freund] [uns$_{-str}$ angerufen hat]$_{-ia}$

b.

daß [ein Freund] [[den lokalen Fernsehsender] [angerufen hat]$_{-ia}$]$_{+ia}$

(*)

(37)
a. ?von dem$_i$ [[ein Freund e$_i$] [uns angerufen hat]$_{-ia}$]
b. *von dem$_i$ [[ein Freund e$_i$] [[den lokalen Fernsehsender] [angerufen hat]]$_{+ia}$]

Thus, many interesting predictions can be derived when we combine the list of prerequisites of nonautonomy with our ideas about the role of autonomy in different parts of the grammar.[17] Nevertheless, the list is somewhat unsatisfactory. In clause c it stipulates a precondition of nonautonomy that on the basis of a more principled approach would probably follow from the compositional construction of the relevant semantic representations; compare 3. Furthermore, certain phenomena have not been taken into account at all, such as *quantifiers*, which tend to resist integration. Maybe this could be explained by a proper generalization of condition (b.i),[18] but this would require additional research.

Finally, the conditions in the list are *necessary but not sufficient* for nonautonomy (neither alone nor in conjunction). The reason is that even when all the conditions are met, speakers sometimes still have the option to make a head informationally autonomous. Especially, sentences can be split into a *topic* and a *comment* (which implies informational autonomy of the latter) even when the comment obeys all our conditions. For example, whether a speaker will say (38a) (without topic-comment structure) or (38b) (with the subject as topic)

(38)   a. [The políce] [are coming]$_{-ia}$
         b. [The polìce] [are cóming]$_{+ia}$

seems to depend on purely pragmatic factors, such as the extent to which information about the police can be expected by the hearer.[19] Of course we could add to our list a fourth condition prohibiting X from being a comment. But such a move would only obscure the fact that in addition to research on the grammatical conditions of informational autonomy an investigation of its *pragmatical* prerequisites is on the agenda.[20]

5   A Syntactic Alternative?

The most unattractive feature of our theory of nonautonomy, however, is the fact that it is based on a complex condition consisting of several more or less unrelated parts.[21] Certainly it would be more attractive to have a notion that does the job of informational autonomy without requiring such a complex condition. Indeed, there is a candidate for such a more elegant notion. One might suspect that what is really crucial for the phenomena we have tried to explain is *how deeply the head is syntactically embedded*. In fact, for some of these phenomena, explanations have been proposed that rely exclusively on depth of syntactic embedding. An example is Cinque's (1993) theory of phrasal and compound stress, which is based on the idea that neutral stress directly reflects depth of embedding, with the most deeply embedded constituent becoming rhythmically most prominent through cyclical assignment of metrical grids. But unfortunately, this elegant theory makes incorrect predictions (even if we take into account that Cinque already assumes exceptions[22]). For example, (39a, b) (= Cinque's (24c) and (37b)) are predicted to have main stress on the adjunct (unless something else is in focus):

(39)   a. daß Karl ein Buch mit   Múhe   lesen kann
            that K.   a   book with difficulty read can
         b. weil   Fritz gút   kochen kann
            because F.   well cook   can

However, the correct neutral stress pattern of these sentences is (40),

(40)   a. daß Karl ein Buch mit Mühe lésen kann
         b. weil Fritz gut kóchen kann

in accordance with our proposals, which entail that heads having a (nonfunctional) modifier are autonomous.[23]

Of course we could try to save Cinque's theory by adding conditions to the effect that sentences like (40a, b) cease to be counterexamples. One way to do this would be to make sure that the procedure assigning grids cyclically to syntactic structures not only overlooks specifiers (cf. note 22) but also adjuncts. But this modification, besides further weakening the plausibility of Cinque's basic idea, would not help in other cases, such as (31). Here we have a direct object that undoubtedly is the most deeply embedded constituent.[24] Nevertheless, the main neutral stress goes to the verb, as a consequence of the fact that the object lacks protopatient properties. Examples like these show clearly that what is at the bottom of neutral stress (and, as I have argued, of valency projection, extraction, and possibly other phenomena) is not syntax, but semantics, more precisely, that level of semantic structure on which informational autonomy is situated.

Notes

1 I consider only the thetic reading of this sentence, which is marked by main stress on the subject.
2 A plus-minus pattern dominating sister constituents X and Y means that X is more prominent than Y. A metrical grid corresponding to the metrical tree and to the lexical stress patterns involved is added. (Remember that the grid has to reflect the prominence relations in the tree for each pair of sister nodes.)
3 (6b) is borrowed from Vallduvi (1993).
4 This context is used by Vallduvi (1993:5) to illustrate the all focus reading of (6b). Although it is certainly true that the sentence in this context does not contain any narrow foci, it is also clear that the contextually given conjunction of 'brown water' and 'pipes' makes 'rusty' highly predictable.
5 A more detailed description of the interaction between grids and pitch accents in German can be found in Uhmann (1991).
6 The question which *kinds* of pitch accent can be chosen in German is discussed extensively in Uhmann (1991). See also Gussenhoven's contribution to this volume.
7 But many languages have certain weak pronouns that cannot be stressed even when they are in narrow focus, for example, the German neuter pronoun *es* 'it'; cf. ?? *Er hat es gesehen* 'He has seen [it]$_F$'.
8 The most famous example of this is the Nuclear Stress Rule of Chomsky and Halle (1968).
9 There are languages without a phonological marking of informational nonautonomy, such as the Romance languages. Moreover, there are languages that strengthen the *first* strongest syllable, which makes them sound dramatically different even if they have a minus-marking of nonautonomy. An example is Hungarian, as argued in Jacobs (1992a).
10 Again, the most famous example is Chomsky and Halle's analysis.
11 Of course there are many questions that this analysis of movement does not answer. Especially, in addition to our autonomy-based identification of extraction domains we need a theory of the possible chains linking antecedents with their traces, perhaps some suitable adaptation of Müller and Sternefeld's (1993) Principle of Unambiguous Binding.
12 Compare, for example, Jacobs (1983, 1984).

13 But note that in the stress rules proposed in Section 2.1, the feature F neutralizes ±ia. Whether this points to a deeper connection between F and ±ia is not clear to me.

14 For example, it is unclear which (if any) of the protopatient entailments apply to the verbal arguments serving as the logical objects of control verbs like *versuchen* 'to try'. (Remember that we should be able to treat these arguments as being integrated; compare (18).)

15 I assume that the mental affectedness typical of this role is not an instance of protopatient entailment c.

16 Of course, (b.ii) also blocks integration of stage level *subjects*, for example, in *weil Gäste hungrig waren* 'because guests were hungry'; cf. *[weil Gäste hungrig waren]ꜰ (no focus projection), *??Wasᵢ waren eᵢ für Gäste hungrig* (no extraction from the subject). The subject of *hungrig waren* again is an experiencer and therefore isn't associated with protopatient entailments.

17 Probably, autonomy or integration is influential in more areas than those mentioned in the preceding discussion. For example, the question of whether *indefinites* are interpreted existentially or not (cf. Diesing 1992) seems to depend at least partially on whether they are integrated or not: An indefinite (e.g. bare plural) argument that is integrated into a verbal head is always interpreted existentially (provided that the verb and its argument are not contained in a larger phrase serving as the restrictor of a quantifier or of another operator). This explains, among other things, why the verbal head sisters of indefinite objects that are interpreted nonexistentially fail to meet at least one of the conditions b and c of nonautonomy (or are part of a restrictor phrase). Typical examples are verbs with indefinite objects not carrying any protopatient entailments, e.g., in *weil er Politikern mißtraut* 'because he distrusts politicians.' (Note that Diesing's theory of indefinites has problems explaining such cases; cf. also É. Kiss 1994.)

18 Note that a sentence like *Jeder hat angerufen* 'Everyone has called' does not specify an event with clear spatiotemporal boundaries, but rather a whole collection of such events.

19 This does not require the subject to be in the background of a focus-background structure. Topics often are part of the "new information" in the sentence.

20 But note that the grammatical conditions will strongly restrict the pragmatic options. For example, in a typical thetic assertion (i.e. one without topic-comment structure, as described in Sasse 1987), all verbal projections of the sentence have to meet our conditions a.–c.

21 But remember that clause c. can probably be eliminated in a more principled account.

22 He stipulates that syntactic specifiers do not fully count in the calculation of stress patterns.

23 Surprisingly, Cinque cites (39a, b) as evidence in favor of his theory.

24 Note that this object is indefinite and – in at least one of relevant readings – nongeneric and unspecific. Thus it would be extremely implausible to assume that it has been invisibly moved into a higher position.

References

Chomsky, N. 1986. *Barriers*, MIT Press, Cambridge, Mass.

Chomsky, N., and M. Halle 1968. *The Sound Pattern of English*, Harper & Row, New York.

Cinque, G. 1993. A null theory of phrase and compound stress, *Linguistic Inquiry* 24, 239–298.

Diesing, M. 1992. *Indefinites*, MIT Press, Cambridge, Mass.

Dowty, D. 1991. Thematic proto-roles and argument selection, *Language* 67, 547–619.

É. Kiss, K. 1994. Generic and existential bare plurals and the classification of predicates. *Working Papers in the Theory of Grammar.* Vol. 7, No. 2. Theoretical Linguistics Programme. Budapest.

Jacobs, J. 1983. *Fokus und Skalen. Zur Syntax und Semantik der Gradpartikeln im Deutschen,* Niemeyer, Tübingen.

Jacobs, J. 1984. Funktionale Satzperspektive und Illokutionssemantik, *Linguistische Berichte* 91, 25–58.

Jacobs, J. 1991. Focus ambiguities, *Journal of Semantics* 8, 1–36.

Jacobs, J. 1992a. Neutral stress and the position of heads. In J. Jacobs (ed.), *Informationsstruktur und Grammatik,* Westdeutscher Verlag, Opladen, 220–244.

Jacobs, J. 1992b. Bewegung als Valenzvererbung, *Linguistische Berichte* 138, 85–122.

Jacobs, J. 1993a. Integration. In M. Reis (ed.), *Wortstellung und Informationsstruktur,* Niemeyer, Tübingen, 64–116.

Jacobs, J. 1993b. Syntaktischer und morphologischer Akzent-(k)ein Gegensatz. Ms. Wuppertal. (Unpublished)

Lang, E. 1988. *The Semantics of Coordination,* Benjamins, Amsterdam.

Liberman, M., and A. Prince 1977. On stress and linguistic rhythm, *Linguistic Inquiry* 8, 249–336.

Müller, G., and W. Sternefeld 1993. Unambiguous binding and improper movement, *Linguistic Inquiry* 24, 461–507.

Primus, B. 1994. *Cases and Thematic Roles,* University of Munich.

Sasse, H.-J. 1987. The thetic/categorical distinction revisited, *Linguistics* 25, 511–580.

Uhmann, S. 1991. *Fokusphonologie,* Niemeyer, Tübingen.

Vallduví, E. 1993. *Information Packaging: A Survey,* HCRC Publications, University of Edinburgh.

5   Subject-Prodrop in Yiddish

ELLEN F. PRINCE

Abstract

An empirical quantitative study is presented that argues that Subject-Prodrop in Yiddish is not a unitary phenomenon. Rather, the data are first partitioned according to whether the referent of the zero subject is a discourse entity or propositionally introduced, the two types being subject to different syntactic constraints; then, those whose referent is a discourse entity are partitioned into two groups according to whether the referent is the second person singular or not, the second group but not the first being subject to discourse constraints statable in terms of Centering Theory.

1   Introduction

Much work has been done in recent years on Subject-Prodrop in a number of languages, both from a syntactic perspective (Jaeggli 1980, Huang 1984, 1989, Bouchard 1985, Shlonsky 1987, Jaeggli and Safir 1989, Kayne 1991, among others) and from a discourse perspective (Li and Thompson 1979, Gundel 1980, Kameyama 1985, Di Eugenio 1990, Walker, Iida, and Cote 1990, 1994, Cameron 1992, among others). To my knowledge, however, virtually none of this work has been based on a corpus of naturally occurring data, and, perhaps relatedly, all have found Subject-Prodrop to be a unitary phenomenon in the language studied, although significant differences have been noted cross-linguistically. In this chapter, I present a corpus-based analysis of Subject-Prodrop in Yiddish, a language in which Subject-Prodrop has not yet been analyzed, and I show that, at least in this corpus of this language, the term Subject-Prodrop is a rubric covering phenomena that have diverse syntactic and discourse constraints.

In what follows, I first describe the corpus and present the syntactic constraints

An earlier version of the chapter was presented at the Focus Conference, Schloss Wolfsbrunnen, Germany, June 12–15, 1994, for which opportunity I should like to thank Peter Bosch, the organizer. I should also like to thank him and the other participants, as well as Breck Baldwin, Robert Rothstein, Beatrice Santorini, Umit Turan, and Lyn Walker for their help. Thanks are also due my Yiddish informants, especially Masha Benya, Marvin Herzog, and Nanca and the late Alex Meilijson, for their time and trouble. This research was partially funded by NSF-STC Center Grant SBR9347355 to the Institute for Research in Cognitive Science, University of Pennsylvania.

found. Then I present the results of a discourse analysis of Subject-Prodrop in Yiddish with respect to Centering Theory. Finally, I discuss the implications of these findings.

2 Yiddish Subject-Prodrop: The Facts

In this section, I first describe the corpus on which this study was based and then present the syntactic constraints on Subject-Prodrop found in the corpus.

2.1 *The Corpus*

The corpus for this study is the 1923 Yiddish three-act play *Grine Felder* by Peretz Hirschbein, transcribed in Romanized form into an Emacs file by Beatrice Santorini and me and consisting of 2091 clauses. For this study, each clause was coded for 12 variables: clause type (declarative, imperative, interrogative), V/1 or V/2, position of subject (initial, medial, final, ambiguous between medial and final), overt presence/absence of subject, occupant of initial (preverbal) position, main versus subordinate clause, subject type (full NP, personal pronoun, demonstrative pronoun, zero, *men* 'one', clause, *wh*-trace, etc.), subject referent (dummy – no referent, discourse entity, discourse deixis (Webber 1991), etc.), provenance (stage direction vs. character's speech), and three centering-related variables, which are discussed later.

2.2 *Preliminary Findings: Syntactic Constraints*

A preliminary analysis of the corpus by VARBRUL revealed, first, that Yiddish Subject-Prodrop is not "telegraphic" but is in fact perfectly well-formed in the colloquial language.[1] Examples are presented in (1):[2]

(1)   a.   [0 = Ikh] Bin opgeven a khoydesh, efsher shoyn mer vi a khoydesh tsayt – genug. (GF.II.83)
             '[I] have been [here] a month, maybe already more than a month's time – enough.'
       b.   [0 = Du] Veyst, az ikh bin dir mekane. (GF.1.69)
             '[You] know that I envy you.'
       c.   [0 = Zi] Horevet iber di koykhes. (GF.III.97)
             '[She] Works too hard.'
       d.   [0 = Ir] Badarft bentshn goyml. (GF.III.92)
             '[You] Should say a prayer of thanks.'
       e.   Vazhne oysyes; (0 = zey) kukn poshet fun bretl arop. (GF.II.82)
             'Wonderful letters; [they] just look down from the blackboard.'

Note that pronouns of any person and either number may be dropped, contra the claim made by traditional Yiddish grammarians and teachers that only *du*, the second person singular pronoun, is deletable (Kagarov 1929, Zaretski 1929, Katz 1987). Later I speculate on why they might think this.

At the same time, the preliminary statistical analysis revealed that Yiddish Subject-Prodrop is subject to an important syntactic constraint, from which follow a number of other syntactic constraints, to which we now turn.

2.2.1   Clause-Initial Constraint

The zero pronoun in a Yiddish Subject-Prodrop sentence must be clause-initial in that it must be preverbal and it may not follow a filled Comp. From this one constraint, a great many syntactic facts about its distribution follow.

2.2.1.1 No Zero Subject in Clauses with Lexically Realized 'Initial Field'. First, Subject-Prodrop does not occur in topicalized sentences (2a–d), or in sentences with an initial expletive (2e); that is, they do not occur in any sentence with a lexically realized preverbal, or *initial field*, constituent:[3]

(2)   a. Aza shayle kenst du/*0 mir oykh paskenen. (GF.III.94)
           'Such a question you can also answer for me.'
       b. Shoyn lang bist du/*0 aza khakhome? (GF.I.73)
           'For a long time already you've been such a wise woman?'
       c. Ver ken er take zayn, der mentsh? Efsher hot er/*0 gehert, az ikh hob gelakht? (GF.I.71)
           'Who can he be, that guy? Maybe he/*0 heard that I was laughing?'
       d. Oyb du vilst im zen, kenst du/*0 ariberkumen tsu undz. (GF.I.72)
           'If you want to see him, you/*0 can come over to us.'
       e. Dos, Elkone, tust du/*0 an avle. (GF.II.83)
           'It's you/*0, Elkone, who's committing a mistreatment.'

Note the following sequence of sentences, both of which have *du* 'you' as subject. The first, where the subject can be initial, has undergone Subject-Prodrop; the second, where the subject must be postverbal, has not and cannot:

(3)   [0 = Du] Host ongeton shikh? Gut host du/*0 geton, mayn kind. (GF.II.91)
       'You/0 have put on shoes? You/*0 have done well, my child.'

Note, however, that zero subjects may be preceded by a pre-S constituent, as in (4), but these are the same type of pre-S constituents that could precede an overt preverbal subject, as in (5), and thus do not contradict the generalization that zero subjects must be clause-initial, in the sense of occupying *initial field*:

(4)   a. Hersh-Ber, [0 = du] bist a lekish. (GF.I.71)
           'Hersh-Ber, you are a fool.'
       b. Kind mayns, [0 = du] bist dokh a kale gevorn. (GF.III.106)
           'My child, you've become a bride.'

    c. Take, [0 = du] meynst mit an emes? (GF.I.65)
       'Indeed, you really mean it?'
    d. Azoy gor, [0 = du] kukst zikh shoyn unter tsu azoyne zakhn, vos men
       badarf nisht? (GF.I.67)
       'Just like that, you pry into things that you shouldn't?'

(5)   a. Hersh-Ber, du bist a lekish! (GF.I.72)
       'Hersh-Ber, you are a fool!'
    b. Nar, 's makht nisht oys. (GF.I.68)
       'Fool, it doesn't matter.'
    c. Avade, keyner badarf nisht visn. (GF.II.80)
       'Of course, no one needs to know.'
    d. Ot azoy, me shmuest. (GF.III.97)
       'Just like that, we're chatting.'

Note, by the way, that data like (4) provide evidence against a claim that Subject-Prodrop in Yiddish is some sort of 'phonological deletion' affecting only initial segments of a sentence (see Napoli 1982).

2.2.1.2 Main Clause Constraint. In contrast to Subject-Prodrop in the Romance languages, Turkish, and Japanese, inter alia, Yiddish Subject-Prodrop is confined to main clauses, which follows of course from the Clause-Initial Constraint:[4]

(6)   a. Ikh ken gantsene nekht mit an oyg nisht tsumakhn, zint du/*0 host
       mir dertseylt. (GF.II.86)
       'I can't sleep a wink all night since you/*0 told me.'
    b. Vorem Gitl iz take gerekht, vos zi/*0 zogt, az du/*0 tselozt Steren.
       (GF.I.67)
       'Because Gitl is indeed right when she/*0 says that you/*0 spoil Stere.'
    c. 'Kh veys nisht farvos du/*0 host do moyre tsu hobn. (GF.III.98)
       'I don't know why you/*0 are afraid.'

2.2.1.3 Declarative Clause Constraint. If we assume that the deletion of subjects in imperatives is a different phenomenon from the one we are considering here, then Yiddish Subject-Prodrop occurs in declaratives only, again following from the Clause-Initial Constraint.[5] That is, while we find sentences functioning as questions with zero subjects, they are never unambiguously V/1 interrogatives but rather may always be paraphrased felicitously in context by declaratives with question intonation:

(7)   a. [0 = Du] Host zikh geshtayert mit im? (GF.I.68)
       '[You] have wrestled with him?'
    b. [0 = Du] Bist mir moykhl, Sterele? (GF.I.69)
       '[You] forgive me, Sterele?'

c. [0 = Du] Kenst nisht opesn keyn vetshere un geyn ahin? (GF.II.88)
'[You] Can't have supper and go over?'

Questions that are unambiguously interrogative (V/1) in form due to Wh-movement may not occur with Subject-Prodrop:[6]

(8)   a. Tsi veyst ir/*0 gor, vos far a goldn kind dos iz? (GF.I.64)
'Do you/*0 really know what a wonderful child this is?'
        b. To vos zhe redst du/*0? (GF.I.74)
'Then what on earth are you/*0 saying?'
        c. Vu bist du/*0, Rokhl? (GF.I.74)
'Where are you/*0, Rachel?'
        d. Fun vanen veyst du/*0 es alts? (GF.II.89)
'How do you/*0 know it all?'

2.2.1.4 V/2 Declarative Clause Constraint.

Not only may Yiddish Subject-Prodrop occur only in declaratives but it is further constrained to occur only in overt V/2 declaratives, again following from the Clause-Initial Constraint. That is, since the zero pronoun must occur preverbally, it may not occur in apparent V/1 declaratives, called 'consecutive sentences' (see Weinreich 1981, Miner 1990; see also Thrainsson 1985), where there is no preverbal position available. This is of course not obvious from the occurring data but can be seen by taking felicitous Subject-Prodrop tokens in their contexts and having native informants supply the missing pronouns; the resultant clauses have the pronouns in preverbal position only, for example:

(9)   a. Nem dir a shtikl broyt mit puter. [0 = Du] Bist [#du] dokh avade hungerik. (GF.I.66)
'Take yourself a piece of bread and butter. You must be hungry.'
        b. Rokhl: Du host gebetn, oder Hersh-Ber?
'Rachel: You invited [him], or Hersh-Ber?'
            Tsine: [0 = Er] Iz [#er] aleyn gekumen. (GF.I.67)
'Tsine: He came himself.'
        c. Doved-Noyekh: Vu iz der mentsh?
'David-Noah: Where is the person?'
            Rokhl: [0 = Er] Iz [#er] in shtub. (GF.I.71)
'Rachel: He's in the house.'

Conversely, given naturally occurring V/1 declaratives in context, native informants reject Subject-Prodrop versions of them:

(10)   a. Der tate hot im gefregt, vi azoy men ruft im, hot er/#0 gezogt. (GF.I.74)
'Dad asked him what he was called, so he/#0 told [him].'
        b. 'Kh hob gehert vi ir lernt, bin ikh/#0 gegangen aykh onraysn epl. (GF.III.92)
'I heard how you were studying, so I/#0 went to pick apples for you.'

c. Kum, yidene, 0 vest nokh lenger blaybn, vest du/#0 nokh mer narishkaytn redn. (GF.I.65)
'Come, woman, [you] stay any longer, you/#0 will say more foolish things.'

2.2.2 Exceptions

There are several classes of exceptions to the constraint(s) listed above that must be mentioned here, discourse deictic and "ambient" subjects and frozen parenthetical expressions.

2.2.2.1 Discourse Deictic and 'Ambient' Subjects. All of what has been said involves cases where the zero subject refers to an already evoked discourse entity and does not apply to discourse deixis, where the zero subject refers either to something introduced as a clause or a non-nominal part thereof (Webber 1991) or else to what Bolinger (1977) has referred to for English as 'ambient' *it*, the subject of time/place/weather expressions, and which I refer to for Yiddish as 'ambient' *es*. Of course, whether these 'ambient' cases are instances of some kind of Subject-Prodrop or are simply subjectless sentences is not obvious, but, in any event, we find sentences where a discourse deictic subject pronoun, if one were present, would occur non-initially in V/1 interrogatives (11a) and hortatives (11b), and in apparent V/1 'consecutive' declaratives (11c), and we find sentences where an 'ambient' *es* subject, if one were present, would occur both postverbally and in insubordinate clauses (11d, e):

(11)   a. Un az zi iz gekumen helfn Hersh-Bern, to vos zhe iz [0 = es]? (GF.I.67)
'And if she's come to help Hersh-Ber, so what is [it]?'
b. Zol [0 = es] shoyn zayn vi 's iz. (GF.III.104)
'May [it] be already as it is.'
c. Ir vilt nisht. Iz [0 = es] nisht. Iz [0 = es] vi ir vilt zikh. (GF.III.100)
'You don't want [that]. So [it] won't be. So [it] is the way you want.'
d. O, ven ikh volt es gekent makhn azoy, az aykh zol (0 = es?) zayn gut bay undz! (GF.II.81)
'Oh, if I could have made it so that [it] was pleasant for you here!'
e. 'Kh hob gevolt, az dir zol (0 = es?) ton hanoe. (GF.II.88)
'I wanted [it] to give you pleasure.'

I suspect that discourse deixis and 'ambient' *es* are different, not only from the usual case of Subject-Prodrop but also from each other, with discourse deictic subjects being 'real' in some sense but deletable postverbally as well as preverbally (although perhaps only in main clauses) but with 'ambient' subjects being in fact nonexistent, the ambient sentences in question actually being subjectless. However, evidence for such an analysis awaits further investigation. For the present study, I have simply considered both phenomena as not involving ordinary Subject-Prodrop and have excluded them from the final statistical analysis.

2.2.2.2 Exclusion of men *'one'.* In a different vein, it turns out that Subject-Prodrop applies only to true personal pronouns and not to *men* 'one'. Thus, we find *men* 'one' present even when it has recently occurred coreferentially, as in 12:[7]

(12) a. Me fort in shtot arayn, me/*0 fregt zikh nokh. (GF.III.96)
          'One goes into town, one [*0] asks around.'
      b. Me nemt nisht un me/*0 farshemt a dorfishn mentshn. (GF.II.83)
          'One refuses and one [*0] embarrasses a village person.'
      c. Khe-khe, me vert a bisl fargrebt oyfn yishev; ober, az es kumt tsu an avle ton – khapt men zikh. Men/*0 veyst, geloybt iz der Eybershter, fun danen ahin. (GF.III.104)
          'Ha ha, one gets a bit boorish on the farm; however, when it comes to mistreatment – one notices. One [*0] knows, praised be the Eternal One, one's way around.'

Note that this prohibition against zero occurrences of *men* 'one' is not a constraint against subjects whose referent is nonspecific, as such subjects may in principle be dropped, so long as the pronoun that would be present is a personal pronoun in what Donnellan (1978) has called an "anaphoric chain":

(13) a. A shtot-yid iz take a yid. [0 = Er] Redt oys a vort mit a rov; [0 = er] hert a kdushe in der tsayt un [0 = er] ken gebn a nedove, az der vos in himl helft. (GF.III.104)
          'A city Jew is indeed a Jew. [He] discusses things with a big rabbi; [he] hears a holiness from time to time and [he] can give alms, with God's help.'
      b. Modne mentshn do oyf der velt. [0 = Zey] Zeen gor oys andersh vi mir. (GF.I.71)
          'Strange people there [are] in the world. [0 = They] look totally different from us.'

That is, whether the antecedent refers to some particular discourse entity (as in specific reference) or to some arbitrary one (as in a subclass of nonspecific reference), subsequent references may be made by zero subjects, assuming all other conditions are met, just in case the zero subject, if overt, would be a personal pronoun referring to that particular or arbitrary entity.

The constraint against deleting *men* 'one' may be related to the different behavior shown above of discourse deictic subjects in that Subject-Prodrop may involve only pronouns that refer directly to discourse entities already evoked in the discourse-model by nominal means. We shall return to this below.

2.2.2.3 Frozen Expressions. Finally, there is another small class of exceptions involving certain hortative, that is, V/1, frozen expressions that therefore do not obey the Clause-Initial Constraint, even though the referent of the zero subject may be a bona fide discourse entity. Although these occur quite frequently in the language in general, there is only one example in the corpus involving a discourse entity subject, by chance in a sentence without a main-clause finite verb, given in (14a); an example involving such a construction with a discourse deictic subject is given in (14b):[8]

(14)   a. Mayn tate, zol [0 = er] zayn in Gan-Edn, oykh a dorf-mentsh geven. (GF.III.104)
        'My father, may [he] be in paradise, [was] also a village person.'
    b. Elkone vil zikh krign mit undz – zol [0 = es] zayn azoy. (GF.II.83)
       'Elkone wants to fight with us – so be [it].'

3   Yiddish Subject-Prodrop in Discourse

I have described briefly the syntactic constraints on the occurrence of zero subjects in Yiddish. However, it is clear that, even when the syntactic conditions are met, a great number of subject pronouns are not dropped; the phenomenon is far less frequent than in Japanese or Korean, rarer even than in Spanish or Italian. One thing is clear: the occurrence of a zero pronoun, given the right syntactic conditions, is not random and is not governed exclusively (if at all) by social or superficial stylistic factors. That is, a single sentence with a pronominal subject in a single social situation may occur felicitously with a zero pronoun in one discourse context but require an overt pronoun in another discourse context:

(15)   a. Doved hot geredt fun di kale$_i$? Oy, vest du zi$_i$ lib hobn! [0$_i$ = Zi$_i$] Iz efsher nokh a mol azoy shtark vi er. (Adapted from GF.II.88)
        'David talked about the bride$_i$? Oh, are you going to love her$_i$! [She$_i$] is maybe twice as strong as he.'
    b. Ir veyst, az Dovid vet khasene hobn. Er hot geredt fun di kale$_i$? Zi$_i$ [#0$_i$] iz efsher nokh a mol azoy shtark vi er.
       'You know that David is getting married. He talked about the bride$_i$? She$_i$[#0$_i$] is maybe twice as strong as he.'

This suggests that Subject-Prodrop has some substantive discourse function, the appropriateness of which constrains the felicitous occurrence of zero subjects in discourse, even when the syntactic constraints are met. To see what this function might be, we turn to a study of the behavior of Subject-Prodrop in discourse.

3.1   *Centering Theory: An Overview*

The study reported here is based on Centering Theory, which turns out to be very useful in that it partitions the data in an intuitively reasonable way and permits a straightforward account of the facts. Before turning to the results, however, a brief overview of Centering Theory is in order.

    Centering Theory is a way of modeling attentional state in discourse, a component of a theory of local discourse coherence (Joshi and Weinstein 1981, Grosz, Joshi, and Weinstein 1995). Within Centering Theory, each utterance U_i in a coherent local sequence of utterances (a discourse segment) $U_1 \ldots U_m$ affects the structure of the discourse model as follows:

First, each utterance evokes, explicitly and implicitly, a set of discourse entities ('file cards', following Heim 1983) called *forward-looking centers*, or {Cf}.

Second, this set is ranked according to various formal (e.g., syntactic, morphological, theta role, prosodic) features, the rankings being determined language-specifically.

Third, the highest-ranked Cf in the {Cf} of some utterance U_i is called the *preferred center*, or Cp, of U_i. The Cp is a prediction about what the next utterance, U_{i+1}, will be 'about', although this prediction may of course prove wrong much of the time, with certain predicted results.

Fourth, the highest-ranked Cf in the {Cf} of utterance U_{i-1} that appears as well in the {Cf} of the subsequent utterance U_i is the *backward-looking center*, or Cb, of U_i. Note that, if there is no U_{i-1}, as in the case of a discourse-initial U_i, or, if there is a U_{i-1} but no Cf in U_{i-1} occurs in U_i, then U_i lacks a Cb. Thus an utterance has no or exactly one Cb. The Cb is predicted to correlate with what at least some have meant by *topic* or *theme*, that is, what the utterance is "about" (e.g. Reinhart 1981). This distinction between looking back to the previous discourse-part with the Cb and projecting preferences for interpretation in the subsequent discourse-part with the Cp is a key aspect of the Centering framework.

In addition, Centering Theory contains one rule, the Pronoun Rule, which gives the model empirical testability:

(16)   **Pronoun Rule:** If any Cf in an utterance is represented by a pronoun, then the Cb must be represented by a pronoun.

It is relevant to note that the Pronoun Rule was formulated on the basis of English and that subsequent analyses of prodrop languages like Japanese (Kameyama 1985, 1988, Walker, Iida, and Cote 1990, 1994) and Turkish (Turan 1995, 1998) show that a distinction must be made between lexically realized pronouns and zero pronouns and that, for Japanese and Turkish at least, the Pronoun Rule must be reformulated as follows:

(17)   **Zero Pronoun Rule (based on Japanese and Turkish):** If any Cf in an utterance is represented by a zero pronoun, then the Cb must be represented by a zero pronoun.

We see later that this rule is not adequate as it stands to capture the facts of Yiddish Subject-Prodrop.

Since Centering is meant to model attentional state, it must model changes or shifts in attentional state, which it does by defining four possible transitions between adjacent utterances, corresponding to the four logical possibilities of two variables: whether the Cb of the current utterance is the same as the Cp of the current utterance and whether the Cb of the current utterance is the same as the Cb of the previous utterance. This is shown in the chart in (18):

(18)   **Centering Transitions**

	$Cb(U_i) = Cb(U_{i-1})$	$Cb(U_i) \neq Cb(U_{i-1})$
$Cb(U_i) = Cp(U_i)$:	Continue	Smooth-shift
$Cb(U_i) \neq Cp(U_i)$:	Retain	Rough-shift

It is assumed that, other things being equal, *Continues* are easier to process and hence more "coherent" than the other three and that *Rough-shifts* are harder to process and hence less "coherent" than the other three. (The ordering, if any, of the ease of processing of *Retains* and *Smooth-shifts* is not obvious.)

3.2   Coding

As mentioned, three variables for which the clauses in the corpus were coded are directly related to Centering Theory: whether or not the subject is the Cp, whether or not the subject is the Cb, and which of the four transitions occurred between the previous utterance and the current one. A few words are in order here about how these codings were done.

3.2.1   Segmentation

One coding concern relates to the problem of segmentation. That is, Centering Theory is a way of modeling local coherence, that is, coherence within a discourse segment, and thus a prior segmentation of the discourse is required for a Centering analysis. However, I did not segment the play, or, rather, simply assumed a flat segmentation, although it is clear that there is internal structure in the play, as in any discourse. My reason was that I had no independent way of doing a fine-grained segmentation of the discourse; also I suspect that hearers are similarly handicapped and no doubt often assume a flat structure until they get evidence to the contrary. Furthermore, I suspect that some of this evidence for segmentation comes in fact from the hearer's Centering analysis (or reasonable facsimile thereof), with segmentation and Centering being in a bootstrapping relation, rather than the former prerequisite to the latter. In any event, I divided the play into three sister-adjoined segments, corresponding to the three acts of the play.

3.2.2   Clauses Omitted from Statistical Analysis

In a different vein, a large number of clauses were eliminated from the statistical analysis, for a number of different reasons.

First, although Subject-Prodrop was very frequent in the stage directions, as exemplified in (19), only tokens taken from the characters' lines were counted, since it was suspected that other principles might be at issue in the stage directions.

(19)   a.   Stere: 'Kh bin a bayln a kuk ton in fentster. {[0 = Zi] Farganvet zikh
            tsum fentster.} (GF.I.70)
            'S.: I'm curious to take a look in the window. {[She] sneaks over to
            the window.}'
       b.   Hersh-Ber$_i$: To hert nisht, oyb ir$_j$ vilt nisht. Kum in shtub arayn, Tsine$_k$.
            {[0$_i$ = Er$_i$] geyt arayn in shtub.} (GF.III.100)
            'H-B$_i$: So don't hear [it], if you$_j$ don't want to. Come into the house,
            Tsine$_k$. {[He$_i$] goes into the house.}'

The reasons for this were that Subject-Prodrop is otherwise found only in registers
more informal than stage directions and, in addition, plays written in English, a
language that lacks an analog of colloquial Yiddish Subject-Prodrop, may also
contain Subject-Prodrop, as exemplified in (20), supporting the conclusion that
another phenomenon entirely may be at issue in stage directions.[9]

(20)   a.   Mary$_i$: {Suddenly [she$_i$] is overcome by guilty confusion – [0$_i$ = she$_i$]
            stammers.} I – Forgive me, dear. You're right. It's useless to be angry
            now. (O'Neill 1956.II.II.75)
       b.   Ben$_i$: Good boy! {[0$_i$ = He$_i$] Suddenly comes in, trips Biff, and stands
            over him, the point of his umbrella poised over Biff's eye.} (Miller
            1949:I.49)

Second, as mentioned above, a preliminary VARBRUL analysis of the corpus
revealed that Yiddish Subject-Prodrop appears to follow different syntactic constraints when the subject is an instance of discourse deixis or of "ambient" *es*.
Thus it was felt that a different phenomenon might be at issue and such cases
were eliminated, leaving only those zero subjects and lexically realized subject
pronouns whose referents were discourse entities.

Third, since the variation is presumably between a zero and a personal pronoun,
all clauses having neither a zero nor a personal pronoun as subject were likewise
eliminated. Included among those eliminated were of course all clauses with full
NP subjects and with clausal subjects but also all clauses with *men* 'one' as subject.

Finally, since all the remaining tokens of Subject-Prodrop in the corpus were in
V/2 declarative main clauses, with the zero pronoun being preverbal, all clauses
with overt pronouns not fitting this description were eliminated as irrelevant.

3.3   Findings

After the exclusions mentioned above, the corpus consisted of a total of 601 subject-
initial declarative main clauses, of which 468 had overt pronominal subjects and
133 zero subjects. These were then analyzed by VARBRUL, a multivariate analysis
program, with the presence or absence of a lexically realized subject pronoun being
the dependent variable.

VARBRUL analyses of the coded data revealed an interesting finding: in virtually all instances of zero pronoun clauses where the zero pronoun would be lexically realized by a first- or third-person pronoun or by a second-person plural pronoun, the zero pronoun was the Cb and the transition-type was *continue*. However, when the zero pronoun would be realized by the second-person singular pronoun, this was very often not the case; the zero pronoun often was not the Cb and, even when it was, the transition-type often was not *continue*.

The figures for all pronouns and transition-types are presented in (21):

(21)   Distribution of main clause-initial subject zero/pronoun in corpus:

		Continue		Retain		Smooth-shift		Rough-shift		Total	
1sg	0	1	1%	0	0%	0	0%	0	0%	1	0%
	pro	127	99%	58	100%	40	100%	67	100%	292	100%
	T	128		58		40		67		293	
1pl	0	0	0%	0	0%	0	0%	0	0%	0	0%
	pro	5	100%	1	100%	2	100%	0	0%	8	100%
	T	5		1		2		0		8	
2sg	0	37	74%	13	71%	20	90%	27	70%	97	76%
	pro	13	26%	5	29%	2	10%	10	30%	30	24%
	T	50		18		22		37		127	
2pl	0	2	10%	0	0%	1	0%	0	0%	3	8%
	pro	19	90%	3	100%	4	100%	10	100%	36	92%
	T	21		3		5		10		39	
3sg	0	18	28%	0	0%	1	5%	1	6%	20	18%
	pro	47	72%	9	100%	21	95%	17	94%	94	82%
	T	65		9		22		18		114	
3pl	0	12	63%	0	0%	0	0%	0	0%	12	60%
	pro	7	37%	0	0%	1	100%	0	0%	8	40%
	T	19		0		1		0		20	
T:	0	70	24%	13	15%	22	24%	28	21%	133	22%
	pro	218	76%	76	85%	70	76%	104	79%	468	78%
	T	288		89		92		132		601	

The figures for all pronouns other than the second-person singular collapsed and all transition-types other than *continue* collapsed are presented in (22). Note that transition-type is not significant when the subject pronoun is or would be the second-person singular, whereas transition-type is highly significant when the subject pronoun is or would be non-second-person singular:

(22)   Distribution of main clause-initial subject zero/pronoun in corpus collapsing all pronouns other than 2sg and all transition-types other than *continue*:

		Continue		Other Trans.		Total		Signif.
2sg	0	37	74%	60	78%	97	76%	$\chi^2 = 0.258$
	pro	13	26%	17	22%	30	24%	$p < 0.70$
	T	50		77		127		[n.s.]
Other pronouns	0	33	14%	3	1%	36	7%	$\chi^2 = 26.782$
	pro	205	86%	233	99%	438	92%	$p < .001$
	T	238		236		474		
Total	0	70	24%	63	20%	133	22%	$\chi^2 = 1.519$
	pro	218	76%	250	80%	468	78%	$p < .30$
	T	288		313		601		[n.s.]
Significance		$\chi^2 = 81.214$		$\chi^2 = 212.178$		$\chi^2 = 274.993$		
		$p < .001$		$p < .001$		$p < .001$		

The multivariate analysis (VARBRUL) probabilities are presented in (23):

(23)   VARBRUL probabilities for main clause-initial subject zero pronoun in corpus, collapsing all pronouns other than 2sg and all transition-types other than *continue*:

Input 0.14		
Pronouns	2sg = 0.96	Other pronouns = 0.30
Transitions	Continue = 0.65	Other Transitions = 0.37
Both variables found to be significant after step-up, step-down analysis.		

Thus we find two different partitions of the data, one made by syntax and one by discourse.

Syntactic constraints partition the distribution of zero subjects into those whose referents are nominally introduced discourse entities and those whose referents are not nominally introduced discourse entities, with the possibility remaining that at least some of the clauses assumed here to have zero subjects that do not refer to nominally introduced discourse entities are in fact subjectless. In any event, zero subjects whose referents are nominally introduced discourse entities may occur only preverbally and only in main clauses; the others, if they in fact exist, may occur postverbally and in subordinate clauses as well. I reserve the term 'Subject-Prodrop' for the first kind, those instances involving zero subjects whose referents are nominally introduced discourse entities.

Discourse constraints, captured here by Centering Theory, then partition the distribution of (this delimited sense of) Subject-Prodrop zero subjects into cases involving *du* 'you', that is, the pronoun referring to the singular familiar addressee, and all others, which I refer to as *Du-Drop* and *Discourse-constrained Subject-Prodrop*, or *Subject-Prodrop$_{DC}$*, respectively, since Du-Drop seems not to be sensitive to discourse constraints and may occur wherever the syntactic constraints are met, while all other instances of Subject-Prodrop are tightly constrained to represent the already-established topic, which is what I take the Cb after a *continue* transition to be.[10]

4   Discussion

The dual partitioning of the data shown here suggests that there are at least three levels of salience that must be recognized for Yiddish: one for entities created on the fly from propositional material; one for a distinguished participant in the speech situation, the addressee; and one for all other non-propositional entities. How these levels should be handled in a theory of discourse is of course not immediately apparent. One possibility, that the entity representing the distinguished participant, the referent of *du*, be simply added to each {Cf} as a 'phantom' Cp, making it the Cb of any subsequent utterance in which it occurs, is not satisfactory, since it turns out that, even when Du-Drop has occurred, *du* does not 'bump' out the previous Cp or current Cb, as illustrated in (24):

(24) i = Stere, i' = Stere's hands, j = Hersh-Ber, k = Tsine, k' = Tsine's hands
(a) ... Az zi$_i$ vet zayn dayn$_j$ vayb, (b) vet zi$_i$ dir$_j$ krikhn unter di negl.
(c) [0$_i$] Iz efsher nokh a mol azoy shtark vi ikh$_k$. (d) [0$_j$] Host gezen ire$_i$ hent$_{i'}$? (e) [0$_{i'}$] zaynen efsher nokh a mol azoy grob vi mayne$_{k'}$. (GF.II.88)
(a) '...If she$_i$'s your wife,' (b) 'she$_i$'ll drive you$_j$ crazy.' (c) '[0$_i$] is perhaps twice as strong as I$_k$.' (d) '[0$_j$] have seen her$_i$ hands$_{i'}$?' (e) '[0$_{i'}$] are perhaps twice as thick as mine$_{k'}$.'

The Centering analysis of (24) is given in (25):

(25)
Clause	Cp	Cb	Transition
(a)	i	i	Continue
(b)	i	i	Continue
(c)	i	i	Continue
(d)	j	i'	Retain
(e)	i'	i'	Continue

Thus it appears that the salience of the distinguished participant does not affect or interact with the salience of the other discourse entities, the distinguished participant always retaining a very high level of salience, the other discourse entities varying in salience along the lines laid out by Centering Theory.

In a different vein, it is interesting that zero subjects with a propositional antecedent distinguish themselves even on the syntactic level in Yiddish, since their treatment in Centering Theory has long been a puzzle, in that indefinitely many propositional antecedents are available for subsequent reference, making their prior addition to the {Cf} unfeasible, and the discourse constraints on their occurrence in English at least seems to be fairly clearly statable without reference to Centering issues. (See Webber 1991 and Embick and Meyerhoff 1994 for discussion.)

5   Future Research

The work reported here is part of a larger ongoing study on zero anaphora in Yiddish. Questions to be dealt with are (1) What evidence can be brought to bear for deciding whether a sentence has a zero subject or is subjectless, especially insofar as it relates to the "ambient" cases discussed? (2) What are the constraints, if any, on discourse deictic zero subjects, and how do they correlate with constraints on the form and distribution of discourse deictic subjects reported for English (Webber 1991) and Italian (Di Eugenio 1990)? (3) What are the constraints, if any, on Yiddish Object-Drop and how does it interact, if it does, with Subject-Prodrop? Questions that remain for future work include cross-linguistic analyses, the most interesting ones, to my mind, comparing Yiddish with German and with the Slavic languages, as well as with Biblical, Medieval, and Modern Hebrew.

6   Afterword on Meta-Intuitions

I should like here to return briefly to the point made earlier that it is thought by many native speakers, Yiddish teachers, and traditional Yiddishists that only *du* 'you' may be occur as a zero subject. The reasons they give are the usual traditional functional ones invoking redundancy: Yiddish verb morphology is such that only the second-person singular ending is unique, as exemplified in (26); since the morphology uniquely identifies the subject for the second-person singular, the second-person singular subject pronoun is redundant and hence deletable. (Cf. more recent arguments presented for Romance, e.g. Rizzi 1986, Kayne 1991.)

(26)   **kukn 'look'; stem: kuk-**

	Singular	**Plural**
1	kuk-0	kuk-n
2	kuk-st	kuk-t
3	kuk-t	kuk-n

Of course, redundancy cannot be the whole answer, since *du* 'you' is just as redundant in noninitial position as in initial and in subordinate clauses as in main yet it is not deletable in those positions. Furthermore, if the stem of the verb ends in a sibilant, the form of the second-person singular is identical to that of the third-person singular and the second-person plural, as is exemplified in (27) with a high frequency verb that often occurs with a zero subject:

(27)   **visn 'know'; stem: veys-**
         Singular   **Plural**
1   veys-0   veys-n
2   veys-st = veyst   veys-t
3   veys-t   veys-n

In fact, we have seen that it is not true that only *du* 'you' may occur as zero, but I believe there is an interesting story for why people might think so. The reason, I believe, lies in certain limitations on our metalinguistic competence, more specifically in our (meta-)intuitions about our (primary) intuitions. When faced with a linguistic form out of context, speakers can logically do one of two things: they can judge that sentence in the null context or they can create an appropriate context in which to judge it. I believe the first is impossible and the second is what speakers do, though of course they do it automatically and unconsciously. Furthermore, I believe we can be fairly specific about certain properties of the created context.

Consider the fact that, when faced with the question of whether zero subjects are possible in Yiddish, speakers call to mind Du-Drop. This suggests immediately that they are creating a discourse context in which to judge the sentences they are judging, since Du-Drop and Subject-Prodrop$_{DC}$ are syntactically identical and differ only in the constraints on their prior discourse context. As for what kind of prior context they are creating, the facts strongly suggest that they create an *unmarked* discourse context. That is, they create a context where there are no constraints on the presence and salience of the referent of the zero subject in the immediately preceding utterance (i.e., it did not have to be the Cp of the previous {Cf} and hence need not be the Cb of the current {Cf}), much less constraints on its presence and salience in the more remote prior context (i.e. it did not have to be the Cb of the previous {Cf} and hence there need not have just been a Continue Transition).

If this were just an isolated instance, one would not conclude that it reflects limitations on metalinguistic competence. However, it is not. Schmerling 1978 reports a very different but entirely parallel phenomenon with respect to the English *do*-imperative. In particular, she reports that speakers judge *do*-imperatives to be markedly "female". At the same time, she shows that *do*-imperatives are not in fact limited to "female" speech. However, it turns out that there are two different functions associated with the form: one, which she calls *polite*, is exemplified in (28a); the other, which she labels a *reprise*, is exemplified in (28b):

(28)   a.   [To visitor at door] Oh, hello! *Do come in!*
         b.   . . .I'm sending over some papers for you to look at. They show some
              interesting trends that no one's predicted, so far as I know. [Discussion
              re: trends.] Ok, gotta run. Take care. And *do have a look at those
              papers.*

The *do*-imperative in (28a) has a *social* function: it conveys politeness and, therefore, femaleness. Note that it is, for all intents and purposes, discourse-initial and in fact could occur felicitously in any discourse context, given that the social function is appropriately served. We could say therefore that it has no *discourse* function, in the strict sense. Note furthermore that this is the *do*-imperative that Schmerling's informants presumably had in mind when they reported that it is said only by women.

In contrast, *do*-imperatives like the one in (28b) have a *discourse* function: they mark that they are reiterating a command/suggestion made earlier in the discourse, prior to intervening material. Therefore, their felicitous occurrence is constrained by the prior discourse context. They do not share the social function of the first type and hence are not stereotypically female, occurring equally, so far as Schmerling could tell, in the speech of both sexes. Therefore, they are presumably not the ones that the informants were thinking of when they reported that only women use this form.

Thus we see that, in two otherwise very dissimilar cases, speakers' judgments can be predicted if we assume that they invent contexts for the forms they are judging and if the contexts they invent are unmarked, that is, if there are no substantive *discourse* constraints on the felicitous occurrence of the form. In contrast, syntactic constraints, for example, those on Du-Drop, and social constraints, such as those on the 'polite' *do*-imperatives, do in fact seem to be accessible to metalinguistic reasoning.

Notes

1   Subject-Prodrop in Yiddish appears to be restricted to the colloquial register, in contrast to Object-Prodrop, which occurs in all registers.

2   In (1) and all following examples, Subject-Prodrop is indicated by $[0 = X]$ in the position in which an overt pronoun would be felicitous in the context provided, where X is the pronoun that would occur, were there one. Each naturally occurring example is followed by its address: G[rine] F[elder], act, page in edition used.

3   The starred examples in this chapter were checked with two to seven native Yiddish speakers and were unanimously judged to be impossible. However, I suspect that there are different dialects with different constraints, since noninitial Subject-Prodrop sites have been collected outside the corpus analyzed here, for example,

(i)   a. A por ritmen volst $[0 = du]$ antlign, bay dayn tsarter shvester-fleyt. . .
             (*Katerinke* (song))
             'A few rhythms would [you] set here, by your sweet sister-flute. . .'

         b. Un az du vest zikh svabodyen fun fovenen, oy zogn vest $[0 = du]$ ikh bin an alte moyd. (*Zog mir tsu* (song))
             'And when you free yourself from regiment, oh say will [you] I am an old maid'.

         c. Dem tsveytn mol hob $[0 = ikh]$ zikh mitn yeger azoy getrofn. (Der Nister, cited in Zaretski 1929)
             'The second time did [I] meet this way with the hunter'.

4 However, outside the corpus isolated instances of Subject-Prodrop in subordinate clauses have been found:

(i)   Berele, shpring nit, vorem [0 = du] vest araynfaln un [0 = du] vest zikh tsebrekhn ruk un hent. (RP:4)

'Little Barry, don't jump, because [you] will fall in and [you] will break your neck'.

(ii)   Gelt iz dokh kaylekhdik, un vibald az aroys kayklt 0 zikh yo, un arayn kayklt 0 zikh nit, iz dokh shlekht. (RP:145)

'Money is after all round, and as soon as [it] rolls out and [it] doesn't roll in, it's bad'.

I suspect these two examples reflect two different phenomena. The zero subject in (i) is in a syntactically subordinate clause but one that is asserted, that is, the sort of subordinate clause that manifests main clause properties in many languages. The zero subject in (ii) is construed here as referring to the discourse entity evoked by *gelt* 'money' in the previous clause; however, it may possibly have a more 'ambient' reference, discussed below, in which case it obeys different syntactic constraints from the 'entity' reference Subject-Prodrop at issue here. Note that the zero subjects in (ii) are also not clause-initial, another indication that different constraints may be operating.

5 Whether the deletion of subjects in imperatives can be subsumed under Yiddish Subject-Prodrop is not obvious. One reason for not subsuming it thus is the register difference: zero-subject imperatives occur in all registers, while (non-imperative) Subject-Prodrop is confined to the colloquial register, as noted above.

6 Note that this falsifies traditional accounts like that of Katz (1987), where not only is it thought that only *du* 'you' is deletable but also that this occurs only in questions, via a sort of truncation of the pronoun encliticized onto the finite verb and where it is not noticed that the pronoun is never absent when the clause is unambiguously V/1, that is, where the pronoun *must* be so encliticized.

7 Note that a series of occurrences of *men* 'one' may in fact be noncoreferential, as in

(i)   Az me vet mir zogn vi azoy me badarf zayn frum – vel ikh. (GF.II.86)

'If one [= you] tells me how one [= I] should be pious – I will'.

8 Outside the corpus, examples of such hortative expressions with zero subjects abound, for example,

(i)   Mit mayn tatn, zol[0 = er] gezunt zayn, hot zikh amol getrofn punkt aza mayse. (RP:208)

'With my father, may [he] be well, just such a story once occurred.'

(ii)   A nar filt nit, ober ayer vayb, zol [0 = zi] gezunt zayn, filt gut. (RP:24)

'A fool doesn't feel(/fill), but your wife, may [she] be well, fills(/feels) well.'

9 In fact, the treatment of pronominal subjects in stage directions is quite interesting, in both Yiddish and English, and varies somewhat from author to author, although a detailed discussion is beyond the scope of this chapter.

10 Whether or not there are discourse constraints on discourse deictic or "ambient" zero subjects is not obvious from the present study and awaits further research. Similarly, it is possible that Du-Drop is in fact constrained by some discourse factors to which a Centering analysis is not sensitive.

References

Bolinger, D. 1977. *Meaning and Form*, Longman, London.

Bouchard, D. 1985. PRO, pronominal oranaphor. *Linguistic Inquiry* 16(3), 471–477.

Cameron, R. 1992. Pronominal and null subject variation in Spanish: Constraints, dialects, and functional compensation, Ph.D. Dissertation, University of Pennsylvania.

Di Eugenio, B. 1990. Centering and the Italian pronominal system. Presented at the 13th International Conference on Computational Linguistics, COLING 90, Helsinki, Finland, August 20–25.

Donnellan, K. 1978. Speaker references, descriptions and anaphora. In P. Cole, (ed.), *Syntax and Semantics*, 9, Pragmatics, Academic Press, New York, 47–68.

Embick, D., and M. Meyerhoff. 1994. It's it, that's that, and this is something else. Ms., University of Pennsylvania.

Grosz, B. J., A. K. Joshi, and S. Weinstein. 1995. Centering: A framework for modelling the local coherence of discourse. Computational Linguistics 21(2), 203–225.

Gundel, J. K. 1980. Zero NP-anaphora in Russian: A case of topic-prominence. In *Papers from the Parasession on Pronouns and Anaphora*, Chicago Linguistic Society, Chicago.

Heim, I. 1983. File change semantics and the theory of definiteness. In R. Bauerle, C. Schwarze, and A. von Stechow (eds.), *Meaning, use, and the interpretation of language*, Walter de Gruyter, Berlin.

Hirschbein, P. 1923. Grinefelder. In *Di yidishe drame fun 20stn yorhundert.*, Alveltlekhn Yidishn Kultur-Kongres, 1977, Band 2, 61–106.

Huang, C. T. J. 1984. On the distribution and reference of empty pronouns. *Linguistic Inquiry* 15(4), 531–574.

Huang, C. T. J. 1989. Pro-drop in Chinese: a generalized control theory. In O. Jaeggli and K. J. Safir (eds.), *The Null Subject Parameter*, Kluwer, Dordrecht.

Jaeggli, O. 1980. On some phonologically-null elements in syntax. Ph.D. Dissertation, M.I.T.

Jaeggli, O., and K. Safir (eds.). 1989. *The Null Subject Parameter, Studies in Natural Language and Linguistic Theory*, 15.

Joshi, A. K., and S. Weinstein. 1981. Control of inference: Role of some aspects of discourse structure—Centering. In: *Proceeding of the International Joint Conference on Artificial Intelligence*. Vancouver, B.C., 385–387.

Kagarov, E. 1929. Eynige akhtungen oyfn gebit fun yidishn sintaksis. *Filologishe shriftn fun YIVO* 3, 467–472.

Kameyama, M. 1985. Zero anaphora: The case of Japanese. Ph.D. dissertation, Stanford University.

Kameyama, M. 1988. Japanese zero pronominal binding: Where syntax and discourse meet. In W. Poser (ed.), *Papers from the 2nd International Workshop on Japanese Syntax*, CSLI, Stanford, Calif.

Katz, D. 1987. *Grammar of the Yiddish language*, Duckworth, London.

Kayne, R. S. 1991. Romance clitics, verb movement, and PRO. *Linguistic Inquiry* 22(4), 647–686.

Li, C., and S. Thompson. 1979. Third person pronouns and zero-anaphora in Chinese discourse. In T. Givón (ed.), *Discourse and syntax*, Academic Press, New York, 311–335.

Miner, K. 1990. Yiddish V/1 declarative clauses in discourse. *IRPA Papers in Pragmatics* 4(1/2), 122–149.

Napoli, D. J. 1982. Initial material deletion in English. *Glossa* 16(1), 5–111.

Reinhart, T. 1981. Pragmatics and linguistics: An analysis of sentence topics. *Philosophica* 27, 53–94.

Rizzi, L. 1986. Null objects in Italian and the theory of pro. *Linguistic Inquiry* 17(3), 501–557.

Shlonsky, U. 1987. Null and displaced subjects. Ph.D. Dissertation, M.I.T.

Thrainsson, H. 1985. V/1, V/2, V/3 in Icelandic. In H. Haider and M. Prinzhorn (eds.), *Verb Second Phenomena in Germanic languages*, Foris, Dordrecht, 169–194.

Turan, U. 1995. Null vs. overt subjects in Turkish discourse: A Centering analysis. Ph.D. Dissertation, University of Pennsylvania.

Turan, U. 1998. Ranking forward-looking centers in Turkish: Universal and language-specific properties. In Walker, M. A., A. K. Joshi, and E. F. Prince, (eds.), Centering Theory in discourse. Oxford University Press, Oxford, 139–160.

Walker, M. A., M. Iida, and S. Cote. 1990. Centering in Japanese discourse. *Proceedings of the 13th International Conference on Computational Linguistics*, COLING 90, Helsinki, Finland, August 20–25.

Walker, M. A., M. Iida, and S. Cote. 1994. Japanese discourse and the process of centering. *Computational Linguistics* 20(2), 193–232.

Webber, B. 1991. Structure and ostension in the interpretation of discourse deixis. *Language and Cognitive Processes* 6(2), 107–135.

Weinreich, U. 1981. *College Yiddish: An introduction to the Yiddish language and to Jewish life and culture*, 5th revised edition, YIVO, New York.

Zaretski, A. 1929. *Yidishe gramatik*, Vilner Farlag fun B. Kletskin, Vilna.

PART II

Semantic Interpretation of Focus Phenomena

6   What Is the Alternative? The Computation of Focus Alternatives from Lexical and Sortal Information

PETER I. BLOK AND KURT EBERLE

Abstract

A focused constituent of a sentence is generally interpreted as the denotation of the unfocused constituent together with a set of (excluded) alternatives to that denotation. The determination of the relevant set of alternatives is a problem. We present an approach to focus interpretation that is syntactic in nature: alternatives for constituents are defined syntactically, in terms of a hierarchy of similarity of lexical items. This hierarchy is inferred from a semantically justified sort hierarchy. We show the impact of this theory on the resolution of specific desambiguation problems in Machine Translation. Our approach is designed for incorporation within the *logic-programming-based machine translation* system LMT, currently under development at the Scientific Center of IBM at Heidelberg.

In Section 1 we present a relevant desambiguation problem. In Section 2 the concept of *alternative* is briefly discussed. In Section 3 the essentials of a suitable sort hierarchy are introduced. In Section 4, using this hierarchy, we formulate a basic heuristics for the computation of alternatives. In Section 5 we deal with more troublesome cases, where contextual information has to be taken into account. We finally give a solution for the translation mismatch presented in section 1 and discuss further refinements to the proposal made.

1   Introduction

The concept of *alternative* in focus theory can often be of crucial importance for desambiguation in computational applications; in particular a number of translation mismatches (cf. Kameyama et al. 1991) a machine translation system is confronted with can be resolved by the impact of this concept on the semantic evaluation of texts. Consider the following example from Dutch:

(1)   De vader VERGEEFT zijn dochter haar aanstaande niet.[1]

    a.   'The father FORGIVES his daughter her fiancé not.'
        The father won't FORGIVE his daughter (for the choice of) her fiancé.

    b.   'The father GIVES AWAY his daughter her fiancé not.'
        The father does not GIVE AWAY his daughter to her fiancé.

Vergeven is ambiguous, and neither the arity (valence) nor the type of the verb arguments (i.e. *selectional restrictions* (cf. Lehmann and Ott 1992)) can disambiguate the sentence. Now, consider the following possible continuations of the text:

105

(1)   a.′ Hij TOLEREERT het paar slechts.
           'He TOLERATES the couple only.'
           He only TOLERATES the couple.
       b.′ Hij zal ze slechts NAAR DE KERK BRENGEN.
           '*He will them only* to the church bring.'
           He will only TAKE them TO THE CHURCH.

Slechts in (1a′) associates with the focus on the verb. The *tolerating* of the father is contrasted with other attitudes that refer to the same situation paradigm the *tolerating* refers to. *Slechts* excludes the applicability of these attitudes to the father. Thus, we learn from (1a′) that there was no other moral or social attitude the father showed with respect to daughter and fiancé, in particular no forgiving his daughter the fiancé. With respect to (1b′) similarly, we conclude that there was no other conventionalized physical action of the marriage frame the father undertook other than taking the daughter and the fiancé to the church, in particular no giving away of the daughter to the fiancé. Given (1a′) one cannot interpret (1) as (1b), because no suitable rhetorical or discourse relation could be found that links up the information of (1b) and (1a′), which aims at rather different scenarios: one at physical actions in the context of *marriage* and the other at attitudes. In contrast, when interpreting (1) as (1a), the discourse relation is obvious: the function of (1a′) is to *elaborate* the theme introduced by (1a); this theme is the *attitude of the father* and the exclusion of one specific subtype of this semantic action- or situation-class.[2] Similarly, the sequence of sentences (1), (1b′) presupposes the interpretation (1b) of (1) in order to establish a coherent text. Then (1b′) elaborates (1) by presenting an alternative to the excluded action of (1) within the paradigm of marriage preparation actions.

    In order to resolve the translation mismatch, the system must be able to exploit the contextual clues described; that is, it must be able to make a connection between *vergeven* in the sense of (1a) and *tolereren* as in (1a′), on the one hand, and between *vergeven* in the sense of (1b) and *naar de kerk brengen* as in (1b′), on the other, and it must realize that no similarly reasonable connection holds in the opposite arrangement. The specific connection is given as a relation between alternatives with respect to a common semantic paradigm.

2   Focus and Alternatives

As pointed out by Gabbay and Moravcsik (1978), Rooth (1985), and others, a sentence with a focused constituent, S_F, should be interpreted as relating the meaning of the corresponding sentence without focus, S, to a set of alternatives that develop from the interpretation of S by exchanging the denotation of the focused constituent by other suitable denotations. With this we agree. In Rooth (1985), on the basis of Montagovian-style interpretations, the alternatives to the denotation D of a constituent are taken to be the objects of the type of D. The set of these objects is called the *p-set*. However, as pointed out by Rooth (1985, 1992), Blok (1993a, b), and others, the *p-set* is, on principle, too big in number, if the focused constituent has a type higher than *e*.

(2)   John only SWIMS.

The alternatives to *swim* that (2) excludes are certainly not all remaining properties of John. Since the examples (1):(1a′) and (1):(1b′) show that a set of alternatives is not necessarily homogeneous with respect to the type of its members – *vergeven* is a 3-place verb; *tolereren* and *brengen* are 2-place verbs – we can say that the p-set also often is too small. We conclude from this that focused constituents must be evaluated with respect to some limited domain, where, nevertheless, it must be allowed what, in terms of the Montagovian interpretation, would result in a certain variability of the type of the denotations.

How can we obtain reasonable limits for the set of alternatives? Blok (1994) proposes a semantics for (2) involving sets of "aware" properties. The term *awareness* is borrowed from epistemic logic for the following reason: *awareness* aims at the shape of formulas, not at their meaning.[3] In the same way as the form-oriented awareness prevents belief states from being logically closed (normally believers are not logically omniscient!), it also allows for reasonable restrictions on the range of properties one wants to quantify over in order to get the set of alternatives of focused properties. In the following we assume that, with respect to focus examples like (1) and (2), awareness is restricted to a limited set of syntactic objects the author or the recipient of the text has access to, namely, the signs of the lexicon. The claim is to compute the set of alternatives, depending on lexically driven classifications. With respect to interpretations the theoretical background is provided by an event semantics as developed in Eberle (1991).

The problem is that the lexicon only provides the background against which specific contextual clues trigger the choice of the exact domain of quantification. To say (2) of a triathlete may be quite something else than saying it of some hotel guest. Moreover, as the example (1) shows, the set of relevant alternatives may go beyond word class boundaries. What we need, then, is a flexible system in which basic relations between words and concepts are expressed and from which more general relations can be deduced.

3   A Sort Hierarchy for LMT

In Eberle (in prep.) a sort hierarchy is designed that is suited for the purposes of a machine translation system like LMT (cf. McCord 1989). Formally the hierarchy consists of a set of primitive sort symbols S that are structured by means of a decidable partial order $\leq$. This hierarchy can be understood as a weak version of a *signature* in the sense of Smolka's *feature logic with subsorts* (cf. Smolka 1988).[4] The meaning of the primitive sort symbols are subsets of the domain D of an interpreting model. The hierarchy comprises symbols for top and bottom:

TRUE and FALSE, that is, of each (canonical) interpretation M with domain D it holds:

$$\|[\text{TRUE}]\|_M = D$$
$$\|[\text{FALSE}]\|_M = \emptyset$$

The *upper structure* of the hierarchy is stored in a knowledge base to which the components of LMT for parsing, semantic construction, and transfer have access. The *lower structure* of the sort hierarchy is built up dynamically from the information contained in the lexicon by the lexical lookup of the parsing process.[5] Some of the facts of the upper structure present a rather canonical and common structuring of the domain of text interpreting models.

In the following we use *part_partition* $(S, [S_1, \ldots, S_n])$ as an abbreviation for $S_i \leq S$ for all $1 \leq i \leq n$ and $S_i \sqcap S_j = \text{FALSE}$ for all $1 \leq i, j \leq n$ with $i \neq j$:

> *part_partition* (TRUE,[TIME,SPACE,SITUATION,MATERIAL])
> *part_partition* (MATERIAL,[OBJECT,SUBSTANCE])
> ANIMATE $\leq$ OBJECT
> *part_partition* (ANIMATE,[ANIMAL,PLANT])
> *part_partition* (ANIMAL,[HUMAN,NHANIMAL])[6]

The interpretation of such statements in a model M is as follows:

$$S_i \leq S_j \text{ is true in } M \text{ iff } \|[S_i]\|_M \subseteq \|[S_j]\|_M$$
$$S_i \sqcap S_j = S_k \text{ is true in } M \text{ iff } \|[S_i]\|_M \cap \|[S_j]\|_M = \|[S_k]\|_M$$

The idea underlying the sort hierarchy proposed for LMT is to provide subsumption relations between both semantic and syntactic sorts by one unique taxonomy. The maximal sort of syntactic sorts is L_ELEM (for *language element*). The maximal sort of semantic sorts is NL_ELEM (for *nonlanguage element*). There are statements like the following:

> *part_partition* (TRUE,[L_ELEM,NL_ELEM])
> *part_partition* (L_ELEM,[VERB,NOUN])
> *part_partition* (NOUN,[MNOUN,CNOUN])
> *part_partition* (VERB,[SS,SO])
> *part_partition* (VERB,[A1,A2,A3])

This says that L_ELEM and NL_ELEM are disjoint classes, that verbs and nouns are disjoint subsorts of L_ELEM, that there are mass nouns (MNOUN) and count nouns (CNOUN), that there are verbs that control the subject of embedded infinitival VPs such that the embedded subject is equivalent to the higher subject (ss) or such that the embedded subject is equivalent to the higher object (SO), and that there are verbs of arity 1, of arity 2, and of arity 3. In a model the extension of NL_ELEM comprises objects (the classic individuals), times, spaces, situations, and so on, and the extension of L_ELEM consists of the equivalence classes of instances of word(-stem)s (or specific constituents) that appear in natural language texts.

LMT uses the slot grammar formalism of McCord (1991), which provides slots for the *sense* and the *type* of words, which the parsing routine fills by means of the lexical lookup. Normally the sense is a complex term $s(W,N)$, where W is the word(-stem) as a string and N a number that refers to that lexical entry of the word that reflects (syntactically and semantically) the use of the word in the sentence. In the existing LMT the type is a conjunction of upper structure sorts. In order to obtain precise characterizations of the LMT-sense in terms of primitive sort symbols, we deviate from this by also allowing for types that are conjunctions of upper and lower structure sorts. For instance, for the German word *Pils* (which describes a specific kind of beer) parts of the result of the lexical lookup might look as follows (rendered as a feature structure):

a. *Pils* $\begin{bmatrix} sense : s(pils, 1) \\ type : \text{MNOUN} \cap \text{BIER} \end{bmatrix}$

b. *Pils* $\begin{bmatrix} sense : s(pils, 2) \\ type : \text{CNOUN} \cap \text{BIER} \end{bmatrix}$

These alternative results will trigger the dynamic updating of the lower structure of the sort hierarchy, resulting in the following new facts:

$$s(pils,1) \leq \text{MNOUN} \qquad s(pils, 2) \leq \text{CNOUN}$$
$$s(pils,1) \leq \text{BIER} \qquad s(pils, 2) \leq \text{BIER}$$

In order for the LMT-sense to be anchored in the upper structure by each of the branches that are designated by the conjuncts of its type, recursive calls of the lexical lookup may be necessary, as in the preceding example, where BIER, of course, will be a lower structure sort.[7] The lexical lookup for *Bier* and, perhaps, further lookups will provide us, for instance, with the following information:

$$s(pils,1), s(pils,2) \leq \text{BIER} \leq \ldots \leq \text{ALC\_LIQUID}$$

where ALC_LIQUID is an upper structure sort.

In a model, the extension of an LMT-sense, that is, of a $s(W,N)$-sort, is the set that contains as unique element the class of those NL-sentences that use W in the sense of the lexicon entry N of W, or, roughly, identifying this class with its representative:

$\|[s(W,N)]\|_M$: the "word" W in the sense of the lexicon entry N of W

Thus, roughly, $s(pils,1)$ denotes the word *Pils* used as a mass noun, and $s(pils,2)$ denotes the word *Pils* used as a count noun. LMT-senses (which are syntactic sorts) are assigned semantic sort symbols via the symbol transformation $ST: s(W,N) \rightarrow WN$. We could say that the sort for the *signifiant*, $s(W,N)$, is assigned the sort for the *signifié*, WN, with

$\|[WN]\|_M$: a subset of the NL_ELEM-domain of M[8]

For instance, $\|[\text{PILS2}]\|_M$ is the set of quantities of pils seen as objects, and $\|[\text{PILS1}]\|_M$ is the set of the corresponding portions of matter.[9] By means of the further symbol transformation *STw: s(W,N)* → W^N we combine the syntactic sort *s(W,N)* and the corresponding semantic sort *WN*, *signifiant* and *signifié*, so to speak, within the sort W^N that we call a WAO-sort, that is, a *Word- and Object*-sort.

$$\|[W^N]\|_M := \|[s(W,N)]\|_M \cup \|[WN]\|_M \cup (\bigcup_{\{s(V,M)|ST(s(V,M))<WN\}} \|[s(V,M)]\|_M)$$

Of course, we call a sort of the form W^N "*Word-and-Object*," because it denotes both "words" and objects (the representative for *W* and the representatives for all words of the considered language that are more specific than *W*, the *W*-words, and the objects that are denoted by *W* and the *W*-words). Figure 6.1 illustrates the essential features of the sort hierarchy for LMT, including the WAO-branch.

Lower WAO-sorts reflect the organization of the world relative to a specific language. In Figure 6.1, (part of) the German categorization of beer is given:

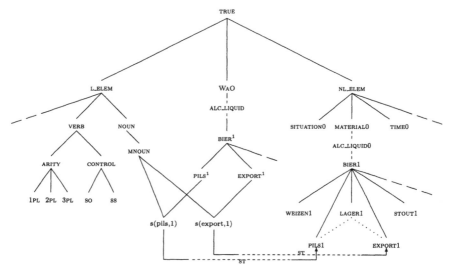

Fig. 6.1.

$$\|[ALC\_LIQUID]\|_M \supseteq \|[BIER]\|_M = \|[BIER^1]\|_M \cup \|[BIER^2]\|_M$$
$$\|[BIER^1]\|_M = \|[s(bier,1)]\|_M \cup \|[PILS^1]\|_M \cup \|[EXPORT^1]\|_M \cup \|[KÖLSCH^1]\|_M \cup$$
$$\|[WEIZEN^1]\|_M \cup \ldots$$

For English we would obtain something like the following:

$$\|[ALC\_LIQUID]\|_M \supseteq \|[BEER]\|_M = \|[BEER^1]\|_M \cup \|[BEER^2]\|_M$$
$$\|[BEER^1]\|_M = \|[s(beer,1)]\|_M \cup \|[LAGER^1]\|_M \cup \|[STOUT^1]\|_M \cup \|[ALE^1]\|_M \cup$$
$$\ldots \text{etc.}$$

This results in the use of different *hierarchies of primitive sorts (PSH)* in the machine translation system. However, the assumption is that the different PSHs (we use subscripts to mark the specific language) are identical with respect to the upper structure and, in addition, with respect to the complete NL_ELEM branch, which we can call the *concept hierarchy*. The concept hierarchy must be understood as a categorization of the world that is at least as fine-grained as needed in order to reflect all the categories that are made available by at least one of the natural languages involved in the system. Therefore, in Figure 6.1, which relates to PSH_{german}, we nevertheless find concepts for the English WAO sorts LAGER[1] and STOUT[1], that is, LAGER1 and STOUT1.[10] The dotted lines refer to the information from the German/English transfer lexicon; both *Pils* and *Export* translate into *lager* (the dotted lines in the picture at hand may also be taken to describe a subset relation).

We stress that in the system sketched, sorts like ALC_LIQUID classify objects, substances, *and* nouns (noun senses), though the naming might suggest the misleading assumption that such sorts are part of the NL_ELEM branch. In order to construct the corresponding concept sort, we make use of the symbol transformation $STO{:}W \rightarrow WO$, which only applies to upper WAO sorts W, returning sorts WO, that denote the intersection of W with NL_ELEM. With this transformation, and with filtering out of WAO sorts from the type description of the LMT-sense, the semantic component of the LMT system produces updates of the NL_ELEM-branch – the concept lexicon – from the lexical lookup. It computes conceptual statements like the following, which relates to the Pils example:

$$PILS1 \leq BIER1 \leq ALC\_LIQUID0$$

The integrated representation of syntactic and semantic knowledge that is used in the type description of lexicon entries (for denoting expressions) and that presupposes sorts that are unspecified with respect to the word/object difference, that is, WAO sorts, helps to control the parser in search of a possible syntactic analysis. It controls the semantic outcome as well, especially with respect to the impact of selectional restrictions on the resolution of semantic ambiguities. In addition, it helps, as we see in the next section, to compute sets of alternatives in the presence of focused elements.

4   Computing Alternatives

It is our main claim that alternatives should be looked for on the level of WAO sorts.

(3)   a. John trinkt nur PILS.
         b. John only drinks LAGER.

All our German and English informants confirmed that, even if we accept *lager* as translation of *Pils*, (3a) and its possible translation (3b) differ with respect to the alternatives of the focused constituent. Assuming the empty context, the alternatives of which the native speaker is aware of in (3a) are those kinds of beer that have a name in German, and correspondingly for (3b). Normally, neither is *Kölsch* an alternative of *lager*, nor is *ale* an alternative of *Pils*. Therefore, in order to compute the set of alternatives, it is incorrect and too general to point to all denotations that are of the same semantic type as the focused element, a subset of the NL_ELEM domain, even if we restrict the domain to the denotation of the concept sorts BIER1 or BEER1, respectively. Also it is not correct to point to the immediate, primitive subsorts of the concept sort that describes the reference domain, BEER1 or BIER1, because the structuring of the concept hierarchy is language independent, such that there might be neighbors of an immediate primitive subsort S that are not alternatives of S and such that correct alternatives are subsumed by such neighbors. If we interpret the dotted line relation of Figure 6.1 between PILS1 and LAGER1 and between EXPORT1 and LAGER1 as subsumption, WEIZEN1, PILS1, and EXPORT1 are alternatives of each other, though only WEIZEN1 is an immediate primitive subsort of the reference sort BIER1. The picture is different if the intermediate sort between alternative candidate and reference sort has a name in the language considered. WEIZEN1 is an alternative of PILS1, EXPORT1, KÖLSCH1, and so on, not the more specific RAUCHWEIZEN1. Thus, on the level of conceptual alternatives, we should take into consideration only these sorts that, with respect to the specific PSH_L used, have names, that is, that are images of LMT-senses. Because under the given interpretation of the word senses the set of word senses cannot be structured by the subsumption relation, the determination of the alternatives has to take place on the language specific level WAO. It is the only level that directly provides the relevant information: subsumption relations of the language specific granularity. With respect to the empty context, we suggest the following heuristics:

> BASIC STRATEGY FOR THE DETERMINATION OF THE ALTERNATIVES OF AN LMT-SENSE $s(W,N)$:
> - Choose the appropriate sort hierarchy for the L-specific LMT-sense $s(W,N)$: PSH_L
> - Determine the unique primitive WAO sort that immediately dominates $s(W,N)$: $idw_{PSH_L}(s(W, N))$
> $(= \{W^N\}$, with idw_{PSH_L} for *immediately dominating* $\underline{W}$AO *sort in* PSH_L).
> - Choose a WAO-sort that immediately dominates W^N:
> $Rnode_{sem,PSH_L}(s(W,N)) \in idw_{PSH_L}(W^N)$
> $(= \text{BIER}^1$, for $s(pils,1)$, with $Rnode_{sem,PSH_L}$ for *semantic reference node in* PSH_L).
> - Determine the set of alternatives for $s(W,N)$ as those LMT-senses whose idw-sort contrasts with W^N within $Rnode_{sem}$ and is maximal in this respect:
>
> $$SA^s_{PSH_L}(s(W, N))$$
> $$= \left\{ s(V, M) \mid \begin{array}{l} \neg(W^N \leq V^M) \\ \wedge\ V^M < Rnode_{sem,PSH_L}(s(W, N)) \\ \wedge\ \neg\exists U, L \quad (V^M < U^L < Rnode_{sem,PSH_L}(s(W, N))) \\ \wedge\ \forall S \in \text{LUS} \quad (s(V, M) \leq S \leftrightarrow s(W, N) \leq S) \end{array} \right\}$$

LUS stands for the set of upper structure sorts subsumed by L_ELEM. We assume here that $s(W,N)$ and its alternatives are equivalent modulo the upper structure descriptions of L_ELEM.

The SA-superscript points to the ambiguous use of *alternative* as a "*word*" (s, here, for a word sense), a *predicate* (an ST-image), or an *extension*, respectively (we mark the predicate use by p and the extension use by e). From the word sense alternatives $SA^s_{PSH_L}$ we easily define the sets $SA^p_{PSH_L}$ and $SA^e_{PSH_L}$ as follows:

$$SA^p_{PSH_L}(s(W, N)) = \{ST(V, M)) \mid s(V, M) \in SA^s_{PSH_L}(s(W, N))\}$$
$$SA^e_{PSH_L}(s(W, N)) = \{\|[ST(V, M))]\|_M \mid s(V, M) \in SA^s_{PSH_L}(s(W, N))\}$$

The transition from $SA^s_{PSH_L}$ to $SA^p_{PSH_L}$ and $SA^e_{PSH_L}$, respectively, corresponds to the transition from evaluating synonyms as independent alternatives, as in examples like (4a), where the focused constituent is used in a quoting sense, to evaluating synonyms on the semantic level, as in (4b), where the focused constituent is *used*, not *mentioned*.

(4)   a. John sagt, daß Peter nur GEIGE spielt (nicht VIOLINE, . . .).
           John says that Peter only plays FIDDLE (not VIOLIN, . . .).
    b. John denkt, daß Peter nur GEIGE spielt (nicht CELLO, . . .).
           John thinks that Peter only plays FIDDLE (not CELLO, . . .).

With respect to PHS$_{german}$, the heuristics entails that $s(weizenbier, 1)$, $s(kölsch, 1)$, $s(export, 1)$, and so on, are the alternatives of $s(pils, 1)$, and, with respect to PHS$_{english}$, that $s(stout, 1)$, $s(ale, 1)$, and so on, are the alternatives of $s(lager, 1)$ (or the corresponding ST-sorts or the corresponding denotations, respectively). This is as desired. Of course, the quality of the outcome depends on the structuring capacity of the sort hierarchy used: a coarse grained PHS$_{german}$ that omits the BIER level means that the maxima of all available named alcoholic liquids different from pils are enumerated.

5   Refinements

(5)   a. Mary does not LIKE to swim.
    b. She HATES to swim.
    c. She HAS to swim.

In (5) we understand (b) and (c) as possible continuations of the text (a). Similar to example (1) the continuations present alternatives to the focused constituent of the first sentence. Figure 6.2 presents the relevant parts of a suited reference PSH$_{english}$. With respect to this PHS, the basic heuristics entails correctly that $s(hate, 1)$ functions as an alternative to $s(like, 1)$. However, (5c) shows that this heuristics has to be modified in the presence of particular contexts. In order that $s(have, 3)$ be included within the set of alternatives, the mark $Rnode_{sem}$ has to be pushed onto the next higher level, as illustrated in Figure 6.2.

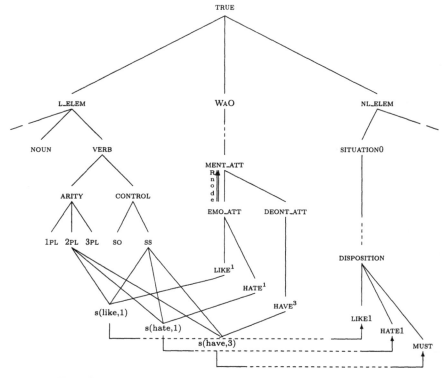

Fig. 6.2.

We encounter another type of problem in (6):

(6)   a. John only SWIMS.
       b. John is a triathlete, but today he only SWIMS.

Obviously, in (6a) the alternatives are other sports, whereas in (6b) the context restricts this set to the triathlon sports. A sufficiently fine-grained PSH for English contains the node TRIATHLON_SPORT. However, it seems that the normal language user is not aware of this node, at least with respect to neutral contexts. The structure in the middle of Figure 6.3 tries to render this situation. The fact that SPORT is framed means that, with respect to the leave nodes, it is a possible candidate for $Rnode_{sem}$, whereas the dashed TRIATHLON_SPORT is not. Frames visualize *labels*. The assumption is that only some of the nodes of the neutral lexicon/hierarchy are *labeled* (framed), that is, visible or accessible as $Rnode_{sem}$ candidates. The structure to the left in Figure 6.3 represents the situation of the structure in the middle from the perspective of the language user: the hierarchy of which the normal user is aware in the neutral context. From this we obtain the correct set of alternatives for (6a): all (basic) kinds of sport. The structure to the right in Figure 6.3 represents the impact of the context information on the neutral lexicon/hierarchy: the first sentence of

(6b) causes the labeling of the TRIATHLON_SPORT node in PHS. Therefore, with respect to (6b) the *biking/running/swimming* set seems to be preferred to the bigger set of alternatives of the empty context case.

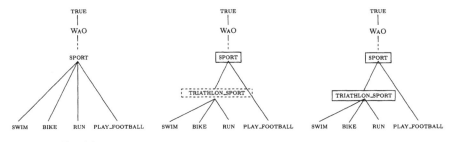

Fig. 6.3.

Summarizing, we conclude that the context can label nodes of the PSH that otherwise would be invisible with respect to the $Rnode_{sem}$-determination. In addition, it seems that climbing up the hierarchy step by step diminishes the likelihood that nodes are chosen as *Rnodes*.

We turn to a solution of our introductory example (1); compare Figure 6.4:

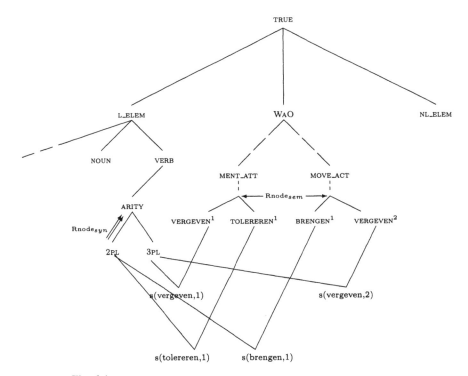

Fig. 6.4.

In example (1), $s(tolereren,1)$ and $s(vergeven,1)$ are alternatives of each other, and similarly for $s(brengen,1)$ and $s(vergeven,2)$. In order to be able to predict this, we must modify our heuristics of the last section in another respect. We introduce $Rnode_{syn}$ and weaken the condition of syntactic identity between focused constituent and alternative to the condition of being alternatives of each other with respect to $Rnode_{syn}$. (Note that $s(tolereren,1)$ and $s(brengen,1)$ are 2PL-, whereas $s(vergeven,1)$ and $s(vergeven,2)$ are 3PL-verbs). We obtain the following:

> INFORMAL STRATEGY FOR THE DETERMINATION OF THE ALTERNATIVES OF AN LMT-SENSE $s(W,N)$:
> - Taking the context into account, revise the labeling of PSH.
> - Choose a nonredundant conjunction of L_ELEM-sorts that characterizes $s(W,N)$ as $Rnode_{syn}$, where the subsumption relation '>' reflects decreasing preference.
> - Choose a labeled WAO-sort S with $S > W^N$ as $Rnode_{sem}$. Here, too, the subsumption relation '>' reflects decreasing preference.
> - Determine the set of alternatives as in the fourth step of the basic routine of the last section (weakening the requirement for LUS equivalence to $Rnode_{syn}$ restrictedness).

Of course, the preference relation for the different sets of alternatives follows the preference relation for the set of the corresponding Rnode-pairs.

6   Outlook

We have outlined an algorithm that computes sets of alternatives for focused constituents. This algorithm operates over language-specific sort hierarchies that share essential parts: the complete upper structure and the concept hierarchy. Depending on the contextually determined distribution of labels over the nodes of the hierarchy, different sets of alternatives are entailed. With respect to a specific contextual constellation, that is, a specific labeling, sets of alternatives that follow from more specific syntactic and semantic paradigms are normally preferred to sets that follow from more general ones.

The techniques of labeling and of choosing paradigms as they are described in this chapter allow the (canonical) reference nodes of the initial neutral setting to be pushed upward (toward TRUE) or to be pushed downward (toward the LMT-sense). However, we can also navigate differently in the labeled hierarchy:

(7)   What does John do, does he swim, work, or drink wine?
       Oh, of course, he only SWIMS.

In (7) the context introduces and labels the union of SWIM, WORK, and DRINK_WINE. In order to prefer this node to SPORT, we must allow that the semantic Rnode of the initial setting can be shifted *sideward*, so to speak, and that it can be shifted to a node that is not a *primitive sort symbol*. Empirical studies must show whether there are still other possibilities of Rnode shifts. We hope that on the basis of such studies we will be able to turn the heuristics that we have suggested in this chapter into an exact algorithm that keeps track of the decisive contextual features and of their effects on the initial setting with respect to the changing of labelings, the introduction of new nodes, and specific preference scales.

Since, in the semantic component of LMT, the PSHs are embedded as partial descriptions of signatures into corresponding feature logics, we can use *features* in order to handle more complex cases of focusing via more analytic descriptions of the focused constituent, its alternatives, and the corresponding paradigms. For instance, instead of the atom DRINK_WINE, we would obtain DRINK $\cap$ object: WINE, where the semantic paradigms can be automatically deduced from the paradigms of DRINK and WINE.

Though our approach was designed for the specific settings of the slot grammar implementation of LMT, it can be made available for other grammar formalisms. Instead of further concluding remarks, using the example of HPSG (Pollard and Sag 1994), we sketch the adaptation we have in mind for unification grammar formalisms that, via features, describe syntactic and semantic information about the structures analyzed.

The basic idea is to spell out the quantification over LMT-senses that is restricted by $Rnode_{syn}$ and $Rnode_{sem}$ as quantifications over accordingly restricted feature structures, that is, over HPSG-word-signs that are restricted by feature terms like

$$Rnode'_{sem}[\text{SYNSEM:LOCAL: [CATEGORY: } Rnode'_{syn}]]$$

where $Rnode'_{syn}$ is a suitable translation of $Rnode_{syn}$ into the HPSG framework: that is, a specific feature description of type *cat*. $Rnode'_{sem}$ is an element of a hierarchy of subtypes WAO' of the HPSG type *word* that has to be introduced into the HPSG framework as a homomorphic image of the WAO-hierarchy. Thus, we assume that the adaptation translates

- a word sense $s(W,N)$ ($<Rnode_{syn} \cap Rnode_{sem}$) into a feature structure that satisfies the description

$$W^{N'} \begin{bmatrix} \text{PHON:} & W \\ \text{SYNSEM:LOCAL:} & \begin{bmatrix} \text{CATEGORY:} & Rnode'_{syn} \\ \text{CONTENT: RELN: } WN' \end{bmatrix} \end{bmatrix}$$

with $W^{N'} < Rnode'_{sem}$,
- a concept sort into a one-place relation type that is admitted in content restrictions, in particular the ST-image WN of the sense $s(W,N)$ into the noun content relation type WN',
(where, of course, the function " ' " is order preserving with respect to the concept hierarchy),
- a primitive upper WAO-sort S into the word subtype S',
where the HPSG type system is constrained by the subsumption schemas

$WN' \leq [$ SYNSEM:LOCAL:CONTENT: RELN: WN'], if W^N a STw-image in WAO, $US' \leq [$ SYNSEM:LOCAL:CONTENT: RELN: $US0'$], if US a upper structure element of WAO.

The argument for the necessity of a hierarchy that structures the *word* type into a homomorphic picture of the WAO-hierarchy parallels the argument introduced in the beginning of Section 4 in favor of the WAO-hierarchy: we need a representation level where subsumption relations of the language specific granularity are available. This level cannot be provided (at least not directly) by the domain of the feature structures that are assigned to nouns or verbs, nor by the domain of *content* restricting relations, but by the domain of WAO'-determined classes of feature structures.

Notes

1 We thank Jack Hoeksema for providing us with this example.
2 Note that the function of negated focused sentences such as (1) often is to cause the recipient of the text to expect the presentation of an alternative to the excluded action or the presentation of an action that shows somehow weaker consequences than the excluded one does. For *rhetorical relations* or *discourse relations* like *elaboration*, compare the work on rhetorical structure theory and on discourse structure respectively, for instance Mann and Thompson 1987, Polanyi and Scha 1988, Lascarides and Asher 1991, Eberle 1992.
3 Compare Fagin and Halpern 1988.
4 Whereas a signature of feature logic is a complete join semilattice over a set of primitive sort symbols where the corresponding partial order is decidable, our sort hierarchy also makes use of a join operation, but the set of primitive sort symbols is not necessarily closed with respect to this operation. This weakening seems justified by the properties of the structured domain of natural language motivated concepts.
5 Here, *upper* and *lower structure* both represent knowledge that in the KL-One tradition would be called T-box knowledge, that is, *terminological knowledge* (cf. Brachman and Schmolze 1985, Brachman et al. 1985; in particular the lower structure is not *assertional knowledge*. It structures sorts that stem directly from verbs and nouns along the lines of the terminological classes provided by the upper structure.
6 With *nhanimal* (for nonhuman animal) we distinguish the use of *animal* as opposed to *human being* from the class of biological *animals* that subsumes the class of human beings.
7 Compare Véronis and Ide 1992 for a discussion of the problems connected to the more ambitious task of automatically deducing inheritance hierarchies from machine-readable dictionaries.
8 Of course, here we allude to the well-known distinction introduced by Saussure (1967). In this chapter we must avoid saying something specific about *signifiants* with more complex extensions: the idea is to introduce reductions via specific thematic roles.
9 Here, we adopt the distinction between object and its constitutive substance that was proposed by Link, Bach, and others (cf. Link 1983, Bach 1986, Eberle 1991 with regard to the domain of text interpreting models.
10 Of course, since the different PSHs share the concept hierarchy, the concepts must be named without reference to a specific language. Therefore, precisely speaking, the descriptions *WN* are pointers that refer to ST(s(W,N)), where ST is not a simple symbol transformation but a function whose extension can be dynamically built up by

consulting the transfer lexica. For reasons of simplicity we continue to abstract from these more precise specifications however.

References

Bach, E. 1986. The Algebra of Events. *Linguistics and Philosophy*, 9:5–16.

Blok, P. I. 1993a. The Interpretation of Focus: An Epistemic Approach to Pragmatics. Ph.D. thesis, University of Groningen.

Blok, P. I. 1993b. Two Dogmas of Focusism. In: P. Ackema and M. Schoorlemmer (eds.), *Proceedings of the Workshop on the Semantic and Syntactic Analysis of Focus: OTS Working Papers*, Utrecht.

Blok, P. I. 1994. On the Contribution of Contextual Information to the Semantics and Pragmatics of Focus. In: F. van Eijnde (ed.), *Final Report of the et-10/61 Project "Formal Semantics for Discourse."* Centrum voor Computerlinguistiek, University of Leuven.

Brachman, R. J.; Gilbert, V. P.; and Levesque, H. J. 1985. An Essential and Hybrid Reasoning System: Knowledge and Symbol Level Accounts of Krypton. In: *Proceedings of the Ninth International Joint Conference on Artificial Intelligence*, pp. 532–539.

Brachman, R. J., and Schmolze, J. G. 1985. An Overview of the KL-ONE Knowledge Representation System. *Cognitive Science*, 9(2):171–216.

Eberle, K. 1991. Ereignisse: Ihre Logik und Ontologie aus textsemantischer Sicht. Ph.D. thesis, University of Stuttgart.

Eberle, K. 1992. On Representing the Temporal Structure of a Natural Language Text. In: *Proceedings of Coling92*, Nantes.

Eberle, K. in preparation. A Semantic Component for LMT.

Fagin, R., and Halpern, J. 1988. Belief, Awareness and Limited Reasoning. *Artificial Intelligence*, 34:39–76.

Gabbay, D. M., and Moravcsik, J. M. 1978. Negation and Denial. In: F. Guenthner and C. Rohrer (eds.), *Studies in Formal Semantics*, pp. 251–265. North Holland, Amsterdam.

Kameyama, M., Ochitani, R., and Peters, S. 1991. Resolving Translation Mismatches with Information Flow. In: *Proceedings of the 29th Annual Meeting of the Association for Computational Linguistics*, Berkeley.

Lascarides, A., and Asher, N. 1991. Discourse Relations and Common Sense Entailment. DYANA deliverable 2.5b, Centre for Cognitive Science, University of Edinburgh, Edinburgh.

Lehmann, H., and Ott, N. 1992. Translation Relations and the Combination of Analytical and Statistical Methods in Machine Translation. In: *4th International Conference on Theoretical and Methodological Issues in Machine Translation*, Montreal.

Link, G. 1983. The Logical Analysis of Plurals and Mass Terms: A Lattice-Theoretical Approach. In: R. Bäuerle, R. Schwarze, and A. von Stechow (eds.), *Meaning, Use and Interpretation of Language*, pp. 302–323. de Gruyter, Berlin.

Mann, W., and Thompson, S. 1987. Rhetorical Structure Theory: A Theory of Text Organization. Technical Report ISI RS-87-190, USC/ISI.

McCord, M. 1989. A New Version of the Machine Translation System *LMT*. *Journal of Literary and Linguistic Computing*, 4:218–299.

McCord, M. 1991. The Slot Grammar System. In: J. Wedekind and C. Rohrer (eds.), *Unification in Grammar*. MIT Press, Cambridge.

Polanyi, L., and Scha, R. 1988. An Augmented Context Free Grammar for Discourse. In: *Proceedings of Coling*, pp. 573–577, Budapest.

Pollard, C., and Sag, I. 1994. *Head-Driven Phrase Structure Grammar*. Chicago University Press, Chicago.

Rooth, M. E. 1985. Association with Focus. Ph.D. thesis, University of Massachusetts, Amherst.

Rooth, M. E. 1992. A Theory of Focus Interpretation. *Natural Language Semantics*, 1(1): 75–117.

Saussure, F. de 1967. *Cours de Linguistique Générale*. Payot, Paris.

Smolka, G. 1988. A Feature Logic with Subsorts. LILOG Report 33, IBM Deutschland, WT LILOG, Stuttgart.

Véronis, J., and Ide, N. 1992. A Feature-Based Model for Lexical Databasis. In: *Proceedings of Coling92*, pp. 588–594, Nantes.

7 The Treatment of Focusing Particles in Underspecified Discourse Representations

JOHAN BOS

Abstract

I present a formalism that allows composition of semantic representations of natural language expressions that are underspecified with respect to scope and focus. Explicitly labeling semantic substructures provides means to put constraints on scopal and focus relations while maintaining ambiguities that are known in natural language. The formalism is applied to a small fragment of English and shows how scopal and focus ambiguities are dealt with in an underspecified fashion. Attention is particularly paid to the scopal and presuppositional properties of the particles *only* and *too*. The object language with which I work is defined by the discourse representation structures of Kamp's Discourse Representation Theory.

1 Introduction

This chapter presents a description language for underspecified discourse representations. The reason for exploring *underspecified representations* as suitable semantic representations for natural language expressions emerges directly from practical natural language processing applications. The so-called Combinatorial Explosion Puzzle, a well-known problem in this area, can be tackled successfully by using underspecified representations. The source of this problem is ambiguities that appear in natural language expressions, particularly if they appear without context.

The chapter covers scope and focus ambiguities with respect to underspecification. Concerning approaches that use *underspecification* to handle scope ambiguities the reader is referred to the rich literature on this topic, for example, Quasi Logical Forms (Alshawi 1992, Alshawi and Crouch 1992), Underspecified Discourse Representation Structures (UDRSs) (Reyle 1993), Minimal Recursion Semantics (Egg and Lebeth 1995), and others (Poesio 1994, Muskens 1995, Bos 1995, Pinkal 1995). Focus ambiguities are illustrated in section 2. Particular attention is paid to the interpretation of the English adverbs *only* and *too*.

The core of the chapter is a discussion of LUD, a description language for underspecified Discourse Representation Structures (from Kamp's DRT). Therefore, the reader is assumed to be more or less familiar with Discourse Representation Theory (Kamp and Reyle 1993). The syntax, resolution, and interpretation of underspecified representations in LUD are discussed in general and are specifically applied to a small fragment of English. It is shown how ambiguities introduced by focusing particles can be treated.

2   Focusing, Meaning, and Presupposition

Focusing particles are characterized by the fact that their interpretation normally follows from the accentual pattern of the utterance in which they occur. Semanticists say that they are associated with *focus*, which is often that part of the utterance that bears intonational stress. Focus has effects on the interpretation of the meaning and presuppositions of utterances with focusing particles.

In general, there are two kinds of focusing effects. In the first, focus determines the *meaning* of an utterance; in the second, focus determines the *presuppositions* of the utterance (and not the meaning). Examples of the first kind correspond to what König (König 1981) classifies as *exclusive* particles: the English *alone, just, only* and the German *bloß, erst, gleich, lediglich, nur, wenigstens, zumindest*, to name just a few. Examples of the second kind, the so-called inclusive particles, are in English *also, even, too* and in German *auch, noch, sogar*. This list is not exhaustive; more can be found in König's papers (König 1981, 1991) that discuss the syntax and semantics of scalar particles.

Let us consider some examples in a context where two people try to arrange an appointment. The utterances in (1) and (2) have the same syntactic surface structure, but different prosodic patterns (stressed constituents are capitalized in these and the following examples). The meaning of (1) is that the speaker is not available on Tuesday afternoon, Wednesday afternoon, Thursday afternoon, and so on. The meaning of (2) is that the speaker is not available on Monday, except in the afternoon. Both utterances have as presupposition that the current speaker is available on Monday afternoon.

(1)   I am only available on MONday afternoon

(2)   I am only available on Monday afterNOON

In contrast, examples with the German adverb *auch* (3) and (4) show that the meaning of both utterances is 'Dienstag geht bei mir' (i.e., the meaning of the utterances without the occurrences of *auch*). The presupposition triggered by the focusing particle of (3) is that there is a day different from Tuesday on which the current speaker is available. An appropriate context for (3) would be one where, for example, the current speaker is available on Monday. The presupposition of (4), however, is that the current *hearer* is available on Tuesday.

(3)   Dienstag geht AUCH bei mir

(4)   Dienstag geht auch bei MIR

If we assume that the syntactic analyses for (1) and (2), respectively (3) and (4), are identical, then semantic interpretation of these utterances in a natural language processing system cannot rely on syntax alone. It is clear that without context prosodic information should be accessible to obtain satisfying semantic representations for utterances that contain focusing particles.

Apart from the particle itself and its focus, its scope is the third essential feature needed for interpretation. In (5) the scope of the inclusive focus particle *too* can either be the entire utterance or the embedded sentence only.

(5)   I believe that BILL is coming too

In the reading where *too* takes scope over the entire sentence, the triggered presupposition is 'I believe that someone (not Bill) is coming'; however, when *too* takes scope only over the subordinated sentence, the involved presupposition is just 'Someone (but not Bill) is coming'.

In summary, by interpreting focusing particles three ingredients are of importance: the particle itself, its focus, and its scope. Focusing particles refer to a set of alternatives for the focus. The members of this set are of the same type as the focus and sometimes given by context. A final remark on focusing particles: we restrict our analysis to the nonscalar use of focusing particles.

We assume the following about *presuppositions*. First, presuppositions are all lexically triggered; second, they are of propositional type; third, they are defined with respect to a certain proposition, the one that contains the relevant presupposition trigger. Presupposition triggers are (apart from the already discussed focusing particles), for example, definite noun phrases, proper names, aspectual verbs, and factive verbs.

As is well known, presuppositions seem to survive in some contexts, whereas in others they are "cancelled". In the following examples about the twin sisters Mary and Sue utterance (6) presupposes (triggered by the focusing particle *too*) that someone, but not Mary, is sleeping. In contrast, (7) shows no presupposition for the entire utterance, although exactly the same presupposition trigger appears here, too.

(6)   Mary is sleeping, too

(7)   If Sue is sleeping, then Mary is sleeping, too

Here we see the projection problem for presupposition. There are quite a number of strategies in the literature on presupposition to attack this problem. Probably the most accurate and strikingly intuitive approach is that of van der Sandt (van der Sandt 1992), who treats presupposition on a par with anaphora. In his view, a presuppositional expression is actually the same as an anaphoric expression. The only difference is of semantic nature: that is to say, presuppositions have more descriptive content than anaphors do.

Resolution of presupposition in this picture takes place in the same way as one would expect for anaphora. Discourse structure constrains resolution, not only for anaphora but also for presupposition. Moreover, van der Sandt's resolution procedure has the ability to *accommodate* presuppositions. In cases where presuppositions fail to find a proper antecedent, accommodation is put to work. This adds the propositions that were presupposed to the established discourse. Accommodation can be performed on the global level of discourse, as well as in local (subordinated) contexts. This is the "Presupposition as Anaphora" theory in a nutshell; for a complete overview the reader is referred to van der Sandt's article (van der Sandt 1992).

3   DRT Unplugged: LUD

To compute the contribution of focusing particles to the meaning of an utterance we need a framework that formalizes discourse semantics including presupposition phenomena, moreover one that deals with scopal ambiguities and allows for different focusing possibilities. We present a description language for underspecified discourse representation structures (Language for Underspecified DRSs [LUD]) that has these properties. First, it has means to underspecify the scope of basically all kinds of operators that introduce scope. Second, it includes a treatment of focusing particles and allows underspecification of focus. Third, the object language of LUD is Kamp's well known Discourse Representation Structures. LUD is based on *Hole Semantics*, a general framework for underspecified semantic representations (Bos 1995).

Semantic representations of natural language expressions are traditionally constructed on the basis of their syntactic analyses. Since expressions can be semantically ambiguous, this is a one-to-many mapping. The idea of underspecified representations is to make this mapping functional, that is, a one-to-one mapping from syntactic to semantic structure. The interpretation of an underspecified semantic representation is (hence) the set of interpretations that are expressed in it.

We define underspecified representations as follows: We take as object language the Discourse Representation Structures (DRSs) of an extended version of Kamp's Discourse Representation Theory (Kamp and Reyle 1993). Then we define a description language that we call LUD, which is able to describe several DRSs in one compact, underspecified representation. Our interest is in scope and focus ambiguities.

A representation in LUD has three components. It consists of a set of labeled conditions (a label-condition pair; *labels* are constants), a set of variables over labels (*holes*), and a set of constraints. We label conditions for an obvious reason: it will be very easy to talk about them. Holes are lexically introduced as arguments of scope bearing operators. Constraints on the labels and holes tell us how the different conditions fit together to form a well formed DRS. They obey relations between the different conditions in a LUD-Representation (LR) with respect to scope. For example, it is possible to express that a condition (annotated with label l) is outscoped by a certain operator with scope h by a constraint of the form $l \leq h$.

This constraint forces l to be directly or indirectly in the scope of h of the relevant operator (e.g., indirectly in the case where l is in the scope of some operator with label l', where l' is in the scope of h).

So, metaphorically speaking, *holes* underspecify scope in an LR. In order to give LRs a nonambiguous interpretation, the holes should be "plugged" with the (labeled) conditions of UR in such a way that all the constraints of the LR are satisfied. A *plugging* is a mapping from holes to labels. For each plugging there is corresponding DRS, as we see later in this section, when we define LRs as well as their mapping to DRSs more precisely.

A LUD-Representation (LR) is a triple $U = \langle H, L, C \rangle$, where H_U is a set of holes (variables over labels), L_U is a set of labeled LUD-conditions, and C_U is a set of LUD-constraints on $H \cup L$. We use t, t', t'' (sometimes indexed) for *terms* that refer to either labels or holes. Discourse markers are written as x, y, z (possibly indexed), and the symbols Q, Q' are used for predicate symbols. Constants of the domain of the model of interest are written as D, D'.

Definition 1: **Syntax of LUD-conditions**

1. If x is a discourse marker, then $dm(x)$ is a LUD-condition;
2. If Q is a symbol for an n-place relation, $x_1, \ldots, x_n$ are discourse markers, then $pred(Q, x_1, \ldots, x_n)$ is a LUD-condition;
3. If D is a constant, x a discourse marker, then $named(x, D)$ is a LUD-condition;
4. If t and t' are terms, then $neg(t)$, $imp(t, t')$, $and(t, t')$, and $or(t, t')$ are LUD-conditions;
5. If t is a term, then $too(t)$ and $only(t)$ are LUD-conditions;
6. Nothing else is a LUD-condition.

Clauses 1 and 2 define descriptions of discourse markers and predicates; clause 3 handles representations of proper names. The boolean operators are defined in clause 4. These ingredients are exactly those that we need to describe a standard DRS-syntax. Finally, clause 5 defines meta-representations for focusing particles. We continue by defining the syntax of constraints within LRs.

Definition 2: **LUD-constraints**

1. If t, t' are terms, then $t \leq t'$ and $t \alpha t'$ are LUD-constraints;
2. Nothing else is a LUD-constraint.

There are two types of constraints. The $\leq$ type is used to constrain subordination and is transitive, reflexive, and antisymmetric. The α type represents anaphora and presupposition and is transitive but not reflexive. A constraint $l \alpha l'$ states that the DRS associated to l is a presupposition for the one of l', or to put it differently, l' presupposes l.

Definition 3: **Presuppositions (PRE)** $\text{PRE}(t)_U = \{l \mid l\alpha t \in C_U\}$

We define subordination for terms in U as $\text{SUB}(t, t')$, meaning t is subordinated to t', or putting it differently, t' subordinates t. SUB is used to define properness and consistency in LUD.

Definition 4: **Subordination (SUB)** Let l be a label, h a hole, t a term of an LR U. Then:

1. $\text{SUB}(t, t)_U$;
2. $\text{SUB}(t, t')_U$ if there is some t' such that $t \leq t' \in C_U$;
3. $\text{SUB}(h, l)_U$ if there is some ϕ such that $l{:}\phi \in L_U$, h is an argument of $l : \phi$, and it is not the case that $\text{SUB}(l, h)_U$;
4. $\text{SUB}(t, t')_U$ if there is some t', t'' such that $\text{SUB}(t, t'')_U$ and $\text{SUB}(t'', t')_U$;
5. SUB is only defined on the basis of 1–4.

The first clause represents reflexivity. The second clause is the explicit definition of subordination: if there is a constraint $\leq$ present in U. The third clause defines subordination on labeled LUD-conditions that have holes as arguments. The fourth clause expresses transitivity. With SUB we continue to define a *proper* LR.

Definition 5: **Properness** An LR U is *proper* iff for all $t, t': t, t' \in H_U \cup L_U$ it is the case that there is some t'' such that $\text{SUB}(t, t'')_U$ and $\text{SUB}(t', t'')_U$.

A proper LR is one that describes a join semilattice. Yet we are able to define what, with respect to a plugging P, a *consistent* LR U is, using the following notational convention: for any $k \in H_U \cup L_U$, we define $I_P(k) = P(k)$ iff $k \in H_U$, and $I_P(k) = k$ iff $k \in L_U$. A consistent LR is an LR that is proper, taking pluggings into account.

Definition 6: **Consistency (CONS)** $\text{CONS}_{U,P}$ iff for all t, t', such that $\text{SUB}(t, t')_U$, it is the case that either $I_P(t) = I_P(t')$ or $I_P(t) \neq I_P(k')$ and $\text{SUB}(t', t)_U$ is not supported.

We have not yet defined what possible pluggings are about. Pluggings are, as we have discussed in the previous section, bi-jective functions from holes to labels. A plugging for an LR U is *possible* if the LR, with respect to this plugging, is consistent: in other words, when the underspecified representation, taking the plugging into account, has the properties of a join semilattice. Since we have already defined what a consistent LR is, defining possible pluggings is an easy job.

Definition 7: **Possible Plugging (PP)** $\text{PP}_U = \{P \mid \text{CONS}_{U,P}\}$

A plugging is possible if U is consistent with respect to this plugging.[1] For the interpretation and construction of LRs we need to refer to the top and bottom elements of the lattice that the LR of interest describes. Top ($\top$) is the label or hole that subordinates all others. Bottom ($\perp$), on the other hand, is a term that is subordinated by all other labels and holes.

Definition 8: **Top and Bottom** Let t, t' be terms such that $t, t' \in H_U \cup L_U$. Then:

1. $\top_U = t$ iff there is no $t', t \neq t'$ such that $\text{SUB}_U(t, t')$.
2. $\perp_U = t$ iff there is no $t', t \neq t'$ such that $\text{SUB}_U(t', t)$.

The object language of LUD is the language of Discourse Representation Structures (DRSs). Before we define the interpretation function from LRs to DRSs, we define the syntax of DRSs. We use boldface **K** (indexed when needed) as a symbol denoting DRSs.

Definition 9: **Syntax of DRSs**

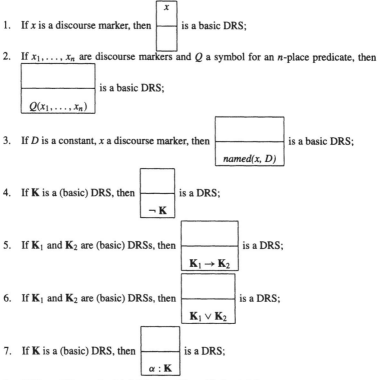

1. If x is a discourse marker, then [diagram with x] is a basic DRS;

2. If $x_1, \ldots, x_n$ are discourse markers and Q a symbol for an n-place predicate, then [diagram with $Q(x_1, \ldots, x_n)$] is a basic DRS;

3. If D is a constant, x a discourse marker, then [diagram with $named(x, D)$] is a basic DRS;

4. If **K** is a (basic) DRS, then [diagram with $\neg\,\mathbf{K}$] is a DRS;

5. If $\mathbf{K}_1$ and $\mathbf{K}_2$ are (basic) DRSs, then [diagram with $\mathbf{K}_1 \to \mathbf{K}_2$] is a DRS;

6. If $\mathbf{K}_1$ and $\mathbf{K}_2$ are (basic) DRSs, then [diagram with $\mathbf{K}_1 \vee \mathbf{K}_2$] is a DRS;

7. If **K** is a (basic) DRS, then [diagram with $\alpha : \mathbf{K}$] is a DRS;

8. If $\mathbf{K}_1$ and $\mathbf{K}_2$ are (basic) DRSs, then $\mathbf{K}_1 \otimes \mathbf{K}_2$ is a DRS;

9. Nothing else is a (basic) DRS.

Clauses 1–3 introduce basic DRSs, representing discourse markers, basic conditions, and conditions for proper names, respectively. Clauses 4, 5, and 6 define the boolean operators in DRT. In clause 8 $\otimes$ represents the merging of DRSs, which operates on two DRSs $\mathbf{K}_1$ and $\mathbf{K}_2$ and returns a DRS with the union of the domains of $\mathbf{K}_1$ and $\mathbf{K}_2$ as domain, and as conditions the union of the conditions of $\mathbf{K}_1$ and $\mathbf{K}_2$ conform with λ-DRT (Bos et al. 1994, Kohlhase et al. 1995). Presuppositions and anaphora are represented as α-conditions (clause 7), along the lines of van der Sandt's Presupposition as Anaphora Theory and Krahmer's *Presuppositional DRT* (van der Sandt 1992, Krahmer 1995).

The interpretation of an LR is defined as the set of DRS interpretation results of the LR's top term. The following defines an interpretation function $[\![.]\!]$ for LRs. The interpretation of an LR U yields a set of DRSs, as many as there are possible pluggings (PP) and possible focus structures (PF) for it:

$$[\![U]\!] = \{\text{DRS}(\top_U)_{U,P,F} \mid P \in \text{PP}_U \;\&\; F \in \text{PF}_U\}$$

The interpretation of focus in LUD is controlled by the function PF_U, the possible focus structures for the LR U of our interest. A focus structure is here a set of terms, a subset of $H_U \cup L_U$, and those that are in "focus" position. We will not formally define this function, since this involves (a possible complex) interaction with prosodic and syntactic information and is outside the scope of the present topic. In any case, PF should never denote an empty set. If accentual information is absent, PF contains all possible focus structures. If accentual information is present, PF should exclude certain focus structures. This is exemplified in the examples that are given later.

Inspired by Rooth's Alternative Semantics (Rooth 1992), we have, in addition to a DRS interpretation function (DRS), a so-called Focus-DRS interpretation function (FDRS). The two interpretation functions are defined for LUD-terms and LUD-conditions; the first yields a DRS, the second a set of DRSs. Both functions are defined with respect to an LR U, a plugging P, and a focus structure F. Subscripts are omitted in the definitions if this causes no confusion. We use the notation $\bigotimes\{\mathbf{K}_1, \ldots, \mathbf{K}_n\}$ as an abbreviation for $\mathbf{K}_1\otimes, \ldots, \otimes\mathbf{K}_n$.

Definition 10: **LR to DRS mapping (DRS)**

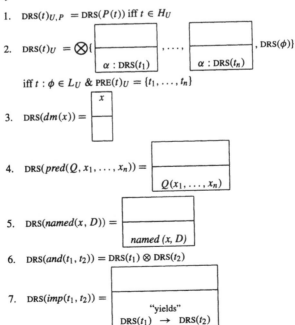

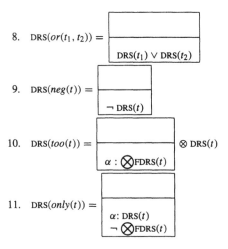

8. DRS($or(t_1, t_2)$) =

DRS(t_1) ∨ DRS(t_2)

9. DRS($neg(t)$) =

¬ DRS(t)

10. DRS($too(t)$) =   ⊗ DRS(t)

α : ⊗FDRS(t)

11. DRS($only(t)$) =

α: DRS(t)
¬ ⊗FDRS(t)

The first clause covers the case when an LUD-term is a hole, and the second the case when it is a label. Clause 3 handles the translation of a discourse marker to a DRS, and clauses 4 and 5 handle the basic predicates and proper names in the same manner. Clauses 6–9 cover the boolean operators. Clause 10 translates *too* into a DRS where the ordinary DRS corresponding to the scope of *too* is asserted and the focus DRS is presupposed. Finally, clause 11 states that the focus DRS of the scope of *only* is negated, and the ordinary DRS is presupposed.[2]

Definition 11: **LR to Focus DRS mapping (FDRS)**

1. FDRS(t)$_{U,P}$ = FDRS($P(t)$) iff $t \in H_U$

2. FDRS(t)$_{U,F}$ = {⊗{ ... , K} |

α : $\mathbf{K}_1$

... ,

α : $\mathbf{K}_n$

$\mathbf{K}_1 \in$ FDRS(t_1), ..., $\mathbf{K}_n \in$ FDRS(t_n) & $\mathbf{K} \in$ FDRS(ϕ)}
iff $t : \phi \in L_U$ & PRE(t)$_U$ = {$t_1, ..., t_n$} & $t \in F$

3. FDRS(t)$_{U,F}$ = {⊗{ ... , DRS(ϕ)} |

α : $\mathbf{K}_1$

... ,

α : $\mathbf{K}_n$

$\mathbf{K}_1 \in$ FDRS(t_1), ..., $\mathbf{K}_n \in$ FDRS(t_n)}
iff $t : \phi \in L_U$ & PRE(t)$_U$ = {$t_1, ..., t_n$} & $t \notin F$

4. FDRS($dm(x)$) = {

x

}

5. FDRS($pred(Q, x_1, ..., x_n)$) = {

$Q'(x_1, ..., x_n)$

| (Q', n) $\in$ SIG & $Q \neq Q'$}

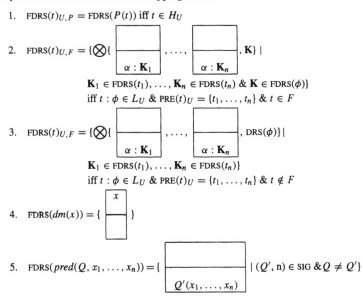

6. FDRS($named(x, D)$) = { [DRS box: $named(x, D')$] $|(D', 0) \in$ SIG & $D \neq D'$}

7. FDRS($and(t_1, t_2)$) = {$\mathbf{K}_1 \otimes \mathbf{K}_2 \mid \mathbf{K}_1 \in$ FDRS(t_1) & $\mathbf{K}_2 \in$ FDRS(t_2)}

8. FDRS($imp(t_1, t_2)$) = { [box: $\mathbf{K}_1 \rightarrow \mathbf{K}_2$] $\mid \mathbf{K}_1 \in$ FDRS(t_1) & $\mathbf{K}_2 \in$ FDRS(t_2)}

9. FDRS($or(t_1, t_2)$) = { [box: $\mathbf{K}_1 \vee \mathbf{K}_2$] $\mid \mathbf{K}_1 \in$ FDRS(t_1) & $\mathbf{K}_2 \in$ FDRS(t_2)}

10. FDRS($neg(t)$) = { [box: $\neg \mathbf{K}$] $\mid \mathbf{K} \in$ FDRS(t)}

11. FDRS($too(t)$) = { [box: $\alpha : \bigotimes$FDRS(t)] $\otimes \mathbf{K} \mid \mathbf{K} \in$ FDRS(t)}

12. FDRS($only(t)$) = { [box: $\alpha : \mathbf{K}$ / $\neg \bigotimes$FDRS(t)] $\mid \mathbf{K} \in$ FDRS(t)}

Most of the clauses in the definition of FDRS mirror those in the definition of DRS and need no extra attention, apart from the fact that sets of DRSs are yielded. Clause 2 and 3 are crucial, since at this point it is decided whether recursion remains at the FDRS definitional level (clause 2) or switches to that of DRS. This decision is, as expected, dependent on the focus structure *F*.

Clauses 5 and 6 are of special interest, since here "alternative" DRSs are defined. As a bookkeeping device, here we use a signature, which contains the information of interest (the relevant domain) and information about the kind of language we use. We use the signature here for generating "alternatives". A signature (SIG) is represented as a set of pairs, for example (8):

(8)   {(love,2), (name,2), (whistle,1), (walk,1), (mary,0), (john,0)}

The first instance of a pair is the name of the relation; the second instance says something about the arity of the relation. Constants are represented as 0-place relations.[3] Note that we deviate from Rooth's Alternative Semantics (Rooth 1992), since we *exclude* the relevant item itself from the set of its alternatives.

4   The Lexicon and Composition in LUD

To derive LRs for complex expressions, such as constructing compositionally semantic representations for natural language expressions, LUD has two operations. The first is functional application for LRs (⊙) followed by a sequence of β-reduction steps, which is the basic composition operation in LUD (we allow λ-abstraction over LRs). The second is merge for LRs (⊕), which the reader shouldn't confuse with the merge operation for DRSs (⊗). We redefine the syntax of LUD-Representations in the following way:

Definition 12: **Syntax of LUD-Representations**

1. If H is a set of holes, L is a set of LUD-conditions, and C is a set of LUD-constraints, then $\langle H, L, C \rangle$ is a basic LR;
2. If U and U' are basic LRs, then $U \oplus U'$ is a basic LR;
3. If φ is a discourse marker or a variable for a (basic) LR, then $U \odot \varphi$ and $\lambda\varphi.U$ are LRs;
4. A (basic) LR is only defined on the basis of 1–3.

The interpretation of a simple LUD-R was given in the previous section. We extend it as follows:

Definition 13: **Interpretation of LUD-Representations**

1. $[\![U]\!] = \{\text{DRS}(\top_U)_{U,P,F} \mid P \in \text{PP}_U \ \& \ F \in \text{PF}_U\}$
2. $[\![U \oplus U']\!] = [\![\langle H_U \cup H_{U'}, L_U \cup L_{U'}, C_U \cup C_{U'}\rangle]\!]$
3. $[\![\lambda\varphi.U \odot \psi]\!] = [\![U[\psi/\varphi]]\!]$
4. $[\![\lambda x.U]\!] = \{\lambda x.\mathbf{K} \mid \mathbf{K} \in [\![U]\!]\}$
5. $[\![\lambda Q.U]\!] = \{\lambda\mathbf{Q}.\mathbf{K} \mid \mathbf{Q} \in [\![Q]\!] \ \& \ \mathbf{K} \in [\![U]\!]\}$

The first clause has not changed with respect to the definition given earlier. Merging (clause 2) of two LRs (⊕) involves taking the unions of the holes, labeled conditions, and constraints, respectively. Composition (⊙), in clause 3, is read as $\lambda\varphi.U \odot \psi$ is equal to U with ψ substituted for all occurrences of φ. Clauses 4 and 5 indicate how λ-LRs can be mapped to λ-DRSs, assuming DRSs along the lines of λ-DRT (Bos et al. 1994, Kohlhase et al. 1995) or Compositional DRT (Muskens 1993), that is, DRSs in a Montague-style Extended Type Theory.

With *composition*, *merging*, and the ability to abstract over representations in LUD, we are able to construct LRs compositionally for a small fragment of English. The fragment of interest is described in the appendix to this chapter. To get a taste of it we go through two sample derivations, starting with the analysis of (9), where *walks* is focus of the particle *too*. We assume a (very simple) syntactic analysis (10) for this utterance.

(9)   Every man walks, too.

(10) $s : (s' : (np : (det : every), vp : vp' : iv : walks), too)$

This syntactic tree allows us to construct a LUD-R compositionally for the whole utterance in a bottom up way. We start with the lexical entry for the intransitive verb *walks* (11).

(11) $\lambda y.\langle\{h_0\}, \{l_0 : pred(walk, y)\}, \{l_0 \leq h_0\}\rangle$

In LUD, the main verb of a sentence introduces a hole, which is $\top$ with respect to the other ingredients of the sentence. The variable y of the predicate *walks* is abstracted over by the lambda operator, and the predicate itself is subordinated to the top hole, via the $\leq$ constraint.

The LR for the noun phrase *every man*, which can be composed by combining the LR for *every* and *man*, is shown in (12). The scope of the quantifier is underspecified by h_1. The variable Q, ranging over an LR, is the abstraction of the property that is applied to x, the discourse marker introduced by *every man*.

$$
(12) \quad \lambda Q. \left\langle \{h_1\} \begin{cases} l_1 : dm(x) \\ l_2 : pred(man, x) \\ l_3 : l_1 \wedge l_2 \\ l_4 : l_3 \rightarrow h_1 \end{cases}, \begin{cases} l_4 \leq \top_Q \\ \bot_Q \leq h_1 \end{cases} \right\rangle \oplus Q \odot x
$$

Combining the expressions in (11) and (12) results in (13), the LR for the sentence *every man walks*.

$$
(13) \quad \left\langle \begin{cases} h_0 \\ h_1 \end{cases}, \begin{cases} l_1 : dm(x) \\ l_2 : pred(man, x) \\ l_3 : l_1 \wedge l_2 \\ l_4 : l_3 \rightarrow h_1 \\ l_0 : pred(walk, x) \end{cases}, \begin{cases} l_4 \leq h_0 \\ l_0 \leq h_0 \\ l_0 \leq h_1 \end{cases} \right\rangle
$$

The lexical entry for *too* is (14), where the scope h_2 of *too* is underspecified.

$$
(14) \quad \lambda U. \left\langle \{h_2\}, \{l_5 : too(h_2)\}, \begin{cases} l_5 \leq \top_U, \\ \bot_U \leq h_2 \end{cases} \right\rangle \oplus U
$$

With (13) and (14) we construct the LR for *every man walks too* (15).

$$
(15) \quad \left\langle \begin{cases} h_0 \\ h_1 \\ h_2 \end{cases}, \begin{cases} l_1 : dm(x) \\ l_2 : pred(man, x) \\ l_3 : l_1 \wedge l_2 \\ l_4 : l_3 \rightarrow h_1 \\ l_0 : pred(walk, x) \\ l_5 : too(h_2) \end{cases}, \begin{cases} l_4 \leq h_0 \\ l_0 \leq h_1 \\ l_0 \leq h_2 \\ l_0 \leq h_0 \\ l_5 \leq h_0 \end{cases} \right\rangle
$$

Since there are two scope bearing operators in (15), the universal quantifier and the focus particle, there are two corresponding readings and DRSs. The two possible pluggings are P_1 $(P_1(h_0) = l_4, P_1(h_1) = l_5, P_1(h_2) = l_0)$, where the universal quantifier outscopes the focusing adverb *too*, and P_2 $(P_1(h_0) = l_5,$ $P_1(h_1) = l_0, P_1(h_2) = l_4)$, where the focusing adverb has scope over the universal quantifier.

Possibly foci for *too* are in the first case *walks* or *man*, *every man*, or *every man walks*. We do not give all DRSs here, but restrict ourselves to the case where the focus is *walks*, with corresponding label l_0. Correspondingly, the focus structure F in that case should contain l_0, as well as l_3, and the holes in (15), the terms that subordinate the element in focus.

Let us assume *whistles* is the only appropriate alternative for *walks*; then the corresponding DRSs for P_1 and P_2 are (16) and (17), respectively (skipping the steps of mapping the LR to the DRSs):

(16)

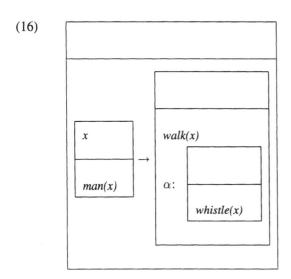

Consider the DRS in (16). According to van der Sandt's presupposition projection algorithm, global accommodation (i.e., moving the presupposed information to the main DRS) is prevented, since this will result in a DRS with a free variable. Local accommodation (storing the presupposed DRS in the consequent of the implication) is possible and paraphrases the reading "every man whistles and walks," which is certainly too strong a reading for (9). Intermediate accommodation, which involves moving the presupposed information to the antecedent DRS of the implication, is derived in a reading that one could paraphrase as *every man that whistles, walks.*

(17)

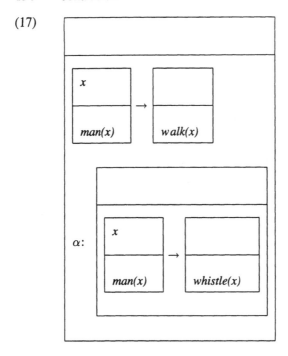

The DRS in (17) is the one where *too* outscopes the universal quantifier. The presuppositional part of this DRS will be accommodated globally according to van der Sandt's projection mechanism. This results in a reading that is true in a model where there are no men that do not walk, and there are no men that do not whistle, in contrast to the two possible interpretations of the DRS (16).

Note that this example involved accommodation in both cases. Example (18), in which we assume *whistles* as the focus of *too*, shows that accommodation is not needed here because the context is rich enough to perform anaphora resolution.

(18)   Every man that walks, whistles, too.

In example (18) a proper antecedent for the triggered presupposition is accessible from the antecedent part of the conditional, and this is the case where the universal quantifier has scope over the focusing particle. Actually under this reading (18) has no presuppositions. The picture changes where *too* outscopes the quantifier; in this case (18) presupposes 'every man that walks, does *P*' where *P* is a proper alternative for whistling. Since resolution normally seems to be "cheaper" than accommodation, the first scope reading is probably preferable.

The second example that we will discuss involves the focusing particle *only* (19), with underlying syntactic analysis as shown in (20). The LR for *only* is represented in (21). As was the case with *too*, the scope of *only* is underspecified.

(19)   John only walks.

(20) $s : s' : (np : pn : john, vp : (only, vp' : iv : walks))$

(21) $\lambda U. \left\langle \{h_1\}, \{l_1 : only(h_1)\}, \begin{Bmatrix} l_1 \leq \top_U \\ \bot_U \leq h_1 \end{Bmatrix} \right\rangle \oplus U$

In our fragment of English that we wish to cover we assume *only* to be a verb phrase modifier. Combining *only* with *walks* (11) results in the LR (22).

(22) $\lambda y. \left\langle \begin{Bmatrix} h_0 \\ h_1 \end{Bmatrix}, \begin{Bmatrix} l_2 : pred(walk, y) \\ l_1 : only(h_1) \end{Bmatrix}, \begin{Bmatrix} l_1 \leq h_0 \\ l_2 \leq h_1 \\ l_2 \leq h_0 \end{Bmatrix} \right\rangle$

Finally, we apply *John* to *only walks* and derive an LR for *John only walks*. The lexical entry for *John* is shown in (23). Combining (23) and (22) will give the LUD-Representation in (24).

(23) $\lambda P. \left\langle \{\}, \begin{Bmatrix} l_5 : dm(x) \\ l_6 : named(x, john) \\ l_4 : and(l_5, l_6) \end{Bmatrix}, \{l_4 \, \alpha \bot_P\} \right\rangle \oplus (P \odot x)$

(24) $\left\langle \begin{Bmatrix} h_0 \\ h_1 \end{Bmatrix}, \begin{Bmatrix} l_5 : dm(x) \\ l_6 : named(x, john) \\ l_4 : and(l_5, l_6) \\ l_2 : pred(walk, x) \\ l_1 : only(h_1) \end{Bmatrix}, \begin{Bmatrix} l_1 \leq h_0 \\ l_4 \, \alpha \, l_2 \\ l_2 \leq h_1 \\ l_2 \leq h_0 \end{Bmatrix} \right\rangle$

Since there is only one scope bearing operator, that is, *only*, the sentence represented by (24) is not scopally ambiguous. Accordingly, there is only one possible plugging $P : P(h_0) = l_1$ and $P(h_1) = l_2$. Nevertheless, the sentence is ambiguous with respect to focus. The focus of *only* can be either l_6 (*John*) or l_2 (*walks*). So there should be two possible focus structures.

If we take *walks* as focus for *only*, and if we assume again that the proper alternative for *walks* in the relevant context is *whistles*, the DRS of (24) is (25).

(25)

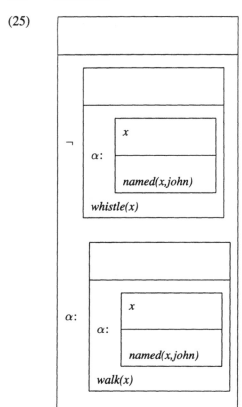

This DRS has as presupposition that John walks and asserts that it is not the case that John whistles. And this is exactly what we want. Van der Sandt's presupposition projection algorithm would accommodate the DRS containing the proper name in the main DRS, and, second, accommodate that John walks. The resulting DRS would be (26):

(26)

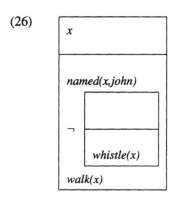

If we take as focus for *only* in (19) not *walks*, but *John*, in a context where the issue is whether Mary or John is walking, and hence *Mary* counts as the (one and only) proper alternative for *John*, we derive the following DRS:

(27)

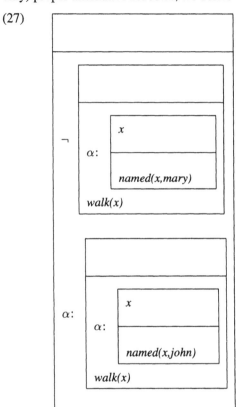

The DRS in (27) expresses the presupposition that 'John walks', and asserts that it is not the case that 'Mary walks'. After accommodation the resulting DRS is (28):[4]

(28)

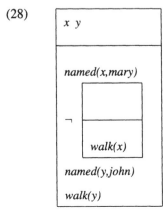

An example discourse where accommodation does not occur is one like (29). The available context in this example includes the presupposition of the antecedent sentence of the conditional.

(29)   John likes Mary. If John only likes Mary, Sue would be unhappy.

A context where John likes Mary is established by the first sentence. The second sentence triggers the presupposition that John likes Mary. Since this information is available as antecedent, the presupposition is resolved. As a consequence, the entire discourse (29) does not retain the presupposition triggered by *only*.

5   Conclusion

We have presented LUD, a description language for underspecified discourse representations. The key feature of this formalism is that it allows composition of representations of natural language expressions that are underspecified with respect to scope and focus. This is realized using a labeling device that first enables us to express something about scope constraints and second gives us means to refer to the semantic focus of natural language expressions. The general idea is applied to a (very) small fragment of English.

Appendix A: LUD for a Fragment of English

A.1   Syntax Rules

Syntactic categories are s (sentence), np (noun phrase), pn (proper name), det (determiner), cn (common noun), vp (verb phrase), iv (intransitive verb), and tv (transitive verb). LRs, for which we use α and β, are related to their syntactic category using a colon; that is, $c : \alpha$ means α is the LR for some syntactic category c. A rule $c \to c', \ldots, c''$ means that a category c can be derived from a sequence of categories or lexical entries $c', \ldots, c''$.

$$s : \alpha \to s' : \alpha$$
$$s : (\alpha \odot \beta) \to s' : \beta, \ too : \alpha$$
$$s' : (\alpha \odot \beta) \to np : \alpha, \ vp : \beta$$
$$np : \alpha \to pn : \alpha$$
$$pn : \alpha \to john : \alpha$$
$$pn : \alpha \to mary : \alpha$$
$$np : (\alpha \odot \beta) \to det : \alpha, \ cn : \beta$$
$$det : \alpha \to every : \alpha$$
$$det : \alpha \to a : \alpha$$
$$det : \alpha \to the : \alpha$$
$$cn : \alpha \to man : \alpha$$
$$cn : \alpha \to woman : \alpha$$
$$vp : \alpha \to vp' : \alpha$$
$$vp : (\alpha \odot \beta) \to only : \alpha, \ vp' : \beta$$

$vp : (\alpha \odot \beta) \rightarrow doesn't : \alpha, \; vp' : \beta$

$vp' : \alpha \rightarrow iv : \alpha$

$vp : (\alpha \odot \beta) \rightarrow tv : \alpha, np : \beta$

$tv : \alpha \rightarrow likes : \alpha$

$tv : \alpha \rightarrow loves : \alpha$

$iv : \alpha \rightarrow walks : \alpha$

$iv : \alpha \rightarrow whistles : \alpha$

A.2   Lexical Entries

Here we list sample lexical entries for some proper names, common nouns, determiners, transitive and intransitive verbs, and adverbs.

$$john: \lambda P. \left\langle \{\}, \left\{ \begin{array}{l} l_1 : dm(x) \\ l_2 : named(x, john) \\ l_3 : and(l_1, l_2) \end{array} \right\}, \{l_3 \; \alpha \; \bot_P)\} \right\rangle (P \odot x)$$

$$mary: \lambda P. \left\langle \{\}, \left\{ \begin{array}{l} l_1 : dm(x) \\ l_2 : named(x, mary) \\ l_3 : and(l_1, l_2) \end{array} \right\}, \{l_3 \; \alpha \; \bot_P\} \right\rangle (P \odot x)$$

$$every: \lambda P.\lambda Q. \left\langle \{h_1\}, \left\{ \begin{array}{l} l_1 : dm(x) \\ l_2 : and(l_1, \bot_P) \\ l_3 : imp(l_2, h_1) \end{array} \right\}, \left\{ \begin{array}{l} l_3 \leq \top_\varrho \\ \bot_\varrho \leq h_1 \end{array} \right\} \right\rangle \oplus (P \odot x) \oplus (Q \odot x)$$

$$a: \lambda P.\lambda Q. \left\langle \{h_1\}, \left\{ \begin{array}{l} l_1 : dm(x) \\ l_2 : and(l_1, \bot_P) \\ l_3 : and(l_2, h_1) \end{array} \right\}, \left\{ \begin{array}{l} l_3 \leq \top_\varrho \\ \bot_\varrho \leq h_1 \end{array} \right\} \right\rangle \oplus (P \odot x) \oplus (Q \odot x)$$

$$the: \lambda P.\lambda Q. \left\langle \{\}, \left\{ \begin{array}{l} l_1 : dm(x) \\ l_2 : and(l_1, \bot_P) \end{array} \right\}, \{l_2 \; \alpha \; \bot_\varrho\} \right\rangle \oplus (P \odot x) \oplus (Q \odot x)$$

$walks: \lambda y, \langle \{h_0\}, \{l_0 : pred(walk, y)\}, \{l_0 \leq h_0\} \rangle$

$whistles: \lambda y. \langle \{h_0\}, \{l_0 : pred(whistle, y)\}, \{l_0 \leq h_0\} \rangle$

$likes: \lambda U.\lambda y.(U \odot \lambda z. \langle \{h_0\}, \{l_0 : pred(like, y, z)\} \{l_0 \leq h_0\} \rangle)$

$loves: \lambda U.\lambda y.(U \odot \lambda z. \langle \{h_0\}, \{l_0 : pred(love, y, z)\} \{l_0 \leq h_0\} \rangle)$

$man: \lambda x. \langle \{\}, \{l_1 : pred(man, x)\}, \{\} \rangle$

$woman: \lambda x. \langle \{\}, \{l_1 : pred(woman, x)\}, \{\} \rangle$

$$too: \lambda U. \left\langle \{h_2\}, \{l_2 : too(h_2)\}, \left\{ \begin{array}{l} l_2 \leq \top_U \\ \bot_U \leq h_2 \end{array} \right\} \right\rangle \oplus U$$

$$only: \lambda U. \left\langle \{h_2\}, \{l_2 : only(h_2)\}, \left\{ \begin{array}{l} l_2 \leq \top_U \\ \bot_U \leq h_2 \end{array} \right\} \right\rangle \oplus U$$

$$doesn't: \lambda U. \left\langle \{h_2\}, \{l_2 : neg(h_2)\}, \left\{ \begin{array}{l} l_2 \leq \top_U \\ \bot_U \leq h_2 \end{array} \right\} \right\rangle \oplus U$$

Notes

1   This is illustrated by the following two examples. First, suppose that

$$U = \langle\{h_0\}, \{l_1 : \phi\}, \{l_1 \leq h_0\}\rangle$$

for some formula ϕ. Hence, SUB(l_1, l_1), SUB(h_1, h_1), and SUB(l_1, h_1) are valid. Then a possible plugging P for U is one such that $P(h_0) = l_1$, since CONS$_{U,P}$ holds. In the second example we consider an LR with the following constraints:

$$\{h_1 \leq l_1, h_2 \leq l_2, l_2 \leq h_0, l_1 \leq h_0, l_3 \leq h_1, l_3 \leq h_2\}$$

Here, a plugging P where $P(h_0) = l_3$, $P(h_1) = l_2$, and $P(h_2) = l_1$ is not possible. The LR to which these constraints belong is not consistent, since SUB(l_3, h_2) and SUB(h_2, h_0) are valid and with P lead to "SUB(l_3, l_1)" and "SUB(l_1, l_3)," violating antisymmetry.

2   Since discourse markers in focus DRSs are not renamed, there is a slight technical problem on the DRS level. This problem surfaces when the accommodation procedure is put to work at a DRS level where discourse markers with the same names are already present. A straightforward solution would be to extend accommodation by refreshing the discourse markers of the presuppositional DRS.

3   We are aware that following this procedure of generating alternatives is a very simple way of looking at it. Cases where (correct) alternatives for complex expressions in focus are needed are not covered and require a revised approach to generating alternative DRSs. However, the procedure outlined here works for the linguistic data we are interested in.

4   And this is actually a case where accommodation requires renaming of discourse markers, a technical issue mentioned earlier but not dealt with in this chapter.

References

Alshawi, H., ed. 1992. *The Core Language Engine*. MIT Press, Cambridge, Mass.

Alshawi, H., and R. Crouch. 1992. Monotonic Semantic Interpretation. In *Proceedings of the 30th Annual Meeting of the ACL*, 32–39.

Bos, J. 1995. Predicate Logic Unplugged. *Proceedings of the Tenth Amsterdam Colloquium*.

Bos, J., E. Mastenbroek, S. McGlashan, S. Millies, and M. Pinkal. 1994. A compositional drs-based formalism for nlp applications. In H. Bunt, R. Muskens, and G. Rentier (eds.), *International Workshop on Computational Semantics*. University of Tilburg.

Egg, M., and K. Lebeth. 1995. Semantic underspecification and modifier attachment ambiguities. In J. Kilbury and R. Wiese (eds.), *Integrative Ansätze in der Computerlinguistik*, pp. 19–24. Düsseldorf, Seminar für Allgemeine Sprachwissenschaft.

Kamp, H., and U. Reyle. 1993. *From Discourse to Logic: An Introduction to Modeltheoretic Semantics of Natural Language, Formal Logic and DRT*. Kluwer, Dordrecht.

Kohlhase, M., S. Kuschert, and M. Pinkal. 1995. A Type-Theoretic Semantics for λ-DRT. In *Proceedings of the Tenth Amsterdam Colloquium*.

König, E. 1981. Scalar Particles in German and their English Equivalents. In *Contrastive Aspects of English and German*, pp. 116–158. Julius Groos, Heidelberg.

König, E. 1991. Gradpartikeln. In *Semantik/Semantics: An International Handbook of Contemporary Research*, pp. 786–803. De Gruyter, Berlin.

Krahmer, E. 1995. *Discourse and Presupposition*. Ph.D. thesis, University of Tilburg.

Muskens, R. 1993. A Compositional Discourse Representation Theory. In *Proceedings of the Ninth Amsterdam Colloquium*.

Muskens, R. A. 1995. Order-independence and underspecification. In J. Groenendijk (ed.), *Ellipsis, Underspecification, Events and More in Dynamic Semantics*, pp. 17–34. Dyana Deliverable R2.2.C.

Pinkal, M. 1995. Radical underspecification. In *Proceedings of the Tenth Amsterdam Colloquium*.

Poesio, M. 1994. Ambiguity, underspecification and discourse interpretation. In H. Bunt, R. Muskens, and G. Rentier (eds.), *International Workshop on Computational Semantics*, University of Tilburg.

Reyle, U. 1993. Dealing with ambiguities by underspecification: Construction, representation and deduction. *Journal of Semantics* 10, 123–179.

Rooth, M. 1992. A theory of focus interpretation. *Natural Language Semantics* 1, 75–116.

Sandt, R. A. van der. 1992. Presupposition projection as anaphora resolution. *Journal of Semantics* 9, 333–377.

8   Topic

DANIEL BÜRING

Abstract

In this chapter I show how the formal treatment of focus as developed in Rooth 1985 can be extended so as to capture not only focus but also sentence topics. Sentence topics, like focus, are realized phonologically in the form of a specific pitch accent. Semantically, I claim that a simple formal characterization of the appropriateness conditions and the implicatures of sentence topics suffices to explain their different usages. In the final part of the chapter, I show how the interpretation of focus and sentence topics interacts with the semantics of adnominal quantifiers to yield effects such as partitive, proportional, and focus-affected readings. I argue that these phenomena follow entirely from the compositional semantics in tandem with the effects of topic/focus/background structure.

1   Focus and Topic

1.1   Focus and Question/Answer Pairs

Before I introduce the concept of topic, let me briefly outline the assumptions about focus I am presupposing. Syntactic focus is represented by labeled brackets around the focused part. The material outside the focus is called the background. In English and German, the languages I am concerned with here, focus is realized by an accent (represented by capitals) on the so-called focus exponent. From the focus exponent, focus may project onto higher nodes. Because of the optional nature of focus projection, a sentence like (1a) might yield any of the bracketings in (1b).

(1)   a.   All the pop stars wore dark CAFTANS.
       b.   [all the pop stars [wore [dark [CAFTANS]$_F$

Each focus/background structure is especially suited to an appropriate utterance of (1) in a specific discourse setting. Among other things, each of the structures in (1b) answers a specific question, for example: *What was the consequence of that? What did the pop stars have in common? What did the pop stars wear?* or *Did the pop stars wear anything dark?*

I thank Regine Eckardt, Katharina Hartmann, Gerhard Jäger, Renate Musan, Inga Kohlhof, Arnim von Stechow, and Hubert Truckenbrodt for discussion.

Let us say that at any stage of a discourse there is not only a common ground (of beliefs and knowledge agreed upon by the participants) but also a certain restricted range of possibilities as to where the conversation might move to next. We may view this range of possibilities as a set of sentences/propositions with which the conversation might be continued. Technically, we call this set a D(iscourse)-topic, and the most straightforward way to establish a D-topic – that is to set course for the next utterance – is to ask a question. The different bracketings in (1b) then indicate different focus/background structures, which in turn match with different D-topics.

In a question/answer sequence the focused part within the answer must be the information asked for by the question (i.e., usually the part corresponding to the question word); conversely, the background must only consist of information that the D-topic – and thus the person asking – already takes for granted. Following Rooth's (1985) idea, we can formalize this by deriving from a sentence S a second semantic value, its *focus value*, $[\![S]\!]^f$ for short. If the focus is on the object NP in (1), $[\![(1)]\!]^f$ is the set of propositions we get by sticking in alternatives for the focus.

(2)   all the pop stars wore dark caftans/suit and tie/ dresses/ Rococo costumes. . .

We can transform $[\![S]\!]^f$ into a proposition by conjoining each of the propositions by *or*. Set theoretically, the meaning of this big disjunction is the union of all the propositions denoted by $[\![S]\!]^f$, that is, $\cup[\![S]\!]^f$. Not surprisingly, $\cup[\![S]\!]^f$ – sometimes called the *trivialization* of $[\![S]\!]^f$ – is just as informative as the question that S was supposed to answer. For we said that all the new information conveyed by S is within the focus part. So replacing the focus part by all its alternatives will again get us where we started, with nothing but the D-topic, namely, the question.

Notice that a question Q, being represented as a set of propositions, can be trivialized too, again giving us a single set of worlds, $\cup[\![Q]\!]^o$. We can thus formulate the relation that has to hold between a question and an answer as the following rule of thumb:

(3)   A sentence A can appropriately be uttered as an answer to a question Q iff $\cup[\![A]\!]^f = \cup[\![Q]\!]^o$

This then readily explains why for example the following sequence is ill formed:

(4)   A: What kind of caftans did the pop stars wear?
        B: All the pop stars wore [dark CAFTANS]$_F$.

The trivialization of B's answer will be something like *all the pop stars wore dark caftans or suit and tie or dresses or Rococo costumes or. . .* But that is not what A considered for she already knew that what they wore were caftans. In a sense, B is trying to sell as new what is really old, namely, the fact that they were wearing caftans. In order to answer A's question appropriately, it would have been better had B said something like

(5)   All the pop stars wore [DARK]$_F$ caftans.

Here the trivialization of the answer – 'all the pop stars were wearing *X-colored* caftans' – is just what the question is asking.

By a similar token the following sequence is ill formed:

(6)   A: What did the pop stars wear?
       B: All the pop stars wore [DARK]$_F$ caftans.

It should be clear what went wrong here: A didn't presuppose that the pop stars wore caftans. The D-topic hence contains all sorts of clothes such as those in (2). But B's answer is constructed as if only the color of caftans had been under dispute. The focus is thus too narrow, leaving new information (*caftans*) within the background part. So much for focus.

1.2   Sentence Internal Topics

The general phenomenon of what I call topics is illustrated by sentence (7):

(7)   a. Auf der /NEUNundfünfzigsten Straße habe ich die SCHUHE\ gekauft.
       b. On fiftyNINTH Street I bought the SHOES.

Take (7): The sentence contains two intonationally marked constituents, the fronted PP *auf der 59ten Straße*, 'on 59th Street,' and the direct object *die Schuhe*, 'the shoes.' The former is marked by a rising pitch contour, L*H, the latter by a falling one, H*L.[1] I occasionally refer to these accents as rise and fall, respectively. Semantically, the constituent marked by the fall corresponds to the focus in the sense of subsection 1.1.

(8)   A: What did you buy on 59th Street?
       B: Auf der /NEUNundfünfzigsten Straße habe ich [die SCHUHE\]$_F$ gekauft.

(9)   A: Where did you buy the shoes?
       B:# [Auf der /NEUNundfünfzigsten Straße]$_{*F}$ habe ich die SCHUHE\ gekauft.

Text (9) is meant to show that the PP bearing the rise cannot be understood as marking the focus of the sentence. Accordingly the question-answer sequence is ill formed. By analogy with our notational convention for focus marking, I indicate topic marked constituents by brackets subscripted with a T, for topic:

(10)   [Auf der /NEUNundfünfzigsten Straße]$_T$ habe ich [die SCHUHE\]$_F$ gekauft.

The PP in (10) is called the Topic. Accordingly, we might refer to the rise accent as *topic accent*. To avoid confusion, we must differentiate between such sentence internal, or S-topics (e.g., *[on 59th Street]$_T$* in (7)) as opposed to d(iscourse)-topics (established for example by a preceding question, as discussed in subsection 1.1.).

How do S-topics relate to the focus/background structure of a sentence? There are several types of answers to this question that have been proposed in the literature. The answer that I subscribe to is that the topic is simply an (im-proper) part of the nonfocus. Topics may or may not be present in a given sentence; that is, sentences are either bipartite or tripartite from the point of view of topic/focus/background structure. I call the *background* that part of the sentence that is neither topic nor focus. In (7) *on 59th Street* is the (S-) topic, *the shoes* is the focus, and *I bought* is the background. If a sentence contains no topic, background and focus are complementary, as before.

1.3   *The Meaning and Use of Topics*

As indicated in example (8), repeated here, the topic is not new information. It is given in the context, in this case in the question.

(11)   A: What did you buy on 59th Street?
        B: Auf der /NEUNundfünfzigsten Straße habe ich [die SCHUHE\]$_F$ gekauft.
               'On 59th Street I bought the shoes.'

However, the topic is not just an arbitrarily selected part of the given information. It is understood as "what the rest of the sentence is about," or "the entity anchoring the sentence to the previous discourse." A common syntactic means to signal topichood is by an initial *as for...* phrase:

(12)   As for 59th Street, that's where I bought the shoes.

However, this is not the only use of S-topics. It has sometimes been noticed that an S-topic can be used to move the conversation away from an entity given in the previous discourse. This is called a *contrastive topic*:

(13)   A: Do you think that Fritz would buy this suit?
        B: Well [I]$_T$ certainly [WOULDN'T]$_F$.

(14)   A: Glaubst Du, Fritz würde diesen Anzug kaufen?
        B: [ICH]$_T$ würde ihn sicher [NICHT]$_F$ kaufen.

Speaker B obviously doesn't answer A's question. Instead, she gives a different, though related statement. The constituent that is "replaced" (i.e., *I* instead of *Fritz*) is marked as topic.

Moreover, S-topics might be used to "narrow down" a given D(iscourse)-topic. Take examples (15) and (16):

(15)   A: What did the pop stars wear?
        B: The [female]$_T$ pop stars wore [caftans]$_F$.

(16)   A: Was hatten die Popstars an?
        B: Die [weiblichen]$_T$ Popstars trugen [Kaftane]$_F$.

Again, speaker B does not really answer A's question, at least not exhaustively. The part where she deviates from the original question is marked by the topic accent. Let us call this a *partial topic*.

Finally, S-topics can be used to indicate that the speaker would like to discuss alternative issues:

(17)   A: Did your wife kiss other men?
        B: [My]$_T$ wife [didn't]$_F$ kiss other men.

(18)   A: Hat deine Frau fremde Männer geküßt?
        B: [Meine]$_T$ Frau hat [keine]$_F$ fremden Männer geküßt.

B literally answers A's questions. However, that would not have required the topic accent on the possessive. What B expresses by this additional accent is that he considers other wives to be relevant in the given context. For example, he might intend his answer to make A think about his own wife. For reasons that should become clear later, I call this the *purely implicational topic*.

In this chapter I sketch a formal account of how S-topics are interpreted. I then show that the proposed semantics can in fact handle the different uses of S-topics – contrastive topics, partial topics, and purely implicational topics – just discussed (section 2). That means that "contrastive Topic," "partial Topic," and "purely implicational Topic" are just convenient descriptive labels without any theoretical significance. They are just more or less different uses of S-topics. In section 3 I discuss another effect of topic marking connected with adnominal quantifiers.

I give examples both in English and in German, although the discussion (and the conclusions drawn) is based on the German examples mainly. Although I tend to think that the semantic aspects of the examples – but not the phonological ones – are basically the same, the gentle reader is asked to understand the English examples merely as convenient means of explanation where this is not the case. Furthermore, I do not think that the treatment to be proposed here can be adapted to cases of rise contours not followed by a fall (which would be topics without foci in our terms) as discussed in Cutler 1977, Ladd 1980, and Ward and Hirschberg 1985, among others, which – to the best of my knowledge – have no corresponding counterpart in German.

2   The Semantics of S-Topics

2.1   *Presuppositions*

Let us start by considering examples of contrastive and partial topics. Why? Because it seems that the S-topic is necessary in order to warrant the well-formedness of the discourse in these cases:

(19) a. A: What did the pop stars wear?
           B: The [female]$_T$ pop stars wore [caftans]$_F$.
           B': # The female pop stars wore [caftans]$_F$.
      b. A: Was hatten die Popstars an?
           B: Die [weiblichen]$_T$ Popstars trugen [Kaftane]$_F$.
           B': # Die weiblichen Popstars trugen [Kaftane]$_F$.

(20) a. A: Which book would Fritz buy?
           B: Well, [I]$_T$ would buy [*The Hotel New HAMPshire*]$_F$.
           B': # Well, I would buy [*The Hotel New HAMPshire*]$_F$.
      b. A: Welches Buch würde Fritz kaufen?
           B: [ICH]$_T$ würde [*Das Hotel New HAMPshire*]$_F$ kaufen.
           B': # Ich würde [*Das Hotel New HAMPshire*]$_F$ kaufen.

The answers (B') are not appropriate in the given contexts. In (19) it seems as if B' tries to sell a part of the story (what the women wore) as the whole (what the pop stars wore). In (20) she even tries to sell an entirely different story (what she would buy) for the one A is asking for (what Fritz would buy). And obviously, the laws of discourse don't allow for this kind of betrayal.

Let us therefore try to revise the condition on question/answer pairs given in subsection 1.1, repeated here.

(21)   A sentence A can appropriately be uttered as answer to a question Q iff the question meaning matches the focus value of the answer ($\cup[\![S]\!]^f = \cup[\![Q]\!]^o$).

Obviously the A–B' sequences in (19) and (20) violate this condition. Question (19A) denotes a set of propositions of the type 'the pop stars wore ____' while the focus value of the answer consists of propositions like 'the female pop stars wore ____.' The situation is similar in (20). The question would contain propositions like 'Fritz would buy ____.' But the answer's focus value consists of things like 'I would buy ____.' The mismatch is obvious.

Now, what does the S-topic marking do to prevent this mismatch? The idea is to let the S-topic induce alternatives, in a way very similar to the focus. But these alternatives do not have any impact on the focus value. Instead, we introduce a third semantic object important to the meaning of a sentence, its *topic value*. The topic value is basically a 'typed up' focus value, that is, a set of sets of propositions; or, as one might put it more perspicuously, a set of questions. How is this set arrived at? Take (a.B) as an example:

(22) a. [ICH]$_T$ würde [*Das Hotel New HAMPshire*]$_F$ kaufen.
      b. [I]$_T$ would buy [*The Hotel New HAMPshire*]$_F$.

The focus value of (22) might be a set like (23):

(23)   {I would buy *War and Peace*, I would buy *The Hotel New Hampshire*, I would buy *The World According to Garp*, . . .}

The topic value is a set of such sets, with alternatives to the S-topic I replacing I:

(24)   {{I would buy *War and Peace*, I would buy *The Hotel New Hampshire*,
         I would buy *The World According to Garp*, ...}, {Rufus would buy *War
         and Peace*, Rufus would buy *The Hotel New Hampshire*, Rufus would
         buy *The World According to Garp*, ...},
         {Fritz would buy *War and Peace*, Fritz would buy *The Hotel New Hamp-
         shire*, Fritz would buy *The World According to Garp*, ...},
         {Fritz's brother would buy *War and Peace*, Fritz's brother would buy *The
         Hotel New Hampshire*, Fritz's brother would buy *The World According
         to Garp*, ...}, ...}

The alternatives to I in (24) are thrown in arbitrarily, as are the ones to *The Hotel New Hampshire*. The important point is that (24) consists of sets of propositions, each set with a fixed subject – the S-topic – but varying with respect to the object – the focus. As before, (24) can be understood as a set of questions:

(25)   {which book would you/I buy, which book would Rufus buy, which book
         would Fritz buy, which book would Fritz's brother buy, ...}

Let us write $[\![S]\!]^t$ for the topic value of a sentence. Hence (24) $= [\![(22)]\!]^t$. What will $[\![(22)]\!]^t$ do for us? Notice that the original question *What would Fritz buy?* is an element of (25) (alias (24) alias $[\![(22)]\!]^t$). Let us assume that this is the effect of the S-topic in this example: It induces alternative focus values for the sentence, and one of these must match the original question. Accordingly, we replace (21) by (26):

(26)   *Question/Answer Condition, revised*:
         The meaning of the question Q must match one element in the topic value
         of the answer A ($[\![Q]\!]^\circ \in [\![A]\!]^t$).

Obviously, the sequence (20A/B), repeated here, meets this condition.

(27)   A: Which book would Fritz buy?
         B: Well, $[I]_T$ would buy ["The Hotel New HAMPshire"]$_F$.
         B: $[ICH]_T$ würde ["Das Hotel New HAMPshire"]$_F$ kaufen.

The meaning of (27A) is an element of $[\![(27B)]\!]^t (=(24)/(25))$. Next, what about the illicit answer B′?

         B′: # Well, I would buy [*The Hotel New HAMPshire*]$_F$.
         B′: # Ich würde [*Das Hotel New HAMPshire*]$_F$ kaufen.

The sentences do not contain an S-topic. So what will their topic value be? Let us assume that the Topic value of a topicless sentence is the singleton set containing its focus value. Hence $[\![B′]\!]^t = (28)$:

(28)   {{I would buy *War and Peace*, I would buy *The Hotel New Hampshire*, I
         would buy *The World According to Garp*, ...}}

(Note that (28) is not *identical* to the focus value of B′ but to the set containing
it.) Does the sequence (27A–B′) meet the revised Question/Answer Condition in
(26)? Of course not! The only element in the topic value of the answer corresponds
to the question *Which book would I buy?* And that one does not match the original
question *Which book would Fritz buy?* This is a typical example of a contrastive
topic in the sense we discussed. Given an original D-topic, such as a question, the
person answering does not answer that question but another, related one. And to
do so, she has to use the appropriate intonational marking, for example, a topic
accent on the constituent that differs from the original question. The meaning of
that constituent might then be called the 'contrastive topic.'
    What about the partial topic, for example (19), repeated here?

(29)   a.   A: What did the pop stars wear?
               B: The [female]$_T$ pop stars wore [caftans]$_F$.
               B′: #The female pop stars wore [caftans]$_F$.
         b.   A: Was hatten die Popstars an?
               B: Die [weiblichen]$_T$ Popstars trugen [Kaftane]$_F$.
               B′: #Die weiblichen Popstars trugen [Kaftane]$_F$.

It is easy to see what explains the mismatch found with the B′ answers: the
answer just doesn't match the question. What we should do now is look for a
replacement for *female* that would make the answer match the question. If we
succeed in that, we have explained why the topic marking on the adjective makes
the sequence come out fine. Such an alternative is readily found, although not
easily expressed. It is simply the trivial property; or the property *male or female*
for that matter. So we assume that the topic value of (29B) looks like (30):

(30)   {{the female pop stars wore caftans, the female pop stars wore dresses,
         the female pop stars wore overalls, ...},
         {the male pop stars wore caftans, the male pop stars wore dresses, the
         male pop stars wore overalls, ...},
         {the female or male pop stars wore caftans, the female or male pop stars
         wore dresses, the female or male pop stars wore overalls, ...},
         {the Italian pop stars wore caftans, the Italian pop stars wore dresses, the
         Italian pop stars wore overalls, ...}, ...}

The third element in (30) (excuse me for numbering set members) is the set we are
looking for: it matches with the meaning of the question *What did the pop stars
wear?*
    Examples with trivial properties might strike the reader as far-fetched (though I
can find nothing wrong with them). But notice that partial topics can also be found
without such properties:

(31)   A: What did the German musicians wear?

       B: The [Bavarian]$_T$ musicians wore ["Lederhosen"]$_F$.

       B′: Die [bayerischen]$_T$ Musiker trugen [Lederhosen]$_F$.

Although there is evidence to the contrary, Bavaria is a part of Germany. So (31) is an instance of a partial topic, too: speaker A asks for all the German musicians, but speaker B only answers about some of them, the Bavarians. But this time, we don't need other properties but those expressible by ordinary adjectives: *Bavarian, Swabian, German, Flemish, Dutch*, and so on.

So we have seen that the treatment of S-topics proposed here can quite naturally account for both contrastive topics and partial topics. What about the purely implicational topics? To account for these, we have to look at the semantic effects of S-topics from another point of view. Instead of exploring what effects they have with respect to the previous discourse, we have to check out how they affect the utterances to follow.

2.2   Implicatures

I assume that there is an implicature carried by the S-topic, which we might characterize as follows:

(32)   Given a sentence A, containing an S-topic, there is an element Q in $[\![A]\!]^t$ such that Q is still under consideration after uttering A.

If we again regard $[\![A]\!]^t$ as a set of questions, as we did earlier, we say that there is a question in the set of questions denoted by $[\![A]\!]^t$ that is still disputable. This remnant question we call a *residual topic*. For example, in (29), repeated here, (33b) might be a residual topic.

(33)   a.   Die [weiblichen]$_T$ Popstars trugen [Kaftane]$_F$.

          'The [female]$_T$ pop stars wore [caftans]$_F$'.

      b.   What did the male pop stars wear?

Note that (33b) – or, rather, its meaning – is an element of $[\![(33a)]\!]^t$ as given in (30). So (33a) meets (32). The residual topic might also be the "original" topic, provided of course that it has not been resolved. This happens with contrastive topics such as (27), repeated here:

(34)   a.   A: Which book would Fritz buy?

          B: Well, [I]$_T$ would buy [*The Hotel New HAMPshire*]$_F$.

             [ICH]$_T$ würde [*Das Hotel New HAMPshire*]$_F$ kaufen.

      b.   Yeah, but what would Fritz buy?

Here A's first question comes back as a residual topic since B hasn't answered it (it is still disputable which book Fritz would buy). We already know that the meaning of A's question must be in the topic value of B's answer. Otherwise the sequence in (34) wouldn't be well formed to begin with (as a result of condition (26)). Accordingly, (34b) is licensed as a residual topic to B's answer.

Let us next ask, What does *disputable* mean? Naturally we would want to say that a question is disputable if the answer to the question is not yet known. So let us say that a question (a set of propositions, more generally) is disputable if there are informative but nonabsurd answers to it. As already said, this notion of disputability must be relativized to the current common ground:

(35)   *Disputability*:
       A set of propositions P is disputable given a common ground CG, DISP (P,CG), iff there are propositions $p \in P$ such that p is informative and nonabsurd with respect to CG; formally DISP(Q,CG) iff $\exists p \in Q : p \cap CG \neq CG$ & $p \cap CG \neq \emptyset$.[2]

Now that we know what a disputable question looks like, we can formalize the implicature connected with the S-topic, given as (32) earlier:

(36)   Implicature connected with S-topic in a sentence A: $\exists q[q \in [\![A]\!]^t$ & DISP(q, CG $\cap [\![A]\!]^\circ)]$

We are now ready to give an account of purely implicational topics. Consider (17), repeated here:

(37)   a.   A: Did your wife kiss other men?
            B: [My]$_T$ wife [didn't]$_F$ kiss other men.
       b.   A: Hat deine Frau fremde Männer geküßt?
            B: [Meine]$_T$ Frau hat [keine]$_F$ fremden Männer geküßt.

In (37) the topic accent doesn't seem to serve any particular purpose. Note that the question-answer sequence would be well formed without it as well. On the other hand it doesn't do any harm. Since everything is an alternative to itself, the original focus value will necessarily be an element of the topic value. As we have already suggested, $[\![(37B)]\!]^t$ could look like (38):

(38)   {{my wife kissed other men, my wife didn't kiss other men}, {your wife kissed other men, your wife didn't kiss other men}, {Rufus's wife kissed other men, Rufus's wife didn't kiss other men}, {Fritz's wife kissed other men, Fritz's wife didn't kiss other men}, . . .}

The question meaning $[\![(37A)]\!]^\circ$ is an element of (38), so (26) is met. By (36), the topic implicature, at least one element in (38) is disputable and can serve as a residual topic. So speaker B can use his utterance to signal that – according to his knowledge – there is at least one person whose wife might or might not have kissed other men. Depending on the choice of contextually salient alternatives, speaker A might understand it that his wife is the one in question.

The S-topic in (37) then serves the sole purpose of implicating the existence of a residual topic. This is why I call this use of the S-topic the purely implicational topic.

This completes my account of the semantics of S-topics. We have seen that the basic cases discussed in subsection 1.2 are readily explained. We understand why S-topics can help to maintain discourse appropriateness even in cases where the answer doesn't seem to match the question. And we have modeled the implicational effects of the S-topics, namely, to establish a residual topic. The remainder of this paper explores a particular usage of S-topics more thoroughly, namely, topic marking on quantifiers. Other applications of the theory presented can be found in Büring 1995, 1995/6, and 1996.

3   Quantifiers as S-Topics

The phenomena to be discussed in this section have received some attention in the literature, though the – as I argue – crucial role of the accent patterns has not always been recognized. The first set of data consists of sentences with a topic accent on a weak quantifier, a phenomenon that has sometimes been described as a strong or partitive reading of these quantifiers. The second set of data concerns the interplay of topic on (weak or strong) quantifiers and narrow focus on adjuncts.

I try to show that the semantic and pragmatic effects noticed in the literature follow straightforwardly from the treatment of S-topics developed in section 2. No further assumptions are needed.

3.1   *Strong Readings for Weak Quantifiers*

Since Milsark (1974) it is well known that the class of natural language quantifiers is lexically divided into two disjoint sets called weak and strong quantifiers; however, it is also well known that weak quantifiers may have what is called a strong reading, in particular one that is presuppositional (other terms have been used in this connection, for example, partitive, proportional, or truly quantifying, to name just a few). A number of researchers have taken this to indicate a true ambiguity in lexical type. While weak quantifiers on their weak (or cardinal) reading are taken to denote individuals (type $\langle e \rangle$) or predicates (type $\langle et \rangle$), they are supposed to be true quantifiers or properties of properties (type $\langle et, \langle et, t \rangle \rangle$) on their strong reading. This ambiguity has been taken to be either lexical (Diesing 1992) or derived by rules of semantic interpretation (de Hoop 1992). Finally, weak quantifiers on their strong reading always come with a special intonational pattern. As we will see, this special intonational pattern is in fact the rising accent indicating an S-topic.

The claim I want to defend in this section is that the strong reading for weak quantifiers is just a natural consequence of their being the S-topic. In other words, we might get by without type shifting or lexical ambiguity. Let us inspect a run-of-the-mill example of a so-called partitive weak quantifier:

(39)   a. Ein /PAAR Cowboys beschlossen, zu HAUSE\ zu bleiben.
        b. [Some]$_T$ cowboys decided [to stay home]$_F$.

In (39) we have the falling stress on *home* project its focus up to the embedded infinitival clause node. What then would the D-topic for (39) look like? Let us look at $[[(39)]]^t$:

(40) $\left\{ \begin{array}{l} \text{the} \\ \text{all} \\ \text{many} \\ \text{some} \\ \text{two} \end{array} \right\}$ cowboys decided $\left\{ \begin{array}{l} \text{to stay home} \\ \text{to go to the saloon} \\ \text{to go gambling} \\ \text{to read Hegel} \\ \text{to shave} \end{array} \right\}$

Simplifying a little, (40) is the set of questions of the form 'What did Q cowboys decide on?' with Q some quantifier. What (40) shows is that there is a set of cowboys around in the discourse. Whatever element of (40) may be the actual D-topic, it has to be a cowboy issue.

Note a slight shift in perspective: in sections 1 and 2 we have looked at the effects that the S-topic has on the (in)appropriateness of question-answer sequences. In this chapter we look at the "answers" in isolation and ask, What does the answer – in particular its focus/background structure – tell us about the possible contexts? Since any sentence with a given focus/background structure defines the set of contexts it can be used in, we can infer from the sentence alone which kind of contexts it is suited to. Earlier I called this the presupposition of the sentence. Strictly speaking, this terminology is a bit misleading: presuppositions are propositional in nature. What we deal with here are not propositions but sets of sets of propositions, or – as I will continue to say – sets of questions. No doubt, we can derive from such a set a "classical" presupposition (such as the existence of a group of cowboys in (39)), but the object of inquiry is of a different kind. It is not a statement of facts, but a set of potential issues.

With this in mind, let us return to our cowboy example. The S-topic in (39) allows for the calculation of a set of possible D-topics, such as possible preceding questions. This set is given in (40). The elements in that set have certain things in common. Here they are all statements about cowboys and the decisions they made. Since all possible D-topics for (39) are statements of that kind, we infer upon hearing (39) out of the blue that there must be cowboys at stake.

Maybe this is all we have to say here. Taking this set to be a superset of the set of cowboys who decided to stay home will give us the partitive reading.

This story might sound simplistic. For one thing, it explains why we *can* get a partitive reading, but not why we *must* get it. True enough, but it seems that this is just what we need. Consider the following texts:

(41)   a.   The town was bursting with tension. A cowboy was standing next to the door of the saloon, nervously playing with his gun. [TWO]$_T$ cowboys were posted next to each window.

       b.   The town was bursting with tension. Ten or more cowboys were standing next to the door of the saloon, nervously playing with their guns. [TWO]$_T$ cowboys were posted next to each window.

In (41a), the partitive reading is excluded, for two cowboys can hardly be a subset of one cowboy. But in (41b) this obstacle is no longer present. If the saloon is relatively small, so small in fact that we might say that the windows all are next to the door, (41b) can be read partitively: The ten (or more) cowboys are standing close to the door, split up into groups of two, each group observing one window. Still, (41b) has another reading – I believe the more plausible one – in which *two cowboys* is not read partitively. If the saloon has five windows, then there are at least twenty cowboys in there. Nonetheless, the last sentence in (41b) requires that there be previously mentioned cowboys. So, the partitive reading might be possible in these cases, but it is not obligatory.

Another objection might be that the partitive reading seems to violate the Familiarity Condition of Heim (1982), according to which an indefinite NP (and cardinal NPs clearly count as indefinite in this sense) may not refer to a familiar discourse referent. In fact, this is what distinguishes them from definites, who have to find a previously introduced referent. But it is important to separate the notions of discourse referents from the notion of 'present in the discourse' or 'discourse inferable.' Introducing a group of cowboys, for example by saying *There were ten cowboys loitering around the saloon*, tells us that a set of ten cowboys is part of the universe of discourse. And of course, we can infer that there is also a set of nine, five, or two cowboys. However, the only discourse *referent* introduced is the set of ten, none of its subsets. This can be seen easily in the following sequences:

(42)   There were ten cowboys loitering around the saloon.
    a. They were nervously playing with their guns.
    b. The (ten) cowboys were nervously playing with their guns.
    c. #Ten cowboys were nervously playing with their guns.
    d. #The three cowboys were nervously playing with their guns.
    e. /THREE cowboys were nervously playing with their guns.
    f. /TEN cowboys were nervously playing with their guns.

First, sentence (42) introduces a discourse referent, a group of ten cowboys. As a result we find the contrast between (b) and (c): The definite article has to be used in order to refer to that group. Second, there is no smaller group available as a discourse referent, as the impossibility of (d) shows. Rather, we have to use another indefinite in order to introduce a subset of the ten, as in (e). Again, (e) may be partitive, but it doesn't have to be; remember the examples in (41). Finally, partitivity is not an option in (f). The ten cowboys mentioned in (f) must be a different group than those we know from (42). Understanding the indefinite in (f) as partitive would violate the Familiarity Condition, for this time part and whole would be identical, thereby introducing the same discourse entity twice.

Let me sum up briefly. I have argued that the so-called strong or partitive reading of NPs with weak quantifiers is just a consequence of the quantifier's being the S-topic. In general, the topic accent on the determiner of an NP signals that another NP*, which differs from NP only in the determiner, has previously been used, namely, in the D-topic. In full accord with Heim's (1982) Familiarity Condition, the referent of NP must be different from that of NP*, either a subset of NP*'s referent or an entirely different group. The former case will result in a true partitive reading. Let us call these *token partitives*. The latter case, such as in (41), is not truly partitive. Rather, the discourse referent introduced by the second NP is just another token of the same type as NP*. This we might call a *type partitive*.

It is worthwhile to stress that token partitivity is arrived at purely epiphenomenally. No modifications in the theory of discourse representation are needed. This crucially distinguishes the approach developed here from treatments such as the one developed by G. Jäger (1994; this volume). In Jäger's system, the representation of discourse referents is explicitly refined so as to allow for the notion "part of" directly. In a nutshell, Jäger's approach has it that a topic NP that introduces a discourse referent can only introduce a referent that is part of an already existing one. Importantly Jäger's account fails to generalize to the cases I have called type partitives, that is, cases in which the second discourse referent is related to the first only in terms of membership in an even bigger group, the type, or kind.

There are two more cases in which the alleged strong reading of weak quantifiers cannot be constructed as a relation among individuals and groups. First, we have only said that the sequence 'determiner-noun' must have been previously mentioned. But that does not imply that the existence of an individual has been asserted. Consider the following sequence:

(43)   Q: Are there dealers in this part of town?
        A: [TWO]$_T$ dealers have just been arrested.

In (43Q) the existence of dealers is not asserted but merely considered. Accordingly, the answer does not establish any subset relation (how could it?) but nevertheless picks up the topic '____ dealers VP' in the same way as before.

As for the second case, note that quantifiers bearing a topic accent are not restricted to referential uses. One case in question involves generic uses of topic marked quantifiers. These we discuss next.

Let us ignore the question what exactly is responsible for whether or not an indefinite is or can be interpreted generically for the moment. Sentences like (44) – with a sole focus accent – have a generic reading for the indefinite *two books*.

(44)   Er schickt zwei Bücher immer [mit der POST]$_F$.
        he sends two books always with the mail
        'He always sends two books by mail.'

What if we place a topic accent on the generic indefinite?

(45)   Er schickt /ZWEI Bücher immer mit der POST\.
        a. 'If the cardinality of the books is two, he always sends them by mail.'
        b. 'There are two books which he always sends by mail.'

As suggested by the paraphrases, (45) is ambiguous between a generic and an existential statement. Let us concentrate on the generic reading (45a) first. The only thing that makes (45) in this reading different from (44) is that the latter requires *two books* to be part of the topic, while the former – by virtue of the topic accent – requires only that *books* have been mentioned. A possible D-topic for (44) would be the question *How does he transport two books?* (the reading becomes easier after substituting *many for two*). A possible D-topic for (45) – on the generic reading – would be any question of the form 'How does he transport _____ books?' for example, *How does he transport more than one book?* Answer: *Sets of two books he always sends by mail.*

Note that this is not a partitive reading in the literal sense, because there is no given set of books out of which subsets of two are always sent by mail. However, remember that we derived the partitive reading as a relation between a D-topic (a set of propositions) and the topic value of a sentence (a set of sets of propositions) rather than between sets of individuals. And this is just what goes on here: The S-topic indicates a D-topic like 'How does he transport (sets of) books?' and answers the question 'How does he transport (sets of) two books?' And as before it holds that the (reconstructed) D-topic is an element of the topic value of the sentence. Note again that this cannot be represented in a theory that assumes the part-of relation between sets or groups of individuals to be at the heart of these readings. Furthermore, theories that assume a dichotomy between quantificational and cardinal uses of weak quantifiers must assume that (45a,b) feature two different quantifiers, the cardinal one (on its generic reading) in (45a), the strong one in (45b). The relation between the actual readings and the accenting remains unaccounted for.

The theory proposed here can handle these cases without lexical ambiguity. Since 'partitivity' is reconstructed as a relation among propositions (rather than individuals), it naturally carries over to cases of topic marked generic indefinites. All semantic effects are attributed to the interpretation of topic marking. Hence we arrive at a true cross-classification for indefinite NPs as [±existential] and [±topic], where partitive indefinites are simply [+existential] and [+topic]. Since topic marking is supposed to lie at the heart of these facts, no further stipulations regarding interpretation and intonation are required.

Let us finally turn to the second reading, (45b). Here the indefinite is interpreted as an existential quantifier, despite preceding the focus. Since the indefinite itself is existential, we understand reading (45b) to presuppose that there were other books whose possible transportation was being discussed, that is, type or token partitivity.

3.2   *Proportional Readings*

In the preceding section we have seen that a topic accent on a lexically weak quantifier has the effect of strong or partitive readings. It should again be stressed that there is nothing in the meaning of the quantifier that makes it inherently partitive or focus sensitive. And accordingly, the nominal complement to the quantifier has no designated status within the semantic representation. The fact that a lot of the cases discussed seem to express partitivity with respect to the set denoted by the noun (e.g., *books*, *cowboys*) is just a result of the fact that those nouns were the sole background elements in their respective sentences. We thus predict the partitive effects to switch with a shift in focus. There are two ways in which we can do so. First we may enlarge the background, making the focus narrower. This is done below. We shall discuss cases like (46), with a narrow focus and both weak and strong quantifiers.

(46)   a. [THREE]$_T$ boys [WALKED]$_F$ to the station.
       b. [MOST]$_T$ boys [WALKED]$_F$ to the station.

Second we may remove the nominal complement from the background by making it focus. This yields sentences like (47).

(47)   [MANY]$_T$ [SCANDINAVIANS]$_F$ won the Nobel Prize.

These so-called focus affected readings are briefly discussed at the end of this section (see Büring 1995/6:chap.4 and 1996 for more discussion). But first the cases with narrow focus: in a sentence like (48a), a 'partial indefinite' case, everything but the subject noun is either topic or focus. Accordingly, the existence of an appropriate D-topic boils down to '____ boys did something', that is, the mere existence of other boys.[3]

(48)   a. [THREE]$_T$ boys [walked to the STATION]$_F$.
       b. [THREE]$_T$ boys [WALKED]$_F$ to the station.

In (48b), on the other hand, the D-topic whose existence we can infer from the focus/topic/background structure is much more specific. It is about boys getting to the station in one way or other. By the familiarity condition we know that the three boys mentioned in (48a) cannot be those mentioned in the D-topic. Hence there must be more boys than those three (or at least the existence of such boys was under debate). If those other boys walked to the station as well and the speaker knows that, she violated the Gricean Maxim of Quantity in saying (48a). So either the speaker doesn't know about the others' transfer to the station at all, or she knows that they didn't walk. The latter case licenses an inference that the other boys got to the station in some alternative way. It is exactly this amalgam of truth conditions and contextual restrictions that I claim is expressed by a sentence like (48a).

One could try to build the effects of focus directly into the meaning of the quantifier, similar to the alternative analysis of partitives discussed. Such a theory wouldn't restrict the quantifier by its syntactic complement but by the trivialization of the focus value. In other words, (48a) would be made literally to mean

(49)   Three *boys who somehow got to the station* walked there,

where the restrictor (printed in italics) is the focus value of the entire sentence (minus the quantifier). Treatments along these lines have been proposed by Eckardt

(1993, 1994, this volume), Geilfuß (1993), Herburger (1992), and de Hoop and Solà (1996).

It is, however, hard to prove the correctness of such an approach with examples like these, where weak quantifiers are involved. The reason is that weak quantifiers such as *three* are both symmetric and conservative; that is, it holds that $Q(A)(B) \leftrightarrow Q(B)(A)$ and $Q(A)(B) \leftrightarrow Q(A)(A \& B)$. From these properties it follows that the truth conditions for a conservative symmetric determiner cannot change by copying clause internal material into the restrictor.[4] So there is no case for such a "direct association approach" to focus effects, as opposed to the more roundabout treatment that follows from the general semantics of focus and topic advocated here.

Things change if we bring strong determiners into the picture. Strong determiners are conservative but not symmetric. Therefore, it should make a truth conditional difference if material from the matrix (e.g., *get to the station*) appears in the restrictor. Of course, this won't happen if focus projects:

(50)   MOST$_T$ boys [walked to the STATION]$_F$.

Suppose we trivialize focus and topic. This gives us *boys* as the previously mentioned group from which the boys in (50) should be a subset. But this again is irrelevant, for boyhood is already part of the restrictor (assuming that both the focus value *and* the meaning of the syntactic complement provide the restrictor). Now consider our case where only part of VP is nonfocused.

(51)   MOST$_T$ boys WALKED$_F$ to the station.

By trivialization we get '___ boys ___ to the station', that is, the set of boys who got to the station. Accordingly, the meaning of (51) could be paraphrased as in (52).

(52)   Most of the boys who somehow got to the station walked to the station.

And in fact this seems to be the reading that (51) has. One might conclude that these cases provide evidence in favor of directly associating the adnominal quantifier with focus, that is, giving focus direct impact on truth conditions as done in Eckardt (1993, 1994, this volume), and in Geilfuß (1993). In what follows I present an analysis that preserves the insights of the Eckardt/Geilfuß analysis but reduces the specific mechanisms put to use there to the general properties of topics.

The key to analyzing examples such as (51) lies, I believe, in the fact that strong quantifiers are contextually restricted, and that this restriction affects the truth conditions of sentences with strong quantifiers in them.[5] Quantified NPs like *all boys* or *most boys* do not usually mean all or most of the boys in the universe, but only all or most boys of a contextually given set. And it is in fact crucial for determining the truth conditions to know what this set looks like (note that sentences like *all/most boys are blond* would always be true if the choice of domain were entirely free). A straightforward way of implementing this is proposed in Westerståhl (1985) and further elaborated in Geilfuß (1993), von Fintel (1994), Musan (1995), and van Deemter (1992), among others. According to this treatment, strong quantifiers come with a *Resource Domain Variable*, which can be written as a superscript on the quantifier.

(53)   Most^C boys walked to the station.

The variable C denotes a property, which is intersected with the syntactic restrictor of the quantifier. Hence, (53) is interpreted as (54).

(54)   most($[\![$boy$]\!]$ ∩ C)($[\![$walk to the station$]\!]$)

As Westerståhl points out, C is not identical to the domain of individuals but can be smaller. In many cases, C is provided by a preceding NP. Take example (55).

(55)   There were dozens of people in the marketplace. [Most^C WOmen]$_T$ were standing next to the stage.

Here C is presumably the property of standing in the marketplace. As a result, the second sentence in (55) is interpreted as 'most women who stood in the marketplace stood next to the stage'. C is not always unambiguously determined by the context:

(56)   There were dozens of people in the marketplace. Fifteen women entered the stage. MOST^C women waved their hands.

Here, *most women* might relate either to those on the stage or to all women in the marketplace, depending on the choice of C.

Finally, note that the resource domain variable is not necessarily dependent on a preceding NP.

(57)   Let us next turn to the village Simmersbach. Most^C men over 55 are unemployed.

Here, *most men* clearly denotes most men in the village of Simmersbach, although there is no preceding NP such as *the men from Simmersbach*.

This last example shows that those readings are not just token partitives. The resource domain variable is not always a set corresponding to a discourse referent. Instead I would like to pursue the following picture: Resource domain variables are provided by the context in quite a flexible fashion. If we encounter a sentence out of the blue, the only information about the context that we have is again provided by the focus/background structure. If the sentence has a wide Focus, little information is won. This is what happens in (50), repeated here.

(58)   [most^C]$_T$ boys [walked to the STATION]$_F$.

After trivializing we only know that the previous discourse must have been about boys. Now, even if we take boyhood to be the property denoted by C, no change in truth conditions arises. But let us look at (51) again, repeated as (59).

(59)   [most^C]$_T$ boys WALKED$_F$ to the station.

As stated, the D-topic, whatever it may be exactly, is about boys getting to the station. Accordingly the property of being a boy who gets to the station is a good guess regarding the resource domain variable of *most*. We thus interpret (59) as (60).

(60)   most([[boy]] ∩ C)([[walk to the station]])

λx.x is a boy who gets to the station somehow

By intersecting the syntactic restrictor of *most* with *C* we actually get the property 'be a boy getting to the station' as the semantic restrictor of **most**. At the same time we have maintained that there is no direct influence of topic or focus on truth conditions. Truth conditional effects only obtain via the resource domain variable *C*. The only influence that focus/background structure has on truth conditions is that it helps us guess the context if we hear a sentence out of the blue, just as it was.

Let us compare this approach to the more semanticized original in Eckardt (1993) and Geilfuß (1993). According to Geilfuß (1993), focus directly restricts the resource domain variable. For example, (59) is now interpreted as (61):

(61)   most([[boys]]^o ∩ ∪[[WALKED$_F$ to the station]]^f)([[WALKED$_F$ to the station]]^o)

The trivialization of [[WALKED$_F$ to the station]]^f is of course the property of getting to the station somehow, which – intersected with the syntactic restrictor [[boys]]^o – gives us again the pertinent set of boys who target the rails. Since – as Geilfuß notes – this procedure resembles association with focus in the sense of Jackendoff (1972) and, especially, Rooth (1985) (for adverbial quantifiers), let us call it the *direct association approach*.

The problem with this approach is that the predicted truth conditions are sometimes too liberal. Consider the following examples from Eckardt (1993).

(62)   Max had to polish ten cars this afternoon. When I came back, six cars still stood in front of the garage, not even touched by Max. He had polished MOST$_T$ cars CAREFULLY$_F$.

Here *most cars* is quantifier raised and adjoined to S. The trivialization of the S node's focus value – ∪[[he polished *t* CAREFULLY]]^f – is the property of having polished the cars somehow. This property inserted as the resource domain variable of *most* results in reading (63).

(63)   Most cars Max polished he polished carefully.

Again this reading might well be true in the context provided by (62) (imagine that Max has polished three of the remaining four cars excessively), but intuitively it is not available. The topic approach fares better here: The only resource domains contextually available are the ten cars or the six untouched cars, but not the relative complement of both. Accordingly, (62) appears contradictory on any interpretation.[6]

It thus turns out that the rather loose relation between focus/background structure and resource domain proposed here is indeed needed in these cases.

One might try to rescue the direct association approach by invoking an additional presupposition, namely, that in a sentence like (64), all cars must have been polished to begin with.[7]

(64)   Max polished MOST cars carefully.

More generally, $MOST^C(A)(B)$ would have the presupposition $ALL(A)(C)$. Since this presupposition is explicitly contradicted in (62), where it is stated that six cars were left untouched, the presupposition of (64) (all cars have been polished) is clearly not warranted, so (62) is predicted to be unacceptable.

The question is whether we can generally defend such a strong presupposition. For example, it seems perfectly fine to say (65).

(65)   I was curious whether the boys would make it to the station. As it turned out, $MOST_T$ boys $WALKED_F$ to the station, but the others didn't get there at all.

Obviously the last sentence in (65) contradicts the alleged presupposition (furthermore the second sentence might be argued to violate the Gricean Maxim of Quantity, since the stronger *ALL boys* could have been used according to that theory). Matters are even clearer if the speaker expresses uncertainty, as in (66).

(66)   a. Max polished $MOST_T$ cars $CAREFULLY_F$, but I am not sure whether he polished all of them.
         b. All the boys wanted to kiss Amalie. $MOST_T$ boys kissed her $PASSIONATELY_F$. As for the others, I am not sure whether they kissed her at all.

Obviously, the speaker of (66a) does not presuppose that Max polished all cars. Likewise, (66b) does not presuppose that every boy was lucky enough to kiss Amalie (the example is again adapted from Eckardt 1993). The only thing that has to be guaranteed is that Max polishing cars and boys kissing Amalie have been under discussion.[8]

So while the presuppositional version of the direct association approach can presumably handle (62), it is not generally tenable. I conclude that the topic treatment argued for here accounts for the entire range of data more satisfactorily.

Let us finally look at cases of focus within the subject NP. Again, we can regard cases involving weak and strong quantifiers:

(67)   a. $[MOST]_T$ $[inCOMpetent]_F$ cooks applied.
         b. $[FEW]_T$ $[inCOMpetent]_F$ cooks applied.

As noted in Eckardt (1993), cases like (67a) pose a serious problem for the direct association approach. Why? Because the trivialization of the focus value of (67a) is '____cooks applied', which – taken as a restrictor – yields the truth conditions (68) for (67a).

(68)   Most cooks that applied were incompetent.

But (67a) doesn't have this meaning. Rather it seems that – in accordance with the treatment proposed here – the resource domain variable is not provided by any sentence internal material. It therefore seems necessary to block the association of the quantifier with the focus in these cases. However, as Herburger (1992) claims, this very association seems necessary in (67b), which she interprets as (69). She calls this a *focus affected reading*.

(69)   Few cooks that applied were incompetent.

Now, we already saw that this kind of restriction cannot make a truth conditional difference with symmetric determiners. So – given Herburger's analysis – **few(A)(B)** cannot be taken to mean 'the number of x which are both A and B is small'. Rather, one would have to interpret *few* as a nonsymmetric determiner, where the standard of comparison is the first argument. On that interpretation **few(A)(B)** is true if only a small number of A's are also B's, say less than 20 percent. Thus (69) is true if among the applying cooks there are less than 20 percent that are incompetent. If we apply this meaning to the syntactic structure of (a) directly – having A = [incompetent cooks] and B = [applied] – we would have it that less than 20 percent of the incompetent cooks applied. But as Herburger points out, (a) might be true even if almost every incompetent cook applied, provided their overall number is small.

One can object to this analysis that the intended interpretation of *few* is not the only one possible. One might as well think that *few* is in fact a symmetric determiner and that the standard of comparison is not determined sentence internally but pragmatically. Thus there would be no truth conditional effect with *few* and focus at all.[9] One argument in favor of such an analysis comes from the treatment of *many*, which seems to behave in basically the same way as *few*. Consider example (70).

(70)   Many [SWEDISH] models were at my birthday party.

Suppose that among the two hundred guests at my party there were three models, two of them from Sweden. According to the treatment envisioned by Herburger, (70) would mean 'a high percentage of models at Daniel's birthday party were Swedish', which is true in the given scenario. But (70) would be odd – to say the least – if uttered under these circumstances. So it seems that although there must be an external standard of comparison with *few* and *many*, it is not as directly related to the focus/background structure as the structural analysis claims it to be. Accordingly we conclude with de Hoop (1995) that there are no truth conditional effects with weak determiners at all, not even in cases where the focus sits in the nominal argument.

The general claim of this section then is that there are no semantic (let alone syntactic) peculiarities to partitive, proportional, or focus affected readings of adnominal quantifers, be they weak or strong. The effects observed in the literature were shown to be mostly weaker than claimed, usually non–truth-conditional. Let me briefly sum up the cases discussed:

- **Partitive readings of weak quantifiers** result from the fact that the noun, but not the quantifier, is part of the background. Hence an NP containing that noun must have been in the D-topic. This also holds for cases of type partitives and generic partitive not analyzable by using a mereological analysis of "partitivity."
- **Proportional readings of weak quantifiers** are just a special case of partitives, namely, one where the background is bigger than just the nominal argument to the quantifier.
- **Proportional readings of strong quantifiers** result from the interplay of topics and the pragmatic process of finding a resource domain variable. There is no direct association of the focus value with the resource domain variable, which would yield inappropriate truth conditions.
- **Focus affected readings with *few* and *many* and NP internal focus** are again not due to direct association with focus but result from the pragmatic process of finding a standard of comparison.

In general then the theory of topics proposed characterizes sentence internal topics as a quite general phenomenon, which can be formally characterized in terms of (i) its effects on discourse appropriateness and (ii) its implicatures. Apart from its effects in question/answer pairs it could also be shown to figure prominently in a number of puzzling constructions around adnominal quantification. The proposed analysis reduces all these effects to the general semantics of S-topics, thereby simplifying the syntax-semantics mapping.

It was demonstrated that an appropriately weak characterization of these phenomena can be arrived at using only two devices: topic/focus semantics and resource domain variables.

Notes

1 This analysis is taken from Féry (1993), which adopts in turn the framework of Pierrehumbert (1980). The star is associated with the strongest syllable of the pertinent domain. The intonational facts in English are more complicated and will not be discussed here. See also the discussion of B- (as opposed to A-) accents of Jackendoff (1972:258ff.), whose insights lie at the heart of the treatment proposed here.
2 As the editors pointed out to me, these conditions correspond to the first principle of Stalnaker (1978:325).

3   As we have seen, even this is too strong. It suffices that some property of some boys has been discussed, even if that property is (non)existence.

4   Here, Q is the determiner, for example, *three*. A is the first argument of Q, here [[boys]], B the second argument, that is, [[walked to the station]]. Consider (i) as an illustration:
   (i)   Three boys walked to the station.
   (ii)   Three persons who walked to the station were boys. (from (i) by symmetry)
   (iii)   Three persons who walked to the station were boys/persons who walked to the station. (from (ii) by conservativity)

5   This is not to say that weak quantifiers cannot be contextually restricted, but only that this will not make a truth conditional difference. A recent discussion of these issues can be found in Musan 1995.

6   De Hoop (1995:9) claims that a similar example, namely, (i) (her (24b)), is in fact true if six linguists don't drink, five do, and three of them drink at night.
   (i)   Most linguists drink [at NIGHT]$_F$.
   However, this doesn't seem to be correct. (i) presupposes talk about (potentially) drinking linguists; compare.
   (ii)   Most linguists don't drink and most linguists drink at NIGHT.
   Sentence (ii) is clearly odd, though it precisely characterizes de Hoop's scenario. So again, I don't think that the focus restricts anything but the set of possible contexts. Truth conditions remain constant.

7   This solution is also discussed by Eckardt (1993, this volume).

8   One might argue, though, that (i) is decidedly odd:
   (i)   Vladimir saw NO$_T$ movie ENTIRELY$_F$, and in fact he hasn't seen any at all.
   However, this presumably follows from the fact that the sequel *he hasn't seen any at all* implies the first sentence *he saw no movie entirely*. If the speaker knows that he didn't see any movie, she violates the Maxim of Quantity in making the inappropriately weak statement that he saw none entirely. If the speaker is uncertain, the weaker statement is of course licit:
   (ii)   Vladimir saw NO$_T$ movie ENTIRELY$_F$, and I am not certain whether he's seen any at all.
   So again, neither (i) nor (ii) indicates a presupposition such as 'he saw the movies'.

9   This line of reasoning is pursued in de Hoop 1995.

References

Ackema, Peter, and Maaike Schoorlemmer, eds. 1993. *Proceedings of the Workshop on the Syntactic and Semantic Analysis of Focus.* Utrecht: OTS (=OTS Working Papers TL-93-012).

Büring, Daniel. 1995. The great scope inversion conspiracy. In Mandy Simons and Teresa Galloway (eds.), *Proceedings of SALT V.* Ithaca, N.Y.: Cornell University Linguistic Publications, 37–53.

Büring, Daniel. 1995/6. The 59th Street Bridge Accent. Ph.D. dissertation, Tübingen. (Published 1997. Routledge.)

Büring, Daniel. 1996. A weak theory of strong readings. In *Proceedings of SALT VI.* Ithaca, N.Y.: Cornell University Linguistic Publications.

Cuttler, Anne. 1977. The Context Dependence of "Intonational Meanings." *CLS* 13, 104–115.

Deemter, Kees van. 1992. Towards a generalization of anaphora. *Journal of Semantics* 9(1), 27–51.

Diesing, Molly. 1992. *Indefinites*. Cambridge, Mass.: MIT Press.

Eckardt, Regine. 1993. Adverbialsemantik und Fokusse, und wieso sie nicht zu trennen sind. Ms., Stuttgart University.

Eckardt, Regine. 1994. Adverbs in Focus. ESPRIT Basic Research Project 6852 "DYANA", DYANA deliverable R2.2.B, 289–333, IMS, University of Stuttgart.

Féry, Caroline. 1993. *German Intonational Patterns*. Tübingen: Niemeyer.

Fintel, Kai von. 1994. Restrictions on Quantifier Domains. Ph.D. dissertation, University of Massachusetts, Amherst.

Geilfuß, Jochen. 1993. Nominal quantifiers and association with focus. In Ackema, P. and M. Schoorlemmer (eds).

Heim, Irene. 1982. The Semantics of Definite and Indefinite Noun Phrases. Ph.D. dissertation, University of Massachusetts, Amherst.

Herburger, Elena. 1992. Focus and the LF of NP quantification. In *Proceedings of SALT III*.

Hoop, Helen de. 1992. Case Configuration and Noun Phrase Interpretation. Ph.D. dissertation, Rijksuniversiteit Groningen.

Hoop, Helen de. 1995. *Only* a matter of context? In Marcel den Dikken and Kees Hengeveld (eds.), *Linguistics in the Netherlands 1995*. Amsterdam/Philadelphia: John Benjamins Publishing Company, 113–124.

Hoop, Helen de, and Jaume Solà. 1996. Determiners, context sets, and focus. In José Camacho, Lina Choueiri, and Maki Watanabe (eds.), *The Proceedings of the Fourteenth West Coast Conference on Formal Linguistics*. Stanford: CSLI, 155–167.

Jackendoff, Ray. 1972. *Semantic Interpretation in Generative Grammar*. Cambridge, Mass.: MIT Press.

Jäger, Gerhard. 1994. Topic, scrambling and aktionsart. In *Proceedings of CONSOLE*, Venice.

Ladd, D. Robert. 1980. *The Structure of Intonational Meaning*. Bloomington: Indiana University Press.

Milsark, Gary. 1974. Existential Sentences in English. Ph.D. dissertation, MIT.

Musan, Renate. 1995. On the Temporal Interpretation of Noun Phrases. Ph.D. dissertation, MIT.

Pierrehumbert, Janet. 1980. The Phonology and Phonetics of English Intonation. Ph.D. dissertation, MIT.

Rooth, Mats. 1985. Association with Focus. Ph.D. dissertation, University of Massachusetts, Amherst.

Stalnaker, Robert. 1978. Assertion. In Peter Cole (ed.), *Syntax & Semantics 9: Pragmatics*. New York: Academic Press, 315–332.

Ward, G., and J. Hirschberg. 1985. Implicating uncertainty. *Language* 61, 747–776.

Westerståhl, D. 1985. Logical constants in quantifier languages. *Linguistics & Philosophy* 8, 387–413.

9   Focus with Nominal Quantifiers

REGINE ECKARDT

Abstract

I draw attention to examples where nominal quantifiers associate with focus in the same way as adverbial quantifiers, in classical examples studied by Rooth, Krifka, and others. I show that nominal quantifiers become like adverbial quantifiers in such constructions. Indirect evidence involving E-type anaphora suggests that full unselective binding takes place. The behavior of weak determiners shows that focus (instead of syntax) drives the computation of the arguments of the quantifier. Finally, I present a formal account for the examples under investigation.

1   Nominal Quantifiers in Interaction with Focus

It is by now well known that adverbial quantifiers like *always* or *normally* associate with focus. The focus structure of a sentence is the crucial factor in the computation of restrictor and scope argument of the respective quantifiers. This is illustrated by the following minimal pair, which has been treated in Krifka (1991b) and Rooth (1995), among others.

(1)   In St. Petersburg, [OFFICERS]$_F$ always accompany ballerinas.

(2)   In St. Petersburg, officers always accompany [BALLERINAS]$_F$.

Words in capital letters are to be read with an accent, while the brackets with index F indicate the focus domain(s) involved.

Rooth (1995) assumes that the restrictor R of the adverbial quantifier is computed by taking the *union of the focus semantic value* of the sentence (in terms of Rooth 1985, 1995). The scope S consists of the *ordinary semantic value* of the sentence, and the adverbial quantifier binds *unselectively* over the free variables in the restrictor. Without going into the details, this will essentially yield the following analysis for sentence (1):

(3)   R = {x, y, t | x accompanies ballerina y at time t, where x is an officer or anyone else who is appropriate in the context}
         S = {x, y, t | x accompanies ballerina y at time t, and x is an officer}
         ALWAYS(R,S) ($\Leftrightarrow$ R $\subseteq$ S)
         'Always if *someone* x accompanies a ballerina at t, then this someone is an officer'[1]

The representation of (2) will differ in the appropriate way from (3), reflecting the different meaning of the example. Moreover, the differences between (1) and (2) will be due to the different focus semantic values of the sentences.

It is not surprising to find that a certain amount of pragmatics is involved in the interpretation of adverbial quantifiers. However, it may be less well known that very similar processes influence the interpretation of nominal quantifiers. This is illustrated by examples (4) to (6), where the symbols "/" and "\" indicate a *rise accent* and a *fall accent*.

(4)   Ludwig washed most/ cars with X-polish\.

(5)   Almost all/ tickets were sold at checker 4\.

(6)   Alma sliced no/ bagel carefully\.

Let me first show that the meaning of (4) in the indicated intonation pattern indeed differs from the meaning predicted by an ordinary semantic representation. Classical treatments will give a representation for sentence (4) that can be paraphrased as in (7)

(7)   Of a contextually given set of cars M, Ludwig washed more than half and, by the way, with X-polish.

Sentence (4), however, is understood differently. We take it to say that

(8)   Looking at the set N of cars washed by Ludwig, we find that more than half of N were washed with X-polish. (It does not matter how many more overall cars are around.)

In a situation where Ludwig washed four out of ten cars, and three of those four cars with X-polish, sentence (4) will be true, but paraphrase (7) will be false. This demonstrates that these two representations differ, and that (8) reflects the actual reading of (4). Similarly, sentence (5) quantifies over the set of sold tickets, instead of the set of tickets in general. Sentence (6), although not differing in truth value behavior from its nonfocused counterpart, carries the presupposition that Alma actually *did* slice some bagels – a presupposition not shared by the nonfocused variant.

Accidentally, I found a nice example in real life that toys with this difference between a classical interpretation and a focus driven reading. The following advertisment for the WDR 2 radio station could be found in Düsseldorf, spring 1997:

> WDR 2-Hörer wissen auch nicht alles. Aber alles sofort.
> ('Listeners to WDR 2 don't know everything either. But, they know everything immediately.')

Superficially looking at these data, we can give the following diagnosis: While the semantic effect of the rise accent still has to be found out, the fall accent seems to signal an ordinary semantic focus. The indicated focus structure influences the interpretation of the nominal quantifier (carrying the rise accent) insofar as it shapes the restrictor and scope of the quantifier. Moreover, it does so in a way similar to the analysis in (3). The paraphrase (8) could satisfyingly be made precise as in (9):

(9)   R = {x, e | x is a car washed by Ludwig in e, using X-polish or anything else instead}
       S = {x, e | x is a car washed by Ludwig in e, using X-polish in e}
       MOST(R,S) (⇔ S comprises more than half of R)

Before spelling out a mechanism that yields a representation as in (9) for a sentence like (4), I want to discuss some questions in order to clarify the nature of the processes involved.

   (I)   What exactly are the variables quantified over?
   (II)   Can nominal quantifiers bind unselectively, in the same way as adverbial quantifiers do?
   (III) What is the division of labor between syntax and focus, when it comes to the computation of the two arguments of the nominal quantifier?

Questions (I) and (II) are addressed in the next section, while Section 3 is devoted to (III). In the final section I give a formal treatment of the examples in question.

2   What Do We Count?

Let us have a closer look at the world where Ludwig is washing cars. We systematically go through all possible choices of parameters to quantify over with *most* in sentence (4). It turns out that neither choice is completely satisfying. I then argue that the truth lies in a further restriction of the contexts involved, one that is not yet captured by a semantic treatment of focus. The relevant kind of restriction in fact does not only arise in examples involving focus, but has been noted in the study of so-called donkey sentences. Thus, examples like (4) may provide further data for the underlying phenomenon, but I do not intend to give a comprehensive explanation of this further "factor X" here.

2.1   Counting Individuals

The first choice for the variable to be bound by *most* in (4) is, of course, the variable that is introduced by the noun phrase. *Most* normally counts cars, and why should it not continue doing so in (4)? All other variables involved must then be bound existentially. In example (4), this is first of all the respective event variable. The instrumental *with*-PP refers to an optional participant of the washings, and we should thus leave it open whether the overall washings were all done with an instrument participant, or some of them were "just ordinary washings." The corresponding restrictor and scope arguments then look as follows:

(10)   R = {x | ∃e (x is a car washed by Ludwig in e)}

$S = \{x \mid \exists e \, (x \text{ is a car washed by Ludwig in } e, \text{ using X-polish in } e)\}$
(4) says: 'S comprises more than half of R'

The representation in (10) is true in a situation like the one in (11), where C1–C5 are cars and e_i are washings by Ludwig, executed in the indicated manners:

(11)   C1 – e_1: with X   C2 – e_4: with X   C3 – e_6: without
              – e_2: without X   – e_5: without   – e_7: without
              – e_3: without X   – e_8: with X
         C4 – e_9: without   C5 – e_{11}: without
              – e_{10}: with X   – e_{12}: without

Although more washings have been done without X-polish than with X-polish, we find that Ludwig has, for a majority of cars, washed them with X-polish at least *once*. This is enough to satisfy (10). Sentence (4), however, looks a bit odd in a situation like the one depicted in (11) because we would not expect there to be so many spurious washings around. In fact, we expect the washings executed with X-polish in some way to be among the overall washings suggested by the focus structure. Sentence (4) seems to say, 'For most of the cars Ludwig washed, *the* washing was done with X-polish.' Can we capture this kind of paraphrase?

2.2   *Counting Events*

Does it make sense to assume that the nominal quantifier can choose to quantify over washing events, instead of cars, in an example like (4)? Although this may look odd at first sight, a suggestion to this end has been made by Krifka (1991a). Krifka investigates sentences like the one given in (12).

(12)   Four thousand ships passed the lock.

Krifka argues that (12) can be uttered truthfully in situations where the lock-keeper counts four thousand passages although she is very well aware of the fact that the overall number of ships ever using the river may not exceed two hundred. Krifka concludes that the determiner *four thousand* does not bind ships in that case, but is reinterpreted so as to count passages, shipwise (I do not recapitulate the actual formalism). Krifka also notes that his treatment of cardinals carries over to quantifiers like *most* and makes sense in examples like (13):

(13)   Most ships passed the lock at NIGHT$_F$.

Should we count events? The corresponding representation is given under (14):

(14) $R = \{e \mid \exists x(x \text{ is a car washed by Ludwig in } e)\}$
         $S = \{e \mid \exists x(x \text{ is a car washed by Ludwig in } e, \text{ using X-polish in } e)\}$
         (4) says: 'S comprises more than half of R'

Again, representation (14) can't do full justice to sentence (4). Although there might be cases where Ludwig is a serial car washer and we only are interested in washings, not cars, this still is not the standard reading of sentence (4). Nevertheless, reading (14) is unrestrictedly true in a situation like the one in (15).

(15)   C1 – e1 : with X   C2 – e4 : without   C3 – e7 : without
              – e2 : with X   – e5 : with X
              – e3 : with X   – e6 : with X
         C4 – e8: without   C5 – e9: without

Six out of nine washings are done with X-polish, undoubtedly a majority of washings. Nevertheless, X-polish never has touched three out of five cars and therefore we feel (4) to be false in scenario (15).

2.3   *Counting Pairs of Individuals and Events*

The final possible choice of parameters is full unselective binding. The nominal quantifier behaves as an adverbial one, binding more than one fixed parameter. In the case of example (4), this means that *most* count pairs of individuals and events. The corresponding representation is the one in (16):

(16) $R = \{\langle x, e \rangle \mid x$ is a car washed by Ludwig in $e)\}$
         $S = \{\langle x, e \rangle \mid x$ is a car washed by Ludwig in e, using X-polish in $e)\}$
         (4) says: 'S comprises more than half of R'

As long as we are talking about simple events of car washings, we know that the patient participant in the washing is unique. For this reason, we have a one-to-one relation between washing events and pairs of washing events and cars washed therein. This leads to the conclusion that the representations in (14) and (16) are in fact equivalent, and thus (16) cannot be more appropriate than (14). The format in (16) bears a certain resemblance to another counting problem known in the literature: the problem of counting farmers, donkeys, or pairs of farmers and donkeys in "donkey sentences" (see Heim 1982, 1990, Kamp 1981). This similarity will lead us to the "one-to-one reading."

2.4   *One Washing per Car*

Various discourse semantic accounts have been given to treat sentences like those under (17).

(17)   a. Mostly, if a farmer owns a donkey, he beats it.
         b. Most farmers who own a donkey beat it.

A notorious problem is this: What happens in a village where nine farmers own one donkey each, which they treat with great care, and one very rich farmer owns twenty donkeys and beats all of them? Are the sentences in (17) true in this village or not? If we count farmer-donkey pairs, we predict that the sentences are true in such a village. This seems, however, inappropriate. If we only count farmers who beat *some* of the donkeys they own, the sentences become false. The same strategy, however, would predict that a village with ten farmers, each owning ten donkeys, and each of them beating only one of these ten donkeys, will be a village where sentences (18a, b) are true. Nevertheless, the farmers of that village seem to have the right to complain that this characterization of their behavior with respect to donkeys is too negative.

(18)   a. Always if a farmer owns a donkey, he beats it.
       b. All farmers who own a donkey beat it.

The following suggestion might be a solution to this puzzle beyond the range of factors mentioned so far: Sentences like (17a, b) and (18a, b) simply are *inappropriate* in a situation where there are farmers who own more than one donkey. As soon as there is a one-to-one relation between farmers and donkeys, it doesn't matter anymore what we count. Sets of donkeys, sets of farmers, or sets of pairs of them all will yield one appropriate representation.

I want to suggest that the same observation holds for sentences like (4) to (6). It seems that we only would use sentence (4) in a situation where it is clear that Ludwig washed each car exactly once. Such a situation is depicted in (19). In these situations the representation strategies in (10), (14), and (16) all are equivalent.

(19)   C1 – e1: with X   C2 – e2: without   C3 – e3: with X
        C4 – e4: without   C5 – e5: with X

Sentence (4) is predicted to be true in situation (19), which is correct.

2.5   Summary

Sections 2.1 to 2.4 have shown the following: It is inappropriate to assume that the nominal quantifier binds the NP variable – as long as no further qualifications are made. However, it is equally inappropriate to assume that the nominal quantifier binds anything else available, let it be events, or pairs of events and individuals (=unselective binding). There is a requirement to the "context of utterance" in the sense of "what do I want to describe with the sentence" that there should be a one-to-one relation between events involved and individuals quantified over. This requirement is already known from the discussion of "donkey sentences."

Sentences like (4) to (6) involve focus. Focusing is known to be a device to relate an utterance to certain contexts – for instance, by suggesting that the context provides salient alternatives for the expression in focus. The relation between context and focusing has been studied extensively in Rooth (1995). However, the presence of a one-to-one function that relates objects and events in contexts where (4) can be uttered felicitously can't be due to focusing. We derive this from the observation that exactly the same type of proportion problems arise in cases like (17) and (18) where no focus or topics are in play.

These latter examples also support the view that the phenomenon in question has nothing to do with the presence of events. I want to stress this point for the following reason: Krifka (1991a) *does* sketch a way to encode the one-to-one relation between individuals and events (that is, ships and passings in example (13)). Qualifying the nature of the sum of all passing events, Krifka suggests the following representation:

> "There was a global NONITERATIVE event of passings of shipsize n, with a subevent of passings of shipsize m, such that m/n > 1/2."

The predicate NONITERATIVE as it is defined in Krifka (1991a) checks that no two of the atomic subevents of passing were done by the same ship, such that indeed there were as many ships as passings, such that what we count are indeed individuals. If we make sure that the "global noniterative event of passing ships" does not secretly miss any passings that would be relevant in the situation (and moreover destroy NONITERATIVITY), this will give a one-to-one-relation. But this way to reconstruct one-to-one relations attributes all relevant properties to the event involved. It can't do justice to (17) and (18).

As soon as the required one-to-one relation is present, we might use either of the representation formats in 2.1, 2.2, or 2.3. However, the representation in 2.3 is the only one that gives us a basis to spell out the one-to-one requirement, a basis that is in line with the observations concerning donkey sentences: The one-to-one relation has to hold between the objects that instantiate the variables that are unselectively bound. Conditions (20) and (21) contain the respective qualifications for sentence (4) (on the basis of representation (16)) and sentence (17).

(20) $R = \{\langle x, e \rangle \mid x \text{ is a car washed by Ludwig in } e\}$
       $S = \{\langle x, e \rangle \mid x \text{ is a car washed by Ludwig in } e, \text{ using X-polish in } e\}$
       $\forall x \forall y (x \in R \ \& \ y \in R \rightarrow \pi_i(x) \neq \pi_i(y))$ for all projection functions π_i on the ith place that are defined for R.
       (4) says: S 'comprises more than half of R'

(21) $R = \{\langle x, y \rangle \mid y \text{ is a donkey owned by farmer } x\}$
       $S = \{\langle x, y \rangle \mid y \text{ is a donkey that is beaten by farmer } x\}$
       $\forall x \forall y (x \in R \ \& \ y \in R \rightarrow \pi_i(x) \neq \pi_i(y))$ for all projection functions π_i on the ith place that are defined for R.

(17)   says: S 'comprises more than half of R'

Therefore I conclude that the nominal quantifiers in sentences (4) to (6) that carry a rise accent

> – associate with the focus indicated by the fall accent (in the sense of Rooth 1995)

– can do unselective binding over other indefinite NPs in their scope (see Kamp (1981), Heim (1982), Rooth (1995)).

– where a one-to-one requirement has to hold between the variables bound (as exemplified in (20), (21)).

I do not discuss the conceptual nature and origin of the one-to-one relation.

A final qualification of the one-to-one relation yet has to be made. Note that proper names and definite NPs also introduce discourse referents (in terms of DRT) or file cards (in terms of file change semantics). These discourse referents, although being active at that stage, are of course not quantified over with the nominal quantifier, and not mentioned in the one-to-one requirement. Example (22) demonstrates that *Ludwig* is accessible for further anaphoric reference. Moreover, if (20) was formulated on the basis of sets $R' = \{\langle L, x, e \rangle \mid x \text{ is a car washed by L}$ in e)$\}$ and $S' = \{\langle L, x, e \rangle \mid x \text{ is a car washed by L in e, using X-polish in e}\}$, the one-to-one requirement will state that exactly one person ($=$ Ludwig) has washed exactly one car exactly once – and that is too strong.

(22)   Ludwig$_1$ washed most/ cars with X-polish\. He$_1$ knew that this brand was the best.

Definite NPs show mixed behavior. Some can depend functionally on other items in the sentence, as the tractors depend on the farmers in (24). Then they are included in the one-to-one requirement and inaccessible for further reference. Others are absolute NPs, like the *Madonna of Szenstochau* in (23). They are independent as proper names are.

(23)   Most/ farmers visited the black Madonna$_1$ of Szenstochau in DECEM-BER\. She$_1$ is over 500 years old.

(24)   Most/ farmers drove the tractor$_1$ to PAUL'S\ garage. *It$_1$ is red.

DRT does justice to these observations by giving highest scope to definite NPs and names. The formalism in Section 4 will adopt this strategy. It is important because the spelling out of an appropriate one-to-one relation hinges on it.

3   The Division of Labor Between Syntax and Focus

In this section, we investigate whether another feature of "adverbial quantifiers associating with focus" as analyzed in Rooth (1995) carries over to the nominal case. Remember my preformal description of Rooth's semantic representation of example (1), which led to the quantification in (3). I repeat it for convenience: "The restrictor R of the adverbial quantifier is computed by taking the *union of the focus semantic value* of the sentence (in terms of Rooth 1995, 1985). The scope S consists of the *ordinary semantic value* of the sentence, and the adverbial quantifier binds *unselectively* over the free variables in the restrictor." This instruction does not mention the syntactic position of the adverbial quantifier at all. Thus, syntax can at most play an indirect role in the phenomenon in question: There might be syntactic restrictions as to the relative positions of focus and adverbial quantifier – we know such restrictions for German, for example – but syntax in and of itself does not say anything about the two arguments of the quantifier.

Nominal quantifiers, on the other hand, have never been suspected of getting their arguments from anywhere but syntax: The quantifier's restrictor *is* the N of the NP, and the scope *is* the denotation of the right sister node in the syntactic tree. Geilfuß (1995) develops a formal account for the examples in (4) to (6) that models the effects of focusing but remains conservative with respect to the influence of syntax. His account predicts that focusing like that in (4) to (6) can *restrict* the original restrictor (denoted by the N in NP), but cannot change it completely.[2] Roughly, the following steps take place:

(5)   Almost all/ tickets were sold at checker 4\.

(25) $R = [[\text{ticket}]]$ (= original restrictor)
$R' = [[\text{tickets}]] \cap \lambda x.$ x is something sold at checker 1, or 2, or 3, or 4, or. . .
$S = \lambda x.$ x is someting sold at checker 4
ALMOST-ALL(R',S)

The instructions in (25) rely on syntax in order to derive R and S and use focus in order to get the restriction R'. Can we find examples where the primacy of syntax over focus structure is challenged? The following examples, raised in Westerståhl (1985), seem to be of the relevant kind.

(26)   Many/ Scandinavians\ won the Nobel Prize in literature.

(27)   Three/ Chinese\ people were at the party.

(28)   No/ women\ were in the team.

Westerståhl notes that (26) does not state that a number of Scandinavians that would count as *many* Scandinavians have won the Nobel Prize in literature. Intuitively, (26) expresses that among those who won the Nobel Prize in literature we find comparatively many Scandinavians. One might suspect that *many* is always 'many relative to a given standard', and that the odd reading of (26) is due to the fact that already very few people are enough to be *many* winners of a Nobel Prize. However, this can't be the solution of the puzzle proposed by (26), for various reasons.

The first reason is that this can't explain why (29) differs in reading from (26). (29) states exactly what a traditional account of *many* will expect: The ratio of Scandinavians with a Nobel Prize per Scandinavians is big – compared to what would be normal (i.e. maybe 1 percent instead of 0.1 percent).

(29)   MANY Scandinavians [have won the Nobel Prize in LITERATURE]$_F$.
(Read the accents as in the sentence "MANY Russians are SMOKERS")

In contrast (26) measures a different ratio – the one we'd expect with the restrictor *people who won the Nobel Prize* and the scope *Scandinavians who won the Nobel Prize*.

Second, sentence (26) is even true if the nation in question is the biggest on earth, and the ratio of winners per nation is even rather bad. Imagine that five Scandinavians have won the Nobel Prize, one American, and one French person. Imagine moreover – counterfactually – that there are fifty million Scandinavians, one million Americans, and one million French people. Sentence (26) would still be true, although the national ratio of winners in Scandinavia is worse than the one for France and America.

Third, we actually *do* have to compute a ratio. We can't claim that (26) simply means that the size of the set of Scandinavians with a Nobel Prize in literature was big, maybe in comparison to the sizes of other sets of Nobel Prize winners. This is somewhat more tricky to see. Let me develop a scenario for an appropriate minimal pair. Imagine that I went to a party on Saturday. On Sunday, I can truthfully tell you about the *very same* party with the discourses (30–30a) and (30–30b).[3] It may be a bit tricky to keep in mind that the same accent patterns are to reflect different focused domains in (30a) and (30b), but longer reflection will show the difference in question.

(30)   Last Saturday I was at a party of Anthroposophers.
   a.   Many/ drunk [women\]$_F$ were at the party.
   b.   Few/ [drunk women\]$_F$ were at the party.

Imagine that Anthroposophers are sober people who do not tend to consume alcohol excessively, even on festive occasions. So the percentage of drunk people, and also of drunk women, compared to the overall number of guests was low. This is what sentence (30b) would report. Nevertheless the female Anthroposophers still lead a more frustrating life than their male companions, such that the percentage of drunk women among the drunk guests was higher than was to be expected – as is reported by (30a). What would an existential interpretation of *many* and *few* give us for these sentences? In both cases it comes down to saying something about the size of the set of drunk female guests at the party. (30a) would report that this set was bigger than expected. (30b) would say that this set was smaller than expected. Both sentences are true descriptions of the same world. But this is not possible. Examples (30a) and (30b) show that we have to compare the size of certain sets. The overall data suggest that the relevant sets can very easily be derived from the focus structure of the respective sentence. So, why shouldn't we simply adopt this solution?

Finally, example (27) shows that we do not face a topical contrast between *many* and other quantifiers, as has been suggested by Büring (this volume). According to Büring's theory of raise-fall accents, the raise accented item is contrasted with other contextual "topic objects" with respect to the property expressed by the focused part. Büring will predict that sentence (27) excludes the possibility that any other nation was represented by three visitors at the party. This, however, is not true.

In contrast to the previous suggestions, which either are vague or make incorrect predictions, we get perfectly correct representations if we assume that focus structure alone is what determines restrictor and scope in (26), (27), and (28). Let me make the point for (26), because it gives rise to the most distinctive effects on meaning. (31) is built up using the focus structure of (26), in the same way as we derived (25) for sentence (4).

(31) $R = \{x \mid x \text{ is a Scandinavian OR American OR Russian OR French OR} \ldots \text{ who won the Nobel Prize}\}$
         $S = \{x \mid x \text{ is a Scandinavian who won the Nobel Prize}\}$
         $\forall x \forall y (x \in R \ \& \ y \in R \rightarrow \pi_i(x) \neq \pi_i(y))$ for all projection functions π_i on the ith place that are defined for R (trivial in this case)

         (26) says: 'The ratio $|S|/|R|$ is big for what is to be expected in the context'[4]

It is important to note that the restrictor R is not gained by intersecting the denotation of the N of NP (*Scandinavians*) with anything derived from the focus structure, but in fact can only be computed as the union of the focus semantic value of the sentence in the sense of Rooth (1985, 1995). I call this process the *fully focus driven computation of arguments*.

Do all nominal quantifiers allow this radical influence of focusing? Interestingly, this is not the case. It is by now well known that determiners can be divided into two classes with different characteristics: the so-called weak and strong determiners. Strong determiners are those that presuppose the existence of an appropriate domain of quantification, introduced by the noun of NP, in the way illustrated in (32). Weak determiners, in contrast, do not carry any presuppositions about the extension of the denotation of N in their NP. I follow Partee's classification (1988) of determiners as "strong" and "weak."

(32)   Examples of strong quantifiers:
         all A's (of a given totality of A's)
         most A's (of a given totality of A's)
         half of the A's (of a given totality of A's)
         none of the A's . . .
         Examples of weak determiners:
         many A's, *some* A's, *an* A, A's, . . .

I do not want to take a stand about how far the position of an NP determines or is connected with the status of its determiner (see de Hoop 1992, Reinhart 1995).

The distinction between weak and strong determiners is essential when it comes to interaction of focus with nominal quantifiers. We get fully focus driven computation of arguments only for weak determiners, not for strong ones. This is demonstrated by examples (33) and (34), which I contrast with (26) and (28). I give the respective focus driven paraphrases for the meanings of (26) and (28) and the paraphrases that we would expect for (33) and (34). The crucial observation is that (26a) and (28a) reflect the meaning of (26) and (28), but not (33a) and (34a), for (33) and (34):

(26)   Many/ Scandinavians\ won the Nobel Prize in literature.
        a. 'Many of the (Scandinavian, American, French, Russian, . . .) winners of the Nobel Prize were Scandinavians.'

(28)   No/ women\ were in the team.
        a. 'None of the (male, female) members of the team were women'

(33)   All/ Chinese\ were at the party
        a. *'All of the (Chinese, German, French, . . .) guests at the party were Chinese'

(34)   Most/ students\ demonstrated against the new law.
        a. *'Most of the (student, laborer, jobless, professionals) demonstrators were students'

The initial examples have shown that (33)/(34) can't be because strong nominal quantifiers do not interact with focus at all. They simply pose syntactic restrictions on the position of a focus they want to interact with, while weak determiners are more liberal in that respect. (35) summarizes the results of the present section.

(35)   Weak determiners can interact with focus in any position.
        Strong determiners may not c-command the focus they interact with.

A more thorough discussion of the nature of the weak/strong distinction in relation to focus phenomena can be found in Eckardt (1994).

Appendix A: A Formal Account

The previous discussion has shown that we have to provide an interpretation of focus plus a compositional dynamic semantic framework (including unselective binding) in order to treat the data. Essentially, I use a refined version of the formalism in Rooth (1995). Sentences of English will first be translated into formulae of DPL+, a version of the logic of Groenendijk and Stokhof (1991), where I have added lambda abstraction over variables of type e. The denotations of these formulas are the meaning of expressions of English. The resulting formalism allows more elaborated definitions of generalized quantifiers than Rooth's original account, and moreover, scoping of proper names and definites. Other dynamic frameworks that account for focus interpretation can be found in Chierchia (1995).

A.1   The Logic DPL+

We assume a logical language L based on constants $C = \{c_1, c, c', \ldots\}$, variables $V = \{v, v_1, v', \ldots\}$ and discourse referents $D = \{d, d_1, d', \ldots\}$. Constants, variables, and discourse referents are called *terms* of L. Moreover we have n-ary predicate constants $P = \{Q_n, R_n, S_n, \ldots\}$ and n-ary predicate variables $X = \{X_{1,n}, X_{2,n}, X_{3,n}, \ldots\}$ for all $n > 0$. (I usually omit the arity subscript n.) The following expressions are defined in L:

A.1.1   Formulas

(1) If R is an n-ary relation then $R(t_1, \ldots, t_n)$ is a formula of L, where $t_1, \ldots, t_n$ are terms.

(2) If Φ is a formula in L, then $\forall d_i(\Phi)$, $\exists d_i(\Phi)$, $\neg\Phi$ are formulae, where d_i is a discourse referent.

(3) If Φ and Ψ are formulas, then $\Phi \,\&\, \Psi$, Φ/Ψ, $\Phi \rightarrow \Psi$ are formulas.

(4) If Φ and Ψ are formulas, then $MOSTd_i(\Phi, \Psi)$, $MOST(\Phi, \Psi)$, $MANY$ (Φ, Ψ), $ALL(\Phi, \Psi)$ are formulas.

A.1.2   Relations

(1) If R is a predicate symbol of arity n, then R is an n-ary relation.

(2) If X_i is a predicate variable of arity n, then X_i is an n-ary relation.

(3) Any formula is a relation of arity 0.

(4) If Δ is an n-ary relation, then $\lambda v_i.\Delta$ is a relation of arity $n + 1$.

A.1.3   Models for DPL+ Languages

A model **M** of a DPL+ language L consists of the following ingredients:

- A domain M of individuals
- The set ASS of mappings of discourse referents into M. These mappings are denoted as G, H, K, . . .
- Sets $M^n \times ASS^2 := \{\langle m_1, \ldots, m_n, \langle G, G\rangle\rangle \mid G \in ASS \,\&\, m_i \in M\}$ for $n > 0$.
- An interpretation function F, mapping constants, and n-ary predicate constants of L onto individuals and sets in M^n, respectively.
- The set of variable assignments $M^V = \{g, g', h, \ldots\}$ for L.
- The set $C = \{c, c', c1, \ldots\}$ of "context" functions mapping variables $X_{i,n}$ into $M^n \times ASS^2$.

We assume that the domain of individuals can also include event objects (like washings, sellings, and so on).

A.1.4   Interpretation of L in Models **M**

Each formula and relation Π receive an interpretation $[[\Pi]]^{M,g,c}$ in **M** relative to a variable assignment g and a "context" assignment c.

(1) If R is an n-ary relation symbol, then

$$[[R]]^{M,g,c} = \{\langle m_1, \ldots, m_n, \langle G, G \rangle\rangle \mid G \in ASS \ \& \ \langle m_1, \ldots, m_n \rangle \in F(R)\}$$

(2) If X_i is an n-ary relation symbol, then $[[X_i]]^{M,g,c} = c(X_i)$

(3) If R is an n-ary relation (with n > 0), then
  - $[[R(c)]]^{M,g,c} = \{\langle m_1, \ldots, m_n, \langle G, H \rangle\rangle \mid \langle F(c), m_1, \ldots, m_n, \langle G, H \rangle\rangle$
    $\in [[R]]^{M,g,c}\}$
  - $[[R(v)]]^{M,g,c} = \{\langle m_1, \ldots, m_n, \langle G, H \rangle\rangle \mid \langle g(v), m_1, \ldots, m_n, \langle G, H \rangle\rangle$
    $\in [[R]]^{M,g,c}\}$
  - $[[R(d)]]^{M,g,c} = \{\langle m_1, \ldots, m_n, \langle G, H \rangle\rangle \mid \langle G(d), m_1, \ldots, m_n, \langle G, H \rangle\rangle$
    $\in [[R]]^{M,g,c}\}$

  (Application to constants, variables, and discourse referents)

(4) If Δ is an n-ary relation (with n $\geq$ 0), then

$$[[\lambda v.\Delta]]^{M,g,c} = \{\langle m_1, \ldots, m_n, \langle G, H \rangle\rangle \mid \langle m_2, \ldots, m_n, \langle G, H \rangle\rangle$$
$$\in [[\Delta]]^{M,g:v \to m1,c}\}$$

(5) If Φ and Ψ are formulas, then
  - $[[\neg\Phi]]^{M,g,c} = \{\langle G, G \rangle \mid \neg\exists K(\langle G, K \rangle \in [[\Phi]]^{M,g,c})\}$
  - $[[\Phi \ \& \ Y]]^{M,g,c} = \{\langle G, H \rangle \mid \exists K(\langle G, K \rangle \in [[\Phi]]^{M,g} \ \& \ \langle K, H \rangle$
    $\in [[\Psi]]^{M,g,c})\}$
  - $[[\Phi \lor \Psi]]^{M,g,c} = \{\langle G, G \rangle \mid \exists K(\langle G, K \rangle \in [[\Phi]]^{M,g,c} \lor \langle G, K \rangle$
    $\in [[\Psi]]^{M,g,c})\}$
  - $[[\Phi \to \Psi]]^{M,g,c} = \{\langle G, G \rangle \mid \forall K(\langle G, K \rangle \in [[\Phi]]^{M,g,c} \to \exists L(\langle K, L \rangle$
    $\in [[\Psi]]^{M,g,c}))\}$
  - $[[\exists d_i(\Phi)]]^{M,g,c} = \{\langle G, H \rangle \mid \exists K(G = K|_{di} \ \& \ \langle K, H \rangle \in [[\Phi]]^{M,g,c})\}$
  - $[[\forall d_i(\Phi)]]^{M,g,c} = \{\langle G, G \rangle \mid \forall K(G = K|_{di} \to \exists H(\langle K, H \rangle$
    $\in [[\Phi]]^{M,g,c}))\}$
  - $[[MOSTd_i(\Phi, \Psi)]]^{M,g,c} = \{\langle G, G \rangle \mid \mathbf{A}/\mathbf{B} > 1/2\}$ where $\mathbf{A}$ and $\mathbf{B}$
    abbreviate the following:
    $\mathbf{A} := |\{\langle K, H \rangle \mid G = K|_{di} \ \& \ \langle K, H \rangle \in [[\Phi]]^{M,g,c} \ \& \ \exists L(\langle H, L \rangle$
    $\in [[\Psi]]^{M,g,c})\}|$
    $\mathbf{B} := |\{\langle K, H \rangle \mid G = K|_{di} \ \& \ \langle K, H \rangle \in [[\Phi]]^{M,g,c}\}|$

(6)
  - $[[ALL(\Phi, \Psi)]]^{M,g,c} = \{\langle G, G \rangle \mid \mathbf{A} = \mathbf{B}\}$
  - $[[MOST(\Phi, \Psi)]]^{M,g,c} = \{\langle G, G \rangle \mid |\mathbf{A}| \div |\mathbf{B}| > 1/2\}$
  - $[[MANY(\Phi, \Psi)]]^{M,g,c} = \{\langle G, G \rangle \mid |\mathbf{A}| \div |\mathbf{B}| > z\}$

  where z is a contextually given expected value, and $\mathbf{A}$ and $\mathbf{B}$ stand for the
  following:
  $\mathbf{A} := \{\langle G, H \rangle \mid H \in ASS\} \cap ([[\Phi]]^{M,g,c} \cap [[\Psi]]^{M,g,c})$
  $\mathbf{B} := \{\langle G, H \rangle \mid H \in ASS\} \cap [[\Phi]]^{M,g,c}$

Notation: $G = K|_{di}$ abbreviates $G(d) = K(d)$ for all d except d_i.

A more thorough discussion of the interpretation of formulas can be found in Groenendijk and Stokhof (1991). The generalized quantifiers and lambda abstraction are additional features of the present logic. Lambda abstraction is a spellout of the semantic combination operations in Rooth (1995) and Krifka (1991b). Lambda abstraction necessitates the distinction between variables and discourse referents, a distinction that was not included in Groenendijk/Stokhof's original account.

Groenendijk and Stokhof give a recursive definition for actively bound variables in their paper. This definition can be modified into a definition for actively bound discourse referents in the present framework. This notion is important in order to account for the data: The actively bound discourse referents in an unselective quantification are the basis for the one-to-one relation of the contextual restriction to certain uses of unselective binding (see Section 2). I do not spell out the respective definitions here.

A.2   *Semantic Representation*

We now interpret sentences of English or German as objects in DPL+ models. These sentences are assumed to have undergone an appropriate standard adaption before semantic interpretation (LF). Especially, I assume that all NPs have been raised, leaving behind a coindexed trace, which is used to instantiate the appropriate parameter in the verbal predicate. It is important to remember that proper names and absolute definite NPs (in the sense of section 2.5) are raised above all other quantifications. Finally, I assume a tacit existential quantifier $\mathbf{E}$ for event arguments, having the same meaning as the indefinite article a.

A rise accent on a determiner has the following effect at LF:

> The determiner is adjoined to the node dominating the NP and its sister node: $[[\text{Det}/\text{N}]_{\text{NPi}}\text{XP}] \rightarrow [\text{Det}/[[- \text{N}]_{\text{NPi}}\text{XP}]]$

The rise accented determiner is later interpreted in association with a focus in N or XP. The determinerless NP is interpreted as if an indefinite article were in place of the empty bit "$-$".

A.2.1   *Ordinary Semantic Values $\|.\|_o$ for Lexical Items in DPL+*

(1) For nouns N, $\|N\|_o$ is a unary relation symbol N' of L.

(2) For intransitive verbs V, $\|V\|_o$ is a binary relation symbol V' of L (relation between individual and event)

(3) For transitive verbs V, $\|V\|_o$ is a ternary relation symbol V' of L (relation between subject, object, and event)

(4) For adverbs A, $\|A\|_o$ is a unary relation symbol A' in L (predicate over adverbs)

(5) For proper names P, $\|P\|_o$ is a constant in L.

(6) For traces t_i, we have $\|t_i\|_o = v_i$, the variable with index i in L.

(7) We assume a distinguished event trace t_e in the appropriate position and $\|t_e\|_o = v_e$.[5]

A.2.2   Ordinary Semantic Values for Complex Expressions

Remark: We treat the interpretation of NPs syncategorematically, as this spares us the introduction of higher order functors in DPL+.

(8)   Variables and relations are combined by functional application.

(9)   If P is a proper name, we interpret $[P_i \; XP]$ as follows:

(10) $\| [P_i \; XP] \|_o = \exists d_i (\|P\|_o = d_i \; \& \; [\lambda x_i. \|XP\|_o(d_i)])$
      $\| [a \; N]_i \; XP \|_o = \exists d_i (\|N\|_o(d_i) \; \& \; [\lambda x_i. \|XP\|_o(d_i)])$

(11) $\| [\text{every } N]_i \; XP \|_o = \forall d_i (\|N\|_o(d_i) \; \to \; [\lambda x_i. \|XP\|_o(d_i)])$

(12) $\| [\text{most } N]_i \; XP \|_o = \text{MOST} d_i (\|N\|_o(d_i); [\lambda x_i. \|XP\|_o(d_i)])$

(13) $\| \mathbf{E} \; XP \|_o = \exists d_e (\lambda x_e. \|XP\|_o(d_e))$

(14) $\| [-N]_i \; XP \|_o = \exists d_i (\|N\|_o(d_i) \; \& \; \lambda x_i. \|XP\|_o(d_i))$

A.3   Focus Semantic Representation

We make use of the strategy of Rooth (1985), where focusing evokes a set of alternative values that might have replaced the actual one in the present context. Due to the parsimony of the present formalism, our possibilities are limited to give alternatives for all kinds of relations of arity n and for individuals. This is enough for all examples discussed in the text. We are, however, not able to focus full NPs and get contrasting NP meanings. Eventually, the use of a fully compositional formalism like DMG (Groenendijk and Stokhof 1990) can overcome this limitation.

A.3.1   Focus Semantic Value $\|.\|_f$ for Unfocused Lexical Items

For all unfocused lexical items α, we assume that $\|\alpha\|_f := \{\|\alpha\|_o\}$

A.3.2   Focus Semantic Value $\|.\|_f$ for a Focused Constituent α_f

(1)   For nouns N, $\|N_f\|_f = \{\|N\|_o, X_{k1}, X_{k2}, X_{k3}, \ldots\}$ where $X_{k1}, X_{k2}, X_{k3}, \ldots$ are relation variables of arity 1, and the relevant context function c maps X_{ki} to salient alternatives of $\|N\|_o$.

(2)   For intransitive verbs V, $\|V_f\|_f = \{\|V\|_o, X_{k1}, X_{k2}, X_{k3}, \ldots\}$ where $X_{k1}, X_{k2}, X_{k3}, \ldots$ are relation variables of arity 2, and the relevant context function c maps X_{ki} to salient alternatives of $\|V\|_o$.

(3)   For transitive verbs V, $\|V_f\|_f = \{\|V\|_o, X_{k1}, X_{k2}, X_{k3}, \ldots\}$ where $X_{k1}, X_{k2}, X_{k3}, \ldots$ are relation variables of arity 3, and the relevant context function c maps X_{ki} to salient alternatives of $\|V\|_o$.

(4)   For adverbs A, $\|A_f\|_f = \{\|A\|_o, X_{k1}, X_{k2}, X_{k3}, \ldots\}$ where $X_{k1}, X_{k2}, X_{k3}, \ldots$ are relation variables of arity 1, and the relevant context function c maps X_{ki} to salient alternatives of $\|A\|_o$.

(5) For proper names P, $\|P_f\|_f = \{\|P\|_o\} \cup \{m \mid m$ in M is a contextual alternative individual for $F(\|P\|_o)\}$

(6) For VP projections VP′ next to an NP with index i, $\|VP'_f\|_f = \{\|VP'\|_o,$ $X_{k1}, X_{k2}, X_{k3}, \ldots\}$ where $X_{k1}, X_{k2}, X_{k3}, \ldots$ are relation variables of arity 1, and the relevant context function c maps X_{ki} to salient alternatives of $\|N\|_o$.

A.3.3   Combination of Focus Semantic Values

$\|\alpha\beta\|_f = \{\alpha_1 \infty \beta_1 \mid \alpha_1 \in \|\alpha\|_f \,\&\, \beta_1 \in \|\beta\|_f$ and ∞ is the mode of combination one would use to compute $\|\alpha\beta\|_o\}$

A.3.4   Interpretation of Focus Sensitive Nominal Quantifiers Det/

The nodes [Det/ X] are assigned the following semantic interpretation:

$\|[\text{every}/X]\|_o := \text{ALL}(\cup\|X\|_f; \|X\|_o)$
$\|[\text{most}/X]\|_o := \text{MOST}(\cup\|X\|_f; \|X\|_o)$
$\|[\text{many}/X]\|_o := \text{MANY}(\cup\|X\|_f; \|X\|_o)$

A.4   An Example

In order to see the mechanism at work, we derive the representation of sentence (A):

(A)   Ludwig washed most/ cars carefully\.

The fall accent is interpreted as a focus. The rise accent has been accounted for in A.3. The input structure of semantic interpretation essentially appears as in (A.1).

(A.1) $[\text{Ludwig}_1[\text{most}/[[- \text{car}]_2[\mathbf{E}[[\text{wash } t_e\, t_2\, t_1] \text{ carefully}_f]]]]]$

I give translations of the nodes of this tree, and moreover the interpretations of the respective DPL+ expressions in a model M relative to an assignment g and a context function c.

(A.2) $\|\text{wash}\|_o = \text{WASH}$
$[[\text{WASH}]]^{M,g,c} = \{\langle e, b, a, \langle G, G\rangle\rangle \mid a \text{ washes } b \text{ in } e\}$

(A.3) $\|\text{wash } t_e\|_o = \text{WASH}(v_e)$
$[[\text{WASH}(v_e)]]^{M,g,c}$
$= \{\langle b, a, \langle G, G\rangle\rangle \mid \langle g(v_e), b, a, \langle G, G\rangle\rangle \in [[\text{WASH}]]^{M,g,c}\}$
$= \{\langle b, a, \langle G, G\rangle\rangle \mid a \text{ washes } b \text{ in } g(v_e)\}$

(A.4) $\|\text{wash } t_e\, t_2\, t_1\|_o = \text{WASH}(v_e, v_2, v_1)$
$[[\text{WASH}(v_e, v_2, v_1)]]^{M,g,c}$
$= \{\langle G, G\rangle \mid \langle g(v_e), g(v_2), g(v_1), \langle G, G\rangle\rangle \in [[\text{WASH}]]^{M,g,c}\}$
$= \{\langle G, G\rangle \mid g(v_1) \text{washes } g(v_2) \text{in } g(v_e)\}$

(A.5) $\|[[$wash $t_e\, t_2\, t_1]$carefully$_f]\|_o =$ WASH (v_e, v_2, v_1) & CAREFUL(v_e)

[[WASH (v_e, v_2, v_1) & CAREFUL $(v_e)]]^{M,g,c}$

$= \{\langle G, G\rangle \mid \langle g(v_e), g(v_2), g(v_1), \langle G, G\rangle\rangle \in [[$WASH$]]^{M,g,c}$ &

$\langle g(v_e), \langle G, G\rangle\rangle \in [[$CAREFUL$]]^{M,g,c}\}$

$= \{\langle G, G\rangle \mid g(v_1)$washes $g(v_2)$ in $g(v_e)$, and $g(v_e)$ is performed carefully$\}$

(We have omitted the reduction of dynamic conjunction to this simple form. This is trivial in the present case, as the conjuncts bear no dynamic potential.)

(A.6) $\|[\mathbf{E}[[$wash $t_e\, t_2\, t_1]$carefully$_f]]\|_o$

$= \exists \mathbf{d_e}(\lambda \mathbf{v_e}($WASH$(v_e, v_2, v_1)$ & CAREFUL$(v_e))(\mathbf{d_e}))$

$[[\lambda v_e($WASH (v_e, v_2, v_1) & CAREFUL$(v_e))(d_e)]]^{M,g,c}$

$= \{\langle G, G\rangle \mid \langle G(d_e), \langle G, G\rangle\rangle \in [[\lambda v_e($WASH$(v_e, v_2, v_1)$ &

CAREFUL$(v_e))]]^{M,g,c}\}$

$= \{\langle G, G\rangle \mid g(v_1)$washes $g(v_2)$in $G(d_e)$, and $G(d_e)$ is performed carefully$\}$

$[[\exists \mathbf{d_e}(\lambda \mathbf{v_e}($WASH$(v_e, v_2, v_1)$ & CAREFUL$(v_e))(\mathbf{d_e}))]]^{M,g,c}$

$= \{\langle G, H\rangle \mid G = H|_{d_e}$ & $\exists K(\langle H, K\rangle \in$

$[[\lambda v_e($WASH(v_e, v_2, v_1) & CAREFUL$(v_e))(d_e)]]^{M,g,c}\}$

$= \{\langle G, H\rangle \mid G = H|_{d_e}$ & $\langle H, H\rangle \in$

$[[\lambda v_e($WASH(v_e, v_2, v_1) & CAREFUL$(v_e))(d_e)]]^{M,g,c}\}$

$= \{\langle G, H\rangle \mid G = H|_{de}$ & $g(v_1)$ washes $g(v_2)$ in $H(d_e)$, and $H(d_e)$ is performed carefully$\}$

(A.7) $\|[[- car]_2[\mathbf{E}[[$wash $t_e\, t_2\, t_1]$carefully$_f]]]\|_o$

$= \exists \mathbf{d_2}(\mathbf{CAR(d_2)}$& $\lambda \mathbf{v_2}[\exists \mathbf{d_e}(\lambda \mathbf{v_e}($WASH$(v_e, v_2, v_1)$ & CAREFUL$(v_e))$

$(\mathbf{d_e}))](\mathbf{d_2}))$

$[[\exists d_2($CAR(d_2) & $\lambda v_2[\exists d_e(\lambda v_e($WASH$(v_e, v_2, v_1)$ & CAREFUL$(v_e))$

$(d_e))](d_2))]]^{M,g,c}$

$= \{\langle G, H\rangle \mid \exists K(G = K|_{d2}$ & $\langle K, H\rangle \in [[\mathbf{CAR(d_2)}$ &

$\lambda \mathbf{v_2}[\exists \mathbf{d_e}(\lambda \mathbf{v_e}($WASH$(v_e, v_2, v_1)$ & CAREFUL$(v_e))(d_e))](\mathbf{d_2}))]]^{M,g,c})\}$

$= \{\langle G, H\rangle \mid \exists K(G = K|_{d2}$ & $\exists J(\langle K, J\rangle \in [[CAR(d_2)]]^{M,g,c}$ &

$\langle J, H\rangle \in [[\lambda v_2[\exists d_e(\lambda v_e($WASH$(v_e, v_2, v_1)$ & CAREFUL$(v_e))(d_e))]$

$(d_2))]]^{M,g,c})\}$

$= \{\langle G, H\rangle \mid \exists K(G = K|_{d2}$ & $\langle K, K\rangle \in [[$CAR $(d_2)]]^{M,g,c}$ &

$\langle K, H\rangle \in [[\lambda v_2[\exists d_e(\lambda v_e($WASH$(v_e, v_2, v_1)$ & CAREFUL$(v_e))(d_e))]$

$(d_2))]]^{M,g,c})\}$

$= \{\langle G, H\rangle \mid \exists K(G = K|_{d2}$ & $K(d_2)$is a car &

$K = H|_{de}$ & $g(v1)$ washes $H(d_2)$ in $H(d_e)$ and $H(d_e)$ is performed carefully$)\}$

$= \{\langle G, H\rangle \mid G = H|_{d2, de}$ & $H(d_2)$ is a car & $g(v1)$ washes $H(d_2)$ in $H(d_e)$ and $H(d_e)$ is performed carefully$)\}$

The next step consists of the interpretation of the rise-accented quantifier, which involves focus. Therefore we have to compute the focus semantic value of the node reached so far. We start at the lexical level with the focused item "carefully":

(A.8) $\|[\text{carefully}_f]\|_f = \{\|\text{carefully}\|_o, X1, X2, X3, \ldots\}$
A sensible context gives a set like the following:
$\{\{\langle e, \langle G, G \rangle\rangle \mid e$ is performed carefully$\}$,
$\{\langle e, \langle G, G \rangle\rangle \mid e$ is performed normally$\}$,
$\{\langle e, \langle G, G \rangle\rangle \mid e$ is performed sloppily$\}$,
$\{\langle e, \langle G, G \rangle\rangle \mid e$ is performed thoughtlessly$\}, \ldots\}$

(A.9) $\|\text{wash } t_e\, t_2\, t_1\|_f = \{\text{WASH}(v_e, v_2, v_1)\}$
because no focusing was involved in the derivation of this value.

(A.10) $\|[[\text{wash } t_e\, t_2\, t_1]\ \text{carefully}_f]\|_f = \{\text{WASH}(v_e, v_2, v_1)\ \&\ \text{CAREFUL}(v_e),$
$\text{WASH}(v_e, v_2, v_1)\ \&\ X1(v_e),\ \text{WASH}(v_e, v_2, v_1)\ \&\ X2(v_e), \ldots\}$

In the model, we get the following set (by computations analogous to (A.5)):

$\{\{\langle G, G\rangle \mid g(v_1)$ washes $g(v_2)$ in $g(v_e)$, and $g(v_e)$ is performed **carefully**$\}$,
$\{\langle G, G\rangle \mid g(v_1)$ washes $g(v_2)$ in $g(v_e)$, and $g(v_e)$ is performed **normally**$\}$,
$\{\langle G, G\rangle \mid g(v_1)$ washes $g(v_2)$ in $g(v_e)$, and $g(v_e)$ is performed **sloppily**$\}$,
$\ldots\}$

(A.11) $\|[[\,-\text{car}]_2[\mathbf{E}[[\text{wash } t_e\, t_2\, t_1]\ \text{carefully}_f]]]\|_f =$
$\{\exists d_2(\text{CAR}(d_2)\ \&\ \lambda v_2[\exists d_e(\lambda v_e(\text{WASH}(v_e, v_2, v_1)\ \&\ \mathbf{CAREFUL}(v_e))$
$(d_e))](d_2)),$
$\exists d_2(\text{CAR}(d_2)\ \&\ \lambda v_2[\exists d_e(\lambda v_e(\text{WASH}(v_e, v_2, v_1)\ \&\ \mathbf{X1}(v_e))(d_e))](d_2)),$
$\exists d_2(\text{CAR}(d_2)\ \&\ \lambda v_2[\exists d_e(\lambda v_e(\text{WASH}(v_e, v_2, v_1)\ \&\ \mathbf{X2}(v_e))(d_e))](d_2)),$
$\ldots\}$

In model M with context c and assignment g, this will yield the set

$\{\{\langle G, H\rangle \mid G = H|_{d2,de}\ \&\ H(d_2)$ is a car $\&\ g(v1)$ washes $H(d_2)$ in $H(d_e)$
and $H(d_e)$ is performed **carefully**$)\}$,
$\{\langle G, H\rangle \mid G = H|_{d2,de}\ \&\ H(d_2)$ is a car $\&\ g(v1)$ washes $H(d_2)$ in $H(d_e)$
and $H(d_e)$ is performed **normally**$)\}$,
$\{\langle G, H\rangle \mid G = H|_{d2,de}\ \&\ H(d_2)$ is a car $\&\ g(v_1)$ washes $H(d_2)$ in $H(d_e)$
and $H(d_e)$ is performed **sloppily**$)\}, \ldots\}$

(A.12) $\|[\text{most}/[[\,-\text{car}]_2[\mathbf{E}[[\text{wash } t_e\, t_2\, t_1]\ \text{carefully}_f]]]]\|_o =$
$\text{MOST}(A, B)$ where
$A = \cup\|[[\,-\text{car}]_2[\mathbf{E}[[\text{wash } t_e\, t_2\, t_1]\ \text{carefully}_f]]]\|_f$
$= \{\langle G'H'\rangle \mid G' = H'|_{d2,de}\ \&\ H'(d_2)$ is a car $\&\ g(v1)$ washes $H'(d_2)$ in
$H'(d_e)$ and $H'(d_e)$ is performed **somehow**$)\}$
$B = \|[[\,-\text{car}]_2[\mathbf{E}[[\text{wash } t_e\, t_2\, t_1]\ \text{carefully}_f]]]\|_o$
$[[\text{MOST}(A, B)]]^{M,g,c}$
$= \{\langle G, G\rangle;\ |\{\langle G, H\rangle;\ H \in \text{ASS}\} \cap (A \cap B)| \div |\{\langle G, H\rangle;\ H \in \text{ASS}\} \cap A| >$
$1/2\}$
$= \{\langle G, G\rangle;\ |\{\langle G, H'\rangle | G' = H'|_{d2,de}\ \&\ H'(d_2)$ is a car $\&\ g(v_1)$ washes
$H'(d_2)$ in $H'(d_e)$ and

$H'(d_e)$ is performed **carefully**)$\} \mid \div$
$\mid\{\langle G, H'\rangle \mid G = H'\mid_{d2,de} \,\& \, H(d_2)$ is a car $\& \, g(v_1)$ washes $H'(d_2)$ in $H'(d_e)$
and $H'(d_e)$ is performed **somehow**)$\}\}\mid > 1/2\}$

This says that $g(v_1)$ has washed more cars carefully than otherwise. Note that the one-to-one requirement discussed in section 2 can now be imposed on the pairs of objects denoted by d_2 and d_e, the actively bound variables in the quantification. The final step consists of transporting the value of $g(v_1)$ to the value of the input assignment for d_1.

(A.13) $\|[\text{Ludwig}_1 \, [\text{most}/[[- \text{car}]_2[\mathbf{E}[[\text{wash } t_e \, t_2 \, t_1] \, \text{carefully}_f]]]]]\|_0$
    $= \exists d_1(d_1 = \text{LUDWIG} \,\& \, (\lambda v_1.\text{MOST}(\Phi, \Psi))(d_1))$ with Φ and Ψ
    as in (A.11) and (A.7).

This denotes the following set in model M, context c, and assignment g:

$\{\langle G, G\rangle \mid G(d_1) = \text{Ludwig} \,\&$
$\mid\{\langle G, H'\rangle \mid G = H'\mid_{d2,de} \,\& \, H'(d_2)$ is a car $\& \, G(d_1)$ washes $H'(d_2)$ in $H'(d_e)$
and $H'(d_e)$ is performed **carefully**)$\} \mid \div$
$\mid\{\langle G, H'\rangle \mid G = H'\mid_{d2,de} \,\& \, H(d_2)$ is a car $\& \, G(d_1)$ washes $H'(d_2)$ in $H'(d_e)$
and $H'(d_e)$ is performed **somehow**)$\}\}\mid > 1/2\}$

The denotation of (A) is thus nonempty iff there are more cars plus washings that Ludwig performed carefully than there were overall car washings by Ludwig. With a one-to-one qualification, this means that Ludwig has washed each one of the cars involved once, and most of them carefully. Ludwig is still available for further anaphoric reference, while cars and washings are not. This matches the data in question.

Notes

1   The semiformal paraphrases given in the text differ from Rooth's and my own later treatment insofar as I suppress all technicalities of the dynamic representation format that is necessary for Rooth (1995) and the present data.
2   Apart from that, he doesn't consider unselective binding, which section 2 shows to be necessary.
3   I am not allowed to utter (30–30a–30b), though, for reasons of overall discourse coherence.
4   This treatment of *many* has been suggested by Partee (1988), although she would never let focus govern syntax, (personal communication).
5   Admittedly this way to account for the introduction of the event parameter may be a bit crude, but it will do for the present purpose.

References

Chierchia, G. 1995. *Dynamics of Meaning*. University of Chicago Press, Chicago.
Eckardt, R. 1994. Adverbs in Focus, ESPRIT Basic Research Project 6852 "DYANA", DYANA deliverable R2.2.B, 289-333, IMS, University of Stuttgart.

Geilfuß, J. 1992. Nominal Quantifiers and Association with Focus. ConSole I proceedings. Sole Publications, Amsterdam.

Groenendijk, J., and Stokhof, M. 1990. Dynamic Montague Grammar. In: Kálmán, L., Pólos, L. (eds.), *Proceedings of the Second Symposium on Logic and Language*. Akadémiai Kiadó, Budapest.

Groenendijk, J., and Stokhof, M. 1991. Dynamic Predicate Logic. In: *Linguistics and Philosophy* 14, 39–100.

Heim, I. 1982. The Semantics of Definite and Indefinte Noun Phrases. Ph.D. dissertation, University of Massachusetts, Amherst.

Heim, I. 1990. E-type pronouns and donkey anaphora, *Linguistics and Philosophy*, 13, 137–177.

Hoop, H. de. 1992. Case configuration and NP interpretation. Ph.D. dissertation. University of Groningen.

Kamp, J. A. W. 1981. "A theory of truth and semantic representation." In J. Groenendijk, T. Janssen, and M. Stokhof (eds.), *Formal Methods in the Study of Language*, 277–321. Mathematical Centre, Amsterdam.

Krifka, M. 1991a. 4000 ships passed through the lock. *Linguistics and Philosophy*, 13, 487–520.

Krifka, M. 1991b. A framework for focus-sensitive quantification. *SALT* 2, 215–236.

Partee, B. H. 1988. Many Quantifiers. In *Proceedings of ESCOL 1988*. Department of Linguistics, Ohio State University.

Reinhart, T. 1995. Interface strategies. OTS Working Paper TL 95-002, OTS, Utrecht University, Utrecht.

Rooth, M. 1985. Association with Focus. Ph.D. dissertation, University of Massachusetts, Amherst.

Rooth, M. 1995. Indefinites, adverbs of quantification and focus semantics. In Carlson, G., and Pelletier, J. (eds.), *The Generic Book*. University of Chicago Press, Chicago.

Westerståhl, D. 1985. Determiners and context sets. In van Benthem, J., and ter Meulen, A. (eds.), *Generalized quantifiers in natural language*, Foris, Dordrecht, 47–71.

10   Topic, Focus, and Weak Quantifiers

GERHARD JÄGER

Abstract

This chapter is an attempt to establish dynamic semantics, in particular the Dynamic Modal Predicate Logic of Groenendijk et al. (1996), as a tool for the analysis of information structure phenomena. It is argued that the common distinction between familiar and novel discourse referents/file cards that can be found in DRT, File Change Semantics, or Dynamic Predicate Logic is not fine-grained enough to cover a certain "quasi-anaphoric" behavior of weak quantifiers in one of their readings. First, it is investigated under which syntactic and prosodic circumstances this reading arises. Second, the usage of two distinct layers of discourse entities is explained and justified. It turns out that this gives us the appropriate tool to account for the observed phenomena. Finally, a tentative proposal is made as to how this analysis can be extended in such a way that it covers certain aspects of the stage level–individual level distinction.

1   Introduction: The Phenomenon

In certain languages like Dutch, German, or English, weak quantifiers (WQ henceforth) show a certain ambiguity that is linked to specific intonational patterns. The most obvious cases of what I call the existential reading of weak quantifiers are those where they occur in existential sentences and bear the nuclear stress of the sentence.

(1)   There are three UNIcorns \ in the garden.

Capital letters indicate a pitch accent. The shape of the accent (rising of falling) is sketched by "/" (rising) and "\" (falling). This sentence is perfect as an out-of-the-blue utterance. It states the existence of three unicorns having a certain property without making reference to specific contextual information (as long as we ignore tense). The same characterization holds for sentences without *there*-insertion.

(2)   Three UNIcorns \ are in the garden.

If the head-noun of the WQ bears the sentence accent, the interpretation of (2) is

I am indebted to Kai Alter, Reinhard Blutner, Daniel Büring, Caroline Heycock, Manfred Krifka, Inga Kohlhof, André Meinunger, Tolja Strigin, Enric Vallduví, Rob van der Sandt, Henk Zeevat, and Ede Zimmermann for interesting discussions and comments on earlier versions of this chapter.

more or less synonymous with (1). The second reading arises if the clause as a whole shows a hat-pattern; that is, the WQ-subject bears a secondary rising accent and the VP a nuclear falling one. Intuitions are most clear-cut if the first stress is realized at the quantifying expression.

(3)   THREE / unicorns are in the GARden \

This sentence is infelicitous as an out-of-the-blue utterance. The WQ behaves in some respect as an anaphor in that it looks for a linguistic antecedent denoting a superset of the set of three unicorns.

(4)   There is a whole herd of UNICORNS all around. (...)
       THREE / unicorns are in the GARden \

Note that the denotation of the superset-antecedent (*a whole herd of unicorns* in the example) falls under the same predicate (*unicorns*) as the denotation of the WQ itself. Otherwise the discourse would sound rather odd.

(5)   There is a whole herd of unusual animals all around. (...)
       ⁽?⁾THREE / unicorns are in the GARden \

Nevertheless, an anaphoric relationship between *a herd of unusual animals* and *three unicorns* is possible. We get it if we shift the rising accent on the WQ from *three* to *unicorns*.

(6)   There is a whole herd of unusual animals all around. (...)
       Three UNicorns / are in the GARden \

This proves that – contrary to what frequently has been claimed in the literature; compare Löbner 1990, van Deemter 1992, Hoekstra 1992, Jäger 1995 – it is the hat-pattern and not the deaccenting of the noun that triggers the anaphoricity effect. Since the semantic relation between the antecedent and the anaphoric element is a part-of relation here, I call this the *partitive* reading. These results are summarized in Table 10.1.

The basic distinction is the one between existentially and partitively interpreted WQs. This dichotomy corresponds to a contrast between a single falling accent on

Table 10.1.

Semantics		Accent pattern	
	single falling tone on:	hat-contour rising tone on:	
	head noun	quantity expression	head noun
INTERPRETATION	existential	partitive	
Sortal property of the antecedent		given by the head noun	hyperonym of the head noun

the head-noun of the WQ (example (2)) and a hat contour. The partitive reading again splits into two variants: if the quantity expression is the exponent of the falling accent, the antecedent belongs to the same category that is defined by the head-noun (in (4), the three unicorns mentioned in the second sentence are part of a larger quantity of individuals that happen to be unicorns, too).[1] If the head-noun itself bears the accent, this antecedent only has to be describable by a hyperonym of the head-noun (in (6), *unusual animals* is a hyperonym of *unicorns*).

Although the two classes of WQs differ in that partitives show a kind of anaphoric behavior while existentials don't, both completely behave in parallel as soon as we investigate their ability to license subsequent pronominal anaphora.

(7)   a. [Three CHILDren]$_i$ \ are in the garden. They$_i$ are playing.

        b. I have invited a lot of people. [Three CHILDren]$_i$ / are in the GARden \. They$_i$ are playing.

        c. Our son has invited all his friends. [THREE / children]$_i$ are in the garden. They$_i$ are playing.

The WQ *three children* in each example licenses the coindexed anaphoric pronoun *they*, no matter whether the antecedent is existential or partitive.

There are two options to account for such an interrelation between prosody and semantics. Either we assume that there is a direct information flow between these subsystems of grammar, or we let syntax mediate it. The latter view is more restrictive, and hence I adopt it here. Thus we first should investigate the syntactic properties of WQs and the syntax-phonology interface before we start with our major aim, namely, an attempt to account for the semantic observations discussed.

2   Syntax and Phonology

The distribution of weak determiners[2] is nearly identical to that of adjectives. Both kinds of lexical items may occur in combination with the definite determiner.

(8)   a. the little children

        b. the three children

So weak determiners obviously are not determiners in the syntactic sense of the word. Just as bare plurals and adjective + noun construction may, nouns combined with a weak determiner may get a generic reading. This is what we expect in adjunction structures.

(9)   Ten Germans are twice as stupid as five Germans

In German, there are a strong and a weak inflectional paradigm for adjectives, depending on the determiner of the entire DP.

(10)   a. die kleinen Kinder
            the little_weak children
        b. kleine Kinder
            little_strong children

If weak determiners show overt inflection[3] (for example, *viele* 'many' or *wenige* 'few'), they follow the same paradigm as adjectives.

(11)   a. die vielen Kinder
            the many_weak children
        b. viele Kinder
            many_strong children

The remaining differences in the distribution of "common" adjectives and weak determiners (at most one weak determiner may occur in a string of prenominal adjuncts and it must precede the rest of the string) are most likely semantic in nature. I do not pursue this issue further here.

These observations lead to the conclusion that syntactically, German weak determiners are adjectives, at least in one reading. Since bare AP + NP constructions involving common adjectives get an existential interpretation, (2) should be analyzed as follows:

(12) $[_{DP} \emptyset_{indef} [_{NP} [_{AP}$ three$] [_{NP}$ unicorns$]]]$ are in the garden

(I assume an empty indefinite plural determiner on independent grounds.) As mentioned, the difference between (2) and (3) is represented in syntax. One way to account for this would be to assume a different syntactic structure for (3).

But there is evidence against this view. Syntactically complex amount expressions, which combine with mass terms, show exactly the same pattern.

(13)   a. A lot of MOney \ is in your bag. (existential)
        b. A LOT / of money is in your BAG \ (partitive)

Whatever the syntactic structure of such determiner phrases (DPs henceforth) may be, they obviously do not syntactically parallel the subject DPs in (2) and (3), respectively. This forces us to the conclusion that the existential/partitive ambiguity is a property of amount expressions in general and not of a specific syntactic configuration. This apparently contradicts the claim that the relevant information is syntactically represented. But there is a way out of this dilemma.

The prosody of a sentence is determined by three kinds of information:

- lexical information
- syntactic structure
- information structure

Stipulations about different lexical entries for the existential and the partitive reading, respectively, should be excluded by Occam's razor, and additionally, such an assumption would be unable to explain the observation in (6). The syntactic structure of both readings is identical; therefore the different intonation turns out to be a matter of focus. Since focus shows both prosodic and semantic effects, the argumentation at the end of Section 1 leads to the conclusion that focus is syntactically represented. As a minimal assumption, there is a syntactic feature [+F](ocus) that is freely assigned to some node at S-structure. This assignment is arguably restricted to heads and phrases, and [+F] must not dominate [+F]. So (2) and (3) may be distinguished by different locations of [+F].

Let us examine what are the focused constituents in (2) and (3). As an algorithm for the calculation of the position of focal stress, I use a modified version of the rules given in Selkirk 1984:

> (i) Any [+F]-constituent dominates one accented lexical item, and every accented lexical item is dominated by [+F].
>
> (ii) The accented item of a phrase is identical with the accented item of the most deeply embedded semantical argument of the semantical head of the phrase.
>
> (iii) The accented item of a phrase is its head.

(iii) only applies if (ii) is not applicable. (i)–(iii) define a unique one-to-one mapping between occurrences of [+F] and pitch accents. The terms "semantical head" and "semantical argument" are adopted from Abney 1987; in the present context it only matters that the verb is the semantical head of the clause, and that the subject is a semantic argument of the verb. This accounts for the fact that in sentences with an intransitive verb and global focus, the subject receives the sentence accent. Of course, this proposal is simplified in certain respects, but it will do for our purposes here.

(i)–(iii) immediately entail that in the DP

(14) $[_{DP} [_{NP} [_{AP}$ THREE] $[_{NP}$ unicorns]]]

with an accent on the adjective *three* either A^0 or AP must bear [+F]. Any other assignment of [+F] (including [+F] on a node dominating DP) yields an accent on the noun. Since AP is not branching, the question whether the head or the phrase is focused makes no difference here. This leads us to the following focus-structures for (2) and (3):

(15)   a. $[_{+F}$ Three unicorns are in the garden]
        b. $[_{+F}$ Three] unicorns are in the garden

However, the focus assignment in (15b) is not sufficient to get the partitive reading.

(16)   THREE \ unicorns are in the garden

is interpreted as contrastive (for example, *THREE unicorns are in the garden and not FOUR*).

(3) differs from (16) in that there is additional stress on the predicative PP *in the garden*. So we get the focus structure

(17)   a. [$_{+F}$ Three] unicorns [$_{+F}$ are in the garden]
        b. [$_{+F}$ Three unicorns] [$_{+F}$ are in the garden]

for (3) and (6). This clearly shows that the partitive reading is not a property of the DP but of the entire sentence, a further argument against the assumption of different lexical entries.

But how shall we interpret (17)? As it stands, it is not sufficient for the partitive interpretation either, since one may interpret it as a multiple contrastive focus construction. The structure indicated in (17a) would be something like

(18)   THREE \ unicorns$_i$ are$_j$ in the GARden \
        (and not: FOUR \ $\_i$ $\_j$ on the STREET \ )

which may receive an existential interpretation.

The crucial point that distinguishes (3) and (18) is that in (3), the first accent is realized as a rising and the second as a falling tone. In (18), both accents are falling. What determines whether a given focus is realized as a falling or a rising accent? To answer this question, I adopt a proposal by Krifka 1992, who claims that a sentence is partitioned in a first step into a topic part and a comment part. Both parts may contain a focus part (and the comment presumably even has to) and a background part (possibly empty). *Comment* and *background* are purely descriptive notions here, names for the material in the domain that does not belong to topic or focus, respectively. Topic is syntactically represented as a feature [+T], similar to focus. The assignment of these features is governed by the following principles:

(a) At least one constituent (head or phrase) per clause bears the feature [+T].
(b) [+T] must not dominate [+T] except when a CP-node intervenes.
(c) Every [+T]-constituent c-commands one [+F]-constituent.
(d) [+F] must not dominate [+F] except when a CP-node intervenes.

For the sake of simplicity, I identify comment with the c-command-domain of the topic. Most likely, this cross-linguistically works only at LF, but in the examples discussed here, S-structure and LF are more or less identical as far as topic is concerned. Most importantly for the syntax-phonology interface, the stress assignment rules given in (i)–(iii) do not apply to the entire sentence but to the focus domains topic and comment. An immediate consequence of these rules is the fact that the entire focus domain (topic or comment, respectively) may be focused as a whole, which is a reconstruction of the pretheoretic notion of neutral stress. For the prosodic interpretation of [+T], we have to replace (ii) by (ii′), and we need two additional rules besides (i)–(iii):

(ii′) The accented item of a phrase is identical with the accented item of the most deeply embedded [−T]-argument of the semantic head of the phrase.

(iv) If a [+T]-constituent contains a [+F], the latter is mapped to a rising pitch accent.

(v) A [+F] not dominated by [+T] is mapped to a falling pitch accent.[4]

Now we are ready to give the necessary and sufficient structure for the partitive readings.

(19) a. $[_{+T} [_{+F}$ Three] unicorns] $[_{+F}$ are in the garden]
       b. $[_{+T} [_{+F}$ Three unicorns]] $[_{+F}$ are in the garden]

It is easy to see that this is the only way to get the observed intonation of the respective WQs.[5] To sum up, the partitive reading of a weak quantifier arises if and only if the quantifier is a topic. This generalization presumably holds for any language where such an ambiguity is observed.

3   Semantics

It is obvious that some contextual information is necessary to account for the semantic impact of information structure. Instead of extending traditional semantic frameworks with more or less arbitrary tools for the treatment of contextual information, it is reasonable to use a dynamic setup, where context is the basic notion of semantic analysis. In dynamic semantics, the meaning of a sentence is generally seen as an update function, which maps an input epistemic state (or, equivalently, an input context) to an output state. An epistemic state is (or represents) partial knowledge about the world. In the first place, a context contains only information about a subset of the individuals in the domain of the model. This partial domain is sometimes called the *universe of discourse*. In the second place, the knowledge about the properties of and the relation among these individuals is partial, too. Following Groenendijk et al. 1996, complete knowledge about a given contextual domain is called a "possibility." To account for the partiality of this kind of information, a context is a *set of possibilities* that share a domain.

Sentences are interpreted as *updates* or functions over contexts. An update may either introduce new discourse referents into the context domain or eliminate possibilities and therefore increase the knowledge about the domain. In recent dynamic theories like DRT or Dynamic Predicate Logic, it is assumed that indefinites introduce new elements ("discourse referents") into the context domain, while definites or pronouns pick up referents already present in the input context. On the other hand, the intuitive content of the notion *topic* is that the interpretation of the respective constituent ranges over objects that are familiar in the context. This suggests that the topic/comment dichotomy can be reduced to the notion of (in-)definiteness (or vice versa) in some way or another. But this assumption is not supported by the facts. Both definite and indefinite DPs may occur in either the topic part or the comment part of a sentence.

(20)   a. [*Topic* The printer] [*Comment* is out of ORder]
        b. [*Comment* The PRINter is out of order]

(21)   a. [*Topic* THREE children] [*Comment* are in the GARden]
        b. [*Comment* Three CHILDren are in the garden]

In (20) the subject is definite, in (21) indefinite. The (a) examples are categorical (subject = Topic), the (b) examples thetic statements. Each of the four possible combinations is fully acceptable. But although the indefinite *three children* in (21a) is a topic, it is able to license a subsequent pronoun just as any other indefinite.

(22)   THREE children$_i$ are in the GARden. They$_i$ are happy.

On the one hand, the referents of *three children* belong to the entities familiar in the context. On the other hand, you cannot refer to them by means of a pronominal anaphor before they are explicitly mentioned by an indefinite DP. So in a sense indefinite topics merely *activate* old discourse-referents instead of introducing them. The old/new dichotomy in connection with (in)definiteness and in connection with topic and comment applies at different levels. Therefore we have to distinguish between two nested contextual domains. Similar proposals were made in the literature several times, for instance, the distinction between prominent file cards and file cards in general made in Heim 1982, or the dichotomy between discourse referents that are in focus or not (cf. Grosz et al. 1983, Bosch 1988, among many others). In this chapter, I adopt the basic ideas of Groenendijk et al. 1996. The authors mentioned present a dynamic semantics for modal predicate logic. Since we are primarily interested in the compositional semantics of natural language here, it is raised to a type theoretic language called "Dynamic Intensional Type Theory" (DITT). However, the concrete technical implementation is of minor importance for the linguistic argumentation, and thus I leave it to the appendix and only give a semiformal version here.

As mentioned, a context in DITT defines two domains. First, we have the domain of all entities that were either previously mentioned in the discourse or whose existence can be inferred from the discourse information. We follow Groenendijk et al. 1996 in calling these entities pegs (the term is due to Landman 1986, but the underlying idea here is quite different). Second, there is the domain of discourse markers that coincide with the syntactic indices of DPs and that provide the appropriate anchors for the interpretation of anaphoric pronouns. The different status of these discourse entities can be illustrated with the help of Partee's famous marble example.

(23)   a. I lost ten marbles and found only nine of them.
            ???It is probably under the sofa.
        b. I lost ten marbles and found only nine of them.
            The missing one is probably under the sofa.

There is no discourse marker available after processing the first sentence that corresponds to the tenth marble. Hence it is impossible to refer to it by means of an anaphoric pronoun in (23a). Nevertheless, an anaphoric definite description is able to do so. This phenomenon is accounted for by means of the assumptions that

- there are only those discourse markers in the context that are linguistically licensed,
- if the existence of an object not explicitly mentioned in the discourse can be inferred, a corresponding peg is generated, and (c) anaphoric definites do have access to the domain of pegs, while pronouns can only refer to discourse markers.

Of course, anaphoric definites also have access to all entities that a pronoun can refer to. This is explained by the assumption that there is a function that links every discourse marker to a certain peg, but not the other way round; that is, there may be pegs that do not correspond to any discourse marker. The peg representing the tenth marble in the example is a case at hand. The interpretation of a pronoun now works in three steps:

(a) link the pronoun to a discourse marker
(b) map the discourse marker to a peg
(c) interpret the peg in the model

To make what is going on more transparent, we use a graphical representation for contexts. Though it is quite similar to DRS-boxes in DRT, it is purely illustrative, similar to Heim's file-metaphor. Our ultimate goal is a compositional and nonrepresentational semantics. *A context representation structure* (CRS) consists of four parts:

(a) a set of discourse markers,
(b) a set of pegs,
(c) a mapping from the former to the latter, called *referent function*, and
(d) a set of CRS-conditions that restrict the interpretation of the pegs.

(24)

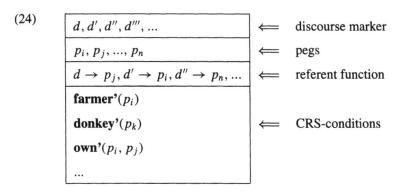

It is important to note that a CRS like (24) does **not** represent the meaning of a sentence but a *context*, that is, the input or output before or after the processing of a sentence. The well-formedness-conditions of CRSs are only informally given here. The domain of the referent function in the third line is the set of the discourse markers in the first line, its range has to be a *subset* of the set of pegs in the second line, and the pegs used as arguments in the CRS-conditions have to be elements of the set of pegs in the second line. The set of pegs corresponds to Heim's file cards and the image of the set of discourse markers under the referent function to the prominent file cards. Since there may be nonprominent file cards, the referent function is an into-function.

To illustrate the update potential of a sentence, we have to give two CRSs, one representing the conditions every legitimate input context of the sentence must meet and one representing the corresponding output conditions. We start with a simple example only involving a pronoun and a predicate.

(25)   a. He$_d$ walks.

b.

d
p_i
$d \to p_i$

$\Longrightarrow$

d
p_i
$d \to p_i$
walk'(p_i)

The index of an anaphoric pronoun has to be a familiar discourse marker as in DRT or File Change Semantics. Therefore "d" is present in the first line of the box on the left, representing the input context. Since every discourse marker has to be mapped to a peg, there is already a peg in the input too – call it p_i – and d is mapped to p_i. There is nothing more about the input we can infer from (25a). Hence the body of the box is empty. Updating with the sentence only means introducing a CRS-condition into the context, namely, that the individual *he* refers to via the peg p_i walks.

(26)   a. A$_d$ man walks.

b.

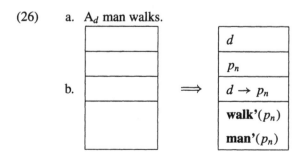

$\Longrightarrow$

d
p_n
$d \to p_n$
walk'(p_n)
man'(p_n)

Updating with an indefinite is even simpler: There are no conditions on the input. The discourse marker of the indefinite, a corresponding peg, and the conditions of NP and VP are introduced. Note that we do not demand that d is new. A transition as in (27) is completely legitimate.

(27)

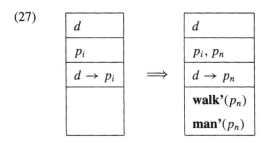

If d is already present in the input, only a new peg is introduced and d is reset to this new peg. The former image of d (p_i in the example) changes, so to speak, from a prominent to a nonprominent file card, but it remains present. Hence the intuition that indefinites introduce something new remains valid, but nevertheless we do not have a *novelty condition* with its shortcomings. This advantage over File Change Semantics is Groenendijk et al. 1996's main motivation for proposing a peg system.

Following Vallduví 1992, I assume that information structure does not affect truth conditions. The notion of truth is not crucial in dynamic semantics, but there is a kind of counterpart, namely, the output conditions of a sentence/update. Its input conditions correspond to the traditional notion of a presupposition. Claiming that (28a) and (28b) have the same truth conditions amounts to saying that they have identical output conditions. They are given in the following.

(28)   a. [*Topic* THREE children]$_d$ [*Comment* are in the GARden]
        b. [*Comment* Three CHILDren$_d$ are in the garden]

        c.

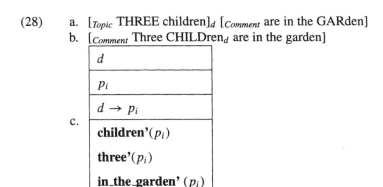

To paraphrase its content briefly, the indefinite subject introduces the discourse marker d that is linked to a peg p_i. This peg must fulfill the condition that its interpretation is a group of children with the cardinality three, and that this group of children is in the garden.

The topic-feature requires that the material in its scope introduce neither new pegs nor new conditions. The only novel entities permitted are discourse markers. Therefore in (28a) both the peg p_i and the condition that it represents three children must be part of the input information. According to this, the minimal input for (28a) is the following:

(29)

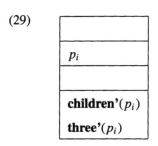

The peg p_i is inactive here and cannot be picked up by a pronominal anaphor. In (28b), we do not have a topic at all. Hence this sentence (or the update corresponding to it) does not state particular conditions at the input context. This corresponds to the observation that the sentence is perfect as an out-of-the-blue utterance.

(30)

The CRS in (28c) represents the result of updating either (29) with (28a) or the empty context (30) with (28b). As far as the existential reading (28b) is concerned, this is a satisfactory result, and nothing more needs to be said about it. Matters are more complicated when we consider the partitive readings more closely.

Let us see whether a sentence like

(31)   There are some children.

in fact provides an output that contains the necessary input conditions of (28a). It is obvious that the sentence introduces a pluralic discourse marker and a corresponding pluralic peg into the context. But there is much more to be said about plural. What does it mean that we know an entity to be pluralic? The most important feature that distinguishes it from singularic entities is the fact that it contains a proper part. Since entities whose existence can be inferred from the previous discourse are represented as newly introduced pegs, the sentence introduces only one discourse marker, but two pegs. Hence (31) corresponds to a transition as follows:

(32)

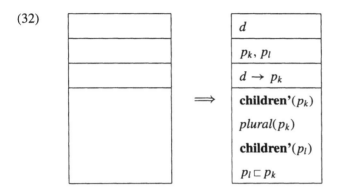

The output of (32) contains (at least) two children-pegs, one representing the entire group of children, the other one an unspecified part of it. Hence it comes quite close to the conditions a suitable input for (28a) has to meet, but it does not completely match it. To be a legitimate anchor for the subject of (28a), a children-peg has to be specified as having the cardinality three. Hence the discourse following is predicted to be unacceptable.

(33)   There are children. [$_{+T}$ Three children] are in the garden.

This is not an undesired result. Without focus-marking of *three* in the second sentence, a partitive reading is indeed not possible. Note that it is just the focused part of the topic that makes the input conditions of the second sentence too strong. Thus we conclude that the update properties we have assumed are not entirely correct. Besides picking up an old peg, topic-DPs presuppose their background, while the focus-part of the topic is a part of the assertion of the sentence as well as the comment part. Technically, we refine our assumptions in two respects:

(a)   [+T] is a head-feature that is shared by a DP and its head. Only its occurrences at a D^0 have semantic impact. It acts as an operator that shifts a determiner-meaning to another determiner-meaning.

(b) This operator is focus-sensitive. The discourse marker introduced by a [+T]-determiner is linked to a familiar peg that has to fulfill the conditions given by the background-part of the NP already in the input context, while the focus-part is added during the updating.

With this proviso, the output of (32) now fulfills the input conditions of (28a), which is repeated here for convenience. (The focus of the comment is ignored in the rest of the chapter, since it does not have any importance for the semantic aspects of the problem discussed.)

(34)   a. $[_{DP} [_{D,+T} \emptyset] [_{NP} [_{AP,+F}$ Three] children]] are in the garden.

b.

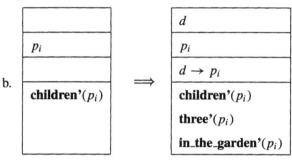

But there is still a problem, however. The left-handed CRS in (32) contains two children-pegs, p_k and p_l, the first representing the entire group of children introduced by (31), and the second an unspecified part of it. The input in (34a) requires there to be one children-peg only. Hence we expect that the output of the conjunction of (31) and (34a) is underspecified with respect to the issue whether the three children mentioned in the second sentence are a part of the group of children mentioned in the first or whether there are only three children all over, depending on whether p_i in (34b) is unified with p_k or p_l in (32). Both provide a legitimate anchor. On the other hand, we have clear intuitions that only the properly partitive reading is available. Well, I wonder whether this really is a matter of semantics proper. Take a look at the discourse in (35).

(35)   A: There are some students at the party. TEN / students are DANcing \.
       B: Actually, these ten are the only students here.

The example shows that an improper-part reading is indeed possible, although it is usually not preferred. Maybe this phenomenon is a consequence of the opposition of the indefinite with the definite article. *The three children* instead of *three children* could only pick up the peg representing the sum of all children in the context. Thus this option, although possible, is canceled out as a conversational implicature if we choose an indefinite in this place. Taking this into account, the whole two-sentence discourse gives the following update:

(36) a. There are children. THREE / children are in the GARden \.

b.

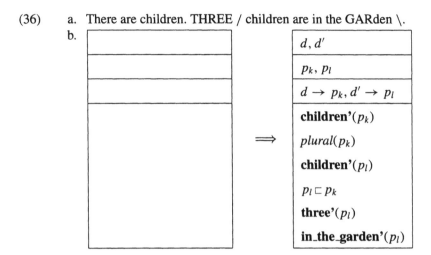

$$
\begin{array}{|l|}
\hline
d, d' \\
\hline
p_k, p_l \\
\hline
d \to p_k, d' \to p_l \\
\hline
\textbf{children'}(p_k) \\
plural(p_k) \\
\textbf{children'}(p_l) \\
p_l \sqsubseteq p_k \\
\textbf{three'}(p_l) \\
\textbf{in\_the\_garden'}(p_l) \\
\hline
\end{array}
$$

Now let us turn to the second version of partitive WQs, those where the entire NP is focused.

(37) There are many people. Three CHILDren / are in the GARden \.

Ignoring the semantic impact of *many* and tense, the first sentence defines a transition as in (38).

(38)

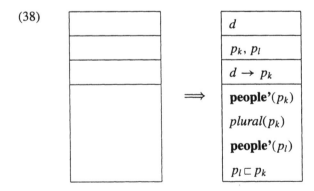

$$
\begin{array}{|l|}
\hline
d \\
\hline
p_k, p_l \\
\hline
d \to p_k \\
\hline
\textbf{people'}(p_k) \\
plural(p_k) \\
\textbf{people'}(p_l) \\
p_l \sqsubseteq p_k \\
\hline
\end{array}
$$

According to the analysis proposed here, in the second sentence, the silent indefinite article carries the feature [+T], and the NP *three children* is in focus.

(39)   a.   [_DP_ [Ø_D,+T_] [_NP,+F_ [_AP_ Three] children]] are in the garden

b.

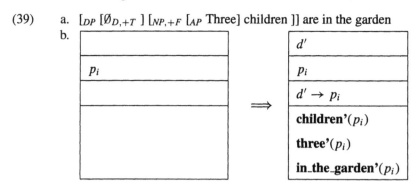

Here the presupposition triggered by the topic-feature is much weaker. Since the whole descriptive content of the DP *three children* is in focus, the only effect of [+T] is the fact that the peg picked up is a familiar one. The output of (38) again presents two options, p_k and p_l, and again, the latter is pragmatically preferred. Hence we have (40) as the update defined by the discourse in (37).

(40)

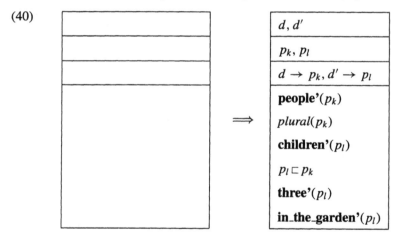

Hence the assumptions about the prosodic and semantic impact of topic and focus made previously are able to account for both kinds of partitive WQs.

Note that although the presupposition of the second sentence of (37) is predicted to be pretty weak (only the presence of one familiar peg is required), it is not empty. This explains the fact that the sentence cannot constitute an appropriate answer to a question like "What's the matter?" This distinguishes this approach from the one advocated by D. Büring (compare Büring 1995 and this volume). In his view, the semantics of topics has nothing in common with discourse entities of whatever kind. Instead, topic and focus (to be understood as the focus of the comment in my terminology) merely serve to define a set of abstract questions, one of which has to be salient in the context of utterance. In slightly more detail, replacing the interpretation of the focus by appropriate alternatives gives us the focus value $\|\phi\|^f$ of the sentence ϕ (compare Rooth 1992), which has the semantic type of a question. By applying the same procedure to the topic-part, we end up with the topic value $\|\phi\|^t$ of ϕ, namely, a set of questions. Applied to the sentence in (41a) with the indicated topic-focus structure, we get the focus value (41c) and the topic value in (41d).

(41) a. $\phi = [_T$ Three children $]$ $[_F$ are in the garden$]$
      b. $\|\phi\|^0 = \|$three children$\|^0(\|^\wedge$are in the garden$\|^0)$
      c. $\|\phi\|^f = \{p \mid \exists x[x \sim \|^\wedge$are in the garden$\|^0 \wedge p = \|$three children$\|^0(x)]\}$
      d. $\|\phi\|^t = \{q \mid \exists y[y \sim \|^\wedge$three children$\|^0 \wedge q = \{p \mid \exists x[x \sim \|^\wedge$are in the garden$\|^0 \wedge p = y\{x\}]\}]\}$

The relation $\alpha \sim \beta$ should be read as "α is a contextually salient alternative to β." At the beginning of a discourse, there are surely no restrictions on the possible alternatives to a certain semantic object besides the fact that alternatives should belong to the same type. Under these conditions, (41c) is the set of propositions that entail that there are three children, and (41d) is just the set of all sets of propositions:

(42) a. $\|\phi\|^f = POW\{w \in W \mid w \in \|$three children$\|^0(\|^\wedge$exist$\|)\}$
      b. $\|\phi\|^t = POW(POW(W))$

Since the set of abstract questions in (42b) is entirely trivial, Büring wrongly predicts that (41a) can be uttered out of the blue. As far as I can see, a notion of topic that is based on considerations concerning discourse objects therefore comes closer to intuitions.

Let me finally make some rather tentative remarks concerning a certain asymmetry in the distribution of partitive and existential WQs (or actually of topic DPs and nontopic DPs in general). Quite unexpectedly, in combination with individual level predicates in the sense of Kratzer 1995, only existential WQs are admitted, while stage level predicates are not sensitive for the contrast (the latter fact is sufficiently illustrated by our previous examples).

(43) a. TWO / students are inTELligent \ (while the rest of the course is quite simple-minded).
      b. Two STUdents / are inTELligent \ (but neither the other students nor the professors are).
      c. *Two STUdents \ are intelligent.

The first step toward an explanation concerns the information structure of thetic sentences, that is, sentences lacking an overtly realized topic. It is questionable whether they are really all-comment sentences. According to Chierchia 1992, topic-comment structuring is responsible for the symmetric-asymmetric ambiguity of donkey sentences.

(44) a. Usually, if $[_{+T}$ a farmer] owns a DONkey, he beats it. (subject-asymmetric reading)

    b. Usually, if a FARmer owns [$_{+T}$ a donkey], he beats it. (object-asymmetric reading)

    c. Usually, if [$_{+T}$ a farmer] OWNS [$_{+T}$ a donkey], he beats it. (symmetric reading)

If this analysis is correct, adverbs of quantification always quantify over instances of the topic-part of the antecedent of the conditional. Let us take this for granted. Now one might wonder what happens if the antecedent is thetic. Actually, we are forced to expect ungrammaticality because of vacuous quantification, but such sentences are perfectly acceptable.

(45)   Usually, if three CHILdren are in the garden, every plant is in danger.

In its most prominent reading, (45) does not quantify over groups of three children as predicted under the unselective-binding approach but over time slices. The sentence may be paraphrased as *For most times t such that three children are in the garden at t, every plant is in danger at t.* It is reasonable to assume that the meaning of the tense morpheme is comparable to the meaning of an indefinite DP, with the exception that tense introduces a *temporal* discourse entity. Hence we may hypothesize that in thetic sentences, the tense morpheme is marked as [+topic].

    As a second step to account for the contrast in (43), we have to ask what it means for an item to be a topic. There are two basic pretheoretic intuitions about this concept. The first one, namely, that topics represent old information, is accounted for by the assumptions made earlier. Besides this, it is frequently assumed that the comment of a sentence makes a certain statement *about* the topic (that's why just those words were chosen). It is quite difficult to fill this aboutness-concept with content. But anyway, you only learn something *about* an object if you learn something that distinguishes this object from other entities. Hence a certain kind of contingency requirement seems to be linked to the topic-comment dichotomy. To make this slightly more precise, a sentence with a given topic-comment structure is only legitimate or felicitous if the interpretation of the comment does not hold for all objects in the domain the interpretation of the topic belongs to.

(46)   [$_{+T}$ tense] Two students be intelligent.

At some level of representation, (43c) has a structure as indicated in (46). Since *intelligent* is an individual level predicate, the comment of the sentence either holds at any time or never holds. But this is just in contradiction to the mentioned contingency requirement. If tense is a topic here, the sentence has to be temporally contingent. Hence we may conclude that individual level predicates are excluded in thetic statements. This kind of explanation, tentative though it may be, has the advantage over competing ones that it only relies on the defining property of individual level predicates to be temporally unrestricted, without making further stipulation about argument structure of syntax (cf. Diesing 1988, 1992, Kratzer 1995).

Appendix A: Dynamic Intensional Type Theory (DITT)[6]

Definition 1 (Types). The set TYPE of types in DITT is the smallest set such that

   (i)   e, t, up are types.
   (ii) if α is a type, $\langle s, \alpha \rangle$ is a type.
   (iii) if α and β are types, $\langle \alpha, \beta \rangle$ is a type.

Definition 2 (Vocabulary).

   (i)   For any type $\tau \in TYPE$, $Con_\tau = \{c_\tau, c'_\tau, c''_\tau, ...\}$ are the constants of type τ.
   (ii) $Con = \cup_{\tau \in TYPE} Con_\tau$.
   (iii) For any type $\tau \in TYPE$, $Var_\tau = \{v_\tau, v'_\tau, v''_\tau, ...\}$ are the variables of type τ.
   (iv) $Var = \cup_{\tau \in TYPE} Var_\tau$
       $DM = N$ is the set of discourse markers.
   (v) $DITT = Con \cup Var \cup DM \cup \{=, \wedge, \neg, \uparrow, \downarrow, {}^\wedge, {}^\vee, \lambda, \Diamond, \mathbf{T}, \exists, \mathcal{E}, (,), .\}$

Definition 3 (The Syntax of DITT). Exp_{DITT}, the set of well-formed expressions of DITT, is the smallest set such that

   (i)   If $\alpha \in VAR_\tau \cup CON_\tau$, $\alpha \in Exp_\tau$
   (ii) If $\alpha \in DM$, $\alpha \in Exp_e$
   (iii) If $\alpha \in Exp_{\langle \sigma, \tau \rangle}$ and $\beta \in Exp_\sigma$, $(\alpha(\beta)) \in Exp_\tau$
   (iv) If $\alpha \in Exp_\tau$ and $v \in VAR_\sigma$, $(\lambda v.\alpha) \in Exp_{\langle \sigma, \tau \rangle}$
   (v) If $\alpha \in Exp_\tau$ and $\beta \in Exp_\tau$, $(\alpha = \beta) \in Exp_{up}$
   (vi) If ϕ, $\psi \in Exp_{up}$, $d \in DM$, and $v \in Var$, $(\neg\phi)$, $(\Diamond\phi)$, $(\mathbf{T}\phi)$, $(\mathcal{E}d.\phi)$, $(\exists v.\phi)$, $(\phi \wedge \psi) \in Exp_{up}$
   (vii) If $\phi \in Exp_t$, $\uparrow \phi \in Exp_{up}$
   (viii) If $\phi \in Exp_{up}$, $\downarrow \phi \in Exp_t$
   (ix) If $\phi \in Exp_\tau$, ${}^\wedge \phi \in Exp_{\langle s, \tau \rangle}$
   (x) If $\phi \in Exp_{\langle s, \tau \rangle}$, ${}^\vee \phi \in Exp_\tau$
   (xi) For all $\tau \in TYPE$, if $\alpha \in Exp_\tau$, $\alpha \in Exp_{DITT}$

Definition 4 (Inference Rules). $\forall x_1, ..., x_n [\Box\phi_1, ..., \Box\phi_i \rightarrow \exists y_1, ..., y_m \Box\psi_1, ..., \Box\psi_j]$ is called an inference rule iff

   (i) $0 \leq i, m, n, 1 \leq j$,
   (ii) $\phi_1, ..., \phi_i, \psi_1, ..., \psi_j$ are literals consisting of first-order DITT-predicate-constant, variables and possibly negation, and
   (iii) all variables are bound.

Definition 5 (Model of DITT). A model $\mathcal{M}$ for DITT is a quadruple $\langle E, W, F, MP \rangle$, such that

   (i) E is a denumerable infinite set (the individual domain),
   (ii) F is an Interpretation Function that maps each constant to a function from W into the domain of the type of that constant,
   (iii) W is nonempty (the set of "possible worlds"),
   (iv) MP, the set of Meaning Postulates, is a set of inference rules,
   (v) all elements of MP are true in $\langle E, W, =, F' \rangle$ under static modal predicate logic interpretation, where $F'(P)(w) =_{def} F(P)(w)$ for all first-order predicate constants P and worlds w.

Definition 6 (Discourse Markers, Pegs, and Sequences).

   (i) $DM =_{def} N$ % Discourse Markers
   (ii) $P_n =_{def} \{p_i \mid 0 \leq i < n\}$ % The first n pegs

(iii) $P_\omega =_{def} \{p_i \mid i \in N\}$ % The set of pegs

(iv) $S =_{def} E^{DM}$

The set of pegs is linearly ordered by means of their indices. Discourse markers are mapped to pegs by means of referent functions.

Definition 7 (Referent Functions). $R =_{def} \cup_{D \subseteq DM} \cup_{n \in N} P_n^D$

Peg interpretations map a sequence of n pegs to the elements of domain of the model.

Definition 8 (Peg Interpretations). $PI_n =_{def} E^{P_n}$

Definition 9 (Possibilities). $Pos =_{def} \{\langle D, n, r, i, w\rangle \mid D \subseteq DM \wedge n \in N \cup \{\omega\} \wedge r \in P_n^D \wedge i \in PI_n \wedge w \in W\}$

Definition 10 (Contexts). $CT =_{def} \cup_{D \subseteq DM} \cup n \in N\ POW(\{D\} \times \{n\} \times P_n^D \times PI_n \times W)$

Definition 11 (Domains of a Context). Let *ct* be a context, $D \subseteq DM$, and $n \in N$, such that $ct \subseteq POW(\{D\} \times \{n\} \times P_n^D \times PI_n \times W)$

(i) $Ddom(ct) =_{def} D$

(ii) $Pdom(ct) =_{def} P_n$

(iii) $Wdom(ct) =_{def} \{w \mid \exists r, i : \langle D, n, r, i, w\rangle \in ct\}$

Definition 12 (Informativity).

(i) $\langle D, n, r, i, v\rangle \le \langle D', m, r', j, w\rangle$ iff $D \subseteq D' \wedge n \le m \wedge i \subseteq j \wedge v = w$

(ii) $\langle D, n, r, i, v\rangle \sqsubseteq \langle D', m, r', j, w\rangle$ iff $D \subseteq D' \wedge n \le m \wedge r \subseteq r' \wedge i \subseteq j \wedge v = w$

(iii) $ct \le ct'$ iff $\forall k[k \in ct' \rightarrow \exists l[l \in ct \wedge l \le k]]$

(iv) $ct \sqsubseteq ct'$ iff $\forall k[k \in ct' \rightarrow \exists l[l \in ct \wedge l \sqsubseteq k]]$

Definition 13 (Join, Meet, Empty, and Inconsistent Context).

$$\{\langle D, n, r, i, v\rangle\} \sqcup \{\langle D', m, s, j, w\rangle\} =_{def} Pos \cap \{\langle D \cap D', min(\{n, m'\}), t, k, u\rangle \mid t \subseteq r \wedge k \subseteq i \wedge u = v \vee t \subseteq s \wedge k \subseteq j \wedge u = w\}$$

$$\{\langle D, n, r, i, v\rangle\} \sqcap \{\langle D', m, s, j, w\rangle\} =_{def} Pos \cap \{\langle D \cup D', max(\{n, m'\}), t, k, v\rangle \mid r, s \subseteq t \wedge i, j \subseteq k \wedge v = w\}$$

$$ct \sqcup ct' =_{def} \cup_{k \in ct} \cup_{l \in ct'} \{k\} \sqcup \{l\}$$

$$ct \sqcap ct' =_{def} \bigcap_{k \in ct} \bigcap_{l \in ct'} \{k\} \sqcap \{l\}$$

$$\mathbf{1} =_{def} \sqcup CT = \{\langle \emptyset, 0, \emptyset, \emptyset, w\rangle \mid w \in W\}$$

$$\mathbf{0} =_{def} \sqcap CT = \emptyset$$

Definition 14 (Context-Model). Let $\mathcal{M} = \langle E, W, F, MP\rangle$ be a *DITT*-model, *ct* a context such that each of its possibilities contains *n* pegs, and P^m an *m*-ary first-order predicate constant from *DITT*. The Modal Predicate Logic Model corresponding to *ct* is defined as follows:

$M_{ct} =_{def} \langle P_N, ct, ct \times ct, G\rangle$, such that

$G(P^m)(\langle D, n, r, i, w\rangle) = \{\langle p_1, ..., p_m\rangle \in (Pdom(ct))^m \mid \langle i(p_1), ..., i(p_m)\rangle \in F(P^m)(w)\}$

Definition 15 (Realistic Contexts).

$$CTR =_{def} \{ct \in CT \mid M_{ct} \models MP\}$$

Definition 16 (Realistic Extension of a Context).

$$rex(ct) =_{def} \sqcup \{ct' \mid ct \sqsubseteq ct' \wedge \forall k \in ct \exists l \in ct'[k \leq l] \wedge ct' \in CTR\}$$

Definition 17 (Open Discourse Markers).

$$\forall s, s', d[s \sim_d s' \equiv_{def} Dom(s - s') = Dom(s' - s) = \{d\}]$$

$$\forall d, g, w[d \in od(\alpha) \equiv_{def} \exists s, s'[s \sim_d s' \wedge \|\alpha\|_{g,s,w} \neq \|\alpha\|_{g,s',w}]]$$

Definition 18 (Updates). $UP = \cup_{C \subseteq CT} CTR^C \cap POW(\leq)$

Definition 19 (Peg Deletion). Let $ct \in CT$.

$$ct[p_n = p_i] =_{def} \{\langle D, n, r, i, w\rangle \mid \exists s, j[\langle D, n+1, s, j, w\rangle \in ct \wedge i \subset j \wedge$$
$$\forall d \in D[[s(d) \neq p_n \rightarrow r(d) = s(d)] \wedge$$
$$[s(d) = p_n \rightarrow r(d) = p_i]]]\}$$

if $Pdom(ct) = P_{d+1} \wedge p_i \in Pdom(ct)$, undefined else.

Definition 20 (Domains).

$$
\begin{aligned}
Dom(e) &=_{def} E \\
Dom(t) &=_{def} \{0, 1\} \\
Dom(up) &=_{def} UP \\
Dom(\langle\alpha, \beta\rangle) &=_{def} Dom(\beta)^{Dom(\alpha)} \\
Dom(\langle s, \alpha\rangle) &=_{def} Dom(\alpha)^{S \times W}
\end{aligned}
$$

Definition 21 (The Semantics of DITT). For any model $\mathcal{M} = \langle E, W, F, MP\rangle$, world w, total sequence s, and assignment g, it holds that

$$
\begin{aligned}
\|c\|_{g,s,w} &=_{def} F(c)(w) \text{ iff } c \in Con, \\
\|v\|_{g,s,w} &=_{def} g(v) \text{ iff } v \in Var, \\
\|d\|_{g,s,w} &=_{def} s(d) \text{ iff } d \in DM, \\
\|\alpha(\beta)\|_{g,s,w} &=_{def} \|\alpha\|_{g,s,w}(\|\beta\|_{g,s,w}), \\
\|\lambda v_\tau.\alpha_\sigma\|_{g,s,w} &=_{def} \iota f(f \in Dom(\langle\tau, \sigma\rangle) \wedge \forall x : f(x) = \|\alpha\|_{g[v/x],s,w}), \\
\|{}^\wedge\alpha_\tau\|_{g,s,w} &=_{def} \iota f(f \in Dom(\langle s, \tau\rangle) \wedge \forall t \in S \forall v \in W : f(\langle t, v\rangle) = \|\alpha\|_{g,t,v}), \\
\|{}^\vee\alpha\|_{g,s,w} &=_{def} \|\alpha\|_{g,s,w}(\langle s, w\rangle), \\
ct[\alpha = \beta]_{g,s,w} &=_{def} rex(\{\langle D, n, r, i, v\rangle \in ct \mid \forall s'[r \circ i \subseteq s' \rightarrow \|\alpha\|_{g,s',v} = \|\beta\|_{g,s',v}]\}) \\
&\quad \text{iff } od(\alpha) \cup od(\beta) \subseteq Ddom(ct), \text{ undefined else,} \\
ct[\neg\phi]_{g,s,w} &=_{def} rex(\{k \in ct \mid \neg\exists l[l \in ct[\phi]_{g,s,w} \wedge k \leq l]\}) \\
ct[\phi \wedge \psi]_{g,s,w} &=_{def} ct[\phi]_{g,s,w}[\psi]_{g,s,w}, \\
ct[\exists v_\tau.\phi]_{g,s,w} &=_{def} rex(\sqcup_{x \in Dom(\tau)} ct[\phi]_{g[v/x],s,w}), \\
ct[\mathcal{E}d.\phi]_{g,s,w} &=_{def} (Pos \cap \{\langle D \cup \{d\}, n+1, r[d/p_n], i \cup \{\langle p_n, e\rangle\}, v\rangle \mid \\
&\qquad \langle D, n, r, i, v\rangle \in ct \wedge e \in E\})[\phi]_{g,s,w}, \\
&\quad \text{where } r[d/p_n] \text{ is exactly like } r \text{ except that it maps } d \text{ to } p_n, \\
ct[\uparrow \alpha]_{g,s,w} &=_{def} rex(\{\langle D, n, r, i, v\rangle \in ct \mid \forall s'[r \circ i \subseteq s' \rightarrow \|\alpha\|_{g,s',v} = 1]\}) \\
&\quad \text{iff } od(\alpha) \subseteq Ddom(ct), \text{ undefined else,} \\
\|\downarrow\phi\|_{g,s,w} &=_{def} 1 \text{ iff} \\
&\quad \forall D, n, r, i[\langle D, n, r, i, w\rangle \in Pos \wedge r \circ i \subseteq s \wedge \\
&\quad \{\langle D, n, r, i, w\rangle\}[\phi]_{g,s,w} \text{ is defined } \rightarrow \{\langle D, n, r, i, w\rangle\}[\phi]_{g,s,w} \neq \mathbf{0}] \\
ct[\Diamond\phi]_{g,s,w} &=_{def} \{k \in ct \mid ct[\phi]_{g,s,w} \neq \mathbf{0}.\} \\
ct[\mathbf{T}]_{g,s,w} &=_{def} \cup p \in Pdom(ct) ct[p_n = p]_{g,s,w} \\
&\quad \text{iff } \exists p \in Pdom(ct) : ct[p_n = p][\phi]_{g,s,w} \neq \mathbf{0} \text{ undefined else.}
\end{aligned}
$$

Appendix B: DITT with Structured Meanings (DITTSM)

Definition 22 (Types). $TYPE_{DITTSM}$ is the smallest set such that

   (i)   Every type of *DITT* is a type of *DITTSM* (simply "type" henceforth).
   (ii) If τ is a type of *DITT*, $sm(\tau)$ is a type.
  (iii) If σ and τ are types, $\langle \sigma, \tau \rangle$ is a type.

Definition 23 (Domains).

   (i)   If τ is a type of *DITT*, its domain is as under *DITT*
   (ii) If τ is a type, $Dom(sm(\tau)) =_{def} \bigcup_{\sigma \in TYPE}(Dom(\langle \sigma, \tau \rangle) \times Dom(\langle s, \sigma \rangle))$
  (iii) If σ and τ are types, $Dom(\langle sm(\sigma), \tau \rangle) =_{def} Dom(\langle \sigma, \tau \rangle) \cup Dom(\tau)^{Dom(sm(\sigma))}$

Definition 24 (Syntax of DITTSM). Exp_{DITTSM} is the smallest set such that

    (i)   If $\alpha \in Exp_{DITT}$, $\alpha \in Exp_{DITTSM}$.
   (ii) If $\alpha \in Exp_{\langle \sigma, \tau \rangle}$ and $\beta \in Exp_{\sigma}$, $\langle {}_F\alpha, \beta \rangle \in Exp_{sm(\tau)}$
  (iii) If $\alpha \in Exp_{\langle \sigma, \tau \rangle}$ and $\beta \in Exp_{sm(\sigma)}$, $\alpha(\beta) \in Exp_{sm(\tau)}$
  (iv) If $\alpha \in Exp_{sm(\langle \sigma, \tau \rangle)}$ and $\beta \in Exp_{\sigma}$, $\alpha(\beta) \in Exp_{sm(\tau)}$,
   (v) If $\alpha \in Exp_{\langle sm(\sigma), \tau \rangle}$ and $\beta \in Exp_{\sigma}$, $\alpha(\beta) \in Exp_{\tau}$
  (vi) If $\alpha \in Exp_{sm(\tau)}$, ${}^{\wedge}\alpha \in Exp_{sm(\langle s, \tau \rangle)}$
 (vii) If $\alpha \in Exp_{sm(\langle s, \tau \rangle)}$, ${}^{\vee}\alpha \in Exp_{sm(\tau)}$
(viii) If $\alpha \in Exp_{sm(\tau)}$ and $v \in Con_{\sigma}$, $\lambda v.\alpha \in Exp_{sm(\langle \sigma, \tau \rangle)}$
  (ix) If $\phi \in Exp_{sm(t)}$, $\uparrow \phi \in Exp_{sm(up)}$
   (x) If $\psi \in Exp_{sm(up)}$, $\downarrow \phi \in Exp_{sm(t)}$
  (xi) If $\alpha \in Exp_{sm(\tau)}$ and $\beta \in Exp_{\tau}$, $(\alpha = \beta)$, $(\beta = \alpha) \in Exp_{sm(up)}$
 (xii) If $\phi \in Exp_{sm(up)}$, $\psi \in Exp_{up} \cup Exp_{sm(up)}$, $d \in DM$ and $v \in VAR$,
       $(\neg \phi)$, $(\phi \wedge \psi)$, $(\psi \wedge \phi)$, $(\psi \wedge \phi)$, $(\mathcal{E}d.\phi)$, $(\Diamond \phi)$, $(\mathbf{T}\phi)$ and $(\exists v.\phi) \in Exp_{sm(up)}$
(xiii) If $\alpha \in Exp_{\tau}$, $\alpha \in Exp_{DITTSM}$.

Definition 25 (Semantics of DITTSM).

    (i)   If α is an expression of *DITT*, its interpretation is the same as under *DITT*.
   (ii) $\| \langle {}_F\alpha, \beta \rangle \| =_{def} \langle \| \lambda v.\alpha(v) \|, \| \beta \| \rangle$,
  (iii) If $\alpha \in Exp_{\langle \sigma, \tau \rangle}$ and $\langle {}_F\beta, \gamma \rangle \in Exp_{sm(\sigma)}$, $\| \alpha(\langle {}_F\beta, \gamma \rangle) \| =_{def} \| \langle \lambda v.\alpha(\beta(v)), \gamma \rangle \|$,
  (iv) If $\langle {}_F\alpha, \beta \rangle \in Exp_{sm(\langle \sigma, \tau \rangle)}$ and $\gamma \in Exp_{\sigma}$, $\| \langle {}_F\alpha, \beta \rangle(\gamma) \| =_{def} \| \langle {}_F\lambda v.(\alpha(v)(\gamma)), \beta \rangle \|$,
   (v) If $\alpha \in Exp_{\langle sm(\sigma), \tau \rangle}$ and $\beta \in Exp_{\sigma}$, $\| \alpha(\beta) \| =_{def} \| \alpha \|(\| \beta \|)$
  (vi) $\| {}^{\wedge} \langle {}_F\alpha, \beta \rangle \| =_{def} \| \langle {}_F\lambda v.{}^{\wedge}\alpha, \beta \rangle \|$
 (vii) $\| {}^{\vee} \langle {}_F\alpha, \beta \rangle \| =_{def} \| \langle {}_F\lambda v.{}^{\vee}\alpha, \beta \rangle \|$
(viii) $\| \langle {}_F\alpha, \beta \rangle \wedge \phi \| =_{def} \| \langle {}_F\lambda v.(\alpha(v) \wedge \phi), \beta \rangle \|$
  (ix) $\| \phi \wedge \langle {}_F\alpha, \beta \rangle \| =_{def} \| \langle {}_F\lambda v.(\phi \wedge \alpha(v)), \beta \rangle \|$
   (x) $\| \neg \langle {}_F\alpha, \beta \rangle \| =_{def} \| \langle {}_F\lambda v.(\neg \alpha(v)), \beta \rangle \|$
  (xi) $\| \mathcal{E}d.\langle {}_F\alpha, \beta \rangle \| =_{def} \| \langle {}_F\lambda v.(\mathcal{E}d.\alpha(v)), \beta \rangle \|$
 (xii) $\| \exists x.\langle {}_F\alpha, \beta \rangle \| =_{def} \| \langle {}_F\lambda v.(\exists x.\alpha(v)), \beta \rangle \|$
(xiii) $\| \uparrow \langle {}_F\alpha, \beta \rangle \| =_{def} \| \langle {}_F\lambda v.(\uparrow \alpha(v)), \beta \rangle \|$
(xiv) $\| \downarrow \langle {}_F\alpha, \beta \rangle \| =_{def} \| \langle {}_F\lambda v.(\downarrow \alpha(v)), \beta \rangle \|$
 (xv) $\| \langle {}_F\alpha, \beta \rangle = \gamma \| =_{def} \| \langle {}_F\lambda v.(\alpha(v) = \gamma), \beta \rangle \|$
(xvi) $\| \Diamond \langle {}_F\alpha, \beta \rangle \| =_{def} \| \langle {}_F\lambda v.(\Diamond \alpha(v)), \beta \rangle \|$

Definition 26 (The Topic-Operator).

Let *"top"* be a *DITTSM*-constant, $top \in Exp_{\langle \langle s, det \rangle, \langle sm(\langle s, pred \rangle), \langle \langle s, pred \rangle, up \rangle \rangle \rangle}$.[7]
For every *DITT*-model $\mathcal{M}$, sequence s, world w, and assignment g, it holds that

   (i)   If $P \in Exp_{\langle s, pred \rangle}$ and $D \in Exp_{det}$, $\| top(D)(P) \|_{\mathcal{M}, s, g, w} =$
       $D\{{}^{\wedge}\lambda x.\mathbf{T}P\{x\}\}\|_{\mathcal{M}, s, g, w}$
   (ii) If $\langle {}_F\lambda X.B(X), F \rangle \in Exp_{sm(\langle s, pred \rangle)}$ and $D \in Exp_{det}$,
       $\| top(D)(\langle {}_F B, F \rangle) \|_{\mathcal{M}, s, g, w} = \| D\{{}^{\wedge}\lambda x.(\mathbf{T}\exists v.B(v)\{x\} \wedge B(F)\{x\})\}\|_{\mathcal{M}, s, g, w}$

Appendix C: A Fragment of English

Definition 27 (Syntax and Semantics). $[X]$ denotes the *DITTSM*-translation of X.

$$
\begin{array}{llll}
\text{(i)} & T & \Longrightarrow S & :: [T] = [S] \\
\text{(ii)} & T_1 & \Longrightarrow T_2, S & :: [T_1] = [T_2] \wedge [S] \\
\text{(iii)} & S & \Longrightarrow DP, VP & :: [S] = [DP](^\wedge[VP]) \\
\text{(iv)} & S & \Longrightarrow \text{There are } DP & :: [S] = [DP](^\wedge \lambda x. x = x) \\
\text{(v)} & DP & \Longrightarrow D, NP & :: [DP] = [D](^\wedge[NP]) \\
\text{(vi)} & NP_1 & \Longrightarrow AP, NP_2 & :: [NP_1] = \lambda x.[AP](x) \wedge [NP_2](x) \\
\text{(vii)} & VP & \Longrightarrow V, XP & :: [VP] = [V](^\wedge[XP]) \\
\text{(viii)} & D_1 & \Longrightarrow [_{+T}D_2] & :: [D_1] = top(^\wedge[D_2]) \\
\text{(ix)} & C_1 & \Longrightarrow [_{+F}C_2] & :: [C_1] = \langle_F \lambda X.X, [C_2] \rangle
\end{array}
$$

where C is an arbitrary category.

Definition 28 (Lexicon).

$$
\begin{array}{lll}
\text{(i)} & D \Longrightarrow a_d, \emptyset_d & \%d \in DM \\
\text{(ii)} & AP \Longrightarrow \{\text{three}, ...\} & \\
\text{(iii)} & NP \Longrightarrow \{\text{children}, ...\} & \\
\text{(iv)} & XP \Longrightarrow \{\text{in the garden}, ...\} & \\
\text{(v)} & V \Longrightarrow \{\text{are}, ...\} &
\end{array}
$$

Definition 29 (Singular, Plural, and Sum Operator).

$$sing =_{def} c_{\langle e, t \rangle}$$
$$plural =_{def} c'_{\langle e, t \rangle}$$
$$\oplus =_{def} c_{\langle e, \langle e, e \rangle \rangle}$$

Definition 30 (Rigidity of $\oplus$). For every *DITT*-Model $\mathcal{M} = \langle E, W, F, MP \rangle$, there is a two-place operation "+" in E^3 such that

$$\forall w \in W[F(\oplus)(w) = +]$$

Definition 31 (Meaning Postulates). Let the set of Meaning Postulates contain at least the following formulas:

$$
\begin{array}{ll}
MP_\oplus 1: & \forall x \forall y [\Box x \oplus y = y \oplus x] \\
MP_\oplus 2: & \forall x \forall y \forall z [\Box((x \oplus y) \oplus z) = (x \oplus (y \oplus z))] \\
MP_\oplus 3: & \forall x [\Box x \oplus x = x] \\
MP_\oplus 4: & \forall x \forall y [\Box x \leq y \wedge \Box x \neq y \rightarrow \exists z [\Box y \neq z \wedge \Box y = x \oplus z]] \\
MP_{sing}: & \forall x \forall y [\Box sing(x) \wedge \Box y \leq x \rightarrow \Box x = y] \\
MP_{plural}1: & \forall x [\Box plural(x) \rightarrow \exists y [\Box y \neq x \wedge y \leq x]] \\
MP_{plural}2: & \forall x \forall y [\Box x \neq y \rightarrow \exists z [\Box plural(z) \wedge \Box x \oplus y = z]] \\
MP_{three}1: & \forall x [\Box \mathbf{three}'(x) \rightarrow \exists y \exists z \exists w [\Box sing(y) \wedge \Box sing(z) \wedge \Box sing(w) \wedge \\
& \quad \Box x = y \oplus z \oplus w \wedge \Box y \neq z \wedge \Box y \neq w \wedge \Box z \neq w]] \\
MP_{three}2: & \forall x \forall y \forall z [\Box sing(x) \wedge \Box sing(y) \wedge \Box sing(z) \wedge \Box x \neq y \wedge \Box x \neq z \wedge \\
& \quad \Box y \neq z \rightarrow \mathbf{three}'(x \oplus y \oplus z)]
\end{array}
$$

(47)   a. $\emptyset_d$ Three CHILDren are in the garden.

b.   three :: AP :: $\lambda x. \uparrow \mathbf{three'}\, (^\vee x)$

children :: NP :: $\lambda x. \uparrow \mathbf{child'}\, (^\vee x)$

three children :: NP :: $\lambda x. \uparrow$ **three'**$(^{\vee}x) \wedge \uparrow$ **child'**$(^{\vee}x)$

> $\emptyset_d$ :: D :: $\lambda P \lambda Q.\mathcal{E}d.P\{^{\wedge}d\} \wedge plural(d) \wedge Q\{^{\wedge}d\}$
> /

three children :: DP ::
$\lambda Q.\mathcal{E}d. \uparrow$ **three'** $(d) \wedge \uparrow$ **child'** $(d) \wedge plural(d) \wedge Q\{^{\wedge}d\}$

> are in the garden :: VP :: $\lambda x. \uparrow$ **in_the_garden'**$(^{\vee}x)$
> /

three children are in the garden :: S ::
$\mathcal{E}d. \uparrow$ **three'**$(d) \wedge \uparrow$ **child'**$(d) \wedge plural(d) \wedge \uparrow$ **in_the_garden'**(d)

c. $ct[\mathcal{E}d. \uparrow$ **three'**$(d) \wedge \uparrow$ **child'**$(d) \wedge plural(d) \wedge \uparrow$ **in_the_garden'**
   $(d)]_{g,s,w} = \{\langle D \cup \{d\}, n+3, r[d/p_n], i \cup \{\langle p_n, e\rangle, \langle p_{n+1}, f\rangle, \langle p_{n+2},$
   $g\rangle\}, v\rangle | \langle D, n, r, i, v\rangle \in ct \wedge \{f, g\} \subseteq F(sing)(v) \cap F($**child'**$)(v) \wedge$
   $f + g = e \wedge e \in F($**in_the_garden'**$)(v)\}$

d. $\|\downarrow\mathcal{E}d. \uparrow$**three'**$(d) \wedge \uparrow$**child'**$(d) \wedge plural(d) \wedge \uparrow$**in_the_garden'**
   $(d)\|_{g,s,w} = 1$
   iff $|F($**child**$)(w) \cap F(sing)(w) \cap F($**in_the_garden'**$)(w)| \geq 3$

e. $\exists x \exists y \exists z[x \neq y \wedge x \neq y \wedge y \neq z \wedge sing(x) \wedge sing(y) \wedge sing(z)$
   $\wedge$**child'**$(x \oplus y \oplus z) \wedge$**in_the_garden'**$(x \oplus y \oplus z)]$

(48) a. There are $\emptyset_d$ children. $[_{+T}\emptyset_{d'}]$ Three children are in the garden.
      b. $\mathcal{E}d. \uparrow$**child'**$(d) \wedge plural(d) \wedge \mathcal{E}d'.T(\uparrow$**three'**$(d') \wedge \uparrow$**child'**$(d')) \wedge$
         $plural(d') \wedge$**in_the_garden'**$(d')(=\mathbf{A})$
      c. $\mathbf{1}[\mathbf{A}] = $ undefined

(49) a. $[_{+T}\emptyset_d][_{+F}$ three$]$ children are in the garden.
      b. three :: AP :: $\lambda x. \uparrow$ **three'**$(^{\vee}x)$

      > three :: $[_{+F}AP]$ :: $\langle_F \lambda P.P, \lambda x. \uparrow$**three'**$(^{\vee}x)\rangle$

      >> children :: NP :: $\lambda x. \uparrow$**child'**$(^{\vee}x)$
      >> /

      three children :: NP :: $\langle_F \lambda P \lambda x.(P(x) \wedge \uparrow$ **child'**$(^{\vee}x)), \uparrow$ **three'**$(^{\vee}x)\rangle$

      >> $\emptyset_d$ :: D :: $\lambda Q \lambda R.\mathcal{E}d.Q\{^{\wedge}d\} \wedge plural(d) \wedge R\{^{\wedge}d\}$
      >> |
      >> $\emptyset_d$ :: $[_{+T}D]$ :: $top(^{\wedge}\lambda Q \lambda R.\mathcal{E}d.Q\{^{\wedge}d\} \wedge plural(d) \wedge R\{^{\wedge}d\})$
      >> /

      $\emptyset_d$ three children :: DP :: $top(^{\wedge}\lambda Q \lambda R.\mathcal{E}d.Q\{^{\wedge}d\} \wedge plural(d) \wedge$
      $R\{^{\wedge}d\})$
      $(\langle_F \lambda P^{\wedge}\lambda x.(P(x) \wedge \uparrow$**child'**$(^{\vee}x)), \uparrow$**three'**$(^{\vee}x)\rangle) (= \mathbf{B})$

      > are in the garden :: VP :: $\lambda x. \uparrow$**in_the_garden'**$(^{\vee}x)$
      > /

$[_{+T}\emptyset_d]$ $[_{+F}$ three] children are in the garden :: S

$\mathcal{E}d.\mathbf{T}\uparrow\mathbf{child'}(d)\wedge\uparrow\mathbf{three'}(d)\wedge plural(d)\wedge\uparrow\mathbf{in\_the\_garden'}(d)$

c. $\mathbf{B} = \lambda Q\lambda R.\mathcal{E}d.Q\{^\wedge d\}\wedge plural(d)\wedge R\{^\wedge d\}$

$(^\wedge\lambda x.(\mathbf{T}\exists P(P(x)\wedge\uparrow\mathbf{child'}(^\vee x))\wedge\uparrow\mathbf{three'}(^\vee x)\wedge\uparrow\mathbf{child'}$
$(^\vee x)))$

$= \lambda R.\mathcal{E}d.\mathbf{T}\exists P(P(^\wedge d)\wedge\uparrow\mathbf{child'}(d))\wedge\uparrow\mathbf{three'}(d)\wedge\uparrow\mathbf{child'}$
$(d)\wedge plural(d)\wedge R\{^\wedge d\}$

$= \lambda R.\mathcal{E}d.\mathbf{T}\uparrow\mathbf{child'}(d)\wedge\uparrow\mathbf{three'}(d)\wedge plural(d)\wedge R\{^\wedge d\}$

d. $ct[\mathcal{E}d.\mathbf{T}\uparrow\mathbf{child'}(d)\wedge\uparrow\mathbf{three'}(d)\wedge plural(d)\wedge\uparrow\mathbf{in\_the\_garden'}$
$(d)]_{g,s,w}$

$= rex\{\langle D\cup\{d\}, n+1, r[d/p], i, v\rangle | \langle D, n, r, i, v\rangle \in ct\wedge p\in$
$Pdom(ct)$

$\wedge i(p)\in F(\mathbf{three'})(v)\cap F(\mathbf{in\_the\_garden'})(v)\}$

iff $\forall\langle D, n, r', i', v'\rangle\in ct : i'(p)\in F(\mathbf{child'})(v')$, undefined
else.

Notes

1 Note that this class-membership can be a consequence of inferences driven by extralinguistic knowledge. In (7c), the fact that the friends of our son are children is an example at hand.

2 Following Milsark 1977, I call the quantity expressions inside WQs weak determiners. No implications about their syntactic properties are intended by this terminology.

3 The cardinal numbers do not inflect at all.

4 Actually, the shape of the accent corresponding to the comment-focus is determined by several factors. In simple declarative sentences, it is a falling one.

5 Of course there is an ambiguity concerning the stress of *garden*, since it may be an exponent of foci on *garden*, *in the garden*, and *are in the garden*. As we see later, the comment-focus does not matter for our analysis, such that for our purposes, these different locations of it count as one.

6 For reasons of space, I restrict myself to giving only the plain definitions necessary for the "official" compositional theory. DITT extends the skeleton of the Dynamic Modal Predicate Logic from Groenendijk et al. 1996 to a fully-fledged type theory. DITTSM incorporates the basic ideas of Krifka's structured-meaning approach (cf. Krifka 1992) to focus semantics, although technical details are slightly modified. The interested reader is referred to Jäger 1996 for an extensive introduction and discussion.

7 *pred* abbreviates $\langle\langle s, e\rangle, up\rangle$, and *det* $\langle\langle s, pred\rangle, \langle\langle s, pred\rangle, up\rangle\rangle$.

References

Abney, S. P. 1987. The English Noun Phrase in Its Sentential Aspects, Ph.D. thesis, MIT.

Blutner, R. 1990. *Dynamic Generalized Quantifiers and Natural Language*, ZIfS, Berlin.

Bosch, P. 1988. Representing and accessing focussed referents. *Language and Cognitive Processes* 3(3), 207–231.

Büring, D. 1995. The 59th Street Bridge Accent. Ph.D. thesis, University of Tübingen.

Chierchia, G. 1992. Anaphora and dynamic binding. *Linguistics and Philosophy* 15(2), 111–184.

Deemter, K. van 1992. Towards a generalization of anaphora. *Journal of Semantics* 9(1), 27–52.

Diesing, M. 1988. Bare plural subjects and the stage/individual contrast. In M. Krifka (ed.), *Genericity in Natural Language. Proceedings of the 1988 Tübingen Conference*, Tübingen.

Diesing, M. 1992. *Indefinites*, MIT Press, Cambridge, Mass.

Enç, M. 1991. The semantics of specificity. *Linguistic Inquiry* 22(1), 1–25.

Grice, H. 1957. Meaning. *Philosophical Review* 66, 377–388.

Groenendijk, J., and Stokhof, M. 1991a. Dynamic Montague Grammar. In J. Groenendijk, M. Stokhof, and D. I. Beaver (eds.), *Quantification and Anaphora I*, DYANA deliverable R2.2a, Amsterdam.

Groenendijk, J., and Stokhof, M. 1991b. Dynamic predicate logic. *Linguistics and Philosophy* 14(1).

Groenendijk, J., Stokhof, M., and Veltman, F. 1996. Coreference and modality. In S. Lappin (ed.), *Handbook of Contemporary Semantic Theories*, pp. 179–213, Blackwell, Oxford.

Grosz, B., Joshi, A., and Weinstein, S. 1983. Providing a unified account of definite noun phrases in discourse. In *Proceedings of the 21st Meeting of ACL*, pp. 44–50, Cambridge, Mass.

Grosz, B. J., and Sidner, C. L. 1986. Attention, intentions, and the structure of discourse. *Computational Linguistics* 12(3), 175–204.

Heim, I. 1982. The Semantics of Definite and Indefinite Noun Phrases. Ph.D. thesis, University of Massachusetts, Amherst.

Hoekstra, H. 1992. Subsectional anaphora in DRT. In M. Evergest et al. (eds.), *OTS Yearbook 1992*, pp. 53–62.

Jäger, G. 1992. Diskurs-Verknüpfung und der Stadien-/Individuen-Kontrast, Master's thesis, Universität Leipzig.

Jäger, G. 1995. Weak quantifiers and information structure. In J. N. Beckman (ed.), *Proceedings of NELS 25*, Vol. 1, pp. 303–318, GLSA, Amherst.

Jäger, G. 1996. Topics in Dynamic Semantics. Ph.D. thesis, Humboldt-Universität zu Berlin.

Kamp, H. 1981. A theory of truth and semantic representation. In J. Groenendijk, T. Janssen, and M. Stokhof (eds.), *Formal Methods in the Study of Language*, University of Amsterdam Mathematical Centre, Amsterdam.

Kamp, H., and Reyle, U. 1993. *From Discourse to Logic: Introduction to Modeltheoretic Semantics of Natural Language, Formal Logic and Discourse Representation Theory*. Kluwer, Dordrecht.

Kratzer, A. 1995. Stage-level and individual-level predicates. In G. Carlson and F. Pelletier (eds.), *The Generic Book*, pp. 125–175, University of Chicago Press.

Krifka, M. 1992. A compositional semantics for multiple focus constructions. In J. Jacobs (ed.), *Informationsstruktur und Grammatik*. Linguistische Berichte, Sonderheft 4.

Landman, F. 1986. *Towards a Theory of Information*. Foris, Dordrecht.

Link, G. 1983. The logical analysis of plurals and mass terms: A lattice-theoretical approach. In R. Bäuerle, C. Schwarze, and A. von Stechow (eds.), *Meaning, Use, and Interpretation of Language*. de Gruyter, Berlin.

Löbner, S. 1990. *Wahr neben Falsch. Duale Operatoren als die Quantoren natürlicher Sprache*. Niemeyer, Tübingen.

Milsark, G. L. 1977. Towards an explanation of certain peculiarities of the existential construction in English. *Linguistic Analysis* 3, 1–29.

Rooth, M. 1992. A theory of focus interpretation. *Natural Language Semantics* 1, 75–116.

Sasse, H.-J. 1987. The thetic/categorical distinction revisited. *Linguistics* 25, 511–580.

Selkirk, E. 1984. *Phonology and Syntax. The Relation between Sound and Structure*, MIT Press, Cambridge, Mass.

Vallduví, E. 1992. *The Informational Component*. Garland Publishing, New York.

Veltman, F. 1996. Defaults in update semantics. *Journal of Philosophical Logic* 25.

11 Focus, Quantification, and Semantics-Pragmatics Issues

BARBARA H. PARTEE

Abstract

It is understood that focus can affect pragmatic aspects of interpretation; more controversial is the question of whether focus phenomena may have a direct semantic interpretation and, if so, what the relation is between semantic and pragmatic focus effects. Recent work shows two extremes (though substantively similar on many issues): (1) the "structured meaning" approach of von Stechow, Krifka, and others, a grammaticized approach that puts much of focus into syntax and semantics proper, and (2) the approach of Rooth (1992), removing focus as far as possible from the grammar proper.

The approach of the Prague school theorists Sgall and Hajičová offers a differently unified perspective on the semantics-pragmatics interface: their interpretation of focus might be said to give semantic status to what in some approaches would be considered purely pragmatic or contextual contributions, since theme-rheme structure is always considered an aspect of linguistic meaning, whether it has any observable truth-conditional effects or not.

Here I reexamine some of the issues concerning focus and quantificational structures (Partee 1991) in the light of questions that have arisen in working

I am grateful first of all to Eva Hajičová and Petr Sgall for many long and stimulating hours of discussion on issues of topic and focus, focus-sensitive operators, and tripartite structures, including most of the issues raised in this chapter, which has grown directly out of our joint research and is partly parasitic on our joint book in press. At the same time, it is written from my own point of view and I take responsibility for the views not expressly attributed to others or to our joint work, as well as for remaining shortcomings. Besides Professors Hajičová and Sgall, my greatest debts for discussions on various of these issues are to Jaroslav Peregrin, Manfred Krifka, Mats Rooth, and Kai von Fintel; thanks also for helpful discussions to Christine Bartels, Angelika Kratzer, Elisabeth Selkirk, Mark Steedman, Satoshi Tomioka, and Elena Benedicto. Emmon Bach read the manuscript and made valuable suggestions. Thanks also to Peter Bosch and Rob van der Sandt for their excellent organizing of the very fruitful conference on focus at which this chapter was presented, and to the other participants for ideas and discussion. Support for the research reported herein was provided principally by a grant to Eva Hajičová and the author under the U.S.-Czech Science and Technology Program for the period December 1992–September 1995 for the project "Semantics of English and Czech Sentence Structure and Word Order: Contributions to a Theory of Formal Semantics and Information Structure." The research was initiated with support in part by an earlier grant in 1989–90 from the International Research and Exchanges Board (IREX), with funds provided by the National Endowment for the Humanities and the United States Information Agency. None of these organizations is responsible for the views expressed.

on Hajičová, Partee, and Sgall (in press). Among the problematic cases that get particular attention are (1) the status of "second occurrence" expressions, (2) the distinction between the role of focus in determiner quantification and that in adverbial quantification, and (3) Taglicht examples: issues of scope and scope-islands.

The chapter concludes on a positive note with examples of tentative joint generalizations that reflect the emerging synthesis aimed at in Hajičová, Partee, and Sgall (in press).

1   Issues

It has always been understood that focus can affect pragmatic aspects of interpretation; recent investigations of the interaction of focus structure with semantic interpretation have brought increasing attention to the controversial question of whether focus phenomena may also have a direct semantic interpretation and, if so, what the relation is between the way focus interacts with pragmatics and the way it interacts with semantics. These issues also connect with the issue of how focus is treated (if at all) in the syntax.

Recent work in formal semantics shows two extremes on this issue (though highly compatible, and substantively very similar, on many issues): (a) the "structured meaning" approach of von Stechow (1991), Krifka (1991, 1992), and others provides a highly grammaticized approach that puts much of focus into the syntax and semantics proper; traditionally pragmatic uses of focus are assimilated to semantic ones via such things as the overt ASSERT operator of Jacobs (1983) and Krifka; and (b) the approach advocated by Rooth (1992), largely removing from the grammar proper the connection between (intonational) focus and focus-sensitive particles and constructions, attempting to unify and explain the diverse range of apparent contributions of focus to semantic interpretation via the uniform interpretation of focus as signaling the presence in the context of a certain kind of presupposition, to which "focus-sensitive" items might be anaphorically or presuppositionally related, unifying semantic and pragmatic effects in a more pragmatic dimension.

The approach of the Prague school theorists Sgall and Hajičová (Hajičová 1983, Sgall (ed) 1984, Hajičová 1984, Sgall et al. 1986, Peregrin and Sgall 1986, Materna et al. 1987) offers a unified view that suggests a different perspective on the semantics-pragmatics interface: the division of the sentence into topic and focus has something in common with the more recent structured meanings approach, and the interpretation of focus might be said to give semantic status to what in some approaches would be considered purely pragmatic or contextual contributions, since theme-rheme structure is always considered an aspect of linguistic meaning, whether it has any observable truth-conditional effects or not.

The process of working on a joint project that aims to integrate Praguean and formal semantics perspectives (see Hajičová, Partee, and Sgall, in press) has led me to question some of the ideas about the role of focus in the interpretation of quantificational structures expressed in Partee 1991 (influenced by work of Rooth, Krifka, Kratzer, von Stechow, Hajičová, Sgall, and others). This chapter contains more questions than answers; some of the questions arose from straight puzzlement, some from playing devil's advocate and discovering that I didn't always know how to answer the devil, and therefore couldn't be so sure whether the position in question should be regarded as so fiendish after all. The principal quandary that I remain in results from the tension in the following state of affairs: (1) Some of the questions that follow, like recent arguments of Rooth and others, seem to favor strongly a relatively strong "degrammaticization" of the effect of focus on semantics; (2) the Praguean approach, which obligatorily grammaticizes the topic-focus articulation of a sentence, though in a rather different way from the "focus-marking" approach common in Chomskyan and formal semantics traditions, seems to be able to offer potential answers to challenges of the sort raised in Section 4 concerning focus and scope, although the Praguean approach does not include any level or representation corresponding to truth-conditionally disambiguated semantic interpretation per se; (3) if the foregoing suggests that there is a direct connection between syntax and pragmatics in the case of focus but no direct connection between syntax and (truth-conditional) semantics, then something basic (I'm not sure what) about the way I have been accustomed to thinking about syntax, semantics, and pragmatics has to be rethought.

Some of these issues are also mentioned (but not resolved) in Hajičová, Partee, and Sgall (in press); in that work our principal goals are comparison of theories and analyses and first steps toward integration, and I conclude this chapter with some examples of tentative joint generalizations that reflect our emerging synthesis.

2   "Second Occurrence" Expressions

The first puzzle concerns the status of what is sometimes referred to in Prague school discussions of focus as "second occurrence" expressions, examples whose puzzling status might be highlighted if we called them examples of "backgrounded focus" or "deaccented focus." The following example is from Hajičová, Partee, and Sgall (in press); similar examples are discussed in Gussenhoven 1984, Koktová 1986, Rooth 1992, Krifka 1991, and Partee 1991. The two sentences are to be read as a dialogue between speakers A and B.

(1)   A: Everyone already knew that Mary only eats VEGETABLES.
        B: If even Paul knew that Mary only eats vegetables, then he should have
            suggested a different RESTAURANT.

If "only" is a focus-sensitive operator, then it would seem that the two occurrences of "only eats vegetables" should have the same analysis, but if there really is no phonological reflex of focus on the second occurrence, then that leads to the notion of "phonologically invisible focus," which at best would force the recognition of a multiplicity of different notions of "focus" and at worst might lead to a fundamentally incoherent notion of focus.

Intuitively it is clear enough what is going on here. In the first sentence, on its most straightforward interpretation, we have a normal occurrence of a focus-sensitive operator (or focalizer, in Praguean terminology), *only*, associated with focus on *vegetables*. In B's reply, the whole embedded clause containing the focalizer is repeated, and since it is all now familiar, it can be deaccented; the association of *only* with *vegetables* can be "carried over" in interpreting the second occurrence of the clause, whether or not there is any kind of intonational prominence of *vegetables*.

There are other examples of a similar sort that show that overt repetition is not required for this phenomenon; implicit inferrability is often enough to make it clear that a particular element is to be associated with a focus-sensitive operator in the absence of any explicit focus-marking by intonation, word order, or whatever device or devices a given language uses. In fact, example (1) can be readily converted into such an example simply by converting A's sentence into something known by the discussants but not uttered aloud; B's sentence could then still be uttered with the only marked focus on *Paul* but with *vegetables* clearly understood as the "focus" associated with *only*.

Partee (1991) described this phenomenon as "inheritance of focus structure" from an earlier part of a discourse, illustrating it with example (2). Here too the two sentences are to be read as a dialogue.

(2)   A: Eva only gave xerox copies to the GRADUATE STUDENTS.
       B: No, PETR only gave xerox copies to the graduate students.

Rooth's (1992) example (3) is another example of "deaccented focus", one with a slightly different source: there is competition here between contrastive focus and focalizer-associated focus, and one possible resolution of the competition is to omit any marking of focus on the element *rice* associated with the focalizer *only*. (See also Schwarzschild 1993.) (The resulting string with the intonation informally indicated below is of course ambiguous; there is also a reading on which *eat* is the element associated with *only* in addition to being contrasted with *grow*. But that reading does not exemplify the puzzle we are looking at.)

(3)   Farmers who GROW rice often only EAT rice.

The puzzle, a dilemma for a "grammaticized" account of topic-focus structure and of the association of focus-sensitive operators like *only* with their associated foci, is the following: Is the semantic relation of *only* to *vegetables* the same in the A and B sentences of (1)? (It certainly seems so.) If so, does that require the positing of "inaudible focus" on (the backgrounded or contextually bound) *vegetables* in (1B)? That is, does a uniform syntax-semantics relation require a non-uniform relation between syntax and phonology?

If we assume a commitment to a grammaticized account, requiring that both the phonology-syntax relation involved in the representation and realization of focus and the syntax-semantic relation involved in the association of focalizers with focused elements be characterized in the grammar, then we are faced with a serious conflict between phonologists and semanticists, one that already exists implicitly in some of the literature but that may not have been confronted directly. In the rich literature that investigates the phonological phenomena of English pitch accent and phrasal boundary tones (as in the work of Pierrehumbert, Hirschberg, Selkirk, and others), the distribution of accents together with syntactic structure are critical determinants of the possible assignments of focus-marking to pieces of the sentence; from a phonology-centered perspective, if everything following *only* in (2B) is deaccented, then there is no focus other than that on PETR in that sentence, and this would be an example of an occurrence of *only* that is not associating with focus in its sentence; similarly for *vegetables* in (1B). On the other hand, in a semantics-centered theory, if it is decided that *only* is a focus-sensitive operator, or focalizer, it would presumably be preferable to say that *vegetables* receives a secondary or embedded focus in (1B) by virtue of the anaphoric relations holding between (1B) and (1A), and that *only* associates with the focused *vegetables* in (1B) just as it does in (1A). From one perspective, the idea of a deaccented focused element is quite nonsensical, while from the other perspective, that notion is much more tolerable (just appeal to "abstract accent") than the notion of a focus-sensitive operator without a focused element to associate with.

Rooth (1992) and von Fintel (1994) offer perspectives that help to resolve such tensions in an explanatory direction. While neither pretends to be able to account for all potentially relevant cases in their heavily degrammaticized theories of association with focus, both relieve the tension generated by examples like (11) by making the focus-sensitivity of focalizers like *only* less direct than in some other accounts; the semantics of *only* requires that the context in which it is interpreted provide a set of alternatives of a narrowly specifiable sort. A focused element may help signal a presupposition of the existence of a relevant set of alternatives (with the semantics of focus providing the specification of the alternatives, given a particular choice of focus), and that may be the core case; but it is also possible for a relevant set of alternatives already to exist in the given context (as it does when 1B is uttered), in which case no focus is required. On this view, the semantic and the phonological perspectives are then perfectly compatible.

The kind of "degrammaticized" or "pragmatic" account advocated by Rooth (1992) and Fintel (1994) therefore does not face this dilemma, and that could be an argument in its favor. It is conceivable that an advocate of a more grammaticized account might be able to find some way to finesse the dilemma by making use of the same insights concerning context, somehow appealing to pragmatic effects on choices among potentially available semantic structures (whether these are cast in terms of recursive tripartite structures, or structured meanings, or Praguean tectogrammatical representations with their explicit representation of topic-focus articulation). But it is not clear at this point how this could be done, so it seems to me that the only choice is between a degrammaticized account of association with focus and a head-on confrontation between a phonologically based and a semantically based characterization of focus.[1]

3   D-Quantification and A-Quantification Effects

The second puzzle is similar. The question this time is whether focus contributes to the determination of the domain of quantification in the same way or in different ways with respect to determiner quantifiers and adverbs of quantification (*D-quantification* versus *A-quantification* in the terminology of Partee, Bach, and Kratzer 1987, Bach et al. (eds.) 1995). Prima facie, adverbs of quantification (Lewis 1975, Schwarzschild 1989) are focus-sensitive; determiner quantifiers are not. Let me review where I have previously stood on this issue before raising a new puzzle about it. Partee (1991) used this contrast in discussing the status of the hypothesized correlation F regarding topic-focus structure and tripartite quantificational structures (Heim 1982) involving operator, restrictive clause (domain restriction), and nuclear scope:

> F: Topic (or background) corresponds to restrictive clause; focus, or the combination of topic with focus, corresponds to nuclear scope.

Partee (1991) argued that correlation F in languages like English has the status of a default strategy that can be overridden by explicit syntactic rules, as in the case of the determiner quantifiers. Example (4), from Rooth (1985), is a familiar example of the contribution of focus to the determination of the domain of quantification for an adverb of quantification; the analysis of (4a) is given informally in (5).

(4)   a. Mary always took JOHN to the movies.
         b. Mary always took John to the MOVIES.
         c. MARY always took John to the movies.

(5)   Analysis of (4a)
         a. Mary always took [John]$_F$ to the movies
         b. Tripartite structure

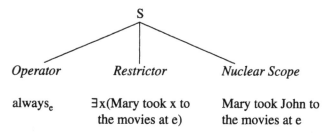

The contrasting behavior of determiner quantifiers is illustrated in (6); the grammar of NPs explicitly requires that the common noun phrase be interpreted as the restrictive clause, and the VP or sentence abstract with which the NP is in construction be interpreted as the nuclear scope: that is the heart of the interpretation of NPs as generalized quantifiers. Sentence (6A) is straightforward, with *logicians* interpreted as the domain of quantification. If we add a focused item within the common noun phrase, there is no tendency at all to interpret the focused item as belonging to the nuclear scope as it was in the sentences in (4): if that happened here, the sentence should mean something like 'most logicians who like linguistics are nice,' or 'most logicians like linguistics and are nice,' or the like, and it is clear that no such reading is possible.

(6)   D-quantifier: Tripartite structure determined by syntax:
        A: Most logicians like linguistics.
        B: Most NICE logicians like linguistics.

But focus can contribute domain restrictions to D-quantification constructions via effects that would most naturally be considered pragmatic effects on context. Example (7) is from Krifka (1990); ignoring the interesting phenomenon of event-induced measures of quantification discussed in his article (and analyzed further in the chapter by Regine Eckardt, this volume, which is highly relevant to the issues discussed here), let us just pay attention to the ambiguity represented by (7a) versus (7b). The reading (7a) is the one that the grammar gives directly. The reading (7b) is also possible and in many contexts would be the more natural one.

(7)   Most ships pass through the lock at NIGHT.
        a. MOST (ships) (pass through the lock at night)
        b. MOST (ships that pass through the lock) (pass through the lock at night)

It is doubtful that anyone would want to propose that a structure like (7b) is syntactically constructed at LF or any other "grammatical" level; for one thing, it is still the case for all possible readings of (7) that the common noun phrase with which the determiner is in construction must go into the restrictive clause and the whole verb phrase goes into the nuclear scope. Rather, as Krifka and others have noted, it seems to be the case that the "backgrounded" part of the verb phrase interpretation is accommodated into the restrictive clause as a further restriction; this makes it similar to normal contextual narrowing of domains and to examples of domain restriction via accommodation of presuppositions (Heim 1983, Schubert and Pelletier 1988, Partee 1993). The exact principles at work in such cases may not be entirely understood, but the classification of these effects as indirect or "pragmatic", rather than grammatical, seems uncontroversial.

Now this time let's not stop here; having seen this interaction of grammatical and nongrammatical effects in the case of D-quantification, let's reexamine A-quantification. What if we just said that the grammatical difference between them is that the grammar does not specify any restrictor clause in the case of A-quantification? If in the case of D-quantification we say that the grammar gives the common noun phrase as restrictor and pragmatic effects such as the focus effects in (7) can add further restrictions, then why couldn't and shouldn't we make a similar analysis of the effects of focus with A-quantification? Why can't adverbs of quantification just take their whole clause as nuclear scope, with no restrictor clause provided by grammar, all the rest of the understood restrictor provided indirectly as in the D-quantifier case (7)?

In an example like (4a), for instance, we would then have the grammar specifying the operator and its nuclear scope, and no restrictor (perhaps more precisely a trivial restrictor; in any case, not limiting the domain at all); if we then intersect the trivial restrictor with the set of alternatives provided by the focus structure (analogously to what happens in (7)), we obtain exactly the analysis in (5).

There may be independent reasons for making the focus-sensitivity of A-quantification a matter of grammar, unlike the "secondary" focus-sensitivity of D-quantification as illustrated in (7). But it needs to be argued. Otherwise this may be a further argument for the Rooth-von Fintel program of degrammaticizing the phenomena of focus-sensitivity.

4   Focus and Scope

The other puzzle or puzzles (it's not clear to me whether these should be considered two aspects of a single phenomenon or not) that I want to discuss also concern the interplay of semantic structure and pragmatic factors, this time in the determination of the scope and domain restriction of focus-sensitive operators.

Examples of the following kind from Taglicht (1984) were discussed by Rooth (1985) and provided some of the important arguments for Rooth's analysis of the behavior of focus-sensitive *only*. Example (8) is an example with unambiguous focus, but ambiguous scope; example (9) has ambiguous focus but unambiguous scope. The meanings these examples can have in English are spelled out below.

(8)   We are required to study only SYNTAX.

(9)   We are only required to study SYNTAX.

The data are as follows. Sentence (8) has two possible interpretations, as indicated in (8.i, ii):

(8)   i. narrow scope: there is a requirement: "study only syntax."
        ii. wide scope: only for syntax is there a requirement to study it, while other subjects are optional.

In both cases, the focused expression is *syntax*; the scope of *only* may be either the lower clause (or VP) or the whole sentence (or VP; I am not trying to distinguish between sentence scope and VP scope here). The first question or subpuzzle concerns the explanation of these facts: must this scope ambiguity be analyzed, as in Rooth (1985), as a case of NP (quantifier) scope ambiguity? I don't know of any direct arguments against such an account, which has always seemed quite satisfying to me, but such an analysis turns out to present a serious obstacle to synthesis of work in the formal semantics tradition with work in the Prague school tradition, which disambiguates topic-focus structure but does not in the grammar disambiguate typical quantifier scope ambiguities.

The second subpuzzle starts from sentence (9), in which the scope of *only* is unambiguously the whole sentence (or VP); the associated focus must contain *syntax* and may contain various amounts more; what should the grammar say about the range of possibilities for the focus? In this case the puzzle concerns two possible claims concerning the position of the focalizer: that its position marks the boundary of its scope, or that its position marks the boundary of the focused part. Rooth (1985) argued for the former; Hajičová (1983), Sgall, Hajičová, and Panevová (1986) and Koktová (1986, 1987) have argued for the latter. Is (9) really clear evidence that the position of "only" marks its scope and not its focus?

We consider these two (sub?)puzzles in turn.

4.1 *"Ambiguous scope" in (8): via NP-Attachment?*

When can an embedded clause *only* have main clause scope as in (8)? Let us consider two hypotheses, the first corresponding to the analysis in Rooth (1985), the second a possible alternative that would be consistent with the Praguean preference not to consider *only* to be part of the NP in (8).[2]

> *Hypothesis (i): NP-attachment:* only if it is attached to an NP that can have main clause scope.

Hypothesis (i) subsumes the explanation of *only*'s scope under principles for possible scopes of NPs when (and only when) *only* is attached to an NP; the assumption is that only NPs (more or less) undergo Quantifying In (or QR, or Cooper Storage, or whatever device one uses to account for NP scope).

> *Hypothesis (ii): Clause-union:* only if at some relevant level there is, or it is as if there is, only one clause.

According to the alternative hypothesis (ii), a possibility suggested in Hajičová, Partee, and Sgall (1997), a focalizer and its focus must be in the same clause; when the focus of *only* depends on a given verb (in dependency grammar terms), so does *only*. So the possibility of main clause scope in (8) is a result of a possible "verb cluster" or clause-union-like interpretation.

Let us work back up to example (8) starting from some simpler Taglicht-type examples.

(10)   Adam ate only an APPLE.

(11)   Adam only ate an APPLE.

The data for English are that (10) is unambiguous: Adam ate nothing other than an apple; while (11) is ambiguous: it can mean the same as (10), or it can mean that Adam did nothing other/more than eat an apple.

There are competing accounts of the synonymy of (10) with one reading of (11).

(i) On the analysis of Rooth (1985) this is an interesting case of the same reading resulting from quite different sources: NP-attachment in (10) versus focus-sensitivity in (11).

(ii) On a Praguean analysis, (10) and (11) have the same "semantically relevant syntax,"[3] *only* having S-scope or VP-scope in both; they differ in surface form because English has a shallow rule optionally moving *only* before the verb even if the verb is less dynamic than *only*.

One interesting query that we might raise at this point concerns the differences in intuitions about the possibility of NP-attachment of *only*, reported in note 2. Might there be differences from language to language concerning the possible analyses of a word like *only* immediately preceding an NP? Are there languages in which *only* is more clearly an adverb and in which adverbs can relatively easily intervene between verb and object, so that an adverbial analysis of *only* in a sentence resembling (10) is more defensible than an ad-NP analysis? (Might Czech be such a language?)

A related query concerning English that has arisen in the course of the Hajičová, Partee, and Sgall discussions of these matters is the question, "What is *mostly* in English, as in *Mary writes mostly poetry?*" Also sharing some but not all properties of *mostly* is one use of *all*, as in *Last year she wrote all poetry, no prose*. The status of "polymorphic" or "cross-categorial" particles, like *only*, *even*, *all*, and *mostly*, clearly needs further work, especially cross-linguistically, as does the notion of an adverb; these elements are not so neatly cross-categorial as the boolean *and*, *or*, and (maybe) *not* have seemed to be.

Returning to the main thread of our argument, let us now consider an example with two clauses, but with no site for NP-attachment.

(12)   Jim said that Peter only WALKED.

In (12) there is no wide scope reading analogous to that in (8). Focus is unambiguous, and scope is likewise unambiguous. The kind of scope ambiguity seen in (8) arises only in sentences in which *only* is adjacent to an NP. How could a clause-union kind of account predict that (12) is less ambiguous than (8)?

But not so fast; we need to test for islandhood. And when we do, we discover a similar lack of a wide scope reading for *only* + *NP* in a comparable construction:

(12′)   Jim said that Peter studied only SYNTAX.

And if islandhood correlates with lack of clause-union effects, it may turn out that the two accounts make similar predictions. This is an interesting state of affairs worth deeper investigation; it could be a case where two structurally quite different mechanisms can produce identical or nearly identical phenomena, and it will take careful research to determine whether we are dealing with competing theories about the same phenomenon or with a subtle typological difference between languages.

Let us return to the Taglicht example (8) that began this discussion:

(8)   We are required to study only SYNTAX.

In support of Hypothesis (i) (NP-attachment), there is independent evidence that a full NP can take wide scope in a sentence like (8), though not in all sentences. Consider the following paradigm:

(8)   We are required to study only SYNTAX. (ambiguous scope)

(13)   It is required that we study only SYNTAX. (unambiguous scope.)

(14)   We are required to study almost no foreign languages. (ambiguous scope)

(15)   It is required that we study almost no foreign languages. (unambiguous scope)

The interpretations of the quantifier sentences in (14)–(15) closely match the available interpretations of the *only*-sentences in (8) and (13). (15) shares only the "narrow scope" reading of (14), in which what is required is that we study very few languages. (14) also has a "wide scope" reading, in which we could be required to study many, but with the choice of which ones left almost entirely to us.

We note that it is the embedded infinitive construction in (8) and (14) that permits the NP to have wide scope, whereas the embedded finite clause construction in (13) and (15) makes it impossible (or at least very difficult) for the NP to take wide scope. This is also suggestive of "clause union" phenomena; witness the extended debates about whether NP-scope is "clause-bound" or not. Thus if islandhood for NP-scope correlates with lack of clause-union effects, the two accounts make similar predictions in this case as well as in the case of sentence (12), discussed earlier.

This leaves us with questions such as the following: How strong are the arguments for NP-attachment in (8) if one is not already presupposing heavily binary-branching structures? What is the correlation between structures that permit higher scope than surface position for *only* and structures that permit clause-union sorts of phenomena? I have no answers to these questions now, but I raise them to suggest that the study of focus has much both to offer to and to gain from debates about whether NP-scope should be analyzed as clause-bound or not (in certain languages or in all languages).

4.2   *Does the Focalizer Mark Boundary of Scope or Boundary of Focus?*

The second subpuzzle of this section, raised by the Taglicht example (9), also arises principally in two-clause sentences. As noted, the principal question here is, Does the position of a focalizer mark the boundary of the scope (Rooth 1985) or the boundary of the focus (Hajičová, Sgall, Koktová)? (And/or do different conceptions of focus go with different positions on this question?)

Let us start the discussion with an example in which the focused item is not an NP, to make it clear that NP-scope is not a necessary ingredient of this puzzle.

(16)   Jim only said that Peter WALKED.

With scope *said that Peter walked*, and focus constrained to include *walked*, Rooth's alternative semantics distinguishes the following readings for (16) (both here and later, "alternative sets" are indicated informally by mentioning sample alternatives):

(16′)   a. $_F$[WALKED] Alternatives: said that Peter Xed (e.g. said that Peter ran)
         b. $_F$[Peter WALKED] Alternatives: said that p (e.g. said that Mary danced)
         c. $_F$[said that Peter WALKED] Alternatives: X'd (e.g. force Peter to confess to treason)

The Prague school analysis does not allow (a) in this case, because the focalizer must normally occur at topic-focus boundary, but does make further distinctions within (b) and (c) that allow the same empirical coverage. *Within* the focus, some subparts may be contextually bound (as exemplified, for instance, by *Peter* in (16′c)). Supposing that we all agree that the interpretation of focus somehow involves a set of alternatives to the focused material: it may nevertheless be the case that contextually bound elements within the focused part may (perhaps optionally) be taken as invariant aspects of the alternatives. Contextually bound elements within the focus may thus have (via a different route) the same effects as elements within the topic, as we illustrate below. In this linearization of Praguean dependency trees with their topic-focus articulation, parenthesization marks dependency structure (so that, for example, in (16″b), *said* has three dependents: *Jim*, *only*, and *walked*; *walked* has one dependent, *Peter*; grammatical morphemes like the complementizer *that* are being ignored here). Subscripted numbers mark relative degree of communicative dynamism, with lower numbers for less dynamic (more topiclike), higher for more dynamic (more focuslike), and the exclamation point marking the boundary between the topic part of the sentence and the focus part.

(16″)   b. (i) (Jim$_1$) (only$_3$!) said$_2$ (that (Peter$_4$) walked$_5$)
             (ii) (Jim$_1$) (only$_3$!) said$_2$ (that (Peter$_5$) walked$_4$)

In both, *Peter walked* is the focus, but in (i), *Peter*, as a dependent less dynamic than its head, must be contextually bound. Similarly in (c.i–ii): in both, *said that Peter walked* is the focus, but within the focus in (c.i), *Peter* is contextually bound.

         c. (i) (Jim$_1$) (only$_2$!) said$_3$ (that (Peter$_4$) walked$_5$)
             (ii) (Jim$_1$) (only$_2$!) said$_3$ (that (Peter$_5$) walked$_4$)

On this analysis, the relevant alternatives are as follows:

for (b.i): e.g. Jim said that Peter ran
for (b.ii): e.g. Jim said that Mary danced
for (c.i): e.g. Jim suspected that Peter ran away
for (c.ii): e.g. Jim filed an official complaint

The Rooth-style analysis[4] (16′a–c) conforms to the generalization of Rooth (1985) that *only* occurs at the boundary of its scope. The competing analysis (16″b–c) conforms to the competing Praguean generalization that *only* (in underlying structure) normally occurs at the boundary of topic and focus; the notion of scope is not normally considered to be a grammaticized notion at all on that approach, but, if needed, it would be defined as the maximal projection of the head (normally verb) on which the focalizer depends.

If these analyses can cover the same empirical data (as suggested but not established by consideration of example (16)), how can one choose between them? What independent evidence is there for the necessity of taking just "walk" as a possible focus? Is that required by a theory like Rooth's, or is it just common practice that has been followed because within that paradigm there was no reason not to?[5]

If we return to our second Taglicht example, (9), repeated here, we see that the same considerations apply here as in (16).

(9)   We are only required to study SYNTAX. (ambiguous focus, unambiguous scope.)

If just "syntax" can be focus, then we clearly need to distinguish focus from scope. But if the same effect can be achieved by taking the focus to be at least "study syntax" with the possibility of "study" being contextually bound and hence pragmatically invariant in the alternative-set, then the Praguean hypothesis that "only" normally marks the topic-focus boundary (in underlying word order) (Hajičová and Sgall 1987) could be maintained (and compare Peregrin's (1994, 1996) generalization). In general, then, how strong are the arguments for distinguishing the focus of a focus-sensitive operator from its scope? This distinction was not commonly drawn before the work of Rooth (1985), and although nothing I have said here constitutes a theory-internal objection, the question needs reexamination in the context of broader theory comparisons.

The issues raised here include points that are currently debated within various frameworks as well as across them; in particular, the question of whether sentence structure per se contributes directly to the determination of the scope and the domain specification of the operator is certainly a matter for debate. Within the formal semantics community, it is normally assumed, I would say, that the determination of the possible scopes of an operator is indeed a matter of grammar (with nonlinguistic factors playing their role in selection of preferred readings from among the grammatically available possibilities), but there is not yet consensus concerning the interplay of linguistic and nonlinguistic factors in the delimitation of the domain (restrictive clause) of the operator. Rooth (1992) and von Fintel (1994) represent moves in a direction more compatible with the Praguean approach described earlier in the sense that they treat quantifier domain selection as a largely implicit, contextually driven matter for operators such as *only* and the adverbs of quantification; the contribution of focus to the determination of logical form is indirect on this kind of approach.

5   Preliminary Generalizations in Two Versions

All of the puzzles discussed previously have arisen in the course of attempting to work out the relation between topic-focus articulation and tripartite structures for adverbs of quantification and other focus-sensitive operators (Hajičová, Partee, and Sgall, in press). Some major differences in theoretical frameworks and some serious substantive disagreements such as the issue of possible NP-attachment of *only* (discussed in section 4), which we have been trying to elucidate as we progress, increase the challenge of reaching joint conclusions. In this section I report an example of some preliminary joint generalizations. These general-izations concern the basic notions connected with tripartite structures – the no-tions of scope, focus, and background of a focus-sensitive operator. They do not directly cover all the potential counterexamples, which we believe can be described as resulting from interacting effects and/or with refinements of these principles.

The notion of the scope of a focalizer, while not uniformly used in the focus literature and, as noted, not a notion that is indigenous to the Praguean approach, is one about which we have been able to maintain relatively easy agreement. We have not always been in agreement about the necessity for or criteria for distinguishing scope from ("broad") focus, and/or "broad" focus from the "focus of a focalizer", but those problematic distinctions have been addressed from within fairly easy agreement about what we want to call scope if we need such a notion at all. We have normally simply taken the scope to be the relevant clausal domain; we have not tried to distinguish clausal scope from VP scope (in part because dependency grammar does not recognize a category of VP, and in part because those issues are in flux within other frameworks as well); and we have not gone very far into the examination of possible cases of NP scope.

The hard work has all centered around identifying the focus of a focalizer. Given that, the notion of "background" (the part that contributes its value to the restrictor clause) is just scope minus that focus.

In the generalizations that follow, we use "f" for focalizer or focus-sensitive operator, "ff" for focus of (associated with) a focalizer, and F or simply "focus" for ("broad") focus in the sense of Praguean topic-focus articulation. Degrees of dynamism are to be understood in terms of the Praguean notion of *scale of communicative dynamism.*

(17)   *Scope, focus, and background of a focalizer.*
     i. The *scope* of a focalizer f is the complete projection (in dependency syntax) of the head on which it depends (that is, the head and all its dependents).
    i'. In "LF" terms, the scope of a focalizer is its c-command domain at LF. In terms of function-argument structure and "f-command" (Bach and Partee 1980), the scope of a focalizer is its f-command domain.
    ii. The *focus ff of a focalizer f* :
       a. Core generalization: ff of f consists of the elements of the scope of f that are more dynamic than f.
       b. Subgeneralizations:
          b1: The prototypical (unmarked) position of f is that of the least dynamic element of the focus of the sentence (clause); the ff then consists of those elements of the scope of f that are more dynamic than f, which should normally be exactly F (the Praguean focus);
          b2: if f occurs in the topic of a sentence or clause, its scope will be limited to the topic; the focus of f will consist of those elements of its scope that are more dynamic than f;
          b3: if f is stressed (carries the intonation center), then it constitutes the whole focus F of the sentence; its own focus ff may be reconstructable from degrees of dynamism in the topic.
    iii. The *background* of a focalizer equals its scope minus its focus.

(18)   *Tripartite structures.*
     The counterpart of the focalizer is the operator, that of its background is the restrictor, and that of its focus is the nuclear scope.

The generalization in (18) has played a partly methodological role in our debates, the issue being whether we can agree on analyses that meet the conditions that have motivated both tripartite structure analyses and Praguean analyses of topic-focus articulation.

The generalizations in (17) do not assume a Roothian NP-attachment and NP-scope account of the Taglicht examples discussed in section 4. To clarify the points at which that difference has an impact on our generalizations, we restate the central part of (17) in two versions, as (19). *Version A*, a streamlining of what we presented in (17), is compatible with a dependency grammar in which *only* in the controversial examples above attaches to the verb, not to the NP, and in which quantifier scopes are not disambiguated at the semantically relevant syntactic level. *Version B* is compatible with a Montague grammar or other disambiguated syntax, assuming that *only* attaches to NP in the controversial cases above and that NP scopes are disambiguated at the semantically relevant syntactic level.

(19)   *Scope, focus, and background of a focalizer.*

    (i) (A) The scope of a focus-sensitive operator (focalizer) is the complete projection of the head on which it depends (that is, the head and all its dependents).

         (B) The scope of a focalizer is its f-command domain (or c-command at LF).

    (ii) (A) The focus of a focalizer is the focus of that projection.

         (B) The focus of a focalizer is the focus of its immediate argument. (Note that if the immediate argument is an NP whose f-command domain is enlarged by QR, the focus of the focalizer still must be within the NP.)

    (iii) (A) Background = scope minus focus. (There may of course also be pragmatic additions to background.)

         (B) Same.

Discussion surrounding these hypothesized generalizations is found in the aforementioned joint book in press. All of the puzzles raised earlier in this chapter are related to points that arose as we struggled to analyze the sources of various difficulties that were impeding a smooth synthesis of our respective approaches. Solutions to those puzzles might very well affect the extent to which the hypothesized generalizations, or some modification of them, can be fleshed out in a manner that covers all of the challenges we know of in ways compatible with our rather different theoretical frameworks. Perhaps some of these puzzles are old and I am just having to restate them for myself at this stage in my progress in this difficult domain. In any case, I do not myself have answers to offer, and answers may not be very quick in coming, but I hope that articulating them in this way and presenting them to others working on focus may help to move the inquiry forward.

Notes

1   This chapter was written in 1994, immediately after the conference in which it was presented. Since then, and partly in response to the issues raised here, there has been important work done on the problem of second-occurrence focus by Christine Bartels (1997) and Manfred Krifka (1997). Bartels presents preliminary evidence suggesting that there may well be significant acoustic correlates of second-occurrence focus, even though they are clearly not intonationally marked in the same way as normal occurrences of focus. Krifka argues for a serious consideration of the possibility that second-occurrence focus may need to be subdivided into two types. One type, proper second-occurrence focus, has complete segmental identity and hence is "deaccented"; this may reflect a special sort of "economy" anaphora that allows previously computed semantic values to be transferred to the deaccented constituent, including any previously computed focus value. The other type, improper second occurrence focus, has

less than complete segmental identity and may show remaining acoustic correlates of focus. Neither author claims to have settled the issue, and I leave the original discussion intact here because it is referred to in some of the subsequent literature.

2   The issue of whether *only* is attached to the NP or to the VP (dependent on the noun or on the verb, in dependency grammar terms) is one that has emerged as a surprisingly strong disagreement in the course of writing Hajičová, Partee, and Sgall (in press) and is discussed there; it seems that speakers of first languages other than English and native speakers of English may have quite different intuitions about the structure of the English sentence. This interesting phenomenon deserves explanation; this is just an initial exploration of one aspect of it.

3   This is the level of tectogrammatical representation in Sgall et al. (1986); the same claims could be recast in terms of LF and its relation to surface structure, or homophonous pairs of rules in classical Montague grammar, or the like.

4   The Rooth-style analysis, which in this respect follows the tradition of focus projection that goes back to early work by Jackendoff, Chomsky, and others, should be reexamined to see whether there is a distinction to be made that corresponds to the Praguean distinction between (16″c.i) and (16″c.ii). That analysis clearly has a four-way distinction here, with *Peter* more or less dynamic than *walked* and independently with *said* part of the focus or not. The usual focus-projection analysis, slightly oversimplified, may simply be said to offer three increasingly inclusive domains projected up the tree from *walked*. While there are surely finer-grained distinctions that are drawn when one takes full account of details of timing and intonation, the basic division on the focus-projection account is among the three structures of (16′) rather than the four structures of (16″).

5   Mark Steedman's paper (1994) reminded me that he has already been making a similar argument and for similar reasons, with respect to examples like (i) from Kratzer (1991), discussed by Steedman at the Ninth Amsterdam Colloquium in December 1993.

(i)   They only asked whether I knew the woman who chairs the ZONING board.

For Steedman's treatment of focus in a combinatorial categorial grammar framework, it is also expected that islands for "movement" should also be islands for focus, since both are analyzed by means of nonstandard "constituents" built up using function composition and other combinators, and Steedman has been suggesting that the apparent island-insensitivity of focus should be explained away along much the same lines as (re)suggested here. The suggestion made by Manfred Krifka (1994) for a distinction between *F-marking* (focus) and *A-marking* (what's relevant for alternatives) also seems to be related to this issue.

References

Bach, E., and B. Partee 1980. "Anaphora and semantic structure." In J. Kreiman and A.E. Ojeda (eds.), *Parasession on Pronouns and Anaphora*. Chicago Linguistic Society. Chicago.

Bach, E., E. Jelinek, A. Kratzer, and B. Partee, eds., 1995. *Quantification and Natural Languages*, Kluwer, Dordrecht.

Bartels, C. 1997. "Acoustic Correlates of 'Second Occurrence' Focus: Toward an Experimental Investigation," in H. Kamp and B. Partee (eds.), Proceedings of the Workshop on "Context Dependence in the Analysis of Linguistic Meaning," Prague and Bad Teinach, 1995, Vol. II, University of Stuttgart Working Papers, 11–30.

Bosch, P., and R. van der Sandt (eds.) 1994. *Focus and Natural Language Processing.* Vols. 6–8. *Working Papers of the Institute for Logic and Linguistics.* IBM Deutschland GmbH., Heidelberg.

Fintel, Kai von. 1994. Restrictions on Quantifier Domains, Ph.D. dissertation, distributed by GLSA, University of Massachusetts, Amherst.

Gussenhoven, C. 1984. *On the Grammar and Semantics of Sentence Accents*, Foris, Dordrecht.

Hajičová, E. 1983. "Topic and Focus," *Theoretical Linguistics* 10, 268–276.

Hajičová, E. 1984. "Presupposition and Allegation Revisited," *Journal of Pragmatics* 8, 155–167.

Hajičová, E., B. Partee, and P. Sgall 1997. "Focus, Topic, and Semantics," in E. Benedicto and S. Tomioka, (eds.), *Proceedings of the Workshop on Focus*, University of Massachusetts, Occasional Papers in Linguistics, GLSA.

Hajičová, E., B. Partee, and P. Sgall in press. *Topic-Focus Articulation, Tripartite Structures, and Semantic Content*, Kluwer, Dordrecht, 101–124.

Hajičová, E. and P. Sgall 1987. "The Ordering Principle," *Journal of Pragmatics* 11, 435–454.

Heim, I. R. 1982. The Semantics of Definite and Indefinite Noun Phrases, Ph.D. dissertation, University of Massachusetts, Amherst.

Heim, I. R. 1983. "On the Projection Problem for Presuppositions," WCCFL 2, Stanford Linguistics Association, Stanford, Calif., 114–125.

Jacobs, J. 1983. *Focus und Skalen, Zur Syntax und Semantik von Gradpartikeln im Deutschen*, Niemeyer, Tuebingen.

Koktová, E. 1986. *Sentence Adverbials*, John Benjamins, Amsterdam.

Koktová, E. 1987. "On the Scoping Properties of Negation, Focusing Particles and Sentence Adverbials," *Theoretical Linguistics* 14, 173–226.

Kratzer, A. 1991. "The Representation of Focus," in A. von Stechow and D. Wunderlich, eds., *Semantics*, de Gruyter, 825–834.

Krifka, M. 1990. "4000 Ships Passed through the Lock: Object-Induced Measure Functions on Events," *Linguistics and Philosophy* 13.

Krifka, M. 1991. "A Compositional Semantics for Multiple Focus Constructions," in S. Moore and A. Wyner, (eds.), *Proceedings of SALT I*, Cornell, New York, 127–158.

Krifka, M. 1992. Focus, Quantification, and Dynamic Interpretation, Ms., University of Texas, Austin.

Krifka, M. 1994. "Focus and Operator Scope in German," In P. Bosch and R. van der Sandt (eds.) (1994), 133–152.

Krifka, Manfred 1997. "Focus and/or Context: A Second Look at Second Occurrence Expressions," in H. Kamp and B. Partee (eds.), *Proceedings of the Workshop on "Context Dependence in the Analysis of Linguistic Meaning,"* Prague and Bad Teinach, 1995, Vol. I, University of Stuttgart Working Papers, 253–275.

Lewis, D. 1975. "Adverbs of Quantification," in E. L. Keenan, ed., *Formal Semantics of Natural Language*, Cambridge University Press, Cambridge, 3–15.

Materna, P., Hajičová, E., and Sgall, P. 1987. "Redundant Answers and Topic/Focus Articulation," *Linguistics and Philosophy* 10, 101–113.

Partee, B. 1991. "Topic, Focus and Quantification," in S. Moore and A. Wyner, eds., *Proceedings of SALT I*, Cornell, New York, 159–187.

Partee, B. 1993. "On the 'Scope of Negation' and Polarity Sensitivity," in Eva Hajičová, ed., *Functional Description of Language*, Prague: Faculty of Mathematics and Physics, Charles University, 179–196.

Partee, B., E. Bach, and A. Kratzer 1987. "Quantification: A Cross-Linguistic Perspective," NSF proposal, University of Massachusetts, Amherst.

Peregrin, J. 1994. "Topic-Focus Articulation as Generalized Quantification." In P. Bosch and R. van der Sandt (eds.) (1994), 379–387.

Peregrin, J. 1996. "Topic and Focus in a Formal Framework," in B. Partee and P. Sgall (eds.), *Discourse and Meaning: Papers in Honor of Eva Hajičová*, John Benjamins, Amsterdam, 235–254.

Peregrin, J. and P. Sgall, "An Attempt at a Framework for Semantic Interpretation of Natural Language," *Theoretical Linguistics* 13, 37–73.

Rooth, M. 1985. Association with Focus, Ph.D. dissertation, University of Massachusetts, Amherst.

Rooth, M. 1992. "A Theory of Focus Interpretation," *Natural Language Semantics* 1, 75–116.

Schubert, L. and F. J. Pelletier 1988. "Generically Speaking, or, Using Discourse Representation Theory to Interpret Generics," in Chierchia, Partee, and Turner, (eds.), *Properties, Types, and Meaning*, Vol. 2: *Semantic Issues*, Reidel, Dordrecht, 193–268.

Schwarzschild, R. 1989. "Adverbs of Quantification as Generalized Quantifiers," *NELS 19*.

Schwarzschild, R. 1993. "The Contrastiveness of Associated Foci," Ms, Hebrew University, Jerusalem.

Sgall, P. (ed.) 1984. *Contributions to Functional Syntax, Semantics, and Language Comprehension*, Academia, Praha.

Sgall, P., E. Hajičová, and J. Panevová 1986. *The Meaning of the Sentence in Its Semantic and Pragmatic Aspects*, Academia, Prague and Reidel, Dordrecht.

Stechow, A. von. 1991. "Current Issues in the Theory of Focus," in A. von Stechow and D. Wunderlich, (eds.), *Semantik/Semantics: An International Handbook of Contemporary Research*, de Gruyter, Berlin, 804–825.

Steedman, M. 1994. "Remarks on Intonation and Focus," in P. Bosch and R. van der Sandt (eds.) (1994), 185–204.

Taglicht, J. 1984. *Message and Emphasis*, Longman, London and New York.

12   Association with Focus or Association with Presupposition?

MATS ROOTH

Abstract

According to alternative semantics, focus has the weak semantics of introducing alternatives. But in some association with focus constructions, assuming a semantics of existential presupposition would give us an independently motivated account of the semantic focus effect. I review two such cases. I then give arguments against an existential-presupposition semantics for focus based on flexibility in the licensing of focus.

1   Introduction

Dretske's 1972 paper "Contrastive Statements" discusses semantic effects of contrastive intonation in counterfactuals, statements of reasons, and several similar configurations. Given that Dretske's paper is one of the primary sources for the perspective on the grammar and semantics of focus that is assumed in current work, it is striking that the constructions discussed there have been the subject of comparatively little careful analysis and are comparatively ill understood. In this chapter, I explore the possibility that the semantic effects in Dretske environments do not arise in a way that accords with the general framework of Rooth (1992) but are instead attributable to an interaction between the semantics of counterfactuals and presupposition. This would have important consequences, because it would involve abandoning the very weak semantics for focus proposed in alternative semantics. Although I end up rejecting such an account, the investigation tends to support the view that alternative focus and various presuppositional devices are closely related and interact with discourse and sentence semantics in similar and sometimes identical ways.

Dretske's examples of association with focus in counterfactuals are (1) and (2), where the locus of focus is indicated with an F subscript.

(1)   If Clyde hadn't [married]$_F$ Bertha, he would not have been eligible for the inheritance.

(2)   If Clyde hadn't married [Bertha]$_F$, he would not have been eligible for the inheritance.

The following version of Dretske's scenario for these examples embodies slight modifications made in Rooth (1996).

Clyde, a bachelor, has a relationship with Bertha, a busy academic and confirmed bachelor(ette). They see each other once a week, unless she has to work on a grant proposal or attend an interdisciplinary seminar. He learns that he stands to inherit a great deal of money at the age of thirty if he is married. Clyde finds the relationship he has with Bertha congenial, and would hate to abandon it for a marriage of the conventional sort. Fortunately Bertha agrees to go through with the legal formalities of marriage, it being understood that their relationship will continue exactly as before.

Given this scenario, Dretske's intuitions are that (1) is true and that (2) is false. I find the intuition about (1) rather effervescent. This may have to do with the focus on the transitive verb *married*: because it is hard to figure out what alternatives to marrying are intended, one has no firm intuitions about truth or falsity. This problem is corrected in the following version.

(3)   Pat had two daughters, one named Bertha; the other was named Aretha and was indispensable to him in his business. He had made a commitment to marry one of the daughters to one of the sons of a man who once saved his life. There were two such sons, the elder son Clyde and the younger son Derek. According to a custom of the society and period, an elder son had to marry before his younger brothers; this was known as seniority. Given the contract, seniority, and the desirability of leaving Aretha free to run his business for him, he figured out that the best thing to do was to marry Bertha to Clyde, and that is what he did.

The examples to be evaluated are

(4)   If he hadn't married Bertha$_F$ to Clyde, Aretha couldn't have continued to run the business.   true

(5)   If he hadn't married Bertha to Clyde$_F$, Aretha couldn't have continued to run the business.   false

(6)   If he hadn't married Bertha$_F$ to Clyde, seniority would have been violated.
                                                                                                                          false

(7)   If he hadn't married Bertha to Clyde$_F$, seniority would have been violated.
                                                                                                                          true

In these versions of Dretske's examples, I experience a genuine association with focus effect. For instance (4) and (5) differ only in the locus of intonational focus, and keeping the story firmly in mind, I judge (4) to be true and (5) to be false. As Dretske points out, a similar effect is observed for statements of reason:

(8)   The reason he married Bertha$_F$ to Clyde was that Aretha was indispensable in the business.   true

(9)   The reason he married Bertha to Clyde$_F$ was that Aretha was indispensable in the business.   false

(10)   The reason he married Bertha$_F$ to Clyde was that he wanted to obey seniority.   false

(11)   The reason he married Bertha to Clyde$_F$ was that he wanted to obey seniority.   true

Given the context, I feel there is a compelling truth conditional effect; for me the reason examples are in fact somewhat clearer than the counterfactual ones. There is a link between the statements of reasons and the counterfactuals: Clyde might use first person versions of (4) and (7) as a statement of his reasons for doing what he did. And by embedding a counterfactual, one obtains a more explicit statement of reasons:

(12)   The reason he married Bertha to Clyde$_F$ was that if he hadn't done so, he would have violated seniority.

(13)   The reason he married Bertha to Clyde$_F$ was that if he had married Bertha to Derek$_F$, he would have violated seniority.

2   The Semantics of Clefts and of Focus

The semantics for clefts such as (14a, b) is stated in terms of the denotations of the clefted element (which is *Sue* in (14a)) and of the relative clause following the clefted element (*who loves Mary* in (14a)).

(14)   a. It is Sue who loves Mary.
        b. It is Sue and Tom who love Mary.

Let us assume that the clefted element denotes a group X', and that the relative clause contributes a property P obtained by lambda binding. Then according to the standard analysis, the cleft contributes a presupposition that something has property P and an assertion that X is an exhaustive list of things that have property P.

In the analysis of Rooth (1992), intonational focus has a meaning that is weaker than that of a cleft. Sentence (15), rather than presupposing that someone loves Sue, simply contributes a set C of propositions of the form 'x loves Sue' to the representation. In different cases, this set has different specific functions, but the general idea is that C is a set of alternatives to the assertion 'Sue loves Mary'.

(15)   Sue$_F$ loves Mary.

I use a notation in which the set of propositions introduced by focus, together with the understood alternatives to the focus element, are written into an LF as explicit arguments of the focus feature. Writing A for the alternatives to the focused element in (15) and C for the set of propositions, the LF of (15) is:

(16)   [[Sue F(A, C)] λe_3 [e_3 loves Mary]]

The focus feature is treated as the main function in the following configuration, where d is the focused phrase and Q is the lambda abstract.

[[d F(A, C)]Q]

Focus introduces the presupposition that (the semantic value of) C is the set of propositions obtainable by applying (the semantic value of) Q to (the semantic value of) A, and that (the semantic value of) A contains (the semantic value of) d and something else. In addition, we have the assertion Q(d). Assuming that the set A in (16) consists of Bill, Liz, and Sue, the effect of focus in (16) is to contribute the information that C is a set of three propositions, namely, 'Bill loves Mary', 'Liz loves Mary', and 'Bill loves Mary'. This is a weak semantics for focus, because it is not presupposed that one of the elements of C is true; in this semantics for focus the existential presupposition found with clefts is absent.

     This kind of representation was introduced in Rooth (1996). It might be advisable to take profligate representationalism a bit further, and say that in addition to a set of alternative propositions, focus makes available the union of that set of propositions, the so-called focus closure. In the case of (15), this is the proposition that Bill, Liz, or Sue loves Mary. The focus closure is written as an additional argument of the focus feature, for instance, F(A, C, p). The justification for this move is that, in certain cases, it is the union of C rather than C itself that is used elsewhere in the representation. Rooth (1985) and von Fintel (1994) discuss an analysis of adverbs of quantification where the union of C is an implicit restriction of the adverb. Sentence (17) is given the LF (18).

(17)   John always takes Mary_F to the movies.

(18)   always($\cup$C) [[John always takes Mary_F to the movies] $\sim$ C]

This is interpreted roughly as 'every occasion of John taking someone to the movies is an occasion of John taking Mary to the movies'; see von Fintel (1994) for an improved and carefully motivated formulation along these general lines. In the current notation, the LF for (17) is (19).

(19)   always(p) [[Sue F(A, C, p)] λe_2 [John always takes e_2 to the movies]]

The difference is just that the union operation is packed into the focus feature, rather than being represented separately. The change in the type of F acknowledges the fact that in certain cases the operator (for example, *always*) that interacts with a variable constrained by focus requires an argument with the type of a focus closure rather than a focus alternative set.

     For purposes of comparison between focus and the cleft, it is convenient to assume that the pieces of meaning operated on by the semantic rule for the cleft are the same as those available to the focus feature, and that in the semantics for the cleft the set C is defined in terms of A in the same way as with clefts. Under this assumption, the existential presupposition of the cleft is a presupposition that p is true.

It can be emphasized that at this point it is not being assumed that it-clefts and intonational focus are variant realizations of a single abstract feature or operator. I do wish to assume that it-clefts have the semantics reviewed earlier, that is, a semantics including an existential presupposition and an assertion of exhaustive listing. But pulling back from what is proposed in alternative semantics, the question whether focus has a weak semantics introducing alternatives or a stronger semantics including an existential presupposition should be considered open at this point in the argument.

3   Presuppositional Interactions in Dretske Environments

Dretske examples work just as well with it-clefts as with simple intonational focus:

(20)   If it hadn't been Bertha that he married to Clyde, Aretha couldn't have continued to run the business.   true

(21)   If it hadn't been Clyde that he married Bertha to, Aretha couldn't have continued to run the business.   false

(22)   The reason it was Bertha that he married to Clyde was that Aretha was indispensable in the business.   true

(23)   The reason it was Clyde that he married Bertha to was that Aretha was indispensable in the business.   false

Moreover, presuppositonal particles such as *too* have a particular effect in Dretske environments. Mary is in the elevator, and John is in the snack bar. Is the following sentence true or false?

(24)   If John were in the elevator, Mary and John would be in the same place.

It depends. If Mary always avoids being in confined spaces with other people, she might have left the elevator if John had made a move to enter it. The sequence (25), however, makes it clear that we are to consider counterfactual situations in which Mary and John are both in the elevator.

(25)   a. Mary is in the elevator.
        b. If John were in the elevator too, Mary and John would be in the same place.

I assume that the particle *too* in (25b) has a covert pronominal argument referring to the proposition denoted by the context sentence (25a), and that it introduces the presupposition that this proposition is true, that is, that Mary is in the elevator. An interesting thing about (25) is that this presupposition is satisfied both in the top-level context and in counterfactual situations that are considered in evaluating the truth of (25b).

Following the terminology used for focus, I call the interaction illustrated by (25) association with presupposition in counterfactuals. This is a phenomenon that is to be explained by the semantics of counterfactuals and how it interacts with presupposition. Whatever explains the effect, it is clear that association with presupposition is relevant to the earlier cleft sentences. The cleft *it is Bertha that Pat marries to Clyde* introduces an existential presupposition that Pat marries either Bertha or Aretha to Clyde, assuming that the alternative set A in this case consists of Bertha and Aretha. This presupposition projects through the negation in *it isn't Bertha that Pat marries to Clyde*. The effect is that the if-clause in (20) presupposes that Pat marries either Bertha or Aretha to Clyde. This assimilates the observation that the negated clefts in Dretske's examples interact with the counterfactual to the more general phenomenon of association with presupposition in counterfactuals. Note that on this approach, the fact that the counterfactual situations consulted in evaluating the truth of (20) are ones in which Pat marries someone to Clyde follows from the existential presupposition of the negated cleft. This means that if we wanted to apply the same analysis to association with focus in Dretske environments, we would have to assume that focus introduces an existential presupposition. That is, we would have to strengthen the weak semantics for focus employed in alternative semantics.

4   Deriving Association with Presupposition

The premise semantics is a simple and intuitive semantics for counterfactuals; my discussion of it is based on Kratzer (1978). A set of propositions H that characterize the base world w is given; the only constraint on H is that $\cap$H is the unit set of the base world w. Here is a slightly simplified version of the rule given in Kratzer (1978:271).

(26)   *Semantic rule for counterfactual (version 1)*:
        If φ then ψ is true iff
        for any subset X of H such that $\cap[X \cup \{\varphi\}]$ is nonempty, either
        (i) X is nonmaximal: there is an X' such that $X \subseteq X' \subseteq H$ and
             $\cap[X' \cup \{\varphi\}]$ is nonempty, or
        (ii) $\cap[X \cup \{\varphi\}]$ entails ψ

That is, any way of conjoining as many facts as possible with the if-clause φ while maintaining consistency results in a proposition that entails the main clause ψ.

Suppose that H includes the facts

(27)   Mary is in the elevator.
        John is in the snack bar.
        Mary is never in a confined space with another person.

We want to evaluate the truth of

(28)   If John were in the elevator, Mary and John would be in the same place.

The if-clause of the definition is *John is in the elevator*. Due to the consistency requirement, none of the maximal subsets of the definition contains the fact *John is in the snack bar*. But some of them will contain the fact Mary is never in a confined space with another person, given that this is consistent with *John is in the elevator*. Since John's being in the elevator and Mary's never being in a confined place with another person exclude Mary's being in the elevator, with such a choice for H sentence (28) is false.

How do things change when the presuppositional particle *too* is added to the if-clause? The components to be put together are

φ John were in the elevator too
ψ Mary and John be in the same place

We are assuming that φ and ψ are dynamic propositions (file change potentials) rather than propositions, and that φ is defined only on input files that entail that Mary is in the elevator. To put together these semantic objects, we have to move to a dynamic version of the counterfactual rule. In view of the typical relation between conjunction and dynamic updates, the following revision suggests itself:[1]

(29)   *Semantic rule for counterfactual (version 2)*:
If φ then ψ is true iff
for any subset X of F such that $\cap X + \varphi$ is defined and nonempty, either
(i)   X is nonmaximal: there is an X' such that $X \subseteq X' \subseteq H$ and $\cap X' + \varphi$ is defined and nonempty, or
(ii)   the propositional content of $\cap X + \varphi + \psi$ is the same as the propositional content of $\cap X + \varphi$

The two occurrences of "is defined" seem to be required to prevent presupposition failure in any case where the if-clause φ has any presuppositions at all; this provides some motivation for the particular form of the rule.

Consider the impact of the new rule on the elevator example. Because of the presence of *too* in the antecedent, $\cap X + \varphi$ is defined only if $\cap X$ entails that Mary is in the elevator. It follows that the fact that Mary is in the elevator is included in each of the maximal subsets of the definition. The elements of $\cap X + \varphi$ for the various maximal choices for X constitute the counterfactual worlds considered in evaluating the counterfactual. So, it follows from the dynamic definition that in the counterfactual worlds considered in evaluating the counterfactual, Mary is in the elevator. This agrees with our intuitions about (28).

In general, given the dynamic semantic rule for counterfactuals, only worlds that satisfy the presuppositions of the if-clause are considered in evaluating the truth of the counterfactual. This fills in a gap in the argument of the previous section: the phenomenon of association with presupposition in counterfactuals is a consequence of the dynamic semantic rule for counterfactuals. We also have an explanation for the interesting fact that the presuppositions of the if-clause are imposed on the base world as well as on the counterfactual worlds. The unit set of the base world w is the intersection of the set of facts H, and therefore w is an element of any of the intersections ∩X on which φ is defined. As long as there is such an X, we derive the fact that w must satisfy the presuppositions of the if-clause. See Heim (1992) for related discussion, and for another formulation of semantics of counterfactuals that captures association with presupposition.

5   A Strengthened Semantics for Focus?

Section 1 reviewed association with focus in counterfactual and reason environments. Section 3 pointed out that the examples work just as well when a cleft is substituted for intonational focus and argued that there was a general phenomenon of association with presupposition in Dretske environments. This was analyzed in section 4 using a dynamic semantic rule for counterfactuals; while I have not looked into the matter, it seems likely that this account would generalize to other Dretske environments.

Once we have an account of association with presupposition in counterfactuals, nothing additional need be said about the cleft examples (20)–(23), since these are just particular examples of association with presupposition. What about the focus examples (4)–(7)? Since the presuppositional analysis is independently motivated, it is attractive to try to treat the focus examples in the same way. This would require adding an existential presupposition to the semantics of focus – it would require strengthening the weak semantics for focus that is assumed in alternative semantics.

Because alternative semantics was introduced in Rooth (1985) as an entire framework for semantic interpretation, the question whether the semantics of F should be strengthened might seem a momentous one. The framework aspect had to do with the recursive definition of focus semantic values, with each phrase having a focus semantic value in addition to an ordinary semantic value. But in subsequent work, this part of alternative semantics has been isolated from a separate and more solidly motivated theory of focus-sensitive constructions. In the account of Rooth (1992), the two-dimensional framework plays no essential role. And as shown in Rooth (1996), the argument for the two-dimensional framework having to do with scope islands that was presented in Rooth (1985) does not go through. As an alternative to the two-dimensional framework, I suggested packing the entire theory of alternative semantics into the meaning of the F feature; this is the approach reviewed earlier. If one sets up the theory in this way, the question whether the semantics of F should be strengthened is not a momentous framework question. Rather, it is a local question: "What function is denoted by the intonational prominence morpheme?"

In Section 2, we looked at the following LF for focus:

$$[[\mathrm{d}\,F(A, C, p)]Q]$$

d is the focused phrase, and Q is a property formed by abstracting the focused position in the sentence. A is the set of alternatives to the focused phrase (including the semantic value of the focused phrase and something else), C is the set of propositions obtainable by applying Q to elements of A, and p is the union of C. If we want to strengthen the semantics of focus, it is trivial to do so: we just have to add to the meaning of F a presupposition that the focus closure p is true.

6   Focusing Adverbs

What at first looks like an argument against the strengthened semantics for focus can be based on certain focusing adverbs where a cleft substitution is not possible:

(30)   a. Mary also took John$_F$ to the movies.
        b. Mary even took John$_F$ to the movies.

(31)   a. #It's also John$_F$ that Mary took to the movies.
        b. #It's even John$_F$ that Mary took to the movies.

The cleft versions are completely incoherent; this could be viewed as an argument against giving focus a semantics similar to the cleft. Fairly transparently, though, the problem here has to do with an incompatibility between the exhaustive meaning of the cleft and the presupposition introduced by the focusing adverb. The focusing adverbs in (31) introduce a presupposition that someone other than John was taken to the movies by Mary. If so, the list including just John is not an exhaustive list of people taken to the movies by Mary.

At the price of a good deal of awkwardness, exhaustiveness can be removed by inserting *in part*.

(32)   a. It was on Monday that they worked on the proposal.
        b. It was in part on Monday that they worked on the proposal.

With this modification, a cleft is indeed compatible with *also*:

(33)   A: When did they work on the proposal?
        B: On Sunday.
        C: It was also in part on Monday that they worked on it.

I assume that *also* in C's sentence has maximal scope, and that its argument has an existential presupposition introduced by the cleft, although the exhaustiveness has been eliminated by insertion of the partitive operator *in part*. The fact that the sentence is good shows that *also*, though it is incompatible with a simple cleft argument, is not incompatible with existential presupposition. In fact, since *also* expresses a presuppostion entailing an existential, it would be quite surprising if it were incompatible with an existential presupposition in its argument.

There is an expectation that sentence-internal exploitations of focus should give the most information about the semantics of focus, because sentence-internal semantics is tighter than discourse semantics. However, I have been unable to find an association with focus construction that is incompatible with an existential presupposition and therefore could serve as a test for the presence of such a presupposition in the semantics of the focus feature. I now turn to two arguments that do refute the strengthened semantics for focus.

7   Discourse Focus Effects

This section argues that a systematic semantics of existential presupposition is too strong in certain cases where focus has a discourse-contrastive function. Consider the following discourse:

(34)   A: Did someone borrow my badminton racket?
         B: I don't know. If [John]$_F$ borrowed it, you can forget about getting it back in one piece.

I assume that focus is interpreted at the level of the if-clause; the LF of the if-clause is then

(35)   [[John]F(A, C, p) λe_2 [e_2 borrowed it]]

The proposition p is the proposition that somebody (or rather, some element of A) borrowed the racket. If focus introduced a presupposition that p is true, this would project through the conditional, resulting in incompatibility with the first sentence *I don't know* in B's response. Consider another example. In my department, a football pool is held each week, and people bet on the outcomes of games. It is set up so that at most one person can win; if nobody wins, the prize money is carried over to the next week.

(36)   A: Did anyone win the football pool this week?
         B: Probably not, because it's unlikely that [Mary]$_F$ won it, and she's the only person who ever wins.

(37)   B: Probably not, because it's unlikely that it's [Mary]$_F$ who won it, and she's the only person who ever wins.

B knew that Mary had made a silly bet, and since in the past nobody else ever won, B finds it unlikely that anyone won. In the response in (36), I assume that the focus takes scope at the level of [Mary won it], evoking alternatives of the form 'x won it'. In the cleft variant (37), we get a presupposition that someone won at the same level. Assuming that this presupposition projects through *because it's unlikely* we predict a conflict with the first part of what B said. Here I do find the cleft variant incoherent and contradictory. In contrast, the focus variant is fine.

Notice that the problem with the cleft version could not have to do with the exhaustiveness assertion of the cleft, because the story was set up so that it can be taken for granted that at most one person won.

To complete this argument, we have to explain how the focus in (36) is licensed. The idea is that the clause *anyone win the football pool this week* in A's question is the antecedent for the focus closure variable constrained by the focus feature. That is, p in the representation F(A, C, p) is the referential index of the S *anyone win the football pool this week.*

Summing up, if the focus feature introduced an existential presupposition, we would expect B's answer in (36) to have the same status as B's answer in (37). But the first is fine and the second odd. So these data argue against strengthening the semantics of the focus feature by adding a cleftlike existential presupposition.

8   Flexibility of Focus Licensing

I have the feeling that intuitions about the association-with-cleft examples discussed are systematically firmer than intuitions about association with focus in counterfactual environments. This can be turned into an argument against an existential presupposition expressed by focus. In the counterfactual environment, focus can interact with the counterfactual, but it can also be licensed in other ways:

(38)   If he hadn't married Bertha$_F$, he would not have qualified, because he would not have married anyone.

Here the focus apparently is licensed by the following *he marry anyone*. This can again be formalized in terms of coindexing with the focus closure. I assume an LF along the following lines:

(39)   If not [[Bertha F(A, C, 8) λe_2 [he marry married e_2]], he would not have qualified, because [would [not [he marry anyone]$_8$]]]

Here the referential index of the clause *he marry anyone* appears in the focus closure slot of the focus feature.

Flexibility in the licensing of focus is predicted by the theory of Rooth (1992), where it is treated as an instance of nondeterminism in antecedence for anaphors. The point now is that presuppositions expressed by clefts are not comparably flexible. The following example seems contradictory to me:

(40)   If it hadn't been Bertha that he married, he would not have qualified, because he would not have married anyone.

Contradictoriness is predicted by the theory of association with presupposition I have reviewed, because the existential presupposition is encoded in the semantics of the if-clause, and the presupposition is inevitably captured by the semantic rule for the counterfactual. If my intuition about (40) is right (I actually am not totally firm about this) these examples are an argument against a systematic existential-presupposition semantics for focus. If there was an existential presupposition introduced by the focus in (38), it would project through the negation and interact with the counterfactual, resulting in contradiction.

9   Counterfactual Environments in the Weak Semantics

At this point, I have rejected the idea that an existential presupposition is the explanation for association with focus in the counterfactual environment. Although an existential presupposition would have provided a welcome account of the Dretske environments, it seems that an existential presupposition is not systematically present with focus. Further, putting existential presupposition into the semantics of focus would predict more systematic semantic effects in the counterfactual environment than what is in fact observed.

Given the negative conclusion regarding a presuppositional analysis, one has to opt for a treatment within the standard alternative semantics. Two analyses of association with focus in counterfactuals have been given in the literature. Von Fintel (1994) suggests that *would* has a covert restriction argument, written as a subscript. In my notation, one would assume an LF where the focus closure variable restricted by the focus feature supplies this restriction:

(41)   [would$_p$ [if [not [[Bertha F(A, C, p) λe_2[Clyde marry e_2]]]]]
            [not [he qualify for the inheritance]]]]

This has the effect of conjoining the focus closure 'Clyde marry Aretha or Bertha' with the if-clause.

Rooth (1985) suggested an analysis in terms of the premise semantics. In effect, I said that the set of facts H is an implicit argument of *would*, and that one could freely write into the representation the information that the focus closure is an element of H. Thus the representation is something like

(42)   [would$_H$ [if [not [[Bertha F(A, C, p) λe_2[Clyde marry e_2]]]]]
            [not [he qualify for the inheritance]]]]
        & $p \in H$

This would predict a subtly different meaning than that which follows from von Fintel's representation. It does not follow from the presence of the proposition 'Clyde marries Aretha or Bertha' in the set of facts H that it is in each of the maximal subsets referred to in the counterfactual rule.

Both of these solutions involve a move I used to feel uncomfortable with: the focus closure rather than the alternative set is used as an implicit argument of some other operator. As mentioned earlier, this kind of analysis was also applied to adverbs of quantification in Rooth (1985) and von Fintel (1994). I now feel that this objection is dealt with by making the focus closure one of the arguments of the focus feature, annotating the fact that it is generally available along with the alternative set.

Note

1   As a component of a dynamic semantics, this definition is not quite what is desired, since it defines truth rather than an update.

References

Dretske, F. 1972. "Contrastive Statements," *Philosophical Review* 411–437.

Fintel, Kai von. 1994. *Restrictions on Quantifier Domains*. Ph.D. dissertation, University of Massachusetts, Amherst.

Heim, I. 1992. "Presupposition Projection and the Semantics of Attitude Verbs," *Journal of Semantics* 9, 183–221.

Kratzer, A. 1978. *Semantik der Rede*, Scriptor, Königstein.

Rooth, M. 1985. *Association with Focus*, Ph.D. dissertation, University of Massachusetts, Amherst.

Rooth, M. 1992. "A Theory of Focus Interpretation," *Natural Language Semantics*, 75–116.

Rooth, M. 1996. "Focus," in S. Lappin (ed.) *Handbook of Contemporary Semantic Theory*, Blackwell.

PART III

The Function of Focus in Discourse

13 Discourse and the Focus/Background Distinction

NICHOLAS ASHER

Abstract

My aim in this chapter is to draw a connection between the semantic theory of focus and principles of discourse structure in a formally precise and explicit way. In so doing I show how to account for one phenomenon concerning focus that eludes the purely semantic accounts. This phenomenon concerns the interpretation of VP ellipsis. I also take at least some modest steps toward a unified theory of foregrounding/backgrounding in discourse and within the sentence, in which these distinctions turn out to reflect the same structural phenomenon at different linguistic levels. The sketch of a unified theory that I propose uses minimal semantic assumptions together with a theory of discourse structure that is thoroughly integrated with the semantics.

0 Introduction

In the work of Jacobs, Krifka, Rooth, and von Stechow, formalizations of the focus/background distinction within the sentence have been used with considerable success in the semantic analysis of focus-sensitive operators. Yet the pragmatic and discourse effects of the focus/background distinction, present in the work of Labov (1972), Hopper (1979), Givon (1984), and the Prague school (Sgall 1967), has not received similar formal attention.

1 One Example of Focus and Discourse Interaction: Contrastive Focus

One place to look for an interaction of focus with discourse structure is the phenomenon of *symmetric contrastive focus* – explored, for instance, in Rooth (1992). Symmetric contrastive focus involves two clauses or sentences, or even a single sentence in which there are two elements of the same type in focus – one contrasting with the other. Rooth offers the following example:

(1)   An[American]$_F$ farmer met a [Canadian]$_F$ farmer.

In (1) [α]$_F$ denotes the fact that α is a semantically significant focus (Rooth 1985, 1992, Krifka 1991, 1992) – a convention that I use throughout the chapter.

There are examples of symmetric contrast involving two sentences or clauses that have a very interesting interaction with discourse relations like *Parallel* and

Contrast. On the basis of earlier work (Asher 1993), I suppose that Contrast and Parallel are rhetorical relations between representational instances of propositions that figure as part of discourse structure. Particles like *but* or *too* indicate that Contrast or Parallel, respectively, hold between the proposition expressed by the clause or other semantic element within the scope of the particle and some other element of the same type in antecedent discourse, typically in the preceding clause. (2a) is an example of a discourse where Contrast holds between the propositions expressed by the two sentences in the discourse while (2b) is an example of Parallel.

(2)   a. John said Mary won the race. But she didn't.
        b. John said that Mary won the race. Sam did too.

Without any intonational markings, these sentences are ambiguous. With (2a), for instance, one could either resolve the VP in the second sentence so that it means either that she didn't say that Mary would win the race or that she didn't win the race. When we mark a particular bit of the sentence with an intonational prominence (which I do by putting the bit in uppercase), we not only can disambiguate a discourse but also can indicate Contrast simply by using intonation. The following examples disambiguate the two readings of (2a) just mentioned above.

(3)   a. John SAID Mary won the race. (But) she DIDN'T.
        b. JOHN said that Mary won the competition. (But) SHE didn't. (higher VP)
        c. JOHN said that Mary won the race, and SAM did.

(3a) is naturally interpreted as saying that Mary didn't win the race, while (3b) says that Mary didn't say that she won the race. Both (3a) and (3b) are examples of symmetric contrastive focus. The intonational stress marked by the uppercase serves to mark in this case the semantically significant focus. We can even delete the particle *but*, suggesting that focusing can have the same effect as a contrastive particle. (3a) indicates a Contrast relation between the two claims, John's saying that Mary would win the race and her not winning, while the contrast in (3b) is intuitively between x's saying that Mary would win the race and x's not saying that she would win the race. (3c) indicates that focusing can also have the same effect as a parallelism particle like *too*: Intuitively, there is a common theme to both clauses – x's saying that Mary would win the race – and this common theme is the semantic import of parallelism.

To sharpen our understanding of the link between discourse structure and focus, we can look at our examples from the perspective of VP ellipsis. Although Sag (1976) did not observe this, his examples below reveal that discourse context and in particular Parallel and Contrast relations can affect the recovery of the appropriate VP. As argued in Asher (1993), the Contrast required by the contrastive particle *but* in (4a) is best accommodated by recovering the lower VP (John's saying that Mary hit him versus Sam's really hitting him), while the parallel in (4b) is best accommodated by recovering the higher VP in the ellipsis.

(4)   a. John said that Mary hit him, but Sam did. (lower VP the preferred source)

        b. John said that Mary hit him, and Sam did too. (higher VP the preferred source)

In Asher (1993) I argued that a sort of accommodation of the discourse relations Parallel and Contrast explains the data in (2) and (3). But since we have seen this data also have to do with focus, we will have to redefine the interpretation of focus on structures on which these discourse relations are defined, and in calculating the effects of these discourse relations we also need to take into account the focus/background division on these structures in a particular way. The following examples give further evidence that recovery of the elided VP to the lower VP requires focal stress on the higher verb and the AUX, and so focal stress on these elements must affect the accommodation of Contrast and Parallel in a particular way.

(5)   a. John SAID that Mary won the competition, and she DID. (lower VP)

        b. John SAID that Mary believed that she won the competition. But she DIDN'T. (lower VP)

        c. John DOUBTED that Mary won the competition, but she DIDN'T. (lower VP even though pragmatically odd or incoherent)

        d. JOHN doubted that Mary won the competition, but SHE didn't. (higher VP)

The theory accounting for such examples will also account for some other odd minimal pairs, for which I have found no account in the literature.

(6)   a. ??Mary HIT Sam. And then Fred DID.

        b.   Mary HIT Sam. And then FRED did.

        c.   Mary HIT Sam. FRED did too.

        d. ??Mary HIT Sam. Fred DID too.

1.1   *Rooth's Theory of Contrastive Focus*

Rooth (1992) offers an elegant theory of contrastive focus that appears to predict the right readings of discourses like (3c). With Rooth I assume that while the semantically significant focus may be below the clause, we interpret the semantic effects of the foci at the interpretation of S. At the level of LF, we have two coindexed proposition variables or property variables P_i and P_J adjoined to the S given by the two clauses and each variable coindexed, respectively, with the proposition expressed by the other clause. These two variables are arguments to the focus operator $\sim$. $\sim P_J$ means that the proposition identified with P_J (that is, the proposition expressed by the other clause) must be in the alternative set for the first clause, as it is since it is of the form, x said that Mary won the race. This is where we assume that the ellipsis is reconstructed as intended. If we attempt to reconstruct the ellipsis in the second clause as meaning Sam won the race, then the presupposition for $\sim$ is violated and the logical form is rejected; similarly, for (3c), in which there is a contrast relation rather than a parallel relation. In either case, the explanations for the preferred readings for these sentences seem to have little to do with the particularities of the Parallel and Contrast relations.

This is not always the case, however. Rooth's general constraint on focus, for instance, will not give us the desired results for (3a). It is important to bear in mind what is the semantically significant focused element and at what level it is interpreted in Rooth's analysis. On Rooth's analysis, the presuppositions of ~ are met on neither resolution of the ellipsis if we interpret the focus effects at S as before. For instance, if we pick the unintended reading (3a) on which we resolve the ellipsis so as to have the second clause mean that Mary did not say that she won the competition, then Mary's V-ing that φ is not of the right form for the alternative set of John's [saying]$_F$ that φ – that is, not of the form John V-ing that φ. But if, on the other hand, we resolve the ellipsis so that the second clause means that Mary does not win the race, again it is not of the appropriate form to be an element of the alternative set of John's [saying]$_F$ that φ. To save the theory we might resort to "focus percolation" and say that the focal stress on *said* percolates up to the VP. But this doesn't satisfy the presuppositions of focus, since if we interpret the effects of focus at VP, then we still have the problem of the alternative set being interpreted at S level and they are not of the right form.

Suppose we interpret the symmetric contrastive focus here at VP rather than S. Then, the unintended interpretation is the one that most plausibly falls into the alternative set of V-ing that φ. The focus on the negation in the second clause, however, still isn't of the right type to match with the focused verb phrase in the left. How would $\lambda y \neg\varphi(y)$ fall into the alternative set of $\lambda x \, V(x,\varphi)$? So it seems that Rooth's approach analyzes (3a) in the wrong fashion.

One might try to satisfy Rooth's presupposition for focus in (3a), using a rather unconstrained notion of focus percolation. Suppose that we interpret focus at S level as before but that we allow focus percolation from intonational marking across nonconstituents in the following way:

> SAID $\rightarrow$ [John said]$_F$

In interpreting at S level, we would like to get an alternative set that ranges over attitudes or modalities towards propositions. This is now in the appropriate set of alternatives for the focused negation in the second clause to recover in fact the intended reading. But at what node in LF do we adjoin our presupposition operator ~ and the associated variable? In standard LFs that are closely related to syntactic structures such as those used in Rooth (1992), there is no appropriate node. This is no surprise, since our hypothesis was precisely that we allowed focus to percolate across nonconstituents. To make sense of this sort of focus percolation, we need to change the level of analysis of the discourse at which the presuppositions of focus apply. This level of analysis must be closer to a purely logical structure than standard LFs are, permitting us to correlate propositional operators of different types to form the appropriate alternative sets.

The only way Rooth's purely semantic analysis can treat (3a) is to treat it as a case of nonsymmetric contrastive focus. Then the focused element in the first clause need not be an element of the alternative set for the second. But now we have no constraints concerning the appropriate, recovered VP. For instance, we could interpret the focus in the second discourse at Neg P – and we could take the previous sentence's higher NEG P value (nonnegative) as giving us the contrasting element. This would then force us to recover the higher VP for the interpretation of the VP ellipsis in the second clause, so that the alternatives would have the appropriate form – {X ∈ POLARITY: λx X(x said that Mary would win the race)}. We could equally well allow the lower NEG P value to generate the alternative set, and this would permit the other reading of the elided VP in the clause. But now nothing in the theory of focus constrains which is the appropriate VP to be recovered. And this means for one thing that we can't explain the data in (5). More important, the theory seems to be missing a generalization and an important effect of focus. We can capture the generalization if we make use of discourse information; the discourse relations Parallel and Contrast have systematic effects on truth conditions – the phenomena about focus and VP ellipsis are one example (for others see Asher 1993).

1.2   A Discourse Theory of Contrast and Parallel

To capture the interaction of focus and the intended interpretation of VP ellipses as in (3a), I propose to analyze focus at another level of logical representation of the sentence. Luckily, this level of representation is needed in any case for the analysis of Parallel and Contrast as discourse relations within a theory of discourse structure like Segmented Discourse Representation Theory (SDRT). I now sketch briefly the way SDRT accounts for Parallel and Contrast (this is a simplification of what is a rather complicated story – see Asher 1993).

SDRT is an extension of DRT that attempts to make clear in a precise and systematic way the interactions between semantic content and discourse structure. It provides a formal foundation for discourse structure in the tradition of Grosz and Sidner (1986) and Mann and Thompson's (1987) Rhetorical Structure Theory (RST), in which a text gives rise to a discourse structure that consists of propositions related by discourse relations. Further, SDRT shows how such a structure may be built up in an incremental and logically precise manner. Finally, SDRT offers a detailed integration of semantic and pragmatic phenomena relevant to the interpretation of discourse. SDRT has been used to show how discourse structure affects temporal anaphora (for instance, Lascarides and Asher 1993), the spatiotemporal structure of text (Asher et al. 1993, 1995), and various forms of abstract entity anaphora (Asher 1993). The following description of SDRT comes from Asher (1993).

In SDRT, the basic building blocks or *constituents* of discourse structure are *segmented DRSs* or SDRSs. These are defined recursively out of DRSs and discourse relations, which are taken to be binary relations between constituents, which represent dynamic propositions (many constituents may represent the same proposition).[1] SDRT, like RST, countenances a number of such discourse relations, but only some of these introduce a hierarchical structure (I note the fact that one constituent a dominates another constituent in a discourse structure by means of the condition $\alpha \Downarrow \beta$). Here our interest concerns two particular discourse relations, Parallel and Contrast, but SDRT also makes use of relations like Background, Narration, and Elaboration.[2]

Contrast in SDRT is supported by two constituents just in case they have a particular structured content. The definition of the appropriate structure is somewhat involved for constituents in SDRT, but for our purposes the logical structure of our constituents can be represented by the partially ordered set of their subDRSs, ordered by the relation of subordination. Since every such structure has a maximal or most "superordinate" DRS, every partially ordered set representing the logical structure of a constituent has a maximal element and so is a tree, which in SDRT is known as an *embedding tree*. *Extended embedding trees* include a representation of the VP meanings of constituents. Each constituent has just one embedding tree. For example, the following is the extended embedding tree for the first constituent of (2a), where k_0 is the top DRS, k_1 is the DRS introduced by the *that* clause, and P_1 is the property derived from *said that Mary won the race*, while P_2 is the property derived from the lower VP.

$$
\begin{array}{c}
k_0 \\
| \\
P_1 \\
| \\
k_1 \\
| \\
P_2
\end{array}
$$

The technical definition of the embedding tree for a constituent α is as follows, where $\in_{tc}$ is the transitive closure of the membership relation and subDRS is the DRT relation of subordination:

> **Definition:** The extended embedding tree for α is a structure $\tau(\alpha) = \langle X, Y \rangle$, where: $X = \{y : y \in_{tc} U_\alpha$, or y is a subDRS of α or a discourse referent or lambda-abstracted DRS representing a VP meaning that is part of α or of some $v \in_{tc} U_\alpha\}$ and $Y = (\{\in \upharpoonright X\} \cup \{\Downarrow \upharpoonright X\} \cup \{subDRS \upharpoonright X\} \cup \{\langle x, y \rangle : x$ is a predicative DRS formed from y by lambda-abstracting over the subject argument in skeleton(y) or a discourse referent representing a null VP that is an argument of skeleton(y)$\}$.

Examples of SDRSs in which Parallel and Contrast hold between complex constituents force us to define the semantics of these relations with respect to structures in which distinct nodes in the extended embedding tree are collapsed and some of the structure of the extended embedding tree is ignored. These are known as *modified extended embedding trees* (MEE trees).

> **Definition:** MEE tree for α is a pair (X, Y) such that $\tau(\alpha) = (X', Y')$ and $X \subseteq X'$ and $Y' = Y \upharpoonright > X'$.

Each constituent may have many MEE trees. Here, for example, is an MEE tree for (2a), in which the structure underneath P_1 is collapsed or ignored (this is the signification of the box around that part of the tree):

The intuitive idea for the semantics of Contrast is that two constituents support contrast just in case there is an isomorphism from one MEE tree to another such that the polarities of at least one set of paired nodes are dissimilar. The definition of isomorphism between MEE trees is straightforward.

Definition: $<_\tau = \{\langle K, K'\rangle : \text{for some } X, Y, \tau = (X, Y) \& \langle K, K'\rangle \in Y\}$.

Definition: tc $\leq_\tau$ = the transitive closure of $<_\tau$ and $=$.

Definition: Let $\tau = \langle A, \text{tc} \leq_\alpha\rangle$ and $\tau' = \langle A', \text{tc} \leq_\beta\rangle$ be two MEE trees. $\zeta: \tau \to \tau'$ is a *tree isomorphism* from A onto A' iff ζ is a bijection and $\forall \gamma, \delta \in A(\gamma \text{ tc} \leq_\tau \delta$ iff $\zeta(\gamma)\text{tc} \leq_{\tau'} \zeta(\delta)$.

Here is an example of a tree isomorphism on two MEE trees for the two constituents in (2a):

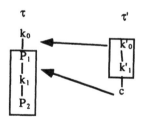

To define polarities, we must introduce another notion, called a *theme*. The most important part of a simple constituent δ – that is, a constituent without subordinate ($<$) constituents – is the condition derived from the main verb or main verbs of the text that yields δ. If we take away the conditions contributed by the verb's arguments, we have the constituent's *skeleton* – it is a DRS containing just those conditions introduced by the main verbs and their logical structure.[3] Note that the skeleton of an atomic condition φ is just φ. The *theme* of a simple constituent δ is just any DRS K such that skeleton(δ) $\in$ K or a generalization of skeleton(δ) $\in$ K (I write this relation as *skeleton(δ)$_G$ $\in$ K*), and every condition in K is either a condition in δ or a generalization of a condition in δ (I write this as K $\subseteq_G \delta$). The full definition of themes is accomplished relative to an MEE tree for the constituent (which is given when an MEE tree for any superordinate constituent is given).

> **Definition:** If K is simple, then $\alpha \subseteq^* \beta$ iff $\alpha \subseteq_G \beta$. If K is complex, then $\alpha \subseteq^* \beta$ iff $\alpha \subseteq G \beta$ and for any $\delta < \alpha$ there is a $\gamma < \beta$ such that $\delta \subseteq^* \gamma$.

> **Definition:** The *matrix* condition of a constituent δ in δ', matrix (δ, δ'), is the condition or operator in δ' of which δ is an argument or term.

> **Definition:** If δ is a simple constituent, a *theme* of δ is any DRS K such that the skeleton$(\delta)_G \in$ K $\subseteq_G \delta$. If δ is not simple, a theme of δ relative to an MEE tree τ for δ is any DRS K such that for any $\gamma <_\tau \delta$, matrix$(\gamma, \delta)_G \in$ K & K $\subseteq_G \delta$.

So, for example, with each of the nodes in the MEE trees for (2a) depicted earlier, we can associate a theme. In the following I associate with each node in the trees the English corresponding to that DRS structure.

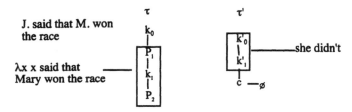

The themes for the uppermost node k_0 in τ could be k_0 itself or any DRS resulting from k_0 by deleting any condition from k_0 with the exception of *said* by generalizing on any of the conditions. So one theme of k_0 is just k_0 itself. Another theme k_0 would be just that someone did something. There are others too: John said something, someone said something, someone said that M. won the race, someone said that someone did something, and so on. Themes of property nodes will be properties, except for the null VP. In Asher (1993) I proposed that the empty VP, when paired with some corresponding property node α under a tree isomorphism, had to be interpreted as having a content identical to that of α. This is part of the SDRT update definition, but it is appealed to in computing the themes of empty nodes.

I have now defined MEE trees, tree isomorphisms, and themes. But to define Parallel and Contrast, I also need to define polarity. Polarity involves a comparison between two themes of nodes in an MEE tree. Themes have a polarity relative to some other theme. For instance, x's not liking Mary does not have the same polarity as x's liking Mary, when they are compared together, though x's not liking Mary and x's hating Mary might have the same polarity. It is the tree isomorphism between two MEE trees that tells us which themes to compare in defining Parallel or Contrast.

> **Definition:** Polarity assignment with respect to a tree isomorphism and a pair of themes
> Let $\zeta : \tau \rightarrow \tau'$ be a tree isomorphism and suppose $\delta < \zeta$.
>
> (a) If there are conditions P and P′ and some substitution of discourse referents Φ such that P is a theme of δ; (ii) P′(Φ) is theme of $\zeta(\delta)$; (iii) P is plausibly equivalent to

P'(Φ) or one is a subsort of the other in the background knowledge base; then
polarity(δ, P) = polarity($\zeta(\delta)$, P').

(b)   If there are conditions P and P' and some substitution of discourse referents Φ such
that P is a theme of δ; (ii) P'(Φ) is theme of $\zeta(\delta)$; (iii) P and P'(Φ) are plausibly
complementary; then
polarity(δ, P) $\neq$ polarity($\zeta(\delta)$, P').

Definition: For α, β constituents of an SDRS $\mathbb{K}_0$, Parallel (α, β) is satisfied in $\mathbb{K}_0$ iff there
are MEE trees τ and τ' for α and β, respectively, and a tree isomorphism $\zeta : \tau' \to \tau$ such
that for all node δ of τ' and there are themes P and P' of δ and $\zeta(\delta)$ such that polarity (δ,
P) = polarity ($\zeta(\delta)$, P').

Definition: For α, β constituents of an SDRS $\mathbb{K}_0$, Contrast (α, β) is satisfied in $\mathbb{K}_0$ iff there
are MEE trees τ and τ' for α and β, respectively, and a tree isomorphism $\zeta : \tau' \to \tau$
such that there is a node δ of τ' and there are themes P and P' of δ and $\zeta(\delta)$ such that
polarity (δ, P) $\neq$ polarity ($\zeta(\delta)$, P').

A couple of facts noted in Asher (1993) are reflected in these definitions. First,
Contrast relations may coexist with Parallel relations as long as the Parallel relations are defined over subconstituents of those for which the Contrast relations are
defined. Second, Contrast or Parallel may be supported between two constituents
by several different tree isomorphisms or different sets of themes. These different
ways of supporting Contrast and Parallel between the same two constituents evoke
intuitively different "contrasts" or "parallels," a fact that we can easily capture by
parameterizing Contrast and Parallel relations to the choice of themes for the pairs
of nodes given by a particular tree isomorphism on two particular MEE trees. These
distinct parallels and contrasts can make a difference to truth conditional interpretation – namely, in the resolution of VP ellipsis or in resolving ambiguity. When
two constituents can support more than one contrast or parallel and it makes a difference to interpretation which contrast or parallel relation is selected, we find that
interpreters pick the interpretation generated by the stronger contrast or parallel.

What does this notion of strength mean? There are, as we have noted, several
degrees of freedom to the way Parallel and Contrast may be supported, reflecting
the fact that Contrast and Parallel are scalar relations. First, the MEE trees used to
define the tree isomorphism and all the rest may involve more or less structure of
the extended embedding trees. In the variant of (2b) without the ellipsis

(2)   c.   John said that Mary won the race. Sam said that Mary won the race
             too.

there is a perfect tree isomorphism between the two embedding trees of the constituents. But this is not always possible. For example, consider (2a) again. The
extended embedding trees of the two constituents are such that there is no perfect
match between the extended embedding trees – some collapse of structure is necessary to establish an isomorphism. We have already seen one pair of MEE trees
that supports Contrast. Below we consider a second.

Another parameter determining the strength of a parallel or contrast is the set of
themes used to establish the polarity. Each node in an MEE tree may have several
themes; different pairs of themes may suggest different contrasts or parallels. Some

themes may entail others. A further degree of freedom consists in the strength of the polarity assignments themselves. For instance, some themes are maximally contrasting in the sense that under a substitution of discourse referents, the two themes are contradictory. On the other hand, two themes may be maximally similar in that under a substitution of discourse referents we get the same theme. The MEE trees of (2a) again with the isomorphism depicted above. k_0 and the collapsed node $k'0$ - $k'1$ are paired, as are P_1 and c. We identify c and P_1 and so we get a common theme. This in turn allows us to get an identical (modulo substitution of discourse referents) theme for k_0 and k'_0 - k'_1: x said that Mary won the race. There is no other common theme for k_0 and k'_0 - k'_1 that entails this one but not vice versa; neither is there a common theme for P_1 and c that entails P_1 but not vice versa. Consequently, we judge this pair of themes for the two pairs of nodes to be maximal or maximally strong relative to this pairing of nodes.

We can sum up the effects of these parameters by defining an ordering on sets of themes – or more precisely sets of common themes supporting Parallel and sets of pairs of contrasting themes supporting Contrast.

> **Definition:** Suppose A and A' are sets of pairs of equivalent or contrasting themes for nodes paired by tree isomorphisms ζ and ζ' on MEE trees for constituents α and β such that A and A' both satisfy Parallel (α, β) (Contrast (α, β)). A is *at least as strong as* A' iff
>
> (i) $\forall x \in \zeta' x \in \zeta$
> (ii) for every pair of themes P'_γ, $P'_{\zeta'(\gamma)}$ in A' for γ and $\zeta'(\gamma)$ (there is a pair of themes in A P_γ, $P_{\zeta(\gamma)}$ such that $P_\gamma \models P'_\gamma$ and $P_{\zeta(\gamma)} \models P'_{\zeta(\gamma)}$)
> (iii) if A and A' satisfy Contrast (α, β) and both (i) and (ii) hold equally for A and A', then for each pair of nodes γ, node $\zeta'(\gamma)$, the polarity assignment for γ and $\zeta'(\gamma)$ relative to the pair of themes in A' is no more plausible than the polarity assignment for γ and $\zeta'(\gamma)$ relative to the pair of themes in A.

Given this ranking, we have a general constraint that says that we prefer polarity assignments to more comprehensive tree isomorphisms and to more comprehensive themes, and if we have two polarity assignments to equivalent pairs of themes, then we prefer the most plausible polarity assignment, if that is appropriate.

Different contrasts or parallels are modeled by different sets of themes. These different sets of themes make a difference to truth conditional interpretation in cases of lexical ambiguity and in VP ellipsis. In Asher (1993) and more systematically in Asher (1996), I define an SDRS update that determines what the output SDRS is given an input SDRS, a new constituent, and a discourse relation attaching the new constituent to some available attachment point in the input SDRS. Part of SDRS update is to determine the values of the empty VPs in VP ellipsis. Empty VPs introduce concept discourse referents into a constituent. I suppose that Contrast or Parallel is always present in VP ellipsis contexts and that when a concept discourse referent c is paired with some property under a particular tree isomorphism, then relative to this tree isomorphism and the contrast or parallel it suggests, c is identified with the property. Since different tree isomorphisms determine different sets of themes, the preference ordering on sets of themes in effect determines an ordering on tree isomorphisms and hence on particular resolutions of VP ellipses.

As an example of how the account works, let us consider the SDRT account of Parallel and Contrast applied to our familiar (2a). We get two readings. Contrast is required because of the presence of the contrastive particle *but*. There are two pairs of maximal, contrasting themes for the root nodes of the two extended embedding trees, the second elements of which are logically independent (neither entails the other): $\langle x$ saying that φ, x¬saying that $\varphi\rangle$ and $\langle x$ saying that φ and $\neg\varphi\rangle$. These themes result from two different pairs of MEE trees and two tree isomorphisms. The first tree isomorphism, depicted on the left, presupposes that the matrix condition of the root node of the first constituent is its implied affirmative modality, and that contrasts maximally with the negation of the second constituent when the concept discourse referent introduced by the null VP node is mapped onto the dynamic property derived from the higher VP, P_1. The second MEE tree, on the right, pairs k'_1 with k_1, contrasting the negation with the modality, saying that.

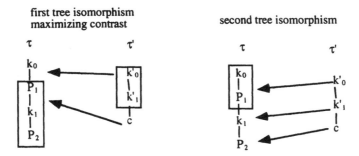

first tree isomorphism
maximizing contrast

second tree isomorphism

I repeatedly refer to these tree isomorphisms later. Of course, when we add a particular stress pattern to (2a) like that given in (3a), there seems to be only one intended reading for the deleted VP. But SDRT has nothing to say about this nor about (3a). We might try simply to say that focus constraints and parallel/contrast effects in discourse are independent and put SDRT's account together with Rooth's analysis of contrastive focus. But matters are not so simple, since as we have seen that barring some account of how to construct the alternatives in the right way here, we get the wrong prediction from Rooth's account, and the account in SDRT of parallel and contrast does not take the patterns of stress and the effects of focus into account.

1.3   Putting SDRT and Focus Together:
A Discourse Based Theory of Focus Interpretation

As the basis of the discourse approach to focus, I use, instead of the logical forms of syntax, MEE trees as the basis of the semantic interpretation of contrastive focus. I suppose the following principles, (0), (3)–(5) are particular to the interpretation of focus at the discourse level and capture explicitly some of the intuitive effects of discourse structure discussed earlier, while (2) is a general constraint on contrastive focus also present in semantic accounts.

Principles of an Account of Symmetric Contrast Focus:

0. Focus applies to conditions on MEE trees.
1. Contrastive focus is interpreted at the level of SDRS construction, and when so interpreted it must exploit either Parallel or Contrast as a discourse relation, relating the two constituents. Which relation is at issue is determined by the SDRT mechanisms.
2. Symmetric contrastive focus must focus distinct elements.
3. The tree isomorphism must respect focus/background structure in target (t) and source (s), if F_t and F_S are of the same SDRS type (symmetric contrastive focus). This means that the tree isomorphism must be extended so that it maps (i) semantic arguments of the one focused element φ to arguments of the other focused element ψ; (ii) constituents containing φ to constituents containing ψ or d-superordinate to that containing ψ; (iii) the constituents d-subordinate to the constituent containing φ must be mapped by the tree isomorphism to constituents d-subordinate to the constituent containing ψ.
4. The maximal contrasting (for Contrast) or equivalent (for Parallel) themes of the source and target constitute the set of alternatives for the focused source clause.
5. The set of alternatives is used in SDRS updating as described in Asher (1993).

To see how this modified SDRT account works, let us look again at our examples. First, let us reconsider (3a). *said* in the first clause and *n't* in the second are both in focus, so an appropriate tree isomorphism for determining parallel or contrast must by constraint (3) map those elements that are arguments of the negation in the source onto elements that are arguments of *said* in the target that are of the appropriate type (symmetric focus on matrix conditions). The second tree isomorphism depicted for (3a) in SDRT without the integration of focus is now, once focus is taken into account, the only possible tree isomorphism. This isomorphism is depicted below.

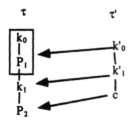

This forces c, the concept discourse referent introduced by the empty VP in the source, to be paired with the dynamic property that results from applying the bottom up DRS construction procedure to the lower VP in the first sentence. SDRS update now forces the identification of c and the dynamic property constructed from the lower VP. This results in the appropriate reading of (3a), and our constraints predict that this is the only possible reading. For the same reasons as with (3a), (5a–c) are all predicted by the theory to only have a reading in which the concept discourse referent c introduced by the null VP in the source is identified with the lower VP property. Given what the focused elements are and our constraints on focus in discourse contexts where the relations Parallel and Contrast are present, only the tree isomorphism given is possible. (5c) is particularly interesting, because while the focus constraints force us to identify c with the property derived from the lower VP, this does not yield a maximal Contrast (the maximal Contrast is present only if we identify c with the higher VP property P_1 in the diagram). With (5c) we must either violate focus constraints or the preference ordering and maximization constraint, and so it is predicted to be incoherent.

In contrast to (3a), nonmatrix conditions are focused in (3b). These conditions occur in the top node of each extended embedding tree, so the requirements of the focus theory on tree isomorphisms (clause 3) impose the constraint that the argument of the one focused semantic structure (a partial DRS in the terms of Asher 1993) that takes a dynamic VP property as an argument) be mapped onto the argument of the other focused semantic structure, which must be of the same type. This leads us to choose the first tree isomorphism for (3b), which I give again in the following.

first tree isomorphism

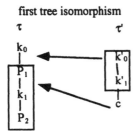

When we apply the SDRT update rule we identify c with P_1 and this predicts that only the higher VP reading is possible for (3b).

In (3b) a contrast relation is required by the presence of *but*, but the theory predicts that this particle is optional. Recall that we pick the tree isomorphism among all those that pass the constraints that maximizes a contrast or parallel relation between the two constituents. So let us first consider pairing c, the discourse referent introduced by the null VP, with the dynamic property P_1 derived from the higher VP; we get a maximally strong polarity assignment contrast – one theme is the negation of the other. Can we maximize parallel with a pair of equivalent that is as strong as the contrast? No. So we predict that (3b), even without the contrast particle, has only one reading (the higher VP reading) and that that reading induces a contrast. Now by SDRS update, we must identify the concept discourse referent introduced by the null VP with the property given by the higher VP in the target. So the SDRT theory of Parallel and Contrast predicts only the higher VP reading for (3b), with or without the contrastive particle.

In example (3c) nonmatrix conditions again are focused, but we do not have a contrast particle. According to the constraint (3), we must map the concept discourse referent c introduced by the null VP onto the higher VP property. This mapping yields maximal common themes under substitution of discourse referents for each pair of nodes – hence a very strong parallel reading. Contrast cannot be generated under this tree isomorphism, and since this is the only possible tree isomorphism given the structural constraints induced by symmetric contrastive focus, the SDRT update of the second constituent predicts only this parallel higher VP reading for (3c), which is intuitively what is desired.

In (6a) and (6d), focus on DR-theoretic elements of the same type but the tree isomorphism constraint (3) forces the concept discourse referent introduced by the null VP to be mapped onto an argument of the condition derived from the main verb in the first clause. But this means that the concept discourse referent is never identified with something of the right type. Consequently, in order to retrieve a VP content for the second sentences of (6a) and (6d), we must violate constraint (3) imposed by the focus background structure on parallel and contrast. In (6b–c), we focus on elements of distinct types, so these discourses are not cases of symmetric contrastive focus.

This theory, integrating focus with the effects of discourse structure, predicts data about VP ellipsis that eludes other theories. It supposes a weak semantic component that is tightly interleaved with a theory of discourse structure. But this theory so far is limited; it speaks only of symmetric contrastive focus across clauses.

A natural extension of this account would answer two questions: (1) What about symmetric contrastive focus within a clause? (2) What about other uses of focus (question answering, focusing adverbs, scalar implicature)? With regard to question (1), if we distinguish symmetric contrastive focus from multiple focus (as the semantics of Rooth (1992) and Krifka (1991, 1992) would strongly suggest), then the function of symmetric contrast focus within the clause seems again to involve contrast – to set up a contrast in further discourse. Consider example (1) again:

(1)   An AMERICAN farmer met a CANADIAN farmer.

This sentence would be most felicitously the beginning of a discourse contrasting attitudes or deeds of American versus Canadian farmers, as Rooth notes. The alternative for each focused element is the other focused element, as Rooth's semantics would have it. The present proposal differs in that it requires contrastive focus to be interpreted at the clausal level. It is at the level of the clause that SDRT takes contrast to be well defined. If we attend to the discourse function of sentences like (1), however, this makes sense. The appropriate set of alternatives is the set of the maximal contrasting themes that will have to do with Americans and Canadians (by clause 4). Since we don't know what the author is going to say about the American and Canadian farmers at this point, we must have as contrast alternatives {[[an American farmer]](P), [[a Canadian farmer]](P)}, where P is a variable over dynamic properties and $[[\alpha]]$ is the partial DRS or dynamic quantifier that results from the bottom up DRS construction procedure applied to α. It is then the function of the ensuing discourse to provide the appropriate values for P and elaborate on the contrast;[4] if ensuing discourse does not provide an appropriate value, then the discourse should be odd or incomplete. I have said that this is the function of ensuing discourse, since it would be hard to imagine how preceding discourse could supply an appropriate topic given the content of (6). So a refinement of clause 4 handles cases of symmetric contrastive focus within one clause:

4′. The maximal contrasting (for Contrast) or equivalent (for Parallel) themes of the source and target constitute the set of alternatives for the focused elements, when the two elements in focus, α and α', are in distinct clauses. When α and α' occur within one clause δ and α and α' are of a type that takes an argument of type τ to yield a DRS or dynamic proposition, then the set of alternatives is {[[α]](P_1^τ), [[α']](P_2^τ), where P_1 and P_2 are to be identified with the appropriate properties φ_1 and φ_2 such that in the discourse in which δ occurs, [[α]](φ_1) and [[α']](φ_2) constitute a pair of maximally contrasting or equivalent themes for two constituents that elaborate δ. When α and α' occur within one clause δ and for something of type τ, $P_\tau(\alpha)$ is a DRS or dynamic proposition, then the set of alternatives is {[[α]](P_1^τ), [[α']](P_2^τ), with the same restrictions on P_1 and P_2 as in the preceding clause.

In the case of two contrasting focused elements within the same clause, the appropriate set of alternatives involves the two maximal contrasting themes each one involving the semantic value of the focused expression together with the appropriate variable to yield an SDRS constituent. Thus, all uses of symmetric contrastive focus have the same discourse oriented explanation.

1.4 A Potential Problem: Nonsymmetric Contrast

Consider again the examples in (3) and (5), but this time with neutral (sentence final) stress on the first element of the pairs.

(3) a′. John said Mary won the race. She DIDN'T.
 b′. John said that Mary won the competition, but SHE didn't. (higher VP)
 c′. John said that Mary won the race, and SAM did.
(5) a′. John said that Mary won the competition, and she DID. (lower VP)

Do we get a difference in judgments? I think not. The reason is that I think we still prefer to map the focused element onto something of the same type if such is available in the corresponding MEE tree. We still prefer strategies for symmetric contrastive focus, when the trees permit.

1.5   *The Pragmatic-Semantic Account of Focus beyond Contrastive Focus*

Not all instances of focus are profitably analyzed as cases of contrastive focus. Certain uses of focus are appropriate to particular discourse contexts – what I have called in another paper (Asher 1995) corrections. These occur frequently in dialogue. Here is an example.

> A: John likes Mary.
> B: No, he DOESN'T.

Further, the present account says nothing about the interaction between other focusing constructions such as questions or focus-sensitive operators and discourse or pragmatics in general, but it is clear that there are interactions that await systematic and formal analysis. One indication that this interaction is worth pursuing is that the logical structure of the SDRS appears to be a factor in determining what is the set of alternatives for a focused element – something that cannot be determined from a semantic account of focus alone.[5] Consider the following examples, in which a set of alternatives is generated for focused elements that are within the scope of a focus-sensitive operator. Note, however, that in all the examples given the focally stressed elements in the discourse also generate symmetric contrastive focus readings for the clauses in which they occur. I again assume that the interpretation of focus may involve constituents larger than those on which the focal stress falls.

(7)   a.   SUSAN kissed Fred. JOAN kissed Fred. MARY kissed Fred too. But only MARY kissed SAM.
       b.   EVERYONE greeted Mary. Only SAM congratulated her on her prize, however.
       c.   MOST of the boys were happy for Mary. Only FRED resented her success.
       d.   FEW boys kissed any girls that they liked. And only MARY got kissed by more than one.

The account of contrastive focus given makes minimal semantic assumptions, and so it is fully compatible with the semantics of focus-sensitive operators such as that given in Rooth (1992) or Krifka (1991, 1992). So we may take *only* and *even* to exploit the set of alternatives of the elements that are semantically interpreted as focused. So, for instance, the truth conditions for the second clauses of (7) could be computed as in Krifka (1992). It is not very difficult to adapt the structured meaning semantics for focus-sensitive operators to the DRT formalism.

An SDRT-based account of focus adds constraints concerning the set of alternatives, if we adopt the following claim: the set of alternatives is *anaphoric* and so obeys the same discourse constraints of availability and accessibility that anaphoric pronouns do in SDRT. This is of a piece with Rooth's claim that the alternative set is a presupposition of the focus construction and so must be either bound anaphorically or accommodated.

The notion of accessibility in SDRT is just that of DRT, and so if we suppose that alternative sets are bound anaphorically in a similar fashion to anaphoric pronouns, as van der Sandt (1992) has suggested, then we would predict that the set of alternatives cannot include elements that are inaccessible or violate the constraints on accessible groups of plural DRT. So, for instance, the set of alternatives to [[Mary]] in (7d) cannot be those girls that the boys liked, since DRT does not license the formation of the group of girls that the boys liked within the scope of a negative determiner like *few*. In cases where we do not have an accesssible anaphoric antecedent, we accommodate – in (7d) we accommodate a general set of girls to serve as the alternative set. There also seem to be cases in which the alternative set is simply conventionally determined – for instance, a focus on *hard liquor* may simply generate the alternative set {beer, wine, hard liquor} but this seems to depend almost completely on extralinguistic knowledge that I cannot take into consideration here.

Besides accessibility, SDRT also imposes the discourse constraint of *availability* on anaphoric antecedents (Asher 1993). A discourse referent introduced in a constituent α by an anaphoric pronoun is *available* to a discourse referent introduced in a constituent β iff α and β are related by some discourse relation.[6] Given the way discourse structures are determined in SDRT, this means that in a discourse like (8a), the man introduced in the second sentence of (8a) does contribute to the alternative set of [[Mary]], while the people introduced in the second sentence of (8b) do not contribute to the alternative set. I assume that in both *a woman* is the interpreted focus element that combines with the focus-sensitive operator [[only]] in the third sentence.

(8)   a. A man and a woman entered the bookstore. There was one other man who was leafing through some magazines on the shelves. Only [the woman]$_F$ bought something, a pocket edition of *du contrat social*.
      b. A man and a woman entered the bookstore. There was one other man who was leafing through some magazines on the shelves, and he was smoking a cigarette. The bookstore was full of shelves with books covered with dust – not much turnover. Only [the woman]$_F$ bought something, a pocket edition of *du contrat social*.

The following is the constituent graph, a schematic representation, of the SDRS for (8b). The second and third sentences generate constituents that serve as background to the constituent k_1 derived from the first sentence. k_1 and its background form a complex structure that is related to a constructed topic by the relation "FBP" or "Foreground-Background Pair." To handle the anaphoric phenomena, SDRT requires that when two constituents are related by the relation background, a particular sort of topic be constructed in which material from the foregrounded constituent is included as well as at least temporarily information from the latest background constituent. This information is removed from the topic and replaced with novel background information, if the backgrounding relation is continued as in (8b) (though it remains in (8a)).[7] Notice finally that in SDRT more than one discourse relation may obtain between two constituents – namely, between k_0 and k_4.[8]

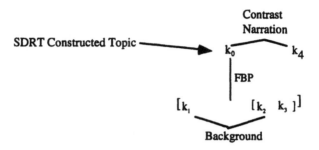

Given this structure SDRT then predicts that the only material anaphorically accessible to the focused expression in k_4 is the material in the constructed topic. This means that in (8a) both the man who entered with the woman and the man reading the magazines are in the alternative set to [[a woman]], whereas in (8b) the intervening background material has forced us to remove the second man from the constructed topic, thus yielding a different alternative set for [[a woman]] in (8b). Though subtle, it seems to me that these predictions are correct.

With other texts like (7a), SDRT predicts that Susan, Fred, Joan, and Mary constitute the contrast set for [Mary]. But this is only because of the way that SDRT constructs topics for narratives – putting the sums of the arguments that play the same role in the constituents related by narration in the topic constituent.[9]

I summarize my claim concerning alternative sets using the terminology of SDRT. Suppose α_0 is an element of a constituent α in an SDRS τ. Then

> *Observation 1:* The alternative set for $[\alpha_0]_F = \{[[\alpha_0]]\} \cup \{[[\gamma_0]] : \gamma_0$ of the same type as α_0 and occurs in γ such that for some discourse relation R $R(\gamma, \alpha)$ is a condition in $\tau\}$, or the alternative set is accommodated from background knowledge.

1.6   Conclusion: There Is a Nontrivial Relation between Sentential Focus and Discourse Focus

The observations of the preceding section bring us back to the discourse distinction between foreground or discourse focus and background. Following (loosely) some of the discussion by Hopper and Givon concerning foreground and background, one could take the *foreground* or "discourse focus" of a particular SDRS prior to the attachment of a new constituent to be the open constituents, shown in the following graph of an SDRS.

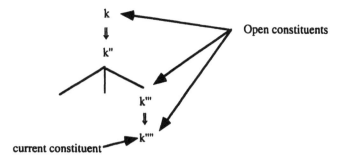

That is, *foreground* = Discourse Focus (α, τ) = the subgraph of τ whose elements are restricted to $\{\beta: \text{Open}(\beta, \alpha, \tau)\}$. Now in SDRT it is just these open constituents to which new information γ can attach by means of some discourse relation, and so it is in fact the Discourse Focus together with the new constituent focus that determines the set of alternatives. Thus, Discourse Focus and the new constituent focus though distinct have an important interaction.

Because of the presuppositional character of anaphoric pronouns, their antecedents must be already part of the discourse context. This explains why anaphoric pronouns in the Discourse Focus cannot be identified with elements in the (sentential) focus, though definites can as the following examples illustrate.

(9)   a. He$_J$ walked in and collapsed on the couch. A man$_J$ was dead tired.
        b. He$_J$ walked in and collapsed on the couch. John$_J$ was dead tired.

Definites like the proper name in (9b) have a presupposition that their referent has already been introduced within the discourse context, so we can in effect assume that it is part of the discourse context of the Discourse Focus and so anaphoric elements within the Discourse Focus can be identified with this referent. Indefinites, however, do not generate such a presupposition and so we cannot assume that the referent of *a man* is part of the discourse context, and so the anaphoric link in (9a) is predicted to be bad.

If we adopt the following conjecture of Givon (1984), reformulated within SDRT,

> *Observation 2:* The background elements δ of a constituent α must be such that for some β such that Open (β, α, τ), δ is part of the topic of β or part of β itself.

we can observe a similar connection between anaphoric pronouns in the sentential background and NPs in sentential focus.

> *Observation 3:* Anaphoric pronouns in the sentential background cannot be identified with discourse referents introduced by NPs in sentential focus, unless the latter generate familiarity presuppositions (e.g., are definites).

As partial confirmation of this prediction, I note an observation of Krifka (personal communication) that (10a) has both a strict and a sloppy reading for the pronoun *his*, while (10b) only has a sloppy reading – namely, a professor was the only one who read his own articles. This observation would follow from Observation 3.

(10)   a. Only[John]$_F$ reviewed his own article.
        b. Only [a professor]$_F$ reviewed his own article.

Notes

1   That many SDRSs represent the same proposition follows from the fact that many DRSs can represent the same proposition. There are infinitely many DRSs that are simply alphabetic variants of one another – a substitution of discourse referents will transform one alphabetic variant into another. But it would be hard to see how alphabetic variants (mere substitution of declared discourse referents) could represent distinct propositions. This will be important in the development of themes below.

2   For a discussion of these relations, their semantics, and how to infer them, see Asher (1993), Lascarides and Asher (1993), Asher et al. (1993).

3   We may apply the same thinning procedure to constituents with a complex logical structure. The definitions that follow are for constituents with an embedding tree that is a singleton.

4   Elaboration is a particular type of discourse relation in SDRT and other discourse theories. In Asher et al. (1993) and Lascarides and Asher (1993), mechanisms are given for calculating discourse relations between constituents. A model-theoretic interpretation for discourse relations and their semantic effects is given in Asher (1993).

5   See Asher (1995) for more details.

6   In which is included the transitive closure of the Elaboration relation – thus a constituent that functions as the topic of a discourse segment may always harbor antecedents for discourse referents introduced by pronouns in the constituents that it dominates.

7   See Asher et al. (1995) for details. Anaphoric pronouns behave similarly with respect to the background relation. Consider the following examples in French, which are of a piece with (8a) and (8b):
   (i)   Marie entra dans un magazin. Un homme était assis derrière le comptoir. Il lisait un journal. Elle s'approcha de lui.
   (ii)   Marie entra dans un magazin. Un homme était assis derrière le comptoir. Il lisait un journal. Le magazin était plein d'étagères avec des livres couverts de poussière. Elle s'approcha de *lui (s'en approcha).
   (iii) Marie entra dans un magazin. Un homme était assis derrière le comptoir. Il lisait un journal. Le magazin était plein d'étagères avec des livres couverts de poussière. Il faisait très sombre. Elle s'approcha de *lui (*s'en approcha).

8   This is due to the fact that SDRT explicitly uses a nonmonotonic logic to infer discourse relations between constituents; any relation that can be consistently inferred to hold will be inferred to hold.

9   It is an SDRT hypothesis that sums or groups of individuals that are not licensed by the syntax or certain sorts of DRS conditions (cf. Kamp and Reyle 1993) are constructed when topics for narrative are built up. See Asher (1993) for details.

References

Asher, N. 1993. *Reference to Abstract Objects in Discourse*, Kluwer Academic Publishers, Amsterdam.

Asher, N. 1995. From Discourse Macro-Structure to Micro-Structure and Back Again: Discourse Semantics and the Focus/Background Distinction, *Proceedings of the Prague and Stuttgart Conferences on Context*, SFB report, University of Stuttgart, Germany.

Asher, N. 1996. Mathematical Treatments of Discourse Contexts, *Proceedings of the Tenth Amsterdam Colloquium*, ILLC Publications, Amsterdam.

Asher, N., M. Aurnague, M. Bras, and L. Vieu. 1993. Space, Time and Discourse, *Proceedings of the Dagstuhl Seminar on Universals in the Lexicon and Proceedings of the Workshop on Temporal and Spatial Reasoning*, IJCAI.

Asher, N., M. Aurnague, M. Bras, and L. Vieu. 1995. L'espace-temps dans l'analyse du discours, IRIT Research Report IRIT/95-08-R, Université Paul Sabatier, Toulouse.

Givon, T. 1984. Prologomena to Discourse Pragmatics, *Journal of Pragmatics* 8.

Grosz, B., and C. Sidner 1986. Attention, Intentions, and the Structure of Discourse, *Computational Linguistics*, 12.

Hopper, P. 1979. Aspect and Foregrounding in Discourse, in T. Givon (ed.), *Discourse and Syntax*, Academic Press, New York.

Kamp, H., and U. Reyle. 1993. *From Discourse to Logic*. Kluwer, Academic Publishers, Amsterdam.

Krifka, M. 1991. A Compositional Semantics for Multiple Focus Constructions, in *Current Issues in Natural Language Processing*, Center for Cognitive Science, University of Texas at Austin.

Krifka, M. 1992. A Framework for Focus Sensitive Quantification, *SALT II Proceedings*, edited by D. Dowty and C. Barker.

Labov, W. 1972. The Transformation of Experience in Narrative Discourse, in *Language in the Inner City*, University of Pennsylvania Press, Philadelphia.

Lascarides, L., and N. Asher. 1993. Temporal Interpretation, Discourse Relations, and Commonsense Entailment, *Linguistics and Philosophy*, 16.

Mann, W. C., and S. A. Thompson. 1987. Rhetorical Structure Theory. In G. Kempen (ed.), *Natural Language Generation*. Martinus Nijhoff, Dordrecht.

Rooth, M. 1985. *Association with Focus*. Ph.D. Thesis. University of Massachusetts, Amherst.

Rooth, M. 1992. A Theory of Focus Interpretation, *Natural Language Semantics* 1.

Sag, I. 1976. *Deletion and Logical Form*. Ph.D. Thesis. MIT.

Sandt, R. van der 1992. 'Presupposition projection as anaphora resolution,' *Journal of Semantics*, 9.

Sgall, P. 1967. Functional Sentence Perspective in a Generative Description, *Prague Studies in Mathematical Linguistics* 2, Academia, Prague.

14   Domain Restriction

BART GEURTS AND ROB VAN DER SANDT

Abstract

Domain restriction can and should be explained in presuppositional terms. In earlier work we presented a theory of presupposition that contains the essential ingredients for an explanatory account of domain restriction. Given certain auxiliary assumptions concerning the representation of quantifiers and the interaction between focusing and presupposition, the theory of presupposition predicts that quantifier domains are restricted in at least three ways: through binding, through (intermediate) accommodation, and through focusing.

1   Introduction

The domain of a quantifying NP is underdetermined by the content of its nominal head and is usually further restricted by pragmatic factors. This much is widely agreed. However, there is a less than perfect consensus on how pragmatic information contributes to domain restriction. In this chapter we view domain restriction as a presuppositional phenomenon. In particular, we claim that domain restriction is, by and large, explained by a theory of presupposition that we presented elsewhere and that we refer to in the following as the 'binding theory' of presupposition projection.[1]

The binding theory is an extension of DRT, whose central tenet is that presuppositions are the kind of entities that must be bound, just as anaphors must be bound. As a matter of fact, we maintain that anaphors *are* presuppositional expressions. The only difference between anaphors and most other varieties of presupposition is that the former must be bound to a given antecedent, whereas the latter generally may be interpreted by way of accommodation. In general, if a presupposition cannot be bound, a suitable antecedent will be accommodated; that is, an antecedent will be set up in some position that is accessible from the DRS in which the presupposition was triggered (its 'home DRS', as we shall say). Accommodation is subject to a number of constraints: accommodation must yield a coherent interpretation and by default a presupposition will be accommodated as closely to the main DRS as is possible while maintaining coherence.

The claim we want to substantiate in the following is that the binding theory, which is amply justified on independent grounds, provides the mechanisms for explaining domain restriction. The only thing we require in addition to these mechanisms is certain assumptions concerning the representation of quantifiers and the interaction between focus and presuppositions. Once these are given, the binding theory predicts that quantifier domains are restricted in at least three ways: through binding, through (intermediate) accommodation, and through focusing.

2   Domain Restriction through Binding

2.1   *Quantifiers as Presupposition Inducers*

In the literature on presupposition it is usually assumed as a matter of course that quantifying NPs are presupposition inducing expressions. According to this view, an NP of the form 'Det$_Q$ N', where Det$_Q$ is a quantifying determiner, triggers the presupposition that there is a nonempty set of Ns.[2] This explains, for example, why one tends to infer from an utterance of (1a) or (1b) that the speaker takes (1c) to be true, as well:

(1)   a. Most passengers survived the crash.
       b. It is likely that most passengers survived the crash.
       c. There were passengers.

These inferences, in particular that from (1b) to (1c), cannot be explained in terms of scope. For, claiming that the quantifier in (1b) induces the presupposition that (1c) is true is something quite different from saying that in (1b) the quantifier takes wide scope. The most likely reading by far of this sentence is (2a):

(2)   a. it is likely that [most x: passenger x](x survived the crash)
       b. [most x: passenger x](it is likely that x survived the crash)

However, the reading on which *most passengers* takes wide scope is hardly plausible for (1b). Similarly, the universal quantifier in (3a) may have narrow or wide scope with respect to the negation operator:

(3)   a. All children weren't asleep.
       b. ¬[all x: child x](asleep x)
       c. [all x: child x]¬(asleep x)

But regardless of whether we construe (3a) as (3b) or (3c), it may still (and typically will) be interpreted as presupposing that there is a given set of children. Evidently, presupposition and scope are distinct phenomena (for further discussion of this difference, see Geurts, in press).

If we adopt the binding theory, the observation that quantifiers are presupposition inducers dovetails nicely with another one, namely, that the domain of a quantifier is normally restricted by contextual factors. Combining the two views, we would expect the domain of a quantifier to be the kind of thing that tends to be bound and, if no suitable antecedent is available, will accommodate at the least embedded level in the discourse representation possible – and that is precisely what we find.

Semantically speaking, a quantifier is a relation between two sets; for example, 'most *A*s are *B*s' says that the majority of *A*s are *B*s. We maintain that, apart from its truth conditional content, a quantifier such as *most* also triggers the presupposition that there are *A*s. Or, to put it differently, a speaker who claims that 'most *A*s are *B*s' indicates that the hearer should be in a position to identify the relevant set of *A*s.

(4)   a. The airplane carried some passengers, and it is likely that most passengers were killed in the crash.
        b. If the airplane carried any passengers, it is likely that most passengers were killed in the crash.

If 'most *A*s are *B*s' induces the domain presupposition that there is a set of *A*s, then at least in outline the binding theory offers a rather plausible construal of examples like these. In (4a) as well as in (4b), the intended domain of *most* is obviously restricted to the set of passengers introduced by the indefinite NP in the first clause. Given an appropriate representation of the presuppositions associated with *most*, *some*, and *any*, the binding theory would actually predict this. In particular it would predict that in (4b) the presupposition will be bound at a subordinate level (in the antecedent of the conditional) and thus account for the fact that, in contradistinction to (4a), (4b) will not normally be taken to imply that there were passengers.

Let us say, following Milsark (1977), that an NP is strong if it is a presupposition inducer, and weak if it is not; if a strong (weak) NP begins with a determiner, then the determiner will be called strong (weak), too. According to this definition, definite NPs (proper names included) are always strong, as are genuinely quantifying NPs.[3] The latter are partitive in the sense that they select a subset of a given domain set; universally quantifying NPs come out as the borderline case in which the domain of the quantifier coincides with the subset it selects. As a rule, this partitive structure can be made explicit (see Löbner 1987). For example, compare (4a, b) with

(4′)   a. The airplane carried some passengers, and it is likely that most *of the* passengers were killed in the crash.
        b. If the airplane carried any passengers, it is likely that most *of the* passengers were killed in the crash.

The following determiners are always strong:

(5)   all, every, each, both, neither, most, . . .

But most determiners allow for strong as well as weak construals:

(6)   some, *n*, at least *n*, at most *n*, few, several, many, . . .

In (4a), *most* is strong, but *some* in (4a) and *any* in (4b) are weak. Intuitively, *some passengers* in (4a) does not require a contextually given set of passengers, and consequently it cannot be paraphrased with an overt partitive:

(7)   The airplane carried some *of the* passengers and it is likely that only few
        passengers survived the crash.

This represents a possible reading of (4a), on which *some passengers* is construed
as a quantifying and, therefore, strong NP, but it is not the first reading to come to
mind when we read this sentence. In other words, there is a strong tendency not to
take this NP as a presupposition-inducing expression.

The fact that the determiners listed in (6) can be either strong or weak might
be explained by assuming that they are lexically ambiguous between these two
readings (this appears to be Milsark's position). We are not convinced that this
would be right, however, and prefer to view the ambiguity in pragmatic terms. For
one thing, we find this ambiguity not only in the determiner system of English
but in other languages as well, which is not what one would expect if it were a
purely lexical matter. For another, the distinction between weak and strong readings
correlates with intonational differences. A strong determiner typically receives a
stress accent (which, incidentally, confirms our suspicion that, for the determiners
listed in (6), this reading is the marked one). This suggests that the distinction
should be accounted for in terms of focusing. We do not pursue this matter further
in this paper but refer instead to the contributions of Büring and Jäger to this volume.

How should the distinction between strong and weak plural NPs be represented
in a DRT framework? We need a representation format that meets at least the
following three requirements. First, it must account for the presuppositions that
quantifiers give rise to. For instance, in

(8)   If the fire started on the top floor, then most (of the) people in the building
        will be rescued.

the domain presupposition of the quantifier *most* will have to be represented in
such a way that it can be accommodated in the main DRS, since normally this
sentence would presuppose that there were people in the building. Second, the
presupposition triggered by a quantifier must be an object that can be bound to an
antecedent, as in

(9)   There are some office workers in the building, but most people will be
        rescued.

On the most obvious reading of (9), the domain of *most* is the group introduced
by the existential NP in the first conjunct, so the presupposition triggered by the
quantifier should be able to pick up this object. Third, when a quantifier links up
in this way to a prior NP α, the scope of α is in a sense drawn out, as the following
example illustrates:

(10)   The mayor awarded all firemen a silver medal. Some (of the) men sold it
        right away.

The most likely reading of this discourse is that each fireman received his own
medal (so the universal quantifier has wide scope) and that some of the firemen

immediately sold the silver medal they had been given. Intuitively, what happens in this case is that the quantifying NP *some (of the) men* picks up the set of firemen-cum-silver-medals introduced in the first sentence, so that in the scope of *some (of the) men* each man is correlated with a medal, which can therefore be picked up anaphorically.

This telescoping effect is not confined to quantifying NPs, of course. First, it also occurs when a plural object is picked up by a pronoun, as can be seen when we replace the subject of the second sentence in (10) with *they*. Second, it is not only NPs that give rise to telescoping: quantifying adverbials, modals, and attitude verbs produce the same effect, as is illustrated by the following selection from Karttunen's seminal paper on discourse referents (first circulated in 1969 and published as Karttunen 1976):

(11)   a. Every time Bill comes here, he picks up *a book* and wants to borrow *it*. I never let him take *the book*.
        b. Harvey courts *a girl* at every convention. *She* always comes to the banquet with him. *The girl* is usually also very pretty.
        c. You must write *a letter* to your parents. *It* has to be sent by airmail.
        d. Bill says he saw *a lion* on the street. He claims *the lion* had escaped from the zoo.
        e. I wish Mary had *a car*. She would take me to work in *it*.

(11a–d) illustrate the telescoping effect in adverbial, modal, and attitude contexts. (11e) is a mixed case, in which the hypothetical state of affairs introduced by the attitude verb *wish* is picked up by the modal *would*.

In our opinion, the same mechanism underlies the phenomena illustrated by (10) and (11). That telescoping may occur in all these cases is a reflection of the fact that similar semantic structures are associated with nominal and adverbial quantifiers, modals, and attitude verbs. And although the account presented in this chapter is focused on quantification, essentially the same analysis applies to modals and attitude reports, too, as is shown by Geurts (1995, in press).

2.2   Duplex Conditions

In the previous section we discussed three desiderata that an adequate representation of strong and weak plural NPs should satisfy. It has to account for the presuppositions quantified NPs give rise to; these presuppositions should be the kind of object that can be bound to an antecedent, and it has to explain the telescoping effect. In Section 2.3 we put forward a proposal that achieves just this, but first we want to discuss briefly an alternative analysis proposed by Kamp and Reyle (1993), which fails to meet these desiderata.[4]

In Kamp and Reyle's version of DRT, NPs are interpreted in one of two ways; their distinction is motivated on quite different grounds, but it is evidently related to the strong/weak distinction we have adopted. According to Kamp and Reyle, a quantifier gives rise to a tripartite structure, which is represented by a so-called duplex condition of the form $\varphi\langle Q\,u\rangle\psi$, where φ and ψ are DRSs, Q is a quantifier, and u is a reference marker. For instance, (12a) is represented by (12b):

(12)   a. Most soldiers surrendered.
         b. [: [x: soldier x]⟨most x⟩[: x surrendered]]

The interpretation of duplex conditions is treated along the following lines. If Q is a quantifier expression, then Q* is the generalized quantifier associated with Q; so Q* is a relation between sets of individuals. Then an embedding function f verifies a duplex condition $\varphi\langle Q\,u\rangle\psi$ in a model M iff $\langle A, B\rangle \in$ Q*, where $A = \{g(x)\colon g$ extends f and g embeds φ in M$\}$ and $B = \{h(x)\colon h$ extends f and h embeds $\varphi \oplus \psi$ in M$\}$, where $\varphi \oplus \psi$ denotes the merge of φ and ψ.[5] Let us adopt for convenience the standard definition of the generalized quantifier associated with *most*, that is, most*(A, B) iff $|A \cap B| > |A - B|$. Then (12b) is true in a model M, on the interpretation given by Kamp and Reyle, iff the soldiers in M that surrendered outnumbered those who fought on.

Observe that the interpretation of duplex conditions $\varphi\langle Q\,u\rangle\psi$ is dynamic in the sense that reference markers introduced in φ may be picked up in ψ. Thus the following type of 'donkey anaphora' is accounted for:[6]

(13)   a. Most professors who own a Porsche wash it once a week.
         b. [: [x, y: prof x, Porsche y, x owns y]⟨most x⟩[: x weekly washes y]]

If an NP is weak, it does not directly give rise to a duplex condition, but to a rather simpler representation, as illustrated by the following:

(14)   a. Harry glued together some butterflies.
         b. [X: butterflies X, some X, Harry glued X together]

Here the plural reference marker X represents a set of butterflies, which Harry treats collectively.[7] This is the default representation for a weak NP; if such an NP is to be construed distributively, a special rule is called upon, which applies in the case of (15a), for example, to yield (15b):

(15)   a. Harry dissected some butterflies.
         b. [X: butterflies X, some X, [x: x ∈ X]⟨all x⟩[Harry dissected x]]

Since we are not concerned in this chapter with collective interpretations this is the only type of structure that is relevant to our purposes. Let us compare, then, Kamp and Reyle's representation of weak NPs as exemplified by (15b) with their representation of strong NPs employed in (13b). Formally, the two representations are rather similar, but there is one salient difference: the former uses, and the latter does not use, a plural reference marker to represent a set object. Without further provisions it is predicted, therefore, that the anaphoric potential of (15b) is greater than that of (13b). This is false: it is true that a plural pronoun, for example, might be used to refer back to *some butterflies* in (15b), but the same holds for *most professors* in (13b). To circumvent this problem, Kamp and Reyle introduce an 'abstraction rule' that, given a duplex condition of the form $\varphi \langle Q\,u \rangle \psi$, generates a plural reference marker that stands for the set of individuals ν that satisfy φ as well as ψ, where ν is a reference marker that is introduced in φ. When applied to (13b), this rule yields, abstracting over x,

(16)   [X: X = $\sum$x[x, y: prof x, Porsche y, x owns y, x weekly washes y],
         [x, y: prof x, Porsche y, x owns y]⟨most x⟩[: x weekly washes y]]

Here a plural reference marker that represents the set of professors that own a Porsche and wash it once a week has been created.

The DRS in (16) provides a suitable object to be picked up by a plural pronoun, but this is not yet sufficient to account for the telescoping phenomenon. Suppose, for instance, that the discourse in (13a) is continued with (17a):

(17)   a.   . . .and they allow nobody else to drive in *it*.
         b.   [X, Z: X = $\sum$ x[x, y: prof x, Porsche y, x owns y, x weekly washes y],
             [x, y: prof x, Porsche y, x owns y]⟨most x⟩[: x weekly washes y],
             Z = X, [z: z ∈ Z]⟨all z⟩[u: z allows nobody else to drive in u]]

Corresponding to the plural pronoun in (17a), the DRS in (17b) features a plural reference marker, Z, which picks up X, that is, the set of professors that own a Porsche and wash it once a week. Since, obviously, *they* is to be read distributively, the distribution rule applies, producing a duplex condition that quantifies over Z, and the reference marker correlated with *it* in (17a), that is, u, is in the nuclear scope of this duplex condition. Now the problem is that there is no suitable antecedent accessible to u:[8] despite the fact that Z = X, there is nothing in either the formal or the informal semantics of (17b) to guarantee that the reference marker y that is in the scope of the abstraction operator is accessible to the reference marker u that is in the scope of the duplex condition quantifying over Z. More generally speaking, in a DRS of the form

(18)   [X, Y: X = $\sum$ xφ, X = Y, [y: y ∈ Y]⟨Q z⟩ψ]

φ is not accessible from ψ, and therefore reference markers occurring in ψ can never be 'bound' in φ.

Kamp and Reyle propose to deal with this problem by allowing the material in φ to be copied into ψ whenever a configuration like (18) arises. This solution is quite clearly ad hoc. In the original version of DRT there is a match between the interpretation of DRSs on the one hand and the notion of accessibility on the other (a match that is akin to, though not quite the same as, the correspondence between the semantics of, say, predicate logic and the metalogical notion of variable binding). Roughly speaking, if a DRS φ is accessible from ψ, then ψ carries at least as much information as φ does, and as a rule the converse holds as well. To illustrate, consider a DRS of the form

(19) $[: \varphi_1 \Rightarrow \varphi_2, \psi_1 \Rightarrow \psi_2]$

In (19), φ_2 and ψ_2 contain at least as much information as φ_1 and ψ_1, respectively, and accordingly φ_1 is accessible from φ_2 and ψ_1 is accessible from ψ_2. A marginal case occurs if φ_1 and ψ_1 are (type-) identical, for then we are forced to admit that φ_2 is at least as informative as ψ_1 and that ψ_2 is at least as informative as ψ_1, although φ_1 isn't accessible from ψ_2 and ψ_1 isn't accessible from φ_2. But save for such coincidences, accessibility may be taken to coincide with an information ordering on DRSs.

In Kamp and Reyle's version of DRT, this correspondence is forsaken. In their system, the relation between φ and ψ in (18) is the same as that between φ_1 and ψ_2 (or ψ_1 and φ_2) in (19) in the marginal case in which $\varphi_1 = \psi_1$ happens to hold: in (18) ψ augments the information in φ, but φ is not accessible from ψ. This leads one to expect that it is an accident that φ is more informative than ψ, just as it is accident if in (19) ψ_2 is more informative than φ_1. But of course such a comparison would be quite inappropriate. And this is not just a technical matter. Intuitively, too, we should expect that, in a constellation like (18), φ is accessible from ψ because the latter serves to select part of the set specified by the former, and it is precisely this property that Kamp and Reyle call upon to justify their copying rule. In our view, however, their solution cures the symptoms but not the disease, for it does nothing to repair the mismatch between the notion of accessibility and the interpretation of structures like (18).

A further problem with Kamp and Reyle's proposal, as it stands, is that it doesn't take into account the presuppositions triggered by quantifying NPs.[9] We saw that a strong NP induces a domain presupposition, which means that, for example, (20a) (=(12a)) presupposes that there is a (salient) set of soldiers. However, this set is not represented in the DRS associated with (20a).

(20)   a.   Most soldiers surrendered.
         b. $[X: X = \sum x[x: \text{soldier } x, x \text{ surrendered}],$
              $[x: \text{soldier } x] \langle \text{most } x \rangle [: x \text{ surrendered}]]$

(20b) is the result of applying the abstraction rule to the sentential DRS correlated with (20a) (that is, (12b)). The resulting object is the set of soldiers who surrendered, which corresponds with the second argument of the quantifier. However, its first argument is not represented by a reference marker, and therefore this representation does not provide a suitable object for the projection algoritm to apply to: the domain argument of the quantifier is represented in such a way that it cannot be detached and moved about. It might seem that this defect can be remedied in a straightforward manner: one could introduce a second abstraction rule that is restricted to the domain of a quantifier. In the previous example this rule would license the following extension of (20b):

(20)   c. [X, Y: X = $\sum$x[x: soldier x, surrendered x], Y = $\sum$x[x: soldier x],
        [x: soldier x]$\langle$most x$\rangle$[: surrendered x]]

However, apart from the general problem with Kamp and Reyle's notion of abstraction, this does not yield a suitable representation of presupposed domains, because of the way the abstraction operator is defined. In general, $\sum u\varphi$ denotes the set of all *u*s in the model that satisfy φ, and thus the semantic value of Y in (20c) is the set of all soldiers in the model. Normally speaking this set will be too large, as Y must be able to denote a contextually restricted set of military, and therefore the new abstraction rule will have to generate a different type of object.

We do not pursue this line of argument further because what we have said suffices for our purposes. The foregoing discussion does not purport to demonstrate that there is no way Kamp and Reyle's version of DRT can be made to account for the presuppositions of quantifiers. What it means to show, rather, is that if one undertakes to make the required revisions the theory tends to become quite unwieldy: one has to add new rules that produce new kinds of structure. This prospect and our qualms about Kamp and Reyle's use of abstraction lead us to propose an alternative theory, which we outline in the remainder of this section. This account is based on Geurts (1996b), to which we refer for a more detailed exposition.

2.3   *Propositional Reference Markers*

Traditionally, the semantics of the DRS language is specified by stating what it means for a function to embed a DRS in a model. Given this notion, we may say that, relative to an embedding function f, each DRS denotes a set of functions g that extend f and that embed φ in a given model. For instance, $\|[x: \text{pumpkin } x]\|_f$ (the denotation of the DRS [x: pumpkin x] relative to the function f) is the set of functions that extend f, whose domain is {x}, and that map x onto a pumpkin.[10] We now introduce into the DRS language a new type of reference markers, which, just like DRSs, denote sets of embedding functions; we call these new objects *propositional reference markers*. If p is a propositional reference marker and φ is a DRS, then $p + \varphi$ is a (complex) propositional term. Intuitively, the content of $p + \varphi$ consists of the content of p plus the information in φ. Formally, $\|p + \varphi\|_f$ denotes the set of embedding functions h that extend some $g \in \|p + \varphi\|_f$ and verify φ. If it so happens that $p = p + \varphi$, then φ doesn't add anything new to the content of p; in this case we say that p *supports* φ, which we abbreviate as $p \vdash \varphi$:

(21) $p \vdash \varphi =_{def} p = p + \varphi$

With the help of propositional terms, a sentence like (22a) is represented as in (22b), assuming that *two raisins* receives a weak construal:

(22) a. There are two raisins in the pudding.

  b. [p: p ⊢ [x: raisin x, x is in the pudding], two$_x$ p]

Informally, this may be read as saying that p supports the proposition that there are raisins in the pudding and that there are two individuals that make p true when assigned to x.[11] Formally, p denotes a set of embedding functions σ, all of which are defined for x, and the condition 'two$_x$ p' requires that the set $\{f(x) : f \in \sigma\}$ contains two elements. That is, for each individual reference marker u there is a relational constant 'two$_u$,' which is interpreted as follows:

(23) If I is an interpretation function, then $I(\text{two}_u)(\sigma)$ iff $|\sum u\sigma| = 2$, where $\sum u\sigma = \{f(u) : f \in \sigma \ \& \ u \in \text{dom}(f)\}$

A strong quantifier like *most* in (20a) requires that two propositional reference markers be set up:

(24) [p, q: p ⊢ [x: soldier x], q = p + [: x surrendered], most$_x$ p q]

The representation of the first argument of *most* parallels that of the weak NP in (22): it is correlated with a reference marker, p, which supports the proposition that there is at least one x who is a soldier. The quantifier's second argument is represented by the reference marker q, which contains the information in p plus the information that x surrendered. The interpretation of 'most$_u$' is as follows:

(25) If I is an interpretation function, then $I(\text{most}_u)(\sigma, \sigma')$ iff $|\sum u\sigma'| > |\sum u\sigma - \sum u\sigma'|$, with '$\sum u\sigma$' as in (23)

And thus (24) says that more than half of the individuals in p are in q, as well.

  A crucial feature of the representation in (24) is that the first embedded DRS in this structure is accessible from the second, and that, therefore, the reference marker in [: x surrendered] is in effect bound in [x: soldier x]. Thus the accessibility relation is in line with the interpretation of the DRS language, and that, we have argued, is as it should be. This is one respect in which the present proposal diverges from Kamp and Reyle's. Another is that the two arguments of a quantifier enjoy the same status: both are explicitly represented by reference markers and don't have to be derived by some sort of abstraction rule, and since both arguments are correlated with reference markers, they may be linked up to other reference markers. Furthermore, if two propositional reference markers are thus linked, the telescoping phenomenon is automatically accounted for. To elucidate this point, let us consider the example in (26). On the reading of (26a) that we are interested in here, this sentence reports that two sailors each ordered a hamburger, and that each ingested his or her hamburger within a few seconds (compare the pair (13a)–(17a) discussed earlier):

(26) a. Two sailors ordered a hamburger. They gobbled it up in a couple of seconds.

  b. [p: p ⊢ [$_A$ x, y: sailor x, hamburger y, x ordered y], two$_x$ p]

c. $[\underline{r}, q: \underline{r} \vdash [_B \underline{u}:], q = r + [_C \underline{z}: u \text{ quickly ate } z], \text{all}_u r q]$

d. $[p, r, q: r = p,$

$\qquad p \vdash [_A x, y, u, z: u = x, z = y, \text{sailor } x, \text{hamburger } y, x \text{ ordered } y],$

$\qquad \text{two}_x p, r \vdash [_B :], q = r + [_C : u \text{ quickly ate } z], \text{all}_u r q]$

e. $[p, q: p \vdash [x, y: \text{sailor } x, \text{hamburger } y, x \text{ ordered } y], \text{two}_x p,$

$\qquad q = p + [: x \text{ quickly ate } y], \text{all}_x p q]$

The first sentence in (26a) is represented by (26b), the second by (26c). We have labeled the sub-DRSs of (26b–d) for ease of reference. In (26c), there are three anaphoric reference markers, which are underlined. We assume that the plural pronoun *they* is interpreted distributively, and therefore it is correlated in (26c) with two reference markers: the propositional marker r and the individual marker u.[12] The only restriction that is imposed upon the former is that it support the empty DRS B; this reflects the fact that the pronoun *they* is semantically inane. After the DRSs in (26b) and (26c) have been merged, r is equated with its antecedent p, and thus the two DRSs supported by p and r, that is, A and B, are mutually accessible: in general, if $p \vdash \varphi$, $q \vdash \psi$, and $p = q$, then evidently φ should be accessible from ψ, and vice versa. So now u can be linked up to x. Furthermore, DRS B is accessible from C (in general, if $p \vdash \varphi$ and $q = p + \psi$, then φ is accessible from ψ), and since A and B are mutually accessible, A is accessible from C. Thus y is a potential antecedent for z. Once all suitable equations have been made, the resulting interpretation of (26a) is (26d), which is equivalent to (26e).

Of course, the analysis we propose for the plural pronoun in (26a) applies to the presuppositions triggered by strong quantifiers, too. There are no relevant differences between (26a) and the following discourse, for example:

(27)   a. The mayor awarded all firemen a silver medal. Some (of the) men sold it right away. (=(10))

   b. $[\underline{p}, p', \underline{q}, q':$

$\qquad \underline{p} \vdash [\underline{x}: \text{fireman } \underline{x}], p' = p + [y: \text{medal } y, x \text{ got } y], \text{all}_x p p',$

$\qquad \underline{q} \vdash [\underline{u}: \text{man } \underline{u}], q' = q + [\underline{z}: u \text{ sold } z], \text{some}_u q q']$

   c. $[p, p', q, q': q = p', p \vdash [x, u: u = x, \text{fireman } x, \text{man } u],$

$\qquad p' = p + [y, z: z = y, \text{medal } y, x \text{ got } y], \text{all}_x p p',$

$\qquad q \vdash [:], q' = q + [: u \text{ sold } z], \text{some}_u q q']$

   d. $[p, q, q':$

$\qquad p \vdash [x: \text{fireman } x, \text{man } x], q = p + [y: \text{medal } y, x \text{ got } y], \text{all}_x p q,$

$\qquad q' = q + [: x \text{ sold } y], \text{some}_x q q']$

The initial representation of (27a) is (27b). In this DRS, the domains of the quantifiers *all* and *some* are represented by the reference markers p and q, respectively. The first of these cannot be bound to a suitable antecedent, so it is accommodated. The second can be bound and is equated with p', as a result of which the individual reference markers u and z obtain access to their antecedents, that is, x and y. The resulting DRS is (27c), which is equivalent to (27d).

It should be noted that (27d) is weaker than the intuitive interpretation of (27a), because this DRS imposes no constraints on the propositional reference marker p, save for the fact that it is extended by q: as it stands, (27d) is verified by *any* nonempty set of firemen who received a medal and sold it. That is to say, the actual truth conditions of (27a) are underdetermined by (27d). We don't think that this is a defect of our analysis, but there is admittedly a problem here, which is caused by the fact that our concept of accommodation is an idealized one, because it captures (and is intended to capture) only part of what actually happens when a presupposition cannot be bound.

Technically speaking, accommodation is a very simple affair: accommodating a presupposition just means that it is inserted in some suitable DRS. But obviously, this is not intended as anything like a full account of what happens when a presupposition is accommodated. Accommodation is by no means an automatic process (compare Heim 1982, Geurts 1995, van der Sandt 1995). Even if the resulting DRS is guaranteed to be well formed and coherent, a presupposition is practically *never* accommodated without further ado. Presupposed information is supposed to be unremarkable and, therefore, is expected to cohere with the context in which it occurs (for, clearly, an incoherent presupposition would not be unremarkable). However, in order to establish coherence it is often necessary to go beyond the information explicitly conveyed by the speaker. This is what happens, for instance, when the hearer imports 'bridging information' into his interpretation of the discourse. The term is due to Haviland and Clark (1974), of course, as is the following well-known illustration of the phenomenon:

(28)   Mary got some picnic supplies out of the car. The beer was warm.
        (Haviland and Clark 1974:514–515)

On the strategy adopted here the presupposition triggered by the definite NP *the beer* must be interpreted by way of accommodation, for the simple reason that there is no suitable antecedent available. But it is evident that just accommodating a reference marker *u* along with a restriction to the effect that *u* is a six-pack of beers (say), will not suffice to do full justice to our ordinary understanding of this discourse. Clearly, someone processing (28) would normally assume that, according to the speaker, the beer was part of the picnic supplies, and not flown in by an obliging fairy, for example. Equally clearly, this assumption is made on the basis of extralinguistic knowledge the hearer has at his disposal. But, crucially, it is only by bringing this extralinguistic knowledge to bear upon the interpretation of *the beer* that the hearer can ascertain that the presupposition he is expected to accommodate is, indeed, unremarkable.

So *in order to* secure the presumption that the presupposition triggered by *the beer* is unremarkable, the hearer has to make further assumptions, uncontroversial though they may be, about the situation described by the speaker. Much of this story is itself uncontroversial, but an important aspect of it is not: it is the division of labor between accommodation on the one hand and world knowledge on the other. We prefer to distinguish accommodation from other factors involved in the interpretation of presuppositions that cannot be bound, but there doesn't seem to be a consensus that this is the right way to go.[13] In the next section we expatiate on our concept of accommodation.

To return to our analysis in (27), there are two possible reasons why (27d) does not completely specify the truth conditional content of (27a). This sentence is normally uttered in a situation in which the audience will be able to figure out which firemen are being referred to. This can mean either of two things. On the one hand, the intended antecedent of *all firemen* may have been mentioned explicitly, in which case the presupposition is bound. On the other hand, the hearer may have to accommodate the presupposition that there were firemen, but in that case he has to make additional plausibility inferences about these firemen. Either way, the interpretation of (27a) as given by (27d) is further restricted. So, although this analysis is incomplete as it stands, it is correct as far as it goes.

3   Domain Restriction through Intermediate Accommodation

In the foregoing section we discussed one way in which, according to the binding theory, the domain of a quantifier may be restricted. In an example like (27) the quantificational domain is restricted because a domain presupposition is bound to a given object in the discourse representation. In this section we are concerned with another way in which domain restriction may occur. The binding theory predicts that the domain of a quantifier may also be restricted through intermediate accommodation, when a presupposition triggered in the quantifier's nuclear scope is accommodated in the restrictor. It has been claimed by Beaver (1994) and von Fintel (1994), among others, that this prediction is wrong, and in the following we want to refute this objection.

According to the binding theory, presupposition projection is constrained by a number of principles, three of which are listed below:[14]

(29)   *Well-formedness*
        A presupposition must be resolved in such a way that the resulting DRS is a proper one (that is, it may not contain any free reference markers).

(30)   *Coherence*
        A presupposition must be resolved in such a way that the resulting interpretation is a coherent one.

(31)   *Maximality*
        If a presupposition cannot be bound it must be accommodated as closely to the main DRS as is possible (in view of other constraints on projection).

These constraints entail that accommodation is not guaranteed to succeed. If no way of accommodating a presupposition yields an interpretation that is well formed and coherent, then the discourse is infelicitous. It is a matter of debate whether, in such cases, accommodation fails altogether or succeeds but fosters a weird interpretation. The difference between these two views is not crucial, however, because either way the resulting discourse is predicted to be awkward.

Maximality implies that, other things being equal, accommodation will be *global*: by default, a presupposition is accommodated in the principal DRS. However, not all other things may be equal, and a presupposition may be forced to accommodate either in a DRS that lies between the principal DRS and the presupposition's home DRS or, as a last resort, in the home DRS itself. In the former case, we speak of *intermediate*, in the latter of *local* accommodation.[15] Thus all three varieties of accommodation (global, intermediate, and local) are governed by the maximality principle. In the following we concentrate our attention on the notion of intermediate accommodation.

The following examples show that intermediate accommodation is not a spurious option:

(32)   a. Maybe Wilma believes that her husband is deceiving her.
        b. Either Wilma isn't married or she believes that her husband is deceiving her.

These are two examples in which an intermediate accommodation reading is at least possible; in (32b) it is even the most likely one. In (32a), the definite NP *her husband* induces the presupposition that Wilma has a husband; this presupposition is triggered within a belief context that, in its turn, is embedded under a modal operator. Maximality predicts that in the absence of a suitable antecedent this presupposition will by default be accommodated in the main DRS, which yields a reading that may be paraphrased as follows: *Mary has a husband$_i$ and maybe she believes that he$_i$ is deceiving her*. If for some reason this reading is not preferred, then the second option is intermediate accommodation, which results in the following: *Maybe Mary has a husband$_i$ and believes that he$_i$ is deceiving her* (we leave it to the reader to construct a context in which this interpretation would be preferred). Analogous remarks apply to (32b), but there is an important difference between this case and the previous one. For reasons we have discussed elsewhere (van der Sandt 1992, Geurts 1995), a global accommodation reading is not possible in (32b), and therefore we predict that intermediate accommodation is preferred, yielding the following paraphrase: *Either Wilma isn't married or she has a husband$_i$ and believes that he$_i$ is deceiving her*. This prediction is clearly correct.

The variety of intermediate accommodation we are interested in here occurs whenever a presupposition α is triggered in the scope of a quantifying expression β and α contains a reference marker bound by β. The binding theory predicts that in such an event global accommodation is excluded (well-formedness) and ceteris paribus a reading is preferred on which α restricts β's domain (maximality). The following is a case in point:

(33)   a. Every German is proud of his car.
        b. Every German who owns a car is proud of it.

The presupposition triggered by *his car* in (33a) contains a reference marker that is bound by the quantifier, and therefore the presupposition cannot be accommodated globally. Hence we predict that, by default, it will be accommodated one level down, that is, in the quantifier's restrictor. The reading thus obtained is roughly (but *only* roughly, as we will see) paraphrased by (33b). We believe that this is a gratifying result, but it has been argued by Beaver and von Fintel that this prediction is false.[16] Beaver's objection is based upon the mistaken assumption that, according to the binding theory, there is no relevant difference at all between (33a) and (33b).

The following are slightly simplified versions of Beaver's examples:[17]

(34)   a. Few of the team members can drive, but every team member will come
            to the match in her car.
        b. Few of the team members can drive, but every team member who
            owns a car will come to the match in her car.

Beaver reasons as follows: The binding theory predicts that (34a) will give rise to a reading that is paraphrased by (34b): the presupposition triggered by *her car* cannot be bound to a suitable antecedent, global accommodation is not possible because this would violate the well-formedness constraint, and so the presupposition is accommodated in the restrictor of *few*. However, (34b) is a perfectly acceptable sentence, and if our analysis is correct, then (34a) should be equally acceptable. But it isn't. Hence, the prediction that a presuppositional expression in the scope of a quantifier can give rise to domain restriction is wrong.

In order to see what is wrong with Beaver's objection, let us go through the interpretation of (34a) step by step, starting out from the following representation:

(35) $[p, q, \underline{p}', q' : p \vdash [x : \text{team member } x], q = p + [: x \text{ can drive}], \text{few}_x \, p \, q,$
        $\underline{p}' \vdash [z : \text{team member } z],$
        $q' = p' + [\underline{w : w \text{ is } z\text{'s car}}, z \text{ comes to the match in } w], \text{every}_z \, p' \, q']$

The quantifier in the first sentence of (34a) induces the presupposition that there is a given set of team members, represented here by p. We assume that this presupposition has already been dealt with. Besides presupposing a set of team members, the first conjunct of (34a) also introduces the subset of team members that can drive, represented by q. In more than one respect these two sets differ in status. In the first place, p is presupposed while q is not. In the second place, p is more salient in the sense that the first conjunct of (34a) will be interpreted as being about the team members rather than about the team members that can drive. It is immaterial to our purposes how this observation is spelled out in detail. What matters is the fact that the first sentence of (34a) sets up a context in which expressions that are anaphorically dependent upon *few of the team members* are much more likely to be construed as referring back to p than to q (see Moxey and Sanford 1993 for discussion). What is more, it seems that a *quantifier* that is anaphorically dependent upon *few of the team members* can *only* pick up p. In (36), for example, *every team member* cannot be construed as 'every team member that can drive':

(36)   Few of the team member can drive, but every team member will arrive in time.

The second conjunct of (34a) introduces two presuppositions that are relevant to our concerns, which are triggered by *every team member* and her car, respectively. The former induces the presupposition that there is a set of team members, represented in (35) by p'. The latter in fact triggers two presuppositions, one of which has already been dealt with by assuming that z is the female person whose existence is presupposed by *her car*. We may assume that the presupposition triggered by the quantified NP *every team member* will be processed first,[18] and that the hearer must first identify a suitable set of team members. There are two such sets available, p and q, but as we have seen the hearer will decide to bind the presupposition triggered by *every team member* to p, equating p' with p (and z with x). The outcome of this decision is (37a), which is equivalent to (37b):

(37)   a. $[p, q, p', q': p' = p, p \vdash [x: \text{team member } x], q = p + [: x \text{ can drive}],$
             $\text{few}_x \, p \, q, p' \vdash [z: z = x, \text{team member } z],$
             $q' = p' + [\underline{w: w \text{ is } z\text{'s car}}, z \text{ comes to the match in } w],$
             $\text{every}_z \, p' \, q']$
        b. $[p, q, q': p \vdash [x: \text{team member } x], q = p + [: x \text{ can drive}], \text{few}_x \, p \, q,$
             $q' = p + [\underline{w: w \text{ is } x\text{'s car}}, x \text{ comes to the match in } w],$
             $\text{every}_x \, p \, q']$

Next, the presupposition triggered by *her car*, represented here by [w: w is x's car], comes up for processing. This presupposition cannot be bound, hence must be accommodated, and there are two DRSs in which it could be accommodated, in principle: the DRS [x: team member x] (intermediate accommodation) and the presupposition's home DRS (local accommodation). The global option is excluded by the well-formedness constraint, because the x in the presupposition [w: w is x's car] would then become unbound. Local accommodation gives (37b) as the final interpretation of (34a). Intermediate accommodation leaves us with the following:

(38) $[p, q, q': p \vdash [x, w: \text{team member } x, w \text{ is } x\text{'s car}], q = p + [: x \text{ can drive}],$
         $\text{few}_x \, p \, q, q' = p + [: x \text{ comes to the match in } w], \text{every}_x \, p \, q']$

The maximality principle predicts that, ceteris paribus, intermediate accommodation will be preferred to local accommodation, but in this particular case either choice will result in an incoherent discourse. To see this, suppose that the hearer opts for local accommodation. Then (34a) is interpreted as implying that, although few members of p can drive, all of them own cars. This might be true, of course, but it is so unlikely that it can be safely dismissed as a possible reading of (34a).[19]

Suppose, on the other hand, that the speaker opts for intermediate accommodation. We then get basically the same result, but via a somewhat different route. For according to this interpretation the speaker, who has just claimed that few of the members of p can drive, is now *presupposing* that the members of p have cars. This is so because the domain of *every team member*, represented in (35) by p′, has been bound to, and thus equated with, p. So in this case there really isn't much to choose between intermediate and local accommodation: they give rise to very similar, and equally weird, interpretations. Consequently, accommodation actually *fails*, and the binding theory thus predicts that the discourse in (34a) is unacceptable, as it is.

It is not hard to see what must have led Beaver to think that (34a) presents a problem for the binding theory. Starting out from the fact that the theory predicts a general preference for intermediate as opposed to local accommodation, he concludes that it cannot tell the difference between (34a) and (34b), because there can be no difference between explicit domain restriction by a relative clause, for example, and implicit domain restriction by a presupposition triggered outside the quantified NP.[20] But as a matter of fact there is a difference and the binding theory accounts for it in what we take to be just the right way, namely, on the basis of the fact that in one case a piece of information is presupposed that is not presupposed in the other case. (34b) presupposes that there is a set of team members who own a car. This presupposition cannot be bound and therefore has to be accommodated, and in order to establish a coherent discourse representation, the hearer will infer that this presupposed set is part of the set of team members introduced in the first sentence of the discourse. However, (34a), as we have seen, is a different matter altogether, for here the speaker first presupposes the existence of a set of team members and then goes on either to presuppose that they own cars (intermediate accommodation) or to assert that they do (local accommodation).

Beaver's approach is exceptional in that he confines his attention to instances of domain restriction, or rather attempts at domain restriction, that are properly contextualized. However, most of the discussion of this phenomenon has revolved around sentences presented 'in isolation,' like (33a). When judged 'in isolation,' does (33a) presuppose that every German has a car, does it entail that every German has a car, or does it merely assert that every German who has a car is proud of it? Intuitions vary on this score, and we believe we can explain why. But first let us consider a few more examples:

(39)   a.   Every German is proud of his $\left\{ \begin{array}{ll} i. & \text{car} \\ ii. & \text{bicycle} \\ iii. & \text{kangaroo} \end{array} \right\}$.

    b.   Every German who has a $\left\{ \begin{array}{ll} i. & \text{car} \\ ii. & \text{bicycle} \\ iii. & \text{kangaroo} \end{array} \right\}$ is proud of it.

According to our judgments, (39a.*i*) is fine, (39a.*ii*) is less so, and (39a.*iii*) is weird.

The differences between the examples in (39b) are less pronounced, but still to us (39b.*i*) sounds somewhat pedantic, (39b.*ii*) is okay, and (39b.*iii*) is strange, though not as strange as (39a.*iii*). Let us consider the second set of examples first.

Of course, our intuitions about these examples are intimately tied up with the cultural prejudices we share with many other people. Germans own cars almost by definition, some of them own bicycles, and the number of German kangaroo owners is negligible. These prejudices explain why (39b.*i*) has an air of redundancy about it: someone who uses *every German who has a car* instead of *every German* simpliciter is being overly explicit. In contrast to this, (39b.*ii*) is perfectly okay, because we assume that it is quite normal, though not virtually necessary, for a German to own a bicycle. (39b.*iii*), finally, is strange because it presupposes a set of Germans who own kangaroos, and although on reflection it is likely that there is a nonempty set that fits this description, the notion is so remarkable that it cannot simply be presupposed.

According to the binding theory, a hearer who must process any of the variants of (39a) 'in isolation' will go about it as follows: Given that this sentence has no context, there is no suitable antecedent for the presupposition triggered by the universal quantifier, so he will have to accommodate a set of Germans (call it 'G'). It seems reasonable to suppose that there is a strong tendency to equate G with the set of all Germans, or perhaps with the set of typical Germans, but this assumption is not crucial. Now the only presupposition that remains to be interpreted is the one triggered by *his N*. Assuming that *his* is bound by *every German*, this results in intermediate accommodation and thus in domain restriction. So if we construe (39a) this way, we take the speaker to be conveying that it may be assumed *as a matter of course* that the members of G own *N*s. However, given our cultural prejudices, we are bound to feel that this assumption is fully justified only in (39a.*i*): in the case of (39a.*ii*) it is more remarkable already, and in the case of (39a.*iii*) it is rash. Needless to say, this matches with our judgments about these variants.

The binding theory correctly predicts that none of the sentences in (39a) presupposes that every German has a {car/bicycle/kangaroo}. Nor do we believe that this follows from any of these sentences. Admittedly, people do tend to associate the claim that every German has a {car/bicycle/kangaroo} with these sentences (for example, Heim 1983, van Eijck 1993). Somehow it seems that (39a.*ii*), for example, suggests that all or nearly all Germans own bicycles, but this suggestion is to be expected on the view we defend here. We have mentioned in the foregoing that if (39a.*ii*) is presented in the absence of a specific context, hearers will tend to identify G, that is, the set presupposed by the subject term, with the set of Germans – or, what seems even more likely, with the set of typical Germans. If this happens, intermediate accommodation of the second presupposition in (39a.*ii*) will convey, in effect, that according to the speaker there is nothing remarkable about the assumption that (typical) Germans have bicycles. This is rather close to, but not the same as, saying or presupposing that all Germans have bicycles. So the binding theory helps to explain both the inference associated with (39b.*ii*) and the fact that it is not more than a strong suggestion. Intermediate accommodation is a crucial ingredient in this explanation.

4   Domain Restriction through Focusing

It is well known that the focus-background division within a quantifier's nuclear scope affects the interpretation of its domain (see, for example, Rooth 1985, Schubert and Pelletier 1987, Krifka 1990, and the contribution of Partee to this volume). Roughly speaking: backgrounded material in the nuclear scope tends to be interpreted as part of the quantifier's restrictor, while focused information remains part of the nuclear scope. Thus the most likely interpretations of (40a) and (41a) are (40b) and (41b), respectively:[21]

(40)   a.   Fred always drinks [milk]$_F$.
        b.   Always, if Fred drinks something, he drinks milk.

(41)   a.   Most tickets were sold [at counter 4]$_F$.
        b.   Most of the tickets that were sold were sold at counter 4.

There are two plausible lines of explanation of this regularity, which we consider in turn. According to the first, a sentence like (40a) is typically interpreted in a context where there is an issue as to where the tickets were sold. The supposition that there is such an issue is prompted by the focus-background division of this sentence and is taken to be part of the global context. But then the domain presupposition triggered by the quantifier may link up to this issue, thus giving rise to an interpretation that can be paraphrased by (40b). In essence, this is the approach adopted by von Fintel (1994) and Beaver (1995), and it is also in agreement with the proposals by Büring and Jäger in this volume.

In order to implement this idea, two assumptions are required. First, we have to assume that the focus/background dichotomy and the division between presupposition and assertion are mutually independent. Second, we have to assume that the former distinction takes priority over the latter in the sense that focus/background structures are interpreted before presuppositions are resolved, because presuppositions must be able to pick up antecedents established, in effect, through focusing. On this account, focusing and presupposition are separate though related and interacting phenomena. They are related in that both signal that the speaker takes certain pieces of information to be contextually given. They interact in that presuppositions may pick up material from the global context set up by focusing.

There is another explanation of the interaction between focusing and presupposition, which relies almost entirely on the mechanism of presupposition projection. Let us suppose, following Jackendoff (1972), that intonational focusing acts, inter alia, as a presupposition inducer. The binding theory then accounts for the fact that the background tends to be interpreted as part of the restrictor in the same way it accounts for the fact that other presuppositions triggered in the nuclear scope may restrict the domain of a quantifier.

To say that focusing induces presuppositions is not to imply that there is no difference between backgrounds and presuppositions. As in most other contributions to this volume it is assumed here that backgrounds are essentially incomplete. Backgrounds may be thought of as properties obtained by abstracting over focused material, or they may be construed as open propositions or likened to questions. For example, in (42) the background is something like '$\lambda x(x$ stole the tarts)' or '___ stole the tarts' or 'Who stole the tarts?'

(42)   [Barney]$_F$ stole the tarts.

The presupposition is obtained by replacing the focused material by a variable or reference marker. This presupposition is resolved in the usual way, either by binding to a given antecedent or by accommodation.[22] It then follows that an utterance of (42) presupposes that someone stole the tarts just as the corresponding clefted sentence does:[23]

(43)   It is Barney who stole the tarts.

If this account is correct, then focusing should indirectly give rise to the projection behavior that is the hallmark of presuppositions. And this appears to be the case, as the following observations show:

(44)   a. If [Barney]$_F$ stole the tarts, then Fred is innocent.
        b. If Fred is innocent, then [Barney]$_F$ stole the tarts.
        c. If someone stole the tarts, then [Barney]$_F$ stole the tarts.

(45)   a. Maybe [Barney]$_F$ stole the tarts.
        b. Maybe the tarts were stolen and maybe [Barney]$_F$ stole the tarts.

(46)   a. [Barney]$_F$ didn't steal the tarts.
        b. I'm not at all certain that the tarts have been stolen, but (I am absolutely convinced that) [Barney]$_F$ didn't steal the tarts.

Normally, one would infer from (44a) and (44b) that someone stole the tarts, but not from (44c). Similarly, (45a) would and (45b) would not normally license the inference that someone stole the tarts, and the same holds for (46a, b). This is precisely the pattern of inferences that the proposal under consideration leads us to expect.

We started this section with the observation that backgrounded material in the nuclear scope of a quantifier tends to be construed as part of the quantifier's domain. In conjunction with the principle that focusing induces presuppositions, the binding theory allows us to see this phenomenon as a special case of a much larger class of data, exemplified by (44)–(46). For example, (41a) is interpreted as follows:

(47)   a. [p, q: p ⊢ [x: ticket x],
            q = p + [u: place u, x was sold at u, x was sold at counter 4],
            most$_x$ p q]

        b. [p, q: p ⊢ [x, u: ticket x, place u, x was sold at u],
            q = p + [: x was sold at counter 4], most$_x$ p q]

Within the nuclear scope of *most*, intonation indicates that 'λu(x was sold at place u)' is a background, where x is bound by the quantifier. This background corresponds with the underlined presupposition in (47a). In the absence of further contextual information this presupposition cannot be bound. The well-formedness constraint tells us that it cannot be accommodated in the main DRS either, because this would cause the reference marker x to become unbound. The maximality principle predicts, therefore, that by default this presupposition will become part of the quantifier's domain, which gives us the reading we wanted to account for.

Instances of adverbial quantification are amenable to essentially the same treatment. Let us assume for convenience that adverbial quantifiers range over events;[24] then (40a) is interpreted as follows:

(48)   a. [p, q: p ⊢ [e:], q = p + [e: Fred drinks something in e, Fred drinks
            milk in e], all$_e$ p q]

        b. [p, q: p ⊢ [e: Fred drinks something in e], q = p + [: Fred drinks
            milk in e], all$_e$ p q]

In (48a) the domain of the adverbial quantifier merely introduces a new reference marker. We would assume that, as a matter of fact, the lexical semantics of *always* imposes certain rather general restrictions on the possible values this reference marker can take, but these restrictions are left out of account in this representation. In the nuclear scope of *always* 'Fred drinks ___' is the background, and accordingly the underlined presupposition is triggered. The binding theory predicts that this presupposition will be accommodated in the quantifier's domain, which gives us (48b) as the default interpretation of (40a).

There is a tendency in the literature to assume that, whenever focusing seems to affect the interpretation of a given sentence, some form of quantification must be involved. For instance, in an attempt to explain the well-known fact that the interpretation of negation is sensitive to focus, Kratzer (1989) proposes to analyze negation as quantification. The following pair of examples is Kratzer's:

(49)   a. Paula isn't registered in [Paris]$_F$.
        b. [Paula]$_F$ isn't registered in Paris.

(49a) and (49b) have different interpretations, and the difference is best described in presuppositional terms: (49a) presupposes that Paula is registered somewhere, and (49b) presupposes that someone is registered in Paris.[25] Kratzer (1989:647) observes that such presuppositions "are typical for certain quantifier constructions" and argues on this basis that negation is a form of quantification, too, which is to say that *not* has a quantificational domain and a nuclear scope, just as *all* or *most*, for example. This conclusion is easily avoided once it is realized that the presuppositions observed in (49) are *not* peculiar to quantifier constructions but conform to the much more general principles of presupposition projection: on the assumption that focusing induces presuppositions, these observations follow from the binding theory without further ado.

Notes

1 See, in particular, van der Sandt (1992) and Geurts (1995). In the following paragraph, we give only a thumbnail sketch of the theory.

2 Or that there was or will be such a set. Matters concerning the tense of presuppositions are not addressed in this chapter, but to the best of our knowledge they do not present any problems for the theory advocated here. The view that quantifiers are presupposition inducers was already taken by Strawson (1952), and subsequently adopted by Karttunen (1973), Gazdar (1979), Soames (1982), van der Sandt (1988), and Zeevat (1992), among others.

3 Quantifying NPs are sometimes read (quasi-) generically, as in (i):
   (i)   Most men are egoists.
   This may be construed as saying something about the species rather than the set. Such construals will be left out of account in this chapter.

4 For further discussion we refer to the contribution of Sæbø to this volume, who takes a less critical view of Kamp and Reyle's proposal.

5 That is to say, $\varphi \oplus \psi = \langle U(\varphi) \cup U(\psi), \text{Con}(\varphi) \cup \text{Con}(\psi) \rangle$.

6 This example also illustrates one minor problem with Kamp and Reyle's proposal. In (13b) only one reference marker is bound by the quantifier, and accordingly it is predicted that (13a) is true iff the set of professors who own a Porsche and wash it once a week contains more than 50 percent of the professors who own a Porsche. It should be noted that this is only one of the possible readings of (13a). On another possible (though perhaps, in this particular case, less likely) interpretation, (13a) is true iff the set of *pairs* $\langle a, b \rangle$, where a is a professor and b a Porsche owned and weekly washed by a, contains more than 50 percent of the pairs $\langle a', b' \rangle$, where a' is a professor and b' a Porsche owned by a'. It is, however, not difficult to amplify the representation format used in (13b) so as to take into account this reading, too.

7 Actually, in Kamp and Reyle's system plural reference markers denote groups, not sets, but this distinction is irrelevant here.

8 We use the term 'accessibility' in two related ways, namely, as denoting relations between DRSs and between reference markers. These two ways are distinguished by the prepositions subcategorized for by the predicate. Given a pair of (not necessarily distinct) DRSs φ and ψ, φ is accessible *from* ψ iff all reference markers in φ are accessible *to* any reference marker occurring in ψ.

9 But see Sæbø this volume, who develops an analysis based upon Kamp and Reyle's proposal.

10 All of this is relative to a given model, of course, which we prefer to leave implicit.

11 Propositional terms denote sets of embedding functions, but we sometimes allow ourselves to speak sloppily and pretend they denote sets of individuals. For instance, we might say that in (22b) the reference marker p represents a set of raisins. This is, strictly speaking, wrong, but it is conveniently short, and we trust that this abuse is less confusing than the correct terminology.

12 Strictly speaking, this treatment of *they* implies that plural pronouns are ambiguous between a collective and a distributive reading. This, however, is just a consequence

of the fact that in this chapter we don't want to take collective readings into account. If we had chosen to do so, we would have adopted essentially the same approach as Kamp and Reyle, with a single lexical entry for *they* and an optional distribution rule.

13   It is of course possible to analyze bridging as a form of binding – specifically, binding to a nonovert but implied antecedent (see, for example, Bos et al. 1995, Geurts 1995, Krahmer and Piwek 1996). The difference between this type of analysis and the view adopted here is at least in part terminological. In both cases world knowledge is called upon to provide a bridge between discourse entities; the basic difference is that according to the binding analysis bridges are brought into play before presuppositions are handled, whereas on the accommodation view they enter the stage afterwards. It should be noted, however, that a binding analysis of bridging doesn't obviate the notion of accommodation, since not all instances of accommodation involve bridging.

14   See van der Sandt (1992) and Geurts (1995) for further discussion of these constraints.

15   While Beaver adopts this terminology, too, von Fintel doesn't distinguish between local and intermediate accommodation, calling both "local". This usage is potentially misleading, however, because it is specifically the notion of intermediate (and not local) accommodation that is at issue.

16   In the following we focus on Beaver's argument, because the particular notion of accommodation criticized by von Fintel is one we never advocated and have no intention of advocating in the foreseeable future.

17   In particular, these versions leave open the actual number of team members (fifteen in Beaver's examples), and we have dismissed five cheerleaders who didn't play an essential part in the original examples, although they enhanced their naturalness somewhat.

18   To begin with, this assumption is plausible in its own right. Furthermore, it is difficult to *avoid* this assumption, because *her car* is dependent on *every team leader*. In van der Sandt (1992) it is stipulated that presuppositions are processed from left to right, but even without this axiom his theory imposes a sequential order in cases like (34a). The same holds for the theory of Geurts (1995), who does not stipulate that presuppositions are processed in any fixed order.

19   According to Beaver, this reading is contradictory. It is not, but given the fact that most of the people who own a car can drive in it, too, it is such a remarkable thing to want to say that (34a) is just not the right way of saying it.

20   "Clearly, if the explicit addition of a domain restriction produces a coherent discourse, it is not open to claim that without these clauses an implicit domain restriction results in incoherence" (Beaver 1994:38). In our view, however, it is.

21   (41) is inspired by an example of Eckardt's in this volume.

22   This method of deriving presuppositions from focal backgrounds is the same as Jackendoff's, with one crucial exception. On Jackendoff's account a predicate $Presup_s(x)$ is formed by replacing the focus by a variable. From this expression he constructs $\lambda x\, Presup_s(x)$, which is the set of objects of which the presuppositional predicate holds. Then Jackendoff obtains the actual presupposition by stipulating that this set must either be under discussion or otherwise be a well-defined set in the current context. Thus the assertion made by the sentence is that the focus value is a member of this set. It is not implied that the predicate holds of at least one member of this set. Jackendoff's analysis thus gives a semantics for presupposition that is essentially weaker than an account that associates an existential presupposition with focus constructions. See also Rooth (this volume), who argues on different grounds that the interpretation of focus should not be strengthened so as to yield an existential presupposition.

23   Thus intonational focus and clefts induce analogous presuppositions. This does not imply that they are on a par in all respects. Whereas we hold that focusing does not

affect the representation of the asserted content (just as it does not affect the standard semantic value in a theory like Rooth's), we believe that clefting does. Thus while (42) presupposes that some x stole the tarts and asserts that Barney stole the tarts, we suggest that the cleft in (43) has the same presupposition as (42), but asserts only that x is Barney. This distinction is irrelevant in extensional contexts, but it may make a difference in intensional embeddings.

24 This assumption is not crucial. What is crucial is that the presupposition that is triggered in the nuclear scope contains a reference marker that is bound by the quantifier. Hence a treatment of adverbials in terms of unselective quantification, for example, would also be consistent with the account we propose.

25 This is not how Kratzer characterizes the difference between (49a) and (49b). According to Kratzer, "[(49a)] presupposes that Paula is registered at some place *which is not Paris*. And sentence [(49b)] presupposes that some person *who is not Paula* is registered in Paris" [emphasis added]. However, the standard diagnostics prove that the italicized material is not itself presupposed; rather, it is entailed by the asserted and presupposed content taken together.

References

Beaver, D. 1994. Accommodating topics, in P. Bosch and R. van der Sandt (eds.), *Focus and Natural Language Processing*. Vol. 3. *Discourse*. Working Papers of the Institute for Logic and Linguistics Vol. 8. IBM Deutschland GmbH, Heidelberg.

Beaver, D. 1995. *Presupposition and Assertion in Dynamic Semantics*. Ph.D. thesis, University of Edinburgh, Edinburgh.

Bos, J., P. Buitelaar, and M. Mineur 1995. Bridging as coercive accommodation, in E. Klein et al. (eds.), *Working Notes of the Edinburgh Conference on Computational Logic and Natural Language Processing*, HCRC, Edinburgh.

Eijck, J. van 1993. The dynamics of description, *Journal of Semantics* 10, 239–267.

Fintel, K. von 1994. *Restrictions on Quantifier Domains*. Ph.D. thesis, University of Massachusetts, Amherst.

Gazdar, G. 1979. *Pragmatics: Implicature, Presupposition, and Logical Form*. Academic Press, New York.

Geurts, B. 1995. *Presupposing*. Doctoral dissertation, University of Stuttgart.

Geurts, B. 1996a. Local satisfaction guaranteed: a presupposition theory and its problems, *Linguistics and Philosophy* 19, 259–294.

Geurts, B. 1996b. A presuppositional account of domain restriction, in D. Gibbon (ed.), *Natural Language Processing and Speech Technology: Results of the 3rd KONVENS Conference*. Mouton de Gruyter, Berlin, pp. 293–304.

Geurts, B. (in press). Presuppositions and anaphors in attitude contexts, to appear in *Linguistics and Philosophy*.

Haviland, S., and H.H. Clark 1974. What's new? Acquiring new information as a process in comprehension, *Journal of Verbal Learning and Verbal Behavior* 13, 512–521.

Heim, I. 1982. The Semantics of Definite and Indefinite Noun Phrases. Ph.D. thesis, University of Massachusetts, Amherst.

Heim, I. 1983. On the projection problem for presuppositions, *Proceedings of the West Coast Conference on Formal Linguistics* 2, 114–126.

Jackendoff, R. 1972. *Semantic Interpretation in Generative Grammar*. MIT Press, Cambridge, Mass.

Kamp, H., and U. Reyle 1993. *From Discourse to Logic*. Kluwer, Dordrecht.

Karttunen, L. 1973. Presuppositions of compound sentences, *Linguistic Inquiry* 4, 167–193.

Karttunen, L. 1976. Discourse referents, in J. McCawley (ed.), *Syntax and Semantics*, Vol. 7: *Notes from the Linguistic Underground*. Academic Press, New York, pp. 363–385.

Krahmer, E., and P. Piwek 1996. Presupposition projection as proof construction, Technical Report no. 1187, IPO, Eindhoven.

Kratzer, A. 1989. An investigation of the lumps of thought, *Linguistics and Philosophy* 12, 607–653.

Krifka, M. 1990. 4000 ships passed through the lock: object-induced measure functions on events, *Linguistics and Philosophy* 13, 447–520.

Löbner, S. 1987. Natural language and generalized quantifier theory, in P. Gärdenfors (ed.), *Generalized Quantifiers: Linguistic and Logical Approaches*. Reidel, Dordrecht, pp. 181–201.

Milsark, G. 1977. Toward an explanation of certain peculiarities of the existential construction in English, *Linguistic Analysis* 3, 1–30.

Moxey, L.M., and A.J. Sanford 1993. *Communicating Quantities*. Erlbaum, Hove, Hillsdale, N.J.

Rooth, M. 1985. Association with Focus. Ph.D. thesis, University of Massachusetts, Amherst.

Sandt, R.A. van der 1988. *Context and Presupposition*. Routledge, London.

Sandt, R.A. van der 1989. Presupposition and discourse structure, in R. Bartsch, J. van Benthem, and P. van Emde Boas (eds.), *Semantics and Contextual Expresssion*. Foris, Dordrecht, pp. 267–294.

Sandt, R.A. van der 1992. Presupposition projection as anaphora resolution, *Journal of Semantics* 9, 333–377.

Sandt, R.A. van der 1995. The lexical encoding of presupposition inducers, in M. Bierwisch and P. Bosch (eds.), *Semantic and Conceptual Knowledge*. Arbeitspapiere des Sonderforschungbereichs 340, Sprachtheoretische Grundlagen für die Computerlinguistik, Stuttgart, Tübingen.

Sandt, R.A. van der, and B. Geurts 1991. Presupposition, anaphora, and lexical content, in O. Herzog and C.-R. Rollinger (eds.), *Text Understanding in LILOG*. Springer-Verlag, Berlin, pp. 259–296.

Schubert, L.K., and F.K. Pelletier 1987. Problems in the interpretation of the logical form of generics, bare plurals and mass terms, in E. LePore (ed.), *New Directions in Semantics*. Academic Press, London, pp. 387–453.

Soames, S. 1982. How presuppositions are inherited: A solution to the projection problem, *Linguistic Inquiry* 13, 483–545.

Strawson, P.F. 1952. *Introduction to Logical Theory*. Methuen, London.

Zeevat, H. 1992. Presupposition and accommodation in update semantics, *Journal of Semantics* 9, 379–412.

15   On Different Kinds of Focus

JEANETTE K. GUNDEL

Abstract

Three independent senses of focus are distinguished – psychological focus (current center of attention), semantic focus (new information predicated about the topic), and contrastive focus (linguistic prominence for the purpose of contrast or emphasis). It is argued that semantic focus is truth-conditionally relevant, but it does not necessarily bring an entity into psychological focus. Contrastive focus, on the other hand, is not truth-conditionally relevant, but it always brings an entity into psychological focus.

1   Introduction

The last time I taught a course on the syntax-pragmatics interface, my students asked whether I could explain what focus is and how the different papers on focus that we were reading in the class related to each other. I did my best to answer their question. But I was not completely satisfied with the answer. The present chapter was motivated partly by a desire to give a better answer the next time this question arises. It is evident that the term *focus* has been used in a number of different senses in the literature. What is less clear, however, is exactly how many independent, and linguistically relevant, notions of focus there are, what specific linguistic phenomena they are correlated with, and what, if anything, the relation is between the different senses. These are the questions I am concerned with in this chapter.

2   Psychological Focus

At least three linguistically relevant senses of 'focus' can be distinguished. One of these, which I refer to here as *psychological focus*,[1] corresponds to the psychological notion of focus of attention (Bosch 1988, Dahl and Gundel 1981, Garrod and Sanford 1982, Grosz and Sidner 1986, Gundel, Hedberg and Zacharski 1993, Kameyama 1986, inter alia), what Hajičová 1987 calls "AI focus". It is similar to the *backward-looking center* of Centering Theory (Grosz, Joshi, and Weinstein 1986, Brennan, Friedman, and Pollard 1987), though the latter concept is more

I am grateful to Peter Bosch and Michael Hegarty for helpful comments on earlier drafts of this chapter.

restricted in its current formulation. An entity is in (psychological) focus if the attention of both speech participants can be assumed to be focused on it because of its salience at a given point in the discourse. This sense of focus has been shown to correlate with various linguistic forms and properties, notably the appropriateness of unstressed personal pronouns and zero anaphors, and of weakly stressed constituents in general. For example, the entities represented by the italicized forms in (1) and (2) can be assumed to be in psychological focus, thereby licensing the use of an unstressed personal pronoun. As (2) shows, an entity doesn't have to be linguistically introduced to be in psychological focus.

(1)   Emily hasn't changed much. *She* still looks like her mother, doesn't *she*.

(2)   (Speaker sees addressee looking at a picture of a woman and says:) *She* looks just like her mother, doesn't *she*.

Gundel, Hedberg, and Zacharski 1993 distinguish between entities that are activated, that is, in current awareness, and the subset of activated entities that are in focus and thus likely to be continued as topics of subsequent utterances.[2] Activation is a necessary status for appropriate use of all pronominal forms, stressed and unstressed, personal pronouns or demonstratives. But only entities that are in focus can be appropriately coded by unstressed personal pronouns and zeros. This accounts for the contrast between examples like those in (3) and (4).

(3)   a. My neighbor's bull mastiff bit a girl on a bike.

b. $\left\{ \begin{matrix} \text{It's} \\ \text{That's} \end{matrix} \right\}$ the same dog that bit Mary Ben last summer.

(4)   a. Sears delivered new siding to my neighbors with the bull mastiff.

b. $\left\{ \begin{matrix} \text{\#It's} \\ \text{That's} \end{matrix} \right\}$ the same dog that bit Mary Ben last summer.[3]

Before (3a) is uttered, the bull mastiff is not yet in focus (or even activated) because it has not been mentioned in the immediately preceding discourse. But since it is introduced in matrix subject position (and is most likely also the topic) in (3a), it is brought into focus and can therefore be appropriately referred to with either *that* or *it* in (3b). But in (4), where the bull mastiff has been introduced in a prepositional phrase that functions primarily to restrict the referent of the indirect object, it has been activated, but not enough to be in focus; reference with *it* in (4b) is therefore inappropriate.[4]

Psychological focus also appears to be relevant for assigning referents to what Prince (1981) calls 'inferrables', that is, forms that have no direct antecedent in the discourse, and whose interpretation involves a bridging inference (Clark and Haviland 1977) to a recently introduced entity. While the referent of an inferrable is not itself in focus, the inferrable is typically associated with something that is already in focus (see Erkü and Gundel 1988, Bosch and Geurts 1990). For example, as Erkü and Gundel (1988) point out, most speakers associate the waitress in example (5) with the hotel bar rather than with the Thai restaurant, even though general encyclopedic knowledge would favor the restaurant interpretation.

(5)   We stopped for drinks at the hotel bar before going to the Thai restaurant. The waitress was from Bangkok.

Syntactic structure is only one of a number of factors that determine whether an entity will be brought into focus. In general, however, an entity introduced in a main clause is more salient than one that is introduced in a subordinate clause. Someone who hears or reads the first sentence in (5) is thus more likely to expect the next sentence to be about the bar than about the Thai restaurant. That is, the bar is more likely to have been brought into focus here. For the same reason, the bar is the favored interpretation for the unstressed pronoun in (6).

(6)   We stopped for drinks at the hotel bar before going to the Thai restaurant. It was being remodeled.

3   Semantic Focus

Psychological focus refers to the speech participants' attention state in relation to some entity. The term 'focus' has also been used to refer to that part of a sentence that is prosodically (and sometimes also syntactically) prominent. This use was introduced in Halliday 1967 and later developed in the generative literature by Chomsky 1971, Jackendoff 1972, Erteschik-Shir 1979, Rooth 1985, Rochemont 1986, Sgall et al. 1973, 1986, inter alia. But there are different reasons why a speaker might want to call attention to a constituent by making it more prominent, and this use of the term 'focus' thus covers at least two distinct notions (with different semantic and pragmatic correlates), which have often been conflated in the literature. One of these represents the new information that is being asserted (questioned, and so forth) in relation to what has variously been called the topic (for example, Sgall et al. 1973, 1986, Gundel 1974/1989, 1985, 1988), the pre-supposition (Chomsky 1971), the background (Jacobs 1991), and the common ground (Vallduvi 1992). Following Cutler and Fodor (1979), I refer to this type of linguistic focusing as *semantic focus*. Semantic focus is the part of the sentence that answers the relevant wh-question (implicit or explicit) in the particular context in which the sentence is used.[5] Thus *Bill* is semantic focus in (7) and (8) (where capital letters indicate position of prosodic prominence).

(7)   Do you know who called the meeting?
        (It was) BILL (who) called the meeting.
        (topic = x: x called the meeting; comment/focus = x was Bill)

(8)   Every time we get together, I'm the one that has to organize things, but this time
        (It was) BILL(who) called the meeting.
        (topic = x: x called the meeting; comment/focus = x was Bill)

Semantic focus is a relational concept, which reflects the way in which the informational content of a particular event or state of affairs expressed by a sentence is represented, and how its truth value is to be assessed. Semantic focus may be linguistically marked by pitch accent, by word order and other aspects of syntactic structure, by focus marking particles, or by some combination of one or more of these devices, with pitch accent being the most universal.

4   Contrastive Focus

The semantic focus is given linguistic prominence because of its newness in relation to the topic of the sentence. But this is clearly not the only reason for calling attention to some constituent. Constituents may also be made prominent because the speaker/writer doesn't think the addressee's attention is focused on a particular entity and for one reason or another would like it to be, because a new topic is being introduced or reintroduced (topic shift), or because one constituent (topic or semantic focus) is being contrasted, explicitly or implicitly, with something else. (See Zacharski 1993 and Vallduví and Zacharski 1994 for more detailed discussion of reasons for assigning phonological prominence.) I refer to this type of focusing as *contrastive focus*.[6] The intonationally prominent constituents *coat* in (9), *youngest* in (10), and *Rob* and *Christine* in (11) are all examples of purely contrastive focus.

(9)   That COAT you're wearing I don't think will be WARM enough.

(10)   What did Bill's sisters do?
       Bill's YOUNGEST sister kissed JOHN. (Krifka 1991)

(11)   To ROB you can complain about anything having to do with the PRO-GRAM, and to CHRISTINE you can address all the OTHER complaints. (uttered by Peter Bosch, June 12, 1994)

Note that the examples in (9)–(11) each have two focused constituents, that is, two positions with prominent pitch accent: a semantic focus (designated here by large capital letters) and a purely contrastive focus (designated here by small capital letters). This is so because all sentences (at least all sentences used as communicative acts) have a semantic focus, because the distinction between relevant context (topic) and new information predicated in relation to that context (semantic focus/comment) is an essential part of the function of sentences in information processing; but not all sentences have a purely contrastive focus, the latter being determined primarily by a speaker or writer's desire to affect the addressee's attention state at a particular point in the discourse. Like semantic focus, contrastive focus may be marked by virtually any linguistic means (prosodic, syntactic, or morphological) across languages, and the same device may mark both in any given language. For example, in English, placing a constituent in a syntactically prominent, sentence initial position may be used to mark either semantic focus or purely contrastive focus. This has led to some confusion in the literature, with the same term 'topicalization' used to describe sentences with 'preposed' objects as in (12) and (13), where the NP *the coat* is a contrastively focused topic, and sentences with 'preposed' objects as in (14), where *the coat* is a semantic focus.

(12)　A. I can't decide what to take on the trip. Should I take the coat you bought me?
　　　　B. Yes. That COAT I bought you, I think you should TAKE.

(13)　You shouldn't go on the trip without warm clothes.
　　　That COAT I bought you, I think you should TAKE.

(14)　A. What do you think I should take on the camping trip?
　　　　B. That COAT I bought you (I think you should take).

The sentences in question in (12)–(14) are superficially similar in that all three have a prosodically prominent sentence initial object *that coat*. This phrase is also in some sense contrastive in all three examples. But it is only in (12) and (13) that the initial NP *that coat* can be said to be a topic. In (14), it is the semantic focus (that is, part of the comment, or new information being predicated about the topic). The type of pitch accent on the 'preposed' NPs is different as well. The sentence initial NPs in (12) and (13) have what Bolinger (1961) and Jackendoff (1972) refer to as a B accent (Pierrehumbert's complex L + H* tone), which is characteristic of (but not restricted to) contrastive topics; the initial NP in (14) has what Bolinger and Jackendoff call an A accent (Pierrehumbert's simplex H* tone), a pattern characteristic of semantic focus. Note also that the portion of the sentence following the initial NP can be omitted in (14), where it is a contextually recoverable topic, but it cannot be omitted in (12) or (13), where it is part of the semantic focus/comment. Finally, as argued in Gundel (1974/1989) and (1988), the two constructions also have different syntactic and pragmatic properties. To take just one example, a contrastively focused topic cannot have a specific indefinite interpretation, since felicitous topics are necessarily familiar to the addressee.[7] The determiner *this* in (14) must therefore be interpreted as a true proximal demonstrative; for example, the speaker might utter the second sentence as she hands the addressee the new coat. It cannot have an 'indefinite this' interpretation, where the speaker is informing the addressee about the coat for the first time but does not actually produce it.

(15)　I wouldn't go on the trip without any warm clothes.
　　　This COAT I bought you, I think you should TAKE.

But a preposed semantic focus has no such restrictions. Example (16) is thus ambiguous between a demonstrative interpretation, for example, in a context where the speaker hands the addressee the coat while uttering the sentence, as in (15), and an indefinite *this* interpretation, for example, in a context where the speaker is informing the addressee that she bought him a new coat and then goes on to tell him more about it.

(16)   What do you think I should take on the camping trip?
         This COAT I bought you I think you should take.[8]

Linguistic focusing (that is, a prominent pitch accent) in both semantic focus and purely contrastive focus calls attention to the focused constituent, thereby invoking a 'contrast set'. What distinguishes contrastive focus from semantic focus is that contrast is its primary function. Constituents that receive contrastive focus (such as new topics) are emphasized in contrast to other elements that might occupy that position; constituents that receive semantic focus are emphasized because they represent the new information being predicated of the topic. The fact that this new information is (implicitly or explicitly) in contrast with other things that may have been predicated of the topic is a secondary effect.

To sum up so far, I have distinguished three senses of focus: psychological focus – entities in a discourse that both speaker's and addressee's attention is currently focused on; semantic focus – information that is being predicated in relation to the topic; and contrastive focus – imposed salience on a given constituent (often, but not necessarily, a topic) that the speaker wants to call the addressee's attention to in order to contrast it with other potential members of a relevant 'contrast set.[9]' The discourse in (17) contains examples of all three types of focus (psychological focus is indicated here by italics; the intonationally prominent part of the semantic focus is indicated by large capital letters; purely contrastive focus is indicated by small capital letters).

(17)   a. And there was this TEMPORARY when George went over to ECON.[10]
         b. And HE was in my OFFICE when SHE came in to BORROW something.
         c. and *she* said, *she* said, "Georgy-porgy puddin'-an-pie, kissed the girls and made them cry."
         d. And HE got this LOOK on his face and *he* said, "THAT was only the three thousand, eight hundred and ninety-second time I've heard THAT!"

                                                        (Frederickson tapes)[11]

Having established a distinction between psychological, semantic, and contrastive focus, I now address some additional questions concerning the pragmatic and semantic properties of these notions and their relation to one another.

5   Relation between the Three Senses of Focus

Are any of the three senses of focus equivalent? We have seen that while the three senses of focus may sometimes overlap, they are not equivalent. Something can receive purely contrastive focus without being in psychological focus or semantic focus, for example, *this coat* in (15). Something can be in psychological focus without being in semantic focus or contrastive focus, for example, *she* in (17c). And something can be the semantic focus without already being in psychological focus or receiving special contrastive focus, for example, *got this look on his face* in (17d).

Are any of the three senses of focus antithetical? I believe the answer to this question is also no. First let's look at psychological focus and semantic focus. As already noted, semantic focus is the linguistic correlate of the pragmatic notion *comment*, that is, the complement of the topic of the sentence. In coherent discourse, the same topic is typically maintained across a number of utterances. Thus, the prototypical topic is something that the addressee's attention is already focused on at a given point in the discourse, and it is therefore often the case that when a given part of the sentence is in psychological focus, the rest of the sentence is the semantic focus. In (16c), for example, the referent of *she*, the temporary, can be assumed to be in psychological focus since she was mentioned in a prominent position in the immediately preceding sentence. Since the semantic focus (comment) in (16c) includes the whole VP (i.e. *said* ".....") psychological focus and semantic focus are distinct and complementary in this sentence. But psychological focus is not necessarily the antithesis of semantic focus. The two notions are logically and empirically independent of one another. Psychological focus has to do with the status of an entity vis-à-vis an attention state of the addressee, but semantic focus is a relation that holds between the comment of a sentence and its topic (compare the distinction between referential givenness/newness and relational givenness/newness in Gundel 1988). A constituent whose referent is not in psychological focus may be part of the semantic focus, but it doesn't have to be. For example, it would not be if it were a newly introduced topic. More importantly, constituents whose referents *are* in psychological focus may be part, even the main part, of the semantic focus, as is the case for the referent of *she* in (18).

(18)   Mary said that it was SHE (= Mary) who called.

What about psychological focus and contrastive focus? Here, too, one would expect that in the prototypical case, contrastive focus would fall on constituents whose referents are not in psychological focus, as with newly introduced topics such as *that coat I bought you* in (12b) or a topic that is activated but not yet in focus, such as the first occurrence of *he* or of the demonstrative *that* in (17d). But a constituent that represents an entity already in psychological focus *can* receive contrastive focus if the speaker wants to call attention to it for some other reason, for example, to contrast it with something else, as with *she* in (16b) or *he* in (19).

(19)   John won't be at the party tonight either. HE has the FLU.

It is clear then that psychological focus and contrastive focus are not antithetical either.

Finally, what about semantic focus and contrastive focus? Both function to call attention to some part of the sentence, but for different reasons. The primary function of semantic focus is to mark the new information predicated of the topic; the primary function of contrastive focus, on the other hand, is simply to mark contrast or emphasis. Since semantic focus is already inherently contrastive, it is usually topics, that is, the complement of semantic focus, that receive special contrastive focus (hence the term 'contrastive topic'). But again, this is only the prototypical case. A semantic focus may be contrastively focused as well. Consider example (14) again, repeated here for convenience.

(14)   A.   What do you think I should take on the camping trip?
        B.   That COAT I bought you, (I think you should take).

A's question here can be answered with two different intonation patterns: *coat* can receive a simplex H* tone, characteristic of semantic focus, or a complex L + H*, characteristic of contrastive focus. The latter might be followed by something like 'but I wouldn't take the boots'. In both cases, however, the coat is part of the semantic focus.[12]

We have seen then that the three types of focus are logically independent of one another. They are not equivalent; there is no implicational relation between them; and they are not mutually exclusive. Now let's turn to the next question.

6   Does Linguistic Focus (Semantic or Contrastive) Bring an Entity into Psychological Focus?

The factors that determine when an entity is brought into psychological focus are complex and still not completely understood. It is clear, however, that syntactic, prosodic, semantic, and pragmatic factors are all involved. Hajičová (1987) and others have argued convincingly that the semantic focus (Hajičová's 'linguistic focus') is the most highly salient part of a sentence and is thus the most likely to be the psychological focus of the next sentence. To the extent that the semantic focus is more often an object than a subject, research that shows that objects often take precedence over subjects as potential antecedents for pronouns (e.g., Dahl 1996) also supports this view. Proponents of Centering Theory, on the other hand, maintain that the entity referred to by the subject of the main clause is most likely to be the backward center (= psychological focus) of the subsequent utterance. And there is ample evidence in support of this view as well. Whichever of these views turns out to be correct (and possibly both are partly right), it is clear that semantic focus is not in itself sufficient for bringing an entity into psychological focus. Example (4) (on the interpretation where the semantic focus of (4a) includes the phrase *my neighbors with the bull mastiff*) shows that the referent of a constituent that is part of the semantic focus is not always brought into psychological focus. Even a narrow semantic focus doesn't always bring an entity into psychological focus, as seen in (20):

(20)   Mary put the milk in the REFRIGERATOR. It was very cold.

The pronoun *it* in (20) is most easily interpreted as referring to the milk, because the expectation at the end of the first sentence is that one will go on to talk about the milk, or possibly about Mary, not about the refrigerator. That is, the refrigerator is not brought into psychological focus here.[13]

Finally, what about contrastive focus and psychological focus? Since the primary function of contrastive focus is to direct the addressee's attention to something, we would expect contrastive focus always to bring an entity into psychological focus (unless it is already in psychological focus, as in (19)). And I am aware of no examples where this is not the case. But more research obviously needs to be done here.

To sum up this section, as (20) shows, a semantic focus is in itself neither necessary nor sufficient for bringing an entity associated with it into psychological focus. However, contrastive focus may be sufficient for bringing an entity into psychological focus. Let's turn now to the final question.

7   Which Types of Focus Affect Truth-Conditions?

The idea that information structure can affect truth conditions goes back at least to the work of Strawson (1950), who maintained that sentences lack a truth value when their presuppositions are not met and that presuppositions are affected, among other things, by the topic-comment organization of the sentence. The work of a number of researchers over the past thirty years has shown that the focus structure of a sentence can be truth-conditionally relevant in the presence of certain focus-sensitive operators, with different choices of focus determining different truth conditions. Some familiar examples are given in (21)–(25)

(21)   a.   DOGS must be carried.
        b.   Dogs must be CARRIED.

                                                                    (Halliday 1967)

(22)   a.   Only voiceless OBSTRUENTS occur in word final position.
        b.   Only VOICELESS obstruents occur in word final position.

                                                                    (Lakoff 1971)

(23)   a.   Clyde gave me the TICKETS by mistake.
        b.   Clyde gave ME the tickets by mistake.

                                                                    (Dretske 1972)

(24)   a.   The largest demonstrations took place in PRAGUE in November (in) 1989.
        b.   The largest demonstrations took place in Prague in NOVEMBER (in) 1989.

                                                                    (Partee 1991)

In all these examples, it is semantic focus and not purely contrastive focus that is relevant. This is so because semantic focus is a relational notion that determines the main predication in a sentence. Purely contrastive focus, on the other hand, does not have truth-conditional effects, as can be seen by comparing the sentences in (24), which have no purely contrastive focus, with sentence (25), which has contrastive focus on *Prague*.

(25)   The largest demonstrations took place in PRAGUE in NOVEMBER.

Sentence (25), which might be uttered in a context where the size of demonstrations in different cities was being compared, has the same truth conditions as (24b); it does not have the same truth conditions as (24a). For example, (24a) would be false if the city with the largest demonstrations of all in November 1989 had been Budapest. However, both (24b) and (25) would still be true in this situation as long as the largest demonstrations in Prague took place in November 1989. This is so because in (24a) November 1989 is part of the topic and Prague is part of the semantic focus, but in both (24a) and (25) Prague is part of the topic and the semantic focus is November 1989. The fact that (25) has a contrastive focus on Prague, thus overtly contrasting Prague with other cities that had demonstrations, is contextually relevant, but it does not affect the truth conditions of the sentence. For the same reason, purely contrastive focus cannot be within the scope of a focus-sensitive operator. Thus (26), with semantic focus on (a part of) the VP, is unacceptable because a subject that is contrastively focused, but that is not the semantic focus, cannot be in the scope of *only*.

(26)   Only voiceless OBSTRUENTS occur in word final POSITION.

To sum up, of the three types of focus that I have distinguished in this chapter – psychological focus, semantic focus, and contrastive focus – only semantic focus is relevant for truth conditions.

Notes

1   My intention in using this term is simply to distinguish it from the other senses in which the term 'focus' has been used. I am not necessarily recommending adoption of 'psychological focus' or of the terms 'semantic focus' and 'contrastive focus' discussed later, as technical terms for these different senses.
2   A similar distinction is made in Sedivy, Carlson, and Tannenhaus (1994).
3   # here indicates unacceptability in the given context.
4   A similar explanation can be given for examples of situational anaphors (Fraurud 1992) with *it* versus *that*.
5   As I argue in Gundel (1974/1989) this concept of focus (compare also focus versus presupposition in Chomsky 1971) is the linguistic correlate of the pragmatic notion of 'comment' and thus does not have to be distinguished as a separate semantic or pragmatic construct in a framework that incorporates topic-comment structure. Hajičová (1987) apparently intends her term 'linguistic focus' to cover only what I call 'semantic focus', defining it as "that part of the (meaning) of the sentence that conveys some (irrecoverable) information predicating something about the 'given', recoverable, contextually bound part (i.e. of the topic of the sentence), distinguishing thus a dichotomy of topic and focus."

6 In using the term 'contrastive focus' in this way I realize I may be creating additional confusion since this term has also been used to designate narrow semantic focus (see Dretske 1972, as well as more recent work by other authors). Whenever information is predicated of some topic, it is inherently in contrast with everything else that might be predicated of that topic, and the narrower the focus (comment/predication) the more salient the contrast. Thus, elements within the scope of operators like *only* and *even* are always part of the semantic focus, and they also have a highly contrastive interpretation. As Dretske himself points out (p. 411) all contingent statements contrast one state of affairs with another. My intent in using the term 'contrastive focus' here is to distinguish linguistic prominence, which has a purely contrastive function, from semantic focus, both narrow and broad.

7 See Gundel 1988 for an explanation of some possible counterexamples to this generalization provided by Prince 1985 and Reinhart 1981.

8 A similar contrast exists in the following German example from Höhle (1982), where the subject NP can be either topic or semantic focus.
   (i)   Ein Junge WEINT NICHT.
            a   boy   cries   not
   (ii)   Ein JUNGE weint nicht.
   In (i), where semantic focus is on the VP, the subject *ein Junge* can only have a generic interpretation ('Boys don't cry'), since specific indefinites cannot be topics. But in (ii), where semantic focus is on the subject, *ein Junge* can be interpreted either as generic ('BOYS don't cry') or as a specific indefinite ('A BOY isn't crying').

9 See Clamons et al. 1993 for further discussion of the notion 'imposed salience'.

10 I assume here that (17a) has two semantic foci, one in each clause. As Michael Hegarty has pointed out to me, there is an alternative analysis where the first clause is focus and the *when*-clause is a new topic. *Econ* would receive a prominent pitch accent on either interpretation, but the type of accent would be different. Since the transcripts were not annoted for this prosodic distinction, it is unclear which interpretation was intended.

11 The Frederickson tapes are transcribed recordings of conversations during family gatherings (1975–1987), collected by Karen Frederickson, secretary of the University of Minnesota Linguistics Department, from 1979 to 1992.

12 Compare also Rooth's example (1992:82) "Well, I PASSED" as an answer to the question "How did the exam go?" With special contrastive accent on *passed*, the answer strongly implies that the speaker could have done better. However, *passed* is semantic focus here with or without such an accent.

13 A semantic focus that is marked syntactically as well as prosodically (for example, the referent of a clefted or sentence initial focus, as in (7) and (8)) does, however, appear to be enough to bring an entity into psychological focus. See Hedberg 1990 for further discussion of this point.

References

Bosch, P. (1988), Representing and accessing focussed referents, *Language and Cognitive Processes*, 3:207–231.

Bosch, P., and R. van der Sandt, eds. (1994), Focus and Natural Language Processing. IBM Deutschland Information Systeme. GmbH, Heidelberg.

Bolinger, D. (1961), Contrastive accent and contrastive stress, *Language*, 37:87–96.

Brennan, S. E., M. W. Friedman, and C. J. Pollard (1987), A centering approach to pronouns, Proceedings of the 25th Annual Meeting of the Association for Computational Linguistics, Stanford University, 155–162.

Chomsky, N. (1971), Deep structure, surface structure and semantic interpretation, in D. Steinberg and L. Jakobovits (eds.), *Semantics: An Interdisciplinary Reader in Linguistics, Philosophy and Psychology*, Cambridge University Press, Cambridge, 183–216.

Clamons, C. R., A. E. Mulkern, and G. Sanders (1993), Salience signaling in Oromo. *Journal of Pragmatics*, 19:519–536.

Clark, H., and S. Haviland (1977), Comprehension and the given-new contract, in R. Freedle (ed.), *Discourse production and comprehension*, Erlbaum, 1–40.

Cutler, A., and J. A. Fodor (1979), Semantic focus and sentence comprehension, *Cognition*, 7:35–41.

Dahl, D. A. (1986), Focusing and reference resolution in PUNDIT, presented at AAAI-86, Philadelphia.

Dahl, D. A., and J. K. Gundel (1981). The comprehension of focussed and non-focussed pronouns, *Proceedings of the 3rd Annual Meeting of the Cognitive Science Society*, Berkeley, 125–127.

Dretske, F. (1972), Contrastive statements, *Philosophical Review*, 81:411–437.

Erkü, F., and J. K. Gundel (1987), The pragmatics of indirect anaphors, in J.Verschueren and M. Bertuccelli-Papi (eds.) *The pragmatic perspective: selected papers from the 1985 International Pragmatics Conference*, John Benjamins, Amsterdam, 533–545.

Erteschik-Shir, N. (1973), *On the Nature of Island Constraints*. Ph.D. dissertation. Massachusetts Institute of Technology.

Erteschik-Shir, N. (1994), Dependencies in focus-structure, in Bosch, P. and R. van der Sandt (eds.), 1994.

Garrod, S. C., and A. J. Sanford (1982), The mental representation of discourse in a focussed memory system: Implications for the interpretation of anaphoric noun phrases, *Journal of Semantics*, 1:21–41.

Grosz, B., A. K. Joshi, and S. Weinstein. (1986), Towards a computational theory of discourse interpretation, unpublished ms.

Grosz, B., and C. L. Sidner (1986), Attention, intentions, and the structure of discourse, *Computational linguistics*, 12:175–204.

Gundel, J. (1974), *The role of topic and comment in linguistic theory*. Ph.D. dissertation. University of Texas at Austin, published by Garland, New York (1989).

Gundel, J. K. (1985), Shared knowledge and topicality, *Journal of Pragmatics*, 9:83–107.

Gundel, J. K (1988), Universals of topic-comment structure, in M. Hammond et al (eds.), *Studies in Syntactic Typology*, John Benjamins, Amsterdam, 209–239.

Gundel, J. K., N. Hedberg, and R. Zacharski (1993), Cognitive status and the form of referring expressions in discourse, *Language*, 69:274–307.

Hajičová, E. (1987), Focussing – A meeting point of linguistics and artificial intelligence, in P. Jorrand and V. Sgurev (eds.) *Artificial Intelligence II: Methodology, Systems, Applications*, North-Holland, Amsterdam, 311–321.

Halliday, M. A. K. (1967), Notes on transitivity and theme in English II, *Journal of Linguistics*, 3:199–244.

Hedberg, N. (1990), Discourse Pragmatics and Cleft Sentences in English, Ph.D. dissertation, University of Minnesota, Minneapolis.

Höhle, T. (1991), On reconstruction and coordination, in H. Haider and K. Netter (eds.), *Representation and Derivation in the Theory of Grammar*, Reidel, Dordrecht.

Jackendoff, R. (1972), *Semantic interpretation in generative grammar*, MIT Press, Cambridge, Mass.

Jacobs, J. (1991), Focus ambiguities, *Journal of Semantics* 8:1–36.

Kameyama, M. (1986), *Zero-Anaphora: the Case of Japanese*, Ph.D. dissertation, Stanford University.

Krifka, M. (1991), A compositional semantics for multiple focus constructions, *Linguistische Berichte*, Suppl. 4:17–53.

Krifka, M. (1993), Focus and presupposition in dynamic interpretation, *Journal of Semantics* 10:269–300.

Lakoff, G. (1971), On generative semantics, in D. Steinberg and L. Jakobovits, (eds.), *Semantics: An Interdisciplinary Reader in Linguistics, Philosophy and psychology*, Cambridge University Press, Cambridge, 232–296.

Partee, B. (1991), Topic, focus and quantification, *Cornell Working Papers in Linguistics*, 10 (*SALT I*) 159–187.

Prince, E. (1981), Toward a taxonomy of given-new information, in P. Cole (ed.), *Radical Pragmatics*, Academic Press, New York, 223–256.

Prince. E. (1985), Fancy syntax and 'shared knowledge, *Journal of Pragmatics*, 9:65–81.

Reinhart, T. (1981), Pragmatics and linguistics: An analysis of sentence topics, *Philosophica* 27:53–94.

Rochemont, M. S. (1986), *Focus in Generative Grammar*, John Benjamins, Amsterdam.

Rooth, M. (1985), *Association with Focus*, Ph.D. dissertation, University of Massachusetts, Amherst.

Rooth, M. (1992), A theory of focus interpretation, *Natural Language Semantics* 1:75–116.

Sedivy, J., G. Carlson, and M. Tannenhaus (1994), Experimenting with focus: mental accessibility and inference in focus constructions. In P. Bosch and R. van der Sandt (eds.), pp. 457–466.

Sgall, P., E. Hajičová, and E. Benešova (1973), *Topic, focus, and generative semantics*, Scriptor Verlag GmbH, Kronberg.

Sgall, P., E. Hajičová, and J. Panevová (1986), *The Meaning of the Sentence in Its Semantic and Pragmatic Aspects*, Reidel, Dordrecht.

Sperber, D., and D. Wilson (1986), *Relevance: Communication and Cognition*, Harvard University Press, Cambridge, Mass.

Strawson, P. F. (1950), On referring, *Mind*, 61:320–344.

Vallduví, E. (1992), *The informational component*, Ph.D. dissertation, University of Pennsylvania.

Vallduví, E., and R. Zacharski. (1994), Accenting phenomena, association with focus and the recursiveness of focus-ground, in P. Dekker and M. Stokhof (eds.), *Proceedings of the 9th Amsterdam Colloquium*, Institute for Logic, Language and Computation, University of Amsterdam, Amsterdam, 683–702.

Zacharski, R. (1993), *A Discourse Pragmatics Model of English Accent*, Ph.D. dissertation, University of Minnesota, Minneapolis.

16   Stressed and Unstressed Pronouns: Complementary Preferences

MEGUMI KAMEYAMA

Abstract

I present a unified account of interpretation preferences of stressed and unstressed pronouns in discourse. The central intuition is the Complementary Preference Hypothesis, which predicts the interpretation preference of a stressed pronoun from that of an unstressed pronoun in the same discourse position. The base preference must be computed in a *total* pragmatics module including commonsense preferences. The focus constraint in Rooth's theory of semantic focus is interpreted to be the salient subset of the domain in the local attentional state in the discourse context independently motivated for other purposes in Centering Theory.

1   Introduction

Stressed pronouns present a peculiar class of anaphoric expressions. Informally, they communicate "old" as well as "new" information. They are also at odds with the *topic-focus articulation* (TFA) (Sgall, Hajičová, and Panevová 1986) – *contextually bound* – which is typical of *topic*, in spite of being in an intonational focus, which is a defining property of *focus* and common for a *contextually unbound* expression. They can also exemplify the different notions of *focus* – *psychological*, *semantic*, or *contrastive* focus (Gundel, this volume) – and can even combine them all at once. Unstressed pronouns (such as *he, she, it, they*) and their stressed counterparts (for example, *HE, SHE, THAT, THEY*) often lead to drastically different interpretations.[1] (Henceforth, stressed pronouns are written in all uppercase.)

An account of the semantics and pragmatics of stressed pronouns needs to explicate their peculiar hybrid behaviors and relation to unstressed pronouns. Example (1) shows two alternative continuations of the first utterance – using an unstressed *he* and a stressed *HE*. The preferred interpretations indicated in the parentheses are opposites of each other.

(1)   John hit Bill. Then {*he* | *HE*} was injured.
        (*he* := Bill)(*HE* := John)

This work was in part supported by the National Science Foundation and the Advanced Research Projects Agency under Grant IRI-9314961 (Integrated Techniques for Generation and Interpretation). I would like to thank Peter Bosch, Elisabet Engdahl, and Hiroshi Nakagawa for helpful comments on an earlier version.

306

Similarly, variations of Lakoff's (1971) example, (2) and (3), show opposite preferred interpretations.

(2)   Paul called Jim a Republican. Then *he* insulted *him*.
       (Paul insulted Jim)

(3)   Paul called Jim a Republican. Then *HE* insulted *HIM*.
       (Jim insulted Paul)

In (2), the preferred interpretation of the unstressed pronouns establishes grammatical parallelism between the two utterances. In (3), the preferred interpretation of the stressed pronouns is the opposite of (2), and the discourse acquires an additional assumption that 'x insults y' follows from 'x calls y a Republican.'

The present approach focuses on the interpretation differences between the *stressed and unstressed counterparts* – the stressed and unstressed versions of the same pronominal form in the same *position* in discourse as well as in a sentence. I assume that stressed and unstressed counterparts have exactly the same denotational range – the same range of *possible* values. They also share the same interpretation problem of choosing the *preferred* value. The difference then arises from the latter. What is the difference in the preferred values of unstressed and stressed counterparts? Is there a systematic relation between them? Does one preferred value *predict* the other?

I claim that the difference between stressed and unstressed counterparts is in the *presuppositions* and that there is a systematic relation between them coming from the interaction between the *semantic focus interpretation* of the stressed pronoun and the *centering principles* associated with its unstressed counterpart. The centering principles here are extended in the sense that they are part of the *total* pragmatics that includes commonsense preferences. Under this unified approach, the systematic relation between the stressed and unstressed counterparts is that of a *complementary preference* within a suitable subset of the domain.

2   The Stressed Pronoun and Semantic Focus

Rooth (1992) develops a theory of focus interpretation in terms of *restricted alternative semantics*, where the focus semantics introduces a presupposed constraint using a *focus interpretation operator* $\sim$. A focus phrase (or sentence) α has a focus interpretation operator with a variable C ($\sim C$). C may denote either individuals or sets of objects of the same type as the denotation of α, which are the elements or subsets of the *focus semantic value* of α (henceforth $[[\alpha]]^f$). C must contain the *ordinary semantic value* of α (henceforth $[[\alpha]]^o$) and at least one more element or subset of C distinct from $[[\alpha]]^o$, which is the *contrasting element or subset* for $[[\alpha]]^o$. Rooth points out that the value of C is a discourse entity to which C is anaphoric and that the important question is how to constrain it. This opens up focus interpretation to all sorts of discourse-pragmatic effects. In this chapter,

I notationally distinguish two types of presuppositional constraints after Rooth (1993) – C for a set of propositions and F for a set of entities (individuals or groups of individuals).

2.1   *The Semantics of Stressed Pronouns*

According to this theory of semantic focus, a stressed *HE* presupposes a constraint $\sim F$ that there is a contextually determined set of entities ($[[HE]]^f = \{x \mid x \in F \subseteq E\}$ where E is the domain of individuals) with at least two members – the denotation of *HE* ($[[HE]]^o$) and at least one more contrasting individual. F is the *contextually available alternatives* or the *focus semantic value* of HE. $[[HE]]^o$ is an element of F, and F is a subset of E ($[[HE]]^o \in [[HE]]^f = F \subseteq E$). An utterance (i.e., a sentence token in a context) with a focused element presupposes a constraint $\sim C$ that there is a contextually determined set of propositions obtained by instantiating a set abstraction with the alternative values of the focused element – for instance, "*HE* was injured" presupposes a constraint $\sim C$ whose value is a set of propositions obtained by instantiating the focus semantic value $\{injured(x) \mid x \in E\}$ with the alternative values of $[[HE]]^f$. The ordinary semantic value of the utterance is a truth value that is an element of the focus semantic values ($[[HE\ was\ injured]]^o \in \{injured(x) \mid x \in F\} \subseteq \{injured(x) \mid x \in E\}$).

2.2   *The Pragmatics of Stressed Pronouns*

Given the above focus semantics, interpreting a stressed *HE* in an utterance U involves four pragmatic subroutines. These subroutines are listed approximately in the following bottom-up processing order, but no strict sequential order is assumed:

- *Locate* $F \subseteq E$, where F is a contextually determined set of entities that may contain more than one potential referent for *HE*.
- *Choose* a member of F as $[[HE]]^o$.
- *Discharge* $\sim C$ for U (which may contain other focused phrases) in the current discourse context – in terms of a pending question or contrasting proposition.
- *Establish coherence* of $[[U]]^o$ in the current discourse context: that is, the contribution of the utterance content to the evolving information state must somehow make sense.

Each pragmatic subroutine consists of an interacting set of preferences, and the combination of all the subroutines may or may not converge into a single preferred interpretation of U. We focus here on the preferences that affect the *locate* and *choose* subroutines, with illustrations of how they interact with the *discharge* subroutine. How is the relevant set of alternatives located? How is the preferred value chosen? Rooth does not discuss these cases where focus interpretation may also involve choosing among multiple alternatives. This chapter proposes an approach that spells out the missing detail in his notion of restricted alternatives.

3   Three Background Hypotheses

Our present aim is to account for the systematic interpretation difference between the stressed and unstressed counterparts. I motivate here the claim that the interpretation of the *unstressed* counterpart should be the basis from which to predict the interpretation of its stressed counterpart. The claim rests on the following analogous characterization of the semantics and pragmatics of the unstressed pronoun such as *he* and *him*.

An unstressed *he* presupposes a constraint $\sim B$ that there is a contextually determined set of entities ($[[HE]]^{f'} = \{x \mid x \in B \subseteq E\}$) with at least *one* member – the denotation of *he* ($[[HE]]^o$). $[[HE]]^o$ is an element of B and B is a subset of E ($[[HE]]^o \in [[HE]]^{f'} = B \subseteq E$). Given this semantics, interpreting an unstressed *he* in an utterance U involves the following pragmatic subroutines:

- *Locate* $B \subseteq E$, where B is a contextually determined set of entities that may contain more than one potential referent for *he*.
- *Choose* a member of B as $[[HE]]^o$.
- *Establish coherence* of $[[U]]^o$ in the current discourse context.

Note that the sets of pragmatic subroutines for the stressed and unstressed pronouns correspond one-on-one *except* for the additional *discharge* constraint on the utterance containing a stressed pronoun. This indicates that the sum of the pragmatic constraints on the use of stressed pronouns may be greater than on their unstressed counterparts. I therefore hypothesize the following:

> **Hypothesis 1:**   *Given the range β of felicitous uses of* unstressed *pronouns in discourse and the range α of felicitous uses of their* stressed *counterparts, $\alpha \subset \beta$.*

The preceding hypothesis is borne out by examples of *asymmetry* such as the following:

(4)   Babar went to a bakery. *he* greeted the baker.
            {*he* | ??*HE*} pointed at a blueberry pie.

The infelicity of the stressed *HE* is due to the difficulty in discharging the presupposed focus constraint on the utterance ("x pointed at a blueberry pie") in terms of a pending question ("Who pointed at a blueberry pie?") or contrasting proposition (for example, "someone did not point at a blueberry pie").

Assuming Hypothesis 1, we may conclude that if the preferred interpretation of either the stressed or the unstressed counterpart serves as the basis for deriving the other preferred interpretation, the base preference should come from the unstressed counterpart, hence the second background hypothesis:

> **Hypothesis 2:**   *The preferred value of a stressed pronoun can be predicted by the preferred value of its unstressed counterpart.*

There are remaining questions. What is the "contextually relevant subset" B for the unstressed pronoun? What constraint, if any, does an utterance containing an unstressed pronoun presuppose? In other words, is there an unstressed pronoun analogue of $\sim C$? I propose an answer only to the first of these questions. I define the *currently salient subset* of the domain of individuals in terms of the centering model of discourse (see the next section) and motivate the third background hypothesis:

Hypothesis 3: *Stressed and unstressed counterparts choose their values from the* same *salient subset of the domain of individuals* (that is, $F = B$).

If we are lucky, then, what we have is an integrated account of the semantics and pragmatics of stressed and unstressed pronouns. Note that in order for this hypothesis to work, we need to explain the discrepancy that the set F for a stressed pronoun must contain at least two members, whereas B may sometimes contain only one. I argue that when the salient subset is a singleton, the contrasting members are accommodated into the context to satisfy the focus constraint of the stressed pronoun.

4   The Unstressed Pronoun and Centering

The problem of choosing among alternative values for pronouns has been investigated in the framework of Centering Theory (Grosz, Joshi, and Weinstein 1983, 1986, 1995).[2] It is part of an overall theory of discourse structure and meaning (Grosz and Sidner 1986) that distinguishes among three components of discourse structure – a linguistic structure, an intentional structure, and an attentional state – and two levels of discourse coherence – global and local. *Attentional state* models the discourse participants' focus of attention, determined by the intentional and linguistic structures at any given point in the discourse. It has global and local components corresponding to the two levels of discourse coherence. The global-level component is a stack of focus spaces, where each focus space holds entities and propositions associated with a discourse segment, which is associated with a discourse segment purpose in the intentional structure. Centering models the local-level component of attentional state – how the speaker's linguistic choices for describing propositional contents affect the *inference load placed upon the hearer* in discourse processing.

An utterance in discourse (not a sentence in isolation) has entities called *centers* that link the utterance with other utterances in the same discourse segment. They are the set of *forward-looking centers* (Cf) partially ordered by relative prominence. One member of the Cf may be the *backward-looking center* (Cb) that connects with a member of the Cf of the previous utterance. The speaker's linguistic choices define centering transitions that affect the local coherence of the discourse. In English discourse, pronouns and grammatical subjects are the main indicators of centering transitions (Grosz et al. 1983, 1986, 1995; Kameyama 1985, 1986; Brennan, Friedman, and Pollard 1987). *Unstressed* pronouns, in particular, are primarily used to indicate the Cb in English-type languages (Kameyama 1985:Ch.1).

4.1   Dynamic Preference Model

Kameyama (1996) develops an initial model of *interacting preferences* for dynamically updating a multicomponent context data structure in discourse processing. Centering preferences, stated in terms of the attentional notion of *salience*, systematically interact with structural and commonsense preferences to predict the preferred interpretation of unstressed pronouns. The perspective is that of *total pragmatics*, which includes both linguistic and commonsense preferences. This *dynamic preference model* is summarized below. (A preference is stated as a defeasible rule in the form of either "normally *p*" or "if *p* then normally *q*.")

- *Discourse* is a sequence of utterances, $U_1, \ldots, U_n$. Each utterance U_i defines a *transition relation* between the *input context* C_{i-1} and the *output context* C_i.[3]
- Context C is a multicomponent data structure $C_i = \langle \phi_i^k, A_i, D_i, \ldots \rangle$ including[4]
  - ϕ_i^k (LF *register*) – the preferred interpretation k of the last utterance U_i in a logical form that preserves aspects of the syntactic structure of U_i.
  - A_i (*attentional state*) – a set of currently "open" propositions with the associated entities, into which a new utterance content can potentially be integrated. The entities in A_i are partially ordered by *salience*, and the most salient subpart of A_i is the *local attentional state*, A_i^{LOC} (see later discussion).
  - D_i (*discourse model*) – a structured information state for what the discourse has been about (situations, eventualities, entities, and relations among them), including the content of A_i.
- A_i^{LOC} (*local attentional state*)[5] – the entities realized[6] by ϕ_i^k (corresponding to the Cf). One of them may be *Center_i* (corresponding to the Cb)[7] – the entity on which the current discourse subsegment is centered. I assume that *Center_i* may be missing in A_i, especially at the onset of a new discourse segment.
- In utterance interpretation, there are interacting preferences for updating different context components. Some come from the linguistic knowledge, and others come from the world knowledge.

4.2   The Role of the Attentional State

Various factors affect salience dynamics – including utterance forms, discourse participants' purposes and perspectives, and the perceptually salient objects in the utterance situation. Here we focus on the factor of utterance forms.

Two default linguistic hierarchies are relevant to the dynamics of salience – *grammatical function hierarchy* (GF ORDER) and the *nominal expression type hierarchy* (EXP ORDER):[8]

GF ORDER: Given a hierarchy [SUBJECT > OBJECT > OBJECT 2 > OTHERS], an entity realized by a higher-ranked phrase is normally more salient in the *output* attentional state.

EXP ORDER: Given a hierarchy [ZERO PRONOMINAL > PRONOUN > DEFINITE NP > INDEFINITE NP],[9] an entity realized by a higher-ranked expression type is normally more salient in the *input* attentional state.

Since matrix subjects and objects cannot be omitted in English, the highest-ranked expression type is the (unstressed) pronoun (Kameyama 1985:Ch.1). From EXP ORDER, it follows that a pronoun normally realizes a *maximally salient entity* (of an appropriate gender-number-person type) in the input A. This accounts for the preference for a pronoun to corefer with the matrix subject in the previous utterance as in the following example:[10]

(5)   1.   John hit Bill. A_1:[[John > Bill]$_{\phi_1}$ ...]
        2.   Mary told him to go home.   *him* := John $\prec$ Bill

The centering model is reinterpreted as follows:

CENTER: $Center_i \in A_i$ is normally more salient than other entities in A_i.
EXP CENTER: An expression of the highest-ranked type in U_i normally realizes $Center_i$ in the *output* attentional state A_i.[11]

EXP ORDER and EXP CENTER combine to make a pronoun either *establish* or *chain* the Center (Kameyama 1985, 1986).[12] $Center_i$ is "established" ($Center_{i-1} \neq Center_i$) when a pronoun picks a salient non-Center in A_{i-1} and makes it the Center in A_i. It is "chained" ($Center_{i-1} = Center_i$) when a pronoun picks $Center_{i-1}$ and outputs it as $Center_i$.

The *maximally salient entity* may be determinate in some *attentional state* and indeterminate in others, depending on whether the GF-based salience ordering and the Center-based one converge. A highest-ranked GF and the Center may converge or diverge in the *input* A, affecting the preferred interpretation of a pronoun.[13] For instance, the Center realized by a sentence-initial matrix subject pronoun is the single most salient entity, but the Center realized by a nonsubject pronoun competes with the entity realized by the subject, resulting in an indeterminacy.[14] The different effects are illustrated here:

(6)   1.   Babar went to a bakery. A_1:[[Babar > Bakery]$_{\phi_1}$ ...]
        2.   *he* greeted the baker.
             A_2:[[[Babar]$_{Center}^{Subj}$ > Baker]$_{\phi_2}$ > Bakeryts]
        3.   *he* pointed at a blueberry pie.   *he* := Babar $\prec$ Baker

(7)   1.   Babar went to a bakery. A_1:[[Babar > Bakery]$_{\phi_1}$ ...]
        2.   The baker greeted *him*.
             A_2:[[Baker <> [Babar]$_{Center}^{Obj}$]$_{\phi_2}$ > Bakeryts]
        3.   *he* pointed at a blueberry pie.   *he* := Baker $\prec_?$ Babar

Example (6) shows the effects of determinate salience ranking in terms of a chain of subject Centers. The preferred value of *he* in (6.3) is determinate. In contrast, the salience ranking in A_2 is indeterminate in example (7). The weak preference in (7.3) comes from the interaction of attentional preference and the separate preference for grammatical parallelism stated below.

4.3   *The Role of the LF Register*

The grammatical parallelism of two adjacent utterances in discourse affects the preferred interpretation of pronouns (Kameyama 1986), tense (Kameyama, Passonneau, and Poesio 1993), and ellipses (Pruest 1992; Kehler 1993). This general tendency warrants a separate statement. Parallelism is achieved, in the present account, by a computation on the pair of logical forms, one in the LF register in the context and the other being interpreted:

> **PARA:** The LF register in the input context and the utterance being interpreted seek maximal parallelism.[15]

We have observed in example (7) that this parallelism preference kicks in when the salience-based preference is indeterminate.

4.4   *The Role of the Discourse Model*

Both linguistic semantics and commonsense preferences apply on the same discourse model. Lexically triggered conventional presuppositions, for instance, constrain possible discourse models. Preferential rules assign a partial order on these models. Commonsense preferences consist of all that an ordinary speaker knows about the world and life. There will be a relatively small number of linguistic pragmatic rules that systematically interact with and *control* an open-ended mass of commonsense rules. Our aim is to describe the former as fully as possible and specify how the "control mechanism" works. Linguistic rules should be stable across examples and domains, while there will be different commonsense rules for each new example and domain. Example (1) illustrates a type of causal knowledge:

> **HIT:** When an agent x hits an agent y, y is normally hurt.

4.5   *Preference Interactions*

Preferences relevant to unstressed pronoun interpretation fall into three *preference classes* corresponding to the preferred transitions of the three context components. CENTER, GF ORDER, EXP ORDER, and EXP CENTER are defeasible *attentional rules* (ATT) stating the preferred *A*-transitions. PARA is an example of defeasible *LF Rules* (LF) stating the preferred LF-transitions. HIT is an example of defeasible *commonsense rules* (WK) stating the preferred *D*-transitions. These preference classes independently conclude the preferred interpretation of an utterance, and these class-internal conclusions combine in a certain general pattern to produce the final preference. Crucially, preferences *can override* other preferences that contradict them. Ambiguities persist only when mutually contradictory preferences are equally strong.

We have identified the following general patterns of preference interactions in pronoun interpretation:[16]

- Indefeasible syntax and semantics (SYN + SEM) can override all preferences.
- Commonsense preferences can override attentional or parallelism preferences. This overriding can be difficult, however, when the latter is extremely strong, producing garden-path phenomena. Observe the difference between *John hit Bill. He was severely injured* (*he* := Bill ≺ John) and *Tommy came into the classroom. He saw Billy at the door. He hit him on the chin. ??He was severely injured* (*he* := Tommy is first chosen but retracted, and results in Billy).
- Attentional preferences can override parallelism preferences except for the cases of parallelism induced by conventional presuppositions.

This general overriding pattern is schematically shown here, where ≥ represents a "can override" relation:

$$\boxed{\text{SYN} + \text{SEM} \geq \text{WK} \geq \text{ATT} \geq \text{LF}}$$

We have thus a fairly rich theory of interacting preferences in unstressed pronoun interpretation. The question is the following – are they related to, or better predictive of, the preferences relevant to the stressed counterpart?

5   Complementary Preference Hypothesis

I claim that the preferred value of a stressed pronoun in discourse is predictable from the preferred value of its unstressed counterpart, and that they draw their values from the same "currently salient" subset of the domain. This salient subset is the presupposed constraint F for the stressed pronoun and B for the unstressed pronoun in Hypothesis 3.

In this unified view, this salient subset is the *local attentional state*, A^{LOC}, or the "center of attention" in the dynamic context.

> **Salient Subset Hypothesis (SSH):** *An unstressed pronoun and its stressed counterpart in utterance U_i draw their possible values from the input local attentional state* ($A^{LOC}_{i-1} = F = B$).

Although the exact specification of A^{LOC} is still open (see note 5), we take the standard view in Centering Theory as the starting point in this chapter – it is the set of entities realized by the previous utterance in the given discourse segment.

It corresponds to the entities associated with the logical form in the LF register in the present dynamic preference model.

Given the common presupposed subset of the domain, I hypothesize that the preference order among the alternative values for a stressed pronoun is the *complement* of the preference order for its unstressed counterpart:

> **Complementary Preference Hypothesis (CPH):** *A focused pronoun takes the complementary preference of the unstressed counterpart.*

Restricting the salient subset is also crucial in this account, in order to avoid an infinite regression into the least preferred entity in the entire universe of discourse to get at the most preferred value for a stressed pronoun.

5.1 Computation of the Preferred Value

Given the CPH, the preferred value of a stressed pronoun in utterance U_i is computed with the following algorithm:[17]

- *Locate* the local attentional state B_{i-1} in the input context C_{i-1}. B_{i-1} contains a nonempty set of entities partially ordered by *salience* $(B_{i-1}^{salience})$.[18]
- *Compute base preference order* for $B_{i-1}^{salience}$ for the *unstressed counterpart* of the stressed pronoun, in terms of the interaction of LF rules, attentional rules, and commonsense rules.[19] The output is a subset H_{i-1} of B_{i-1} partially ordered by *preference* (H_{i-1}^{pref}), where $H_{i-1} \subseteq B_{i-1}$ contains only the possible values of the pronoun within B_{i-1}.
- *Compute complementary preference order* for H_{i-1}^{pref} as follows: $x \prec y$ becomes $y \prec x$, and $x \prec \succ y$ does not change. With the CPH, this outputs the possible values of the stressed pronoun partially ordered by preference $(H_{i-1}^{pref^{\cup}})$.
- *Discharge* the presupposed constraint $\sim C$ for U_i (which may contain other focused phrases). If B_{i-1} is a singleton set, at least one additional contrasting individual is *accommodated* (see below).
- *Establish coherence* of $[[U_i]]^o$.

The algorithm is illustrated with example (1) with a stressed pronoun in the second utterance (repeated here):

(1) 1. John hit Bill. $C_1: B_1^{salience} = \{John > Bill\}$
   2. Then *HE* was injured.
       $B_1 \supseteq H_1^{pref} = \{Bill \prec John\} \leadsto H_1^{pref^{\cup}} = \{John \prec Bill\}$
       $\leadsto HE := \{John \prec Bill\}$

The local attentional state in the input context for U_2 contains John and Bill, with John more salient than Bill. Both John and Bill are possible values of *he*. The base preference for the unstressed counterpart results from the WK rule (HIT) overriding ATT and LF rules, with Bill preferred to John. The complementary preference makes John preferred to Bill for the stressed pronoun. This preference then survives the presupposition discharging, which recognizes the (indirect) contrast between *John was injured* and *John hit Bill*, and coherence establishing, which recognizes the cause-effect relation between U_1 and U_2.

The following variant of (1) illustrates a case where not all the entities in B are possible values for the pronoun:

(1′)   1.   John hit Bill in front of Mary.
$$C_1: B_1^{salience} = \{\text{John} > \text{Bill} > \text{Mary}\}$$
   2.   Then *HE* was injured.
$$B_1 \supseteq H_1^{pref} = \{\text{Bill} \prec \text{John}\} \rightsquigarrow H_1^{pref^{\cup}} = \{\text{John} \prec \text{Bill}\}$$
$$\rightsquigarrow HE := \{\text{John} \prec \text{Bill}\}$$

Here, B_1 contains three individuals, John, Bill, and Mary, of which only two are possible values of *he*. The interpretation of stressed *HE* in U_2 is exactly the same as in the previous example, however, since the base preference is on the same subset H_1.

Nakatani (1993) found in spontaneous narratives that a stressed subject pronoun tends to signal (1) a *local shift* to a non-Cb in the Cf or (2) a *global shift* to an old Cb within the segment. (1) is highly consistent with the present account. (2) would also follow if the local attentional state contains old Cbs in the segment as well as the Cf.

5.2   *Indeterminate Preferences*

This unified account predicts that when the preferred value of an unstressed pronoun is indeterminate, the preferred value for its stressed counterpart is likewise indeterminate because the complement of an indeterminate order is still indeterminate. This prediction is borne out in the following example:

(8)   Jack and Bob are good friends. {??*he* | ??*HE*} is from Louisiana.

Neither Jack nor Bob is more salient than the other in the conjoined NP, and neither parallelism nor commonsense preferences distinguish them, hence the indeterminate preference for *he*. Its complement for *HE* is also indeterminate.

5.3   *Unambiguous Stressed Pronouns*

The proposed mechanism correctly predicts that when the pronoun in question is unambiguous, stressing does not change its values. Since the stressed and unstressed counterparts draw their possible values from the same singleton set, $|H| = 1$, the complementation operation produces the same possible value for the stressed counterpart. The following examples illustrate such unambiguous pronouns:

(9)   Jack and Mary are good friends. {*he* | *HE*} is from Louisiana.
        {*he* | *HE*} := Jack

(10)   Jack is a physicist. {*he* | *HE*} is from Louisiana.
        {*he* | *H E*} := Jack

The interpretation process of the stressed *HE* in example (9) is illustrated here:

(9)   1. Jack and Mary are good friends.
            C_1: $B_1^{salience}$ = {Jack<>Mary}
        2. *HE* is from Louisiana.
            $B_1 \supseteq H_1^{pref}$ = {Jack} $\rightsquigarrow H_1^{pref^{\cup}}$ = {Jack} $\rightsquigarrow HE$:= {Jack}

The preference complementation operation yields the correct unambiguous value of the stressed pronoun, $[[HE]]^o$, with no additional stipulations. A possible alternative to the CPH such as "rule out the most preferred value in H_1^{pref}" would not naturally extend to an account of unambiguous pronouns.

Recall the focus constraint $\sim F$ on stressed pronouns. The focus semantic value of *HE*, *F*, must have at least two members – the denotation of *HE* ($[[HE]]^o$) and at least one more contrasting individual. These contrasting individuals also instantiate contrasting propositions that discharge the focus constraint $\sim C$ on the utterance as a whole. Under the present proposal, *F* is the set of entities in the local attentional state, which is also presupposed for unstressed pronouns ($F = B = A^{LOC}$), so A^{LOC} must provide the contrasting individuals. The question is – are they always supplied from A^{LOC} rather than A?

The present account makes use of nested subsets of the entities in $A - H \subseteq B = A^{LOC} \subseteq A$. Our examples in this chapter indicate that these regions are all potential sources for the contrasting individuals. We have seen the following three sources for contrasting individuals:

•   Alternative values within $H \subseteq A^{LOC}$ – examples (1) and (3)
•   Individuals in A^{LOC} that are not possible values of the pronoun but belong to a common general class with the pronoun referent such as PERSON – example (9)[20]
•   Not found in A^{LOC} but potentially found in A – example (10)

I will discuss what may happen in the third case.

When A^{LOC} does not provide contrasting individuals, the focus constraint for the stressed pronoun $\sim F$ is satisfied by discharging the focus constraint on the utterance $\sim C$ by *accommodation* (Lewis 1979) into the input attentional state. For example, utterance U_2 with a stressed *HE* in both (9) and (10) generates the same focus constraint $\sim C$ – 'x is from Louisiana.' In (9), A^{LOC} contains the contrasting individual, Mary, and $\sim C$ is discharged by accommodating a contrasting presupposition 'Mary is not from Louisiana.' In (10), A^{LOC} does not contain contrasting individuals, and $\sim C$ is discharged by accommodating a question, *Who is from Louisiana?* This question presupposes other persons in the domain, and if no persons have been explicitly mentioned, a set of persons is implicitly accommodated into the current attentional state *A*. A more precise formulation of this process is left as a future task.

The present framework offers an explicit proposal about how the focus constraints at both the phrase and utterance levels are discharged within the nested structure of attentional state, and how contrasts are accommodated when presuppositions do not immediately follow from the explicit discourse.

6   Further Questions

There are a number of related questions, which I only note here.

- The local attentional state is supposed to be relevant only for utterance processing within a discourse segment. What happens to stressed and unstressed pronouns in a segment-initial utterance? More generally, how does the *discourse structure* affect pronoun interpretation?
- *Intrasentential* pronominal anaphora for both stressed and unstressed pronouns is widely studied in syntax (e.g., Akmajian and Jackendoff 1970, Lakoff 1976, Williams 1980, Lujan 1985, Hirschberg and Ward 1991). How does the present account relate to these syntactic facts? How does it extend to the pragmatics of intrasentential pronominal anaphora (e.g., Kameyama 1998)?

7   Conclusion

I have presented a unified account of interpretation preferences of stressed and unstressed pronouns in discourse. The central intuition is expressed as the Complementary Preference Hypothesis, taking the interpretation preference of the unstressed pronoun as the base from which to predict the interpretation preference of the stressed pronoun in the same discourse position. This base preference must be computed in a *total* pragmatics module including commonsense preferences. I have also made a concrete proposal for the pragmatically determined focus constraint in Rooth's theory of semantic focus. The salient subset of the domain in this proposal makes use of the dynamically updated local attentional state in the discourse context independently motivated for other purposes in Centering Theory. As a consequence, the overall discourse processing can unify the interpretation process for the two kinds of pronouns while explaining the source of the curious complementarity in their interpretation preferences.

Notes

1   Note that *it* cannot be stressed, and its stressed counterpart is *THAT*.
2   Centering Theory synthesizes previous work on discourse focusing (Grosz 1977, 1981), immediate focusing (Sidner 1979, 1983), and discourse centering (Joshi and Kuhn 1979, Joshi and Weinstein 1981).

3   Utterance U need not be a sentence in the standard syntactic sense. In fact, it is more natural to think of U as a tensed clause, allowing multiple intrasentential transitions within a complex sentence (see Kameyama 1998). This chapter focuses only on intersentential anaphora, however.

4   Indexical context is notably omitted here.

5   There are other highly salient entities that we are not considering in this chapter – for instance, the entities associated with the current discourse segment *purpose*, the old *Center* entities in the current discourse segment, and the entities realized by possible antecedents in the current utterance.

6   In the examples in this chapter, *realize* simply means *denote*, but it combines a variety of factors in a full account (see Grosz et al. 1995).

7   *Center* corresponds to "topic proper" in TFA (Sgall et al. 1986).

8   Both linguistic hierarchies are in fact recurrent in functional and typological studies of language. The GF ORDER closely resembles Keenan and Comrie's (1977) *accessibility hierarchy*, Givon's (1979) *topicality hierarchy*, and Kuno's (1987) *thematic hierarchy*, all of which predict the preferred syntactic structure for describing the things that a sentence is "mainly about" within and across languages. The EXP ORDER resembles the linguistic correlates of Gundel, Hedberg, and Zacharski's (1993) *givenness hierarchy*, which is closely related to Prince's (1981) *familiarity scale*, which predicts the relative *degrees* of accessibility of referents. It is of interest that virtually the same hierarchies are relevant to the computational interest in how grammar controls inferences in language use.

9   The distinction between stressed and unstressed pronouns in EXP ORDER in an earlier version (Kameyama 1994) has been removed because the ordering UNSTRESSED PRONOUN > STRESSED PRONOUN follows from the present independent account of stress.

10   I henceforth notate the relation *more-salient-than* with >, indeterminate salience ordering with <>, *preferred-over* with ≺, *weakly-preferred-over* with ≺?, and indeterminate preference ordering with ≺≻. Preferences in the subsequent examples come from the survey data discussed in Kameyama (1996).

11   The "highest-ranked type" in EXP CENTER can be interpreted as either relative to each utterance or absolute in all utterances. Under the relative interpretation, a nonpronominal expression type can also output the Center as long as there are no pronouns in the same utterance. Under the absolute interpretation, only the pronominals (either zero or overt, depending on the syntactic type of the language) can output the Center. I take the absolute interpretation in this chapter following Kameyama (1985, 1986), based on the rationale that the choice of the highest-ranked pronominal forms in a language should reflect a certain absolute sense of salience threshold.

12   *Chain* corresponds to what I have previously called *retain* . It covers both CONTINUE and RETAIN, distinguished in Grosz et al. (1986, 1995).

13   Discussions with Becky Passonneau helped clarify this point.

14   Under the present perspective, the proposal to distinguish between CONTINUE and RETAIN transitions (Grosz et al. 1986, 1995) focuses on the convergence of the highest-ranked GF (Cp) and the Center (Cb) in the *output* attentional state.

15   For a specific definition of parallelism, see, for example, Pruest (1992), Kameyama (1986).

16   See Jaspars and Kameyama (1998) for a model of discourse logic that incorporates the notion of preference classes.

17   The subset H_{i-1} was overlooked in the earlier formulation of the algorithm in Kameyama (1994).

18   Actually, this set can also be empty, in which case a plausible assumption is that an accommodation takes place and obtains an indexically salient entity.

19 The salience order controls this computation.
20 I assume a general sort hierarchy for the domain of individuals as proposed by, for example, Bosch (1988) and Prevost (1996), to compute the notion of *a common general class* under which a contrast is established.

References

Akmajian, Adrian, and Ray Jackendoff. 1970. Coreferentiality and Stress. *Linguistic Inquiry*, 1(1), 124–126.

Bosch, Peter. 1988. Representing and Accessing Focussed Referents. *Language and Cognitive Processes*, 3(3), 207–231.

Brennan, Susan, Lyn Friedman, and Carl Pollard. 1987. A Centering Approach to Pronouns. In *Proceedings of the 25th Annual Meeting of the Association for Computational Linguistics*, 155–162.

Givon, Talmy. 1979. *On Understanding Grammar*. Academic Press, New York.

Grosz, Barbara. 1977. The Representation and Use of Focus in Dialogue Understanding. Technical Report 151, SRI International, Menlo Park, Calif.

Grosz, Barbara. 1981. Focusing and Description in Natual Language Dialogues. In Joshi, Aravind, Bonnie Webber, and Ivan Sag, eds., *Elements of Discourse Understanding*. Cambridge University Press, Cambridge, 85–105.

Grosz, Barbara, Aravind Joshi, and Scott Weinstein. 1983. Providing a Unified Account of Definite Noun Phrases in Discourse. In *Proceedings of the 21st Meeting of the Association of Computational Linguistics*, 44–50.

Grosz, Barbara, Aravind Joshi, and Scott Weinstein. 1986. Towards a Computational Theory of Discourse Interpretation. Unpublished manuscript. [The final version appeared as Grosz et al. 1995.]

Grosz, Barbara, Aravind Joshi, and Scott Weinstein. 1995. Centering: A Framework for Modelling the Local Coherence of Discourse. *Computational Linguistics*, 21(2), 203–226.

Grosz, Barbara, and Candy Sidner. 1986. Attention, Intention, and the Structure of Discourse. *Computational Linguistics*, 12(3), 175–204.

Gundel, Jeanette, Nancy Hedberg, and Ron Zacharski. 1993. Cognitive Status and the Form of Referring Expressions in Discourse. *Language*, 69(2), 274–307.

Hirschberg, Julia, and Gregory Ward. 1991. Accent and Bound Anaphora. *Cognitive Linguistics*, 2(2), 101–121.

Jaspars, Jan, and Megumi Kameyama. 1998. Discourse Preferences in Dynamic Logic. In Aliseda, Atocha, Rob van Glabbeek, and Dag Westerståhl, eds., *Computing Natural Language*, CSLI Lecture Notes Number 81, CSLI Publications, CSLI, Stanford, Calif., 67–96.

Joshi, Aravind, and Steve Kuhn. 1979. Centered Logic: The Role of Entity Centered Sentence Representation in Natural Language Inferencing. In *Proceedings of International Joint Conference on Artificial Intelligence*, Tokyo, Japan.

Joshi, Aravind, and Scott Weinstein. 1981. Control of Inference: Role of Some Aspects of Discourse Structure – Centering. In *Proceedings of International Joint Conference on Artificial Intelligence*, Vancouver, Canada, 385–387.

Kameyama, Megumi. 1985. *Zero Anaphora: The Case of Japanese*. Ph.D. thesis, Stanford University.

Kameyama, Megumi. 1986. A Property-sharing Constraint in Centering. In *Proceedings of the 24th Annual Meeting of the Association for Computational Linguistics*, New York, 200–206.

Kameyama, Megumi. 1994. Stressed and Unstressed Pronouns: Complementary Preferences. In Peter Bosch and Rob van der Sandt, eds., *Focus and Natural Language Processing*. Institute for Logic and Linguistics, IBM, Heidelberg, 475–484.

Kameyama, Megumi. 1996. Indefeasible Semantics and Defeasible Pragmatics. In Kanazawa, Makoto, Christopher Piñon, and Henriëtte de Swart, eds., *Quantifiers, Deduction, and Context*. CSLI, Stanford, Calif., 111–138.

Kameyama, Megumi. 1998. Intrasentential Centering. In Marilyn Walker, Aravind Joshi, and Ellen Prince, eds., *Centering Theory in Discourse*, Oxford University Press, Oxford, 89–112.

Kameyama, Megumi, Rebecca Passonneau, and Massimo Poesio. 1993. Temporal Centering. In *Proceedings of the 31st Meeting of the Association of Computational Linguistics*, Columbus, Ohio, 70–77.

Keenan, Edward, and Bernard Comrie. 1977. Noun Phrase Accessibility and Universal Grammar. *Linguistic Inquiry*, 8(1), 63–100.

Kehler, Andrew. 1993. The Effect of Establishing Coherence in Ellipsis and Anaphora Resolution. In *Proceedings of the 31st Meeting of the Association of Computational Linguistics*, Columbus, Ohio, 62–69.

Kuno, Susumu. 1987. *Functional Syntax*, Chicago University Press, Chicago.

Lakoff, George. 1971. Presupposition and Relative Well-Formedness. In Danny Steinberg and Leon Jakobovits, eds., *Semantics: An Interdisciplinary Reader in Philosophy, Linguistics, and Psychology*. Cambridge University Press, Cambridge.

Lakoff, George. 1976. Pronouns and Reference. In James McCawley, ed., *Syntax and Semantics*, Vol. 7, Academic Press, New York, 275–335.

Lewis, David. 1979. Scorekeeping in a Language Game. *Journal of Philosophical Logic*, 8, 339–359.

Lujan, Marta. 1985. Stress and Binding of Pronouns. *Papers of the 21st Regional Meeting*, Chicago Linguistic Society, Chicago University, 248–262.

Nakatani, Christine. 1993. Accenting on Pronouns and Proper Names in Spontaneous Narrative. In *Proceedings of the ESCA Workshop on Prosody*, Lund, Sweden.

Prevost, Scott. 1996. An Information Structural Approach to Spoken Language Generation. In *Proceedings of the 34th Meeting of the Association of Computational Linguistics*, Santa Cruz, Calif., 294–301.

Prince, Ellen. 1981. Toward a Taxonomy of Given: New Information. In *Radical Pragmatics*. Academic Press, New York, 223–255.

Pruest, Hub. 1992. On Discourse Structuring, VP Anaphora and Gapping. Ph.D. thesis, University of Amsterdam.

Rooth, Mats. 1992. A Theory of Focus Interpretation. *Natural Language Semantics* 1(1), 75–116.

Rooth, Mats. 1993. A Hybrid Architecture for Focus. An invited lecture at the Nineth Amsterdam Colloquium.

Sgall, Petr, Eva Hajičová, and Jarmila Panevová. 1986. *The Meaning of the Sentence in its Semantic and Pragmatics Aspects*, Reidel, Dordrecht and Academia, Prague.

Sidner, Candace. 1983. Focusing in the Comprehension of Definite Anaphora. In M. Brady, and R. Berwick, eds., *Computational Models of Discourse*, MIT Press, Cambridge, Mass., 267–330.

Sidner, Candy. 1979. Towards a Computational Theory of Definite Anaphora Comprehension in English Discourse. Ph.D. thesis, Technical Report 537, Artificial Intelligence Laboratory, MIT.

Williams, Edwin. 1980. Remarks on Stress and Anaphora. *Journal of Linguistic Research*, 1(3).

17   Discourse Linking and Discourse Subordination

KJELL JOHAN SÆBØ

Abstract

Roberts (1989) described subordination phenomena in discourse, where covert restrictors of various quantifiers are somehow copied from prior representations. In connection with plural pronouns, Kamp and Reyle (1993) have proposed a construction rule that can provide the key to a more principled account of discourse subordination, on the basis of a formal analysis of discourse linking as suggested by Enç (1991). The result is a partial answer to a question asked by Partee (1993): How do implicit (parts of or all of) restrictive clauses get introduced into the semantic interpretation? The answer given here is, frequently not by way of accommodation, but through set anaphora and a general set description and reduction rule.

1   Introduction

Restrictive clause formation, or quantificational domain selection, is determined in part by syntax, in part by more pragmatic factors. As it appears, these factors include, on the one hand, *accommodation*, where the presupposition trigger in the nuclear scope may be phonological ("association with focus"), and on the other hand, what may be termed *linking*, where material from the context is incorporated into the restrictor. When this material is apparently inaccessible, we can speak of *subordination*. This chapter, unlike several other contributions to this volume, is concerned with the second form of nonsyntactical restrictive clause formation. The aim is to link recent approaches to three special forms of anaphoric connections with a view to a uniform picture of how material from the context enters into restrictive clauses of quantificational structures: implicit partitivity as defined by Enç (1991), dependent plural pronouns as analyzed by Kamp and Reyle (1993), and discourse subordination as described by Roberts (1989). Specifically, the intention is to develop a precise and general notion of "discourse linking", or specificity, two terms used by Enç to describe the context-dependency of the NP in the second sentence in a discourse like (1), and to apply it to the phenomena termed "discourse subordination" to indicate how the second sentence in a text like (2) is somehow subordinate to the first.

I wrote this as a member of the Oslo participation in the ÉSPRIT BRA project DYANA-2. I benefited from discussions with Trond Kirkeby-Garstad and Margrethe Sveinsdatter Skeie.

(1)   The Swedish team played remarkably well in the humid heat.
        Two attackers were particularly brilliant.

(2)   My mother surprisingly often wins something at bazaars.
        Mostly, it's a teddy bear.

The special context-dependency in the second sentence in (2) is underscored by the fact that the pronoun apparently has no accessible antecedent. Enç accounts for cases like (1) by defining a "specific sense" of noun phrases in terms of "second-order definiteness": The two attackers are required to form a subset of a contextually established set, in this case, the Swedish team. Now this analysis carries over naturally to the so-called pronominal use of determiners (Westerståhl 1985), as in (3). Note that the problem of pronoun resolution from (2) can occur with this use as well, as witnessed by (4).

(3)   The Swedish players did remarkably well in the humid heat.
        Two were particularly brilliant.

(4)   Several women won a teddy bear at the bazaar.
        Most handed it back.

So there is reason to try to develop the analysis of specificity in such a way that it can account for the apparently empty restrictor in the case of determiner quantification (*D-quantification*) as in (4) and in the case of adverb quantification (*A-quantification*) as in (2) alike. Set in DRT, the specificity analysis says that the restrictor in (3) or (4) is represented as $\langle\{u\}, \{u \in U\}\rangle$ where U is anaphoric. By itself, this does not yield a proper antecedent for the pronoun in (4). However, in their theory of plural anaphora Kamp and Reyle have proposed a rather special rule to take care of the anaphoric relationships in cases like (5).

(5)   Several women won a teddy bear at the bazaar.
        They all handed them back.

This rule specifies that when the restrictor of the distribution quantifier contains (just) a condition $u \in U$ where U is anaphoric on a set described in the context, that description can replace U and the resulting condition can be reduced. If this rule is generalized to cover any quantificational force and quantification over events, both *D-subordination* as in (4) and *A-subordination* as in (2) are accounted for in a rule-governed way.

The chapter consists of four further sections. In section 2, I review the analysis of (some) so-called strong readings of weak noun phrases proposed by Enç (1991), rephrase this concept of specificity in discourse representation theory, and relate it to the concept of context sets introduced by Westerståhl (1985), in particular to what he called the pronominal use of determiners. In section 3, I present the *Rule for distribution over a set obtained by Abstraction* proposed by Kamp and Reyle (1993) and show that a similar rule is relevant for all cases of specificity (discourse linking), including the pronominal use of determiners. In the core section 4, I extend the generalized rule to specificity uses of adverbs of quantification and show that this step from objects to events provides exactly an adequate analysis of the phenomena labeled *discourse subordination*. Also in this section, I discuss an interesting case of interaction between focus and subordination, and in a concluding section, I compare the two major nonsyntactical forms of restrictive clause formation, accommodation and linking.

2   Discourse Linking

There has been a renewed interest in the semantics of NPs, in particular, in Milsark's (1977) distinction between a weak and a strong reading of indefinite and cardinal NPs. Partee (1989), Enç (1991), de Hoop (1992), van Deemter (1992), and Diesing (1992) agree that such NPs have beside their weak reading a reading to be characterized as presuppositional, specific, partitive, anaphoric, or quantificational. Milsark noted that on the strong reading the sentence (6a) is "very nearly synonymous with" (6b). In this section, one approach to this and similar forms of implicit partitivity is assessed.

(6)   a.   Some salesmen walked in.
       b.   Some of the salesmen walked in.

2.1   Specificity According to Enç

Enç identifies a certain concept of **specificity** as the crucial characteristic of NP strength, referring to Pesetsky's (1987) notion of *D-linking* (D for discourse): Specifics require that their discourse referents be linked to previously established discourse referents. For the discourse (7a) to be coherent, the NP *two girls* must be read in the specific sense. This sense, Enç claims, is equivalent to the overt partitive construction in (7b).

(7)   a.   Several children entered my room. I knew two girls.
       b.   I knew two of the girls.

Though there is scarce evidence that in English, the specific sense constitutes a separate reading, in Turkish the distinction correlates with case, and even in English, the specific sense is impossible in *there* sentences. Accentuation is another structural constraint: As evident from the contrasts in (8), the specific-nonspecific alternation may correspond to distinct intonational patterns, specific noun phrases showing the characteristic contour of (sentence) topics. They probably count as 'links' in the theory of Vallduví (1992).

(8)   There was a knock at the door. Some SALESmen walked in.
       ? Several people were waiting at the door. Some SALESmen walked in.
       Several people were waiting at the door. Some SALESmen walked IN.

(On the role of intonation in relation to partitive readings, cf. Büring (this volume) and Jäger.) Apart from this, the situation in English resembles the situation in most Slavic languages, with no morphological distinction between definiteness and indefiniteness. And in fact, on Enç's formal analysis, set in an extended *file change semantics* where an NP carries a pair of referential indices, specificity is indirect definiteness, or second-order familiarity:

Specificity according to Enç:

Every $[_{NP}\,\alpha]_{\langle i,j\rangle}$ is interpreted as $\alpha(x_i)$ and
$x_i \subseteq x_j$ if $NP_{\langle i,j\rangle}$ is plural,
$\{x_i\} \subseteq x_j$ if $NP_{\langle i,j\rangle}$ is singular.
An NP is specific if and only if its second index is definite.

2.2 Specificity in Discourse Representation Theory

It is useful to rephrase this analysis of noun phrase specificity in DRT terms. This is straightforward as far as discourse referents are concerned, but in one respect the "second-index definiteness" formulation turns out to be too unspecific: We are faced with the choice of whether to represent the $\overline{N}$ constituent as a condition in the assertion or in the presupposition structure. In the latter case, the specific reading is exactly like the corresponding overt partitive, whereas in the former case, there is a slight difference between (7a) and (7b), the former asserting and the latter presupposing that there were girls (among the children entering). To maybe see the difference more clearly, consider (9), which seems to assert that the Shrove collection included etchings – there is no implication, as there would be with the corresponding overt partitive *some of the etchings*, that not all the etchings were particularly popular:

(9)   The Shrove collection fetched good prices at Sotheby's last Thursday. Some etchings were particularly popular.

On the other hand, if in a sentence like (6a) the noun *salesmen* is deaccented, it is probably better represented as a presupposed condition. Either way, the discourse referent for the specific noun phrase is required to be an element or a subset of a set introduced in the presupposition structure and thus, on an anaphoric account of presupposition as in van der Sandt (1992) or Sæbø (1996), to be identified with another set referent in the discourse. Choosing the former alternative, the assertion part of the second sentence in (7a) can be represented as follows:

$$\langle\{\zeta\}, \{\zeta = \Sigma y : \langle\{y\}, \{girl(y), y \in \xi, I\ knew\ y\}\rangle, |\zeta| = 2\}\rangle$$

The set referent ξ is introduced in the representation of the presupposition of the sentence, so that it must be mapped onto some previously introduced set referent, in this case, the one for the children entering my room.

Specific NPs pattern with strong NPs with regard to structural constraints like case marking in a language like Turkish or the "definiteness effect" in English (though not in Dutch, where even overt partitive NPs can occur in *"er"* constructions). And in fact, Enç regards any proportional NP as partitive ("all quantifiers are specific"). However, this is implausible in the face of discourses like (10), where the NP *"two boys"* in the second sentence is specific but the NP *"most boys"* in the third sentence is not.

(10)   Several children entered the museum. I saw two boys at the movies.
Most boys are bored by museums.

As it appears, the claim that quantificational NPs are inherently specific cannot be substantiated. The structural analogy between proportional and specific (including definite) NPs must be explained at another level. By the same token, some alleged "strong" senses of "weak" NPs seem not to be captured by the Enç notion, notably those triggered by individual-level predicates as in *Some dolphins are intelligent*, which, as pointed out by Abbott (1993), is appropriate in a discourse without a superset.

2.3   *The Pronominal Use of Determiners*

The notion of specificity under discussion is strongly reminiscent of the concept of *context sets* introduced by Westerståhl (1985) to describe how the domains of generalized quantifiers are typically narrowed down intersententially. The most striking instance of the phenomenon is the case of *bare determiners*. Westerståhl called the use of determiners witnessed in (11) the *pronominal* use. On the reasonable assumption that this corresponds to the specific reading of an NP with an empty $\overline{N}$, the empty restrictor of the quantifier is represented as $\langle \{y\}, \{y \in \xi\} \rangle$ where ξ is introduced in the presupposition structure.

(11)   (The park at Shrove was seriously damaged in the hurricane.
Many trees were destroyed.) Most were uprooted, while some were . . .

The assertion part of the sentence *Most were uprooted* could be represented as follows:

$$\langle \emptyset, \{most_y(\langle \{y\}, \{y \in \xi\}\rangle, \langle \emptyset, \{uprooted(y)\}\rangle)\} \rangle$$

Are bare determiners always anaphoric in the sense that the empty restrictor must be filled by a context set – is the pronominal use invariably definite? If so, there ought to be a reason, and it appears that the specific sense prevails with most determiners in English (but note the default 'people' set in cases like *Many are called, but few are chosen*). Now it is generally agreed that the sets denoted by the restrictors of strong determiners like *every* or *most* are presupposed to be nonempty (compare Partee 1989, where strong interpretations of weak noun phrases are attributed to a corresponding presupposition). Thus a sentence *Most*

Grieg symphonies have three movements presupposes that Grieg wrote some symphonies. This does not yet imply that the restrictors are anaphoric; as Abbott (1993) points out, there is a difference between presupposing the nonemptiness of the set and requiring the discourse existence of some group possessing the property. However, according to the theory of anaphoric presuppositions developed in Sæbø (1996), what happens when a presupposition involves a referent that does not act as a constant is that that referent acquires an anaphoric interpretation. This is due to the principle that the presupposition structure is proper (containing no free occurrences of referents) so the referent must be in the presupposition's universe, which is to say that it must be mapped to some previously introduced referent. And this is the case when the restrictor is zero, as in a sentence *Most have three movements*: The variable set referent in the nonemptiness condition must be in the presupposition's universe, the locus for anaphora. Such an explanation would apply to proportional quantifiers, where a tripartite structure with a nonemptiness presupposition associated with the restrictor is unproblematic, but not without qualification to cardinal or indefinite "quantifiers". For the time being, we have to say with Partee (1989) that there is a presuppositional interpretation available for noun phrases with such determiners (even in connection with stage-level predicates), often enough a specific interpretation, and the question remains why this interpretation seems to be systematically selected by bare determiners.

3 Set Description and Reduction in Discourse Representation Theory

In the theory of plural anaphora in Kamp and Reyle (1993), a plural antecedent can take two forms, both of which are relevant for the covert set anaphor involved in specificity:

- A referent introduced as a result of an (in)definite NP or the sum of such referents
- A referent introduced by abstraction on a duplex condition constructed from a (cardinality or proportional) quantifier

3.1 Abstraction

The crucial characteristic of the latter case is that the antecedent set referent, say ζ, is associated with a condition $\zeta = \Sigma y : \langle \{y, \ldots\}, \{\ldots\} \rangle$; that is, the referent is defined as the set of, say y, such that ....[1] The introduction of the referent ζ and its identification with the construct $\Sigma y : \langle \{y, \ldots\}, \{\ldots\} \rangle$ are the result of Abstraction on a duplex condition (or the direct result of construction on the basis of a cardinal NP, cf. Kamp and Reyle, pp. 452ff.). The rule of abstraction says (p. 344) that once a tripartite structure has been constructed from a sentence like (12), the two structures representing the restrictor and the scope may be merged into one structure K and a set referent S with a condition $S = \Sigma y{:}K$ may be introduced for any y in the universe of K.

(12)   Most paintings lost in the art robbery have been recovered.

In this case, Abstraction permits the construction of the set of paintings that have been recovered, and this set can serve as antecedent for a variety of overt and covert anaphors. The discourse can now continue with either one of, for instance, (13a–c), where (13a) contains a plural pronoun, (13b) a 'specific' full NP, and (13c) a bare determiner.

(13)   a. They are now stored in the basement.
         b. Two Munch pieces were purchased back.
         c. Several have suffered minor damage.

3.2   The Rule CR.DA

Now in order to account for the way the *"dependent plural"* pronoun *them* is resolved in a discourse like (14), Kamp and Reyle propose a special construction rule CR.DA, Rule for Distribution over a Set Obtained by Abstraction (p. 389).

(14)   Every director gave a present to a child from the orphanage.
         They opened them right away.

The problem is this. Abstraction on the basis of the first sentence provides both the set of children given a present by a director and the set of presents given to a child by a director, but the intended reading is not that all members of the former set opened some member of the latter set and that all members of the latter set were opened by some member of the former; rather, it is that the children opened their *respective* presents right away. This is accomplished by CR.DA. Informally, the rule prescribes what amounts to a set-theoretical reduction at DRS level: Whenever the restrictive clause of the distribution (*every*) operator has the form $\langle \{\,u\}, \{u \in U\}\rangle$ and U is identified by anaphoric resolution with a set referent Z identified by description, U may be replaced by the description of Z and the resulting condition $u \in \Sigma z{:}\langle \ldots \rangle$ may be reduced. In this way, the representation of *they* in (14) becomes the same as for "every child given a present by a director," so that the atomic present referent becomes accessible to the pronoun *them*.[2]

When a set is introduced via Abstraction over some duplex condition δ, then the information contained in the constituent DRSs of δ is available as information concerning the members of that set. This means that when we distribute over such a set, the DRS occurring on the right-hand side of the Abstraction equation may be "copied" into the left-hand DRS of the duplex condition which the distribution operation introduces. (p. 379)

3.3   *Generalizing CR.DA*

As it stands, the Rule for Distribution over a Set Obtained by Abstraction may seem very limited in scope. It is not obvious that its complexity is entirely justified by the problem it is designed to solve. But the ingredients of the rule may appear as less ad hoc if they can be shown to have a wider field of application. As I believe, the principle of set description and reduction in discourse representation is not necessarily so specialized as one is led to expect by CR.DA. This rule can be generalized to cover a range of problematic phenomena, ultimately that of "modal subordination". Note to begin with that a rule in the spirit of CR.DA is highly relevant not only for distribution in connection with plural pronouns, but also for specific (discourse-linked) NPs:

(15)   Every director gave a present to a child from the orphanage.
       Two boys opened it right away.

(16)   Most books contain a table of contents. In some, it is at the end.
       (Heim 1990)

This shows that Kamp and Reyle's CR.DA is too narrow in scope: The principle that a set referent S may be replaced by the description of S and the resulting condition $u \in \Sigma z : \langle \ldots \rangle$ may be reduced is not confined to distribution. (15) is an example of a specific full NP, and (16) is an example of a bare determiner. (15) resembles (14) closely, but whereas in (14) the condition $u \in U$, where U is anaphoric, is the only condition in the restrictor of the (universal) distribution quantifier applying to the set referent introduced by the anaphor *they*, in (15) it is an extra condition in the restrictor of the quantifier *two* in the specific noun phrase.[3] In (16), that condition is again the only condition in a restrictor, but this time the quantifier is the bare determiner *some* in its pronominal use. Let us focus on the steps in the construction of the representation for this discourse.[4] The first step is the construction of the duplex condition from the first sentence; the second is the application of Abstraction to form the set of books containing a table of contents:

(i) $\text{most}_x(\langle\{x\}, \{book(x)\}\rangle, \langle\{y\}, \{toc(y), x \text{ contains } y\}\rangle)$
(ii) $\zeta = \Sigma x : \langle\{x, y\}, \{book(x), toc(y), x \text{ contains } y\}\rangle$

The third and fourth steps are the construction of the preliminary representation for the second sentence and the resolution of the anaphoric set referent – its identification with the set referent previously introduced through Abstraction:

(iii) $\text{some}_z(\langle\{z\}, \{z \in \xi\}\rangle, \langle\emptyset, \{it \text{ is at the end in } z\}\rangle)$
(iv) $\text{some}_z(\langle\{z\}, \{z \in \zeta\}\rangle, \langle\emptyset, \{it \text{ is at the end in } z\}\rangle)$

The fifth step consists in the replacement of that set referent by its previous description inside the restrictor of condition (iv), and step (vi) consists in the reduction of the resulting condition, raising the referent y into the universe of the restrictor structure, and the resolution of the pronoun – its identification with the now accessible referent y:

(v) $some_z(\langle\{z\}, \{z \in \Sigma x:\langle\{x, y\}, \{book(x), toc(y), x \text{ contains } y\}\rangle\}\rangle,$
        $\langle\emptyset, \{it \text{ is at the end in } z\}\rangle)$
(vi) $some_z(\langle\{z, y\}, \{book(z), toc(y), z \text{ contains } y\}\rangle, \langle\emptyset, \{y \text{ is at the end in } z\}\rangle)$

4   Discourse Subordination

Beside modal subordination in the narrow sense, as in (17), Roberts (1989) treats "quantifier subordination," as in (16), in general, "discourse subordination," where the relevant operator may be a modal, a determiner, or a quantificational adverb, as in (18).

(17)   A thief might break into the house. He would take the silver.

(18)   Mary always wears a dress. Usually, it has polka dots. (Kratzer 1988)

In the formal theory developed here, where accommodation takes place at the DRS level of representation, the requirement under consideration might be expressed as a stipulation that if the accommodated material includes the antecedent of a pronoun in the modally subordinate clause, that material must be borrowed from a prior representation. (p. 705)

In each case, the second sentence in a discourse is interpreted as involving an operator (explicit or implicit) whose force is relativized so that it ranges only over the type of situation given in part by the first sentence. (p. 717)

This is the closest that Roberts in her 1989 paper comes to a precise formulation of the mechanisms underlying discourse subordination. However, a generalization of Kamp and Reyle's DRS set description and reduction rule coupled with a second-order definiteness analysis of (bare determiner) specific NPs can account for cases like (15) and (16) in an explicit way, as the last section was meant to show. And this section is meant to show that a further generalization can provide a fruitful basis for the analysis of cases like (18) as well. A *D-linking* analysis of "bare" adverbs of quantification, without overt restrictors, implies that whatever the adverb quantifies over be drawn from a familiar set, and once this set is identified, its description can be transferred to the restrictive clause to supply pronouns in the nuclear scope with proper antecedents.

4.1   *From Objects to Events*

On the face of it, matters look a bit more complicated with adverbs than with determiners: Possibly they quantify over tuples of various kinds of variables ("cases"), and in that case, one needs "unselective" versions of operations like abstraction. Possibly, however, it suffices to operate with event(uality) variables, as argued in de Swart (1993) and Skeie (1994). Let us look at how a case like (18) could be represented stepwise along the same lines as (16):

(i) $\text{every}_e(\langle\{e, y\}, \{\text{Mary}(x), e: x \text{ wears } y\}\rangle, \langle\varnothing, \{\text{dress}(y)\}\rangle)$

(ii) $\zeta = \Sigma e: \langle\{e, y\}, \{\text{Mary}(x), \text{dress}(y), e: x \text{ wears } y\}\rangle$

(iii) $\text{GEN}_\varepsilon(\langle\{\varepsilon\}, \{\varepsilon \in \xi\}\rangle, \langle\varnothing, \{\text{it has polka dots}\}\rangle)$

(iv) $\text{GEN}_\varepsilon(\langle\{\varepsilon\}, \{\varepsilon \in \zeta\}\rangle, \langle\varnothing, \{\text{it has polka dots}\}\rangle)$

(v) $\text{GEN}_\varepsilon(\langle\{\varepsilon\}, \{\varepsilon \in \Sigma e: \langle\{e, y\}, \{\text{Mary}(x), \text{dress}(y), e: x \text{ wears } y\}\rangle\}\rangle,$
       $\langle\varnothing, \{\text{it has polka dots}\}\rangle)$

(vi) $\text{GEN}_\varepsilon(\langle\{\varepsilon, y\}, \{\text{Mary}(x), \text{dress}(y), \varepsilon: x \text{ wears } y\}\rangle\},$
       $\langle\varnothing, \{y \text{ has polka dots}\}\rangle)$

The first line is the duplex condition constructed from the first sentence in the discourse. (It is assumed that adverbs of quantification quantify over events (or states), that this particular partition of the sentence is determined by focus, and that the scope of the quantifier is interpreted as a set of events in a verification condition.) The second line is (together with the introduction of the set referent ζ) the result of Abstraction on that duplex condition. The third and fourth lines are the duplex condition constructed from the second sentence, before and after resolution of the anaphoric set referent associated with the bare adverb of quantification. The fifth line is the result of substitution of the description of ζ for ζ in the restrictor, and the sixth line is the result of reduction in the restrictor and resolution of the pronoun in the scope made possible by that reduction.

The account of discourse subordination that suggests itself is based on two assumptions: First, a seemingly empty restrictor of a (determiner or adverb) quantifier over, say, u typically contains the condition $u \in U$ where U is anaphoric (and nonempty restrictors can contain this condition). Second, a generalization of Kamp and Reyle's rule CR.DA, like (i) Any set referent Z occurring in a condition can be replaced by $\Sigma z:\langle\ldots\rangle$ given a condition of the form $Z = \Sigma z:\langle\ldots\rangle$; (ii) any condition $u \in \Sigma z:\langle\ldots\rangle$ can be reduced so that u replaces z and $\langle\ldots\rangle$ is merged with the structure where the condition occurs.

Such an account predicts that discourse subordination[5] is only possible when there is a quantifier licensing a condition $u \in U$ and this anaphoric U has an antecedent Z acting as a constant: $Z = \Sigma z:\langle\ldots\rangle$. This means that both the "superordinate" and the "subordinate" clauses (corresponding to the first and second sentences in the discourses considered) must have a quantifier structure, though not necessarily a tripartite one; cardinality quantifier structures provide both a proper antecedent and a proper environment for a $\in$ condition. The relevant quantifier in either clause may be that of distribution; compare (4) and (14). And a $\in$ condition can be licensed by a singular NP (although not strictly a quantifier) in its specific sense – compare (19) – as by an adverb like *once* – compare (20).

(19)   Every director gave a present to a child from the orphanage.
        One boy opened it right away.

(20)   Harvey courts a girl at every convention. Once she came to the banquet with him.

As for modal subordination proper, compare (17), where the quantifier quantifies over possible worlds, world and world set referents are required, the latter representing propositions, in such a way that the set of worlds such that a thief breaks in can be added to the conversational background for the zero antecedent counterfactual operator *would*.

4.2   Telescoping and Conditionals

Thus an account of discourse subordination in terms of set anaphora and set reduction provides an explanation for Roberts's (1989:717) descriptive generalization that "in each case, the second sentence in a discourse is interpreted as involving an operator (explicit or implicit)." There must be something in the second sentence to license a $\in$ condition. In particular, it is predicted that so-called telescoping, where a simple sentence is somehow understood as involving an implicit universal quantifier, is in principle constrained. The nature of the constraints is not well understood, but it seems that the sentence in question must describe a man-made rule and not just an accidental generalization:

(21)   Harvey courts a girl at every convention.
    a.   He takes her to the banquet.
    b.   ? She comes to the banquet with him.

Now implicit universal quantifiers are unproblematic in connection with conditionals. It is commonly assumed that an *if* clause serves to restrict some quantifier in the main clause, and when this quantifier is not overt, it is by default universal (*always* or *must*). Thus (21c) is in order, where the abstracted information from the first sentence is merged with the representation of the *if* clause, supplying the pronoun with an antecedent.

(21)   c.   Harvey courts a girl at every convention.
        If she's from Iowa, she comes to the banquet with him.

4.3   Subordination without Abstraction

Sometimes the antecedent for the set anaphor in a restrictor is a set formed from the restrictor, not the merge of the restrictor and the nuclear scope, of a given quantificational structure. This is particularly evident in cases of narrow, contrastive focus, like:[6]

(22)   a.   Mary usually drives a RED car. But sometimes it is blue.

Informally, the antecedent for the pronoun in the second clause is not the red car Mary drives but just the car Mary drives. Note the oddity of the version where the noun *car* in the first clause is not deaccented:

(22)   b.   ? Mary usually drives a RED CAR. But sometimes it is blue.

On standard assumptions about focus and semantic partition, in (22a) the restrictor for *usually* is *Mary drives a car*, whereas in (22b) it is just *Mary drives* (or, depending on context, *Mary goes to work* or the like). Evidently, in (22a), the restrictor supplied for *sometimes* is *not* the result of Abstraction on the restrictor and scope from the first clause, but just the restrictor from the first clause. It seems that with a monotone decreasing quantifier like *rarely*, there is a strong tendency not to use Abstraction – compare (23a, b) – but also that this tendency can be overridden in the presence of a suitable discourse relation, such as Explanation; compare (23c).

(23)   a. ? Mary rarely bets on a harness horse. It is always an outsider.
        b. Mary rarely bets on a harness horse. If she does, it is always an outsider.
        c. Mary rarely bets on a harness horse. It always gallops.

5   Subordination versus Accommodation

Roberts (1989) described discourse subordination as a form of accommodation, largely induced by pronouns in the subordinate sentence in need of antecedents. On this view, subordination is a special case of the more general phenomenon characterized by Partee (1993) thus: "Some non-overt material appears to be 'accommodated into' the restrictor clause, typically by virtue of being presupposed by something in the nuclear scope." However, on the view of anaphora as presuppositions (van der Sandt 1992), accommodation of a pronoun is considered to consist in the creation of a novel referent and to be practically impossible because pronouns have next to no descriptive content. And in fact, on the account outlined, discourse subordination does not appear as a repair strategy but as a regular form of context-dependency, composed of independently motivated mechanisms: set anaphora, set abstraction, set description, and set reduction. The term accommodation ought to be reserved for those cases where what is "filled into" the restrictor is predictable from the scope context-independently, as in (24), where the restrictor is the presupposition of the scope.

(24)   Hans always answers the phone.

Berman (1991) proposed that the presuppositions of the nuclear scope are accommodated into the restrictor, and if, as considered by Rooth (this volume), the focus constraint is interpreted as an existential presupposition on a par with clefts – compare (25a, b) – semantic partition by association with presupposition and by association with focus can be predicted as instances of the general mechanism of intermediate accommodation in the sense of van der Sandt (1992).

(25)   a. Mary always takes JOHN to the movies.
        b. It is always John that Mary takes to the movies.

However, it has been argued by von Fintel (1994) and, with regard to focus and nominal quantifiers (compare Eckardt [this volume]), by de Hoop and Solà (1995) and Büring (this volume) that focus or presupposition does not affect quantification directly but only indirectly insofar as both the former and the quantifier depend on a discourse antecedent. Similar ideas are pursued by Roberts (1995). On this view, (nonsyntactical) restrictive clause formation is invariably a case of discourse linking. Many cases involve subordination, in the sense that the discourse antecedent is apparently inaccessible, calling for some process of Abstraction.

Summing up, it has been shown that the machinery developed by Kamp and Reyle to give a complete description of plural anaphora can by way of the Enç notion of specificity be generalized to give a precise description of how, in Roberts's terms, material including antecedents for pronouns is borrowed from prior representations. Such a generalization provides a broader motivation for the special distribution rule of Kamp and Reyle and at the same time explicates discourse subordination as a formal procedure. However, it may be felt that the description is overly explicit. It is a central tenet in DRT that any anaphor should be supplied with an accessible antecedent, and if this is upheld, the proposed account is on the right track. But there may be reasons of a more general nature for preferring a less representational approach, maybe along the lines drawn up by Heim (1990). And in fact, there may well be data that after all cannot be handled by the machinery invoked in this chapter, like (26), which does not seem to pose a corresponding problem for an 'E-type' approach.

(26)   Most books contain a table of contents.
         In *War and Peace*, it is at the end.

Notes

1   Actually, in model theory, Kamp and Reyle do not treat plural entities as sets but as nonatoms in a lattice structure. But as far as representations are concerned, they use set terminology for convenience.

2   Note that the result of the rule is in all interesting cases a duplex condition with an indirect binding structure: *Every child given a present opened it* is a donkey sentence. In Kamp and Reyle, although the *donkey* referent in the restrictor is an accessible antecedent for the pronoun in the scope, the determiner quantifies over the *farmer* referent only, and the proportion problem is deferred to the model theory.

3   This cardinal quantifier does not necessarily impose a tripartite structure; if the second sentence in (15) is represented directly as a cardinality structure, the condition $u \in U$ is an extra condition in the description of the set of cardinality two of boys opening *it* right away.

4   It should be said that if *some* is construed as an indefinite NP (compare Kamp and Reyle 1993:332 ff.), the adaptation of the rule is not so straightforward; however, a quantificational structure is perhaps not implausible for this "strong reading" *some* phrase.

5   In the loose sense of material including the antecedent of a pronoun being borrowed from a prior representation.

6   This phenomenon was brought to my attention by David Beaver.

References

Abbott, B. 1993. "Referentiality, specificity, strength, and individual concepts," West Coast Conference on Formal Linguistics 12.

Berman, S. 1991. On the Semantics and Logical Form of Wh-Clauses. Dissertation, University of Massachusetts, Amherst.

Deemter, K. van 1992. "Towards a generalization of anaphora," *Journal of Semantics* 9, 27–51.

Diesing, M. 1992. *Indefinites*. Cambridge, Mass.: MIT Press.

Enç, M. 1991. "The semantics of specificity," *Linguistic Inquiry* 22, 1–25.

Fintel, K. von 1994. *Restrictions on Quantifier Domains*. Dissertation, University of Massachusetts, Amherst.

Heim, I. 1990. "E-type pronouns and donkey anaphora," *Linguistics and Philosophy* 13, 137–177.

Hoop, H. de 1992. Case Configuration and Noun Phrase Interpretation. Dissertation, University of Groningen.

Hoop, H. de, and J. Solà 1995. "Determiners, context sets, and focus," West Coast Conference on Formal Linguistics 14.

Kamp, H., and U. Reyle 1993. *From Discourse to Logic*. Dordrecht: Kluwer.

Kratzer, A. 1988. "Stage-level and individual-level predicates," paper presented at the Tübingen workshop on genericity. Published in G. Carlson and F. Pelletier (eds.) *The Generic Book*. Chicago: The University of Chicago Press, 1995.

Milsark, G. 1977. "Toward an explanation of certain peculiarities of the existential construction in English," *Linguistic Analysis* 3, 1–29.

Partee, B. 1989. "Many quantifiers," Eastern States Conference on Linguistics, 5, 383–402.

Partee, B. 1993. "Towards a typology of quantificational constructions," paper presented at the 9th Amsterdam Colloquium.

Pesetsky, D. 1987. "Wh-in-Situ: Movement and unselective binding," in E. Reuland and A. ter Meulen (eds.) *The Representation of (In)definiteness*. Cambridge, Mass.: MIT Press.

Roberts, C. 1989. "Modal subordination and pronominal anaphora in discourse," *Linguistics and Philosophy* 12, 683–721.

Roberts, C. 1995. "Domain restriction in dynamic semantics," E. Bach, E. Jelinek, A. Kratzer, and B. Partee (eds.) *Quantification in Natural Languages* Vol. II. Dordrecht: Kluwer.

Sæbø, K. 1996. "Anaphoric presuppositions and zero anaphora," *Linguistics and Philosophy* 19.2, 187–209.

Sandt, R. van der 1992. "Presupposition projection as anaphora resolution," *Journal of Semantics* 9, 333–377.

Skeie, M. 1994. Eventer og kvantifikasjon. Om å analysere kvantifikasjonsadverb som kvantorer over eventer. Thesis, University of Oslo.

Swart, H. de 1993. *Adverbs of Quantification: A Generalized Quantifier Approach*. New York: Garland.

Vallduví, E. 1992. *The Informational Component*. New York: Garland.

Westerståhl, D. 1985. "Determiners and context sets," in J. van Benthem and A. ter Meulen (eds.) *Generalized Quantifiers in Natural Language*. Dordrecht: Foris.

18   Position and Meaning: Time Adverbials in Context

HENRIËTTE DE SWART

Abstract

This chapter develops an interpretation of phrasal and clausal time adverbials in a discourse theory without reference times. Since Reichenbach (1947), it has been assumed that these expressions give the reference time of the sentence. I argue that theories that incorporate this Reichenbachian view are inadequate because they do not account for the difference in meaning between preposed and postponed time adverbials. In narrative discourse, this is a pragmatic contrast related to topic/focus structure. Truth-conditional meaning effects arise under quantification. The analysis I develop here builds on work by Lascarides and Oberlander (1993a, b) and Lascarides and Asher (1991, 1993a, b). The key to the interpretation of time adverbials resides in recognizing their presuppositional character, which allows them to be anchored to the time axis without being dependent on the rhetorical structure of the local context.

1   Topic/Focus Structure in Narrative Discourse

1.1   *Background*

Kamp and Rohrer (1983), Hinrichs (1981, 1986), and others have shed new light on the interpretation of tense morphemes, aspectual class, and time adverbials by going beyond the sentence level and focusing on the way these expressions constrain temporal relations in discourse. These approaches follow the Reichenbachian tradition and distinguish among S(peech time), R(eference time), and E(vent time). In narrative texts, the unfolding of the story often corresponds with the feeling of progress in time. One way to handle this moving on in time is to assume that reference times progress with the story line. Compare:

(1)   a. John bought a one-way ticket, hopped on the bus, and bought himself a new pair of shoes.

          b. He went to the window and pulled aside the soft drapes. It was a casement window, and both panels were cranked out to let in the night air.

The research for this chapter was supported by a fellowship from the Royal Netherlands Academy of Arts and Sciences (KNAW), which is hereby gratefully acknowledged. Thanks, to the audiences of the ITK colloquium (Tilburg), the discourse colloquium (Amsterdam), and the workshop on focus and natural language processing (Kassel) for helpful discussion.

All sentences are interpreted with respect to the current reference time in order to fit in with the event structure built up by the discourse so far. This is referred to as the anaphoric nature of independent clauses. Hinrichs proposes that each new past-tense event sentence occurs within the then-current reference time. It subsequently causes the reference time to shift to a new value, later than the original one. The new value of the reference time becomes the current one for the next sentence of the discourse to be processed. States, activities, and sentences in the progressive are required to include the current reference time. Unlike events, states do not shift the reference time to a later time. This accounts for the "dynamics" of event sentences, which carry on the main story line (1a), and it contrasts with the "stative" nature of (1b).

Of course there are also explicit indicators of temporal structure, such as time adverbials. Kamp and Rohrer (1983) and Hinrichs (1981, 1986) assume with Reichenbach (1947) that the function of phrasal and clausal time adverbials is to provide the reference time of the main clause.[1] A stative sentence normally describes a condition prevalent at the time indicated by the reference time given by the preceding context, but it need not do so when the sentence contains its own adverb of temporal location, as in (2), where the time of dying does not overlap with having a drink and going to bed:

(2)   The doctor came home and found his wife waiting for him. They had a drink and went to bed. The next morning, she was dead.

If tense is always anaphoric, a time adverbial is required in cases where the preceding context fails to provide any reference point at all. An example is the first sentence of the discourse. Actually, Kamp and Rohrer point out that it is not uncommon for a story to begin without an adverb of temporal location. They describe this as a stylistic device, which accommodates the presupposition that there be a reference time to which the event or state introduced by the sentence can be anchored. This evokes in the reader a sense of "already being part of the narrative."[2] As an example, Kamp and Rohrer cite the famous opening line of Gustave Flaubert's *Madame Bovary* (3):

(3)   Nous étions à l'étude, quand le Proviseur entra, suivi d'un *nouveau* habillé en bourgeois et d'un garçon de classe qui portait un grand pupitre. 'We were in the preparation room when the head came in followed by a new one dressed in bourgeois clothes, and a school servant carrying a large desk.'

It is rather surprising that Kamp and Rohrer present (3) as an example of an unanchored opening line if time adverbials are supposed to always provide the reference time. (3) contains a so-called "narrative" *when*-clause: the effect is that "suddenly" something happens within the context given by the stative main clause. This interpretation only arises with postponed *when*-clauses, suggesting that the position of time adverbials and temporal clauses is not irrelevant to their interpretation. As we will see, this is not an isolated example. There is a systematic correlation between the position and the meaning of the time adverbial. The question how to analyze these data in a dynamic theory of temporal structure is the subject of investigation of the present chapter.

1.2   *Position and Meaning*

In Hinrichs's system the Reichenbachian assumption that a frame adverbial provides the reference time for the main clause is made explicit by the indexing mechanism. At any point in the processing of the discourse, the sentence with the lowest index is interpreted next. Any sentence receives a higher index than any preceding sentence and a lower index than any following sentence. Frame adverbials and temporal clauses receive an index that is lower than the index of the sentence they modify. This guarantees that the time adverbial is processed before the main clause. A time adverbial introduces its own reference point, so it overrides the current reference time produced by the discourse so far. This creates a "break" in the narrative structure: we can "jump" to a time that is not the time where we "were" in the previous discourse (compare Example 2). The main clause it modifies is anaphoric in the same way an independent clause is, so it is interpreted with respect to the current reference time as usual. As a result, it is automatically interpreted as dependent on the reference time introduced by the time adverbial. As far as preposed time adverbials are concerned, this seems to be an unproblematic assumption. But if we take a closer look at preposed and postponed time adverbials, we realize that there are subtle differences in meaning, which are not captured by this analysis:

(4)   a. At six o'clock, Jane left.
        b. Jane left at six o'clock.

Considered in isolation, (4a) and (4b) describe the same facts, namely, that there is a time interval described as six o'clock and there is an event of Jane's leaving and the two overlap in time. Yet, there are differences at the level of topic/focus structure that come out if we embed the sentences in a larger context. (4a) can answer the question "What happened at six o'clock?" (4b) can also answer this question, especially with the right intonation pattern. But (4b) can also be an appropriate answer to the question "When did Jane leave?" (4a) is not a preferred answer to this question. In (4a), the main clause is interpreted in an event structure enriched with the information conveyed by the time adverbial. (4b) can, but need not, be interpreted in this way. If the "old" information is provided by the main clause and the "new" information by the time adverbial, (4b) provides a more precise location in time for the event of Jane's leaving. Assuming that main clauses are anaphoric in nature, we expect the main clause in (4b) to be dependent for its location in time on the previous discourse, rather than the time adverbial. This correlates with the observation that there is no "break" in narrative structure; compare

(5)   a. Bill went home, had dinner, and left again to go to the meeting.
        b. Bill came home at six o'clock and left again at seven. The inspector did not get there until eight.

In the absence of a time adverbial, the exact time at which the events take place remains vague (5a). Gricean maxims about informativeness guarantee that this is not a problem: knowing that an event is located shortly after the preceding one will usually be sufficient for the coherence of the discourse. But for other purposes (e.g., a detective story), the more specific information may be required. This typically leads to a discourse like (5b): further specification of the location time of the event is realized by means of postponed time adverbials. These meaning effects play an even more prominent role in negative sentences:

(6)   a. At three o'clock, the bomb didn't explode.
        b. The bomb didn't explode at three o'clock.

(6a) only allows for a reading in which the time adverbial is outside the scope of negation: what happened at three o'clock was that the bomb didn't explode (although it had been programmed to do so; what had gone wrong?). This is in accordance with the Reichenbachian analysis: if the time adverbial provides the reference time, it takes wide scope over any operators present in the main clause. This interpretation is represented in (7a):[3]

(7)   a. $\exists t$ [Three o'clock$(t) \land \neg \exists e$ [Explode(the bomb, $e) \land t \circ T(e)$]]
        b. $\exists e$ [Explode(the bomb, $e) \land \neg \exists t$ [Three o'clock$(t) \land T(e) \circ t$]]
        c. $\neg \exists e$ [Explode(the bomb, $e) \land \exists t$ [Three o'clock$(t) \land T(e) \circ t$]]

(6b) allows for the interpretation spelled out in (7a) as well, but there is another reading in which the time adverbial is under the scope of negation: the bomb exploded, but this didn't happen at three o'clock (7b). In (7b), the time adverbial does not provide the reference time for the main clause, and this reading is not generated by (a straightforward extension of) Hinrichs's rules. The representations in (7a) and (7b) can be viewed as different ways to spell out the more general representation in (7c). The semantic scope of negation is the entire proposition, but its pragmatic scope is the part of the sentence that is in focus. Negation bears just on the main clause in (6a), and on the time adverbial in the relevant reading of (6b). The part of the sentence that is not in focus constitutes the background. This information is presupposed to be true and is outside the (pragmatic) scope of negation (cf. Horn 1989:504–528).

The adverb *even* is another expression that is sensitive to the position of the time adverbial:

(8)   a. After midnight, Julia even drinks vodka.
        b. Julia even drinks vodka after midnight.

Even carries a scalar presupposition concerning likelihood. In (8a), the unlikely thing happening is that Julia drinks vodka (and not something lower on the scale like juice or beer). In the relevant reading of (8b), it is Julia's drinking of the vodka after midnight that is unexpected.

Similar observations can be made with respect to clausal time adverbials:

(9)   a. When I was in the kitchen I heard a strange noise.
       b. I heard this strange noise when I was in the kitchen.

(9a) answers the question "What happened when you were in the kitchen?" (9b) can answer the same question but is also appropriate in response to "When did you hear this strange noise?" Again, the effect of position on the meaning of the construction is stronger with negation and *even*:

(10)   a. When Bill left the house, he didn't turn off the stove.
       b. Bill didn't turn off the stove when he left the house.

(11)   a. After Julia has had a glass of wine, she even sings Beatles songs.
       b. Julia even sings Beatles songs before she has had a glass of wine.

The preposed temporal clause in (10a) provides the reference time for the main clause and takes wide scope over negation. (10b) is ambiguous. In addition to the interpretation (10a) has, it allows a reading in which Bill did turn off the stove, but not when he left the house. In this reading of (10b), the subordinate clause is under the scope of the negation, and it does not provide the reference time for the main clause. In (11a), it is Julia's starting to sing Beatles songs that comes as a surprise. In the relevant reading of (11b), the unexpected fact is that her singing takes place before she has had a glass of wine.

The difference in behavior between preposed and postponed time adverbials is rooted in the syntax. Postponed time adverbials and temporal clauses are PPs, which modify the VP, so the sentence-final position is their basic position (Emonds 1985). Preposing of a phrase often has the semantic effect of topicalization (Kuno 1972). The topic is "what the sentence is about" (Reinhart 1982). If preposed time adverbials are topicalized, they provide the temporal frame for the main clause, which means in the current terminology that they provide the reference time. In the case of postponed time adverbials, what is "old" and what is "new" information is not just determined by the syntactic structure of the sentence. Focus comes into play and a wider range of interpretations becomes available.

The meaning effects are stronger with negation and *even*, because these expressions are sensitive to focus and operate on the part of the sentence that constitutes the background to the focused element. A constituent that is topicalized is not readily interpreted as itself being in focus (cf. Partee 1991 and Vallduví 1992 for insightful discussion of the relations between focus/background and topic/comment). Instead, it is normally part of the background of the focus. As a result, the preposed, topicalized time adverbial naturally ends up outside rather than inside the (pragmatic) scope of negation. In this way, we can explain why negated sentences with preposed time adverbials such as (6a) and (10a) do not have the same broad range of interpretations as sentences with postponed ones like (6b) and (10b). Similarly, a focusing adverb like *even* does not associate with a preposed time adverbial in cases like (8a) and (11a), implying that we need to postpone the time adverbial if we want to focus on the unexpectedness of the location in time of the event described by the main clause.

It is not clear how to accommodate these facts in a Reichenbachian theory. Hinrichs's indexing mechanism forces the time adverbial to provide the reference time for the main clause, but in cases where the adverb is postponed, this is not necessarily the right interpretation. Moreover, the combination of this indexing mechanism with the general phenomenon of association with focus only generates the interpretation in which the time adverbial is part of the background. Because the time adverbial is processed prior to the main clause, it automatically gives "old" information that the "new" information provided by the main clause anchors to. This makes it impossible to generate the reading in which the time adverbial is in focus, and under the pragmatic scope of negation (6b, 19b) or *even* (8b, 11b). Of course we could try to modify Hinrichs's analysis. Hornstein (1990) argues that preposed time adverbials systematically introduce a new reference time, whereas postponed adverbials may in addition be interpreted as event modifiers. The contrasts discussed then come out as an ambiguity in the interpretation of postponed time adverbials. Bertinetto (1985) claims that there is not just one notion of reference time, but that we should introduce additional, more or less related notions. I am not convinced that a proliferation of interpretation mechanisms and reference times really helps us understand what is going on, though. I am even less convinced that these solutions extend to all the relevant instances of temporal clauses.

1.3 Temporal Clauses

Phrasal and clausal time adverbials are closely related expressions. There are some obvious differences, though. Unlike phrasal adverbials, clausal adverbials do not give the time reference directly on the time axis, but indirectly, namely, with respect to some other state of affairs. But the location in time of this event is again independent of the current reference time and is recoverable from the general linguistic context: temporal clauses presuppose their event (Heinämäki 1978). Clausal time adverbials come with tense and aspect, and there are differences between stative and event sentences. As far as clauses introduced by *when* are concerned, Heinämäki (1978) observes that the intervals or moments denoted by accomplishments and achievements are included in the intervals referred to by durative sentences (12b–e). Two durative sentences overlap (12a), and two accomplishments happen in succession (12f):

(12) a. It was raining in New Orleans when we were there.
       b. Everybody was away when John destroyed the documents.
       c. They built the wall when bricks were still very cheap.

  d. The balloon broke when Lydia was playing with it.
  e. We were crossing the street when John noticed us.
  f. When John wrecked the car, Bill fixed it.

Heinämäki's judgments of (12a–d) are generally accepted. Note that (12e), which contains a narrative *when*-clause, is unproblematic in Heinämäki's theory, because the only prediction made is that we get a relation of temporal overlap, which seems correct. The claim that two events related by *when* happen in succession has been challenged. Hinrichs provides examples like (13) to support his claim that two event sentences related by *when* can occur in any order:

(13) a. John broke his arm when he wrecked the Pinto.
      b. John built a boat when Bill wrote a novel.
      c. When the Smiths moved in, they threw a party.
      d. When the Smiths threw a party, they invited all their old friends.

According to Hinrichs, the events in (13a, b) are understood as happening simultaneously. In (13c), the event in the main clause is perceived as following the event of the *when*-clause, while (13d) is a mirror image of (13c). This argument has been refuted, as sending out invitations could be interpreted as part of what it is to throw a party (Moens and Steedman, 1988). Moreover, as Partee (1984) points out, such relations obtain between simple sentences as well. So the typical characteristic of *when*-clauses is that they update the reference time, but otherwise *when* remains neutral as to the temporal relation established between the two clauses.

I share Partee's opinion about the role of the subordinate clause insofar as preposed temporal clauses are concerned (13c, d), but her analysis leaves part of the meaning of postponed *when*-clauses unexplained. For instance, the treatment of temporal clauses as providing the reference time does not handle narrative *when*-clauses (12e). Now, we could try to extend Partee's analysis and claim that in postponed *when*-clauses as well as in preposed ones, the relations between the two clauses are just those that govern normal narrative discourse. (12e) would then be accounted for: there is an event happening that is set against the background of a state. Problems would arise in other cases, though. We would predict that the two events related by *when* in (13a) and (13b) describe a sequence of events in which the event of the subordinate clause actually follows the one of the main clause. But this is not what we find: the temporal relation expressed is simultaneity, and in general simultaneity between two events tends to be expressed with postponed, rather than preposed temporal clauses. One might think that the preference for a simultaneity reading is a coincidence of the context in (13a, b), but it is more general than that. Neither preposed nor postponed *when*-clauses express a succession of events in which the event described by the subordinate clause follows the main clause event, even if this is strongly suggested by world knowledge. Compare

(14) a. When the president asked who would support him, Jill raised her hand.
      b. Jill raised her hand when the president asked who would support him.

c. When Jill raised her hand, the president asked who would support him.

d. The president asked who would support him when Jill raised her hand.

e. The president asked who would support him. Jill raised her hand.

(14a) describes the two events as happening in succession: Jill's raising of her hand is interpreted as a response to the president's request for support. The preferred interpretation of (14b) is the same as that of (14a). But there is an alternative interpretation available in which Jill raises her hand just at the moment at which the president asks who would support him. Under this reading there is no causal relation between the two actions. Note that we do not locate the request for support in (14b) after the raising of the hand. But then there is a strong causal connection telling us that the succession relation is the other way around. (14c) gives us the mirror image of (14a): although it is a bit harder to imagine a causal relation, the main clause event is located shortly after the event described by the subordinate clause. The puzzle is (14d). If two events related by *when* could describe the two events as happening in succession independently of subordination, then we would predict that we locate Jill's raising of her hand after the president's request for support, just as in the sequence of two independent sentences in (14e). There is also a strong causal relation between the two events that would support this temporal ordering. Nevertheless, it is not something (14d) can express. So *when* is not neutral concerning the temporal relation between the two clauses when it is postponed.

The picture that arises is that preposed temporal clauses give the reference time for the main clause event. Postponed clauses can have this function as well, but they can also be interpreted after the discourse representation has been enriched with the information conveyed by the main clause. Narrative *when*-clauses such as (12e) illustrate the discourse effects this can have. On the other hand, examples like (14d) show that postponed temporal clauses do not yield the full range of discourse relations a sequence of independent clauses allows for (14e). This puzzle proves hard to solve within a Reichenbachian theory. Modifications to Hinrichs's approach, such as the analyses proposed by Hornstein (1990) or Bertinetto (1985), treat postponed temporal clauses as event modifiers, but this by itself does not explain why event-modifying *when* induces temporal overlap, whereas reference-time-providing *when* allows for a broader range of temporal relations. Moreover, an analysis of postponed subordinate clauses as event modifiers is inadequate for the narrative *when*-clause in (12e). At this point, a unified analysis of these data within a Reichenbachian perspective is not in sight.

2   Truth-Conditional Meaning Effects

One might object that the meaning effects related to position we have observed so far are subtle and pragmatic in nature. Hamann (1989) claims that the uses of postponed temporal clauses that are problematic for the view that they provide the reference time (in particular the narrative *when*-clauses) are exceptional and can be left out of the core theory of temporal reference. But if it is true that the postponed adverbials constitute the basic case, and the more restricted range of interpretations associated with preposed time adverbs and temporal clauses is explained as an effect of topicalization, then such a position is untenable. Even so, it would be nice if we could strengthen the discourse effects to truth-conditional meaning differences. The way to do that is to consider embedding under a semantic operation like quantification.

2.1   *Phrasal Time Adverbials*

If sentence-initial time adverbs are topics that always provide old information with respect to the main clause they modify, we expect them to take wide scope over semantic operators present in the main clause. If postverbal time adverbials can fulfill two different roles, depending on topic/focus structure, they should participate in scope ambiguities. This prediction is borne out:

(15)   a.   On a beautiful Sunday in spring, every student on campus went hiking in the foothills.

       b.   Every student on campus went hiking in the foothills on a beautiful Sunday in spring.

(16)   a. $\exists t\ [\text{Sunday}(t) \wedge \forall x\ [\text{Student}(x) \rightarrow \exists e\ [\text{Hiking}(x, e)\ \wedge t \circ T(e)]]]$

       b. $\forall x\ [\text{Student}(x) \rightarrow \exists e\ [\text{Hiking}(x, e) \wedge \exists t\ [\text{Sunday}(t)\ \wedge T(e) \circ t]]]$

In (15a), the existentially quantified *a Sunday* takes wide scope over the universally quantified *every student*, as spelled out in (16a). The time adverbial provides the reference time, so it takes wide scope over the quantifier in the main clause, and the students must all go hiking on the same Sunday. In (15b) both scope orders are available. If the adverb is processed first, it will yield the same interpretation as (15a). If the main clause is interpreted first, there are two options. If it is read "collectively", it will introduce one big event in which everyone went hiking. If the main clause is read "distributively", it will introduce a collection of events (one for each student) and each of these events will take place on a Sunday. The $\exists \forall$ reading is the only one generated by Hinrichs's rules. The $\forall \exists$ order in (16b) is unavailable in a system in which time adverbials are always processed prior to the main clause they modify, even if they are postverbal. This means that a Reichenbachian approach misses the preferred reading of (15b).[4] Similar problems arise in (17):

(17)   a.   On Sunday morning, Julia only goes to church.

       b.   Julia only goes to church on Sunday morning.

Only cannot associate with *on Sunday morning* in (17a), because the time adverbial is topicalized and focus is naturally on the predicate. C in (18a) is the set of contextually relevant alternatives, which determines the domain of quantification of *only* (Rooth, 1992):

(18)   a. $\forall X [[X \in C \wedge \exists e [X(j, e) \wedge \exists t [\text{Sunday-morning}(t) \wedge t \circ T(e)]]] \rightarrow$
$X = \text{Go-to-church}]$

      b. $\forall X [[X \in C \wedge \exists t [X(t) \wedge \exists e [\text{Go-to-church}(j, e) \wedge T(e) \circ t]]] \rightarrow$
$X = \text{Sunday-morning}]$

X in (18a) is a variable over properties (of individuals), so among all the contextually relevant things Julia could do on Sunday morning, she chooses to go to church. (17b), with its unmarked syntactic order, can get the same interpretation as (17a). It can also mean that the only time Julia goes to church is on Sunday morning. The time adverbial is focused, so X in (18b) is a variable over properties of time intervals. The truth conditions for the two readings given in (18a) and (18b) are different. If Julia goes to church on Thursday as well as Sunday morning, (17b) is falsified, but not necessarily (17a). On the other hand, if Julia goes to the pub right after church on Sunday morning, (17a) will no longer be true, whereas the truth of (17b) need not be affected.

2.2   *Temporal Clauses*

Similar effects can be observed with temporal clauses:

(19)   a. Before she goes to church, Julia only has tea.
      b. Julia only has tea before she goes to church.

(19a) suggests that Julia does not consume anything else but tea before she goes to church. The relevant reading of (19b), on the other hand, claims that the only time Julia has tea is before going to church. The representation of the two readings is similar to (18). Consider further the examples in (20) and (21), already studied in de Swart (1993):

(20)   a. Before he goes to bed, Paul always brushes his teeth.
      b. Paul always brushes his teeth before he goes to bed.

(21)   a. When he is in the shower, John usually shaves.
      b. John usually shaves when he is in the shower.

In (20a), the first argument of the quantifier *always* is the subordinate clause introduced by *before*: all situations of Paul's going to bed have an instance of Paul's brushing his teeth located before them. (20b) is ambiguous. It can have the same interpretation as (20a), but it can also take its arguments in the order of the clauses. In this second reading, *always* quantifies over all situations of Paul's brushing his teeth and requires them to precede an instance of Paul's going to bed. This reading is unavailable for (20a). Similar observations can be made with respect to (21a, b), discussed by Rooth (1985:180).

    The quantificational structure of sentences like (20) and (21) is built up around two sets of events, denoted by the main and subordinate clauses and a two-place relation between events denoted by the temporal connective. The reading of (20b) in which the temporal clause is in focus involves quantification over the set of events corresponding with the main clause. This set is included in the set of events related to the first one by means of the temporal connective. The embedded quantificational structure is represented in a generalized quantifier format, so that extension to cases involving proportional quantifiers such as *usually, often, rarely* (as in 21) is straightforward:

(22)   Paul always brushes his teeth before he goes to bed.
    a. Always $(\{e_1 \mid \text{Brush-his-teeth}(\text{Paul}, e_1)\},$
        $\{e_1 \mid \exists (\{e_2 \mid \text{Go-to-bed } (\text{Paul}, e_2)\}, \{e_2 \mid \text{Before}_{e1}(e_2)\})\})$
    b. $\{e_1 \mid \text{Brush-his-teeth}(\text{Paul}, e_1)\} \subseteq$
        $\{e_1 \mid \exists (\{e_2 \mid \text{Go-to-bed}(\text{Paul}, e_2)\}, \{e_2 \mid \text{Before}_{e1}(e_2)\})\}$
    c. $\text{Before}_{e1} = \{e_2 \mid \langle e_1, e_2 \rangle \in \text{Before}\}$

The analysis appeals to the image set of the two-place relation described by the connective, that is, the set of events that constitutes the range of the *before* relation (22c). The truth conditions in (22b) correctly rule out a context in which Paul brushes his teeth at a different time than before going to bed. In the interpretation of (20b) that it shares with (20a), the subordinate clause provides the first argument. We look at situations of Paul's going to bed and verify that they all have an event of his brushing his teeth located before it:

(23)   Before he goes to bed, Paul always brushes his teeth.
    a. Always $(\{e_2 \mid \text{Go-to-bed}(\text{Paul}, e_2)\},$
        $\{e_2 \mid \exists (\{e_1 \mid \text{Brush-his-teeth}(\text{Paul}, e_1)\}, \{e_1 \mid \text{Before'}_{e2}(e_1)\})\})$
    b. $\{e_2 \mid \text{Go-to-bed } (\text{Paul}, e_2)\} \subseteq$
        $\{e_2 \mid \exists (\{e_1 \mid \text{Brush-his-teeth}(\text{Paul}, e_1)\}, \{e_1 \mid \text{Before}_{e2}(e_1)\})\})$
    c. $\text{Before'}_{e2} = \{e_1 \mid \langle e_2, e_1 \rangle \in \text{Before'}\}$
    d. $\text{Before'} = \{\langle e_2, e_1 \rangle \mid \langle e_1, e_2 \rangle \in \text{Before}\}$

The converse relation *Before'* is defined in terms of the reversal of the arguments of the connective.[5] The corresponding change in the quantificational structure leads to the desired interpretation in which (23) is true iff the set of events in which Paul goes to bed is a subset of the set of events such that Paul brushes his teeth beforehand. The truth conditions in (23b) correctly rule out a context in which Paul goes to bed without brushing his teeth beforehand.

The correlation between position and meaning is thus more than just a pragmatic effect: under quantification, it gives rise to differences in truth conditions. These cases also confirm the hypothesis that topicalization and given/new information play a crucial role in the interpretation. If the preposed temporal clause is topicalized, it is not readily interpreted as itself being in focus, but it is normally part of the background of the focus. If adverbial quantifiers like *only* and *always* associate with focus, and quantify over the part of the sentence that constitutes the background to the focused element, as assumed by Rooth (1985, 1992) and de Swart (1993), we expect the topicalized time adverbial to end up in the restriction on the quantifier, rather than in the second argument. In this way, we can explain why sentences with preposed constituents such as the a-sentences of (15), (17), (19), (20), and (21) do not have the same range of interpretations as their postponed counterparts in the corresponding b-sentences. The postponed time adverbial can be part of the background, if the focus is on the main predicate, but if the temporal clause is itself in focus it will end up as the second argument of *only/always*.

Again, it is hard to account for these meaning effects in a Reichenbachian framework. Partee (1984) shows that an extension of Hinrichs's analysis to quantificational cases has *when-*, *before-*, and *after-*clauses end up as the first argument of the quantifier. This does not lead to an explanation of the entire range of interpretations temporal clauses give rise to under quantification. Alternative analyses developed by Hornstein (1990) and Bertinetto (1985) do not discuss quantificational cases, and it is hard to know how they would extend their proposals to the examples discussed here.

If we want to make the interpretation of time adverbials sensitive to topic/focus structure, we need to have a broader view of the temporal structure of narrative discourse than what a Reichenbachian theory offers us. One such view can be found in a series of papers by Lascarides and Oberlander (1993a, b) and Lascarides and Asher (1991, 1993a, b). Lascarides et al. are not the only ones who appeal to rhetorical relations to describe event structure. However, as we see later, the fact that their framework provides an explicit characterization of temporal anaphora makes it suitable for our purposes of interpreting time adverbials.

3   Rhetorical and Temporal Information

3.1   *Event Structure without Reference Times*

In a series of papers, Lascarides and Oberlander (1993a, b) and Lascarides and Asher (1991, 1993a, b) develop a system DICE – discourse and common sense entailment – to describe the temporal structure of texts that does not rely on the notion of reference time. Temporal relations are derived from rhetorical relations. The triple $\langle \tau, \alpha, \beta \rangle$ expresses that the representation τ of the text so far (of which α is already part) is to be updated with the representation β of the current clause via a rhetorical relation that attaches β to α. α functions as the temporal antecedent for β in the discourse. As the default case, Lascarides et al. assume that the descriptive order of events matches the temporal order, unless there is information to the contrary:

(24)   a.   *Narration*
              $\langle \tau, \alpha, \beta \rangle > \text{Narration}(\alpha, \beta)$
        b.   Axiom on *Narration*
              For α describes e_1 and β describes e_2:
              $\Box (\text{Narration}(\alpha, \beta) \rightarrow e_1 \prec e_2)$

The connective > in (24a) indicates the default character of the implication. (24b) uses the strict inference → and claims that, if Narration(α, β) holds, then the discourse must describe two events happening in succession:

(25)   Max stood up. Bill greeted him.
        α: Max stood up
        β: John greeted him
        Narration(α, β)
        $\exists e_1$ [Stand-up(max, e_1) $\wedge$ $\exists e_2$ [Greet(john, max, e_2) $\wedge$ $e_1 \prec e_2$]]

Other discourse relations overrule the default case and describe more specific cases. These are accounted for by means of (versions of) the Penguin principle:

(26)   Penguin principle
        $\phi > \psi$, $\psi > \chi$, $\phi > \neg\chi$, $\phi \models \neg\chi$
        but not: $\phi > \psi$, $\psi > \chi$, $\phi > \neg\chi$, $\phi \models \chi$

If we know that penguins are birds, that birds fly, and that penguins don't fly, then knowing that Tweety is a penguin will support the (default) inference that Tweety doesn't fly, rather than that Tweety flies. According to the Penguin principle, the more specific relation wins. It is used for cases like (27), which involve *Elaboration*. Elaboration(α, β) holds if the event in β is part of the preparatory phase of the event described by α (Moens and Steedman 1988):

(27)   The council built the bridge. The local architect drew up the plans.
        α: The council built the bridge
        β: The local architect drew up the plans
        Elaboration(α, β)
        $\exists e_1$ [Build(council, bridge, e_1) $\wedge$ $\exists e_2$ [Draw(arch, plans, e_2) $\wedge e_2 \prec e_1$]]

The Penguin principle is also used in other rhetorical relations, such as *Explanation*. Explanation(α, β) holds if the event described in clause β causes the event described in clause α. Typically, causes precede effects:

(28)   Max fell. John pushed him.
        α: Max fell
        β: John pushed him
        Explanation(α, β)
        $\exists e_1$ [Fall(max, e_1) $\wedge \exists e_2$ [Push(john, max, e_2) $\wedge$ Cause(e_2, e_1) $\wedge e_2 \prec e_1$]]

The converse relation of *Explanation* is *Result*; it is exemplified in (29):

(29)   Max switched off the light. The room was pitch dark.
        α: Max switched off the light
        β: The room was pitch dark
        Result(α, β)
        $\exists e_1$ [Switch(max, e_1) $\wedge \exists s_2$ [Dark(room, s_2) $\wedge$ Cause(e_1, s_2) $\wedge e_1 \prec s_2$]]

The resulting state follows the event described by the first sentence, because of the causal relation between switching off the light and a room's being dark. In cases where no such specific information is available, states are interpreted as overlapping the state/event described by the first sentence. If a state takes an event as its temporal antecedent, the default relation is *Background*. Background(α, β) holds if the state in β describes the circumstances under which the event in α holds:

(30)   Max opened the door. The room was pitch dark.
        α: Max opened the door
        β: The room was pitch dark
        Background(α, β)
        $\exists e_1$ [Open(max, door, e_1) $\land$ $\exists s_2$ [Dark(room, s_2) $\land$ $e_1 \subseteq s_2$]]

The system Lascarides and Asher develop is flexible, and more discourse relations can be defined if needed. For instance, the relation between the president's asking for support and Jill's raising her hand is stronger than just *Narration*, but can be defined as *Reaction*, which involves a causal connection. Temporal sequencing is derived as a result of the interpretation of the second event as a reaction to the first one.

Information about causation is not usually encoded in temporal morphemes. DICE is a system that uses a mixture of world knowledge and linguistic knowledge to describe the temporal structure of a text. The notion of reference time is thus not indispensable for a description of the temporal order between independent clauses in a discourse (in the simple past).[6]

In order to analyze time adverbials and temporal clauses in this framework, we need more than discourse relations, because the information expressed by time adverbials and temporal clauses has an explicitly temporal character. So we need to extend the set of rhetorical relations with a set of temporal relations. More specifically, I will incorporate Smith's (1978) relational analysis of time adverbials into the present framework.

3.2   Phrasal Time Adverbials

Syntactically, temporal prepositions like *at*, *before*, *after* combine with a temporal noun to build a time adverbial, which combines with the main clause. Semantically, the temporal preposition denotes an overlap relation, an earlier-than relation, or a later-than relation between the eventuality described by the main clause and the time referred to by the temporal noun (cf. Smith, 1978):

(31)   Semantics of absolute time adverbials:
        For γ a main clause, which describes a set of eventualities $P(e)$, and δ a temporal noun, which denotes a set of times t on the time axis, the temporal connective *at*, *before*, *after* denotes a set of pairs of eventualities e and times t, such that

- At $(\gamma, \delta) \rightarrow \mathcal{T}(e) \circ t$
- Before $(\gamma, \delta) \rightarrow \exists e' [e' \sqsubseteq e \wedge P(e') \wedge \mathcal{T}(e') \prec t]$
- After $(\gamma, \delta) \rightarrow \exists e' [e' \sqsubseteq e \wedge P(e') \wedge \mathcal{T}(e') \succ t]$

The preposition establishes a temporal relation between t and the eventuality described by the main clause.[7] Note that the interpretation given involves strict, and not default inferences: the preposition forces a certain temporal relation between the time interval described by the adverbial and the event given by the main clause. In this sense, explicitly temporal information is stronger than rhetorical information, because it cannot be overruled by world knowledge.

The interpretation given predicts that there are no differences in temporal structure between preposed and postponed time adverbials. This prediction is borne out by the sentences in (32), which get the representations in (33):[8]

(32)   a.   At six o'clock, Jane left.
        b.   Jane left at six o'clock.

(33)   a. $\exists \{t_2 \mid \text{six-o'clock}(t_2)\}, \{t_2 \mid \exists \{e_1 \mid \text{Leave(Jane, } e_1)\}, \{e_1 \mid \text{At}'_{t_2}(e_1)\}\}$
        b. $\exists \{e_1 \mid \text{Leave(Jane, } e_1)\}, \{e_1 \mid \exists \{t_2 \mid \text{six-o'clock}(t_2)\}, \{t_2 \mid \text{At}_{e_1}(t_2)\}\}$

In the absence of an explicit temporal quantifier, we assume that the tense operator induces existential closure over both the e and the t variables. *At* and *At'* are converse relations, which both express temporal overlap. Given that the formulas under (33) are not essentially second-order, we can work them out to give the temporal structures in (34):

(34)   a. $\exists t_2 [\text{Six-o'clock}(t_2) \wedge \exists e_1 [\text{Leave(Jane, } e_1) \wedge t_2 \circ \mathcal{T}(e_1)]]$
        b. $\exists e_1 [\text{Leave(Jane, } e_1) \wedge \exists t_2 [\text{Six-o'clock}(t_2) \wedge \mathcal{T}(e_1) \circ t_2]]$

(34a) and (b) are equivalent under a standard first-order predicate logical interpretation of conjunction. This is in accordance with the view that we desire a unified analysis of preposed and postponed time adverbials. The differences in meaning related to position have to do with the way time adverbials update the event structure built up by the discourse as a whole. Updating is associated with a noncommutative interpretation of conjunction in which the second conjunct is interpreted in the context created by the first (Groenendijk and Stokhof 1991). In narrative discourse, updating is governed by the left-right order in a sequence of sentences. In complex sentences containing time adverbials, the question which conjunct is added first is not purely governed by left-right order, but is dependent on topic/focus structure.

The major difference between main clauses and time adverbials resides in their anaphoric behavior. Unlike independent and main clauses, time adverbials are presuppositional, as argued by Heinämäki (1978). In a dynamic perspective, presuppositional expressions are often characterized as anaphors with semantic content (e.g., van der Sandt 1992). The anaphorical relation a time adverbial establishes with the preceding discourse differs in nature from the one established by a main clause, though. A time adverbial looks for a temporal antecedent it can establish an identity relation with, not one it can establish a rhetorical relation with. That is, the use of a locating time adverbial like *at six o'clock* requires that there is a time of six o'clock either already mentioned or accommodated in the discourse representation built up so far, which the time *t* referred to by the temporal noun identifies with. As a result, the time interval referred to can be attached to the discourse structure *τ* without a rhetorical relation, because its location on the time axis is already known within the general linguistic context. Given that their location in time is independent of the rhetorical structure of the local discourse, time adverbials can function as temporal antecedents for other anaphorical expressions to establish a rhetorical relation with, but they never behave as anaphors in a rhetorical relation and cannot take another expression as their temporal antecedent in such a relation. In the triple $\langle \tau, \alpha, \beta \rangle$, time adverbials can occupy the position of α, but never of β. The impossibility of time adverbials' behaving as anaphors in a rhetorical relation is reflected in the following inference rule:

(35)   For TP a temporal preposition (*at, before, after*), γ a main clause, and δ
a temporal noun:

- $TP(\gamma, \delta) \rightarrow \neg \langle \tau, \alpha, \delta \rangle$

The temporal relation the preposition establishes between the adverbial and the main clause as formulated in (31) overrules all rhetorical relations that might be possible otherwise, so the presuppositional character of the time adverbial does not influence the sentence-internal temporal structure of (32a, b). The differences only come out when we embed these sentences in a broader context. Time adverbials function as temporal antecedents for the main clause when they are preposed, as is clear from (36), which expands (32a):

(36)   Jane went to the shoestore. She tried two pairs of walking shoes, and
bought one. At six o'clock she left the store to go home.
α: Jane went to the shoestore
β: Jane tried two pairs of walking shoes
γ: Jane bought one pair of walking shoes
δ: Six o'clock
ε: Jane leave the store to go home
Narration(α, β), Narration(β, γ), At'(δ, ε)
$\exists e_1 [Go(j, e_1) \wedge \exists e_2 [Try(j, shoes, e_2) \wedge \exists e_3 [Buy(j, shoes, e_3) \wedge$
$e_1 \prec e_2 \wedge e_2 \prec e_3 \wedge \exists t_5 [Six-o'clock(t_5) \wedge \exists e_4 [Leave(j, e_4) \wedge t_5 \circ$
$\mathcal{T}(e_4)]]]]]$

The time adverbial is added to the event structure, without any rhetorical relation to the immediately preceding discourse. This may seem strange: we would expect an incoherent text if no structure $\langle \tau, \alpha, \beta \rangle$ can be created, because we wouldn't know how β relates to the event structure built up so far. Coherence is saved by the presuppositional character of time adverbials: the time adverbial can be attached to τ, because the interval referred to can be located on the time axis within the general linguistic context. This procedure creates a break in narrative structure, though. There is no local temporal antecedent that the time interval is related to, so the rhetorical chain is broken. The main clause is interpreted in the event structure updated with the contribution of the time adverbial. The main clause is anaphoric and takes the adverbial as its temporal antecedent. The default rhetorical relation is overruled by the contribution of the preposition, which is formulated as a strict inference. As a result, temporal relations win over rhetorical relations, and the main clause event is interpreted as overlapping the interval of *six o'clock*.

If we embed (32b) in the larger discourse in (37) and focus on the time adverbial, we get the following event structure:

(37)   Jane quickly packed some clothes. She left at six o'clock.
α: Jane quickly packed some clothes
β: Jane left
γ: Six o'clock
Narration(α, β), At(β, γ)
$\exists e_1$ [Pack(jane, clothes, e_1) $\wedge$ $\exists e_2$ [Leave(Jane, e_2) $\wedge e_1 \prec e_2$ $\wedge$
$\exists t_3$ [six-o'clock(t_3) $\wedge$ $\mathcal{T}(e_2) \circ t_3$]]]

If the time adverbial is in focus, it provides new information in a context enriched with the contribution of the main clause. This requires the main clause to take a preceding sentence as its temporal antecedent, according to the usual rules governing narrative discourse. In the present case, a relation of *Narration* is established between Jane's packing her clothes and her leaving. Given this orientation toward something that is part of the discourse structure already, we have a naturally continuing text, without any break in narrative structure. The time adverbial that follows introduces a point/interval as usual. Because of its presuppositional character, the time adverbial does not need to attach itself to the preceding discourse by means of a rhetorical relation with the main clause, and no structure $\langle \tau, \alpha, \beta \rangle$ is created. But there is of course a temporal relation between the time adverbial and the main clause event, which is governed by the preposition. The result is that the time adverbial in (37) behaves as an event modifier: it provides a more precise location in time for the main clause event, by relating it to an interval the location of which on the time axis is known from the general context. For time adverbials introduced by *before* or *after*, the situation is similar, except that the temporal relation established by the preposition is now precedence or succession instead of overlap.

Not everyone would allow the time referred to by the adverb to be completely independent of the preceding discourse, as I argue here by characterizing the adverb as presuppositional, and independent of the local rhetorical structure. Kamp and Reyle (1993:530) claim that, for sentences in the simple past, we need to conceive of the time referred to by the adverb as later than the event described by the previous sentence. Consider (38a, b):

(38)   a. Fred arrived on Wednesday. He left on Sunday.
       b. Fred left on Wednesday. He arrived on Sunday.

It is certainly true that in these sentences we would need a pluperfect to be able to go back in time and have Fred leave on the Sunday before the Wednesday of the first sentence of (38b). But remember that succession in time is also the default option for two event sentences, yet Lascarides et al. convincingly argue that this should not be built into the semantics of the simple past tense (compare (27) and (28)). Especially in texts with a journalistic style it is easy to find counterexamples to Kamp and Reyle's generalization:

(39)   Former Wall Street financier Sherman McCoy was brought in handcuffs to the Bronx *yesterday* and arraigned on a charge of manslaughter in the death of Henry Lamb, a 19-year-old black honor student. Mr. Lamb died *Monday night* at Lincoln Hospital as a result of cerebral injuries suffered when he was struck by Mr. McCoy's Mercedes-Benz sports car on Bruckner Boulevard in the Bronx thirteen months ago.
       (T. Wolfe (1987). *The Bonfire of the Vanities*, New York: Bantam, p. 686.)

In this context, the time of *Monday night* precedes *yesterday*. I conclude that the default order in (38) falls out as another effect of the Gricean maxim "Be orderly." Causal relations offer the possibility of backshifting and (39) is a case at hand: after being informed of McCoy's return to court, we get further details on the reason of this event, namely, Henry Lamb's death.

3.3   Temporal Clauses

As was pointed out, the interpretation of temporal clauses is more complex, because they describe events or states and do not directly refer to intervals. This is reflected in the unified semantics I propose for preposed and postponed temporal clauses introduced by *before* or *after*:

(40)   Semantics of temporal clauses introduced by *before* or *after*:
       For γ a main clause, which introduces an event/state e_1 such that $P(e_1)$ and δ a subordinate clause, which describes an event/state e_2 such that $Q(e_2)$, the temporal connective denotes a set of pairs of events e_1 and e_2, such that
       - $Before(\gamma, \delta) \rightarrow \exists e' \, [e' \sqsubseteq e_1 \wedge P(e') \wedge e' \prec e_2]$
       - $After(\gamma, \delta) \rightarrow \exists e' \, [e' \sqsubseteq e_1 \wedge P(e') \wedge \exists e'' \, [e'' \sqsubseteq e_2 \wedge Q(e'') \wedge e' \succ e'']]$

Before- and *after*-clauses presuppose the state of affairs they describe. In terms of van der Sandt's theory, they are anaphors that identify with a state or event that is already present in the discourse representation structure. Consequently, the subordinate clause can play the role of a temporal antecedent α in a rhetorical structure $\langle \tau, \alpha, \beta \rangle$, but it never occupies the position β of the anaphor. (41) is a straightforward extension of the inference rule (35) formulated for phrasal time adverbials:

(41)   For TC a temporal connective (*when/before/after*), γ a main clause, and
        δ a subordinate clause:
        • TC (γ, δ) → $\neg \langle \tau, \alpha, \delta \rangle$

Note that the antecedent of a temporal clause is a state or an event, which plays its own role in the rhetorical strucure of the discourse (assuming it is introduced by a main clause, or accommodated as such). This allows the temporal clause to fit in with the rhetorical structure of the discourse built up so far, without being the anaphor in such a rhetorical relation itself. The direct link that Lascarides and Oberlander (1993b) have temporal clauses establish with rhetorical structure is thus replaced by an indirect connection. I think that this is a better reflection of the subordinate and presuppositional nature of temporal clauses. Moreover, it preserves the similarity with phrasal time adverbials.

The differences in meaning related to position now come out as an effect of topic/focus structure on updating:

(42)   a.   Ty and John were good friends, and they often went to the movies
             together. But John's behavior changed quickly after he met Hélène.
             Ty said she bewitched him.
        b.   John had always been rather shy. But after he met Hélène, his behavior
             changed quickly. He was very self-assured now.

In (42a), the main clause is integrated in the existing event structure via a rhetorical relation of *Background* with the preceding sentence. The event described by the temporal clause gives a more precise location in time for the main clause event. The preposed temporal clause in (42b), on the other hand, creates a break in the narrative structure, because its presuppositional character guarantees that the event described by the subordinate clause is added to the event structure without any temporal or rhetorical relation with the immediately preceding discourse. The main clause takes the subordinate clause as its temporal antecedent, but all rhetorical relations are overruled by the information contributed by the temporal connective.

3.4   A Special Case: when-Clauses

The semantics of *before* and *after* as given in (40) predicts no difference in sentence-internal temporal structure between preposed and postponed cases. The strict inference related to the connective overrules all rhetorical relations that could possibly be inferred. This is correct as far as these connectives are concerned, but in the case of *when*, we did notice differences in temporal structure between preposed and postponed clauses. The crucial example was (13), repeated here as (43):

(43)   a. The president asked who would support him when Jill raised her hand.
         b. When the president asked who would support him, Jill raised her hand.
         c. The president asked who would support him. Jill raised her hand.

The temporal relations we want to obtain are simultaneity in (43a) (with raising of the hand followed by the request for support as a pragmatically less interesting case) and succession of events (i.e., raising of the hand as a reaction to the request) in (43b). The question is why succession of events is possible in (43b), just as in the sequence of independent clauses in (43c), but not in (43a).

I propose to account for these data by adopting a very weak semantics for *when*. I assume that *when* essentially describes temporal overlap, just as the prepositions *at, in, on* that we discussed in the previous section. However, *when* differs from the other temporal connectives by the fact that its contribution can be overruled by a rhetorical relation. Only in those cases where no rhetorical relation can be established will the temporal meaning of the connective come out, and an overlap relation is the result. As a first approximation of the semantics of *when*-clauses this can be defined as in (44):

(44)   Semantics of temporal clauses introduced by *when* (first version):
         If the main clause γ introduces an event/state e_1 and the subordinate
         clause δ describes an event/state e_2, we define
         $$\neg [\langle \tau, \gamma, \delta \rangle \vee \langle \tau, \delta, \gamma \rangle] > [when(\gamma, \delta) \rightarrow e_1 \circ e_2]$$

According to (44) *when* establishes a relation of temporal overlap between e_1 and e_2 if there is no way to establish a rhetorical relation between the two clauses. Note that the definition does not appeal to the position of the time adverbial. This is exactly what we expect from a unified semantics of temporal connectives, but then, how does (44) predict that temporal overlap typically arises with postponed time adverbials? The key to the understanding of the behavior of *when*-clauses resides again in the presuppositional character of time adverbials. A rhetorical structure $\langle \tau, \alpha, \beta \rangle$ arises if a new expression β is attached to τ via a rhetorical relation with an expression α that is already part of the discourse structure τ. Although the antecedent of (44) allows two different ways in which a rhetorical relation could arise between the main and the subordinate clause, one of these possibilities is never realized. (41) specifically states that the presupposed event expressed by the subordinate clause δ can be the temporal antecedent (α), but not the anaphor (β) in a rhetorical structure $\langle \tau, \alpha, \beta \rangle$. This means that we can simplify (44) and adopt (45) as the semantics of *when*-clauses:

(45)   Semantics of temporal clauses introduced by *when* (final version):
         If the main clause γ introduces an event/state e_1 and the subordinate
         clause δ describes an event/state e_2, we define
         $$\neg \langle \tau, \delta, \gamma \rangle > [when(\gamma, \delta) \rightarrow e_1 \circ e_2]$$

According to (45), *when* establishes a relation of temporal overlap between e_1 and

e_2 if the subordinate clause does not provide the temporal antecedent for the main clause. This situation arises when the subordinate clause is postponed and focused as in (43a). (45) leads to the following representation of (43a):

(46)   The president asked who would support him when Jill raised her hand.
     a. $\exists\{e_1|\ \text{Ask}(\text{pres}, e_1)\}\{e_1\ |\ \exists e_2\ \text{Raise}(\text{Jill}, \text{hand}, e_2)\}\{e_2\ |\ When_{e1}(e_2)\}\}$
     b. α: the president asked who would support him
          β: Jill raised her hand
          $When(\alpha, \beta)$
          $\exists e_1\ [\text{Ask}(\text{president}, e_1) \wedge \exists e_2\ [\text{Raise}(\text{Jill}, \text{hand}, e_2) \wedge e_1 \circ e_2]]$

In the absence of a rhetorical relation, the two events are interpreted as happening simultaneously. Compare this with the analysis of (43b) in (47):

(47)   When the president asked who would support him, Jill raised her hand.
     a. $\exists\{e_1|\ \text{Ask}(\text{pres}, e_1)\}\{e_1\ |\ \exists\{e_2\ |\ \text{Raise}(\text{Jill}, \text{hand}, e_2)\}\{e_2\ |\ When'_{e_1}(e_2)\}\}$
     b. α: the president asked who would support him
          β: Jill raised her hand
          $Reaction(\alpha, \beta)$
          $\exists e_1\ [\text{Ask}(\text{president}, e_1) \wedge \exists e_2\ [\text{Raise}(\text{Jill}, \text{hand}, e_2) \wedge e_1 \prec e_2]]$

The preposed temporal clause in (47) is topicalized, so it counts as old information with respect to the main clause. Given that the main clause is anaphoric as usual, we want to build a structure $\langle \tau, \alpha, \beta \rangle$. As a result, the antecedent of (45) is not verified, and *when* need not be interpreted as overlap. The raising of the hand is viewed as a reaction to the request for support. Because of the way the semantics of *when* is defined, we end up with a temporal structure of the preposed *when*-clause that is indistinguishable from the one the sequence of two independent sentences in (43c) would lead to. In such cases, the semantic contribution of *when* is indeed empty.

According to (45) the connective only forces an overlap relation if no rhetorical relation can be established. In practice, this means that *when* always expresses overlap between the two events when the temporal clause is postponed and focused. Preposed temporal clauses are topicalized and provide the temporal antecedent of the main clause. The relation between the two events is governed by the defeasible inference rules of DICE (*Elaboration, Background*, etc.). The combination of a general characteristics of time adverbials (namely, their presuppositional nature) with a very weak semantics of the connective *when* thus explains the effects of position of the subordinate clause on the temporal structure of the complex sentence.

The analysis can easily be extended to account for narrative *when*-clauses, an example of which is given in (48a):

(48)   a. We were crossing the street when John noticed us.
      b. When John noticed us, we were crossing the street.
      c. When we were crossing the street, John noticed us.
      d. We were crossing the street. John noticed us.

(48a) is not an answer to the question "When were you crossing the street?" suggesting that the *when*-clause does not function as an event modifier. But the *when*-clause does not provide the temporal frame for the main clause either: we would use a preposed time adverbial as in (48b) or (48c) instead. The meaning of (48a) comes closest to the one in (48d), except that the feeling of sudden interruption that is characteristic of narrative *when*-clauses is missing in the sequence of two independent clauses.

The main difference between the *when*-clause in (48a) and the sequence of independent clauses in (48d) consists in the way the event of John's noticing us is presented: it is asserted in (48d), but presupposed in (48a). Unlike the preposed clause in (48b), however, the *when*-clause in (48a) does not present the event of John's noticing us as old information, familiar to the hearer. On the contrary, the *when*-clause is focused, so the interruption comes as a surprise and introduces a new situation into the context. In theories on presupposition, such a combination of presupposed and new information is treated by appealing to the notion of accommodation.

Lewis (1979) observed that if the context does not yet contain the presupposition, it can simply be adjusted: the presupposition comes into existence so that the utterance is acceptable after all. Accommodation is exploited in examples like (49), uttered by someone who is late for a meeting:

(49)   I am sorry, my car broke down.

The definite NP carries an existential presupposition. For the hearer it may be new information that the person owns a car, which makes this a "new" definite. The contextual parameters are adjusted to accommodate the presupposition, and the discourse proceeds in a felicitous way.

The situation in (48a) is essentially like the new definite in (49). The presupposition is not present in the context yet but is added in order to keep the utterance interpretable. That accommodation is the key to a better understanding of narrative *when*-clauses is confirmed by the fact that the special meaning effects disappear when the event described by the subordinate clause is present in the previous discourse; compare (50a) and (50b):

(50)   a.   We spent the entire afternoon working on our problem sets. We were almost done when the secretary came in. He announced that classes were cancelled until the end of the week.
       b.   Yes, I remember this afternoon when we worked on our problem sets for the semantics class. I think this was the only time the secretary ever came to our office. We were almost done when he came in. He announced that classes were cancelled until the end of the week.

The narrative *when*-clause in (50a) presents the entrance of the secretary as a sudden interruption in an ongoing activity. This effect is lost in (50b), where the event is already present in the preceding discourse. I conclude that exploitation of the accommodation strategy leads to the stylistic effects characteristic of narrative *when*-clauses. Introducing new information by presupposing it is what makes this construction different from preposed *when*-clauses on the one hand and a sequence of independent clauses on the other.

3.5   Constraints on Rhetorical Relations

In principle, we expect all rhetorical relations that are available in a sequence of independent clauses to be available in constructions with a preposed *when*-clause. Compare, for instance, (51a) and (51b):

(51)   a.   When they built the new bridge, a local architect drew up the plans.
        b.   ??When a local architect drew up the plans, they built the bridge.
        c.   ??They built the bridge when a local architect drew up the plans.

The relation established in (51a) is *Elaboration*: drawing up the plans is the preparatory phase of building a bridge. (51b) is strange, because the subordinate clause cannot be the second argument in a rhetorical relation. As a result, it cannot describe an event that elaborates the main clause. It does not help to change the order of the clauses (51c), because the postponed *when*-clause does not enter into rhetorical relations at all.

There are a few apparent counterexamples to the rule that subordinate clauses never provide the second argument in a discourse relation:

(52)   a.   When John pushed him Max fell.
        b.   ??When Max fell John pushed him.
        c.   John pushed Max. He fell.
        d.   Max fell. John pushed him.

The relation established in (52a) is *Result*, which involves a causal relation between pushing and falling. Given that causes precede effects, we end up with a succession of events in (52a) that is similar to the one in (52c). This is as expected. But the converse relation of *Result*, which also involves causation, is *Explanation*. Although *Explanation* can be invoked to explain the temporal order in the discourse (52d), and it would treat the subordinate clause in (52b) as the antecedent of the relation, it is not a relation that can be established in *when*-clause constructions. I think we can treat this as an apparent counterexample if we recognize that the underlying relation in both cases is causation (cf. Lascarides and Oberlander 1993b for a related constraint). If a subordinate clause event were caused by a main clause event, it would be crucially dependent on some rhetorical relation with the main clause for its interpretation. In the model developed here this is of course impossible. Postponed *when*-clauses confirm this pattern:

(53)   a.   Max fell when John pushed him.
        b.   ??John pushed him when Max fell.

No simultaneity relations are established in (53a), because of a conflict with real world knowledge: we tend to view the two events as causally related. The most straightforward interpretation of (53a) is on the model of (52a). (53b) is then strange for the same reason that (52b) is strange.

In general, the relation between a *when*-clause and its main clause is "tighter" than that between two independent clauses. The default rhetorical relation of *Narration* seems to be too weak to operate in *when*-clause constructions, as illustrated by the contrast in (54) (from Sandström 1993):

(54)   a.   John drank his beer. He left the pub.
          b.   ??When John drank his beer he left the pub.

A succession relation based on *Narration* is possible in (54a), but not in (54b). I refer to Sandström (1993) and Glasbey (1995) for further discussion of such constraints on *when*-clause constructions.

4   Conclusion

Although the idea of moving on the current reference time was originally an attractive way of capturing the unfolding of the story line, it turns out to lead to considerable complications, because a Reichenbachian approach does not account for the relation between position and meaning of the time adverbial. As an alternative, I develop an analysis of phrasal and clausal time adverbials in a framework without reference times. I combine a unified semantics of time adverbials and temporal clauses with a general inference rule about the presuppositional character of these expressions in a discourse setting in which topic/focus structure influences the order in which clauses are processed. Preposed time adverbials are topics, so they provide the temporal frame for the main clause and the background of the focus for negation/quantification. Postponed time adverbials can but need not be in focus, creating ambiguities. When they are in focus, they function as event modifiers and provide the second argument for negation/quantification. The same temporal/rhetorical relations we find in narrative discourse are available under negation and quantification, and in the presence of adverbs like *even* and *only*. We keep the same semantics and inference rules, but what comes out only as a pragmatic effect at the discourse level now has a strong sentence-internal effect because the position of the time adverbial leads to different readings of the focus-sensitive operator. Thus all and only the readings for sentences (15), (17), (19), (20), and (21) become available.

Notes

1   Like most adverbials, time adverbials come in many varieties. In this chapter. I only treat locating time adverbials such as *on the first of January*, *in June*, *at six o'clock*, *yesterday*, *last week*, and temporal clauses introduced by *when*, *before*, or *after*.

2   Kamp and Reyle (1993) drop the requirement on the presence of a time adverbial for text-initial sentences. They assume that the time of the eventuality is represented as unspecified except for the information carried by the tense. This change in perspective does not have any consequences for the views defended here.

3   Expressions like *three o'clock* denote predicates over times. All predicates have an extra argument for the event variable, so that propositions denote predicates of events. Tense induces existential closure and introduces location with respect to the speech time. I simplify the formulas by ignoring this information. I use Krifka's (1989) temporal trace function to map events onto their run time. $T(e)$ is the run time of the event e on the time axis. Time adverbials relate the run time of an event to the time denoted by the temporal noun. In (7) the relevant relation is temporal overlap (o). In section 3, I give a generalized interpretation of temporal prepositions and connectives in this style.

4   Note that a collective/distributive ambiguity cannot replace the scope analysis:

(i)   a.   Every Sunday, some students go hiking in the foothills.
       b.   Some students go hiking in the foothills every Sunday.

In (a) the universal quantifier takes wide scope, just as we expect. (b) has the $\exists\forall$ order as its preferred interpretation, but a reading in which the time adverbial takes scope over the main clause is also available. We could not obtain the $\forall\exists$ order if we did not allow the time adverbial to take wide scope over the main clause.

5   Cf. De Mey (1990) for a treatment of the active/passive contrast in terms of converse relations, on which this analysis is based.

6   See Kamp and Reyle (1993:594–595) and Lascarides and Asher (1993b) for discussion of the pluperfect.

7   Overlap is also expressed by *on/in/Ø* in *on Sunday, in June, yesterday.* With Krifka (1989) and others, I assume that the domain of eventualities has the structure of a join semilattice and is ordered by a part-of relation $\sqsubseteq$. For states and activities, there are proper parts of the event that are of the same type; for accomplishments and achievements there are not. The definition of *before* and *after* allows overlap in (i) and (iii), but not in (ii) and (iv):

(i)   Susan was (already) ill before Christmas.
(ii)   Susan wrote the book before Christmas.
(iii) Susan was (still) ill after Christmas.
(iv)   Susan wrote the book after Christmas.

8   With a different focus structure, (32b) can also get the representation given under (33a). In the following, I always assume this as a possibility unless stated otherwise.

References

Bertinetto, P. 1985. Intrinsic and extrinsic temporal references: on restricting the notion of "reference time." In V. Lo Cascio and C. Vet, editors, *Temporal Structure in Sentence and Discourse*, pages 41–78. Foris, Dordrecht.

Emonds, J. 1985. *A Unified Theory of Syntactic Categories*. Foris, Dordrecht.

Glasbey, S. 1995. 'When', discourse relations and the thematic structure of events. In *Proceedings of the Workshop on Time, Space and Movement*, volume 5, pages 91–104. Université Paul Sabatier, Toulouse.

Groenendijk, J. and M. Stokhof 1991. Dynamic predicate logic. *Linguistics and Philosophy*, 14:39–100.

Hamann, C. 1989. English temporal clauses in a reference frame model. In A. Schopf, editor, *Essays on Tensing in English*, volume II, pages 31–153. Niemeyer, Tübingen.

Heinämäki, O. 1978. Semantics of English Temporal Connectives. Ph.D thesis, University of Texas, Austin.

Hinrichs, E. 1981. Temporale Anaphora im Englischen. M.A. thesis, University of Tübingen.

Hinrichs, E. 1986. Temporal anaphora in discourses of English. *Linguistics and Philosophy*, 9:63–82.

Horn, L. 1989. *A Natural History of Negation*. University of Chicago Press, Chicago.

Hornstein, N. 1990. *As Time Goes By*. MIT Press, Cambridge.

Kamp, H., and U. Reyle 1993. *From Discourse to Logic*. Kluwer, Dordrecht.

Kamp, H., and C. Rohrer 1983. Tense in texts. In R. Bäuerle, C. Schwarze, and A. von Stechow, editors, *Meaning, Use and Interpretation of Language*, pages 250–269. de Gruyter, Berlin.

Krifka, M. 1989. Nominal reference, temporal constitution, and quantification in event semantics. In R. Bartsch, J. van Benthem, and P. van Emde Boas, editors, *Semantics and Contextual Expressions*, pages 75–115. Foris, Dordrecht.

Kuno, S. 1972. Functional perspective. *Linguistic Inquiry*, 3:269–320.

Lascarides, A., and N. Asher 1991. Discourse relations and defeasible knowledge. In *Proceedings of ACL*, volume 29, pages 55–62.

Lascarides, A., and N. Asher 1993a. The pluperfect in narrative discourse. In *Proceedings of the 6th European ACL*, pages 252–260.

Lascarides, A., and N. Asher 1993b. Temporal interpretation, discourse relations and commonsense entailment. *Linguistics and Philosophy*, 16:437–493.

Lascarides, A., and J. Oberlander 1993a. Temporal coherence and defeasible knowledge. *Theoretical Linguistics*, 19:1–37.

Lascarides, A., and J. Oberlander 1993b. Temporal connectives in a discourse context. In *Proceedings of the 6th European ACL*, pages 260–268.

Lewis, D. 1979. Scorekeeping in a language game. *Journal of Philosophical Logic*, 8:339–359.

Mey, J. de 1990. Determiner Logic or the Grammar of the NP. Ph.D. thesis, University of Groningen.

Moens, M., and M. Steedman 1988. Temporal ontology and temporal reference. *Computational Linguistics*, 14:15–28.

Partee, B. 1984. Nominal and temporal anaphora. *Linguistics and Philosophy*, 7:243–286.

Partee, B. 1991. Topic, focus and quantification. In *Proceedings of SALT*, volume I, pages 159–188, Cornell University.

Reichenbach, H. 1947. *Elements of Symbolic Logic*. Macmillan, New York.

Reinhart, T. 1982. Pragmatics and linguistics: an analysis of sentence topics. Distributed by Indiana University Linguistics Club, Bloomington, Indiana.

Rooth, M. 1985. Association with Focus. Ph.D. thesis, University of Massachusetts, Amherst.

Rooth, M. 1992. A theory of focus interpretation. *Natural language Semantics*, 1:75–116.

Sandström, G. 1993. When-clauses and the temporal interpretation of narrative discourse. Technical Report 34, Dept. of Linguistics, University of Umeå.

Sandt, R. van der 1992. Presupposition projection as anaphora resolution. *Journal of Semantics*, 9:333–377.

Smith, C. 1978. The syntax and interpretation of temporal expressions in English. *Linguistics and Philosophy*, 2:43–100.

Swart, H. E. de 1993. Adverbs of Quantification: A Generalized Quantifier Approach. Ph.D. thesis, University of Groningen. Published by Garland, New York.

Vallduví, E. 1992. *Information packaging*. Garland, New York.

Name Index

Abb, B., 18, 20, 40
Abbott, B., 326–7
Abney, S., 191
Akmajian, A., 318
Alshawi, H., 121
Appelt, D., 13
Aristotle, 8
Arnold, U., 18
Asher, N., xv–xvi, 191, 247–8, 251, 256, 262, 266, 347

Baart, J., 15, 44
Bach, E., 118, 218, 227
Bartels, C., 14, 37, 228
Beaver, D., 280, 282, 284, 290, 334
Berman, S., 333
Bertinetto, P., 341, 343, 347
Bierwisch, M., 40
Blok, P., xviii, 107
Bolinger, D., 44, 51, 87, 105, 107, 297
Bos, J., xv, 121, 124, 127, 131, 290
Bosch, P., 194, 293, 294, 306, 320
Bouchard, D., 82
Brachman, R., 118
Brennan, S., 293, 310
Büring, D., xvi, 152, 157, 175, 202, 203, 271, 325, 334
Byrd, S., 46

Cameron, R., 82
Carlson, G., 302
Carpenter, W., 20
Chafe, W., 3
Chierchia, G., 177, 203
Chomsky, N., 3, 43, 46, 53, 64, 68, 79, 295, 302
Cinque, G., 15, 46, 78–80
Clamons, J., 303
Clark, H., 279, 294
Clifton, C., Jr., 46, 54
Cohen, A., 15
Collier, R., 14
Comrie, B., 319
Cote, S., 82, 90
Crouch, R., 121

Cruttenden, A., 3
Cutler, A., 146, 295

Dahl, D., 293, 303
Dalrymple, M., 16
Deemter, K. van, xiv, 5, 159, 192, 324
Diesing, M., 80, 152, 204, 324
Di Eugenio, B., 82, 96
Dirksen, A., 15
Donnellan, K., 88
Dowty, D., 74
Dretske, F., 232, 233, 303

Eberle, K., xvii, 105, 107, 118
Eckardt, R., xvii, 157, 160–2, 164, 177, 219, 290, 334
Egg, M., 121
Eijck, J. van, 285
É. Kiss, K., 80
Embick, D., 96
Emonds, J., 340
Enc, M., 322, 324
Engdahl, E., 306
Erkü, F., 294
Erteshik-Shir, N., 295

Fagin, R., 118
Féry, C., 163
Fintel, K. von, 159, 217, 220, 226, 235, 243, 280, 282, 290
Fodor, J. A., 295
Foolen, A., 43
Fraurud, K., 302
Frederickson, K., 303
Frege, G., 10
Friedman, L., 293, 310
Fuchs, A., 44

Gabbay, D., 106
Garrod, S., 293
Gazdar, G., 289
Geilfuß, J., 158–60, 194
Geurts, B., xvii, 269, 272, 276, 279, 281, 289–90, 294

Givón, T., 264, 319
Glasbey, S., 359
Groenendijk, J., 177, 179, 180, 181, 187, 193,
    194, 197, 211, 350
Grosz, B. J., 89, 194, 251, 293, 310, 318, 319
Gundel, J. K., xiii, 82, 293, 294, 297, 299, 302,
    303, 319
Günther, C., xviii, 20, 38, 40, 41
Gussenhoven, C., xiii, 35, 43–6, 49, 51, 53,
    215

Hajičová, E., 213–29, 293, 300, 306
Halle, M., 64, 79
Halliday, M., 3, 295, 301
Halpern, J., 118
Hamann, C., 343
't Hart, J., 15
Haviland, S., 279, 293, 294, 302
Hedberg, N., 293, 294, 319
Hegarty, M., 293, 303
Heim, I., 90, 154–5, 170, 173, 194–5, 218, 219,
    239, 279, 285, 334
Heinämäki, O., 341–2, 350
Herburger, E., 158, 162
Herweg, M., 20, 23, 40
Heuven, V. J. van, 16
Hinrichs, E., 336, 337
Hirschbein, P., 83
Hirschberg, J., 14, 146, 216, 318
Hobbs, J., 13
Hoeksema, J., 118
Hoekstra, T., 188
Hoenkamp, E., 18
Höhle, T., 46, 49, 303
Hoop, H. de, 152, 158, 162, 164, 176, 324, 334
Hopper, P., 264
Horn, L., 339
Hornstein, N., 341, 343, 347
Huang, C. T. J., 82
Hulst, H. van der, 45

Ide, N., 118
Iida, M., 82, 90

Jackendoff, R., xv, 160, 163, 286, 290, 295,
    297, 318
Jacobs, J., xi, 15, 18, 32, 64, 79, 80, 214, 295
Jaeggli, O., 82
Jäger, G., xvi–xvii, 155, 188, 211, 271
Joshi, A. K., 89, 293, 310, 318

Kagarov, E., 84
Kameyama, M., xiv, 82, 90, 105, 293, 310, 311,
    318, 319
Kamp, H., 121, 124, 170, 173, 266, 272–7,
    289–90, 322, 327–30, 334, 336–7, 352
Karttunen, L., 272, 289

Katz, D., 84, 99
Kayne, R. S., 82, 96
Keenan, E., 319
Kehler, A., 313
Kempen, G., 18
Kingston, J., 14, 37
Kirkeby-Garstad, T., 322
Klein, W., 40
Kohlhase, M., 127, 131
Koktová, E., 215, 221, 223
König, E., 53, 122
Krahmer, E., 127, 290
Kratzer, A., 203, 204, 215, 218, 229, 237,
    288, 291
Krifka, M., 56, 166, 169, 172, 177, 180, 192,
    211, 214, 215, 219, 228, 229, 247, 262,
    286
Kuhn, S., 318
Kuno, S., 319, 340
Kuppevelt, J. van, 49

Ladd, D. R., 6, 43, 51, 146
Lakoff, G., 307, 318
Landman, F., 194
Lang, E., 72
Lascarides, A., 118, 251, 266, 347, 354
Lebeth, K., 121
Lehmann, H., 105
Lessen-Kloeke, W., 43
Levelt, W. J., 18, 20
Lewis, D., 218, 317, 357
Li, C., 82
Liberman, M., 64
Link, G., 118
Löbner, S., 188, 270
Lujan, M., 318

Maienborn, C., xviii, 19, 32, 40
Mann, W., 118, 251
Marsi, E., 43, 45, 48
Martin, P., 13
McCord, M., 107, 109
Meyerhoff, M., 96
Milsark, G., 152, 211, 270–1, 324
Miner, K., 86
Moens, M., 342, 348
Montague, R., xi
Moravcsik, J., 106
Moxey, L. M., 283
Müller, G., 79
Musan, R., 159, 164
Muskens, R., 121, 131

Nakagawa, H., 306
Napoli, D. J., 85
Nespor, M., 35

Oberlander, J., 347, 354
Odijk, J., 5
Ott, N., 105

Panevová, J., 221, 306
Partee, B., xiii, 176, 185, 214–16, 218, 286, 301, 324, 326–7, 333, 340, 342
Passonneau, R., 313, 319
Pelletier, F., 219, 286
Peregrin, J., 225
Pesetsky, D., 324
Pierrehumbert, J., 14, 163, 217, 297
Pinkal, M., 56, 121
Piwek, P., 290
Poesio, M., 121, 313
Polanyi, L., 118
Pollard, C., 117, 293, 310
Prevost, S., 320
Primus, B., 56, 74
Prince, A., 64
Prince, E., xiv, 294, 303, 319
Prüst, H., 4, 313, 319

Reichenbach, 337–8
Reinhart, T., 90, 176, 303, 340
Reyle, U., 121, 124, 266, 272–7, 289–90, 322–3, 327–30, 334, 336–7, 352
Rizzi, L., 96
Roberts, C., 322, 330, 332–3
Rochemont, M. S., 295
Rohrer, C., 336–7
Rooth, M., xiv, xv, 4, 19, 106–7, 128, 130, 142, 160, 166, 171–3, 176–7, 180–1, 185, 203, 214–18, 220–1, 223–5, 227, 232, 234, 235, 239, 242–3, 247, 249, 262, 286, 290–1, 295, 303, 344–6
Rumpp, W., 3

Sæbø, K., xvii, 56, 289, 325, 327
Safir, K., 82
Sag, I., 117, 248
Sandström, G., 359
Sandt, R. van der, xvii, 123–4, 127, 136, 263, 279, 281, 289–90, 324, 333, 350
Sanford, A. J., 283, 293
Sasse, H.-J., 80
Saussure, F. de, 118
Scha, R., 118
Schmerling, S., 43, 44, 48, 97
Schmolze, J., 118
Schopp, A., xviii, 20, 23

Schreuder, R., 40
Schröder, I., 18
Schubert, L., 219, 286
Schwarzschild, R., 218
Sedivy, J., 302
Selkirk, E. O., 35, 44, 45, 46, 191, 217
Sgall, P., xiii, 213–29, 295, 306, 319
Shlonsky, U., 82
Sidner, C., 251, 293, 310, 318
Skeie, M., 330
Smith, C., 349
Smolka, G., 107
Soames, S., 289
Solà, J., 158, 334
Stalnaker, R., 163
Stechow, A. von, 45, 214–15
Steedman, M., 4, 44, 229, 342, 348
Sternefeld, W., 79
Stickel, M., 13
Stokhof, M., 177, 179–80, 350
Strawson, P., xv, 289, 301
Stutterheim, C. von, 40
Sveinsdatter Skeie, M., 322
Swart, H. de, xvii, 330, 345, 346

Taglicht, J., 220
Tannenhaus, M., 302
Terken, J., 3
Thompson, S., 82, 118, 251
Thrainsson, H., 86
Turan, U., 90

Uhmann, S., 45, 49, 79

Vallduví, E., 40, 79, 197, 294–5, 324, 340
Véronis, J., 118
Vogel, I., 35

Walker, M. A., 82, 90
Ward, G., 146, 318
Webber, B., 83, 87, 96
Weinreich, U., 86
Weinstein, S., 89, 293, 310, 318
Westerståhl, D., 6, 159, 174, 323, 326
Williams, E., 318

Zacharski, R., 293, 294, 296, 319
Zaretski, A., 84, 98
Zec, D., 35
Zeevat, H., 289
Ziesche, S., 18, 40

Subject Index

abstraction, 274–6, 327
accent, 3–15, 306–20
  contrastive, 3, 30–9
  neutral, 62
  nuclear, 30–9, 79, 145, 167, 173, 188
  prenuclear, 30–9, 45–6
  realization of, 14, 30–9
  rise, 182
  sentence, 30–9, 44, 58–64
  see also compound stress
accommodation, 124, 133–8, 268, 278–89,
  317, 333
  see also domain restriction
activation, 294
  see also focus
also, 240–1
  see also focus particles
alternative semantics, 147–8 , 234–6, 239
alternatives, 19, 105–7, 113, 234–6
  see also contrast set
anaphora, 6, 123, 125, 134, 268, 337,
  350
  discourse, 306–20
  plural, 274, 278, 327
  situational, 302
  see also pronouns
attentional state, 310
autonomy, informational, 56–80
awareness, 107

background, 295
  see also focus/background structure
backward-looking center, 293, 300

centering theory, xiv, 89–91, 293, 300, 310
comment, 296, 299, 301, 303
  see also topic-comment distinction
common ground, 295
communicative dynamism, 224, 227
complementary preference hypothesis, 315
compound stress, 63–4
concept hierarchy, 111
context, 20, 311
context representation, 27

context set, 6
contextually bound elements, 224–5
contrariety, 3–15
contrast
  nonsymmetric, 261
  as rhetorical relation, 251–7
contrast set, 298
  see also alternatives
contrastive stress, *see* accent
contrastive topic, *see* topic
counterfactuals, 232, 235–9, 242

declaratives, 85–6, 92
default accent rule, 6
definiteness, 325–6
  see also determiner
determiner
  pronominal use of, 326
  strong vs. weak, 270–1, 277, 324
  see also quantifier
discontinuous focus, *see* focus
discourse center, 312
discourse coherence, xi
discourse context, 20
discourse deixis, 87, 96, 99
discourse function, 89, 95, 98
discourse linking, 322
discourse referent, 187, 193–4
  see also reference marker
discourse representation theory (DRT), 121,
  124, 187, 193, 195–6, 268, 272–9
discourse structure, 123
discourse subordination, 322
distribution, 328
domain restriction, 218, 220, 226–8
  and accommodation of presuppositions, 219,
  280–6, 322
  contextual narrowing by, 170, 219,
  277–8
  and focusing, 218, 220, 226–8, 286–8
DRT, *see* discourse representation theory
duplex condition, 272–6
dynamic predicate logic, 177–8
dynamic semantics, 187, 193–4, 197

event quantification, *see* quantification
exhaustivity, 235–6
existential reading, 187, 190, 198
extension of concepts, 113
extraction, 68

feature projection, 64–8
file change semantics, 187, 196–7
focalizer, *see* focus-sensitive operator
focus
  association with, 216, 232–43
  broad/narrow, 26–8, 32, 36–8, *see also* focus
    projection
  contrastive, 24–5, 29–30, 32, 247–51, 258,
    296–8, 300–2
  deaccented, 215–17
  degrammaticized vs. grammaticized accounts
    of, 215–17, 220
  discontinuous, 49–50
  and interaction with phonology, 215–17
  and interaction with pragmatic interpretation,
    213, 217, 219, 226
  and interaction with semantic interpretation,
    213–29
  linguistic, 300
  maximal, 24–5
  multiple, 26–7, 49–50
  psychological, 293–4, 298–9, 301–2
  and scope, 218, 220–8
  semantic, 295–6, 298–300, 302, 307
focus accent rule, 36–9
focus accent theory, 3, 6, 11
focus adverbs, 240–1
  see also focus-sensitive operator
focus ambiguity, 60–2, 121, 124
focus/background structure, 18–19, 71, 142–3,
  145, 192, 199–200, 286–9
  see also given-new distinction; theme/rheme
    structure; topic-comment distinction
focus feature, 191–3, 235, 239
focus interpretation, 47–8, 181
focus of attention, xii
  see also activation
focus particles, 122–3, 125
  see also focus adverbs
focus projection, 43–54, 60–2
focus-sensitive operator, 216, 220–8
  see also scope
focus-to-accent view, 44–5
functional elements, 76

given-new distinction, xii, 3–15
  see also focus/background structure;
    theme/rheme structure; topic-comment
    distinction
givenness (referential, relational), 299
grammatical function hierarchy, 311

hortatives, 87
HPSG, 20–3

imperatives, 85, 97, 99
implicature, 13, 150–2
incremental architecture, 18–19, 23–39, 193, 197
indefiniteness, 88, 324
information structure, 18–19, 23–39
  see also focus/background structure
informational autonomy, 56–80
integration, 66
interrogatives, 85–6
intonation, *see* accent
it-cleft, 234–6, 240

lexicon, 109, 114–15
LMT (logic-based machine translation), 107–11

maxim, Gricean, 339
metalinguistic competence, 96–8
modal subordination, *see* subordination
mostly, 222
movement, 66–7

narration, 338, 347
negation,
  and focus, 288–9
  and time adverbials, 339
noun phrase, *see* determiner; indefiniteness;
  quantifier

only, 121–2, 128, 133, 215–16, 220–7

parallel (rhetorical relation), 251–7
parallelism, syntactic, 3–15, 313
partitivity, *see* determiner; quantifier
pitch accent, 59–64, 142, 217
pragmatics, 307
Prague school, xiii, xv, 213–29
preference, commonsense, 313
preference classes, 313
preference model, dynamic, 311
preferences, interaction of, 311
presupposition, 13, 122–3, 197, 202, 237,
  268–91, 295, 301–2, 325, 327, 337,
  339, 350
  binding of, 268–71, 277–89
  existential, 242
  projection, 278
  of quantifier, 269–70, 275
  triggers of, 123, 269–70
pronouns, 93–5, 276–7, 306–20
  see also anaphora
prosody, 189–90
  see also accent
psychological focus, 294
  see also focus

quantification
  adverbial, 166, 218–20, 235, 288, 323, 330
  collective/distributive, 273
  determiner, 218–21, 223
  over events, 169
  and focus, 162, 166
  restriction on, 268–91, 322
  and time adverbials, 344
quantifier
  generalized, 273
  partitive readings of, 152–6, 188–9, 198–204, 270, 324
  presuppositional readings of, 153
  proportional readings of, 156–63, 174
  strong vs. weak, 152–6, 174–7, 187, 189, 193, 201–4, 270–1, 277
question-answer congruence, 142–4, 147

redundancy, 12, 96
reference marker
  event, 288
  plural, 273–4
  propositional, 276–9
reference time, 336
rheme structure, *see* theme/rheme structure
rhetorical relation, 247–66, 347
  see also contrast; discourse structure; parallel

salience, 298, 311
salience dynamics, 311
salient subset hypothesis, 314
scalar particle, 122
scope, 220–8
scope ambiguities, 124, 134
second occurrence expression, 215–17, 228
segmented discourse representation theory (SDRT), 251–61
semantics-pragmatics interface, 213, 214, 226, 306–20
sense of words in LMT, 109
sentence accent assignment rule (SAAR), 45
signature, 107
signifiant/signifié, 109–10
slot grammar, 109
  see also LMT
sort hierarchy, 107–11
specificity, 324
stage level–individual level distinction, 187, 203
statements, categorical vs. thetic, 194
stress, *see* accent

structured meaning, 214
subject prodrop, 82–99
subjects, ambient, 87, 92, 99
subordination
  discourse, 322, 330
  modal, 322, 330, 332
  quantificational, 330
  see also telescoping
substitution identifying, 3, 9, 10, 12
SYNPHONICS, 19–23

Taglicht examples, 220–5, 227
telegraphic speech, 83
telescoping, 270–1, 277–8, 332
theme/rheme structure, 213, 218, 226–8
  see also focus/background structure; topic-comment distinction
theta roles, 71–8
time adverbial, 336–60
  position of, 338
too, 121–2, 129, 134, 236–8, 303
topic, 142–64, 187, 192–3, 198, 202–4
  contrastive, 145, 300
  residual, 150–1
  sentence-internal, 144–5, 152–3
topic-comment distinction, 192–3, 199–200, 202–4
  see also focus/background structure; theme/rheme structure
topic shift, 296
topicalization, 297
translation, 105
  see also LMT
tripartite structure, 218, 226–8
  see also duplex condition
type hierarchy
  of nominal expressions, 311
  see also sort hierarchy
type of words in LMT, 109

underspecification, 121, 124, 132, 138
unselective binding, 170
update function, 193

valency projection, 64–8
VARBRUL, 83, 92–5
verb initial/verb second clauses, 83, 85–7, 99

Yiddish, 82–99

For EU product safety concerns, contact us at Calle de José Abascal, 56–1°,
28003 Madrid, Spain or eugpsr@cambridge.org.

www.ingramcontent.com/pod-product-compliance
Ingram Content Group UK Ltd.
Pitfield, Milton Keynes, MK11 3LW, UK
UKHW042142130625
459647UK00011B/1142